Y0-BCR-581

MODERN ARCHITECTURE

REPRESENTATION & REALITY

YALE UNIVERSITY PRESS NEW HAVEN AND LONDON

NEIL LEVINE

MODERN ARCHITECTURE

REPRESENTATION & REALITY

Published with assistance from the Annie Burr Lewis Fund and the Graham Foundation for Advanced Studies in the Fine Arts.

Designed by Leslie Fitch
Set in Berthold Akzidenz-Grotesk Pro and Emigré Filosofia type by Leslie Fitch
Printed at Tien Wah Press in Singapore

Library of Congress Cataloging-in-Publication Data
Levine, Neil, 1941–
Modern architecture: representation and reality / Neil Levine.
p. cm.
Includes bibliographical references and index.
ISBN 978-0-300-14567-0
(cloth : alk. paper)
1. Architecture, Modern—18th century. 2. Architecture, Modern—19th century. 3. Architecture, Modern—20th century. I. Title.
NA500.L48 2010
724—dc22 2009017329

A catalogue record for this book is available from the British Library.
This paper meets the requirements of ANSI/NISO Z39.48-1992 (Permanence of Paper).

10 9 8 7 6 5 4 3 2 1

Jacket illustrations: (*circular plan, background*) Louis I. Kahn, Trenton Jewish Community Center, Day Camp, 1956–57 (fig. 8.30, detail); (*center*) Etienne-Louis Boullée, cenotaph for Isaac Newton project, 1784; from left, figs. 3.12, 3.10, and 3.11; (*bottom*) Henri Labrouste, Bibliothèque Sainte-Geneviève, Paris, 1838–50, reading room, final study for ironwork, 1846 (fig. 4.38, detail).

Page vi: Fig. 6.42, detail
Below: Fig. 7.6, detail

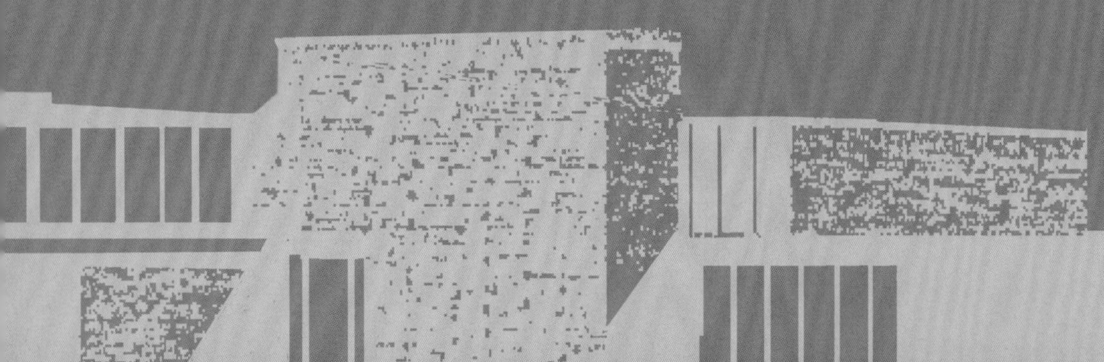

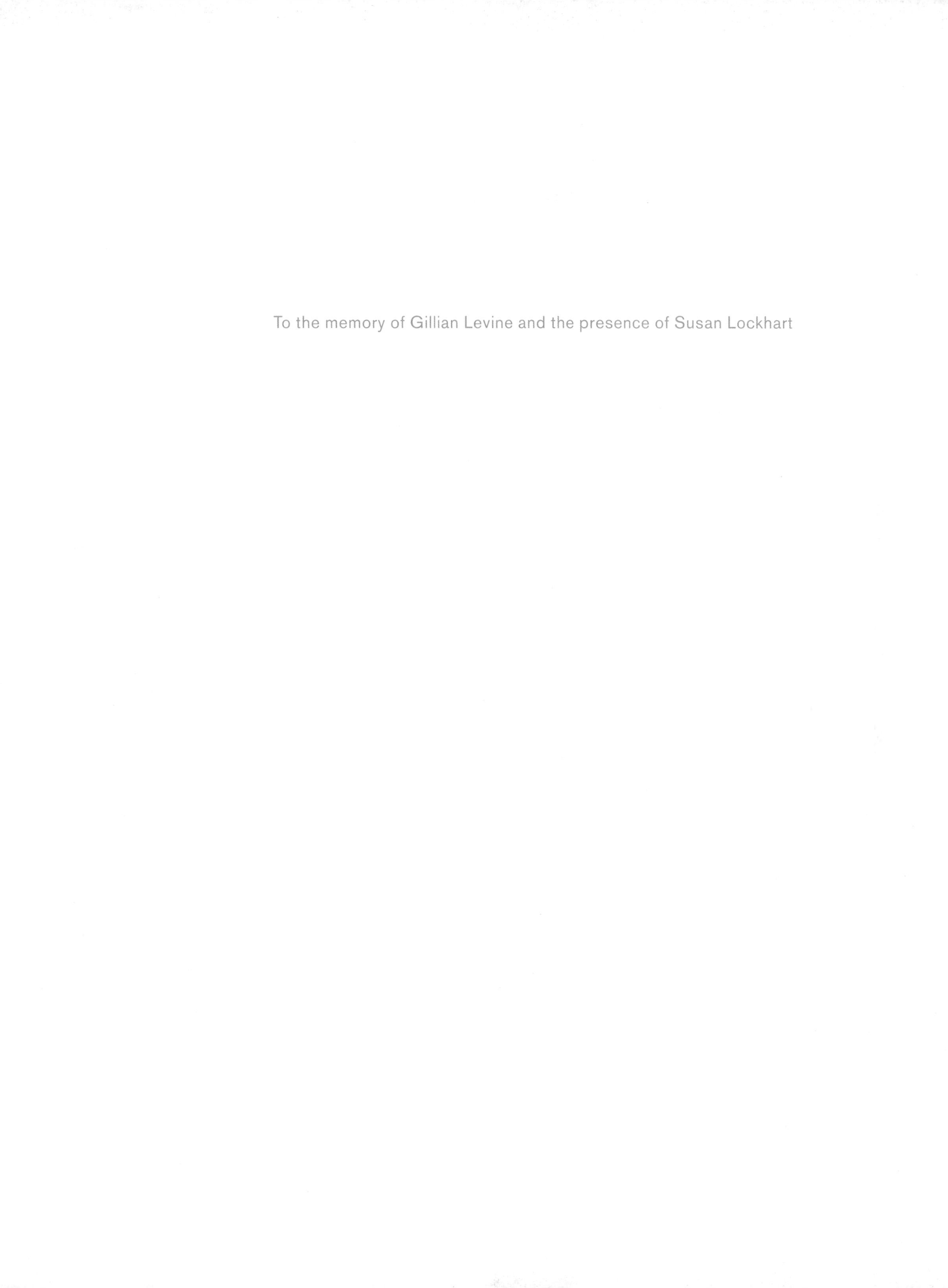

To the memory of Gillian Levine and the presence of Susan Lockhart

Contents

Preface

THIS BOOK BEGAN LIFE as the Slade Lectures on Fine Art, which I was honored to give at Cambridge University in England in 1994–95. Although I had worked on a number of the subjects before bringing them together in the way they were presented there, and now here, the extended format of eight lectures allowed me to develop my thoughts more thoroughly on how the issue of representation could be understood as the underlying factor in the development of modern architecture. Aside from the addition of an introduction and conclusion, plus some rearrangement of the parts along with further research and thinking about matters both general and specific, the eight chapters here fundamentally follow the course outlined in the earlier eight lectures.

Between the delivery of the Slade Lectures and the completion of the book manuscript, I had the opportunity to publish slightly different, stand-alone versions of three of the chapters. The first to appear was an early version of chapter 7, published as "'The Significance of Facts': Mies's Collages Up Close and Personal" in *Assemblage: A Critical Journal of Architecture and Design Culture* 37 (December 1998). Following that, my reading of Castle Howard, which forms the basis of chapter 1, appeared in the September 2003 issue of the *Journal of the Society of Architectural Historians* (vol. 62) as "Castle Howard and the Emergence of the Modern Architectural Subject." Most recently, a condensed version of chapter 8, entitled "The Architecture of the Unfinished and the Example of Louis Kahn," was included in and provided the subtitle for *Fragments: Architecture and the Unfinished: Essays Presented to Robin Middleton*, edited by Barry Bergdoll and Werner Oechslin (London: Thames & Hudson, 2006). I am grateful to the editors of these publications for their often helpful advice. In this regard, I would like to single out K. Michael Hays, Alicia Kennedy, Zeynep Çelik, Nancy Stieber, and Barry Bergdoll.

I have had the fortune to present a good deal of this

material to colleagues who have offered much helpful feedback and criticism. I want to thank, in particular, Ewa Lajer-Burcharth for inviting me to participate in the Seminar on Visual Representation and Cultural History at Harvard University's Humanities Center; Robin Middleton for his invitation to speak in the University Seminar program at the Temple Hoyne Buell Center for the Study of American Architecture at Columbia University; Katherine Fischer-Taylor for asking me to participate in the Chicago Group on Modern France at the University of Chicago; Renzo Dubbini for the invitation to talk in the Henri Labrouste Symposium at the Istituto Universitario di Architettura di Venezia; and Christine Poggi for asking me to present in the session on collage she organized at the College Art Association. In addition, the talks given in the faculty colloquium of my own Department of History of Art and Architecture at Harvard; the History and Theory lecture series in the Architecture School at the Massachusetts Institute of Technology; and, especially, the Interfaculty Colloquium of Harvard's Department of History of Art and Architecture and Graduate School of Design helped me enormously in developing and refining my ideas.

A number of colleagues and friends have, over the years, been of considerable importance to me in this work, most notably Vincent Scully, David Van Zanten, Robin Middleton, Tom Beeby, and Michael Hays. To my colleague Alina Payne I owe a tremendous debt of gratitude for the intelligence and diligence with which she read and criticized the manuscript. Others who have aided in particular ways are James Ackerman, George Baird, Martin Bressani, Effi Casey, David Friedman, Sarah Williams Goldhagen, Antoine Picon, Kathryn Smith, and Sarah Whiting. Cammie McAtee and Erica Allen-Kim proved to be extraordinary researchers. Mary Daniels, Cole Roskam, Gaku Kondo, and Erik Ghenoiu were also very helpful on specific issues. For their help in securing and providing illustrations I am grateful to David R. Phillips, Wim de Wit, Bob Zinck, Steve Sylvester, Susan Palmer, Nabil Boutros, Spruill Harder, Scott Krafft, Adam Kellie, Timothy McCarthy, Barbara Sachäche, Nigel Wilkins, Blanche Legendre, Max Protetch, Stuart Krimko, and Helen Carey.

For the research on Castle Howard, I am particularly grateful to Christopher Ridgway, curator of Castle Howard, for facilitating a second, two-day visit in the fall of 1994 and for his generosity in providing documentary and photographic materials. For their aid in securing illustrations, I also thank Alison Brisby, Castle Howard; Susan Pugh, National Monuments Record, Swindon; Pete Clark, Joe Coagy, Stephen Hayles, Becca Hickman, and Tony Vaughan, Ordnance Survey, Southampton; Camilla Costello, *Country Life;* and Claudia Ponton, Art Resource. To Kerry Downes I owe my initial exposure to Vanbrugh's and Hawksmoor's architecture as well as to the site of Castle Howard.

Access to original drawings and documents of Henri Labrouste was made possible by the extraordinary generosity of Yvonne Labrouste; Léon Malcotte; Madeleine Boy, former administrator, and Marie-Hélène de La Mure, curator of special collections, Bibliothèque Sainte-Geneviève, Paris; and Jean Adhémar, former director, and Yvonne Jestaz, former curator, Cabinet des Estampes, Bibliothèque Nationale, Paris. Access to drawings and documents of Frank Lloyd Wright, not to speak of priceless information and advice, was provided by Bruce Brooks Pfeiffer, Margo Stipe, and Oscar Muñoz of the Frank Lloyd Wright Archives, Frank Lloyd Wright Foundation, Taliesin West, Scottsdale, Arizona. A great debt of gratitude is also owed to the following homeowners and stewards who allowed me to visit the buildings discussed here and provided important documentation. They include Cheryl Bachand, Elaine Harrington, Meg Klinkow, Betty Leigh, Karen McSweeney, Joan Mercuri, John Michiels, Frank Pond, Tom Schmidt, Dale Smirl, Donna Taylor, John Thorpe, and Lynda Waggoner.

Although I did not write about the Heller House, being a house guest there numerous times gave me a special experience of Wright's work of the period. For this opportunity, I especially thank Judith Bromley and Serafino Garella.

For their help in my research on Mies van der Rohe, I should like to thank Paul Campagna and George Danforth, both of whom studied and worked with the architect in the early 1940s and graciously allowed me to interview them. Danforth and Franz Schulze were kind enough to read an early version of this chapter. Although both strongly disagreed with its basic thrust, many of their specific criticisms were extremely helpful. I am also grateful to Pierre Adler of the Mies van der Rohe Archive, Museum of Modern Art, New York, for giving so generously of his time and advice and to Cammie McAtee for reading this chapter in a near final state and providing many important comments.

Anne Tyng was an important source of information on Louis Kahn. Sarah Williams Goldhagen shared with me her knowledge of Kahn and provided a significant critical reading of an early version of chapter 8. Joan Chan helped interpret some of the structural aspects of the initial proposal for the Trenton Bath House roof. Julia Converse of the Architectural Archives, School of Design, University of Pennsylvania, made the important Kahn archives available to me; William Whitaker, curator of the Architectural Archives, was extremely helpful in providing illustrations.

My colleagues at the University of Cambridge were as gracious as hosts as they were helpful intellectually. To John Gage, who was chair of the Department of History of Art, go my warmest thanks. To Peter Carl, Deborah Howard, Jean-Michel Massing, John Sergeant, and Dalibor Vesely go my deep appreciation for their friendship and engagement. I also thank Lord St John of Fawsley, former master of Emmanuel College, along with the other members of Emmanuel's faculty and staff, for all they did to make my stay in Cambridge so enjoyable and productive.

On a more personal, though no less intellectual level, I would like to thank two dear friends, Bénédicte Pesle and Arlette Marchal, for all they have done for me and given to me over the years. As the dedication of this book shows, I feel I owe my deepest sense of gratitude to two special people in my life: my late wife, Gillian Levine, for the untold amount of work, thinking, and criticism we did together on subjects both directly and indirectly related to this book; and my present wife, Susan Jacobs Lockhart, who has shared her ears and her eyes, her wisdom, her knowledge, and her profound critical mind with me in making this manuscript into a book. Finally, I would like to express my great appreciation to Patricia Fidler for standing by this project and helping to see it to completion and to Daniella Berman, Heidi Downey, Leslie Fitch, Duke Johns, John Long, and Mary Mayer for their wonderful efforts in the making of this book.

Introduction

OF ALL THE ARTS, modern architecture has shown itself to be the least comfortable with its own history. In most accounts, there is an assumption of a direct descent from the eighteenth to the twentieth century, yet an almost total disconnect between the early manifestations of formative ideas and their later realization. The schizophrenic nineteenth century occupies a no-man's-land of historical revivalism and eclecticism, where engineering appears temporarily to supersede architecture as the place for experimentation and invention in building. This book proposes a new way to think about modern architecture as a continuous historical development.[1]

Instead of focusing on the issue of style, which has usually served only to isolate one century from another, my emphasis will be placed on the more fundamental question of representation, which will be seen to account for the changing role historical precedent played in the generation of architectural form. The underlying theme is the recognition of the medium's deliberate engagement with the means and purposes of representation at the very beginning of the modern period in the eighteenth century and the vicissitudes of that engagement during the following two centuries under the pressure of new material, functional, and expressive concerns. From this perspective, I hope, will emerge a map of the main outlines of a more unified and coherent history of modern architecture than is now available.

Since the concept of representation as I am using it is far less common in the discussion of architecture than it is in painting and sculpture (where, in modern criticism, it is usually conceived in opposition to abstraction), let me offer a few words about what I do and do not mean by the term. To begin with, I am not using the word in the technical sense of referring to the two- and three-dimensional means employed by architects to convey their ideas on paper, in models, or in digital form. While those media may ultimately have a significant effect on how one reads a design, and may even at times inform the design itself, the illustrative techniques may or may not be used for representational purposes and thus have only limited bearing on any discussion of the origin of forms and their meanings.[2]

Nor am I using the term simply as an equivalent for the concept of sign or symbol. Such uses are common to any semiological system and have no special relevance to the problem of representation as a means or mode of architectural expression. All buildings can be said to represent the ideas of their makers in the same way that a verbal expression is said to represent a thought. In this sense, the tree-lined avenues radiating from the central location of Louis XIV's bedroom at Versailles allow that seventeenth-century palace and its gardens to be read as the representational image of the absolute monarchy of the Sun King, just as the standardized steel sections and factory-like appearance of Ludwig Mies van der Rohe's Minerals and Metals Research Building at the Illinois Institute of Technology in Chicago (1942–43) can be interpreted as a sign of modern industrial conditions and thus as representing the radically altered purpose of architectural design in the machine age (figs. I.1–2).

I.1 Louis LeVau, André Le Nôtre, Jules Hardouin-Mansart, and others. Palace of Versailles, begun 17th century. Aerial view, from southwest

I.2 Ludwig Mies van der Rohe. Minerals and Metals Research Building, Illinois (formerly Armour) Institute of Technology, Chicago, 1942–43. Exterior

Symbolic representations through architecture can range from the abstract to the figurative, which in turn can extend from the sublime—the Gothic cathedral as Heavenly City of Jerusalem or Bible of the Poor; the Byzantine church as Dome of Heaven—to the ridiculous. The pedigree of the latter can also be traced back to the eighteenth century, when the idea of an *architecture parlante*, or "speaking architecture," became somewhat of a fashion.[3] Claude-Nicolas Ledoux's circular design for a house for a barrel maker in the form of a barrel, and his phallus-shaped project for an Oikéma, a public brothel meant to instill the virtue of marriage through an overindulgence in vice, are two notorious examples of this sort of graphic symbolism (fig. I.3). Their twentieth-century progeny can be found in countless buildings for world's fairs—like Walter Dorwin Teague's National Cash Register Building at New York's 1939–40 World of Tomorrow, where the daily and cumulative totals of visitors to the site were rung up on a gigantic cash register that formed the roof of the structure—and in roadside or highway locations, like the Newark, Ohio, corporate headquarters of the Longaberger Basket Company, built in the mid-1990s as a gigantic replica of one of their best-selling products, the medium-sized market basket

I.3 Claude-Nicolas Ledoux. Barrelmaker's House and Workshop project, Ideal City of Chaux, ca. 1784–89. Elevation. From Ledoux, *L'Architecture considérée sous le rapport de l'art, des moeurs et de la législation,* 1804

I.4 NBBJ and Korda/Nemeth Engineering (with Dave Longaberger). Longaberger Company Headquarters, Newark, Ohio, 1995–97. Exterior

(fig. I.4). In giving literal expression to their programs, such structures can be thought of as carrying to an extreme the modern injunction that "form should ever follow function," although Louis Sullivan, whose phrase that is, would certainly turn over in his grave if he were to see to what figurative ends his words were put.

What I shall be examining here, rather, is the more general issue of the use of conventional forms and recognizable objects by architects to create buildings for any and all conceivable expressive purposes. This more categorical concept of representation, which takes into account the process by which conventional forms are generated, speaks to the question of how buildings themselves come to be representational. Such a definition of the term, which has its source in the classical theory of mimesis and its closest analogues in the figural arts of painting and sculpture, can be understood in two somewhat different though related senses. The first has to do with the rhetorical dimension of architecture in its capacity to declare its significance through the spectacle of display.

The early eighteenth-century Blenheim Palace in Woodstock, northwest of London, by John Vanbrugh and Nicholas Hawksmoor, clearly exceeds in size, shape, and decorative elaboration what might have been necessary or even appropriate for a nobleman's country house, for it was meant to be much more than that (fig. I.5). As an expression of the gratitude of the English nation to the Duke of Marlborough for his victory over Louis XIV at Blenheim in the War of the Spanish Succession, the house—as an object of representation—took its name not from its owner but from the battle he won, and its crowning device on the attic of the garden facade not from Marlborough's coat of arms but from a bust of Louis XIV, seized as a trophy from the city gate of Tournai after the British sack of the city in 1709 (fig. I.6).

In seventeenth- and eighteenth-century Europe, a distinction was made in domestic architecture between the state or ceremonial apartments and the private quarters. The first were for show and the others, behind the scenes, were for daily use. The "show" aspect has always been a significant feature of architectural expression and, in most cultures and periods, has been what distinguishes architecture from mere building. Although the distinction between architecture and building has become less clear, or at least less obvious, since the eighteenth century, the differences between the representational and the utilitarian remain just as operative, if only more subtle in the ways they manifest themselves.

I.5 John Vanbrugh and Nicholas Hawksmoor. Blenheim Palace, Woodstock, Oxfordshire, 1705–24. Garden (south) facade

That brings me to the second meaning of the term "representation," the one that will guide the course of my analysis. Representation in this sense concerns the form and structure of rhetoric rather than simply its outward effects. It describes an essentially theatrical situation in which a virtual or ideal set of recognizable figures or elements is perceived as standing for, that is to say, representing, an absent set of real ones to which they are meant and believed to correspond. The success of the rhetoric lies in its power to make the fiction stand for the reality, to convince the viewer of the "truthfulness" of the representational elements. In architecture, as in theater or the other visual arts, the process of deception occurs in the slippage from truth to verisimilitude—from the reality to the appearance of it.

We can see the process at work already in the very beginning of the early modern period, in the architecture of the early Renaissance in Italy. In the unfinished fifteenth-century Rucellai Palace in Florence, usually attributed to Leon Battista Alberti, the real, rubble stone construction of the building is masked by a relatively thin veneer of classical

I.6 Blenheim Palace. Garden (south) facade, central pavilion

I.7 Leon Battista Alberti (attrib. to). Rucellai Palace, Florence, ca. 1455–70. Exterior

I.8 Colosseum, Rome, 72–80. Exterior

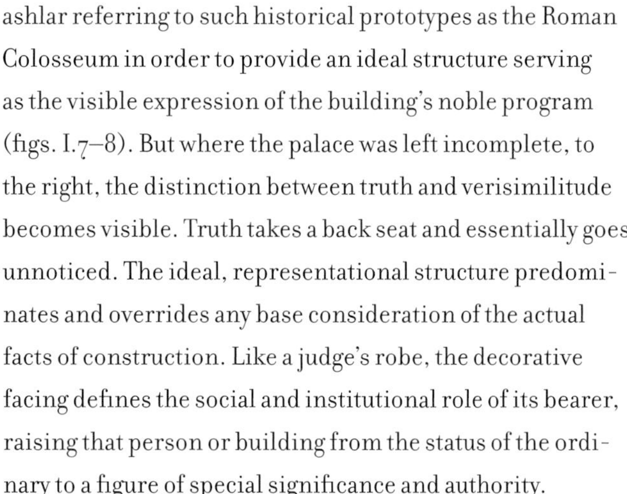

ashlar referring to such historical prototypes as the Roman Colosseum in order to provide an ideal structure serving as the visible expression of the building's noble program (figs. I.7–8). But where the palace was left incomplete, to the right, the distinction between truth and verisimilitude becomes visible. Truth takes a back seat and essentially goes unnoticed. The ideal, representational structure predominates and overrides any base consideration of the actual facts of construction. Like a judge's robe, the decorative facing defines the social and institutional role of its bearer, raising that person or building from the status of the ordinary to a figure of special significance and authority.

The facade of the Rucellai Palace was in fact conceived and built only as a facade, a revetment of the wall enclosing the building's recently completed interior spaces.[4] Yet despite its obvious representationalism, both in the sense of pure "show" and in that of virtuality, the building is rarely described in such terms. The relationship between the decorative elements and the tectonic conditions they articulate are invariably confined to a discussion of the surface revetment itself, as if that virtual structure were the real one and not merely a classical representation supported by it. This is hardly surprising, since architecture by and large is almost never thought of as representational in the same sense that painting and sculpture were and often still are.

Architecture, in contrast to the so-called figurative arts, is generally considered to be inherently abstract and self-referential in its formal language. This perception no doubt arises in large part from the historical identification of representation with the classical concept of the imitation of nature. Where paintings or sculpture might reproduce with a certain degree of exactitude the physical likeness of an existing natural object, architecture, even though included as one of the imitative arts in classical theory, was ordinarily thought to have a more distant, abstract relation to the natural world. It could only imitate the underlying logic or inner workings of nature rather than its outward forms.[5] Reference to preexisting objects was limited to and mediated by human constructions, as in the Rucellai Palace's transformation of the Roman Colosseum prototype.

The rise of a purely abstract, nonrepresentational art in the early twentieth century had, by all accounts, a powerful and formative influence on the development of modern architecture. This is a subject that will be more fully discussed in chapter 7. The reason I mention it here is that, by offering an image of what abstraction in the fullest sense of the word might be, which is to say, the opposite of representational, we are given a basis for understanding the concept of representation outside the theory of imitation of nature and capable of being applied to architecture in the same way it might be to the arts of painting and sculpture. A comparison of Mies van der Rohe's Mosler House, built in Potsdam-Neubabelsberg in 1924–26, with his slightly later German Pavilion for the International Exhibition in Barcelona of 1929 (see figs. 7.8, 7.10) reveals in the most direct and powerful way not just the influence of the new abstraction on the architect's architectural thinking but also, and most critically for us, the representationalism of the earlier building. Its allusion to eighteenth-century German manor houses is no different in kind from the Rucellai Palace's reference to Roman antiquity.

Although it did not take long for historians engaged in the exegesis of the new, abstract architecture of the 1920s to begin to define the antecedent historicism as representational, the long-held belief in the fundamental and universal self-referentiality of architecture as an abstract medium has never quite been relinquished. It also played a significant role in the way representation was judged, giving it a pejorative connotation that also has never quite disappeared. Writing as early as 1928, Henry-Russell Hitchcock spoke of the new architecture as eschewing "the sentimental comfort of representation" and described the characteristic "decorative detail" of representational architecture as "being more or less equivalent to the recognizable elements in painting and sculpture."[6] Twenty years later, he noted that, while "the rather obvious analogy between copying natural forms and re-using architectural motifs—both generally characteristic of the Western European tradition since the Renaissance—may not be exact," "the rejection of the one on the part of modern painters and sculptors and of the other on the part of modern architects . . . has certainly seemed to the public (as to the artists themselves) very closely related. Both represent a refusal to imitate and an emphasis on art as positive creation." But because "the imitation of natural objects" still remained for Hitchcock the defining term of representation, he continued to maintain the customary position that "architecture has always been essentially an abstract art."[7]

Some efforts were made in these same years to interpret premodern architecture in representational terms. The most notable and influential of these was certainly Richard Krautheimer's pioneering essay of 1942 proposing an "Iconography of Medieval Architecture," in which he maintained that a large group of central-plan churches in the Middle Ages were not merely to be thought of as deriving from the Constantinian Church of the Holy Sepulcher in Jerusalem but should be understood as intentional, though for the most part imaginary, representations of the earlier structure.[8] Still, it was not until the 1970s, with the devolution of the historic modern movement and the rise of postmodernism, that the concept of representation, now entirely divorced from classical imitation theory, came to be widely accepted as a way of distinguishing a historically referential mode of design from an abstract or nonreferential one. Paradoxically, such an oppositional positioning came at a time when art itself was blurring the boundaries between abstraction and representation, in part due to the embrace of media such as video, photography, and film.[9]

The two most well-known proponents of the opposing positions were Robert Venturi and Peter Eisenman, whose arguments for an architecture of representation on the one hand and an architecture of abstraction on the other, will be discussed in the book's conclusion. For many architects at the time, such as Richard Meier, the question seemed almost a black-and-white one. "Ornamentation and symbolism are both aspects of representational art," he said in 1987. "As an artist or as an architect one has a choice: representational art or abstract art. Abstraction allows architecture to express its own organisational and spatial consequences, it permits the creation of space without confusing its volume with any superimposed system of meaning or value. It allows architecture to be what it needs to be, namely, tectonic form expressing anti-tectonic concepts."[10]

Despite the clarity with which the issue of representation was articulated in the 1970s, '80s, and '90s, few attempts were made to apply it in a broad or sustained manner to the history of modern architecture as a whole. Mitchell Schwarzer, for instance, used the concept in his close analysis of the theoretical argument advanced by the Berlin architect and historian Karl Bötticher in the 1840s to distinguish between the structural core of Greek buildings, which he called the *werkform*, and its decorative integument, the *kunstform*. The "representational," as the historicizing artistic overlay, was contrasted with the "ontological," the underlying structural reality.[11] Kenneth Frampton, in his *Studies in Tectonic Culture*, which offered a broad overview of significant moments and figures in the evolution of modern architecture and was published the year my work on this book began, used the concept of representation only intermittently and with varying meanings, preferring instead to emphasize the theme of the "poetics of construction" and the expressivity of form it gave rise to in building.[12]

My focus on the issue of representation is not an arbitrary one, nor is the distinction it raises between a referential system of forms based on nature as opposed to one based on history. The concept of representation as I apply it lies at the very foundations of modern architectural thought in the eighteenth century. First with the broadening of the historical horizon in the architecture of the English landscape garden that we will see in Castle Howard and then, even more important, in the postulation by Marc-Antoine Laugier of the primitive hut as the basis for the development of the classical architecture of Greece and Rome, the problem of representation became a fundamental factor in the architecture of the period. In these two occurrences in particular, the historical and the natural were each given new roles to play in the creation of a representational framework for modern architecture to adopt, to react against, to deny, or to transform.

While architects from the fifteenth through the early eighteenth centuries, based on their readings of Vitruvius, often alluded to a source for the classical orders either in the forms and proportions of the human body or in certain parts of the wood huts built by the primitive dwellers of Greece, no comprehensive theory of representation based on a natural or historical model emerged until Laugier made his radical proposition in 1753 that the primitive wood hut, which he described as being of such an originative character as to be deemed natural, was the model that the Greek temple imitated in stone and that all later architecture was bound to represent. Nature and history were thus aligned in a sequential process of transformation from one material to another that spoke of the grander transformation from the transience of nature's forms to the permanent record of history.

I.9 William Chambers. "The Primitive Buildings &c.," *A Treatise on Civil Architecture*, 1759

Needless to say, many immediately contested Laugier's theory. But even among those who did, such as William Chambers, the most important English architectural theorist of the period, the assumption of a comprehensive model for representation proved to be a compelling argument (fig. I.9). Although he rejected the prehistorical aspect of Laugier's mythic source in favor of a more traditional Vitruvian interpretation, Chambers nevertheless fully accepted the illusionism of the representational construct advanced by Laugier, as well as the link between structural form and decorative elaboration it implied. "Nature is the supreme and true model of the imitative arts," he wrote, "and the antique is to the architect, what nature is to the painter or sculptor; the source from which his chief knowledge must be collected; the model upon which his taste must be formed."[13]

The transformation of the primitive forms of wooden shelters into the sophisticated shapes of the ancient Greek temple became the leading edge of critical thought in the Enlightenment as the theory of representation came under intense discussion and scrutiny. But what started as a neoclassical justification for a systematic and rational deployment of the antique orders, based on a thoroughly revised classical notion of mimesis, almost inevitably expanded into the larger questions of the relationship between the ideal and the real, between decoration and construction, between form and function. It is within this continuing discourse of representation that the evolution of modern architectural theory and practice took its bearings.

To trace that evolution as precisely as I would like to, I have adopted a case study method. Each of the eight chapters, which are fairly evenly distributed over the nearly 300-year period from around 1700 to around 1975, will be devoted to a single seminal building, architect, or theoretician, or a small group of closely related individuals or works. The people and the buildings are all well known and form part of the canon of modern architecture. My goal is not to revise or rewrite the history of the period by proposing a new set of landmarks or luminaries. Rather, it is to try to read the existing ones in a new, more insightful way.

The first chapter, as previously mentioned, considers the early eighteenth-century house and gardens of Castle Howard, designed by John Vanbrugh and Nicholas Hawksmoor over the course of the first third of the eighteenth century. Now considered to be the first of the new type of English garden that rewrote the classical rules about how buildings and their landscape settings should relate to one another, Castle Howard provides a remarkable and instructive contrast between the traditional Baroque architecture of the house and the more advanced ideas that govern the landscape and its outbuildings. This contrast reveals not only a move beyond the norms of decorum that controlled and directed the classical system of rhetorical display evident in the house; more important, it displays the first signs of a use of historical forms to serve a representational role comparable to the way images function in paintings.

This introduction of what I call "the subject matter of history" forms the background for my discussion in chapter 2 of Laugier's theory of the primitive hut, which constituted the centerpiece of his widely read text, the *Essai sur l'architecture*. This singular explanation of the origin of the trabeated system of Greek architecture in the natural model of the primitive wood hut was the critical factor in the debate on representation that ensued over the following decades, and it was still seen as the main issue to contest not only by Augustus Welby Pugin at the end of the 1830s but also by Eugène-Emmanuel Viollet-le-Duc as late as the 1860s. The close analysis of Laugier's text, and especially its restructuring of the classical concept of verisimilitude, will be illustrated by Jacques-Germain Soufflot's Parisian Church of Sainte-Geneviève, which Laugier himself believed gave built form to his thoughts. The final section of the chapter will examine Antoine-Chrysostôme Quatremère de Quincy's response to Laugier and his conversion of the theory into a doctrinal position of neoclassicism (the prefix "neo" being understood throughout the book as not simply a way of defining a new style but of generating a radical new meaning, akin to its present-day use in the political label "neoconservative").

Chapter 3 is the longest and most diverse, insofar as it deals with three different architects from three different countries over a period extending from the 1780s through the 1830s. The three are the Frenchman Etienne-Louis Boullée, the Englishman John Soane, and the Prussian Karl Friedrich Schinkel. What links their careers is the shared inheritance of the representational culture of neoclassicism and the desire on the part of each architect to find a way beyond its constraints through the means of abstraction (in the pre-twentieth-century meaning of the term). Boullée, the oldest of the three, took the naturalism of the Laugier model to its extreme, advancing a type of imitation of nature that seemed to fulfill his original intention to become a painter rather than an architect. Soane and Schinkel, on the other hand, developed their different takes on the possibilities of abstracting classical forms and compositions through a broad, synthetic view of history that revealed the diminishing role of neoclassical imitation theory.

If Laugier represents the fundamental premise in the development outlined so far, the writings and work of the two architects discussed in chapter 4 define a turning point that was never reversed. Although the mid-nineteenth-century architects Pugin and Henri Labrouste might seem at first to have almost nothing in common—the one being a Catholic convert single-mindedly devoted to a revival of English Gothic architecture and the other a dispassionate secularist committed to a broad historical inclusivism—the two of them, in their very different ways, developed a new materialist and realist approach to design that undermined the conventional concept of representation by replacing the classical idea of constructing decoration with the post-classical one of decorating construction. Pugin's Church of St. Giles, Cheadle, characterized by its exclusive reliance on preindustrial materials, and Labrouste's Bibliothèque Sainte-Geneviève in Paris, notable for its precocious use of exposed iron, are the buildings on which my analysis will be based.

Once history finally replaced nature as the sole basis for representation, and the new realism of decorated construction undermined the transformational economy of verisimilitude, architects were faced with the pressing questions of not only how to deal with the issue of historical reference but also whether representation as such was a necessary condition of expression. In the fifth chapter, I shall first analyze some of the writings and experimental projects of Viollet-le-Duc that were so important, in the third quarter of the nineteenth century, in showing how one might use historical models without a referential purpose. The resulting "erosion of representation," as I call it, will then be related to the radical theorizing and design of the "tall building" by Louis Sullivan at the turn of the twentieth century. Directly basing his ideas on the new conditions of steel-frame construction and conceiving the problem in typological terms, Sullivan developed a functional definition of form through the proposition that "form ever follows function," which, while not rejecting the representational element in fact certainly allowed for its elimination in theory, thereby serving to redefine how representation might recur in modern terms.

Each of the final three chapters will concentrate on a single architect and group of works that define significant moments in the development of modern architecture in the twentieth century, with the goal of showing how each figure responded to the challenge of the problem of representation and, in turn, offered a quintessentially modern strategy for its resolution. The discussion of Frank Lloyd Wright's work in chapter 6 begins with his translation of Sullivan's ideas regarding the commercial high-rise into the area of domestic architecture, where, through an elaboration of a building's spatial structure, he was able to dissolve and disaggregate the representational indices in a manner akin to contemporaneous Cubist painting in Europe. After this initial phase of work, I will review how the architect regrouped those design elements to reference nature directly and thereby establish a new identity between building and landscape.

With the architecture of Mies van der Rohe as its point of focus, chapter 7 examines the influence of the abstract, nonrepresentational painting and sculpture that developed in Europe in the 1910s and '20s on the so-called Modern Movement in architecture and traces the transformations of that architecture's purist forms through the post–World War II era into a material-based representation of structure that I shall describe, following Clement Greenberg's lead, as a type of "homeless representation." The link between Mies's nonrepresentational work of the 1920s and his use of the applied steel I-beam from the late 1940s on as a kind of surrogate classical order will be seen to lie in the extraordinary series of collages the architect made during the war years, in which he used preexisting, readymade images to create the representational framework of the designs.

I have chosen the architecture of Louis Kahn between 1950 and the early 1970s as the subject for the final chapter, in part because it brings to a conclusion the schema of events that had its start in the eighteenth century and in part because it lies on the cusp of postmodernism and can, indeed, be viewed as opening directly onto that revision of modern architecture's history. The discussion of Kahn's work and thought will move from its early phase, highly influenced by Mies as well as Le Corbusier, to the architect's uniquely intense effort beginning in the mid-1950s to come to terms with the perceived need for a "new monumentality" (the phrase was Sigfried Giedion's) by means of a readjustment of the material forms of architecture to their historical prototypes. Grounded in a theory of design that might be said to reverse the Sullivan formula in its placement of form ahead of function, Kahn was able to reconceptualize the idea of representation in architecture through a reliance on the concept of the "unfinished." This conceit allowed for a clear statement and perception of historical reference, while at the same time taking into account the modern demand for unmitigated material expression and openness to a multiplicity of meanings.

In the brief conclusion to the book, I will first summarize how the discourse of representation revealed through my sequence of case studies informed the evolution of modern architecture and thus provides a coherent way to view that nearly three-century-long development. To highlight that coherency and frame it historically, I shall refer to the events of the mid- to later 1970s that announced a rupture with the immediate past and a new retrospective and critical take on modern architecture. This development almost immediately came to be called postmodernism. While the issue of representation versus abstraction was one of the most important and polemically charged elements in the postmodern debate, I shall focus on the underlying argument over the question of disciplinary self-reflexiveness and autonomy that lay at the heart of the revisionist program and that ushered in the changeover from the term "modern" to that of "modernism." The replacement of the word modern with modernist, which had occurred in the fields of art criticism and art history a good fifteen years before its currency in architectural theory and history, was far from merely a semantic shift. Rather, it signaled a historical realignment that provides an exceptional vantage point from which to review the history of modern architecture as a representational practice.

While this book is about representation as a mode of artistic practice, it is also a representation in itself of the history of modern architecture. And although the meaning of the word representation in the latter case is different from the former, it is still bound to the criterion of verisimilitude, or plausibility, and underwritten by the concept of exemplariness. The case-study method, chosen for the type and depth of analysis it allows, precluded the idea of a survey and mandated a series of decisions about which figures or buildings would best exemplify a moment in time and its major artistic achievements. Fourteen such examples are not many when one considers the span of time covered and the number of possibilities from which the selection had to be made.

These examples were intended to be indisputably significant, which is why they are canonic. I make no excuses for this. Still, many canonic examples were left out. There is no question that Le Corbusier could have taken the place of Mies, or Ledoux that of Boullée. On the other hand, I do not believe that any other English garden could have replaced Castle Howard, any other mid-eighteenth-century figure could have replaced Laugier, any other mid-nineteenth-century figures were as important and influential as Pugin or Labrouste, or any other architect of the turn of the twentieth century was of greater significance than Wright—and that would include Peter Behrens and Auguste Perret. I doubt that anyone would contend that, among post–World War II figures, Eero Saarinen, Jørn Utzon, or Carlo Scarpa were more consequential than Louis Kahn. On the other hand, there might be some who would argue that, as a theorist of the third quarter of the nineteenth century, Gottfried Semper was a more profound and wide-ranging thinker than Viollet-le-Duc; but there is nothing in Semper's design work that comes close to Viollet-le-Duc's either in terms of impact on later generations or in terms of revealing the possibilities inherent in the theory itself.

My choices are also at one level, and a very important one at that, quite personal. The buildings and architects I have chosen to write about are ones I care deeply about and ones about which I feel that I have something particular and original to say. They are buildings I have studied closely over a long period of time and texts that I have read and reread again and again. In addition, that personal engagement no doubt accounts for a relatedness among the examples that provides a sequential character to the story they narrate. While Castle Howard was surely not known to Laugier, the impact of the English garden, which it initiated, was a significant element in the context out of which Laugier's ideas developed. On the other hand, Quatremère, Boullée, and Soane all owed specific debts to Laugier, while Pugin and Viollet-le-Duc both reacted directly to his concept of the imitative basis of the primitive hut. Labrouste not only handed on part of his teaching atelier to Viollet-le-Duc; his work in general also served as a point of departure for the latter. The line from Viollet-le-Duc to Sullivan to Wright, from Wright to Mies, and from the two of them to Kahn can also be easily traced.

The examples of Viollet-le-Duc and Sullivan, not to speak of Laugier, Pugin, and Kahn, also bring up an important aspect of my methodology that is well to mention here. Although theory plays an essential role in this study, the book is in no way a history of theory. The history of architectural theory and the history of architectural design, while they certainly overlap, are two quite different things. Words and objects are not the same. Words have meanings that relate to previous uses of words. While architects may use certain words or phrases to describe an intention or a result, this does not mean that the building or object in question is necessarily similar to or even related to an earlier or later design or theoretical construct described in the same verbal terms. A glaring instance of this is Henri Labrouste's reuse of Quatremère de Quincy's notion of art as "embellishment" to mean something diametrically opposed to what the earlier writer intended.[14] Theory will be used in this study only insofar as it informs or explicates practice. I am interested primarily in what the forms of buildings tell us. Reading texts like those by Laugier, Quatremère, Pugin, Viollet-le-Duc, Sullivan, and Kahn will be undertaken for the sole purpose of being able to read the buildings directly related to them more accurately and more meaningfully.

Not only is this not a history of theory. It is also not a history of how a certain theory played itself out over an extended period of time, such as, for instance, Rudolf Wittkower's *Architectural Principles in the Age of Humanism.*[15] The history I describe, through the rather neutral tool of representation, is a gradual one that reflects significant shifts in emphasis and direction and, most important, major changes in theoretical impulses. While Laugier clearly altered the course of development of European classicism, instituting what we now call neoclassicism, his whole framework of analysis was canceled out by developments in the 1830s and 1840s, so as to render irrelevant any attempt to see his concept of the primitive hut as seriously bearing on events in the twentieth century. I have not attempted any such form of proleptic argument for any of the figures discussed in this book.[16]

The gradualism of my vision of the period 1700–1975 programmatically avoids what I consider to be the most debilitating form of prolepsis that has affected the study of modern architecture, namely, the belief early on voiced by Emil Kaufmann and still fundamentally adhered to by many scholars that there is a direct link between the generation of Ledoux and Boullée and that of Mies and Le Corbusier based on a shared ideal of abstraction and autonomy that had been lost and, even worse, abused for at least a century if not more in between.[17] That epiphanic understanding of modern architecture clearly grew out of the extraordinary innovation of nonrepresentational painting and sculpture in the 1910s and early 1920s and the powerful effects that had on the architecture of the time. It provided modern architecture with a purist historical legacy that preserved it from contamination by the representational divagations of the intervening nineteenth century, what Giedion unforgettably described as the "historicizing masks" of its "stone stage sets."[18]

This study is written from an entirely different perspective. The abstraction that Le Corbusier and Mies supposedly shared with Ledoux and Boullée will be seen to be of an entirely different nature. Nor will these two quite separate generations of architects be seen to share a common idea of the autonomy of the medium of architecture. The main histories of modern architecture since the initial ones of the later 1920s have almost all been based on a teleology of abstraction. That was the direction things had to take, since that is where things had arrived. Since then, however, and especially since the emergence of Pop Art in the early 1960s, the clear-cut distinction between abstraction and representation has broken down, both in real terms and as a definition of modern values.[19] By adopting the expansive and broad-based concept of representation, this book will offer a postmodern view of modern architecture's development.

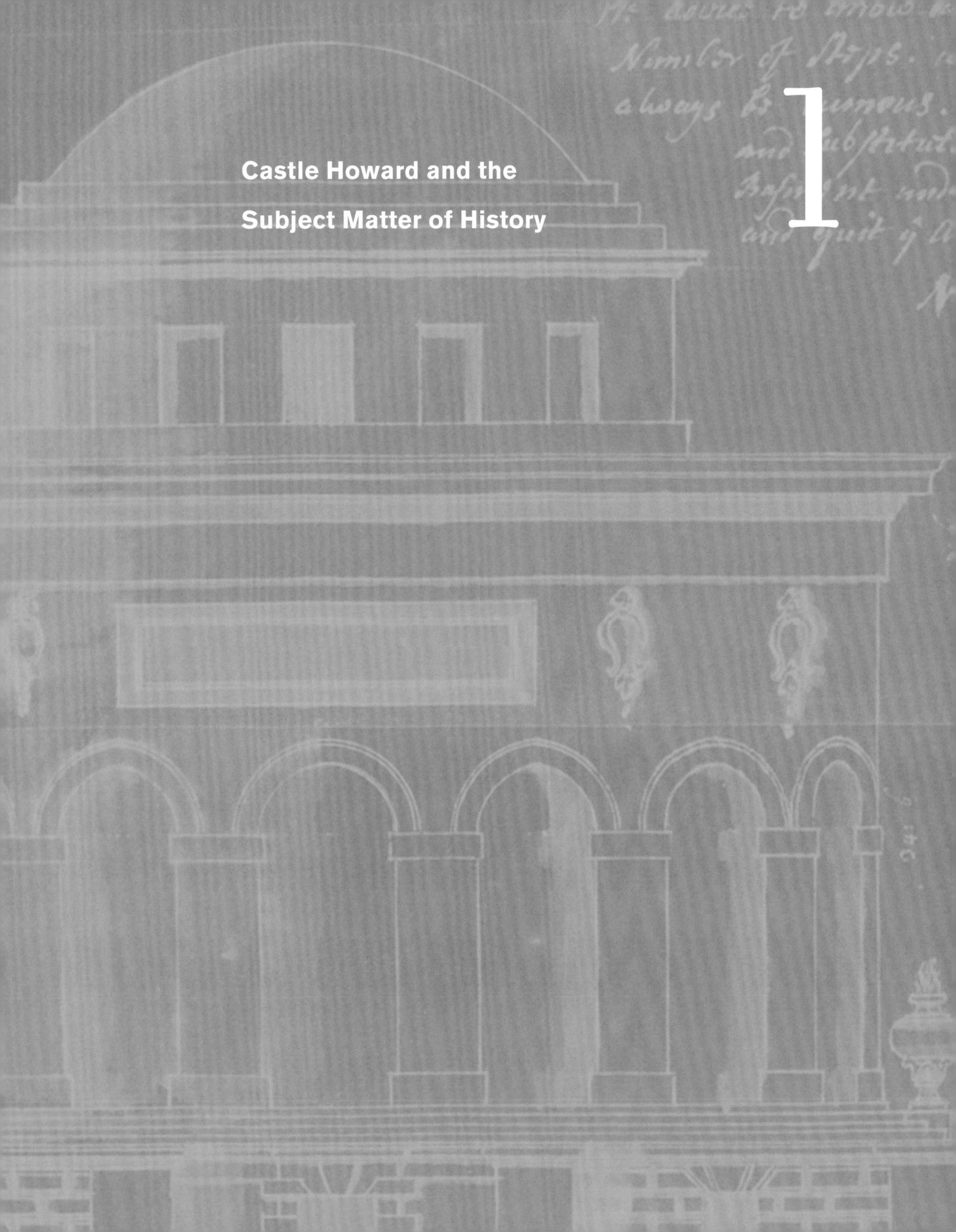

1

Castle Howard and the Subject Matter of History

THE ENGLISH LANDSCAPE GARDEN of the eighteenth century has long been considered the site where the disintegration of what Emil Kaufmann (1891–1953) referred to as the "Renaissance-Baroque system" of classical architecture began and where certain crucial ideas that can be called modern first appeared.[1] The two characteristics most commonly referred to are the naturalistic planning based on an incipient picturesque aesthetic and the eclectic mixture of building styles chosen for the garden structures themselves. Evidencing a new historical relativism, these structures included, most notably, the first experiments in the revival of Gothic architecture. The contrast between the apparent freedom and casualness of the picturesque approach and the geometric regularity and formal order that ruled the earlier Italian and French gardens was interpreted as an explicit sign of the rejection of existing classical conventions of representation and their replacement by something less formulaic and less prescriptive, more open to the variety and indeterminateness of individual experience. These transformations in the realms of architecture and landscape design were seen by the late 1940s as intimately related to the modern politics of liberalism, nascent ideas of nationalism, and the new psychology of perception grounded in the theory of associationism.[2]

Starting in the eighteenth century and up until at least the late 1960s, when the priority of Castle Howard finally began to be recognized, the landscape garden where many of these ideas were thought to have first come together was Stowe.[3] A palimpsest of successive interventions, Stowe was begun by Charles Bridgeman (1690–1738) and John Vanbrugh (1664–1726) in the period from 1713 to 1730, redesigned and enlarged by William Kent (1685–1748) and James Gibbs (1682–1754) in 1730–50, and altered and enlarged once again by Capability Brown (1715–1783) from 1750 to 1780 (fig. 1.1).[4] The earliest stages reveal a certain degree of looseness in the laying out of paths and landscape

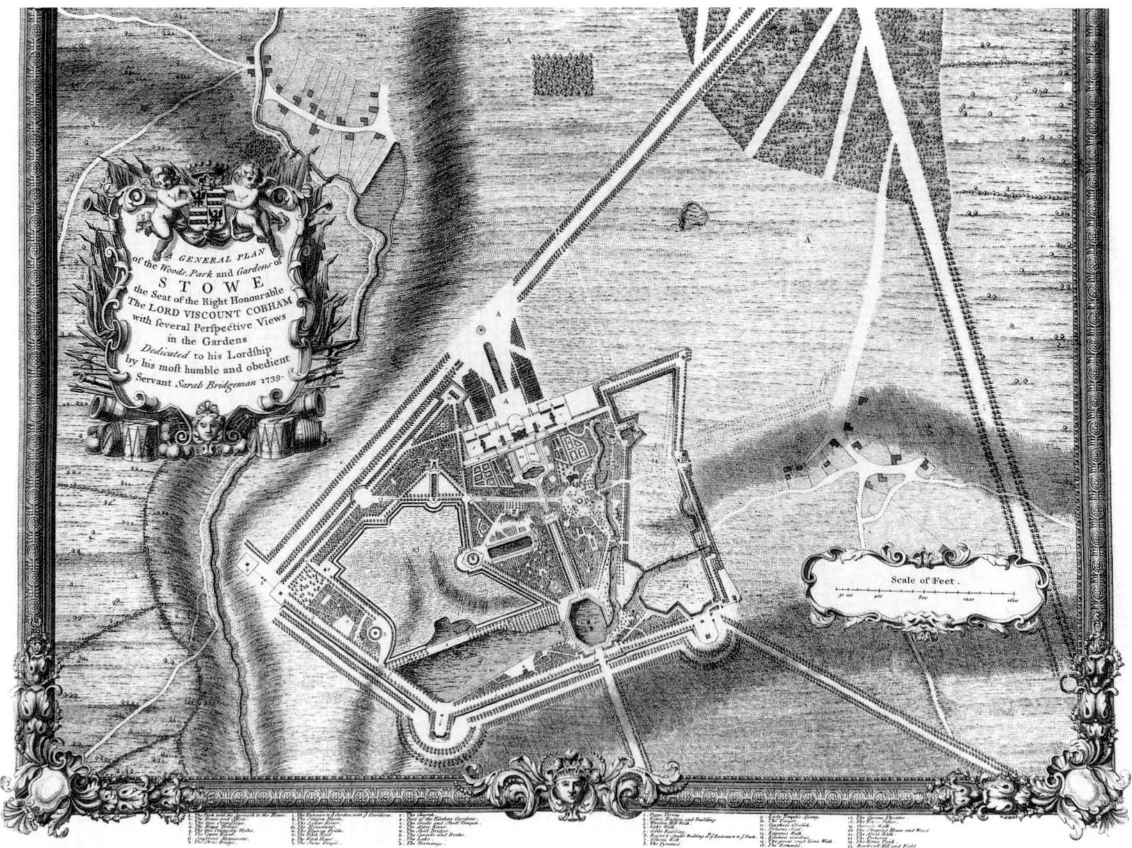

1.1 Stowe, Buckinghamshire. Garden, begun by Charles Bridgeman and John Vanbrugh, 1713–30; enlarged by William Kent and James Gibbs, 1730–50. Plan, 1739, detail. From Jacques Rigaud, *Stowe Gardens in Buckinghamshire,* 1746

elements, although there is little inventiveness in the architecture of the garden pavilions or any significant innovation in the way the buildings, as aspects of the landscape, were meant to be experienced and understood. This changed with the additions of Kent, Gibbs, and Brown. In the area of the gardens known as the Elysian Fields, designed by Kent in the 1730s and including structures by Gibbs, a pictorial grouping of buildings creates an architectural narrative of an allegorical sort, enacted by the individual structures and choreographed by the landscape. Reference and association provide character and meaning.

On an elevated site overlooking the so-called River Styx, a circular peripteral temple, based on the Roman "Temple of Vesta" at Tivoli, was dedicated to the theme of Ancient Virtue. Its meaning was made legible by its proximity to a shabbily and purposely built ruin, designed in a contemporary vernacular and dedicated to Modern Virtue. The allegory of the political ideas of Stowe's Whig owner, Lord Cobham, was completed by the view across the River Styx, from the Temple of Ancient Virtue down to the distant Temple of British Worthies (fig. 1.2). Shaped in the form of an exedra containing busts of figures from British history whose influence it was thought might help redefine the nation's future course, the British Worthies temple gives extension to the ancient idea of Virtue as it captures and reflects the view from on high. On the same side of the river as the British Worthies, across the Elysian Fields, the neo-Gothic Temple of Liberty, designed by Gibbs, provides a point of reference and perspective on England's illustrious medieval past.

Considered in terms of representation, the interventions at Stowe by Kent and Gibbs are interesting in a number

1.2 Stowe. View from Temple of Ancient Virtue to Temple of British Worthies, both by William Kent, 1730s

1.3 Claude Lorrain. *Aeneas at Delos*, 1672

of respects. The use of a relatively wide-ranging historical vocabulary to provide an appropriate associational inflection to each pavilion is an unusually early occurrence of this kind of eclecticism. Even more revolutionary, perhaps, is the relation established between the landscaped groupings and actual pictorial representations of such types of scenes by seventeenth-century painters like Claude Lorrain and Nicolas Poussin (fig. 1.3). Kent's "sequence of three-dimensional paintings," as Christopher Hussey has described them, asserts architecture's right to be considered on equal terms with the other visual arts as an art capable of imitating nature.[5] But, like the paintings the scenes reflect, the sequential views offered at Stowe remain curiously static experiences, framed set pieces of a transparent iconography implying a passive, neutral observer. At Castle Howard, by contrast, where the major work was nearly completed before Kent and Gibbs even began theirs at Stowe, a widely dispersed grouping of three seemingly unrelated structures—a temple, a mausoleum, and a pyramid—establishes distant focal points in the expansive landscape to create a spatial nexus in which the beholder must assume a new subjective stance and a more active role in the determination of meaning. The consequence of a much more profound reworking of the elements and methods of classical representation than Stowe, the combined landscape treatment and outbuildings at Castle Howard offer insights into the changes architecture underwent in the early eighteenth century.

Discussion of Castle Howard since the late 1960s has focused mainly on issues of agency and context: who was responsible for the design, how did the collaboration between architects and client work, what were the intentions of the client, and how did these relate to the specific political, social, cultural, and economic conditions of the period?[6] My purpose here is different. It is to come to terms with effect and experience rather than agency and context. What follows will be a close reading of the garden buildings of Castle Howard in response to the strange and evocative mood they establish within their landscape setting. To that end, I will focus on the three major structures in the extended landscape, but only after describing what preceded them in time and still precedes them in space. Less interested in what is represented than in how and with what consequences representation occurs, I am concerned with the kinds of information the outbuildings disclose and how they affect the beholder as a participant in determining meaning. In lieu of any predetermined, conventional iconographic program, the three outbuildings will be shown to form a coherent and meaningful order in terms of type, geometry, scale, function, and, most notably, historical reference that is radically different from the order of the house itself and that thereby questions the traditional system of classical representation on which the latter was based. At the same time, the undeniably pictorial character of the architecture will help draw out aspects of its signal importance in the prehistory of modernism.

First Phase of Construction: The House and Its Immediate Surrounds

The landscape and garden buildings of Castle Howard were created between about 1705 and the mid-1730s for Charles Howard, the third Earl of Carlisle, by the architects John Vanbrugh and Nicholas Hawksmoor (1661–1736), working in collaboration with the owner.[7] The house itself was begun a few years earlier and gave little indication either in its planning or design of the kind of environment it would end up being part of. Even in the aerial perspective prepared around 1715 and published as late as 1725 (in the third volume of Colen Campbell's [1676–1729] *Vitruvius Britannicus*), Castle Howard appears to be a fairly typical, though by no means uninteresting, late Baroque palace modulated by a good dose of Andrea Palladio (1508–1580) (fig. 1.4).[8]

It is important to keep this discontinuity between house and garden in mind, in order to appreciate fully the unexpected and unprecedented character of the later additions to the estate.

Design of the house began in 1699, and construction started either late that year or early the following one.[9] But Vanbrugh and Hawksmoor were not the first architects to be hired by Carlisle, nor was their building the first to be built on the site. A little over fifteen miles northeast of the city of York, at the edge of the Howardian Hills, the site had been the location of the medieval town and castle of Henderskelfe, both of which can be seen on a map of 1694 (fig. 1.5). The castle had come into the possession of Lord William Howard, the founder of the family dynasty and the third Earl of Carlisle's great-great-great-grandfather, toward the end of the sixteenth century. In the 1680s Carlisle's grandfather rebuilt the ruinous structure; but in 1693, eight years after the first earl's death, it was destroyed by fire. In 1692 Charles Howard succeeded as the third earl and, six years later, made plans to lease the land from his grandmother in order to establish his residence there. Either later that year or in early 1699, he hired the architect William Talman (1650–1719) and the landscape designer George London (1681–1714) to draw up plans.

Before considering what they proposed, it is worth paying some attention to the existing site conditions, for they would play a significant role in later design decisions affecting not just the house but the entire estate. The original Henderskelfe Castle, as shown on the 1694 map, was set on the saddle of a ridge just to the west of the large wooded hill called Ray (sometimes spelled Wray) Wood. The village of Henderskelfe was strung out along the road running east-west just south of the castle and hill. The castle's entrance facade faced west, meaning that views to the rear were blocked by the hill. The Talman-London design replicated the east-west orientation of the castle but obliterated nearly

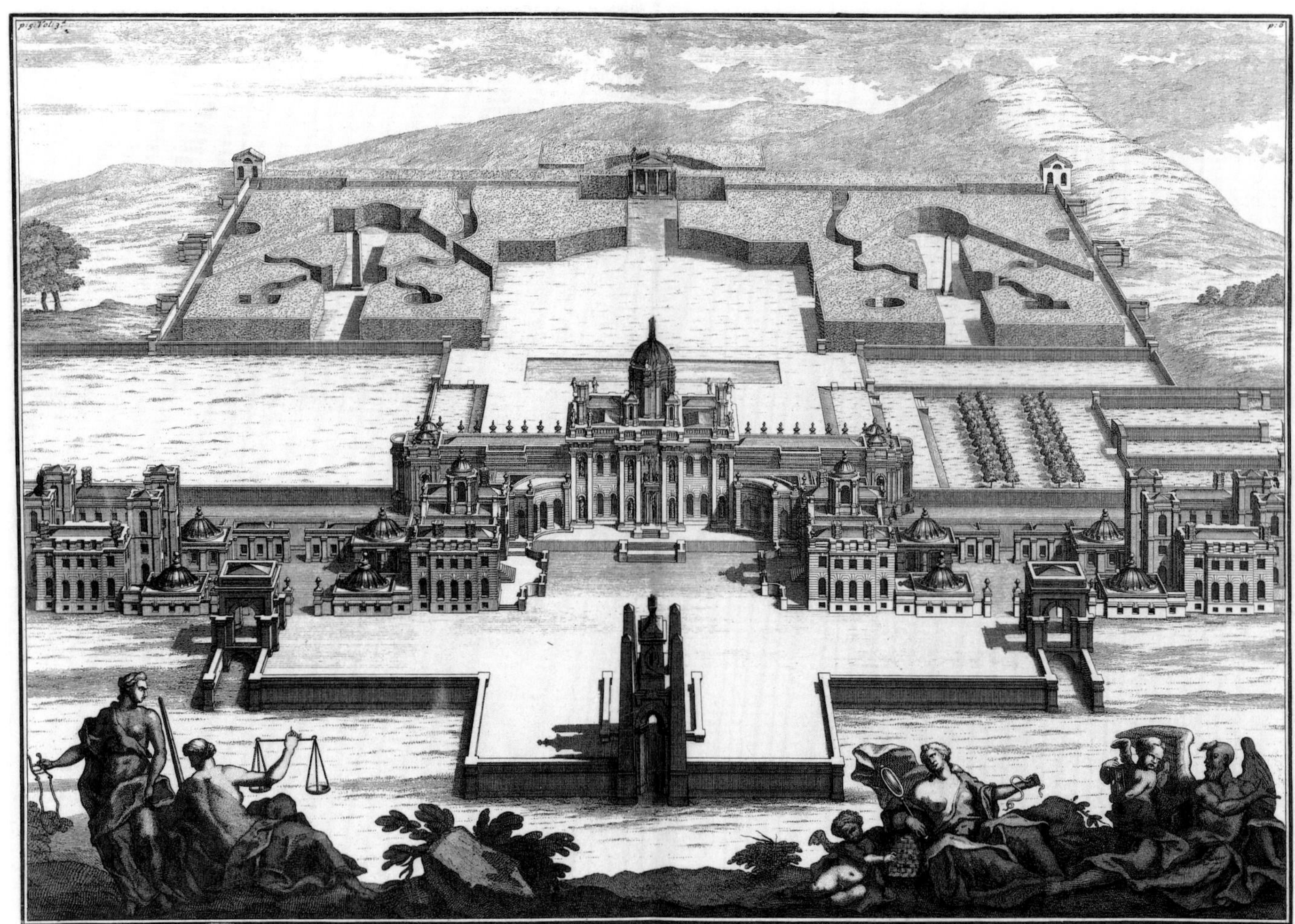

1.4 John Vanbrugh and Nicholas Hawksmoor. Castle Howard, Yorkshire, begun 1699. Aerial perspective, looking south, ca. 1715. From Colen Campbell, *Vitruvius Britannicus*, vol. 3, 1725

everything else, driving Baroque allées through the grounds into Ray Wood and establishing large *étoiles* to punctuate the formal order (fig. 1.6).[10] Gone was any sense of the rise and fall of the land, the picturesque path of the original village lane, and the wild naturalness of the wooded hill to the east. The proposed formal garden to the north, composed of canals crossing at right angles, terminated on the east and west in exedra-shaped water theaters.

Carlisle was not pleased with either Talman's or London's effort, and turned to Vanbrugh, a fellow Whig and member of the Kit-Kat Club, to see whether he could do better. Vanbrugh had been a soldier and more recently had made quite a reputation for himself as a playwright, producing *The Relapse* in 1696 and *The Provok'd Wife* the following year. According to Jonathan Swift, "Van's Genius without Thought or Lecture" then "turnd to Architecture."[11] Perhaps on the advice of Carlisle, who took an enormous interest in the project and played an important role in its design, Vanbrugh reoriented the house on a north-south axis. In addition, he shifted the visual focus of the plan to the south, opening up vistas in that direction and, most significant, leaving Ray Wood as a kind of natural wilderness along the house's east flank (fig. 1.7). At some point in the process, probably early in 1700, Vanbrugh engaged the highly skilled and professionally trained Hawksmoor to collaborate with him on the project. (Hawksmoor had worked with Christopher Wren [1632–1723] for nearly twenty years and been given responsibility for construction at St. Paul's Cathedral [1666–1711].)

It is unclear precisely whose decision it was to treat Ray Wood in such a quasi-naturalistic way, or when that decision was actually made, although it is thought that Carlisle himself was instrumental in the plan and that he may have been independently advised by Stephen Switzer (1682–1745), who extolled the Wood's "intricate mazes" in his *Ichnographia Rustica* (1718), writing that "'Tis there that Nature is truly imitated, if not excell'd."[12] The laying out of

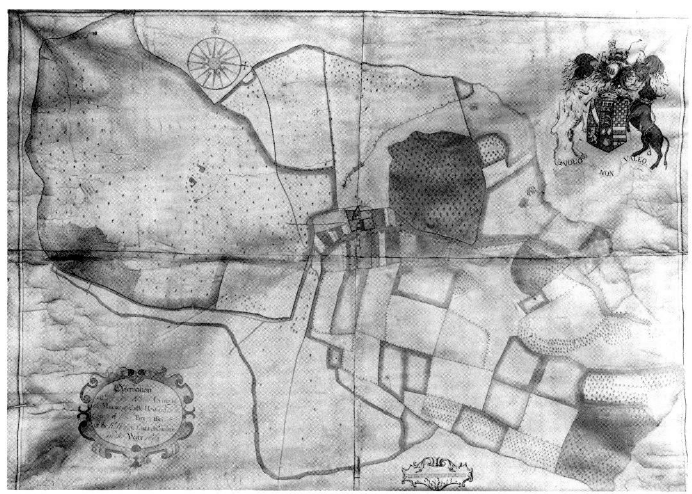

1.5 Henderskelfe Castle and village (site of later Castle Howard). Estate map, 1694

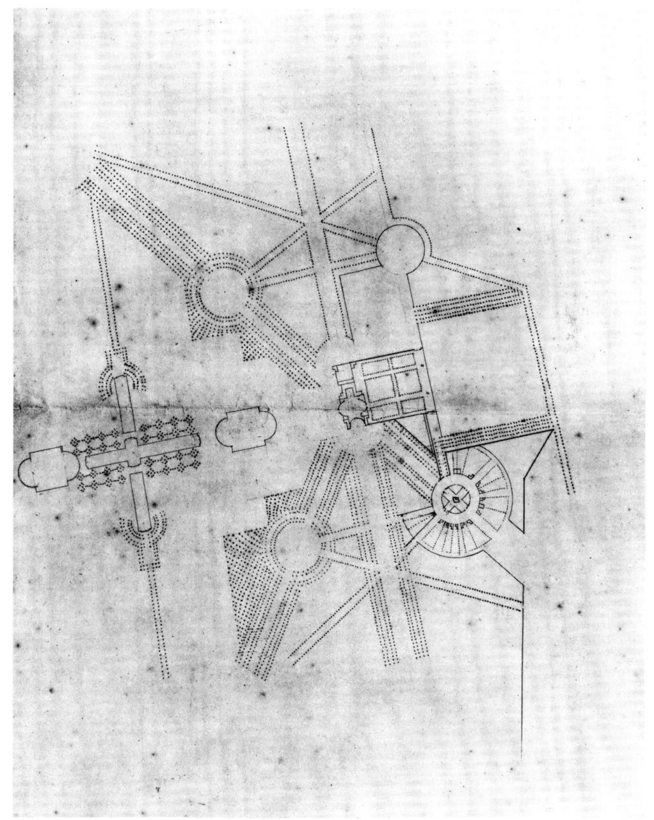

1.6 George London. Castle Howard. Preliminary project, probably 1699. Site plan, showing house design by William Talman (north is to left)

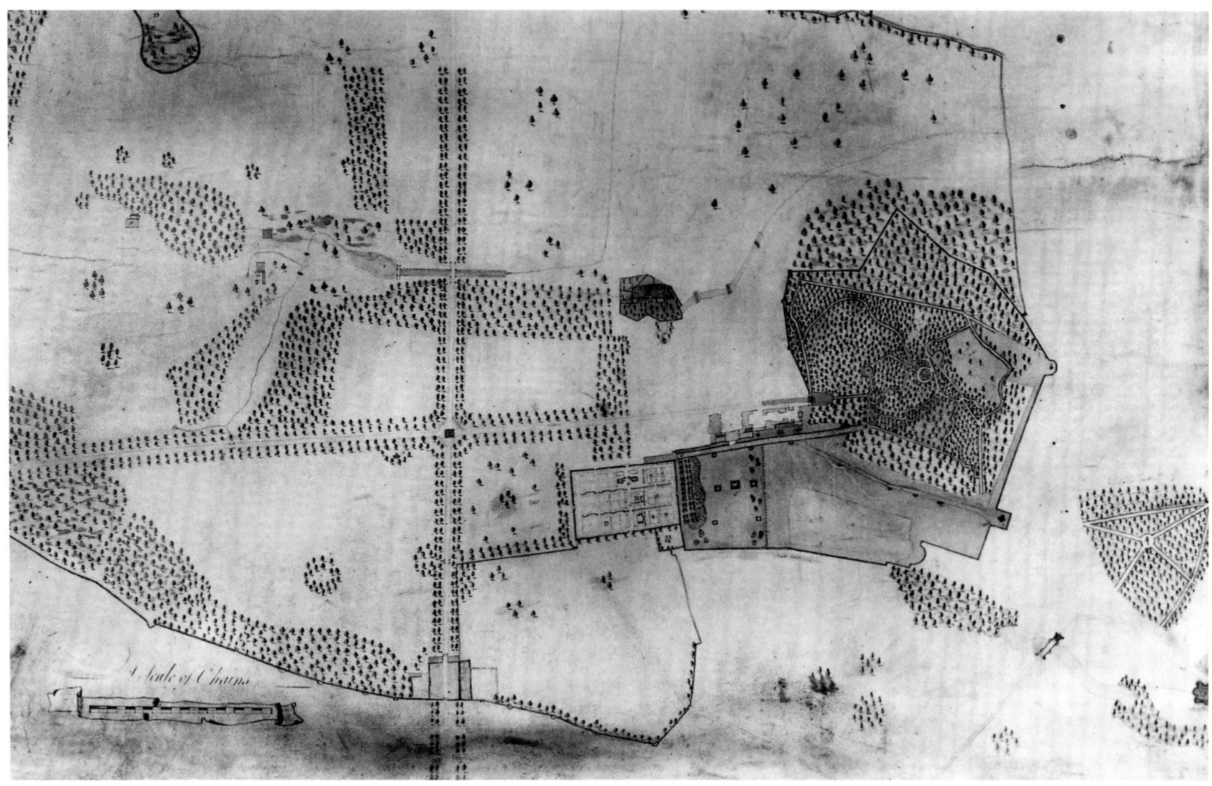

1.7 Castle Howard. Estate map, by Ralph Fowler, 1727

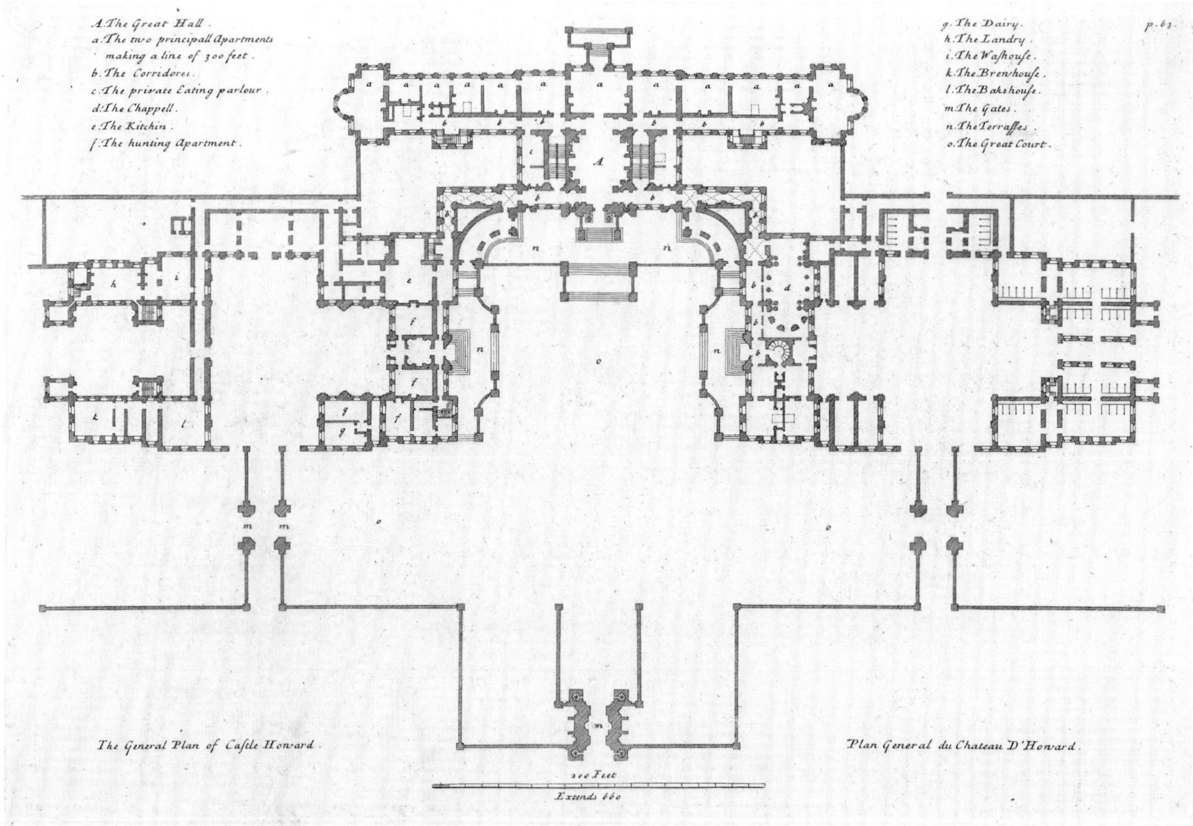

1.8 Vanbrugh and Hawksmoor. Castle Howard. Plan. From Campbell, *Vitruvius Britannicus*, vol. 1, 1715

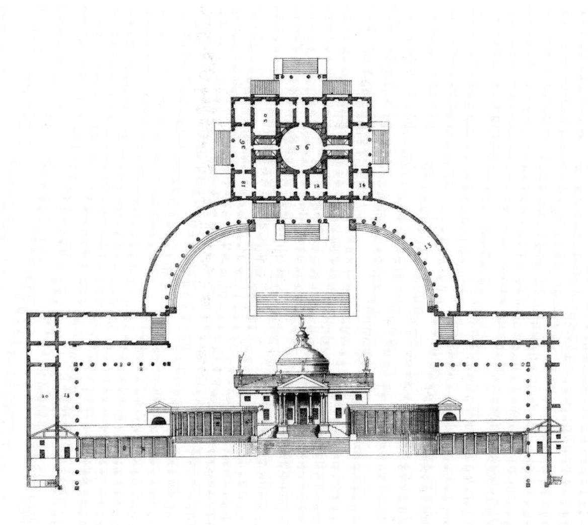

1.9 Andrea Palladio. Villa Trissino project, Meledo, probably 1560s. Plan and elevation. From Palladio, *I quattro libri dell'architettura,* 1570

1.10 Castle Howard. Entrance court, east wing

winding paths, the construction of a system of waterworks, and the placement of seats and statues to bring out the naturalness of the situation probably occurred between 1705 and 1710, at the very time the highly formalized plan of the house itself was being given material shape and before any such picturesque ideas were instituted at Stowe, Chiswick, Rousham, or Alexander Pope's villa at Twickenham.[13]

The Vanbrugh-Hawksmoor plan for the house is composed of a central quadrangular block, raised above the north entrance court and containing en suite a double-height domed hall and a large saloon (fig. 1.8). The latter, which opens onto the formal garden to the south, stretches east and west into wings, each approximately 125 feet long. They contain the main state or ceremonial apartments, with Lord Carlisle's occupying the suite on the east.[14] The dome over the hall is raised on a tall drum that allows it to be read from afar and as part of both the entrance and garden facade compositions. The entrance court is framed by lower wings connected to it by quadrants, as in Palladio's plan for the Villa Trissino at Meledo, which would have been known to Vanbrugh and Hawksmoor through the Renaissance architect's *Quattro libri dell'architettura* (1570) (fig. 1.9). Flanking the wings and masked by them are a kitchen court to the west and a stable court to the east, each terminating in a block dominated by four corner towers. Of the two, only the kitchen court was built according to the Vanbrugh-Hawksmoor plan, but with its position shifted from the west to the east side of the entrance court.[15]

The facades of the lower quadrant wings (only the left, or east, one of which is by Vanbrugh and Hawksmoor) are simply rusticated (fig. 1.10). The importance of the main block is indicated by the colossal order of coupled Doric pilasters supporting an entablature and balustrade beneath the dome (fig. 1.11).[16] The richer Composite order of the central hall (fig. 1.12), which leads to the enfilade of rooms in the garden wing, is complemented by the Corinthian order that decorates the south facade and supports the pedimented temple front that looks out over the formal parterre to the enclosed "Wilderness" of evergreens, or "wood within the walls," as it was called, that carried over the symmetrical arrangement of the house into the landscape (fig. 1.13). The formal garden seen in the drawing published by Campbell was laid out

1.11 Castle Howard. Entrance court, north facade

1.12 Castle Howard. Interior, entrance hall

in the early 1720s, but was removed by the end of the century and restored only in a minimal kind of way in the following century.

The house was finished, as far as it would be in Carlisle's lifetime, by 1712, and he began occupying it the following year. Soon after that, he focused all his attention on the garden and outbuildings, leaving the west wing and stables to be completed by his heirs. This extension of the architecture into the landscape was not a minor effort. In fact, about as much would be spent on this work as on the house itself—and it would be the landscape created by the garden structures, rather than the house, that would reflect Carlisle's ultimate decision to retire from the city to a life of rural pursuits. During the years the house was under construction, Carlisle's life had changed considerably. By the time he was able to move into it, even greater changes were about to occur, all of which affected the function he ascribed to his country estate. When he first began contemplating building on the site outside York, he was barely thirty years old and about to embark on a career in politics. His success and rise to prominence were rapid. After working enthusiastically for the Whigs in the parliamentary elections in 1700–1701, he was made a member of William III's Privy Council in the summer of 1701 and appointed First Lord of the Treasury, the most important political post in England, that December. But when the king died in March of the following year and the Tories came back into power under Queen Anne, Carlisle was dismissed and entered a period of protracted political exile, spending much of his time in Yorkshire overseeing the construction of his country house.

In *The Building of Castle Howard*, Charles Saumarez Smith argues quite compellingly that Carlisle's main reason for building the house was a mixture of political and social ambition.[17] Although the Howard family had significant roots going back to the Middle Ages, Carlisle came from a relatively undistinguished branch whose history in relation to the ownership of Henderskelfe was further compromised by a long-disputed matrilineal inheritance. In addition, Carlisle's title was relatively recent, having been bestowed on his grandfather in 1661, only eight years before he himself had been born. The desire to legitimate and give status to his family coincided with his burgeoning political career. The building of a showy country house was the perfect and completely appropriate rhetorical means to accomplish his end of aggrandizing his family's prestige while displaying his own growing personal power and leadership role. The idea worked very well. Soon after the first plans were completed, a model was shown to the king at Hampton Court in June 1700, following which Carlisle almost immediately received his first political appointment as one of the Gentlemen of His Majesty's Bedchamber.

After his dismissal from the government in 1702, Carlisle kept in touch with political activities at the court and in London, despite his preoccupation with the work at Castle Howard. When Queen Anne died in 1714, he was appointed one of the Lords Justice in the absence of the new king and soon reappointed to the post of First Lord of the Treasury by George I. But he remained in that position for only a few months, deciding of his own accord to leave politics for good. During the years he was obliged to remain out of the government, he had apparently grown too distant from the life of political intrigue not to be disillusioned

1.13 Castle Howard. Garden (south) facade

1.14 Castle Howard. Obelisk, by Vanbrugh, 1714

by what he experienced when he returned to the fray. His own life and ambitions for it also had changed much in the intervening decade. He had separated from his wife and had come to realize that his son and three daughters, none of whom were yet married, needed his support and guidance. His health had begun to deteriorate and would only worsen as time went on. Life in the country, in a place he had created for his family and where he could lay a strong foundation for its future, now seemed to Carlisle, at the age of forty-five, a reason for permanent retirement.

A poem of praise written in 1732 by his second daughter, Lady Anne Irwin, celebrates the creation of Castle Howard as the defining accomplishment of her father's life and explains its significance in terms of his ultimate decision to retire to it:

> Through various Paths to Happiness you've try'd,
> But ever follow'd a falacious Guide,
> Till from the Court and City you withdrew,
> A Life of rural Pleasure to pursue.
> Soon you resign'd what others most desire;
> Nor cou'd Ambition your cool Temper fire:
> The Statesman's Schemes you left to those who
>   durst be great,
> And found joys unmolested in this safe Retreat.[18]

The poem devotes just one stanza to the house but sixteen to the garden and outbuildings. Its descriptions make it evident that, in 1715, once he returned to his estate for good, Carlisle had different purposes from those that initially inspired the construction of the house at the turn of the century. Though no less grandiloquent in many ways, the later work in and on the landscape responded to a more personal and reflective program that could only be expressed in new, more subjective terms, which the subject matter of history was called upon to satisfy.

Second Phase of Construction: The Extended Garden and Outbuildings

The initial step in the creation of the larger context for the house was the erection of an obelisk in 1714, marking the final approach to the house, at the point where the access road from the south turns east toward Ray Wood (figs. 1.14–15). Dedicated to the Duke of Marlborough in commemoration of his war victories, it was still quite conventional in form as well as placement, although its 100-foot height suggested something of the scope of things to come. In fact, Carlisle later added the following inscription to it by way of announcing the more personal intentions his estate had come to embody:

IF TO PERFECTION THESE PLANTATIONS RISE

IF THEY AGREEABLY MY HEIRS SURPRISE

THIS FAITHFUL PILLAR WILL THEIR AGE DECLARE
AS LONG AS TIME THESE CHARACTERS SHALL SPARE
HERE THEN WITH KIND REMEMBRANCE READ HIS NAME
WHO FOR POSTERITY PERFORM'D THE SAME

CHARLES THE III EARL OF CARLISLE
OF THE FAMILY OF THE HOWARDS
ERECTED A CASTLE WHERE THE OLD CASTLE OF
HENDERSKELFE STOOD, AND CALL'D IT CASTLE-HOWARD
HE LIKEWISE MADE THE PLANTATIONS IN THIS PARK
AND ALL THE OUT-WORKS, MONUMENTS AND OTHER
PLANTATIONS BELONGING TO THE SAID SEAT

By 1731, when the above inscription was added, all the major elements in the overall design of the landscape of Castle Howard were in place or under construction. The development of the grounds had reached way beyond the area of Ray Wood and the formal parterre and "wood within the walls" that lay just south of the house. The best way to appreciate the changes in character, scale, and meaning that resulted from these extensions is to tour the grounds as they would have appeared at the time, rather than analyze the individual designs in chronological order, as is often done.

The main avenue of approach, as it was laid out around 1709 and finally completed in the 1730s, runs north from the county road for a little more than a mile, in a perfectly straight line about 500 yards to the west of the house, a gesture that, according to Tom Williamson, "expressed power and control—naked and unashamed—over the surrounding landscape" and thus served immediately to define the domain as a world unto itself.[19] From the turnoff, one can faintly see in the distance (on a sunny day, that is) what looks for all intents and purposes like a vision of a medieval town stretching out along the ridge of the mounting terraces of hills (fig. 1.16). At the point where the avenue dips just before crossing a stream, it is compressed within a strange-looking arched portal, called the Carrmire Gate, marking

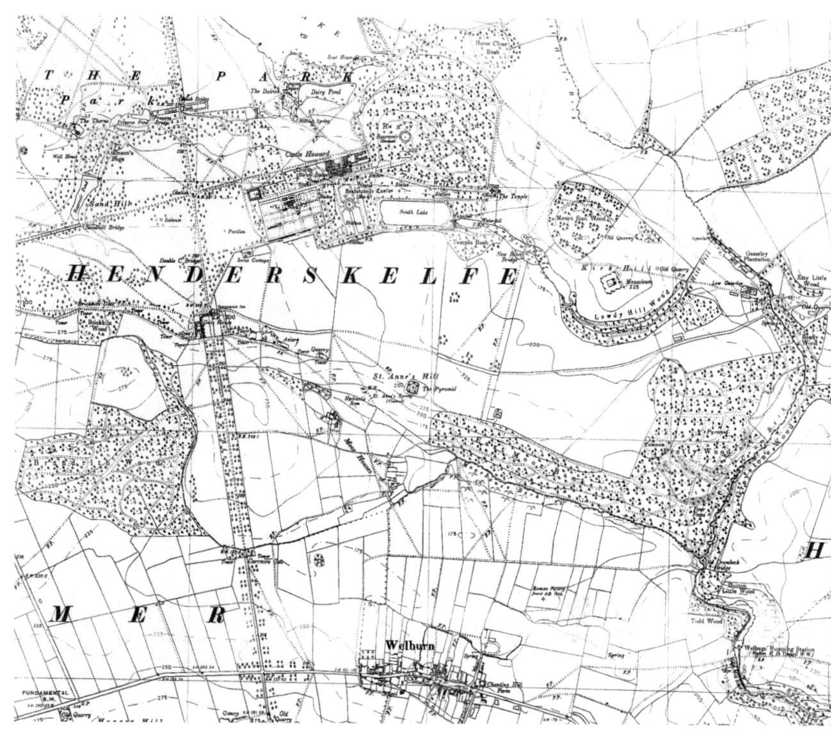

1.15 Castle Howard. Map of estate and surrounding area. Ordnance Survey, Thirsk and Malton Division, Yorkshire (North Riding), provisional edition, 1952, detail

1.16 Castle Howard. Distant view, looking north, from turnoff from county road

1.17 Castle Howard. Carrmire Gate, by Hawksmoor, ca. 1730

1.18 Castle Howard. Carrmire Gate and bastions

and protecting, as it were, the point of entry into the domain (fig. 1.17).

Designed by Hawksmoor around 1730, the Carrmire Gate was built of small, rough-cut blocks of rubble stone that give the appearance of having perhaps once been faced with a more elegant surfacing material that has since disappeared. The implication of change over time is reinforced by the disparity between the classical design of the arch itself and the medieval-looking walls into which the arch seems to have been inserted at a later date (fig. 1.18). The rather forbidding air given to the arch by the diagonally set pyramids protecting its flanks (an idea that may have its source in Christopher Wren's reconstruction of the Etruscan tomb of King Porsenna) was carried further into space by crenellated curtain walls terminating in turreted bastions furnished with Latin cross–shaped machicolations.[20] These are among the earliest such mock-Gothic structures to be built in the eighteenth century. Although it has been suggested that some country estates were still being fortified at the time, the walls at Castle Howard were clearly symbolic.[21] The idea was to give credence to the "castle" part of the name Castle Howard and to cause the visitor, from a distance, to begin to think about the age and extent of the place. Was it, as Strawberry Hill's creator Horace Walpole (1717–1797) wondered after a visit in 1772, "a palace, a town, [or even] a fortified city"?[22]

As the avenue continues north toward the Obelisk, which disappears from view over the following stretch of road, still more signs along the way provide further traces of imagined earlier inhabitation. From the Carrmire Gate, one can see the next point of arrival, located on the high ridge in the distance. The second gate, called the Pyramid Gate (marked "Gate House" in fig. 1.15), was designed by Vanbrugh in 1719 (fig. 1.19). The solid, solemn cubical block forming the body of the structure is built of ashlar in a quasi-utilitarian, quasi-militaristic mode that ultimately derives from late Roman architecture as it might have existed in the far reaches of the empire, perhaps even as far north as here in Yorkshire.[23] Above the round-arched portal, and supported by a deep corbel table of smaller round arches containing the family coat of arms and an inscription to Carlisle, is the distinctive form that gives the gate its name. The reference to Egypt resonates across space as the arch itself frames, and throws into perspective, the pyramid-topped Obelisk seen through it in the distance. The mixture and elision of historical horizons is elaborated by the mock defensive walls that stretch out from the gate in both directions (fig. 1.20). Added sometime in the early 1720s and composed of

1.19 Castle Howard. Pyramid Gate, by Vanbrugh, 1719 (additions, to left and right, by Thomas Robinson, 1756)

stone retrieved from the ruins of the former Henderskelfe Castle, these multibastioned, medievalizing curtain walls reverse the impression given by the Carrmire Gate. Rather than appearing to have been subject to a later intervention, the mock fortifications look as if they had been built, as in fact they were, as an addition to a preexisting structure.

As it stretches into the distance on the right, the curtain wall also directs the eye toward a third pyramidal shape, this one a freestanding example known as the Pyramid, located to the southeast on the same ridge as the Pyramid Gate (see fig. 1.15).[24] The rhyming of the three pyramidal forms across space makes the viewer's mind begin to work in new ways by implying the need to take in the landscape setting as a whole. The visitor also now realizes not only that there is more than just a house to see at the end of the

1.20 Castle Howard. Pyramid Gate, east bastions, early 1720s. View looking east to Pyramid in far distance

1.21 Castle Howard. Temple (later of Four Winds), by Vanbrugh (with Hawksmoor), 1723–39

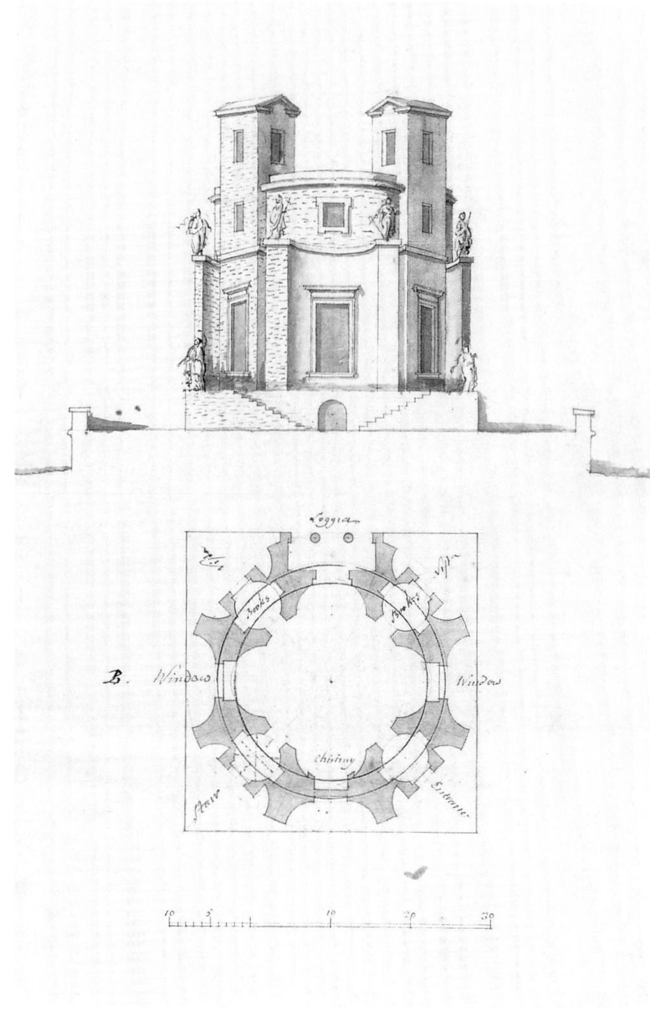

1.22 Castle Howard. Temple. "Turret" project, by Hawksmoor, 1724. Perspective and plan

road, but that the journey will not always follow the straight path of approach the main avenue at first seemed to promise. Indeed, little of what is to be seen at Castle Howard is approached head-on or even, as in the case of the free-standing Pyramid, by a man-made path. In what amounts to a fairly radical departure from standard classical practice of the period, the entrance to the house is neither aligned with the access road nor given much axial definition. Instead it is reached in a rather roundabout way that only serves to reinforce the primacy that the landscape setting acquired after work on the house was aborted. A right turn at the Obelisk, which lines up with the top, or northern edge, of the entrance court, focuses attention on the hill of Ray Wood that terminates the view. The entrance court, set at a right angle to the cross-axis, only gradually appears—and then almost inadvertently—as the house seems to nestle at the edge of the wooded hill.

The preservation of Ray Wood in a relatively naturalistic state was a crucial element in the broader conception of Castle Howard, going back nearly to the very beginning of the building process. Although the symmetrical and hierarchical design of the house may seem to have little to do with the treatment of the wooded area, the forceful presence of the hill cheek by jowl with the house provides a constant reminder of the natural as well as cultural history of the site, what later writers would refer to as the genius loci, or spirit of the place. This role grew exponentially in the years after 1715, when Carlisle and his architects shifted their attention from the house to the estate grounds. Ray Wood served as the catalyst for the first of the three major outbuildings begun in the 1720s, and eventually it became a locus of their intersection.[25]

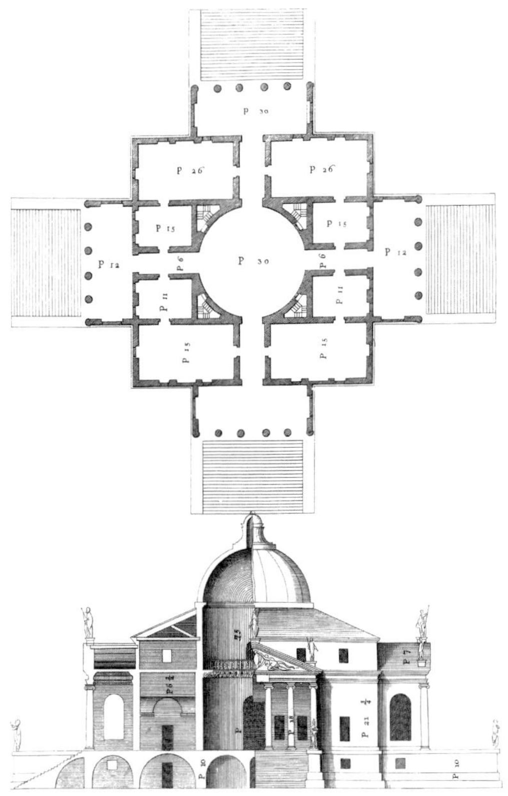

1.23 Palladio. Villa Rotonda, Vicenza, 1560s. Plan and elevation/section. From Palladio, *I quattro libri*

The southern edge of Ray Wood preserved the line of the path that previously joined the town of Henderskelfe to the neighboring one of Malton (see figs. 1.5 and 1.7). When, probably sometime in 1723, Carlisle thought to construct a building at the southeast corner of Ray Wood to serve as a summer house and belvedere, it was decided to make the approach to it follow the original village lane rather than a more axial route leading directly from the house. The result is a curving path bordered by statuary, called the Terrace Walk, that gently rises to the structure designed by Vanbrugh to overlook the valley beyond. Conceived and built in 1723–39, the Temple is a biaxially symmetrical classical structure composed of prismatic geometric units (fig. 1.21). Now known as the Temple of the Four Winds, it was almost always referred to in the eighteenth century simply by its typological referent, although sometimes a functional attribute was added to make it the Belvedere Temple.[26]

Vanbrugh specifically rejected any "Gothick" or rustic-looking design for the site, an idea that was advanced by Hawksmoor in early 1724 in response to a request by Carlisle for a more economical solution. Hawksmoor called his project a "Turret" (fig. 1.22).[27] Its curious, four-towered design, to be built of rubble stone, clearly related to the bastioned walls that surrounded Ray Wood—and that were then being added to the Pyramid Gate—although the only part of this design that could truly be called Gothic was the rather crude juxtaposition of the vertical towers to the circular substructure. Vanbrugh assured Carlisle that what was demanded was an "Italian Building in that Place," meaning a classical design of the modern sort. He said it "Shou'd be Square, not round" and even expressed concern over how the building should be referred to. "I have some doubts about the Name of Belvedere, which is generally given to some high Tower," he wrote to Carlisle. "Such a thing will certainly be right to have some time and in Some Place.... But this Building I fancy wou'd more naturally take the Name of Temple which the Situation likewise is very proper for."[28]

The model for Vanbrugh's Temple was Palladio's Villa Rotonda, a most appropriate choice given the program, the setting, and the desire for views in all four directions (fig. 1.23). Originally built for someone much like Carlisle, who had recently retired from public life, the Villa Rotonda was unique among Palladio's villas in having no agricultural function and being simply a place for pleasurable activities like the entertainment of friends and the enjoyment of nature.[29] It is often thought of as the first Renaissance building to have explicitly appropriated the forms of ancient temples for modern domestic purposes. Like its Palladian prototype, the twenty-six-foot-square block of Vanbrugh's cubic structure is topped by a dome and embellished on all four faces with Ionic porticos, those on the east and west being amplified by paired statues of sibyls. Where Hawksmoor's incurving niches and turreted angles would

1.24 Castle Howard. Temple, looking northeast over landscape

have created a protective shelter from the outside world, the porticos in the Vanbrugh design Carlisle chose open the building's airy and well-lit room to distant views of the surrounding landscape and the Arcadian world of pastoral imagery defined by his estate "improvements" (fig. 1.24).[30]

Views today from the Temple to the north and northeast still provide the visitor with images of animals grazing and farmers working the fields, but those to the south and southeast reveal a scene of a more monumentally constructed order. From the broad terrace surrounding the summer house, one can survey the landscape where Carlisle had Hawksmoor design two other structures between 1726, the year Vanbrugh died, and 1729. Both were dedicated to preserving some aspect of the Carlisle family history and lineage. The first of the two appears on the hill beyond the serpentine river that flows from the lake put in below Ray Wood around the same time the Temple was begun (fig. 1.25). The Mausoleum, as it was called, was built in part to replace the church of the former village of Henderskelfe—and thus sometimes was referred to in the correspondence between Hawksmoor and Carlisle as "the Church" or "y^{r} Chappel"—but its main purpose was to contain the remains of Carlisle and his progeny.[31] The project was discussed as early as 1722, when Vanbrugh was consulted on the subject, but the three-year design process did not begin until 1726. The building took more than fifteen years to construct and was completed in 1745 (fig. 1.26).

Although the idea that the Mausoleum should be circular appears to have governed Hawksmoor's thinking from the very beginning, its specific form only emerged after much discussion with the client and his eldest son, Viscount Morpeth. Carlisle had originally thought that the building should take the "form of a Greek Temple," but Hawksmoor demurred, claiming that "the Gentiles, Jews, or any other polite people had either Magnificent piles for Sepulture, but never buryed near their temples, or built their tombs in the form of any temple dedicated to divine honours."

1.25 Castle Howard. Temple, with view southeast to Mausoleum

Rather than imitating a temple, he strongly advised choosing from among the known examples of "Greek or Latin" tombs.[32] After considering the Mausoleum at Halicarnassus and the tomb of King Porsenna, he decided on the tomb of Caecilia Metella, outside Rome. In order to appropriate the closed exterior of the pagan memorial to the religious faith of a Christian church, Hawksmoor surrounded the blank drum of his model with a continuous open arcade, following the example of Early Christian churches (fig. 1.27). By the spring of 1729, it was decided to replace the arcade with a colonnade, and for this Hawksmoor turned to Palladio's engraving of the early sixteenth-century Tempietto in Rome, the martyrial church of San Pietro in Montorio by Donato Bramante (ca. 1444–1514), which was thought to be so pure a representation of antique architecture that Palladio himself considered it authentic in everything but date (fig. 1.28).[33]

The round cella walls and drum of the Mausoleum rise up through an exceedingly tall Doric colonnade into a dome supported on a clerestory, the crown of the dome reaching a height of ninety feet from the site's already elevated position. The circular superstructure forming the chapel proper is set on a high base containing a crypt large enough to accommodate seventy coffins. The base originally rose directly out of the ground, with the steps leading to the upper chapel concealed within its solid mass. (The elaborate stairway, copied from Lord Burlington's villa at Chiswick, and the bastioned wall surrounding the whole were

1.26 Castle Howard. Mausoleum, by Hawksmoor, 1722–45 (bastioned walls around base and stairway added by Daniel Garrett, 1738–45)

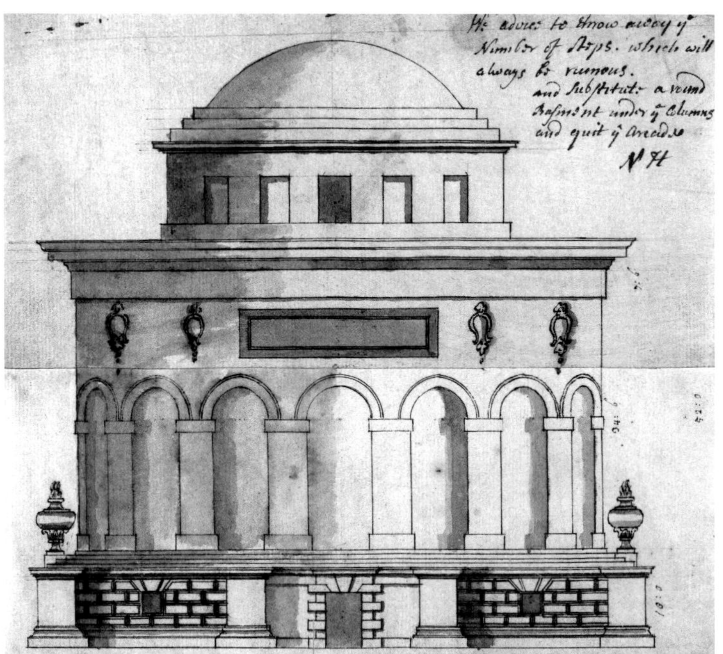

1.27 Castle Howard. Mausoleum. Preliminary project, by Hawksmoor, 1728. Elevation

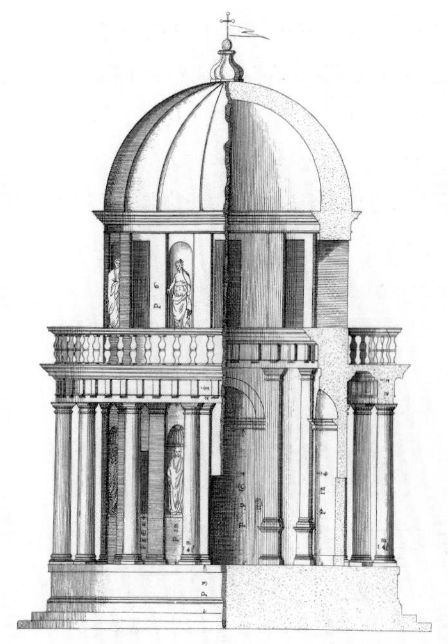

1.28 Donato Bramante. San Pietro in Montorio (Tempietto), Rome, ca. 1502. Elevation/section. From Palladio, *I quattro libri*

1.29 Castle Howard. Pyramid, by Hawksmoor, 1728. View, looking southwest, from Mausoleum

added after Hawksmoor's death by Burlington's protégé Daniel Garrett [d. 1753], under the influence of Carlisle's son-in-law Thomas Robinson.) The tall, closely spaced columns of the Mausoleum give the structure a guarded and forbidding appearance, while the cylindrical shape and dome provide a dour and powerful silhouette.[34] Deriving from the tomb of Caecilia Metella by way of Bramante's Tempietto, the Mausoleum resonates with the ecclesiastical meanings associated from the Early Christian period on, with the arcaded or colonnaded central-plan spaces of martyria.

From the vantage point of the Mausoleum, one can see on the horizon the third in the triad of major monuments in the southeastern quadrant of Castle Howard's extended landscape (fig. 1.29). This is the Pyramid, built in 1728 and dedicated to the memory of William Howard, the Elizabethan founder of the Carlisle line and the one who was responsible for acquiring Henderskelfe (fig. 1.30). The cenotaph is twenty-eight feet high and absolutely blank, except for a small dedicatory marble plaque, set in the low square base on the side facing the house, and a tiny door on the rear, barely visible at first, that opens into the vaulted space of the interior. The highly personal inscription on the plaque reads as follows:

TO THEE O VENERABLE SHADE
WHO LONG HAST IN OBLIVION LAID
A TRIBUTE SMALL FOR WHAT THOU'ST DONE
DEIGN TO ACCEPT THIS MEAN RETURN,

PARDON THE LONG NEGLECT
TO THY LONG LABOURS, TO THY CARE
THY SONS DECEAS'D, THY PRESENT HEIR
THEIR GREAT POSSESSIONS OWE:

1.30 Castle Howard. Pyramid. Exterior

1.31 Castle Howard. Pyramid. Interior, with bust of Lord William Howard

SPIRIT DIVINE WHAT THANKS ARE DUE
THIS WILL THY MEMORY RENEW
IT'S ALL I CAN BESTOW

Under the beehive-shaped dome of the interior is a rough-hewn pedestal base supporting a strange capital, seemingly pieced together from elements of dissimilar origin (fig. 1.31). The lower part contains a ring of degraded vegetal motifs; the upper portion has four consoles attached to a stubby column supporting a ring on which is set, well above eye height, the crudely carved bust of the ancestral figure. As Lord Howard looks out across the gloom with a kind of wide-eyed, late Roman otherworldliness, the visitor is put in mind of another time.[35]

Temple, Mausoleum, and Pyramid: Geometric, Historical, and Typological Correlations

From the Mausoleum, the Pyramid appears unapproachable, sinking into the ground as it directs the eye to the sky. There is no obvious path to it. Indeed, as far as we know, neither Vanbrugh nor Hawksmoor ever drew a plan of the extended landscape garden of Castle Howard, nor was any ever published at the time.[36] The absence of a planned approach to the Pyramid—or from the Temple to the Mausoleum—is less disturbing, however, than its apparent lack of orientation to the formal order of the house and its south parterre (fig. 1.32). The Pyramid is neither axially aligned with the house nor oriented toward it, a dislocation that would not have been as noticeable at ground level when the "wood within the walls" still existed. The Pyramid is shifted well to the east of the house's main north-south axis and rotated in the direction of the Temple and Mausoleum (see fig. 1.15).[37] The significance of these deviations only slowly makes itself felt as one becomes aware of another kind of order they establish. The landscape of the estate's southeastern quadrant is in fact triangulated by the three

1.32 Castle Howard. Pyramid, seen from garden parterre on south side of house

monuments, setting up a series of internal relationships that separates their world from the formal logic of the house and its immediate surrounds.

It is as if the conventional ground of representation has literally shifted beneath one's feet, leaving the visitor to stabilize the floating pieces in his or her own mind. The distances between the three structures are inordinately vast—and there are no visible clues on the ground to indicate how one connects to the other two. Nor can any sense of their interrelationship be gained from the vantage point of the house or, indeed, from any static location, as would normally be the case in the more typical English garden, such as that at Stowe, where house, garden, and garden structures are linked by a system of paths that increasingly came to define a prescribed visual and sometimes even narrative circuit (see fig. 1.1).[38] The order of the landscape at Castle Howard is at first too natural-seeming to appear like order, especially in contrast to the carefully wrought architectural figures in it. And the precisely differentiated character of those figures seems to contradict the apparently unregulated nature of the landscape. A mood is created—as in the setting for a story that is about to unfold—and it is the visitor who is asked to give voice to the action. The life in the landscape is sensed through the perspicuous differentiation of the three figural representations, and this at the level of shape, of source, of type, and of temporal dimension.

One is immediately struck by the obvious distinction of square, circle, and triangle—or cube, sphere, and pyramid—and perhaps even reminded of the famous drawing of Le Corbusier's, showing how the modern mind might abstract such geometric figures from their historical appearance (see fig. 7.5). Indeed, Vanbrugh asserted to

Carlisle that the Temple had to be "Square, not round," and rationalized the economy of using a flat ceiling hiding the dome "because it will shape the Room just to a Cube."[39] Hawksmoor, for his part, specifically rejected Carlisle's desire for a "Greek Temple" for the Mausoleum because he believed the building should be circular rather than rectangular. The Temple, the Mausoleum, and the Pyramid each declare their independence from the other two through their geometry, while relating to the others in the expression of geometry's three primary forms. This is in no way an exercise in abstraction, however, for the three geometric forms all have their source in particular historical traditions, which also relate to building type—and therefore to use or function.[40]

The three distinct historical periods of Egyptian, ancient classical, and Renaissance architecture (what contemporaries would have thought of as Egyptian, Greek, and Roman or Italian architecture) are invoked by the three buildings. The cubic Temple, with its four porticos and central dome, represents, at a diminished scale, the Italian Renaissance Villa Rotonda by Palladio. The Mausoleum refers to ancient Roman and Greek prototypes through its circular shape and Doric order, the intermediary of Bramante serving to assure its ancient pedigree.[41] The Pyramid, though sometimes found in the classical world, as in the tomb of Cestius in Rome, is always read as instantiating an Egyptian type.[42]

The three historical horizons outlined by the structures at Castle Howard also serve to support and to characterize the differential expression of use through type. The three types they illustrate are the domestic, the ecclesiastic, and the sepulchral. The Temple was designed as a summer house, with places for books, wine, spirits, and other such domestic accoutrements provided in its niches, cabinets, and built-in furniture. The identification with the Villa Rotonda as the ideal Renaissance version of the type gives bold emphasis to the building's domestic mien, especially in contrast to the other two structures. The Mausoleum was intended to serve an ecclesiastic function and was referred to by Hawksmoor, as noted previously, as the "Church" or "Chappel." The form of the Early Christian martyrium gave historical validity to the association between church and tomb, and the direct reference to Bramante's Tempietto justified the formal composition of superstructure as chapel, substructure as crypt. This left a purely sepulchral definition for the Pyramid, which assumed the Egyptian tomb type without equivocation.

In their representations as a cubic Renaissance house, a cylindrical antique-style church, and a pyramidal Egyptian tomb, the three garden buildings describe and situate themselves within three different temporal dimensions and thus begin to portray in singularly vivid terms the story embedded in their landscape setting. It is a story that is personal in meaning and improvisational in realization: the story, as both Charles Saumarez Smith and John Dixon Hunt have explained, of Carlisle's relationship to his country retreat, its history, its present welfare, and its future prospects.[43] The Temple, with its open, domestic outlook, is, in effect, all about the present. It speaks of communion with nature, the contemplative life, and pleasure in socializing; the four porticos infer the natural cycle of the day and year. The Pyramid is a monument to the past, dying into the ground and gathering in its secret enclosure a portrait bust of the figure who gave impetus to Carlisle's venture. Finally, the Mausoleum, with its tall, domed cella breaking through the surrounding colonnade, is a statement about the future, a place where Carlisle's children and their children would be reminded of the importance of carrying on the work he began.[44]

There is one final aspect of the coordination of the triad of monuments that is necessary to consider, for it is what assures the intensity, the coherence, and the differential specificity of their combined expression. This is the question of scale, not of the enterprise as a whole, on which I have already commented, but of the relative scale of the individual elements themselves. The changes in scale from model to representation are in large part responsible for turning what could have been merely a rhetorical display into the personal and historical drama the landscape presents. The Pyramid, which by all rights should have been the largest of the three structures, is the smallest and most retiring. The Mausoleum, which, according to the Bramantean version, should have been the smallest, is the largest—and by an exceedingly apparent amount. The house/Temple is thus relatively correct in scale, being midway in size between the other two; but on an absolute scale in relation to the size of its model—the Villa Rotonda—it is touchingly diminutive, one might even say fragile as life itself.

These distortions in scale could be interpreted on purely functional or material grounds as coinciding with the intended use or purpose of each of the structures.[45] While such a reading ultimately serves to reinforce the expressive charge that results, it also points to the question of intention and coherence. The poem about the house and garden written by Carlisle's daughter in 1732 clearly substantiates the preceding reading of the monuments' discrete and collective meanings. Lady Irwin describes how "Buildings…Of *Grecian, Roman,* and *Egyptian* Form"—referring to the Mausoleum, the Temple, and the Pyramid—speak to the visitor of "the immortal Vert'ous dead," the "future Prospects" of Carlisle's "noble Progeny," and "the Harmony of Soul this Place inspires" in "the present Hour." In her assertion that "Carlisle…so early form'd this great Design," the author also suggests, if not a theory of premeditation, then at least a predisposition on the client's part toward a certain end.[46]

Advocacy of such a strong position on the issues of intention and coherence has been questioned by Saumarez Smith and Hunt, who maintain that the development of the estate as a whole was process-driven, with changes constantly occurring and affecting each succeeding stage in the garden's design.[47] But it should be remembered, and constantly kept in mind, that the key structures in question—the Temple, the Mausoleum, and the Pyramid—were all discussed and designed, sometimes simultaneously and in reference to one another, within a very short period of time—approximately five to six years at most.[48] Given the precision with which Vanbrugh defended his idea for an "Italian" design for the Temple—whose cubical form he considered one of its most noteworthy features—over Hawksmoor's turreted, rustic version, and given Hawksmoor's disagreement with Carlisle over what would be an appropriate form for the Mausoleum—in which Hawksmoor maintained that a "Greek Temple" (indicating a rectangular structure) would not be as suitable as a Roman tomb (indicating a circular one)—it is clear that the two architects and their client were convinced, if not from the outset, then certainly through the process itself, that each building should be distinguished from the other two based on typological, geometric, and functional differences encoding specific sets of historical references and meanings.[49]

From the Representation of Distinction to the Representation of Difference

Design by discrimination was one of the basic tenets of classical imitation theory going back to Aristotle's distinctions between the modes of tragedy, comedy, satire, and the like. Each mode was thought to have its own appropriate form and manner relative to the "class" of objects imitated. In Renaissance and Baroque architectural theory, the distinctions among the orders gave expression to distinctions in character of a hierarchical sort (fig. 1.33). The spectrum ranged from the grave, sturdy Doric—usually characterized as male—through the intermediate, delicate, rather matronly Ionic—characterized as female—to the rich and elegant Corinthian—also female in derivation (the later

1.33 Claude Perrault. The Five Orders, *A Treatise of the Five Orders of Columns in Architecture,* orig. pub. as *Ordonnance des cinq espèces de colonnes selon la méthode des anciens,* 1683; English translation, 1708

Composite being essentially an enrichment of the Corinthian).[50] By virtue of this universality, the orders were thought to contain all significant variations of expression. Good taste and training would enable the architect to choose and combine elements to ensure a proper and decorous representation, that is to say, one in accord with the status of the subject. By the same token, an undecorated, astylar design would be suitable for more utilitarian, less representationally significant purposes.[51]

Vanbrugh and Hawksmoor were well aware, if not equally well versed, in this classical system of expression. (The former, it should be recalled, had started out as a playwright.) The gradated effects of hierarchical distinction can be seen quite clearly in the progressive elaboration of the spectacle of the house itself. It starts with the supporting characters around the edges of the scene and proceeds through the main space of the building along its processional axis. The kitchen court to the east of the entrance court (originally mirrored by a stable court to the west) is built of rubble stone, only sparingly relieved by ashlar trim (see fig. 1.4). Its nearly unadorned, medieval-looking towers are masked from view by the east wing of the forecourt, which housed private family living quarters behind a sturdy and elegant (though simple) rusticated facade (see fig. 1.10). This astylar unit turns the corner by means of a curved arcade to rise into the double-height facade of the main entrance block, which is articulated by imposing pairs of colossal Doric pilasters separated by niches containing statues (see fig. 1.11). The relatively small and graceful Ionic columns forming an aedicule around the door create a transition zone between the solemn and imposing exterior and the grandiloquent domed hall to which it gives entry and which, in turn, leads out through the saloon and the richly relieved Corinthian order of the south facade's pedimented temple front to the formal garden (see figs. 1.12–13).[52] Conjoining aspects of the Ionic and the Corinthian, the noble and generous Composite order supporting the coffered dome of the central hall represents the high point of the sequence at its central, culminating moment.[53]

The garden buildings of Castle Howard, by contrast, take us beyond the strict limits of the existing classical system of hierarchical distinction in order to express certain kinds of ideas, more discursive and more subjective in nature, that could only be represented by means of reference. Once differentiation through reference replaced distinction by rank as the basis of representation, a much wider and more clearly defined range of historical types came to form the subject matter of the mimetic operation.[54] A comparison with a more traditional garden pavilion of the period, such as Richard Mique's (1728–1794) Belvedere at the Petit Trianon at Versailles, makes this quite clear (fig. 1.34). Mique's

1.34 Richard Mique. Belvedere, Petit Trianon, Palace of Versailles, 1778–81. View, with Grotto to left

design is essentially a scaled-down, lighthearted version of the main house, while the contiguous grotto acts as a conventional foil of rusticity to highlight the Belvedere's sophistication. Only with the addition of painting or sculpture would such a standard architectural form be able to approach the kind of specificity of expression and meaning present in the outbuildings of Castle Howard.

A key to the referential definition of Castle Howard is its incorporation of the pictorial as an instrumental factor in architectural representation. Rather than simply adding a quality of the "picturesque" in the aesthetic sense of the term, it plays an operational role. Castle Howard is in fact more picturelike in its production of effects than it is in many of those effects themselves. Opinions differ on how to assess what influence the Virgilian and Arcadian worlds painted by Claude and Poussin might have had on Vanbrugh, Hawksmoor, and Carlisle; but there is little question that a significant relationship exists. Vanbrugh, whom Joshua Reynolds praised as "an Architect who composed like a Painter," expressed admiration, as he put it, for the "Objects that the best of Landskip Painters can invent."[55] And in her poem about Castle Howard, Lady Irwin made the parallel between its architecture and narrative landscape painting a major theme. Describing the landscape and the architecture through continual mythological reference, in which poetic, pictorial, and architectural metaphors constantly overlap, she wrote:

> *Virgil* presum'd to paint th' *Elysian* Fields,
> To him my Lays, but not my Subject yields.
> Had *Mantua's* Bard been bless'd with such a Theme,
> He ne'r had form'd a Visionary Dream.
> All that Luxurious Fancy can invent,
> What Poets feign, what Painters represent;
> Not in Imagination here we trace,
> Realities adorn this happy Place.[56]

In this modern replay of the traditional *paragone*, or rivalry of the arts, architecture not only incorporates the representational explicitness of painting and poetry; it achieves a superiority through the very materiality and "reality" that might otherwise have worked to its detriment.[57] Clearly, what was being questioned was the assumption, implicit in the classical distinction between *natura naturata* and *natura naturans*, that architecture, although one of the "arts of imitation," has a less literal, less direct, more generalized relationship to the natural world than do painting, sculpture, or poetry. In other words, architecture at Castle Howard was not simply restricted to the imitation of the principles of harmony, order, or symmetry that underlie and govern the natural world; it could indeed represent, and with even more vividness than painting or sculpture, the physical objects of that world.[58]

Looking at Castle Howard and Claude's painting *Aeneas at Delos* in this light, one might well ask whether there is in fact a critical difference between the painted temple of the ancient oracle and the stone one built for the third Earl of Carlisle. From the point of view of representation as such, I would submit that there is none. In this regard, the issue is hardly whether the architecture imitates the painting or offers a world "parallel" to it, as Christopher Hussey has aptly characterized the relationship between the two media.[59] It is simply that the conventional shapes of the built buildings stand in virtually the same relationship to nature as the shapes of the painted buildings and figures do to the world of reality. Both depend, in more or less equal measure, on the intermediary of historical models in the process of representation that Ernst Gombrich has characterized as the "finding, making, and matching" of art imitating art.[60] Architectural representation thereby achieves in the landscape garden of Castle Howard a kind of parity and identity with pictorial representation that was strikingly new. The overlapping of the two modes is brought into vivid focus in the painting of the house by Hendrik de Cort (1742–1810), commissioned by the fifth Earl of Carlisle, in which an idyllic scene of pastoral life is imagined as taking place in the actual environment of the Yorkshire estate (fig. 1.35).[61]

But the challenge of the pictorial was not as easily won as Lady Irwin thought. While opening up the possibilities for architectural representation beyond the general and universal categories of hierarchical distinction provided by the classical orders, the construction of images through a pictorial form of mimesis necessarily sacrificed something of the "realities" of architecture, as Carlisle's daughter called them, to the "fancy" of painting. And the evidence this now gave of an unavoidable confrontation between the demands of appearance and those of reality—of the desires of the imagination and the needs of material conditions—set into motion a dialectic that came to define modern architecture. At the same time, in picturing the past, present, and future of Carlisle's personal history in three typologically and historically differentiated structures whose only links to one another were to be supplied by the movement of an observer in real space and real time, Vanbrugh and Hawksmoor also suggested in the outbuildings of Castle Howard, a

1.35 Hendrik de Cort. *Castle Howard: Mausoleum and House*, 1800

generation before G. E. Lessing's *Laocoön* (1766) first articulated the modern idea of "truth to medium," how the representations of architecture might find their own means for realization independent of the modalities of painting or sculpture and grounded in a strictly architectural conception of experiential space.

Considered as a whole constructed in two distinct stages—the house coming first and the landscape garden second—Castle Howard provides early evidence of the fundamental shift that occurred in the eighteenth century from a traditional, rhetorically based mode of representation, characteristic of architecture since the Renaissance, to a historically defined one driven by the more explicit, individuated, and descriptive possibilities inherent in a pictorialized mode of composition. Exchanging the exclusive and closed system of representation of the classical orders that gave hierarchical distinction to the various parts of the house for the more open, more varied, more evocative, but also more elusive set of references embodied in the differentiated figures of the garden outbuildings, Vanbrugh and Hawksmoor recalibrated the subject-object mechanism in architectural expression to suit the demands of an unconventional narrative of the self. In the process, and much more important for us, they placed the subject matter of history at the forefront. This set the stage for the more thoroughgoing and deliberate questioning of the classical system of representation that took place beginning at mid-century. This neoclassicism, as we shall see in the following two chapters, used history itself as a way to resolve the confrontation between the demands of appearance and those of reality and thus to ensure a "truth to medium" within the parameters of classical figuration.

2

The Appearance of Truth and the Truth of Appearance in Laugier's Primitive Hut

AROUND 1750, A YOUNG French Jesuit priest began writing a relatively short critique of contemporary architecture, offering his views on how the situation might be reformed. To argue his position, which was decidedly outside the mainstream and had no professional credentials for support, he made use of a mimetic theory of representation, most of the elements of which had been noted before, but which as a whole had never previously been articulated with quite the same sense of purpose or conviction. Marc-Antoine Laugier's (1713–1769) *Essai sur l'architecture* was published anonymously in 1753 and had a veritable succès de scandale. It was translated into English and German within a couple of years.[1] Its main premise was rebutted almost immediately by William Chambers (1723–1796), followed soon thereafter by Johann Wolfgang von Goethe (1749–1832) and later by Jean-Nicolas-Louis Durand (1760–1834); whereas John Soane (1753–1837), who was born the year it first appeared, eventually acquired ten copies of it for his library, and Antoine-Chrysostôme Quatremère de Quincy (1755–1849), the leading French theorist of neoclassicism and the major spokesman for the Academy of Fine Arts during the first third of the nineteenth century, made Laugier's hypothesis the cornerstone of his own definition of architecture.[2] In 1755 the book appeared in a second French edition, this one including the name of the author and containing a number of illustrations. The most significant of these was the frontispiece, an extraordinary engraving that provided one of the boldest and most potent images ever produced of architectural representation as a form of imitation of nature (fig. 2.1). The primitive hut it depicted became the centerpiece around which much of the debate over modern architecture revolved during the succeeding two centuries.[3]

Some of Laugier's contemporaries, like Jacques-François Blondel (1705–1774), the most prominent academic theorist and teacher of architecture of the period, saw a nefarious influence in what he characterized as the enticing sophistry of the book's argument. "Because they have read

2.1 Marc-Antoine Laugier. *Essai sur l'architecture*, orig. pub. 1753; 2nd ed., 1755. Frontispiece, 2nd ed., by Charles Eisen

2.2 Henry Flitcroft, with Henry Hoare. Garden, Stourhead, Wiltshire, 1743–69. View of lake, with Temple of Flora, 1744–46 (on left); medieval Bristol High Cross, transplanted 1765 (in center, beyond Bridge); and Temple of Apollo, 1765 (on right), by Francis Nicholson, ca. 1813

the *Essay of Father Logier* [sic]," he noted, young architects "think themselves well educated." They "are rationalizers, and do not reason."[4] Blondel's former student William Chambers derided "the reverend father's inborn aversion" to most of the commonly accepted classical conventions, declaring that Laugier's "objections ... consist more of words than of meaning." He condescendingly counseled the "French Jesuit" to "give himself the trouble to think again."[5]

The young Goethe was even more defensive and vitriolic. In his essay *Von deutscher Baukunst* (1772) on the nature of German Gothic architecture, in which he extolled the power of Strasbourg Cathedral and the genius of its architect, Erwin von Steinbach, Goethe lashed out at Laugier as the archenemy of artistic freedom and creativity. He rhetorically asked: "What does it profit us, O neo-French philosophizing connoisseurs, that the first man who sensed his needs, rammed in four tree-trunks, joined up four poles on top, and topped all with branches and moss?" Making mockery of Laugier's belief that he could "decide the adequacy of our present-day needs" based on this "primitive discovery," Goethe referred to the hut as a "pigsty" from which one "would be unable [in truth] to abstract a single principle," and characterized Laugier's theory as a pure "protoplastic fable." Objecting, in particular, to its strict construction of the imitative process in terms of Greek trabeation, Goethe struck at the heart of the problem Laugier's proscriptive rationalism raised by admonishing the Frenchman in the following way: "You want to teach us that which we should need because by your principles that which we do not need cannot be justified."[6] We will return to this conundrum later.

Laugier's redefinition of mimesis in strict accord with a natural model for architecture's more sophisticated productions was a trenchant response to the marriage of convenience between need and desire—or truth and appearance—that controlled traditional classical theory and practice and suppressed many of its inherent ambiguities and paradoxes. The proscriptions alluded to by Goethe devolved from Laugier's reformist position, which brought out into the open the negotiation of the relationship between truth and appearance in the concept of *vraisemblance*, or verisimilitude, that lay at the heart of the matter of architectural representation. This chapter will analyze some of the issues raised by Laugier, first in his book and then in a building programmatically intended to embody many of the same ideas: the Parisian Church of Sainte-Geneviève, designed by Jacques-Germain Soufflot (1713–1780) shortly after Laugier's essay was published and completed by the end of the century.

The Translation of the English Garden to Ermenonville and the Idea of the Unfinished

In many ways, the ground for Laugier's critique of Baroque artifice and rhetoric in favor of a stricter and more imitative form of classicism was prepared by events in England over the preceding half century. The naturalism of the English landscape garden and the clarity of neo-Palladianism—not to speak of the tradition of a more bookish classicism that went back from Christopher Wren to Inigo Jones (1610–1660)—have often been acknowledged as playing a role of some significance in the evolution of architectural thought and practice in France (the dependence of Soufflot's dome of Sainte-Geneviève on that of Wren's St. Paul's Cathedral being only the most obvious instance).[7] But the so-called Anglomania of mid-eighteenth-century France should not prevent us from seeing the very different directions that developments took in the two countries.[8] From the point of view of the theory of representation, these differences were crucial—and categorical. And nowhere, perhaps, can they be better seen than in the later history of the English landscape garden as it migrated across the Channel to France.

In England, the pictorialized representation of the outbuildings of Castle Howard evolved at Stowe into a narrative form of expression, allegorical in nature, that emphasized the referential and associational basis of the built forms. Henry Hoare's garden at Stourhead, built from the 1740s through the 1770s, took this idea to its logical conclusion. Now entirely separated from the house, and therefore from any interaction with its obviously man-made formal order, the various garden buildings are linked to one another along a path around a lake (fig. 2.2). The closed circuit sets up a continuous narrative almost novelistic in its exposition of characters and situations. As at Castle Howard, the pictorialized representations rely for their specificity on references to distinct historical models, such as the Roman Pantheon or the Temple of the Sun at Baalbek.[9]

Though at first glance looking quite similar to its English parent, the transplanted *jardin anglais* often had significantly different purposes and effects. The one at the Château of Ermenonville, just north of Paris, designed by its owner, René de Girardin, with the help of the painter Hubert Robert (1733–1808) among others, offers a telling example. Girardin, who was to author the only French book on garden theory translated into English at the time, inherited the property in the early 1760s and developed it over the next ten years or so.[10] One of his final additions was the tomb of Jean-Jacques Rousseau (1712–1778) on the Ile des Peupliers, in the lake in front of the château (fig. 2.3). An ardent admirer of Rousseau, Girardin had invited the author-philosopher to live and work at Ermenonville, where, in the summer of 1778, he spent the last six weeks of his life. (Rousseau's body was moved to Paris in 1794 and interred in the Panthéon, following its conversion from the Church of Sainte-Geneviève.)

The landscaping and garden buildings at Ermenonville reflect Rousseau's philosophy of nature, his social theories, and especially his historiographic treatment of society's institutions in their relation to natural origins and future evolution. The circular Doric Temple of Modern Philosophy, set on a hill overlooking Rousseau's tomb, might at first appear to be a ruin, meant to inspire melancholic thoughts about the past and a golden age that once was (fig. 2.4). Modeled on the so-called Temple of Vesta at Tivoli, it was built, on the contrary, as a deliberately unfinished structure, intended to function as a kind of lapidary blueprint for the future (fig. 2.5). The rubble base is unfaced, as are the cella walls, which are complete only up to the level of the entablature. The door jambs and lintel of the main entrance are blocked out, but only six of the surrounding columns are in place. Each of these is dedicated to a particular modern philosopher or thinker Girardin considered to be unique and prophetic: Descartes, Newton, William Penn, Montesquieu, Voltaire, and Rousseau.[11] Inscribed on the columnless base just to the right of the door is the question, in Latin, "Quis hoc Perficiet?" (Who will finish this?). A number of roughly finished columns lie waiting on the ground nearby. Girardin's idea was that, when modern philosophy found

2.3 Hubert Robert. Rousseau's Tomb, Château of Ermenonville, ca. 1778. View with château in background

2.4 Robert, with René-Louis de Girardin. Temple of Modern Philosophy, Château of Ermenonville, ca. 1770. View from rear, looking down to lake

2.5 Temple of Modern Philosophy, Château of Ermenonville

its future leaders, the remaining columns would be inscribed with their names and raised into place to complete the corpus of the building. In the meantime, the unfinished state of the temple revealed the beginnings of modern thought.

The forms of classical architecture were thus called upon not simply to serve as representational figures in an otherwise independent pictorial or poetic narrative, but rather to function as integral elements of a self-referential architectural construct signifying the evolution from a condition close to nature to one having arrived at a state of highly advanced civilization. Evidence of the importance of architecture's own historiography and role in the development of culture can be seen throughout the grounds. One of the most impressive monuments is an artificial dolmen, or megalithic burial chamber. (It was in fact inspired by the discovery nearby of an authentic prehistoric burial pit.) But the most important and conspicuous example in this history of primitive construction at Ermenonville is the no longer extant Rustic Temple, located on a high point of land, like the Temple of Modern Philosophy, to which it was no doubt meant to be related (fig. 2.6). The open cella containing a statue of a chthonic deity is defined by unhewn tree trunks and covered by a thatched gable roof. An early engraving of the structure portrays a site of Arcadian activities; the altar just below and in front suggests a place of propitiation. The Rustic Temple thus became the primitive precursor and prototype for the as yet incomplete Temple of Modern Philosophy, unsophisticated in form as compared with the latter but, by that very token, uncorrupted and pure in spirit.[12] It was the same scenario that had been played out by the Abbé Laugier about ten to fifteen years before in his *Essai sur l'architecture*, a book that Girardin undoubtedly knew. Whether or not the creator of Ermenonville actually intended his design to echo Laugier's thought is not recorded, but if he did, he certainly would not have been alone.

2.6 Robert, with Girardin (probably). Rustic Temple, Château of Ermenonville, ca. 1770. From *Promenade, ou Itinéraire des jardins d'Ermenonville*, 1788

2.7 François Mansart and Jacques Lemercier. Church of Val de Grâce, Paris, 1646–67. West facade

2.8 Church of Val de Grâce. Interior

Laugier's Argument versus the Vitruvian Convention

Laugier's *Essai* was written as a diatribe against the corruption of modern architecture at the hands of those whom he felt had lost contact with the primitive purity of the art and had thus been led from one abuse to another. As a Jesuit priest, he surely knew well his own mother church in Rome, the late sixteenth-century proto-Baroque Church of the Gesù that was built at the beginning of the final stage in this precipitous state of decline. But it was not the Italian model that he lashed out against as much as it was its French followers. He condemned almost all the seventeenth- and early eighteenth-century classical churches in Paris (figs. 2.7–8). Laugier criticized their heaviness and massiveness, the plasticity of their sculptured surfaces, the multiplication of redundant parts, the lack of calm, quiet planes and clear, distinct, structurally defined shapes. His most acerbic criticism was reserved for the Baroque use of thick piers with attached pilasters to support the heavy arches and barrel vaults that define the typical church's interior space.[13] The resulting oppressiveness was, in his view, diametrically opposed to the kind of spiritually affective and uplifting space appropriate to a place of Christian worship.

In contrast to such decadence, Laugier wrote of the early Imperial Roman temple in Nîmes, known as the Maison Carrée, as a "beautiful" building that "accords with the true principles of architecture" by virtue of "a simplicity and a nobility that strikes everybody" (fig. 2.9).[14] As Wolfgang Herrmann has shown, Laugier knew the Maison Carrée from an early age, having been born in Provence and having spent part of his Jesuit training, in 1742, in the city of Nîmes itself. The two buildings Laugier held up as rare examples of good modern architecture were ones he got to know well when he was transferred from Lyon to Paris two years later. The first of these was the east colonnade of the

2.9 Robert. *The Temple of Augustus (Maison Carrée) in Nîmes,* 1783

2.10 Claude Perrault, Louis Le Vau, and Charles Le Brun. East facade, Louvre, Paris, 1667–70

2.11 Jules Hardouin-Mansart. Chapel, Palace of Versailles, 1688–1703. Interior

Louvre, the facade designed by the team of Claude Perrault (1613–1688), Louis Le Vau (1612–1670), and Charles Le Brun (1619–1690) in the late 1660s, following Gianlorenzo Bernini's (1598–1680) forced withdrawal from the scene, and as a direct criticism of the Italian architect's Baroque projects (fig. 2.10). The second was the Chapel at Versailles, designed by Jules Hardouin-Mansart (1646–1708) at the end of the century and finished in the early 1700s (fig. 2.11).[15] Laugier had in fact preached there on more than one occasion during the time he was writing the *Essai*.

What should be striking is that the three buildings Laugier admired most— the Maison Carrée, the east facade of the Louvre, and the Chapel at Versailles— all have one thing in common: freestanding columns supporting unbroken (or nearly unbroken, in the case of the Louvre) entablatures. This combination, which Laugier called the only true and "essential" form of architecture, established a fundamental criterion for his critique of Renaissance and Baroque classicism and the basis for his proposed reforms.[16] To ground that ideal combination of freestanding column and unbroken entablature (and triangular pediment, in the case of an exterior) in a foolproof argument based on reason and nature, Laugier turned to the myth of the noble savage and rewrote the theory of mimesis around it.

Under the heading "General Principles of Architecture," he began the first chapter of the *Essai* in the following way:

> Architecture is the same as all the other arts: its principles are based on simple nature, and all the rules of architecture are to be found clearly indicated in the way nature proceeds. Let us consider man in his primitive state, without any aid or guidance other than his natural instincts. He is in need of a place to rest. On the banks of a quietly flowing brook, he notices a stretch of grass; its fresh greenness is pleasing to his eyes, its tender down invites him; he is drawn there and, stretched out at leisure on the sparkling carpet, he thinks of nothing else but enjoying the gift of nature; he lacks nothing; he does not wish for anything. But soon the scorching heat of the sun forces him to look for shelter. A nearby forest draws him to its cooling shade; he finds a refuge in its depth, and there he is content. But suddenly, mists swirl around and grow denser, until thick clouds cover the skies; soon torrential rain pours down on this delightful forest. The savage, in his shelter of leaves, does not know how to protect himself from the uncomfortable dampness that penetrates everywhere. Seeing a cave nearby, he creeps into it, and, finding it dry, he praises himself for his discovery. But new sources of unpleasantness make his stay unbearable here. He finds himself in darkness, the air he breathes is foul, and so he leaves, this time resolved to make good, by his own industry, the careless neglect of nature. He wants to make himself a dwelling that would protect him without burying him. Some fallen branches in the forest are the right material for his purpose. He chooses four of the strongest, raises them upright and arranges them in a square. Across their top he lays four other branches; and on these he hoists from two sides yet another row of branches, which incline toward each other and meet at their highest point. He then covers this sort of roof with leaves so tightly compacted that neither rain nor sun can penetrate; and thus the savage is housed [see fig. 2.1]. Admittedly, the cold and heat will make him feel uncomfortable in this house that is open on all sides; but he will soon fill in the space between the parts and feel secure.[17]

So ends the first paragraph of the *Essai*, recounting the narrative of humankind's first construction. At this point, Laugier states the premise of his theory:

> Such is the course of simple nature: it is in the imitation of its ways that art was born. The little rustic hut that I have just described is the model on which all the splendors of architecture have been imagined. It is by approaching the simplicity of this first model that fundamental mistakes are avoided and true perfection is achieved.... It is easy from now on to distinguish between those parts that are essential to the composition of an architectural order, those that have been introduced by need, and, finally, those that have been added only by caprice. It is only in the parts that are essential that one finds beauty; in the parts introduced by need consist all the licenses; and in the parts added by caprice are all the faults.[18]

The previously cited reference to the Maison Carrée directly follows this passage and terminates the section on "General Principles of Architecture."[19] Laugier then turns his attention in the remaining sections of the first chapter to describing the various parts of the classical order and how they are to be used, following the "natural" model of the primitive hut as historically represented in the Greek or early Roman temple.

In a certain sense, there was nothing new, from the point of view of architectural treatises at least, in referring to the primitive hut. Beginning with Vitruvius (ca. 90–ca.

20 B.C.), authors had usually cited the first human efforts at building in their attempts to describe the beginnings of architecture. But rarely, if ever, were those originary events directly connected in an evolutionary continuum with the development of the classical forms of Greek architecture, nor— and this is the really radical step Laugier took— was the example of the primitive hut given priority and used to justify those later sophisticated forms by testifying to their natural origins.[20]

Vitruvius set the conventional pattern, followed more or less faithfully up until Laugier's time. His prehistory of architecture, recounted in the fourth book of his *De architectura,* started not with primitive and isolated individuals living "like animals in forests and caves and woods" but with organized groups of human beings, gifted "beyond the other animals," who, as a result of "the discovery of fire" and the ability to communicate with one another by means of language, began "a life in common" entailing the construction of shelters. These earliest structures varied in materials and techniques: "some [began] to make shelters of leaves, some to dig caves under the hills, some to make of mud and wattles places for shelter, imitating the nests of swallows and their methods of building."[21]

But between those primitive origins and what Vitruvius referred to as "architecture," meaning the much later buildings of Greece and Rome, lay an enormous gulf in time reflecting the passage of humanity "from a savage and rustic life to a peaceful civilisation." During this long period of progress and change, people initially "produced better kinds of huts" as a result of seeing and learning from each other's work.[22] Variations in construction techniques abounded. "First," Vitruvius stated, "with upright forked props and twigs put between, they wove their walls with mud. Others made walls, drying moistened clods which they bound with wood, and covered with reeds and leafage, so as to escape the rain and heat. When in winter-time the roofs could not withstand the rains, they made ridges, and smearing clay down the sloping roofs, they drew off the rainwater."[23] Referencing contemporary practices, Vitruvius continued his historical account of the variety of early types of shelter by noting that, "to this day,"

> In Pontus among the nations of the Colchi, because of their rich forests, two whole trees are laid flat, right and left, on the ground, a space being left between them.... On the furthest parts of them, two others are placed transversely, and these four trees enclose in the middle the space for the dwelling. Then, laying upon them alternate beams from the four sides, they join up the angles. And so constructing the walls with trees, they raise up towers rising perpendicular from the lowest parts.... Further, they raise the roofs by cutting off the cross-beams at the end and gradually narrowing them. And so, from the four sides they raise over the middle a pyramid on high.... But the Phrygians [by contrast], who are dwellers in the plains [and]...lack timber ...choose natural mounds, and dividing them in the middle by a trench and digging tracks through, open out spaces as far as the nature of the place allows. They fasten logs together at the upper end, and so make pyramids. These they cover with reeds and brushwood and pile up very large hillocks from the ground above their dwellings.[24]

All this, in Vitruvius's view, preceded the development of "craftsmen" who "armed their minds with ideas and purposes" and, "building up themselves in spirit, and looking out and forward with larger ideas born from the variety of their crafts and disciplines, ...began to build, not huts, but houses, on foundations, and with brick walls, or built of stone; and with roofs of wood and tiles."[25] Still, none of this, in his view, had any direct bearing on the classical

2.12 Laugier. *An Essay on Architecture,* 1st English edition, 1755. Frontispiece, by Samuel Wale

architecture of Greece and Rome. As he wrote at the end of the account summarized above, his purpose at this point was only to describe "whence the kinds of buildings have originated" and not "whence architecture arises."[26] That discussion was entirely separate and left for book 4, where the author discussed how some of the decorative details of the upper parts of the Doric and Ionic orders such as triglyphs, mutules, and dentils, although never the structure of the temple as a whole, "arose from th[e] imitation of timber work" and thus were to be considered as "representations" of existing techniques of carpentry.[27] Those discrete elements, however, had nothing to do with the primitive huts of "savage and rustic life" that were by then entirely lost to memory.

Vitruvius's historical account allowed for progress and change, which in turn provided the basis for classical theory from the Renaissance through the eighteenth century, which saw Roman and postmedieval European architecture as not only building on the Greek example but improving it in numerous ways. This was the kernel of William Chambers's critique of Laugier's hypothesis. Chambers's illustrations of the "Primitive Buildings" preceding the classical temple in his *Treatise on Civil Architecture* of 1759 show three successive forms of wood huts, only the last of which bears a resemblance to its later masonry counterpart (see fig. I.9). The first, conical in shape, was, in his words, "a form of the simplest structure." "Like the birds" whose "nests...they imitated," these early humans "composed [their huts] of branches of trees, spreading them wide at the bottom, and joining them in a point at the top, covering the whole with reeds, leaves, and clay." The second type, a flat-roofed cubic structure, evolved as dwellers "found the Conic Figure inconvenient, on account of its inclined sides." Over time and "insensibly," Chambers asserted, "mankind improved in the Art of Building, and invented methods to make their huts lasting and handsome, as well as convenient."[28]

The "improvements" that resulted in the third, gabled type ultimately led to "solid and stately edifices of stone [that] imitated the parts which necessity had introduced into the primitive huts." But Chambers argued that even these "first buildings were in all likelihood rough and uncouth" and only after "long experience and reasoning...and by great practice" did architects reach the "perfection...which succeeding ages have regarded with the highest veneration." This evolutionary progress in the prehistoric past foreshadowed the advances monumental architecture itself would undergo from the fifth century B.C. to the present. To condemn pilasters, for example, as Laugier did, because they did not exist in the "pristine simplicity" of the "primitive wooden huts" and were, in effect, "a Roman invention," was therefore to write off the extraordinary achievement of architects like Palladio, Jones, and Vincenzo Scamozzi (1552–1616), something Chambers was absolutely unprepared and unwilling to do.[29]

Unlike the Vitruvian and Vitruvian-derived accounts of architecture's earliest beginnings, Laugier's assumed that the creator of the "model" rustic hut was still living in a "state of nature" and reacting to circumstances "without any aid or guidance other than his natural instincts." As with Rousseau's contemporaneous description of the noble savage in his *Discourse on the Origins of Inequality* (1755), Laugier explained, in the third paragraph of his section on "General Principles," how the primitive hut was not merely the first example of built form but also how it had to be seen as the natural prototype for the Greek temple and the conventional forms of classical architecture that derived from it.[30] Natural origin and historical continuity were essential to his program. "Let us never lose sight of our little rustic hut," he warned his readers. "I can only see columns, a ceiling or entablature, and a pointed roof forming at both ends what is called a pediment. So far, there is no vault, still less an arch, no pedestals, no attic, not even a door or a window. I therefore come to this conclusion: in an architectural order only the column, the entablature, and the pediment may form an essential part of its composition." He concluded that "if each of these parts is suitably placed and suitably formed," meaning in accord with its natural "model," "nothing else need be added to make the work perfect." As a case in point, he referred his readers to the Maison Carrée, "a rectangle where thirty columns support an entablature and a roof— closed at both ends by a pediment— that is all."[31]

Of the many points on which critics could take issue with Laugier, there was one that was fundamental to his argument and absolutely crucial for him to dispose of efficiently and with the least amount of discussion. This was the presumption of the hut's natural origins. Laugier's account surely left the reader in some doubt as to the "naturalness" of what might have taken place when the "savage" emerged from his cave to start the building process. There is no more compelling evidence for such a logical misreading of the author's intention than the frontispiece to the pirated, first English edition of the book, which appeared in early 1755, about the same time the second French edition was published (fig. 2.12). The artist, Samuel Wale (1721–1786), clearly interpreted the originary event quite differently from the way Laugier described it. Instead of a solitary "savage," probably unclothed and, like an animal, working by "instinct" alone, Wale's image depicts a community of laborers in a domesticated environment, each performing a specialized task and using various sophisticated tools to accomplish the desired ends. According to this reading of the event, which is clearly the most reasonable one (and the one that follows Vitruvius most closely), the hut made of four corner posts supporting straight entablatures and a gabled roof is a man-made artifact and in no way a natural occurrence. The attribution of the templelike design to an already advanced stage of human civilization, however, robbed it of a significant aspect of the ideational power Laugier intended it to have.[32]

As previously noted, the first edition of Laugier's *Essai* was unillustrated. This allowed the reader to imagine things in conventional and entirely reasonable terms. For the second edition of 1755, a number of engravings were added, the most important of which is the frontispiece by Charles Eisen (1720–1778) depicting the building of the hut as Laugier imagined the scene and wanted his reader to (see fig. 2.1).[33] The addition of this image serves to preclude a "cultural" reading based on Vitruvius and to reinforce Laugier's belief in the "natural" state of existence of the "savage" in question. The trees forming the four posts of

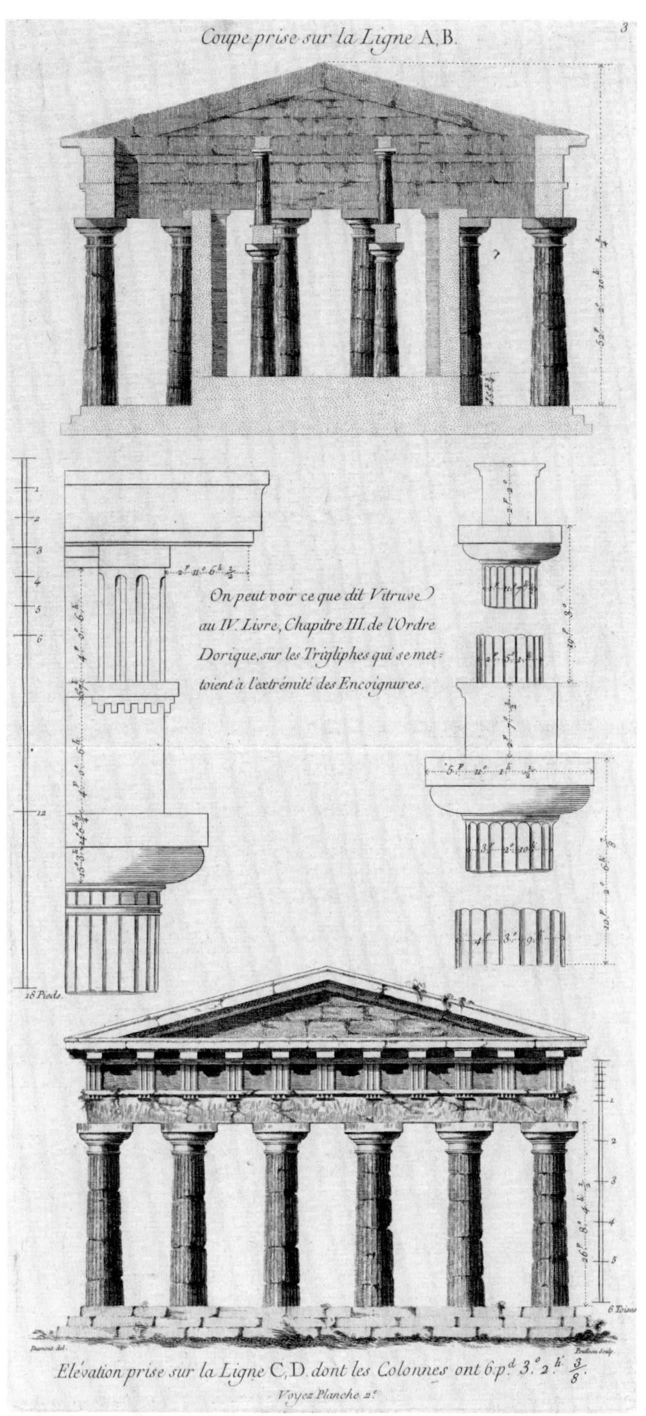

2.13 Gabriel-Pierre-Martin Dumont (based on Jacques-Germain Soufflot). Section, elevation, and details of "Temple Hexastyle" (Temple of Hera II), Paestum, *Les Ruines de Paestum, autrement Posidonia, ville de l'ancienne Grande Grèce, au Royaume de Naples,* 1769

the structure were neither felled nor found lying on the ground. They are rooted in it and apparently still growing. It is also almost impossible to distinguish the constructed parts of the roof from the overhanging boughs of the trees. Most curious is the fact that there is no human in sight. A female muse of architecture points to the hut, and her gaze is reflected by a genie who seems to look on, as Herrmann noted, in wonder and astonishment. The hut is thus presented, even before the text begins, as a kind of miracle of nature. The reader will be hard put to eliminate this picture from his or her mind while attending to the story that follows. In its uncanniness—and still to this day—the image predisposes us to infer what is not actually stated and to accept Laugier's interpolation in the 1755 text explaining that the hut is "a rough sketch that nature offers us" as a model for architecture.[34] The confounding of truth and appearance in the engraved image places new emphasis on the meaning of the concept of verisimilitude, while stretching its power of approximation to new limits.

Laugier's "Graeco-Gothic" Ideal and Soufflot's Church of Sainte-Geneviève

If the primitive hut was the "rough sketch," the finished picture, according to Laugier, was the ancient Greek temple. "Architecture owes all that is perfect to the Greeks," he wrote.[35] It is unclear whether he knew Greek architecture in any detail or had actually seen drawings like the ones Soufflot did at Paestum in 1750 (fig. 2.13), but he did know the Maison Carrée, which was considered at the time to be a fairly accurate reflection of Greek ideals. Based on this, Laugier maintained that the Greeks were the first to understand the significance of the hut, thus initiating the cycle of imitations. They transformed the various parts of the primitive wood structure into stone, turning the tree trunks into columns, the horizontal branches into entablatures, and the angled ones above them into the pediment. In this way the Greek temple as a whole imitated, in permanent materials, the forms of nature and could thus be considered to be a pure representation of the natural prototype of the hut. Being made permanent in stone, the forms of the temple were, in effect, idealized. They became *la belle nature* that later architects would refer to and represent, just as the marble figures of Phidias or Praxiteles would form the images of "ideal nature" for the classically trained painter and sculptor.[36]

The hut, as represented by the Greek temple, was not beautiful in Laugier's eyes for superficial reasons. It was beautiful because it combined rationality with clarity, both of which depended on "naturalness." The key to this rationality and clarity was the distinction Laugier made between those parts of architecture that are "essential" and those that are merely the result of "need" or, worse still, "caprice." Here Laugier's radical move was to bring the issue of structure, however vaguely understood, into the open and make it definitive of the "essential," as opposed to the merely "necessary." In the foreword to the second edition of the *Essai*, he noted that "the parts of an architectural order are the parts of the building itself. They must therefore be applied in such a way that they not only adorn, but actually constitute the building." In a structurally inflected paraphrase of Alberti's definition of beauty, he concluded: "The existence of the building must depend so completely on the union of these parts that not a single one could be taken away without the whole building collapsing."[37]

It was by narrowing the traditional distinction between construction and decoration that Laugier was able to use the argument about the representational form of the Greek temple as a means of critiquing contemporary architecture.[38] If the freestanding column, the unbroken entablature, and the triangular pediment were the only "essential" features of architecture, then most of the things Laugier disliked about contemporary design could be classified as either unnecessary or willfully bizarre, which is to say, unnatural. Walls, doors, windows, pedestals, arches, vaults, domes, pilasters, volutes, even a second or third story—all these were not part of the "essential," representational construct of the hut-temple. Some of these elements, like walls, doors, and windows, not to speak of upper stories, Laugier acknowledged were needed in a climate like that of France and, indeed, had already been granted a "license" by custom and tradition.[39] But broken pediments and entablatures, attached pilasters, pedestals under columns, volutes, and superimposed pediments had no reason whatsoever to exist and therefore should be banned as faults of the grossest kind. The proof of their falsehood was the way in which they contradicted not the rules of *bienséance* and decorum, but those of representation as such, meaning the criterion of verisimilitude. A pediment beneath another pediment implies, as Laugier noted, the "absurd" condition that there are "two roofs one over the other," and thus one building inside the other, since the pediment by definition "represents the gable of the roof." A pilaster, in his view, represented nothing so much as a squared column shorn in half, which could only be interpreted as the result of an exceedingly "bizarre" and "unnatural" act. A pedestal under a column was a tautology that undercut the very function a column was meant to represent, which was to carry the load of a building down to the ground. "Since the columns are the legs of a building," Laugier noted, "it is absurd to give them an additional pair of legs."[40]

The hyperboles, tautologies, redundancies, and other rhetorical figures of speech Laugier found so unnatural and irrational in later Renaissance and Baroque architecture filled pages and pages of his book. But before he could actually offer his own proposal for how to proceed in contemporary France, he had to figure out what to use as a model for the interior space of buildings—and ultimately how to represent that. The primitive hut would obviously not do. Nor, for that matter, would the antique temple, whose dark, narrow, enclosed cella hardly suited most eighteenth-century needs. Rejecting the cavernousness and massiveness of

Renaissance and Baroque churches, Laugier was led, almost by elimination, and like a number of French theorists before him, such as the Abbé de Cordemoy (1631–1713), to the Gothic cathedral.[41]

Despite his absolute animadversion to what he described as the "barbarism" of the Gothic style, "in which the lack of proportions and bizarre and childish ornament produced nothing but a filigree stonework of [an unparalleled] formlessness, grotesqueness, and excessiveness," Laugier declared that "our Gothic churches are still the most acceptable [we have]." He was bowled over by the openness, lightness, structural elegance, and height of the Gothic cathedral's interior space. "I enter Notre-Dame," he wrote, and "at first glance my attention is captured, my imagination is struck by the size, the height and the unobstructed view of the vast nave; for some moments, I am lost in the amazement that the grand effect of the whole stirs in me. Recovering from this initial astonishment and taking note now of the details, I find innumerable absurdities, but I lay the blame for them on the misfortunes of the time [in which the cathedral was built]."[42]

The openness and lightness he admired in Gothic churches clearly derived from the same type of structural precision, clarity, and expressiveness that he believed the Greek temple owed to its origins in the primitive hut. But how could one redeploy such interior effects—what Laugier referred to as the "spirit" of Gothic construction—without reproducing the grotesque "formlessness" of Gothic decoration? The representational identity between decoration and construction, so carefully secured by the reconstruction of the mimetic process based on the prototypical hut, was thus almost immediately called into question. To understand how Laugier resolved the problem and how his interpretation of architectural representation ultimately differed from that of his predecessors, it is useful to turn to the building by Soufflot that echoed his ideas.

In the fourth chapter of the *Essai*, Laugier provided a verbal description of an ideal church in which he tried to combine the effects of a Gothic interior structure, based on the use of arches and rib vaults, with the representational forms of Greek trabeation. The result, though not uninteresting, simply proved to his detractors that he was not an architect. But within less than two years of this effort, the most progressive architect of the period, Jacques-Germain Soufflot, would give a truly professional imprimatur to what Robin Middleton has described as Laugier's "Graeco-Gothic ideal."[43] The building in which Soufflot achieved the desired synthesis of structural and decorative elements is the Parisian Church of Sainte-Geneviève (now known as the Panthéon). Laugier himself recognized it as the expression of his most cherished ideals, writing to the Academy of Lyon in 1761 that "this church will become the true masterpiece of French architecture. It will overshadow all the wonderful works that Italy has produced.... Here all faults common elsewhere are carefully avoided, and of all the refinements of which architecture is capable, none has been forgotten. Here is a genius that aims high without ever missing the natural and the simple."[44]

The church has a complicated history, which need not concern us unduly, so I will merely sketch in the most significant details. Sainte-Geneviève was a votive church dedicated to the patron saint of Paris, whose remains, along with those of the first Christian king and queen of France, Clovis and Clothilde, were buried in the crypt beneath the baldachin at the crossing (figs. 2.14–15). A Church of the Holy Apostles had originally been built on the site by Clovis to contain the remains of Sainte-Geneviève, as well as to serve as a royal mausoleum. Rebuilt in the Middle Ages, it had fallen into disrepair by the mid-eighteenth century. In 1744 Louis XV made a vow to rebuild the church when he was taken grievously ill at Metz during the War of the Austrian Succession. Ten years later, the vow was consummated, and Soufflot was hired as architect in early 1755 by the recently appointed *directeur des bâtiments*, the Marquis de Marigny.[45]

Soufflot had accompanied Marigny on a lengthy educational tour of Italy just a few years before, and it was on that trip that he visited and drew the Greek temples at Paestum, becoming, in effect, the first architect of any note to do so.[46] Aside from the buildings he had designed in Lyon in the interim, including the Hôtel-Dieu (1738–60s) and the Loge du Change (1747–50), he had also made a certain reputation for himself as a critical historian. He lectured in a notably intelligent fashion to the Lyon Academy in 1741 on the positive values of Gothic architecture, pointing to the advances made during the period in the areas of construction and spatial composition. Soufflot therefore brought with him a fairly uncommon knowledge of and sensitivity to the two historical types of architecture Laugier had proposed as constituting the basis for reform. And, according to most recent historians, there is no question that Marigny appointed Soufflot to the job with a program of architectural reform in mind.[47]

The design produced by early 1757 and engraved in that year established the *parti* that remained essentially unchanged despite a number of important alterations made during the nearly thirty-five years that it took to complete the building (fig. 2.16). The perfect biaxial symmetry of the Greek cross plan was compromised, beginning in the very first year or two of construction, by the addition of bays at the west and east ends to lengthen the nave and choir. The height of the dome was raised considerably, with a triple-shell system based on Wren's St. Paul's being substituted for the original double-shell design, and a peripteral colonnade, again like that at St. Paul's, being added to mask the tall exterior drum (see fig. 2.14). To increase the interior's sense of lightness and openness, the rather high pedestal-like bases of the columns in the 1757 project were reduced to mere plinths, and the vaults supporting the cupolas over the arms of the Greek cross were hollowed out to allow for a gallery above the ground-floor peristyle (see fig. 2.15). (In the process of secularization following the Revolution, one of the most significant changes made to the fabric of the structure was the walling in of the expansive ground-floor windows.)

The one aspect of the design that was never changed, however, was the nearly independent, full-height temple portico, following the example set by Hawksmoor and Gibbs in England, though unique in French architecture of the time.[48] This feature of the building, no doubt in large measure a consequence of Soufflot's trip to Italy just a few years before, was in fact considered so significant that a full-scale painting of the portico was set up on the site in 1764 when the king laid the cornerstone after work on the foundations had been completed (fig. 2.17). With its enormous freestanding Corinthian columns, nearly unbroken entablature, and triangular pediment, the portico was literally understood as representing the entire structure. The building that would be erected behind it, on the other hand, had a very different character and issued from quite a different world of ideas.

The centralized, Greek cross plan reflected a long tradition of Renaissance architecture including, most notably, the Basilica of St. Peter in Rome (fig. 2.18).[49] The tradition had its origins in the early medieval period of the East rather than the West. The most celebrated early occurrence of the type was Justinian's sixth-century Church of the Holy Apostles in Constantinople, a most apt choice of model for Soufflot, since the original church built on the Paris site had been dedicated to the apostles Peter and Paul. But probably even more important was the association of the central plan type with martyria. The baldachin under the central dome protected and celebrated the relics of Sainte-Geneviève just below the crossing in the crypt.

Like St. Peter's and Justinian's Holy Apostles, Soufflot's church employs a central dome surrounded by transverse barrel vaults and subsidiary cupolas. But, as can readily be seen in a comparison between it and Michelangelo's design, there is a vast difference in the articulation of the support

2.14 Jacques-Germain Soufflot. Church of Sainte-Geneviève (now Panthéon), Paris, 1755–90. Exterior perspective, by Jean-Jacques Lequeu, 1781

2.15 Church of Sainte-Geneviève. Interior perspective, 1775

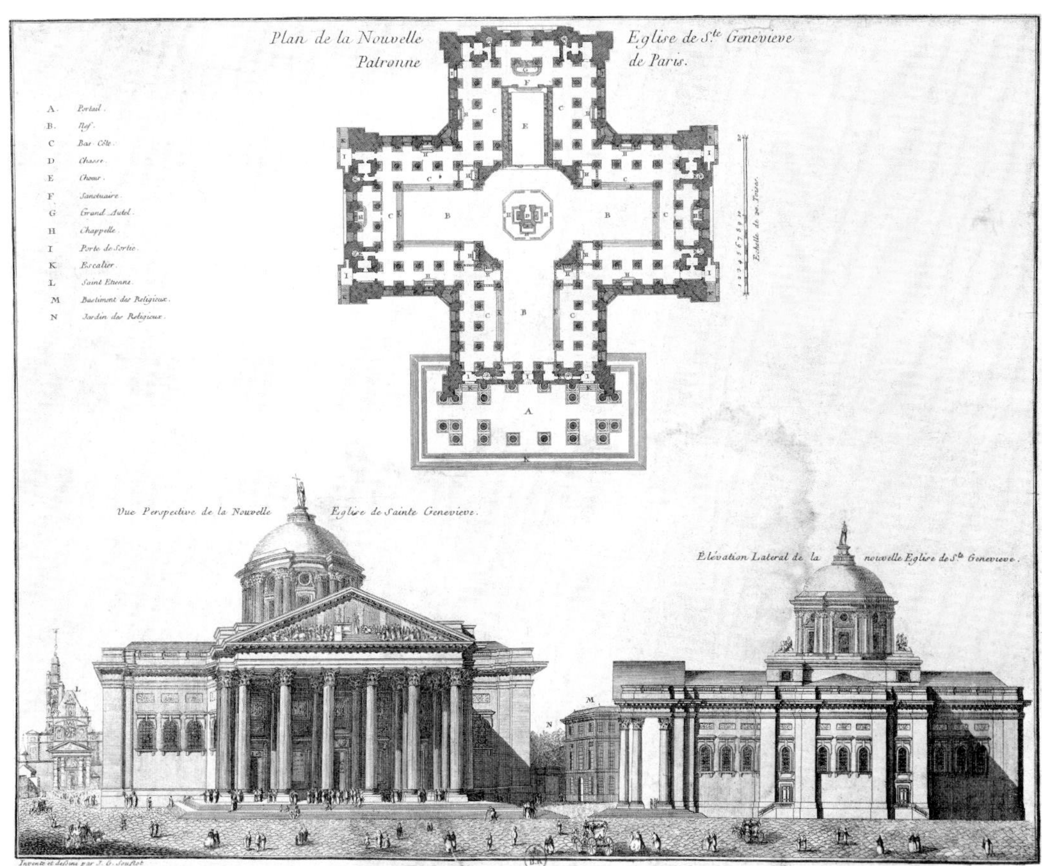

2.16 Church of Sainte-Geneviève. Plan, exterior perspective, and side elevation, 1757

2.17 Pierre-Antoine de Machy. *Cornerstone Laying Ceremony of the New Church of Sainte-Geneviève, September 6, 1764,* 1765

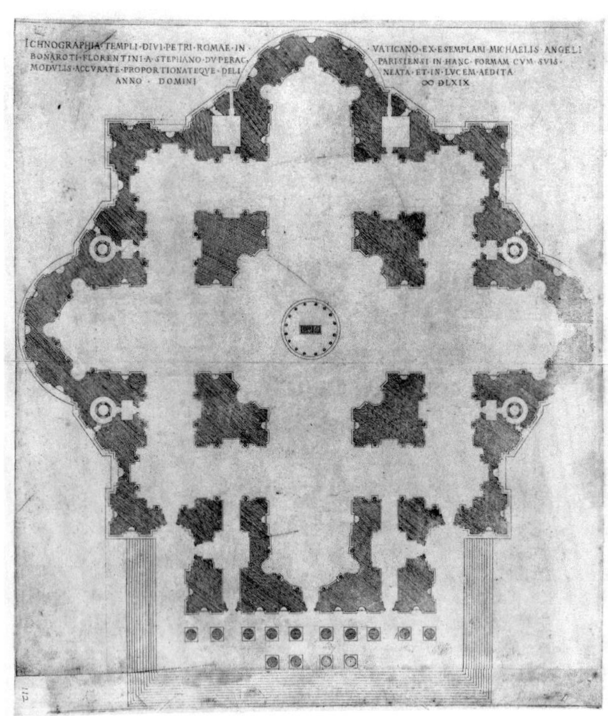

2.18 Michelangelo. Basilica of St. Peter, Rome. Plan, by Etienne Dupérac, 1546

system, so vast in fact that one might be hard put to believe that what happens above ground level is the same in both cases. In Soufflot's design, the massive piers and thick walls of St. Peter's have been completely eliminated, leaving in their place an almost skeletal structure of freestanding point supports.[50] These clearly defined architectonic elements translate the trabeated system of the main portico into the church's interior. At the same time, they provide a reticulated screen of fluted Corinthian columns that is permeated by space, flowing freely in all directions just as Laugier had desired (fig. 2.19).

The classical system of post-and-lintel construction, where freestanding columns carry unbroken entablatures with only the most minimal amount of mass in the corner piers of the crossing to support the dome, is transformed, however, in the upper stages of Soufflot's church, into the categorically different system of arcuated construction that derives not from Greek but from medieval

2.19 Church of Sainte-Geneviève. Interior, north side aisle

2.20 Church of Sainte-Geneviève. Interior, springing of cupola over west end of nave

2.22 Church of Sainte-Geneviève. Flying buttresses, masked by parapets

2.21 Cathedral of Saint-Etienne, Auxerre. Choir, 14th century

reinterpretations of late Imperial Roman construction (fig. 2.20). Just as one can point to the similarity of the final design of Soufflot's triple-shell dome to that of St. Paul's, one can also relate the skeletonized interior construction to the Church of St. Stephen, Walbrook (1672–87), one of the many churches Wren built in London after the fire of 1666. This parallel is particularly intriguing given Wren's interest in medieval architecture and his precocious desire to find a formal solution that would combine the structural elegance and economy of Gothic architecture with the ornamental detailing of the classical orders.

As Soufflot refined the design of Sainte-Geneviève throughout the 1760s and 1770s, he worked toward an even greater sense of dematerialization of the building's mass. The transverse arches supporting the cupolas and central dome were cut into by deep voids to produce the riblike effect of Gothic construction that Soufflot continued to study throughout his career (fig. 2.21). The reduction of

2.23 Place du Panthéon. Aerial view, showing Church of Sainte-Geneviève (now Panthéon) in center; former Abbey of Sainte-Geneviève (now Lycée Henri IV) behind it; Church of Saint-Etienne du Mont to left of Abbey; Bibliothèque Sainte-Geneviève to left of Panthéon; and Law School in lower left

the mass to lines of force ultimately led him to adopt the specifically Gothic device of flying buttresses, which he used to relieve the thrust of the vaults and domes (fig. 2.22). But unlike the exposed exoskeleton of a Gothic cathedral, these props were kept from the observer's view. As in Wren's St. Paul's, they are hidden by the parapet that rises above the walls to the height of the roofline (fig. 2.23). The large openings created by the lunette-shaped clerestory windows are also masked by the masonry screen and thus prevented from disturbing the external appearance of solidity and monumentality.

The exterior of the Church of Sainte-Geneviève thus preserves the classical composure and decorum promised by the representational frontispiece of the Corinthian portico, just as the parapet topping the side walls and the peristyle ringing the dome disguise any evidence of Gothic structural gymnastics. "Soufflot's principal goal," his collaborator Maximilien Brébion (1716–ca. 1792) said on the architect's death in 1780, "was to unite in the most beautiful of forms the lightness of construction of Gothic buildings with the purity and magnificence of Greek architecture."[51] That the word "architecture" in this case meant something more superficial than constitutional is made clear by Charles-Nicolas Cochin's (1715–1790) comment on the same subject ten years before. In defense of his friend Soufflot's design of the dome, which had come under severe criticism from a structural point of view, Cochin remarked that Soufflot had "found a way of uniting the noble decoration of the Greeks with the lightness of the Gothic."[52] Soufflot's intention at synthesis is well known and has often been cited as evidence of his liberalism, even eclecticism. But what is rarely, if ever, remarked is that the marriage of the two historical traditions was of unequal partners: only one of the pair—the classical—was allowed to represent itself; the other—the Gothic—had to remain behind the scenes in the role of servant.

2.24 Leon Battista Alberti. Church of Sant'Andrea, Mantua, begun 1472. Exterior

It should by now be apparent that the union of the Gothic and the classical was not, as Laugier's argument might have suggested, a matter simply of encasing an interior modeled on the former with an exterior representing the latter. The exterior of the interior— meaning the actual decorative appearance of the interior elevations— also had to be represented in Greek or Roman terms, for these were the only valid terms of representation understood as an imitation of nature. In other words, whatever went on behind the scenes (in the conjugal bed, so to speak), was not a matter fit for public display. Only the antique order had a natural (read "divine") right to representation. Well before Soufflot adopted the expedient, Laugier had recommended, in the *Essai,* the use of "flying buttresses, as ... in Gothic churches," as long as they were "so well hidden that nothing appears that indicates the pressure of the vaults."[53] Such "artifice," as he called it, ensured the truth of appearance by a verisimilar appearance of truth.

Putting the larger issue of truth and appearance in terms of the architectural discourse of construction and decoration, Laugier summarized— and predicted— Soufflot's synthesis in the following way:

> The great secret and true perfection of the art [of architecture] consists in joining solidity to delicacy. Whatever our artists say, these two qualities are not at all incompatible. In buildings of the Gothic style, delicacy has sometimes been taken as far as it can go, even beyond the generally accepted limits.... I wish that at least in this respect architects would adopt the spirit of this ridiculous style and study the astonishing workmanship of this way of building.... [Gothic architects] were sparing with the use of stone and lavish with that of iron; in this way ...they succeeded in joining the solid and the delicate. What would be the disadvantage of doing as they did? We understand decoration infinitely better than they did, but they were more skilled in construction than we are. If we want to improve [our architecture], do not let us consult them in matters of decoration but let us never stop consulting them in those of construction.[54]

In distinguishing between construction and decoration in this way, the "Graeco-Gothic" ideal of Laugier not only revealed the inequality of the partners in the marriage it was intended to effect; it also clarified, as perhaps never before, the fundamentally decorative constitution of the classical elements of design. In this regard, Laugier was no different from his critic Blondel, who maintained throughout his *Cours d'architecture, ou Traité de la décoration, distribution & construction des bâtiments* (1771–77) the complete separation of construction from decoration, as well as the priority of decoration as the defining term of architecture in its physical manifestations.[55]

2.25 Church of Sainte-Geneviève. Pediment, detail

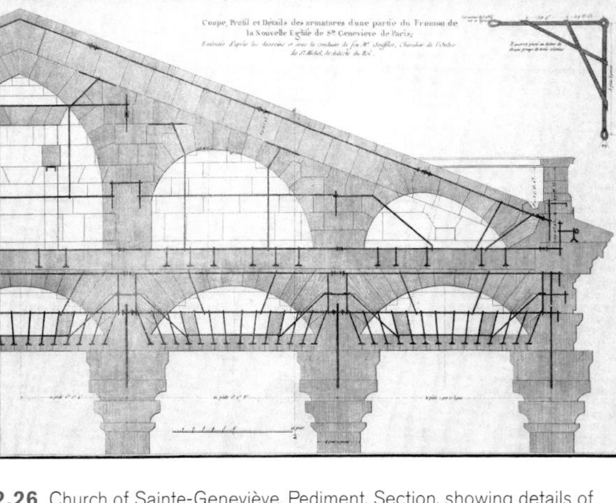

2.26 Church of Sainte-Geneviève. Pediment. Section, showing details of iron reinforcement, by Dumont, 1781

A Degree Zero of Verisimilitude

The relationship between truth and appearance in post-antique European classical architecture had fundamentally devolved from the distinction between decoration and construction. In this sense, Soufflot's church and Laugier's text were part of a long history. Alberti's Church of Sant'Andrea in Mantua, begun in the 1470s, can almost be read as an unsuspecting, or rather unenlightened, precedent (fig. 2.24). Although its interior and exterior are both classical, in contradistinction to the architect's earlier Church of San Francesco in Rimini (ca. 1450), where the exterior columns and arches encase a preexisting Gothic interior, the temple portico cum triumphal arch of Sant'Andrea is essentially a decorative, albeit monumental, frontispiece. Like Soufflot's portico, it stands synecdochically for the whole and thereby represents, in the linguistic sense of the term, the idea of church as temple. To preserve the existing Gothic tower on the left while providing space for a large circular window to light the nave, the portico was designed to front only a portion of the building's facade. Its decorative design appears to reflect the interior space of the nave and side aisles by virtue of the hierarchical division into three distinct vertical units, but the portico is actually only as wide as the nave and not nearly its full height. Moreover, this confusion of truth and appearance— or construction and decoration— permeates the very decorative system itself. In the portico, for instance, Alberti combined a thin and relatively flat post-and-lintel system with arches substantiating the thickness and massiveness of the solid walls.

Following Laugier's rational argument for eliminating any element foreign to the structural components of the Greek temple in its imitation of the primitive hut, Soufflot avoided the contradictions in the appearance of Alberti's facade, though not those that would inhere in the realities of construction. Unlike its antique model, Sainte-Geneviève's entablature is not built of uniform horizontal lintels spanning fully from one column to the next (figs. 2.25–26). Rather, it is made up of voussoirs locked together in flat arches, which, through a hidden and complex deployment of iron cramps and ties, gives the illusion of an antique pediment to a system of counterbalancing arches that even employs a pointed Gothic arch at the apex.[56] The tie-rods were in fact incapable of eliminating all the outward thrust of the arches, which forced Soufflot into devising a method of buttressing that, because it was highly visible, had to be consistent with the decorative system of exterior trabeation. His solution was a pair of columns added to both sides of the portico and joined to the front by means of reentrant angles.

Laugier had no compunction about such expedients as metal cramps and ties. Arguing that Gothic architects made "lavish" use of iron, he recommended its employment as a way to achieve the desired visual ends. It was visual appearance rather than actual constructed fact that was always uppermost in his mind; and it is this that we must keep in mind in assessing the full implication of his theoretical position and its delineation of the mimetic process of representation in the transformation of the primitive hut into the classical temple.[57] In one of his most significant and often quoted propositions, added to the second edition of the *Essai* to bolster and clarify its argument, Laugier wrote that "I should like to convince everybody of a truth in which I myself believe absolutely, namely, that the parts of an architectural order are the parts of a building itself. They must therefore be applied in such a way that they not only adorn but actually constitute the building."[58]

Laugier never for a moment meant that the fictive character of architectural decoration or "display," as he put it, should give way to brute reality. The very idealism of his construct of the primitive hut as imitative model makes this self-evident. Laugier was interested not in the truth of the structural facts of the "freestanding columns that carry entablatures," but rather, as he stated in response to one of the critics of the *Essai*, in "the truth of the architectural display they [re]present." What distinguished nature—that is to say, the hut—from architecture—that is to say, the temple—was not merely the change from wood to stone but, even more, the embellishment, the polish, and the sophistication of the "decoration" that the stone forms themselves received at the hands of art.[59]

For all that, however, Laugier—and, by extension, Soufflot—should in no way be thought of as merely proceeding on the same basis as Alberti and his successors. The differences, though subtle, are profound. The key to understanding them lies in the concept of verisimilitude, or *vraisemblance*, a concept that was central to eighteenth-century artistic theory, though only occasionally applied directly to the discussion of architecture.[60] The idea had its origins in Aristotle's *Poetics*. "It is not the function of the poet to relate what has happened," Aristotle wrote, "but what may happen—what is possible according to the law of probability or necessity." In contrast to the truth of everyday existence, verisimilitude, or that which is made to appear to be likely to be true, defines the "higher" truth of art: "The poet and the historian differ not by writing in verse or prose.... The true difference is that one relates what has happened, the other what may happen. Poetry, therefore, is a more philosophical and a higher thing than history; for poetry tends to express the universal, history the particular. By the universal I mean how a person of a certain type will on occasion speak or act, according to the law of probability or necessity."[61]

Laugier's celebration of the "essential" virtues of the primitive hut served to establish, with greater firmness, more precision, and much greater scope than had previously been attempted, the "law of probability or necessity" for the plausible appearance of truth in architecture.[62] His critique of the "licenses" and "caprices" of the buildings he grew up with derived from a perception of the enormity and incommensurability of the gap between truth and appearance in Renaissance and Baroque architecture and of the need to narrow it to within reason. In Alberti's Church of Sant'Andrea and perhaps even more obviously in the Rucellai Palace (see fig. I.7), the material realities of structure and space are so completely overridden by the representational devices of the decorative facing that one never even thinks to question how what appears to be true relates to what might in fact be true. No matter how forcefully the apparent or virtual structure seems to express the conditions of load and support, appearance is fundamentally what counts. For this reason, arched construction can be mixed with trabeated construction, just as exterior forms of expression can be completely dissociated from the spaces to which, in actuality, they respond. Credibility depends, as it still did in the house at Castle Howard, on the power and display of rhetoric.[63]

While constructing, or at least substantiating, a myth in his own right, Laugier sought a basis for representation in the primitive hut that could be credible in an age of reason and enlightenment. Never once in the *Essai* did he make the obligatory reference to the legendary analogy between the column and the human body, nor did he spend any time on the issue of proportions, the quasi-mystical subject that was generally paramount in earlier architectural theorists' minds.[64] Focusing on the question of imitation and representation, he was able to rationalize the relation between truth and appearance through an understanding of verisimilitude that would give his conclusions a relatively modern ring. The idea, if not the reality, of construction makes itself felt in his argument. Appearance and reality are no longer entirely separate domains but begin to affect one another in a new kind of dialectical relationship. A "law of probability or necessity" based on a structural paradigm, albeit itself a product of fiction, now governs both the kinds of deceptions architecture is allowed to entertain and the manner by which they can to be visualized.

The key to this, in Laugier's thought as in Soufflot's church, is a characteristically modern methodology of reductiveness—the setting of limits in relation to structure. This is what Goethe detested in the "neo-French philosophizing connoisseur." Laugier, for his part, was well aware of what he was doing. An "objection will perhaps be made," he wrote, "that I reduce architecture to almost nothing, since with the exception of columns, entablatures, pediments, doors and windows, I more or less cut out the rest." (One is hard put here not to think of Mies's "beinahe nichts.") "But let there be no mistake about it," Laugier continued, "I do not take away anything from the work or the resources of the architect. I [merely] force him to proceed in a simple and natural manner.... Those belonging to the profession will agree that, far from reducing their work, I sentence them to take great pains and to work with an extraordinary degree of precision."[65]

The representational link Laugier forged between the primitive wood hut and the sophisticated stone temple served to rationalize the relationship between truth and appearance by limiting that which could be represented exclusively to that which might be believed to be the likely structure of the building. Artistic illusion and constructed reality now neatly coincided in the realm of the verisimilar. In drastically reducing the architect's range of decorative/architectural elements to those deriving from the structural paradigm of the hut, Laugier's theoretical construct produced a relative equivalence between decoration and construction that seemed not only "simple and natural" but also "rational" and "precise." In effect, what Laugier did was to make truth approximate appearance so closely that the appearance of truth became one with the truth of appearance; and, for at least a generation or two, the temple portico could be taken for the primitive hut.

From Plausible Fiction to Article of Belief: Quatremère de Quincy's Defense of Imitation

Where Laugier's hypothesis had appeared radical and progressive in terms of mid-eighteenth-century Vitruvian conventions and Baroque practices, it quickly took on a conservative, even reactionary cast once it became dogma. The person most responsible for turning Laugier's concept of verisimilitude into the neoclassical doctrine of imitation was the sculptor, political activist, academician, and theorist Quatremère de Quincy. He used Laugier's theory over the next forty years to affirm an almost religious position that raised the representational model of the hut into an article of neoclassical faith. Quatremère developed his views between 1785 and 1788, first in a prize-winning essay comparing Egyptian architecture with that of Greece and then in the initial volume of entries for the section on architecture in Charles-Joseph Panckoucke's *Encyclopédie méthodique* (1782–1832). Between 1801, when he completed the second of the three architecture volumes for the *Encyclopédie* (the third was published in 1825) and 1832, when he published a two-volume version of the entries as the *Dictionnaire historique d'architecture*, Quatremère reigned supreme as the permanent secretary of the French Academy of Fine Arts and the era's dictator in the domains of criticism and theory.[66]

A major innovation of Quatremère's *De l'architecture égyptienne considérée dans son origine, ses principes et son goût, et comparée sous les mêmes rapports à l'architecture grecque* was to place the concept of a natural model within a comparative framework that historicized Laugier's theory while at the same time taking into account the Vitruvian narrative of origins. In order to prove the independence of Greek architecture from any external influence and thus assert the unique quality of the originary form of classicism, Quatremère defined three historical architectural types relative to the three main stages in human development and claimed that each of these types was founded on the imitation of a distinct natural— or nearly natural— model: the cave, which responded to the needs of hunters and gatherers, was imitated in the architecture of Egypt; the tent, a nomadic form characteristic of a pastoral society, became the model for the architecture of Asia; and the hut, an abode developed by sedentary farmers, was imitated in the buildings of Greece. By definition, these models were not equal, and only one of them, the hut, was articulate enough in and of itself and susceptible to a proportion system derived from the human body that it could serve as the basis for a significant and progressive evolution.[67]

The critical factor in the process of imitation that distinguished Greek architecture from the two others was the transformation from one material to another. This, and this alone, gave rise to a verisimilitude in representation. The cave, considered by Quatremère as already a form of masonry, foreclosed any possibility for "illusion" and thus preordained the static character of its imitations.[68] The tent, by contrast, offered too unstable and capricious a model for permanent and systematic representation. Only the hut, in Quatremère's view, naturally lent itself to the transformational process of imitation from one less permanent material to another more permanent one. The "transposition from wood to stone," he wrote, gave Greek architecture a metaphorical dimension, "associating [it] with the other arts" and endowing it with "the pleasure of imitation." The masonry temple's "imitation at once illusory and real ... of the hut" thus offered a form of representation that "fools us in telling us the truth."[69] "This imitation ... of the hut ... cannot be given up or changed ... without undermining the laws of Nature, of verisimilitude, and destroying all our impressions of pleasure."[70]

Quatremère's article on "Architecture," in particular, in Panckoucke's *Encyclopédie* elaborated the argument of the earlier essay and focused it on the origins of classicism in Greece and the concept of imitation from which it derived. In effect, "only" Greek architecture, in his view, was "worthy of the name of art," and this because of "the advantage it had in finding in its first attempts a simple, rich, and varied model the fruitful imitation of which gave it the means to rise to the level of perfection it attained."[71] This representation of the wood structure of the primitive hut in the monumental masonry of the Greek temple provided Quatremère with the example he needed to explain the meaning and importance of representation for the art of architecture. "Let there be no doubt whatsoever," he wrote, that the "pleasing fiction" maintained by architectural representation offers the same sort of "pleasure that accompanies all the other arts and that constitutes their charm." It is "the pleasure of being semi-deceived, ... of preferring the truth disguised to the naked truth." The "artifice is always to hold as close to the truth as to the lie" in a process in which one becomes "less the dupe than the confidant."[72]

Although the methodology and intention of representation in architecture, painting, and sculpture were fundamentally the same for Quatremère, architecture involved a more complex relationship with nature than either of the other two arts.[73] It had its primary model in the primitive hut, as Laugier had explained; but in order to become the truly expressive art the Greeks created, architecture soon turned to another source, for which the "wood skeleton" of the hut was "the most fortunate preparation" and which functioned, "if not as a new model, at least as a new analogue of a model." This was the "rational imitation of the human body," which allowed architecture, "by the application of its system of proportions and natural relationships," to appear to be "part of Nature." "Broadening to a greater and greater degree the idea of its model, *architecture*," according to Quatremère, ultimately "succeeded in extending the sphere of imitation" to incorporate "the general imitation of Nature in its principles of order, of harmony relative to the affections of our senses, and to the perceptions of our understanding." "No longer a copyist, nor an imitator, but the rival of Nature itself," the art of building, in this sense, took on as its "model ... the order of Nature, [which] exists everywhere without being visible anywhere."[74]

The three stages or levels in architecture's imitative reach—from the hut to the human body and then to the order of nature itself—represented an attempt on Quatremère's part to expand Laugier's reductive position and bring it into line with the history of architectural theory as it had evolved since the Renaissance. Still, the acceptance of the primitive hut as the starting point of the classical development—the "framework of the art," as Quatremère described it—made it the primary factor in the representational apparatus of architecture. This, however, created a major problem for Quatremère. Although convinced of the value and efficacy of the model of the hut as an explanation and justification for the uniqueness of the Greek system of design, he was unable to present Laugier's argument for the direct imitation of nature as naively and as unquestioningly as Laugier himself had done. Quatremère hesitated and wavered, sometimes declaring unequivocally that "the imitation or transposition of the forms of the hut is an actual fact" and the architect nothing "but its copyist." More often, however, he hedged in stating that "the imitation is at once illusory and real," that the mimetic process in architecture is "metaphysical and indirect," and that the model—"real or ideal"—is "much less absolute, much less positive than that of the other arts" and is, in fact, "imaginary."[75]

But Quatremère, like Laugier, had to maintain the reality of the fiction in order for the fiction of representation to attain reality. The evidence he offered bordered on the theological: "I will not attempt ...to prove the reality of the model [of the primitive hut] for Greek architecture. There are two things that it is impossible for one to prove: either some things are so obviously false that they cannot be justified for any reason, or they are so obviously self-evident that they can only be proven by a greater degree of evidence; and it is in this latter group that one must place our certitude that Greek architecture is an imitation of the *rustic hut* and [its] wood-frame type construction."[76]

On the major issue of the naturalness of the model itself, Quatremère had this to say: "It is understood, no doubt, that imitation in *architecture* is less absolute, less positive than in the other arts that model themselves directly on Nature.... However, this model [of the hut] whose authenticity is questioned, if it is not to be found in Nature, it is nonetheless a product of it; if it is not a work of Nature, it is a result of it; if Nature in no way produced it, Nature suggested it: it is so bound to Nature that to deny it would be to deny Nature itself, or at least the impressions of Nature that produced it."[77]

As the frontispiece of the second edition of Laugier's *Essai* proposed, "Nature," Quatremère finally admitted, "undoubtedly did not make the hut; but Nature directed man in its formation, and [this primitive] man, guided by an instinct, crude, if you will, but sure, and by a sentiment that in the beginning of time could not be misled, transmitted in it [the hut] the true impressions of Nature." This "original imprint" of nature thus gave to the hut/temple construct, according to Quatremère, a "basic truth" comparable to an "axiom in ethics."[78]

In historicizing and conventionalizing the natural model of the hut, Quatremère took Laugier's argument to its logical conclusion, irrevocably disconnecting the theory of the hut from any remaining mythological or legendary associations and thereby aligning it with modern reason. To do so, however, he resorted to another kind of mythmaking, this one based on theological models. Quatremère's explanation demanded belief, unqualified and unimpeachable:

> We will go as far as granting that [the primitive hut] is nothing but a fable, an allegory invented to contain this or that meaning and doctrine. One can give up the outside skin if one wants, but the principles it contains will remain nonetheless irrefutable. One will have but chased a shadow, fought a chimera, and one would have gained nothing.
>
> Yes, without a doubt, it is the principles contained in the rustic hut that, independent of all the proofs of its existence, render it unshakable, and make it triumph over all attacks. Those who have wanted to proscribe the imitation of it have not realized that it was no longer possible to repudiate it.[79]

The belief in the theory of the hut was clearly intended by Quatremère to forestall any divergence from the classical system of representation suggested by contemporary ideas of materialism, utilitarianism, and historical relativism. In opposition to those who "find it bad that stone might be the representative of another material," Quatremère claimed that the history of Egyptian architecture proved the contrary: "stone, in copying itself, which is to say, in copying nothing, has never produced any form of art."[80] A strict adherence to the Greek model of imitation would not only ensure a work having the values of classical form; it would prevent the dissolution of classicism itself.[81] Those who had forsaken the "real or fictive imitation of the hut," he stated, had simply proven that one cannot do this "without abandoning at the same time the principles of which it is the demonstration."

Quatremère thus warned architects in words closely recalling those of Laugier:

> Always keep your eyes fixed on the real or ideal model [of the hut] that has given existence to architecture; such that all the constituent parts of your buildings are ... in conformity with the parts of the model they represent; never lose sight of their origin, the needs that motivated their structural relationships, and the reality of the objects of which you are doing nothing but rendering, in a way, the image. This primitive model, of which you are but the copyist, will ... preserve you from those dubious and mongrel forms that leave the spirit in painful doubt about their utility; ... it will distance you, above all, from those irrational forms and ornaments that act in a contrary sense to the imperious forms of construction, creating continual contradictions between the appearance and the reality of objects.[82]

Through his writing, his critical role in architectural production, and perhaps most important, his powerful hold on the education system of the Ecole des Beaux-Arts, Quatremère de Quincy brought Laugier's message from the belle-lettristic circles of the eighteenth-century *amateur* into the nineteenth-century world of professional discourse. From the late 1780s through the mid-1830s, as we shall see in the next chapter, the theory of imitation and the concept of verisimilitude on which it rested would govern architectural thinking and practice in France, as elsewhere, one way or another.

From Imitation to Abstraction in the Neoclassicism of Boullée, Soane, and Schinkel

3

THE REDUCTIONIST LOGIC of Laugier's theory of representation and its promulgation by such influential figures as Quatremère de Quincy underwrote the establishment of a strict form of neoclassicism that became the lingua franca of architectural production from the last quarter of the eighteenth century through the first third of the nineteenth. The equation of truth and appearance believed to be inherent in the imitation of the forms of the antique temple provided the rationale for what can be seen to be the last truly international style prior to the advent of the modern movement in the 1920s and early '30s. Whether in Berlin, Munich, St. Petersburg, Washington, D.C., London, or Paris, buildings of all types and sizes were designed with representational facades based on the post-and-lintel system of Greek and Roman columnar architecture (fig. 3.1). The ubiquity of this neoclassical ideal was matched only by the restricted palette of its characteristic forms and the academic rigor of their application.

Although some refused to accept the myth of origins that provided the rationale for the widespread adoption of neoclassicism, hardly anyone initially thought seriously to substitute a different system of forms for the classical one. Already in 1788, Quatremère noted that "there exist many people who blame [Greek] *architecture* for having reduced itself to imitating the earliest constructions in wood: they find it bad that stone might be the representative of another material.... They would prefer that each material derive its form...from within itself and its own nature."[1] Although he did not mention him by name, it is clear that the person Quatremère had in mind was the Venetian Franciscan monk Carlo Lodoli (1690–1761), who developed a faithful following for his so-called Rigorist ideas in the latter part of the eighteenth century.[2] Lodoli, who left no published record of what he thought, reportedly believed, like Laugier, that Baroque architecture had degenerated to the point that only radical reform could save it. His answer, however, was to forswear the kind of imitation practiced by the Greeks and

3.1 Thomas Jefferson, with Charles-Louis Clérisseau. Virginia State Capitol, Richmond, 1785–89. Exterior

instead to heed only the dictates of materials and purpose. But all he or his followers could envisage, in actuality, was a less elaborately decorated, more stripped-down form of classicism.[3]

In the course of architecture he taught for engineers at the Ecole Polytechnique in Paris from the mid-1790s until his death in 1834, Jean-Nicolas-Louis Durand (b. 1760) professed a similar utilitarian bias and arrived at a similar result. In claiming that "the purpose of architecture cannot be pleasure but utility," he diametrically opposed Quatremère's "pleasing fiction" of imitation with a demand that buildings respond solely to the criteria of "fitness and economy." But because he never questioned the universal value of the conventional forms of classical architecture as a serviceable language of design, he was obliged to undermine the representational content they were thought to have. Not only did he decry the concept of imitation as such; he denied its foundational role in the generation of the Greek orders themselves. "The forms of the orders," he stated in the introduction to his lectures, "were no more imitated from a hut than their proportions were derived from the human body." In any event, he reminded his students, as would their reading of Vitruvius, that "a hut is not a natural object" but just "the inchoate production of the first falterings of art."[4]

In the numerous designs Durand offered his students as models, the classical forms were deployed in a determinedly mechanical manner, denatured and emptied of metaphorical content (fig. 3.2). "The Greeks," he maintained, "saw nothing in what we call the *orders* but supports and parts supported," merely "useful objects, which they proportioned, not in imitation of anything whatever, but in accordance with the eternal fitness of things."[5] The column as point support became the basis for a compositional strategy indebted to a post-and-lintel conception of architecture grounded in a rigorous adherence to the grid. "The unit to which we shall refer all quantities in architecture," he stated, "will be the interaxis: that is to say, the distance between the axes of two columns."[6] Arches and vaults might be used, but they were treated simply as extensions of a general system of trabeation. This apparent interchangeability of parts reinforced the structural definition of the columnar order as a denatured form.

While the "utilitarianism" espoused by Lodoli and Durand may at first seem radical, its effect on neoclassical practices of representation remained purely hypothetical.

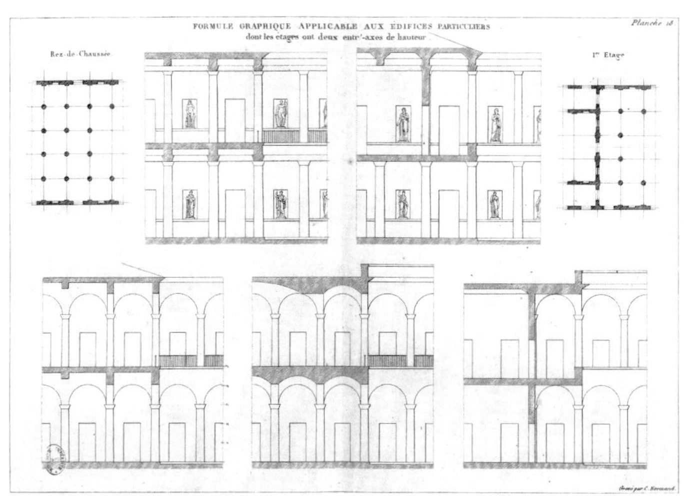

3.2 Jean-Nicolas-Louis Durand. "Graphic Formula Applicable to Private Buildings Whose Floors Are Two Inter-Axes High," *Partie graphique des cours d'architecture faits à l'Ecole Royale Polytechnique depuis sa réorganisation,* 1821. Plans and sections

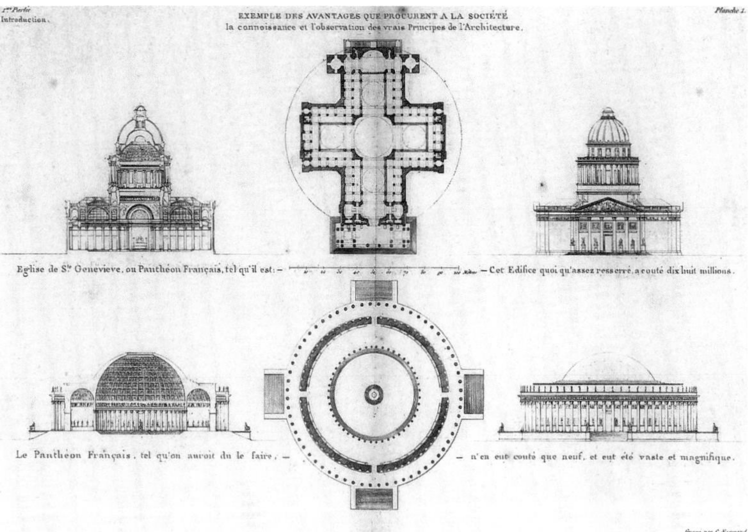

3.3 Durand, "Example of the Advantages That Society Gains from the Knowledge and Observation of the True Principles of Architecture" (comparison of Soufflot's Church of Sainte-Geneviève with an "improved" version), *Précis des leçons d'architecture données à l'Ecole Royale Polytechnique*, vol. 1, 1802. Plans, sections, and elevations

Neither author proposed a new method for recalibrating the language of architecture in terms of materials, techniques of construction, or programmatic demands. No matter how schematically presented, the classical elements were never themselves subjected to an analysis based on the new historical understanding of the period or the new interest in subjective, critical thought. Durand's message was in fact explicitly conservative. He declared that his approach to design would avoid "expensive, unnecessary, bizarre combinations" and return architecture to the "simple, natural combinations—as used by the ancients and by Palladio."[7] Indeed, his suggestions for the "improvement" of the east colonnade of the Louvre and the Church of Sainte-Geneviève read less as a rejection of Laugier's aims than as a continuation of his reductive means.

In the case of the Louvre (see fig. 2.10), Durand opined that, had the upper floor been designed as a continuous colonnade without the interposition of a central pavilion, and the ground floor similarly opened up into a colonnade, the building would have gained not only in "majesty" but in "fitness" and "economy" as well.[8] His redesign of Soufflot's church, presented as the first plate of the *Précis of the Lectures on Architecture,* takes the form of a Roman Pantheon-like domed structure supported by forty-eight freestanding columns surrounded on the exterior by sixty-four freestanding columns, all carrying continuous, unbroken entablatures (fig. 3.3). Again, the reduction of means to what Laugier called the "essential" and "natural" forms of classical representation was justified by a purported gain in "fitness" and "economy," not to speak of "grandeur" and "magnificence."[9]

Others, however, followed a more interesting and innovative path than Durand or Lodoli, taking into account the new pictorialism and historicism that was reflected in the garden buildings at Castle Howard but also, even more important, elaborating and transforming the theory of imitation expounded by Laugier and Quatremère, rather than simply rejecting it. No architectural thinker of the period was more eloquent or more clear-sighted in his promotion of these changes than Etienne-Louis Boullée (1728–1799), whose career as a practitioner, teacher, and theorist marked the final third of the eighteenth century. (Durand, in fact, had been a student of his.) The gist of Boullée's thought has been preserved for us in the manuscript of a theoretical text composed during the latter years of his life, most probably sometime between 1785 and 1793. It is entitled "Architecture: Essai sur l'art."[10] Written in the personal, subjective, and often conversational tone for which Laugier had established a kind of precedent, Boullée's "Essai" uses his own highly imaginative projects for a variety of building types to illustrate the radical redefinition of classical principles he offered in the wake of Laugier's disruptive ideas.

In the section devoted to projects for funerary monuments and cenotaphs, Boullée characteristically describes where his ideas for these designs came from and how he arrived at their forms:

3.4 Etienne-Louis Boullée. Cemetery entrance gate project, early 1780s. Perspective

> I was in the country, walking along the edge of a wood in the moonlight. My effigy produced by the light caught my eye (certainly this was nothing new for me). Because of my particular mood, the effect of this simulacrum seemed to me of an extreme sadness. The shadows of the trees etched on the ground made a most profound impression on me. As my imagination exaggerated this scene [*tableau*], I caught a glimpse of all that is most somber in nature. What did I see there? The mass of objects stood out in black against the extreme wanness of the light. Nature seemed to offer itself to my gaze as if in mourning. Struck by these sensations I was experiencing, I immediately began to wonder how I might apply this in a direct way to architecture. I tried to find a composition made up of the effect of shadows. To achieve this, I pictured the light (as I had observed it in nature) giving back to me all that my imagination had been able to conceive. That was how I proceeded when I was seeking to create this new genre of architecture.[11]

A number of Boullée's designs for cemetery structures, including entrance gates, chapels, and tombs, are directly based on this recollection of his experience in the moonlight (fig. 3.4). To the modern eye, their prismatic, unadorned geometric shapes make them seem like pure abstractions. But one should be careful not to confuse that apparent simplicity with the twentieth-century idea of abstraction as antirepresentational nonobjectivity.[12] On the contrary, from Boullée's point of view, such abstraction was only the result of pushing the imitation of nature to an extreme in an effort to heighten the emotional effects of architectural representation and to bring the medium into closer rapport with painting and sculpture. "The aim of art," Boullée asserted, "is fundamentally the imitation of nature." "If artists in architecture," as he put it, "have not acquired the high degree of perfection that other artists seem to have attained," this may be because "the other arts, being closer to nature, are consequently more likely to move us." "To prove that architecture, in its relations with nature, had perhaps an even greater advantage than the other arts" was "the task" Boullée "set himself."[13]

Boullée's abstraction of shape in the cause of imitation was not the only way in which neoclassical representation evolved. The two most distinguished architects of the generations immediately following him, namely John Soane (1753–1837) and Karl Friedrich Schinkel (1781–1841), advanced the abstraction of classical forms through a broader consideration of historical types, leading to an

3.5 Boullée. Metropolitan Church project, 1781–82. Exterior perspective

emphasis on the structural logic of classicism itself. Where Boullée could be said to have concerned himself essentially with the naturalistic implications of Laugier's French frontispiece (see fig. 2.1), Soane and Schinkel concentrated on the cultural/structural ones at stake in the English version (see fig. 2.12). In his later interiors at London's Bank of England, for example, designed in the 1810s and '20s, Soane reduced the apparent structure to a linear diagram that dematerializes the space and drains the forms of any traditional sense of plasticity. But like Boullée, Soane thought of himself as working within a strictly classical representational framework. This chapter will attempt to clarify how the changes in representational practices evident in the abstractions of Boullée, Soane, and Schinkel set limits on the acceptability of the concept of verisimilitude underlying the relation between illusion and reality in classical architecture, eventuating in a full-scale questioning of the concept of neoclassical representation.

Boullée, Laugier, and Soufflot

To begin with Boullée, one must return to Laugier. His *Essai sur l'architecture* was published when Boullée was twenty-five, having recently finished his architecture studies and having just begun to teach and practice on his own. Boullée would eventually rise to the very top of his profession, being named to Soufflot's seat in the architecture section of the Academy of Fine Arts in 1780 and included as a member of Napoleon's newly founded Institut de France in 1795.[14] Laugier's book would inform Boullée's thought in a number of crucial ways. Laugier's theory of the natural origin of the Greek temple in the primitive hut would provide Boullée with a basis for his own interpretation of the mimetic and would eventually be inscribed in Boullée's pedagogical program as the foundation of architectural education. The immediate effects of Laugier's theory on contemporary architecture would also serve, in a negative way, to inspire Boullée's rethinking of the problem of representation.

The rationale of Laugier's argument was simple and convincing, its target so vulnerable that the fundamental reductiveness of its conclusions was hardly a real problem at first. The freestanding portico became the typical design solution to almost any building facade. Soufflot's Church of Sainte-Geneviève established the type in France. The temple front could be used to decorate the main facade of a professional school, like Jacques Gondoin's (1737–1818) Medical School in Paris (begun 1769), just as well as it could serve as the representational frontispiece of an American state capitol, as it did in the one for Richmond, Virginia, designed by Thomas Jefferson (1743–1826) with the help of Charles-Louis Clérisseau (1721–1820) in the mid-1780s (see fig. 3.1). But the ubiquitousness and conventionality of the type worked to its detriment in Boullée's eyes. He believed that the expression of character should be the paramount concern of architects and that such expression could only effectively be achieved through the creation of "images" that would "arouse in [the beholder] feelings analogous to the use to which the building is to be put."[15] In other words, the expression of character demanded a specificity and individuation of representation that overrode the possibilities contained in the mere application and manipulation of the orders.

While normally as laudatory as Laugier in discussing the achievements of the Greeks, Boullée severely criticized Greek architecture on the issue of expression of character, implying that its inability to express individual character might be held responsible for contemporary failures in the same regard. "It must be admitted," he wrote, "that the Greeks do not appear to have concerned themselves with giving their buildings any individual character. Their temples all have a striking similarity; they are all more or less the same form." He wondered out loud how "such men of genius...could have failed to give evidence of the Poetry of architecture," as he called it, and thus raised the issue, if only by implication, of whether one should continue to imitate them unquestioningly.[16]

Throughout the 1760s and 1770s, Boullée closely followed the Laugier model in the numerous private buildings he built. The Hôtel de Brunoy on the rue du Faubourg Saint-Honoré in Paris (1774–79), to take perhaps the most celebrated example, featured a temple facade of freestanding Ionic columns, dedicated to the goddess Flora, facing the enclosed garden that overlooked the Champs-Elysées. And, when he finally turned his attention in the early 1780s to the design of more theoretical projects that would ultimately illustrate his "Essai sur l'art," Boullée began with a revision of Soufflot's Church of Sainte-Geneviève that was based on a more focused application of Laugier afforded by twenty-five years of hindsight (figs. 3.5–6). It is not known whether Boullée's project of 1781–82 for a Metropolitan Church was a bid for the position of architect of the Church of Sainte-Geneviève following Soufflot's death the year before, or simply an acknowledgment of artistic continuity on taking the older architect's seat at the Academy.[17] What is clear, however, is that the project became a springboard for Boullée's theoretical development of an architecture more closely engaged with the imitation of nature. How this manifests itself in what on first glance would appear to be simply a pastiche is fascinating to study.

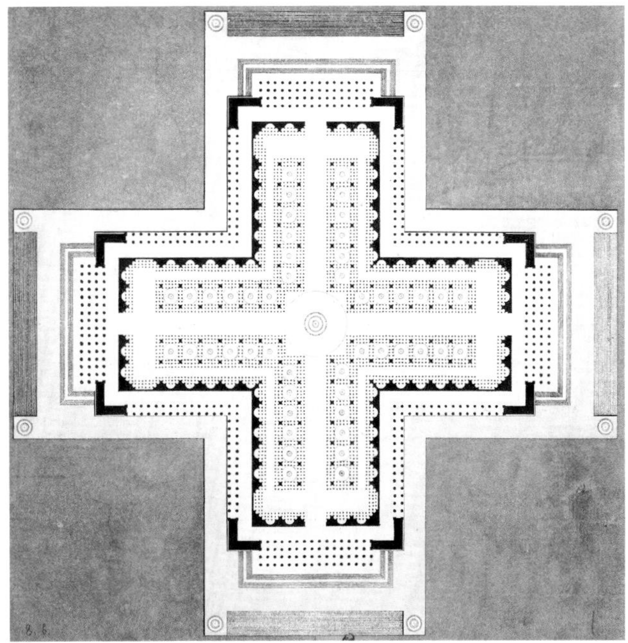

3.6 Metropolitan Church project. Plan

Boullée adopted the Greek cross type of Soufflot's church, then still under construction, along with its freestanding portico (see figs. 2.14–16). Although he based his central dome on Sainte-Geneviève's final, Wren-inspired design, he returned the plan to its original, biaxially symmetrical form. Each arm of the cross was treated equally, and each was given a sixteen-column-wide, four-column-deep portico. The overpowering giant order of the four temple fronts was intended by Boullée to cause the beholder "to experience a feeling of veneration at the mere sight" of the building and "to inspire in him the profound respect that results from religious belief." Though a little exaggerated, this was a distinct echo of Laugier's own reaction to the Cathedral of Notre Dame. Boullée likewise defended

3.7 Metropolitan Church project. Section

3.8 Metropolitan Church project. Interior perspective of variant design

the colossal order of the portico in Laugier's terms, declaring that "two or three orders of architecture, one on top of another," would make the building look as if it "had more than one floor inside." He also based his justification of the inordinate height of the temple fronts on Laugier's redefinition of verisimilitude, maintaining that he "dared to raise the height of the entrance up to the top of the vaulting and to make it as wide as the nave."[18]

One of the most striking features of the exterior of the Metropolitan Church is its complete lack of windows—indeed, any visible openings—which was a further sign of Boullée's correction of Soufflot in terms of Laugier. But it is in the design of the interior that Boullée's debt to Laugier, as well as his extension of the latter's representational model, becomes most evident (fig. 3.7). Boullée began by criticizing "our modern architects" for having substituted for "the magnificent colonnades" of the Greeks "a form of decoration using heavy arcades whose massive piers are ornamented...with pilasters" that carry "vaults pierced by lunettes that resemble basement windows." Looking for a solution for the interior that would be both "magnificent" and "elegant," he stated that he arrived at such a conception based on the ideal union of Greek decoration and Gothic construction—the same idea that Laugier had first proposed and that Soufflot had followed. "For a long time," Boullée wrote, "I had had the idea of joining to the beauties of Greek architecture...the techniques [of construction] only known and employed by the Goths."[19] In Boullée's "Graeco-Gothic" synthesis—much simpler and more "Greek" than Soufflot's, though hardly more "Gothic" in appearance—the long rows of freestanding columns and straight entablatures support continuous, coffered barrel vaults terminating in low saucer domes at the entrances and a high central dome supported by pendentives and encircled both inside and out by unbroken, freestanding colonnades.

Laugier and Soufflot had been amazed by the lightness of Gothic interiors and the ingenuity of the structural techniques they employed, but dismayed by the apparent lack of solidity resulting from the thinness of the supporting piers and the fact that the flying buttresses, which allowed for that thinness, were invisible from inside the building. Boullée, however, saw the matter from an entirely different perspective. He had only praise for the way Gothic architects "introduced magic into art by concealing the buttressing structure of their [cathedrals] so as to make them appear supported by a supernatural power."[20] This rather anticlassical interpretation became the basis for Boullée's major innovation, which is perhaps best appreciated in the interior perspective of the church, taken from one of the vestibules looking down a nave toward the dome (fig. 3.8). (This perspective does not correspond exactly with the plan.) The barrel vaults are supported on square piers, seven along each side of each nave. These in turn are articulated by engaged columns, like those around the triangular piers of Soufflot's central dome. But in Boullée's "corrected" version, the mass of Sainte-Geneviève's solid supporting piers is rendered diaphanous and nearly immaterial by the freestanding colonnade that screens the internalized—and completely hidden—structure. Boullée described his method in the following way:

> Once I had devised the supporting structure and had reinforced it with the number of engaged piers necessary to carry the dome, the vaults of the nave, and those of the side aisles, I surrounded these masses with colonnades on all sides; and it is in this way, by means of all that is most pleasant in architecture, that I have managed to draw the eye of the beholder away from these solid masses.
>
> The result is that, by this arrangement, the supporting structure of my temple [church] is masked in the manner of the Goths and the building appears as if to stand by some miracle while, moreover, being decorated, in imitation of the Greeks, with all the richness architecture has to offer.[21]

Most important to Boullée was how the theatrical solution to structure allowed for a "mysterious diffusion of daylight" producing a "truly enchanting magic quality," as he described it.[22] A careful inspection of the plan reveals how the architect intended to achieve this indirect lighting effect. Circular skylights are set within each group of four piers. Screened by the columns around them, they would allow light to filter in from above and flicker through the structure as if through a forest cover. Boullée stressed the phenomenal aspect of light over the structural one of support. In fact, he explained that it was only when he discovered the natural model of the forest that the design came together. "When I began the project," he wrote,

> I was at first blocked by what appeared to be insurmountable difficulties. How, I asked myself, was I going to be able to give my temple the appropriate character? Did architecture have the technical means necessary to allow one to inspire all the religious feelings appropriate to the worship of the Supreme Being?....
>
> I pondered the question for a long time without any success.... Finally, there was a ray of hope when I recalled the somber or mysterious effects that I had observed in the forest and the various impressions they had made on me. I then saw that if any means existed of putting the ideas that now preoccupied me into effect, it must lie in the way light was filtered into the temple.[23]

It was the effects of light, in Boullée's view, that determined one's emotional reaction to buildings, based on the experience of those same effects in nature. At the crossing,

3.9 Metropolitan Church project. Interior perspective of crossing during celebration of Corpus Christi

under the dome, Boullée's drawings make the light appear, in his word, "celestial"—like an epiphany (fig. 3.9).[24] No windows would be visible, for they were hidden from below by the encircling colonnade. Seen from the distant vantage point of the nave, the light-filled crossing would be more like a miraculous clearing in the "forest" in which Boullée had found his inspiration. Indeed, Boullée thought of the stands of columns marching down the length of the nave in Edmund Burkean terms as disappearing into "infinity" and thereby giving "an impression of immensity" to the church commensurate with God's creation.[25]

In explaining his reliance on nature and his manipulation of light to impart an appropriate character to the church, Boullée used a phrase that he would repeatedly employ to define what he meant by a mimetic architecture. He said that he had been able to "mettre la nature en oeuvre," meaning "to bring nature into play," or implement it in the work.[26] In effect, what Boullée meant in a larger sense, and what he would go on to develop in his theoretical text and in the various other projects that illustrated it, was that he was not simply imitating the effects of nature through the forms of architecture but actually incorporating natural phenomena into the work. The building thus becomes a representation of nature imitating itself, and the architect a kind of director of ceremonies or midwife. This reflexiveness is in large part responsible for the new sense of scale and apparent abstractness of the forms.

Architecture as the Imitation of Nature on the Model of Painting

Just as his Metropolitan Church can be seen as a revision of Laugier's ideas on architectural reform as manifested in the work of Soufflot, so too should Boullée's entire theoretical project be understood as a commentary on and development of the ideas contained in the earlier author's *Essai*. Boullée began his own treatise by asking the question, "What is architecture?"—to which he immediately responded that it was in no sense the "art of building" that Vitruvius had taken it to be. Vitruvius, he said, made the "gross error" of "mistaking the effect for the cause."[27] Architecture, in Boullée's view, was not about building (in the sense of construction) as much as it was about designing (in the sense of conception). The architect had to conceive an image in his mind before he could even think about executing it. And the first proof Boullée offered of this was the statement, clearly supported by the engraving of the hut in the frontispiece to Laugier's book, that "our first forefathers only built their huts after having conceived an image of them." The hut, as Laugier projected it and Boullée revisited it, was a spontaneously generated "production de l'esprit," a product of the mind.[28]

Boullée found this primary image of the primitive hut so compelling that he proposed to use it as the basis for the education of architects. Instead of having young students begin at the end of the process, as he put it, by drawing the orders—the usual method at the time—Boullée suggested that the novice's first exercise should be to draw the primitive hut. The student would start with "the facade of the hut, after which he would be made to understand a plan by showing him how to lay it out. In the same way, by [studying] the profile or section of the hut, he will learn the art of unifying the interior and the exterior."[29] Beginning with this representation of the primitive hut, each student would thus literally imitate, in his own personal development, the development of architecture as a social art and thereby ensure that ontogeny recapitulates phylogeny. He would also ensure what Quatremère had assumed—that whether or not the model of the hut was "real" or "imaginary," it had to be established in the mind for the architecture based on it to flourish (see chapter 2).

Boullée relegated the study of the orders to the final stage of the curriculum. In the "Essai," he never discusses them in any detail nor does he describe, as even Laugier did, the various characteristics of the different orders. This was not out of ignorance, for knowledge of the orders would have been drilled into him when he was a student of Jacques-François Blondel. Boullée's disregard for the orders may have been strategic. He very much believed in "immutable laws" but also considered that it was necessary to find a higher one (or ones) than those contained in the orders. In fact, much of the early part of the "Essai" is devoted to a critique of Claude Perrault's argument for a relative or customary, rather than absolute or natural, interpretation of classical proportions, which had appeared in his *Ordonnance des cinq espèces de colonnes selon la méthode des anciens* (1683) and was played out in his debate with François Blondel (1618–86) in the 1670s and '80s.[30] Boullée disputed Perrault's conclusion that architecture is an art of custom and "invention," maintaining that it is an art of strict "imitation" whose "objects" and "laws" are all "derived from nature."[31]

At the same time, Boullée denied one of the fundamental principles of classical theory since the Renaissance, which maintained that there was an inherent analogy between architecture and music based on the laws of harmonic proportions.[32] "These [two] arts," Boullée asserted, "bear no relation to one another, and have no analogy, and thus their basic principles are totally different." Extending this to the question of proportions themselves, Boullée argued that "although proportion is one of the most important elements constituting beauty in architecture," it is, as Perrault had suggested, a relative rather than an absolute matter, depending essentially on agreement and taste. Consequently, "it is not the primary law from which [architecture's] basic principles derive."[33]

By agreeing with Perrault in this backhand way, Boullée was able to turn the latter's argument on its head. Having dispensed with the notion of proportion as constituting the "primary law" of architecture, Boullée concluded that "the primary law, and the one that establishes the basic principles of architecture, originates in regularity" and is represented by "symmetry," the latter being, in his view, the very "image of order and perfection."[34] Starting from this near tabula rasa, Boullée was then able to erect a new system of constitutive forms that would be at once absolute—and based on nature. These regular, symmetrical, and geometric elements would effectively replace the orders as the fundamental building blocks of his architectural conceptions. Not wishing to have these geometric shapes or masses confused with the purely abstract constructs of mathematics, he referred to them as *corps* (bodies) and to his general theory as "la théorie des corps."[35]

Boullée differentiated between "irregular bodies," which offered merely a "mute and sterile image," and "regular bodies," which "alone could convey to men clear ideas of the[ir] shape" and thus embody the qualities of "regularity, symmetry, and variety." He went to great pains to show how these geometric "bodies" that he substituted for the orders had "analogies" with the human "organism," especially at the level of feeling and sensation. He constantly referred to "the power they have on our senses" to affect our understanding of architectural character.[36] In one particularly descriptive passage, he wrote that regular "bodies that lie low to the ground make us feel sad; those that rise up into the heavens enrapture us; those that we find gentle please us; while those that are angular and hard give us a sensation of repugnance."[37]

By means of this *théorie des corps*, Boullée was able to articulate a mimetic basis for architecture that was as totalizing as Laugier's, if not more so. A building could now be viewed as an entire figure, rather than simply as a composition of proportionally related structural elements. And the figure of the building could then become, by virtue of its organic wholeness, an image of an object in nature, which is precisely what Boullée proposed as a definition of architectural representation. Architecture, he declared, "is the art of presenting images by the arrangement of [regular solid] bodies. But," he continued, "when considered in a larger sense,... it is not only the art of presenting images by the arrangement of [such] bodies, it also consists in knowing how to gather together all the scattered beauties of nature in order to bring them into play ["les mettre en oeuvre"]. I cannot repeat myself often enough. The architect must be the one who brings nature into the act." As the "metteur en oeuvre de la nature," the architect becomes the director of a scene or "tableau" in which nature is the actor representing itself.[38]

Boullée defined the task of the architect as that of creating a "tableau" or "picture of reality" through the "image" represented by his building. He admitted this could lead to accusations of "theatricality."[39] Perhaps for this reason, he stressed the relationship of the architect to the painter rather than to the director or playwright. To leave no doubt in the minds of his readers where his sympathies lay, he chose as an epigraph for the "Essai" Correggio's celebrated pronouncement of faith upon seeing Raphael's work: "Ed io anche son pittore" (I too am a painter).[40] But Boullée asserted that the comparison of the architectural to the pictorial should not lead one to infer a more distant or less positive relation to nature in the mimetic capacity of architecture.

3.10 Boullée. Cenotaph for Isaac Newton project, 1784. Exterior perspective

On the contrary (and almost repeating the same argument put forth by Lady Irwin regarding the garden structures at Castle Howard), Boullée declared: "Architecture, in its relations with nature, has an even greater advantage than the other arts," for the ability to "bring nature actually into play" and "appropriate the effects of nature" gives architecture the possibility of reproducing in reality what painting or "poetry can only describe."[41]

Projects for the Newton Cenotaph and the Royal Library

Of the numerous projects that Boullée described in his "Essai," there are two in particular that illustrate his concept of architectural representation with special force and clarity. The first, in chronological order and in many ways the most striking, is the proposed Memorial or Cenotaph for Isaac Newton. Designed in 1784, it was a consummate expression of the architect's use of primary geometric forms in conjunction with the manipulation of natural effects of light to create a picture of reality that might rival the art of painting (fig. 3.10).[42] The choice of subject was fraught with significance. By the later eighteenth century, Newton had become the symbol par excellence of the Enlightenment. In Boullée's eyes, he was the ultimate expression of the human capacity to understand and control the natural order of the universe. Newton was therefore the perfect subject for an architecture of the totalizing sort Boullée had in mind.

The monument was to be a perfect sphere—the very image of the planet Earth whose "figure," as Boullée put it,

3.11 Cenotaph for Newton project. Section, in daytime

3.12 Cenotaph for Newton project. Section, at night

Newton had "defined."[43] Set within a cutaway base, which rises in stages to about midheight to act as a buttress, the circular "body" would be entered from below through a cavernous half-round arch. The plan shows only a single entrance in front; but the section indicates that at least two, and perhaps four, tunnels were to lead from exedra-like vestibules through long, dark passages up into the sphere at the very center of the monument (fig. 3.11). Here the visitor would emerge, from the underside of an elevated sarcophagus, onto stepped platforms that would rise up to the sepulcher through a vaporous atmosphere at the base of the dome of the sky. Boullée pictured the experience of arrival in this way: "The spectator would find himself, as if by magic, transported through the air, carried on billows of clouds into the immensity of space."[44]

How the clouds were to have been produced was not disclosed by Boullée, although he no doubt had certain theatrical techniques in mind. More strictly architectural was his solution for representing the constellations of stars and planets in the upper half of the sphere. Funnel-like apertures were to be cut through the depth of the upper shell, piercing it to allow the daylight to enter. These are clearly visible in the section drawing. The location of the holes was calculated to reproduce a planetarium. Boullée described the light inside the memorial during the daytime hours as "resembling that of a clear night sky[,]...the arrangement of the stars conforming to nature" and "being a perfectly truthful reproduction" of it.[45]

The reference to the Roman Pantheon is unmistakable, but so is Boullée's attempt to harness the antique monument's symbolic expression of universality to a much more specific and unmediated form of representation. The direct relation to nature in the Newton Cenotaph extends beyond that which is visibly apparent at any one moment in time into the life cycle of the monument itself. The experience of the space was intended to vary according to the amount of natural light that was available, so that what one saw in the daytime was quite different from what one saw at night (fig. 3.12). When it was dark outside, the interior of the memorial would be brilliantly lit (again by means not disclosed by Boullée) to imitate the effects of the sun. The light would emanate from a suspended mobile, looking like an armillary sphere and clearly meant to symbolize Newton's discovery of the law of gravitation that determined the orbits of the earth and moon around the sun. Day and night would therefore each be represented in an inverse relation to its natural referent, and the monument would thus encompass, in its real-time existence, a temporal as well as a spatial continuity with the world around it.

Only such a complete simulacrum of the natural universe could be a suitable representation, in Boullée's view, of the prodigiousness, profundity, and sublimity of Newton's mind: since the enlightened scientist and mathematician had "determined the figure of the earth," the only form of artistic acknowledgment that would be "worthy" of him was to "envelop him in his own discovery." Boullée described the Newton Memorial as, "in a certain sense, enveloping [Newton] in [him]self."[46] The reflexiveness of nature imitating itself, made evident in the natural light creating the night sky, now extended from the level of form to that of content, as the subject of the representation—Newton—was subsumed within its object—the universe. The "body" of the sphere, suggesting completeness and infinitude by its very form, served to contain the expression of the completeness and sublimity of its subject's thought.

The unmediated transparency of the representation in the Newton Cenotaph involved a degree of mimetic realism that ultimately led Boullée to believe that the best expression of his idea of the "tableau" of the interior with the night sky would be in the form of a painted "scene" rather than an architectural section. As a result, the "interior view" of the monument would become one and the same thing as

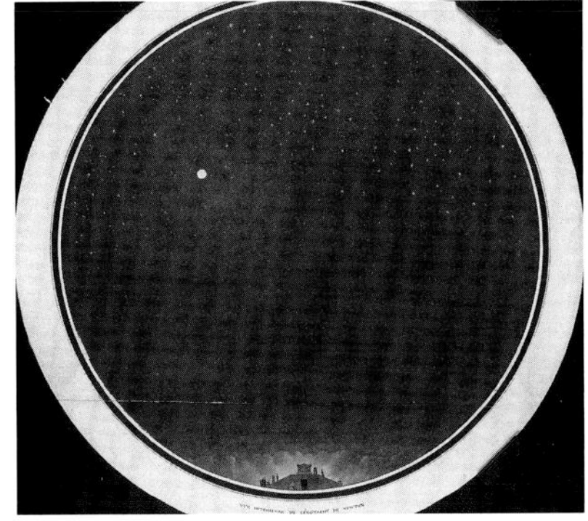

3.13 Cenotaph for Newton project. Interior view

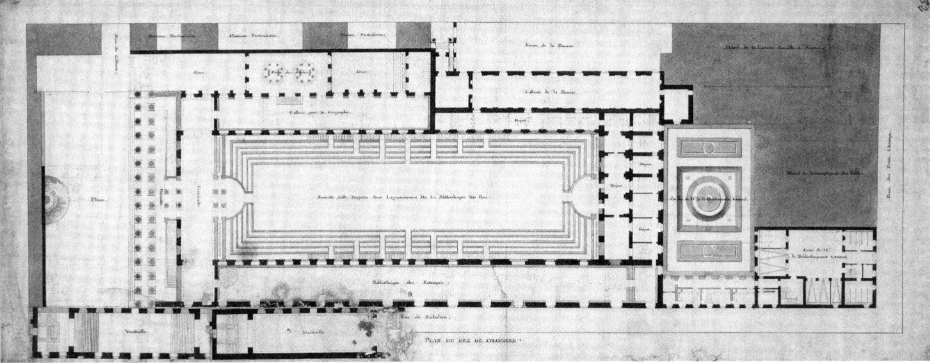

3.14 Boullée. Royal Library project, Paris (rue de Richelieu site), 1785. Plan (north is to left)

its pictorial rendition (fig. 3.13). Characteristically, and significantly, the architect also described the genesis of the design as a kind of architectural painting, although he went to great pains to point out that this was not to be confused with conventional paintings:

> The effects of this great painting [the Newton Cenotaph] are, as can be seen, produced by nature. One could not arrive at them by the conventional means of art. It would be impossible to render in paint the azure of a clear night sky without any clouds, its color barely distinguishable in its lack of any nuance or gradation, the brilliant light of the stars standing out crudely and sharply against the darkened background.
>
> In order to obtain the correctness of tone and effect, . . . it was necessary to employ the magic of art and to paint with nature, that is to say, to implement [nature] in the work.[47]

Boullée's dependence on the critical category of the pictorial, though not on the physical properties of the medium of painting, recalls Castle Howard and the role the pictorial played in that early picturesque landscape garden in helping architecture attain a more positive referential basis. But Boullée's dependence on the pictorial was quite different from Vanbrugh's and Hawksmoor's. One way to describe that difference would be to say that Boullée's use of the pictorial was more intensive. Where the English architects created scenic compositions of multiple elements in their natural environment, Boullée pictorialized the composition of the individual building itself so as to give it a quality of nature. One would therefore suspect that actual paintings sometimes became the direct inspiration for Boullée's architectural representations. And this certainly turns out to have been the case in the second of his projects that I want to discuss.

Unlike many of the projects discussed in the "Essai," the one for the Royal Library in Paris had a real program and a real site. In 1784, the same year he designed the Newton Cenotaph, Boullée was commissioned to study the idea of moving the library from its constricted quarters in the former palace of the Cardinal Mazarin, on the rue de Richelieu, to a new site on the rue Saint-Honoré, near the Place Vendôme. When the costs turned out to be prohibitive, he proposed in the following year to remodel and enlarge the existing structure so as to assure the present and future needs of the library for safety, security, ease of use, and adequate storage space.

Boullée's plan, published though never executed, was to roof over the existing court of the palace to create a large public reading room surrounded by storage and offices. The renewed facility was to be entered from a courtyard extending across the northern end of the building (fig. 3.14). In the original design, a stoalike portico of Corinthian columns,

3.15 Royal Library project. Entrance facade. Elevation, 1785

two rows deep, screening a double flight of stairs leading to an indoor-outdoor, upper-level landing, serves as a monumental frontispiece (fig. 3.15). The reading room could apparently be entered both at the ground level through the door underneath the stairs and, from the upper landing, at the level of the interior colonnade that rises above the tiers of bookshelves on each side of the 300-foot-long, basilica-like space (fig. 3.16). An Ionic colonnade supports the skylit barrel vault that covers the space in a single, uninterrupted sweep.

Boullée likened the space not only to a basilica but also to an arena for intellectual activity, calling it a "vast amphitheater of books."[48] In his perspective view of the interior, numerous figures in togas people the space. One or two stand alone, but the majority are arranged in groups that appear to be discussing weighty intellectual matters inspired by what they have been reading. Many of the antique-garbed figures hold books in their hands, and some are even caught in the act of removing them from the shelves. The perspective depicts the participation of the readers in what Boullée referred to as a "spectacle" of learning. The confusion of dress turns the present-day users into actors who express, through bodily imitation, the building's character and meaning. "In evoking the desire to follow in the footsteps of these great men," Boullée explained, "their masterpieces [the books] inevitably give rise to lofty thoughts; one experiences at that time such noble transports, such sublime bursts of feeling that it seems as if the soul is about to leave; one believes oneself to be inspired by the shades of these celebrated men."[49]

The juxtaposition of images of authors to the actual presence of their books was a common theme in library design, of which Wren's Library at Trinity College, Cambridge (1676–84), is one of the best-known examples and the former Bibliothèque Sainte-Geneviève in Paris (1675–1733) the one that was closest at hand (fig. 3.17). While there can be little doubt that Boullée was alluding to this tradition, he completely transformed it by dispensing with the symbolic intermediary of sculptured busts and suggesting, through a pictorial device, that the readers might think of themselves as representing the authors and thereby actively animating the room with their thoughts. To set the scene for this vicarious experience, he modeled the reading room on a specific painting he believed could infuse the whole with the requisite impression of contemplative activity (fig. 3.18). Struck by the appropriateness of the "sublime conception of

3.16 Royal Library project. Reading room. Perspective

3.17 Former Bibliothèque Sainte-Geneviève, Paris, begun by Claude-Paul de Creil, 1672–75; enlarged 1699; completed by Jacques de la Guépière, 1720–33. Interior perspective, by Pierre-Claude de la Gardette, 1773

3.18 Raphael. *School of Athens,* Stanza della Segnatura, Vatican Palace, 1509–11

3.19 Boullée. Cemetery project with Turenne Cenotaph, ca. 1782. Aerial perspective

Raphael's *School of Athens*," Boullée wrote that he "attempted to realize [or effectuate] it" in architectural terms, that is to say, to turn it into a reality.[50] The virtual world of pictorial representation, with its illusion of real bodies in space, became the basis for a real space that might enforce by analogy, and through a form of sympathetic projection, a similar kind of intellectual and emotional engagement.

Boullée's Poetry of Death

Of all building types, Boullée felt that the funerary offered the greatest need and scope for "the poetry of architecture" and, through the pictorial means available to architecture, could provide the most powerful emotional response.[51] Some sense of this should already be clear from the description of the cemetery entrance quoted at the beginning of this chapter. I would like now to focus on this subject in order to understand more fully how the representational effects of Boullée's architectural work are to be related to and distinguished from those of the pictorial.

Boullée stated that funerary monuments should "chill the heart" and "inspire the horror of death."[52] The purpose was not mere ghoulishness, but to convey the sense of awe and terror the finality of death entails. An expression of such finality could, as in the proposed monument to the great seventeenth-century French military hero the Maréchal de Turenne, serve as an inspiration to emulation (fig. 3.19). Remembrance was fundamental to the type, and thus a geometric form or "body" combining expressions of permanence and grief had to be found. Ancient Egyptian pyramids were the obvious historical source for Boullée "in that they present the sorrowful image of arid mountains and immutability."[53]

But if the funerary monument was to do more than merely represent the dead, it had to affect the living. To this end, Boullée focused on the cemetery's entrance gate as the element to which a synecdochic meaning and power had to be imparted. The gate to the complex containing the Turenne Cenotaph, for example, is depicted in a suitable state of gloom—with a storm temporarily lighting up the surface of the building, which otherwise recedes into darkness (fig. 3.20). The downward-angled, earth-tending lines of the pyramidal cenotaph are exaggerated in the depressed, nearly sunken gable shape of the entrance gate, thus highlighting and foregounding the sense of "sadness" and "expiration" Boullée believed to be inherent in the triangular form. Hardly any detail is allowed to distract the eye from the overall shape. The void over the entrance proper echoes the larger triangle in the hollowness of its darkened interior. But the flat, bare, unadorned surface had another purpose in Boullée's mind: it was meant to give the impression of a body stripped of all life and flesh. He likened the image to a "skeleton of architecture."[54]

The relationship between the building's naked, geometric body and the skeletal remains of the dead was further developed in two ways. The first was the idea that the building itself should appear "buried" or "interred"; the second, as mentioned at the beginning of this chapter, was that the building should look like a "shadow" of itself seen in silhouette in the moonlight. Boullée called the first an "architecture ensevelie," or "buried architecture," the second an "architecture des ombres," or "architecture of shadows." He emphasized the "buried" aspect of the gate for the Turenne complex by juxtaposing it to the funerary monument he described as "characterizing the genre of the architecture of shadows" (fig. 3.21). Because the proportions and shape of the templelike structure "characterizing the genre of the architecture of shadows" are so rude and unfinished, one could only "assume," as Boullée wrote, that, in the "buried"

3.20 Boullée. Cemetery entrance gate project ("characterising the genre of buried architecture"), early 1780s. Elevation

3.21 Boullée. Funerary monument project ("characterising the genre of the architecture of shadows"), early 1780s. Elevation

version, "part of it was concealed underground."[55] The terrifying image of a body returning to the earth, announced in the very entrance to the cemetery, would thus prepare the visitor for the vicarious experience of death that the passage into the cemetery was supposed to entail.

But it was the aspect of being in shadow that defined for Boullée the true character of a cemetery gate (see fig. 3.4). And it is here that the full impact of the pictorialization of architecture on his work can be seen, for only a complete absence of materiality could instantiate the ultimate outcome of burial and death. As previously noted, Boullée claimed that the inspiration for casting the form of the monument in shadow came during a moonlit walk in the woods, when he witnessed the "mournful" sight of his own "effigy"-like shadow appearing to him as a "simulacrum" of himself and thus an uncanny premonition of death. To replicate such an effect in the physical terms of building, he first oriented the entrance gate to face north, so that it would always appear in silhouette. He also specified that the building was to be constructed of a light-absorbent material, so that its surface would become nothing more than "a picture of shadows outlined by still deeper shadows."[56] Nature itself would thus be brought into play in order to represent, through architecture, the image of death suggested by one's own shadow.

Unlike other eighteenth-century architects who imitated the paintings of Claude or Poussin to re-create scenes of an Arcadian landscape, Boullée turned to the pictorial not to reproduce its imagery but rather to invoke its special power to recall emotion through the very act of representation. Like Laugier, who gave new life to a myth of architectural origins in order to reestablish the mimetic foundations of architecture, Boullée also retold a story of origins in support of his pictorial ambitions. In the prefatory remarks to

3.22 Joseph-Benoît Suvée. *Dibutades, or the Origin of Drawing*, 1791

his narrative of the moonlit walk in the woods, he referred to the Greek myth of the origins of painting, a subject that had become quite popular among artists at the time.[57] A contemporary painting by Boullée's fellow academician Joseph Suvée (1743–1807), for example, depicts the Corinthian maiden Dibutades outlining the shadow of her soon-to-depart lover on the wall of her father's pottery studio, her purpose being to retain an image of him while he was away (fig. 3.22). Boullée equated his own "invention" of an "architecture of shadows" with this story. "Everyone knows the effect of bodies seen against the light," he wrote. "Their shadows offer the semblance of these bodies. It is to this natural phenomenon that we owe the birth of the art of painting."[58]

Dibutades' tracing of the outline of her lover's shadow on the wall located the origin of painting in a figure of such abstraction—a mere outline of a shadow—that Boullée could readily appropriate its mimetic implications for his own architectural program, which was no less dependent on drawing out representational effects from natural occurrences for purposes of emotional recall. Drawing was a common denominator of both painting and architecture. But whereas it could eventually be used by the painter to fill in the outlines of the silhouette with enlivening detail and color, the signs of animation in Boullée's architecture would only be those of nature itself. One must therefore read Boullée's turn to the subjectivity of the pictorial in terms of his critique of Vitruvius and Perrault and the expressive limitations of an architecture based on the conventional manipulation of the classical orders. The price of heightened character and representational specificity was paid by Boullée in terms of loss of plastic detail and an ever-increasing geometric abstraction.

John Soane and the Effects of Historical Relativism

The reductiveness of Boullée's formal means was predicted by Laugier. So too was the clarification of the distinction between architecture as preconceived image and architecture as constructed object that Boullée used in his argument against the Vitruvian position. But Laugier's account of the primitive hut could be interpreted, as I have alluded to in the introduction to this chapter, in at least two ways. It could be read, as the frontispiece to the second French edition suggested, as a kind of deistic, immaculate conception (see fig. 2.1). This was Boullée's understanding of the hut's natural status as pure image, fundamentally unaffected by the realities of building. Laugier's narrative could also be read, as the English edition revealed, as a studied act of human construction, wherein materials and forces of load and support come directly into play (see fig. 2.12). It was this second, more pragmatic interpretation, with its view toward a synthesis of history, that underwrote the simplification and abstraction of classical form in the work of Soane and Schinkel.

John Soane was born the year Laugier's *Essai* was first published, and, as previously noted, eventually he acquired ten copies of the Jesuit priest's work for the library of his combined house and studio in Lincoln's Inn Fields in London.[59] Soane's practice, which began in 1780, coincided for nearly its first two decades with the years Boullée, twenty-five years his senior, was preparing the drawings and writing the text of his "Essai." The major work of these early years, and one that preoccupied Soane throughout his career, was the renovation and enlargement of the Bank of England, a job he took over from Robert Taylor (1717–1788) in 1788.[60] In 1796–97, Soane began erecting the first sections of the new facade that would eventually encase the entire block occupied by the bank (fig. 3.23). The detailing of the blank screen walls is subdued, stressing the qualities of solidity and security appropriate to the building's function and avoiding most signs of Baroque rhetorical display. Points of emphasis, like the corner and the entrances, are marked by freestanding columns carrying unbroken entablatures topped by balustrades decorated with elements

3.23 John Soane. Bank of England, London, 1788–1833. Perspective of Lothbury Street and Bartholomew Lane facades, 1796–97

3.24 Soane (with George Dance the Younger). Bank Stock Office, Bank of England, 1791–93. Interior perspective, by Joseph Gandy

imitated from classical sources. The so-called Tivoli corner, built soon after the turn of the century, was a direct representation of the Roman "Temple of Vesta" at Tivoli, a popular model since the early part of the previous century.

The interiors designed in the 1790s are more unusual. The Bank Stock Office, which dates from 1791–93 and was designed with help from his friend and former teacher, George Dance the Younger (1741–1825), is exceedingly restrained, almost schematic in appearance (fig. 3.24). It has been taken by John Summerson (1904–1992) and others following his lead to be the prototype for Soane's personal, abstracting process of design.[61] Compared to the dense enclosure of the exterior facades, the interior is open and light. The interest in the pictorial effect of light reminds

3.25 Soane. Consols Transfer Office, Bank of England. 1797–99. Interior perspective

one of Boullée. But in Soane's design, the source of the natural light is clearly visible, as it filters in through the lunette windows under the arch of the vaults and the clerestory around the base of the shallow dome. More striking is the similarity of the thin, nearly riblike structure to Soufflot's Church of Sainte-Geneviève (see fig. 2.20).[62] But Soane went well beyond his Parisian predecessor in stripping away sculptural effects and limiting the decoration essentially to linear impressions. He also reduced the elements of classical articulation to a minimum and even completely eliminated some in certain key places. The pilaster strips have no actual capitals; they make use of the Greek fret string course for the purpose. In fact, the string course itself is a much reduced version of a classical entablature. The lack of moldings around the lunettes and in the spandrels of the dome offers a further instance of streamlining.[63]

Soane, clearly interested in considering how the underlying structure might affect the decorative surface, had perspectives drawn of the bank's interiors, showing them both under construction and as built (figs. 3.25–26). What a comparison between the unfinished and finished states of the slightly later Consols Transfer Office reveals is not at all a transparent, one-to-one relationship between construction and decoration but rather an extremely subtle adjustment of the classical vocabulary of the latter to the exigencies of the former. The details of the decorative plaster surface do not precisely coincide with the stone and brick construction that supports and lies beneath it, the points where the arches spring being a most obvious indication. As in the Church of Sainte-Geneviève, iron tie-rods are used to contain the thrusts of the vaults.[64] On the other hand, the extraordinarily shallow and thin linear

3.26 Consols Transfer Office, Bank of England. Interior perspective, under construction, by Gandy

network defined by these simplified classical forms allows the surface to appear to be a fairly direct transcription of the underlying structural conditions. The line between truth and the appearance of truth has been drawn very tightly indeed, but it still exists as an operative distinction based on the aesthetic of verisimilitude.

In some of his later interiors for the bank designed in the 1810s and '20s, Soane stressed the continuity of parts to such a degree that he almost dispensed with all vestiges of the differentiation between load and support that was the central fact of the decorative construct of the classical orders (fig. 3.27). In the Five Per Cent Office's nearly thoroughgoing adoption of a round-arched style—a structural idea that was, as will be discussed in the next chapter, promoted by the next generation as a tool of radical reform—he arrived at a medieval sense of linearity and

3.27 Soane. Five Per Cent (later Colonial) Office, Bank of England, 1818–23. Interior perspective

3.28 Soane. Designs for Commissioners' churches, London, ca. 1820–24. Perspective, by Gandy

3.29 Soane. St. John's, Bethnal Green, London, 1826–28. Exterior

dematerialization that Laugier, Soufflot, and Boullée all talked about but were perfectly content to compromise by the devices of classical articulation.[65] Soane's interest in the nonclassical was instrumental in the increasing abstraction of his later work. In 1818, the same year the Five Percent Office was designed, the act providing £1,000,000 for the construction of what came to be known as the Commissioners' churches was passed, and Soane began thinking about designs for them in styles ranging from the Grecian and the Roman to the Romanesque and the Gothic (fig. 3.28).

Holy Trinity, Marylebone, was built in London in 1820–24 as a fairly straightforward version of neoclassical representation. But just a couple of years later, it was followed by St. John's, Bethnal Green, in what can be best described as a synthesis, or reduction in the literal sense of the word, of the various trabeated and round-arched modes the architect had offered as alternatives to the Commissioners in the perspective drawn by Joseph Gandy (1771–1843) (fig. 3.29). The corrosive effect of the historical relativism evident in the perspective gives the suburban church an appearance of decided abstraction, although the organizing principle is still the classical one. The pattern was established in the different Commissioners' designs. All except one of them follow essentially the same classical plan and make use of a common structural division of parts.[66] In fact, Gothic and Greek capitals and moldings are strewn willy-nilly in the foreground, appearing like interchangeable parts.

One is thus led to the conclusion that there is no fixed and "natural" relation between reality and appearance, or construction and decoration, as there was for Laugier. And since the same plan and structure underlie the different forms of appearance, one also is led to believe that there is a general or synthetic order controlling, or at least guiding, them. This is exactly what the church at Bethnal Green substantiates. By taking into account the whole range of historical possibilities and focusing on the shared plan and structure, Soane drained both the classical and nonclassical forms of their plastic force and reduced them to the fundamental elements of design that the frontispiece of the English translation of Laugier had revealed in the ur-construction of the primitive hut. In fact, Soane did not accept Laugier's epiphanic, anti-Vitruvian explanation of the origin of the Greek temple. In the course of lectures on architecture he began giving at London's Royal Academy in 1810 and continued through 1821, he never mentioned Laugier's explanation of the origin of Greek architecture, instead preferring the progressive, evolutionary version that William Chambers had based on Vitruvius (see fig. I.9).[67] His illustrations to the lectures paid special homage to Chambers and the idea of the hut as the man-made source for classical imitation (figs. 3.30–31).[68]

3.30 Soane. Royal Academy lecture 1. Illustration of primitive hut with flat roof, 1807. Perspective

3.31 Royal Academy lecture 1. Illustration of primitive hut with internal pillars and side aisles, 1807. Cutaway perspective and plan

The abstraction of sign from referent in Soane's

3.32 Soane. Soane House, London, begun 1792. Frontispiece added in 1812. Perspective, by Gandy

3.33 Karl Friedrich Schinkel. Design for *The Magic Flute,* act 1: "The Hall of Stars in the Palace of the Queen of the Night," 1815–16

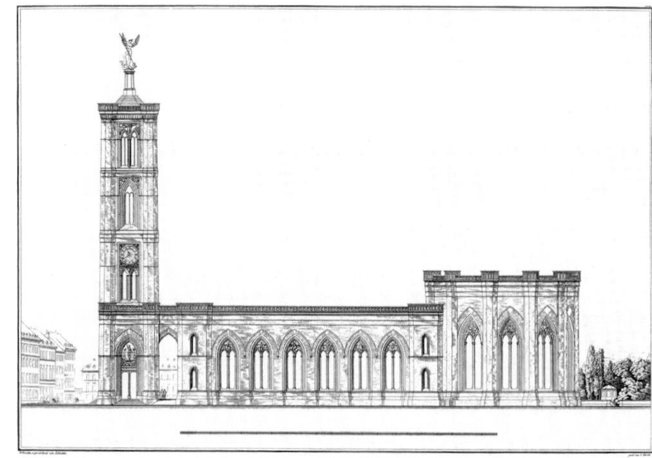

3.34 Schinkel. St. Gertrude's Church project, Berlin, 1819. Side elevation. From Schinkel, *Sammlung architektonischer Entwürfe,* 1819–40

Commissioners' churches indicates a separation of historical cause from effect that forces the image to rely mainly on its own internal structure for coherence and meaning. In the originally unglazed frontispiece the architect added to his London house in 1812, shortly after his first series of Royal Academy lectures, this process of dissociation results in a kind of scaffolding of structural elements that is both subclassical—in the sense of the "constructed" primitive hut—and supraclassical—in the sense of Boullée's abstractions (fig. 3.32). Whichever way we choose to interpret it, and I think both are possible, a new liberal sense of history lies at the core of Soane's synthesis. In the Lincoln's Inn

Fields house, the skylit galleries of the interior teem with sculptural and architectural fragments taken from Egypt, Greece, Rome, and medieval Europe. The portico's exterior framework renders them in abstract terms, outlining a synthetic representation of the fundamental building blocks of architecture. Abstraction and representation thus become synonymous rather than oppositional in the effort to retain a meaningful role for the apparatus of neoclassical display.

Schinkel's Search for Synthesis

Soane's Prussian counterpart in the abstraction of neoclassical representation was Karl Friedrich Schinkel. Born in 1781, the year after Boullée succeeded Soufflot at the French Academy of Architecture and the year after Soane began his practice in London, Schinkel ultimately directed the neoclassical tradition of his predecessors into a form of such "pure radical abstraction," as he put it, that he himself worried about its becoming too "dry and rigid."[69] Fundamental to this development were Schinkel's engagement with medieval architecture (much more serious than either Boullée's or Soane's), as well as his adoption of a utilitarian understanding of the purposes of the art form, which may remind one of Durand but was of an entirely different order in its effect.

Unlike Boullée and Soane, Schinkel was interested in the Gothic not only for romantic and picturesque reasons but also for contextual and, eventually, structural ones. Working mainly as a painter and stage designer until 1815, Schinkel's many pictorial representations of Gothic churches and ruins seen in dramatic settings vie with Boullée's images of funerary monuments in their power to inspire strong emotional reactions, just as a number of his stage sets in a more classical vein recall the earlier French architect's universalizing cosmic imagery (fig. 3.33) The project Schinkel proposed in 1819 for a Gothic-style brick church on Berlin's Spittelmarket, dedicated to St. Gertrude, is one of the earliest indications of his serious consideration of nonclassical models for formal, programmatic, and contextual reasons (fig. 3.34).[70] Designs for medieval and classical structures often went hand in hand in his work, as they did in Soane's Commissioners' church projects. And the increasing simplification and abstraction of form in Schinkel's architecture can similarly be traced to the structural rationalism that evolved from this inclusive, liberal perception of history.[71]

In Schinkel's most important and well-known building, the Altes Museum of 1822–30, the move toward abstraction derives directly from the architect's use of neoclassical representation as referential image and means of rhetorical display (figs. 3.35–36).[72] The building sits on a podium at the rear of a monumental public square and garden in the center of Berlin, facing the former Royal Palace, at the end of the axis of Unter den Linden. The two-story structure contains galleries for sculpture on the lower level and painting on the upper. Following a conventional neoclassical plan for such an institutional program, these spaces surround a central, double-height rotunda (fig. 3.37). Articulated by a ring of twenty Corinthian columns, this space serves as a place of introduction and orientation. In defending it against charges of extravagance and waste, Schinkel argued that "so mighty a building as the Museum...must have a worthy center." This "sanctuary," he continued, which "one first enters...coming from the outer hall," had to offer "the sight of a beautiful and sublime room [that would] make the visitor receptive and create the proper mood for the enjoyment and understanding of the building's overall aims."[73] Intended to display major pieces of antique sculpture in the collection, the space was designed as a representation of the Roman Pantheon.

The plan reveals how Schinkel's overall conception of the building was largely determined by its relation to the public square in front. The outward expression of the museum was reduced to a facade of a simple, unbroken Ionic portico contained at both ends by spur walls terminating in antae.

3.35 Schinkel. Altes Museum (originally Museum), Berlin, 1822–30. Main facade

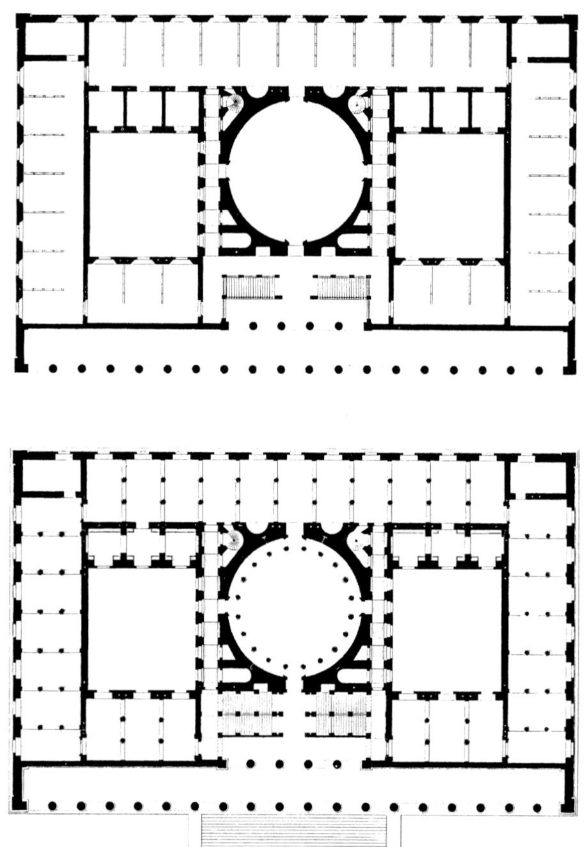

3.36 Altes Museum. Plans, first and second floors. From *Sammlung architektonischer Entwürfe*

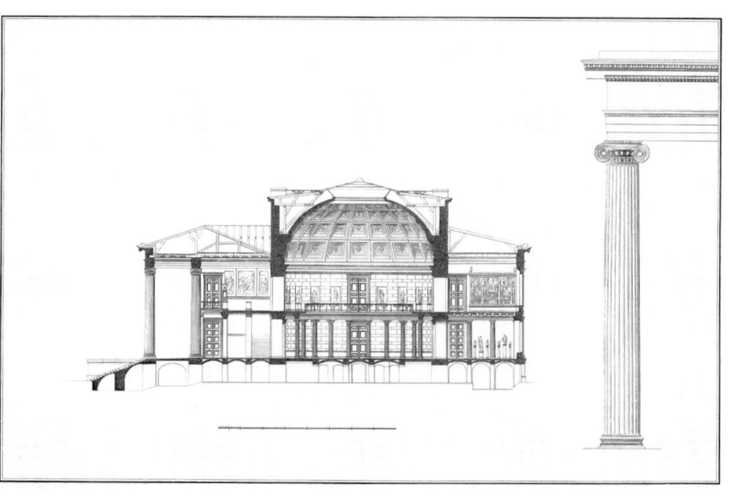

3.37 Altes Museum. Longitudinal section and detail of portico order. From *Sammlung architektonischer Entwürfe*

Representing a classical stoa rather than a temple, the reference to a place for gathering and discussion was especially appropriate for such a cultural institution. To account for the design's stark articulation and strong axiality and symmetry, many scholars have posited the influence of Boullée's student Durand, who was teaching architecture at the Ecole Polytechnique in Paris when Schinkel undertook a study tour to the French city in 1804–5. More intriguing, however, is the obvious connection between Schinkel's stoa-frontispiece/two-level split-stairway design and Boullée's well-publicized and highly regarded project for Paris's Royal Library (see fig. 3.15).[74] In the Berlin museum, the half-indoor, half-outdoor stairway allows the visitor direct access both to the upper-floor painting galleries and, through the door at its base, to the central rotunda and sculpture galleries on the ground floor (see fig. 3.37). The loggia-like upper landing offers a place of respite at the end of a tour of the collections, from which one can contemplate the city outside.[75]

The museum's sharply detailed representational frontispiece is composed of a stately Ionic order based on a deliberate amalgam of elements drawn from both Attic and Asiatic Greek sources, including the North Porch of the Erechtheum in Athens (ca. 421–404 B.C.E.) and the Temple of Athena Polias in Priene (340–334 B.C.E.).[76] This archeological imagery gives way on the side and rear facades to a more matter-of-fact formal organization of surface elements that expresses some of the spatial divisions of the interior not revealed by the colossal order of the representational main facade (fig. 3.38). The brick construction of these less visible faces of the building was rendered in stucco rather than clad in stone. Minimally detailed string courses indicate the floor levels (the lowest being a basement beneath the podium of the front portico), while highly abstracted corner piers, capitals, and entablature contain the block in a flat, gridlike composition that might be understood, in terms of the classical hierarchy of modes, as a kind of serviceable

3.38 Altes Museum. Exterior. Side and rear facades

3.39 Schinkel. Friedrich-Werdersche Church, Berlin, 1821–30. Exterior perspective. From *Sammlung architektonischer Entwürfe*

Doric (in comparison with the more elegant Ionic of the front and the richer Corinthian of the rotunda). The simplified, double-height corner piers are therefore just as representational as the columns across the front; they are simply of a lower order, corresponding to their lesser position in the hierarchy of things.[77]

Contemporary with the Altes Museum, and visible in the perspective from its stairway landing, the Friedrich-Werdersche Church displays the same gridded, structurally rational composition as the sides and rear of the museum on all four of its Gothic-detailed facades (fig. 3.39).[78] The church's rather prosaic, even mundane appearance has

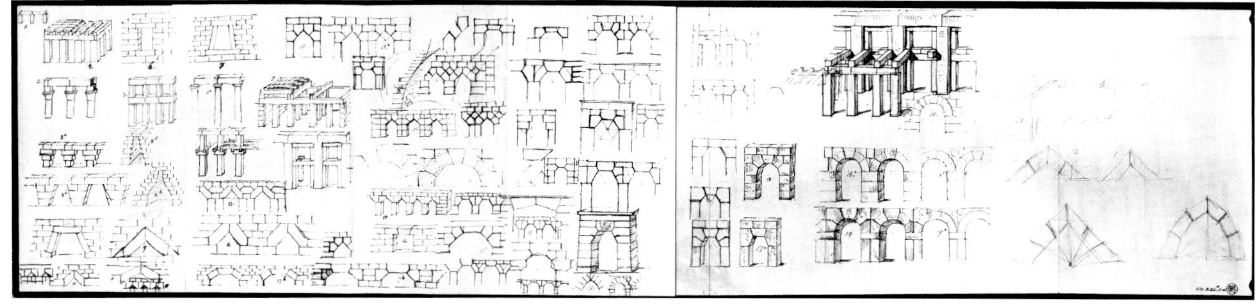

3.40 Schinkel. *Architektonische Lehrbuch*. So-called "Long Sheet," ca. 1825

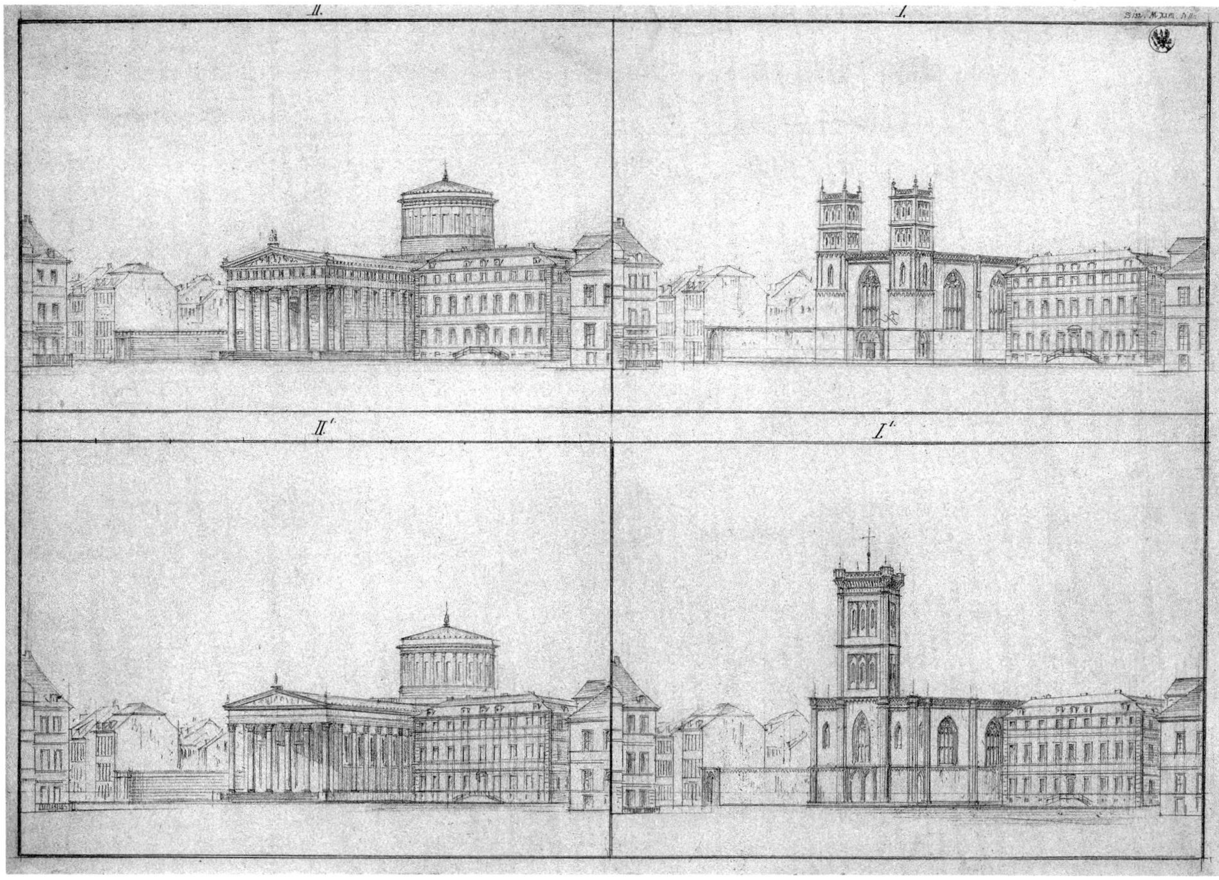

3.41 Friedrich-Werdersche Church. Page of four alternative designs. Perspective sketches, 1824

much to do with the fact that its brick structure was not clad in stone or covered in stucco but left exposed, in the manner of vernacular and commonplace building traditions as well as the historical forms of German and northern Italian late medieval architecture. Like Soane, but with much greater historical attention and analysis, Schinkel had come to believe that underlying all styles were generic structural orders based on material and tectonic conditions and that this very understanding might enable the architect to create a new, synthetic, and thus abstract form language. This is confirmed by the numerous sketches of simple trabeated and arcuated structural combinations and the notes describing them that Schinkel made for a never-published *Architektonische Lehrbuch* (Architectural Textbook) beginning in the early 1820s (fig. 3.40).[79]

As in the case of Soane, a key factor in Schinkel's move

3.42 Friedrich-Werdersche Church. Interior perspective in classical style (project). From *Sammlung architektonischer Entwürfe*

3.43 Friedrich-Werdersche Church. Interior perspective in Gothic style (as built). From *Sammlung architektonischer Entwürfe*

toward abstraction was a willingness to contemplate a variety of stylistic solutions to a single project. Four alternative designs, two in the classical style and two in the Gothic, were in fact presented to Friedrich Wilhelm III as options for the Werdersche Church (fig. 3.41). One of the classical designs is Doric, the other Corinthian; one of the Gothic has a single central tower, the other two towers. A comparison of perspectives of the two interiors reveals how superficial many of the differences are (figs. 3.42–43). Both show a single-nave vessel, covered by vaults in one case and shallow domes in the other, supported by piers acting as interior buttresses cut out to allow for a continuous gallery. The superficiality of these differences in expression was clearly not thought of by Schinkel in pejorative terms, for he published both the classical and the Gothic versions in his *Sammlung architektonischer Entwürfe* (*Collection of Architectural Designs*) before the building was completed.[80] Barry Bergdoll maintains that this was out of a "desire to advocate some equivalence between the various designs."[81] This "equivalence," as we shall see in two of Schinkel's late works, resulted in such a thoroughgoing form of synthesis as nearly to undo the neoclassical ideal of representation first effected in Soufflot's "Graeco-Gothic" compromise of Sainte-Geneviève.

The Bauakademie and the Berlin Royal Library at the Limits of Neoclassical Representation

The Bauakademie, or Allgemeine Bauschule (School of Architecture), as it was called until the late 1840s, was designed by Schinkel in 1831 and built between 1832 and 1836 (figs. 3.44–46).[82] Located on the northeast side of the Werdersche Market, it faced the recently completed Werdersche Church to the southwest as well as the Altes Museum, across the Spree River to the north. Different from both in its foursquare, expressly utilitarian imagery and character, it reveals, perhaps more completely than any other of the architect's works, the expressive potential and limitations of the emphasis on the structure in neoclassical

3.44 Schinkel. Bauakademie (orig. Allgemeine Bauschule), Berlin, 1831–36 (demolished 1961–62). Exterior, ca. 1900. View from east

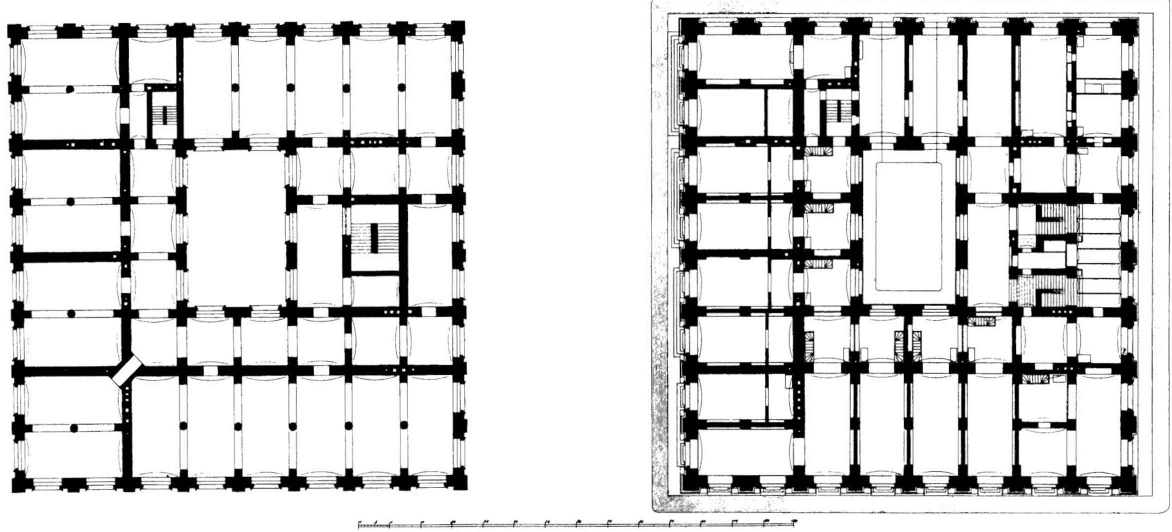

3.45 Bauakademie. Plans, first and second floors. From *Sammlung architektonischer Entwürfe*

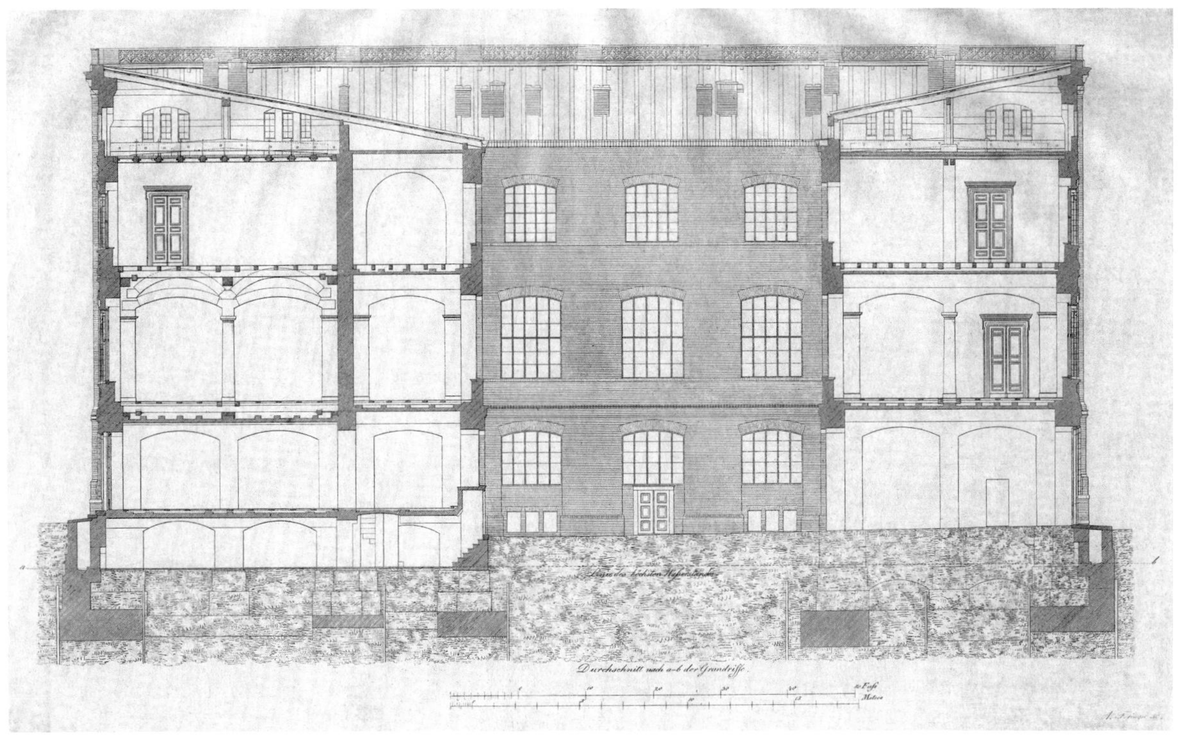

3.46 Bauakademie. Section. From Emil Flaminius, "Ueber den Bau des Hauses für die allgemeine Bauschule in Berlin," *Allgemeine Bauzeitung*, 1836

3.47 Bauakademie. Exterior. Main entrance (north facade), ca. 1900

3.48 Bauakademie. Interior. Drawing studio on northeast side of second floor, during demolition

3.49 Bauakademie. Interior. Classroom at southeast corner of second floor, during demolition

representation that Laugier's reductionism brought into play. Though one might not expect it from the repetitive and seemingly nonhierarchical appearance of the exterior, the building had a rather unusual mixed-use program. The two main components of this were the architecture school itself, which occupied the entire second floor, and the offices of the Oberbaudeputation (State Building Administration), which occupied approximately half of the third floor. Schinkel, who was promoted to Oberbaudirektor in 1830, had his personal apartment and studio in the other half of the third floor. The ground floor had shops on three sides, with direct access from the street on two of them (the stores had been eliminated by the time the photograph in fig. 3.44 was taken). The top floor served merely as an attic, since the inward-sloping, impluvium-like roof rendered it quite useless for any other purpose.

The building's modular design was based on a square structural grid organized around a relatively small, decentered, oblong interior court that functioned mainly as a light well and rain catchment.[83] The court was spatially disconnected from the entrance vestibule, which was reached through two identical and rather understated doors in the center of the building's north facade (fig. 3.47). The door on the left was for the school and the one on the right for the Oberbaudeputation, although both opened into the same space. Overriding all other considerations in the design, it would seem, was the structural system of the grid. That system made use of brick piers, arches, vaults, and wall sections to create a masonry frame structure within which partitions were located and to which the exterior envelope was applied. The brick on the exterior was left exposed, while that of the interior was plastered over to create a smooth, finished appearance.

The best way to visualize the interior construction and space, unfortunately, is, through the photographs that were taken when the building was being demolished in 1961–62 (fig. 3.48).[84] A view of the school's drawing studio, on the northeast side of the second floor, shows the combination of vertical brick piers connected by segmental brick arches resting on stone impost blocks that forms the basic unit of the structural frame. Where piers and partition walls have been eliminated to create double-wide spaces as here, Greek Doric stone columns were inserted as intermediary supports. Against the outer wall, which opens up through a segmentally arched window echoing the shape of the internal arches, one can see the remains of the brick-and-plaster segmental barrel vault that ran from the outside wall to the inside one, defining the studio's overall space as a series of transverse volumes rather than a continuous one (see fig. 3.46). In this case, the low vaults could be read as projections of the window arches, but at the corners of the building the sense of visual consistency was undone by the demands of the grid (fig. 3.49).

The view in fig. 3.46 also shows the solid brick wall on the floor above, separating two of the rooms in Schinkel's own studio. But the most interesting and revelatory aspect of the image is not what it tells us about what could be seen of the building's structure—or at least assumed, since the surfaces were eventually covered in plaster—but what could not be seen. Here the issue is twofold. First, the segmental arches between the bays have relieving arches above them to help distribute the load and diminish the outward thrust. These were entirely hidden from view within the depth of the floor, as was the second expedient Schinkel employed to stabilize the structure and bind it together. Following in the classical tradition exemplified in Soufflot's Church of Sainte-Geneviève (see fig. 2.26), Schinkel secured the vertical piers to one another by wrought iron tie-rods and wood beams that were then anchored into the thickness of the exterior and interior walls (fig. 3.50). He also employed iron alone to tie the outside corners of the building together.

This subordination of reality to appearance in the interior of the Bauakademie carries over into the relationship between interior and exterior to ensure the

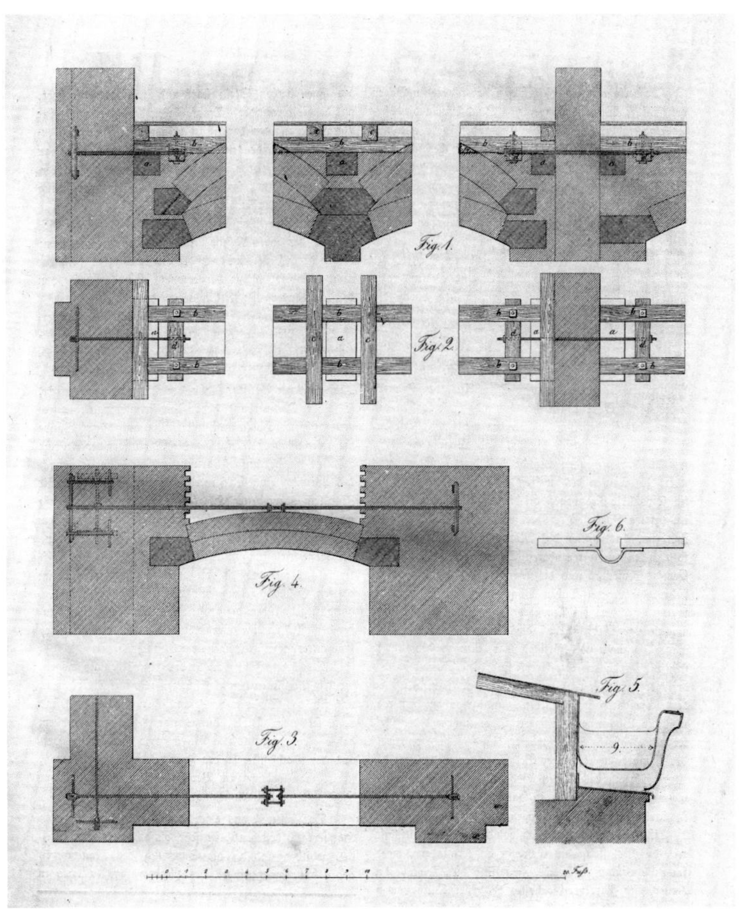

3.50 Bauakademie. Sectional details showing masonry structure with wood connectors and iron tie-rods and anchors. From Flaminius, *Allgemeine Bauzeitung*, 1836

representational integrity of the facades (see fig. 3.44). The four floors were gradated from bottom to top in a classical manner

having nothing necessarily to do with the functions they contained. The ground floor acted as a base, the top floor as an attic. The projecting verticals between the windows of the base were detailed to form pedestals for the attached piers or pilasters rising up through the cornice to punctuate the balustrade that masked the roof, as in a sixteenth-century Renaissance palazzo or public building. Above the ground floor, the diminishing height and width of the windows were made perspicuous by the banding of the brick that substituted for rustication and indicated the coursing of

3.51 Schinkel. Royal Library project, Berlin, 1835–39. First design, 1835. Exterior perspective

the masonry infill, as in the Romanesque architecture of Florence, Pisa, and elsewhere in northern Italy.

The main brick color was red, the horizontal linear bands a glazed violet. On the attached pilasters, the tall open rectangles of glazed brick accentuated the vertical element, while the smaller, nearly square rectangles at the two string course levels represented the anchors of the tie-rods embedded in the masonry behind them (see fig. 3.50). The decorative string courses, window frames, window sills, and main door frames were all made of terra cotta, as were the star-shaped bosses that filled the symbolic anchor frames over the double-door entrance (see fig. 3.47).[85] The panels of reliefs below the second-floor windows (the same on all four facades) told the story, in allegorical terms, of the rebirth of architecture and building trades in the Middle Ages upon the ruins of the golden age of ancient Greece. The panels surrounding the two door frames depicted the spirit of architecture and the origins of the Greek orders in mythological terms that were given a natural referent in the images of plants and botanical processes in the reliefs on the jambs.

The disparity between the Bauakademie's exterior and interior is perhaps most fully evident in the specific expression of use—or, rather, the lack thereof. Here again it is the grid that rules. Clearly unconcerned with the idea of directly relating interior spaces to exterior form or character, Schinkel described the mixed-use building as having "four identical facades."[86] The insistence of the bay system in fact made it virtually impossible to differentiate on the exterior between a six-bay-long, double-depth studio, for instance, and a single-bay-wide office or corridor space. Aside from allowing for a variation in floor heights, it also restricted the means to distinguish between a school, a government office, and a private residence. And while it might have been assumed from the unrelieved mass of the building, the exterior did not indicate the existence of a central court—nor would one have any idea that it was off-center. Finally, the flat, regular, and plaited design of the facade could have led one to conclude that the internal structure was post-and-beam rather than arched and vaulted, the lack of expression of the thrusts exerted by the vaults being only the most obvious cause for such a misperception.

Despite its utilitarian appearance of a straightforward, commonsensical sort—indeed, "functional" in the colloquial sense—the Bauakademie remains representational at the limits of neoclassical thinking. Around the same time he was designing the building, Schinkel wrote the following: "In architecture everything must be true, any masking, concealing of the structure is an error. The real task is to make every part of the construction beautiful."[87] To maintain that the architect was either hypocritical or unable to fulfill his stated intention is clearly untenable. One must therefore accept the fact that, no matter how "structural" the exterior of the Bauakademie looks, it is still only virtual. "Truth" still resides in "appearance," and verisimilitude still governs perception and judgment. It is simply that appearance itself has been reduced to such a structurally rational form that it takes on the character of reality. If Laugier made truth approximate appearance so closely that truth itself became an illusion, Schinkel did the reverse in making appearance seem so much a matter of truth that it could be read as a transparent image of it. In this way, the Bauakademie achieved a "zero degree" of verisimilitude.

This limit condition of neoclassical representation was enabled by the abstraction of tectonic elements resulting in large part from the architect's synthetic reading of history. The plaiting of verticals and horizontals seemed to express a general structural condition of load and support without specific historical reference, although it would be more correct to see it as blending different types into one. Historians have often wavered between describing the verticals of the facade as Gothic-like buttresses or classical pilasters.[88] The brick banding can similarly be read as a medieval correlate of classical rustication. On the other hand, the abstraction in the Bauakademie also owed something to the vernacular, industrial architecture of brick warehouses, factories, and dock buildings that Schinkel sketched on a trip to England in the summer of 1826, while there to research ideas for the installation of the Altes Museum.[89]

In the end, then, the Bauakademie might best be understood as a neoclassical representation of the utilitarian ideal through the creation of a Doric order, such as the one on the rear of the Altes Museum, transfigured by the arch and integrally expressed in brick. Indeed, despite the allusions to the medieval, it is the classical that is privileged and predominates, whether in the specific details of the curved pedimented windows and decorative reliefs of the main entrance or in the more general aspects of overall composition. The disguised brick arches and vaults of the interior—more Roman than Romanesque or Gothic—undergirded the building's Renaissance palazzo–like block, which was clearly articulated in horizontal layers—and in conventional classical terms—by the splayed rusticated base, gradated elevation of windows and attic, and capping cornice masking the roof. In the vertical dimension, the building's "abstracted colossal order," as Jonas Geist described the attached pilasters, provided a uniformity that both controlled the design and endowed it with a formal appearance of decorative unity not unlike that achieved by Michelangelo in the palaces of the Piazza del Campidoglio in Rome.[90]

The extreme abstraction of the Bauakademie revealed significant fissures in the neoclassical economy of representation. I have already noted Schinkel's concern that such "radical abstraction" could have a "dry and rigid" outcome. One of his last major projects, begun while the Bauakademie was nearing completion, attests to this concern and reveals an important way in which the architect felt that the Bauakademie paradigm could be amplified, enriched, and ultimately made less visibly self-contradictory. The initial project for a new Royal Library for Berlin was produced in early 1835 for a somewhat restricted site behind a wing

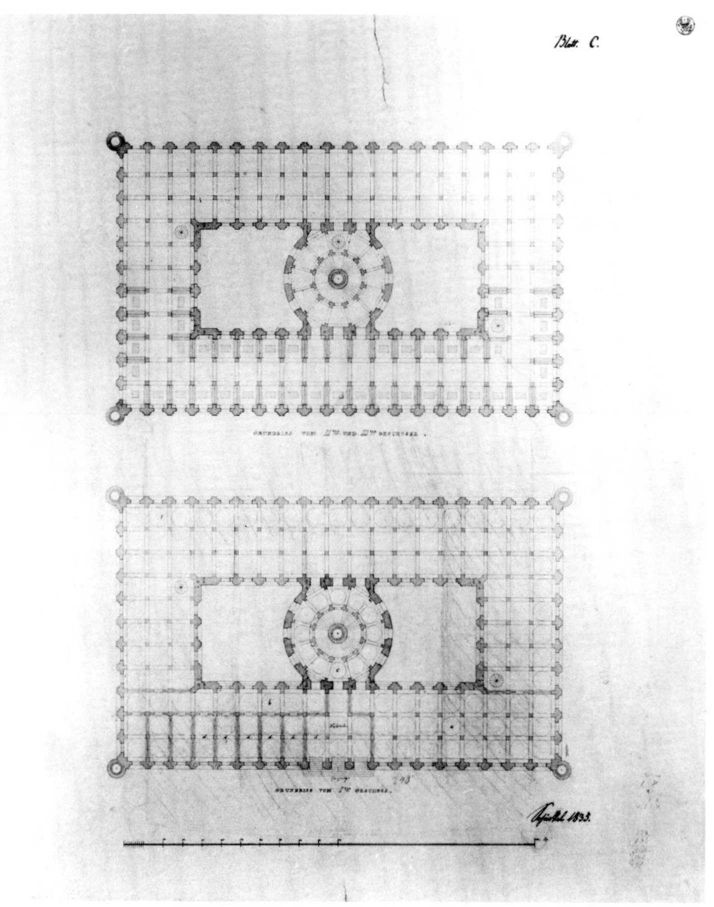

3.52 Royal Library project. First design. Plans, first and second/third floors

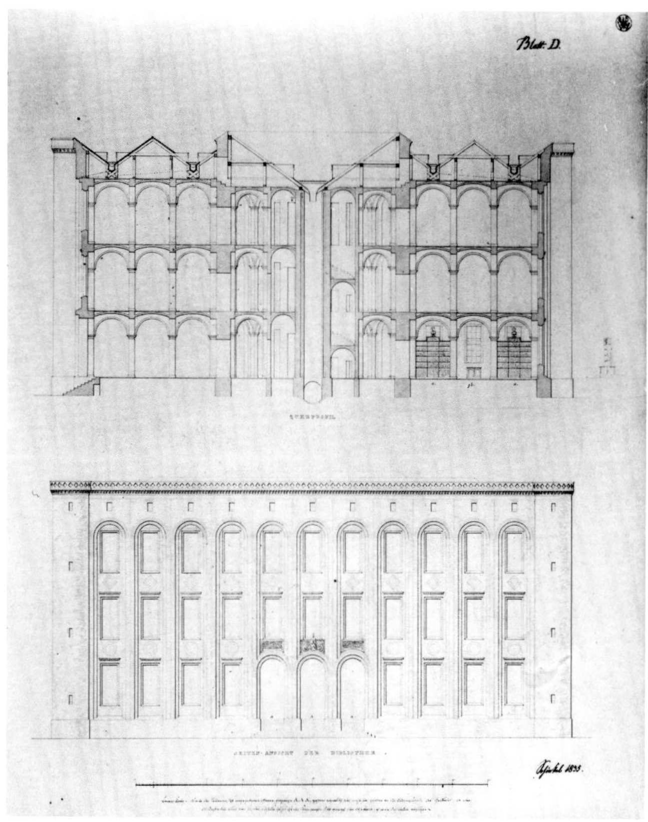

3.53 Royal Library project. First design. Section and elevation

of the University of Berlin, just west of the Altes Museum (figs. 3.51–52). A second design soon followed, intended to take up the entire area to the rear of the university (see fig. 3.54).[91] Had it been built, the new Royal Library would surely have been as significant an addition to Berlin's cultural landscape as the earlier Altes Museum. Planned to be constructed of exposed brick with terra-cotta detailing, the building would also have taken its place as the logical successor to the Bauakademie, further illustrating the architect's thinking on design for public institutions. Schinkel explained that a building for such a purpose as a library called for a "monumental character," but that it should also "have nothing pompous about it; no rooms of a form imposing by their height; nor colonnades; nor a profusion of useless spaces."[92]

The plan for the first project was a revision of the Altes Museum in terms of the Bauakademie. An open, rectangular block, nineteen bays wide as in the museum, surrounds a central rotunda with light courts to either side. Instead of being purely frontal, however, the library has the nonhierarchical bearing of the identically sided architecture school. The entrance colonnade of the museum has been eliminated, and its open stairway has been incorporated into the formerly purely representational and "imposing" space of the central rotunda. Most important from a structural point of view, the columnar order and trabeated structural system of the museum have been replaced by an arcuated one that follows that of the Bauakademie (fig. 3.53). A square grid, as insistent as that of its predecessor, gives rise to a round-arched framework supporting a myriad of small saucer domes that break down the interior space into relatively small units, thus providing for the possibility of numerous small reading rooms and carrels.

Perhaps the most surprising, while also the most telling, aspect of the design is the exterior. Here the superficial differences from the Altes Museum are so great that one might not have suspected the similarity in plan. The differences from the Bauakademie are more discreet. The library's exterior is treated as a continuous three-story arcade. It rises from a low base into a flat attic punctuated by small windows like those that light the service stairs in the round, bastionlike towers, which frame the block and enforce its medieval character as well as its compositional wholeness. Like the antae of the Altes Museum and the colossal order of pilasters of the Bauakademie, these towers, along with the uninterrupted piers of the three-story arcade, provide a decorative unity to the facade. They override the actual conditions of the interior floor levels and thus force one to read the exterior as an independent representational construct analogous to the Altes Museum's neoclassical frontispiece.

Although the triple-height arcade is not a direct translation of the three separate stories of arched and domed interior spaces, it is clear that Schinkel was trying to create a correlation between the two through a kind of structural rhyming. To accomplish this, he resorted to a more figural form of historical reference than he had used in the Bauakademie, as well as one that, at least on the surface, was at the opposite end of the historical spectrum from the antique forms of the Altes Museum. Schinkel's second proposal for the Royal Library added string courses to indicate the different floor levels but did nothing more than the first about expressing the existence of the central rotunda. By contrast, it increased and exaggerated the figural aspects of the initial design so as to make more explicit its representational meaning in the symbolic sense (fig. 3.54). The footprint was more than doubled in size, expanding to a fifteen-by-fifteen-bay square with four

3.54 Royal Library project. Second design, ca. 1835. Plan, ground floor, and elevation

internal courts surrounding the central stairwell rotunda.[93] The triple-arched entrance of the first design was now highlighted by statue columns above the doors, which were reiterated in the four allegorical figures on the balustrade. The machicolated cornice imparted a more plastic sense of definition to the attic story, while the corner turrets were detailed with a spiraling pattern of windows, emphasizing their function as in a medieval tower.

The decorative elaborations in the second design served to characterize the building as a repository of knowledge through an increased use of historical imagery. Where the first project could be read as an imitation of the rather stark, early fourth-century Imperial Roman Basilica at Trier, which Schinkel had drawn in 1816 and revisited ten years later, the second recalled much more forcefully the German Romanesque of the eleventh and twelfth centuries that was, as will be discussed in the next chapter, being promoted by a younger generation of architects as the only solid ground for an authentic modern architecture deriving from the use of the arch.[94] The library's roots in the traditions of medieval scholasticism and learning were thus made evident to its users by its thick, richly detailed historicizing casing.

In rejecting the abstraction of the Bauakademie, Schinkel's Royal Library project reopened the question of historical reference—but now as a source for representation irrespective of and outside of the traditional justification by analogy with nature. Schinkel showed little interest in the Laugier model of the hut, though not in the model of representation it implied. His embrace of the arch and vault in all their historical and structural dimensions took his architecture well beyond the hut's mythological reach. The historical analysis and applications his later work embodied would become a characteristic feature of the architecture of the next few generations. Yet Schinkel's work, even as late as the Royal Library project, was little different from that of Boullée and Soane in one subtle though commanding respect: the adherence to a neoclassical conception of architecture as representation in which the exterior envelope of a building as an independent, self-contained, decorative unity could be believed to stand virtually for the whole.

Pugin, Labrouste, and the New Realism of Decorated Construction

THE 1830S MARKED a change in the modern attitude toward architectural representation as profound and long-lasting as that initiated in the middle of the previous century by Laugier's *Essai*. This change can be characterized most succinctly by the reversal in the relationship between construction and decoration that was expressed in the new concept of decorating construction instead of constructing decoration. In the process, the ruling classical ideal of verisimilitude, or appearance of truth, was replaced by a new standard of realism, or truthfulness as such. As Victor Hugo (1802–1885) put it as early as 1827 in the polemical preface to his play *Cromwell*, it was the direct expression of "the real" that would destroy forever the fictions of "verisimilitude."[1] As Hugo went on to explain in his novel *Notre-Dame de Paris*, published four years later, this transformation in the creative process would have the most devastating effects on the art of architecture in particular. Of all the arts, it was the one most conditioned by functional and material concerns as well as the most public in its form of monumental expression. For it, the loss of representational capacity was a sure sign of meaninglessness and, in Hugo's words, "death."[2]

Surely, any dedicated and intelligent architect reaching maturity in the 1830s would have had to reject Hugo's conclusion, although not necessarily his analysis of the problem. To find one's bearings, however, demanded much original thought plus enormous strength of conviction. A new and broader awareness and understanding of architecture's history had opened up possibilities previously considered only in marginal ways. Combined with this was the now very apparent irrelevancy of the canonical texts of classicism that had previously supported a theory of architecture as a meaningful form of representation. Vitruvius, Alberti, Palladio, and Vignola were no longer read and quoted as almost God-given sources. Nor were the texts of Laugier, Chambers, or even Quatremère de Quincy the objects of serious discussion and debate among younger architects, as they had been through at least the previous decade.[3]

Of the generation of architects that came to prominence in the 1830s and produced their first significant works in the decade following the deaths of Soane and Schinkel, two stand out as the most interesting, the most consequential, and the most representative of the two most important emerging schools of thought. The very fact that the Gothic revivalist Augustus Welby Pugin (1812–1852) and the classical rationalist Henri Labrouste (1801–1875) would appear at first to have so little in common yet ultimately were driven by similar concerns is itself a mark of the changing times to which they responded. Opposites in terms of character, personality, upbringing, training, social status, religious views, and professional affiliations, the pair makes an odd but revealing couple.

Pugin was the son of a French émigré architectural illustrator and book publisher. Although he learned drawing from his father, he received no formal training in architecture, nor did he apprentice in an office. Driven as much by religious as by artistic beliefs, culminating in his conversion to Catholicism in 1835, he remained an outsider to the profession for the relatively short time he lived. Committed to Bethlehem Hospital in 1852 following a severe depression, he was diagnosed as "manic" and died soon thereafter of a seizure at the age of forty, while under heavy sedation at the monastery-like home he had designed and built for himself on the Channel coast at Ramsgate, beginning in 1843. Pugin was a polemicist who advanced and defended his ideas in the public arena of print to such an extent that they were and still are better known than his buildings, to which they are intimately related and by which they can be more precisely understood.[4]

Labrouste, by contrast, was a consummate professional. The son of a barrister who was elected to the Conseil des Cinq-Cents in 1795 and later became a high-ranking official in the July Monarchy, he grew up in a distinguished family of *notables* with strong, liberal, even anticlerical leanings. He went to the state-run Ecole des Beaux-Arts in Paris, where he excelled, winning the Grand Prix in near-record time in 1824. After spending five years as a fellow at the French Academy in Rome, he returned to a career of teaching and building important public works in France, which eventually earned him a coveted seat at the Academy of Fine Arts in 1867. Although radical in his views about how architecture should be taught and made, Labrouste hardly published a word, nor did he ever express his views on design in a public forum. Living in an apartment in Paris to the relatively ripe old age of seventy-five, he did absolutely nothing in his private life that would have compared with Pugin's least eccentricity.[5]

At a superficial level, the two buildings that can be taken as exemplary of their work of the 1840s seem to tell the same story as these brief outlines of the architects' lives. The rich Gothic forms and decorative elaboration of Pugin's Church of St. Giles, Cheadle, built between 1840 and 1846, differ sharply from the lean, ascetic surfaces and skeletal iron structure of Labrouste's Bibliothèque Sainte-Geneviève, built in Paris from 1843 to 1850 (see figs. 4.9 and 4.30).[6] But there is a physical intensity and directness in the expression of both that is similar—and that is different from almost everything else we have considered so far. It can be felt in the material expression of form as well as in the historical imagination underlying it. It is, in effect, an intensity of a profoundly realistic sort about how these two realms—the material and the historical—might be realigned in an age when faith in the classical orders, and the system of representation that faith supported, had disintegrated.

Many explanations for this loss of faith have been proposed, and no doubt one of the most compelling as regards architecture is the impact of new industrial technologies. It was during the latter years of the 1830s, the very moment when Pugin and Labrouste were contemplating the designs for their church and library, that railroads were making their first appearances in England and France and the use of iron in building was becoming relatively widespread. But how each of the two architects reacted to these new technologies would again seem to separate them irrevocably. Where Labrouste embraced the use of iron, and thereby inevitably called into question the masonry-based system of classical proportions embodied in the orders, Pugin rejected any such modern intrusions in his reconstruction of a pre-Renaissance world.

Two Sides of the Same Historical Coin

If any single issue can be said to separate pre-1830 from post-1830 architectural theory, it is surely the role of history. Up until this time, nature, however understood, was thought of as the ground from which form derived. Representation, whether through the model of the hut or not, ultimately always referred back to a natural origin. Symmetry, harmony, proportion, character, and propriety were all thought to be aspects of the natural state of the world. Beginning in the 1830s, as with Schinkel, history replaced nature as the basis for generating architectural forms, relations, and meanings. Both Pugin and Labrouste fully subscribed to this new condition and encapsulated their individual understandings of the issue in images that warrant comparison.

The woodcut Pugin drew for the frontispiece of his master text, *The True Principles of Pointed or Christian Architecture,* published in 1841, gives us his image of the ideal architect: a monk in medieval surroundings drawing figures of Gothic tracery, no doubt to accompany the church whose plan is seen against the wall behind the desk (fig. 4.1). Religious instruments, pictures, and books abound to remind us of the spiritual state in which this mental work is being carried out. We are removed from the modern world to a time stopped somewhere in the fourteenth century.

4.1 A[ugustus] Welby Pugin. *The True Principles of Pointed or Christian Architecture,* orig. pub. 1841; 2nd ed. 1853. Frontispiece of 2nd. ed.

Labrouste depicted his image of architecture, or rather the mind of the architect, in the medal he designed in 1846–47 for the fledgling Société Centrale des Architectes as a token of attendance at board of directors' meetings (fig. 4.2).[7] It is both more abstract and more inclusive than Pugin's woodcut, though no less historicist. Rather than depicting an architect practicing his profession or craft, it illustrates what is going on in his head. Through the conventional symbol of a muse, here wearing a medieval emblem of a city as a crown, Labrouste shows the architect's mind to be crammed with monuments of the past—and not just from a single period in that past, either. Buildings from the Middle Ages vie with those of antiquity for prominence. The only limit placed on the historical imagination is set by the urban confines of the city walls, which seem to provide

4.2 Henri Labrouste. *Jeton de présence* for Société Centrale des Architectes, 1846–47

a much wider scope for development than the four walls of Pugin's monk's study. Yet both images ultimately have the same effect, which is to locate models of architectural thought resolutely within a historical framework now dissociated from nature.[8]

What Pugin's and Labrouste's images have in common is strikingly illustrated by a comparison with the earlier one of Laugier's hut (see fig. 2.1). Laugier presented a mythical image of nature as the source of architectural form through the reinterpretation of a convention that went back to Vitruvius. The implicit transformation of the impermanent materials of nature into the permanent ones of the Greek temple gave the classical orders an ideal and timeless status. Quatremère de Quincy spoke of the "model" of the hut as having "acquired relative to the imitative art [of architecture] the force and the authority of nature," calling the system of representation based on the material transformation a "customary" and "pleasing fiction," resulting in "a deception in which one is less the dupe than the confidant."[9] Pugin and Labrouste, by contrast, confer on the historical imagination a time-bound reality independent of nature.

Equally struck by the problem thus raised of operating in a world without fixed and conventional rules or guideposts, Pugin favored limiting the field of action to a narrowly circumscribed historical period, while Labrouste was willing to open up the area of investigation to the broad range of possibilities that had recently begun to appear on the historical horizon.

Despite the difference in historical scope, the images created by Pugin and Labrouste make it clear that the architects shared a belief that the definition of representation that had surfaced in the eighteenth century had reached the point where an architecture based on the fictive language of the classical orders was no longer a viable proposition—even when, as in the earlier nineteenth century, that language was abstracted into a more openly Graeco-Gothic synthesis. Both architects concluded that (1) only the realities of construction and program could provide a firm ground for truthfulness of expression; and (2) consequently the relationship between construction and decoration that had obtained under the hegemony of verisimilitude would have to be inverted to account for the concept of truth to materials and program. It is one of the great ironies of architectural history that this premonition of modern functionalism would first emerge as an exaggerated form of historicism even more decorative in some respects than its classical predecessor.[10]

Pugin's Polemic and the Church of St. Giles, Cheadle

Pugin was a brilliant polemicist, both in words and in images. This was already abundantly clear in his first major publication, *Contrasts: or, a Parallel between the Noble Edifices of the Fourteenth and Fifteenth Centuries, and Similar Buildings of the Present Day, Shewing the Present Decay of Taste.* Appearing in 1836, the year before Soane died, the book contains a series of plates pairing medieval and contemporary buildings, always to the detriment of the latter. One of the pairs opposes an image of Soane's house in Lincoln's Inn

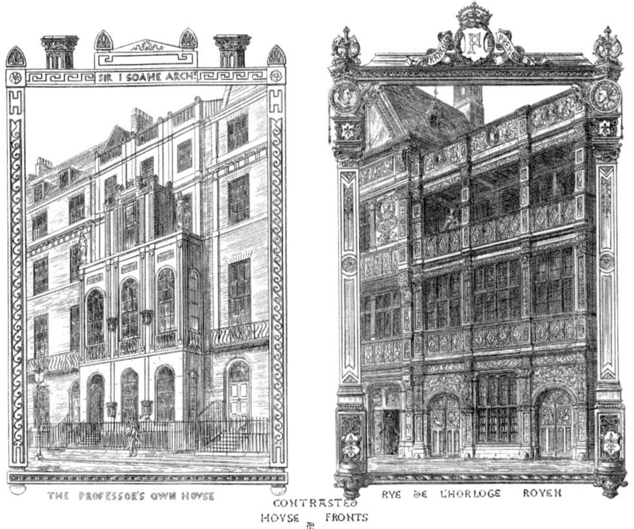

4.3 Pugin. "Contrasted House Fronts: The Professor's Own House/Rue de l'Horloge, Rouen," *Contrasts*, orig. pub. 1836; reprint ed., 1898

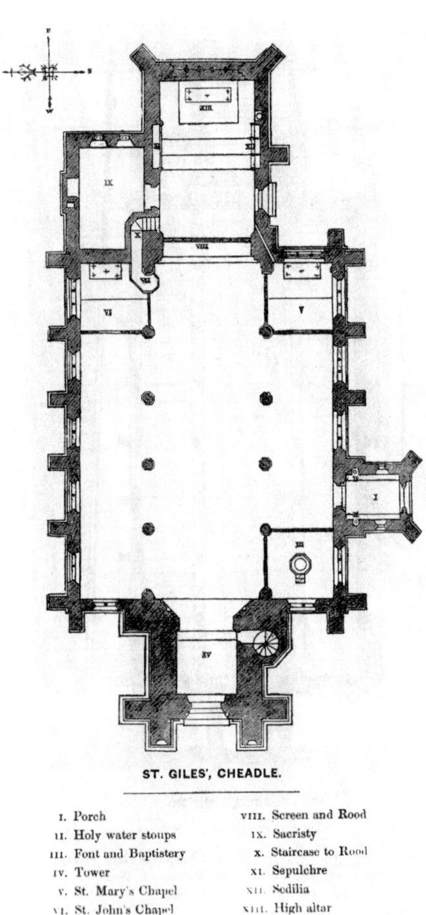

4.4 Pugin. Church of St. Giles, Cheadle, 1840–46. Plan. From Pugin, *The Present State of Ecclesiastical Architecture in England,* 1843

Fields (wryly labeled "The Professor's Own House") to a late medieval French town house (fig. 4.3); another contrasts a mean-looking, early nineteenth-century Gothic-style Commissioners' church in London by William Inwood (ca. 1771–1843) and Henry W. Inwood (1794–1843) to a full-blown fourteenth-century parish church in Yorkshire.[11] Like Labrouste, Pugin had little good to say about the architecture of the seventeenth and eighteenth centuries, calling such buildings as the Louvre, Versailles, and Buckingham Palace "the veriest heathen buildings imaginable."[12] (Labrouste, whose admiration for Greek, even Roman, and especially early Renaissance architecture separated him from Pugin, reportedly refused to visit Versailles for fear of "contagion.")[13]

Yet despite Pugin's general condemnation of postmedieval European architecture, it was the work of the previous three decades or so that was singled out for his most vicious attacks. Designs by Soane and Inwood became easy targets, as they so clearly showed by their flat, abstract imagery and meager, thin lines the degree to which the classical system of representation had lost vitality and conviction. Pugin had only scorn for the relativization and abstraction of historical effect from cause. A major aspect of the power of his critique was to reveal the profound disjunction between form and content that resulted from the loss of faith in the representational power of the classical orders.

Pugin sought to achieve an expression of historical character rooted in local conditions and material facts, based on a methodology meant to subvert the existing classical system of representation. His concept of what I would like to call "architectural realism" was most fully expressed in built form in the Church of St. Giles, Cheadle, begun in 1840, and theorized at precisely the same time in the text of the *True Principles of Pointed or Christian Architecture,* based on lectures given at Saint Mary's College, Oscott, and published in 1841.[14]

St. Giles's Church was intended by Pugin and his patron,

4.5 Church of St. Giles. View from town

the Earl of Shrewsbury, to be a model of its type and thus serve a didactic purpose both in religious and architectural terms, which for Pugin were in fact inseparable.[15] The plan was deliberately designed to follow that of a fourteenth-century, pre-Reformation parish church, with its chancel separated from the nave by a rood screen, its pulpit just off to the side, a south porch for everyday use, and a tall and semi-independent bell tower with spire to announce, from afar, the church's place in the town's physical and spiritual fabric (figs. 4.4–5). The tower is a singular element in this small town in Staffordshire. Its strong and powerful stone shape, dark against the sky, seems to call into question the solidity of the buildings around it, making it seem as if the church was there first and is the very reason for the town's existence.

Closer up, the scale of the tower seems so disproportionate to the rest of the building and town that it becomes embedded in one's mind as an object of special significance (fig. 4.6). In fact, each functionally distinct part of the structure pulls out from the mass to dominate the visual field and declare its individual identity. This gives the plan, in relation to the overall composition, a determinate character. Pugin went to great pains to make each separate element or volume read from a distance as distinguishable in shape, the break in the roofline at the chancel being the most subtle and most important sign (fig. 4.7). But above and beyond this functional expression of separate volumetric units is the sheer physical expression of mass in the stone construction itself (fig. 4.8). Nothing could be further

4.6 Church of St. Giles. West facade and tower

from the abstraction of the classical orders in Soane's church at Bethnal Green, where the building seems drained of materiality and the surface reads as pure representation (see fig. 3.29).

In the church at Cheadle, we are made conscious of the particular color and texture of the stone, its redness deriving from the clay soil of the area, where the Staffordshire potteries are located. The buttresses exhibit the forces coursing through their short, stocky forms, just as the capping stones tell us how they were designed to shed the rain. The contrast between the richly decorated and illuminated surfaces of the interior and the solemn, earthy forms of the exterior describes their different functions and grounds the faith of the user in a reality that has physical bearing on the matter (fig. 4.9). The authenticity of the structure serves to substantiate the authenticity of the religious belief to which it is dedicated.

4.7 Church of St. Giles. View from southeast

Pugin's True Principles of Architecture

Much of Pugin's writing concerned the intimate relationship between the Catholic faith and its expression in Gothic, or what he more often called "Pointed or Christian," architecture. The text of *The True Principles of Pointed or Christian Architecture,* however, speaks directly to the more general questions that concern us here: how could architectural design be reformulated on a more realistic basis, and why should Gothic architecture be the model for that?

In a text that is uncannily reminiscent of Laugier's in terms of clarity, tone, criticism of abuses, and definition of correct procedure, *The True Principles* begins with the following declaration, italicized for emphasis: "The two great rules for design are these: *1st, that there should be no features about a building which are not necessary for convenience, construction, or propriety; 2nd, that all ornament should consist of enrichment of the essential construction of the building.* The neglect of these two rules is the cause of all the bad architecture of the present time. Architectural features are continually tacked on buildings with which they have no connection, merely for the sake of what is termed effect."[16] Indeed, if Pugin had stopped here, one might confuse his position with that of Laugier. The eighteenth-century Jesuit had also called for the necessary and the essential to be the ruling factors in design. But, as Pugin's text continues, it immediately becomes apparent that his definition of "the essential construction of the building" was totally different from Laugier's. It was the real construction Pugin had in mind, not an ideal one.

Pugin's argument involved a radical revision of classical thinking that turned the relation between construction and decoration inside out. Elaborating on what he meant by "architectural features" being added "merely for the sake of what is termed effect," he noted that in classical buildings "ornaments are *actually constructed,* instead of forming the decoration of *construction,* to which ... they should always be subservient." He then went on to say that, "in pure architecture the smallest detail should *have a meaning or serve a purpose;* and...the construction itself *should vary with the material employed,* and the designs should be adapted to the material in which they are executed."[17]

That one should decorate construction rather than construct decoration flew in the face of classical theory and practice. Boullée's Metropolitan Church was only an exaggerated case of the normal process of constructing decoration (see fig. 3.7). Expanding upon Soufflot's attempt to combine in the Church of Sainte-Geneviève "the noble decoration of the Greeks with the lightness [of construction] of the Gothic," Boullée wrote that he "surrounded" the "supporting structure" of his own church "with colonnades on all sides" that "masked" the underlying "masses" so that "the building appears as if to stand by some miracle while, moreover, being decorated, in imitation of the Greeks, with all the richness architecture has to offer."[18]

Building upon a tradition that can be traced back to Alberti, Boullée, as noted in the previous chapter, equated the orders, and architecture by extension, with decoration.[19] "The temples of the Greeks," he stated, "were decorated both outside and within, by colonnades that enveloped the entire edifice." "Our modern authors," on the other hand, "have substituted for these noble resources of architecture a decoration formed by heavy arcades whose massive piers have as their sole ornament a revetment of a few centimeters thick, which we, in architecture, call pilasters."[20] The orders and the elements related to them were thus seen as an autonomous decorative construct having only a metaphoric relation to the actual construction, which was separate from it and subservient to it. In the publication of the lectures on architecture he gave at the Ecole Polytechnique in the first years of the nineteenth century, Durand presciently criticized this conception as "la décoration

4.8 Church of St. Giles. South facade

4.9 Church of St. Giles. Interior. South side aisle

architectonique" (architectonic decoration). He even went so far as to state that "what is generally known by the name of *Architecture,*" as in the "palaces of the Escorial, Versailles, and the Tuileries," is but "decoration."[21]

The general lack of self-consciousness until the turn of the nineteenth century about the identification of architecture with decoration, and the corresponding disregard for the independent role of construction, is evidenced by the change in title that William Chambers's treatise underwent between its first edition in 1759 and its third in 1791. Though initially called *A Treatise on Civil Architecture,* it merely discussed the orders and the decorative elements derived from them in their application to contemporary building programs of a public, monumental sort—to wit, what his teacher, Blondel, had covered in the first three of the six volumes of his *Cours d'architecture.* By the end of the century, however, the original title of Chambers's book no longer appeared self-explanatory, and, despite the actual expansion of the text, the book was given the more restrictive title of *A Treatise on the Decorative Part of Civil Architecture.*[22]

For Pugin, the actual conditions of construction were to serve as the basis for all decorative elaboration. Such decoration was to enhance and give meaning to the building through an expression of its material structure. In the *True Principles,* as elsewhere, Pugin came back repeatedly to this issue, rephrasing it in a variety of ways. He spoke of "the great principle of decorating utility" and of the necessity of "suiting the design to the material and [then] decorating [the] construction." "*Constructing the ornament instead of confining it to the enrichment of its construction,*" he wrote, was always a sign of artistic decadence. This could already be seen, in his view, in the late Gothic architecture of Henry VII's chapel at Westminster Abbey.[23]

The difference between constructing decoration and decorating construction was, in Pugin's estimation, not only the difference between good and bad: it was, in moral terms, the difference between truth and untruth and, in historical terms, the difference between the Gothic and the classical. "Strange as it may appear at first sight," he noted after defining the structural and programmatic principles that constituted what he called "the two great rules for design," "it is in *pointed* [Gothic] *architecture alone that these great principles have been carried out.*" "The architects of the middle ages," he added, "were the first who *turned the natural properties of the various materials* [of construction] to *their full account,* and made *their mechanism a vehicle for their art.*"[24]

The reasons Pugin gave for turning to the Gothic as a model were therefore quite different from those that Laugier, Soufflot, Boullée, and Soane proposed. They responded to the formal "effects" of lightness and openness in Gothic churches, but either abhorred or were ignorant of the physical means by which those effects were achieved. Boullée, as discussed in chapter 3, praised Gothic architects for concealing their structural gymnastics by a kind of magic sleight of hand, which justified, in his view, the imitation of those effects beneath the decoration of the classical orders. And Laugier, as we read, believed that Gothic architects achieved their remarkable spatial effects in part through a "lavish" use of concealed iron. Pugin was quick to point out the flaws, not to say the hypocrisy, in these classical interpretations. "Pointed architecture," he explained, "does *not conceal her construction, but beautifies it,*" whereas "classic architecture seeks to conceal instead of decorating it." The constructed decoration of "screen" walls masking the flying buttresses at St. Paul's Cathedral, which Soufflot also employed at the Church of Sainte-Geneviève, and "the use of engaged columns as breaks for strength and effect" led Pugin to assert that in classical architecture it is more often than not the case that "one half of the edifice is built to conceal the other."[25]

The distinction between the decoration of construction and the construction of decoration thus became a difference between expression and representation, the drawing out of a form from a material object as opposed to the substitution of another figure for it. Where the former process can be likened to extrusion, the latter is more like a transcription. Gothic architecture was, in Pugin's view, fundamentally different from classical architecture by virtue of its expressive nature. To prove this crucial point, he returned to the issue of the origins of Greek architecture in the primitive hut (fig. 4.10). "Grecian architecture is essentially *wooden* in its construction," he remarked. "It originated in wooden buildings, and never did its professors possess either sufficient imagination or skill to conceive any departure from the original type." Unlike Laugier, Chambers, and Quatremère, who lauded the later imitation of these wooden members in stone, Pugin had only scorn for it. "Is it not extraordinary," he asked, "that when the Greeks commenced building in stone, the *properties of this material did not suggest to them some different and improved mode of construction?*"[26]

By the time Pugin made these remarks regarding the origin of Greek architecture in the primitive wood hut, the truth of the theory was hardly any longer taken for granted. We must therefore assume that his unqualified acceptance of it had a rhetorical purpose. As noted in the previous chapter, both Lodoli and Durand dismissed the transmutational hypothesis, although not the classical forms that were supposed to have resulted from it. It was only when architects began to study medieval architecture seriously that the issue of imitation took a different turn.[27] In 1822 the young German architect Heinrich Hübsch (1795–1863) published the essay *Uber griechische Architectur,* in which he turned the critique of the theory of the hut into a much broader argument against the contemporary relevancy of an idealist conception of classical architecture, pointing to the Roman mixture of Greek columnar forms with arched construction as the source of the problem. Hübsch's answer to the historical dead end was to leapfrog over the previous three centuries in order to find a new basis for contemporary design in the integral arcuated system of medieval construction.[28]

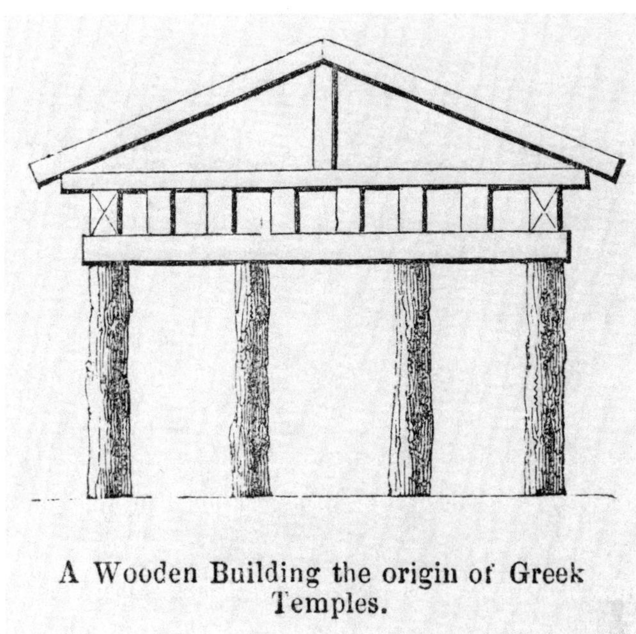

4.10 Pugin, "A Wooden Building the origin of Greek Temples," *True Principles*

In a pathbreaking essay published six years later, provocatively entitled *Im welchem Style sollen wir bauen? (In What Style Should We Build?)*, Hübsch laid out the case for a revival of the round-arched architecture of the early Middle Ages (*Rundbogenstil*), based on a more inclusive view of architectural history than was either available to or acknowledged by earlier writers such as Quatremère or Durand (though soon to be embraced by Schinkel). Referring to the theory of the hut as "the event whereby original sin was fully brought into architecture," Hübsch put forth a purely materialist argument for the origin of architectural forms that enabled him to equate the trabeated system of the Greeks and the arcuated one of the Middle Ages on the basis of their both being derived from the rational use of stone and, more important, to distinguish the latter from the former as a more advanced system of construction, as well as one more appropriate to the material and cultural conditions of northern Europe.[29]

In contrast to these two integral styles, where "sculptural decoration...is almost exclusively an adornment of the essential parts," the Roman application of the Greek orders to a structural framework of arches and vaults, he wrote, resulted in a "mere sham and show architecture," a composition of "feigned constructions."[30]

The irredeemably representational character of post-Greek classical architecture, combined with the "technostatic progress" of medieval vaulting that allowed for the wide spans and lightweight construction demanded by the nineteenth century, inevitably led Hübsch to propose a return to the architecture preceding the Renaissance and postdating the Roman period. In that large span of time, however, there was a choice to be made. The Gothic (*Spitzbogenstil*), he admitted, was the style in which the "forms, down to the smallest detail, derive in a consistent and organic manner from the construction of the vault, completely eliminating those reminiscences of the antique that here and there still disturb us in the *Rundbogenstil*," or earlier Romanesque architecture. Yet Hübsch preferred the latter to the former, and not just for material reasons. While noting that the "exceedingly steep proportions" of the Gothic were "incompatible with our needs" and that round and segmental arches were more adaptable to modern requirements, the choice of one over the other was undoubtedly also a matter of taste. The strong and sober lines of the Romanesque, "governed by the same spirit that gave life to the Greek style," had a "moving simplicity" that led Hübsch to compare buildings in the round-arched style to "a pre-Raphael painting" just as it allowed Schinkel to assimilate it to his late neoclassicism.[31]

While it is not known whether Pugin was aware of Hübsch's essay, his thinking about the relationship between historical style and the need for a new precedent followed a similar pattern of reasoning, but with a much more determined and unequivocal result.[32] Gothic architecture, according to Pugin, was derived from the capacities

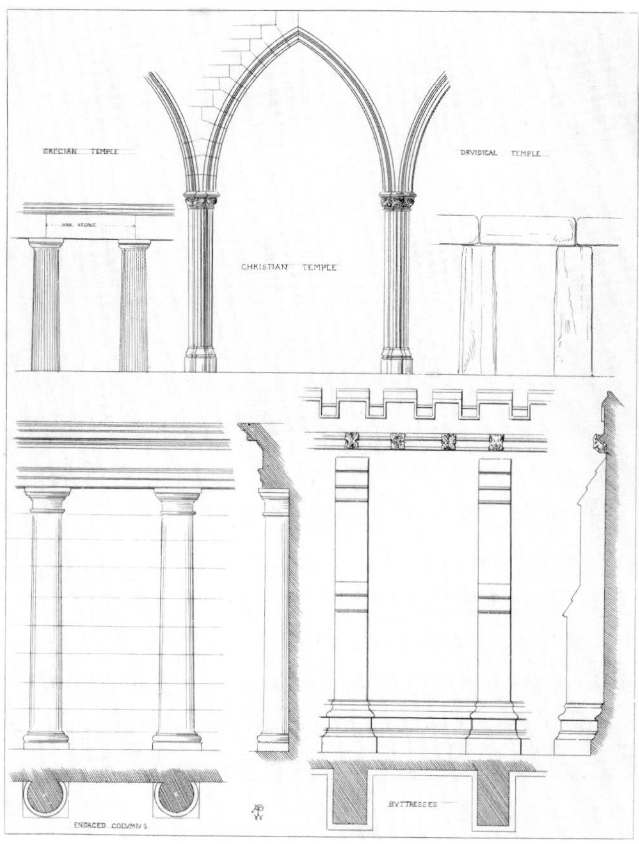

4.11 Pugin. A "Grecian Temple," a "Christian Temple," and a "Druidical Temple," with a comparison of "Engaged Columns" and "Buttresses," *True Principles*

and conditions of masonry construction alone. "A pointed church," he explained, "is the masterpiece of masonry. It is essentially a stone building; its pillars, its arches, its vaults ... are all peculiar to stone, and could not be consistently executed in any other material."[33] Arcuation versus trabeation now became the critical debate in the argument over the significance of the hut. The important issue for Pugin was no longer whether the Greek temple did or did not imitate the hut; it was that the Greek temple adopted the "barbarous" post-and-lintel system characteristic of primitive construction, whether in wood, as in the hut, or in masonry, "like the uprights of Stonehenge," whereas they should have evolved forms more consistent with stone (fig. 4.11).

Arcuated construction, Pugin maintained, was the proper response to building in masonry. It represented a technological advance that could not be abandoned; nor could it be denied without travestying history itself, as Roman and Renaissance architects did through their adoption of the "inconsistent" decorative system of the orders.[34] Turning the mimetic theory of transformation of the primitive hut on itself, Pugin was thus able to claim that the dissimulating character of classical architecture was an inescapable flaw in its very constitution and that only Gothic architecture, by virtue of its nontransformative origins and complete emancipation from classical traditions, was capable of an authentic, expressive realism.[35]

4.12 Church of St. Giles. Main (west) entrance

It is surely ironic that the release from the constraints of classical representation not only placed a greater premium on decoration as the exponent of construction—as manifest in the extraordinary elaboration of the door hinges at St. Giles, which Pugin refused to "conceal" by conventional techniques of mortising (figs. 4.12–13)—but also entailed an even more self-effacing commitment to imitation, in the sense of straightforward copying of the past. In order to reengage with a style of architecture that had gone out of general use centuries earlier and that had not, like classical architecture, been preserved in published treatises, Pugin had to find, draw, and establish the models on which to base new designs.[36] He was quite open about the procedure, maintaining that in St. Giles's Church "every detail of an *old english* [*sic*] *Parish church* [of the Middle Ages] is *restored with scrupulous fedelity* [*sic*]."[37]

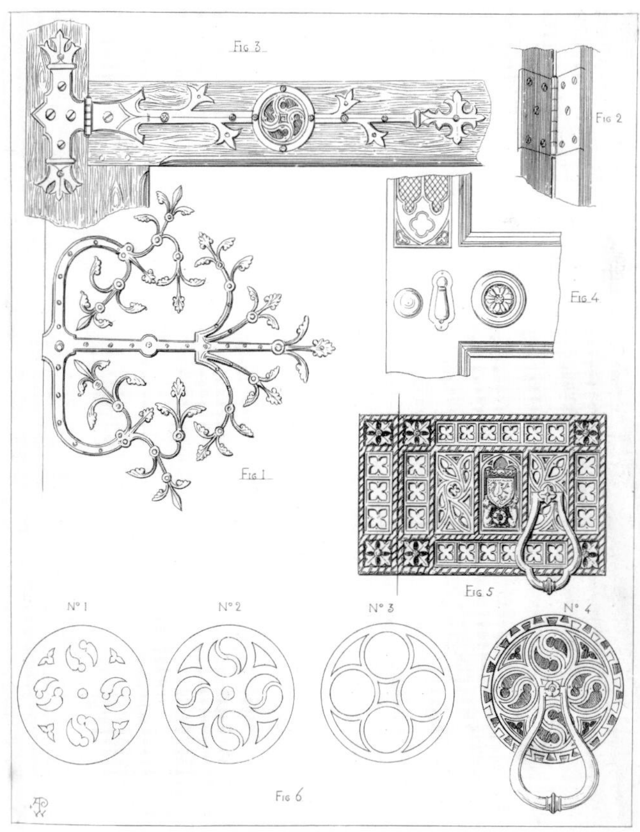

4.13 Pugin. "Metal-Work" (door hardware), *True Principles*

But if Pugin was open about such direct dependence on historical models, he was vague about who he, the living architect, was. The frontispiece of *The True Principles*, as we saw, illustrates a medieval monk in his studio. Is it a self-portrait—or an alter ego? Pugin wrote in *Contrasts* that "*revivals of ancient* [Gothic] *architecture*, although erected in, are not buildings of, the nineteenth century,—[and thus] their merit must be referred back to the period from whence they were copied."[38] But his hope, as he expressed it a couple of years later, was "*not*... *to produce mere servile*

4.14 Henri Labrouste. Bibliothèque Sainte-Geneviève, Paris, 1838–50. View, from southwest, with Panthéon (on right) and Law School (on left), by Soufflot, 1763–74

imitators" of the past "*but men imbued with the consistent spirit of the ancient* [Gothic] *architects, who would work on their principles, and carry them out as the old men would have done, had they been placed in similar circumstances, and with similar wants to ourselves.*"[39] For Pugin, then, the present was to be seen as the perfect conditional of the past, and the purpose of "copying" or imitating Gothic architecture was not simply a matter of representing it but rather of resuming it. In eliminating the illusionistic and idealistic aspect of neoclassical representation (which is to say its material deceptiveness), the expressive realism of the work would guaranty its authenticity and contemporaneity. Now devoid of its metaphoric dimension, representation was reduced to the role of catalyst, thus containing within itself the seeds of its eventual dissolution.

The Design of the Bibliothèque Sainte-Geneviève

If the narrowly sectarian tone of Pugin's polemic, not to speak of the rather insular character of the work, made it difficult for some to see the wider implications of its meaning, such was never the case with Henri Labrouste's Bibliothèque Sainte-Geneviève. Emerging from the mind of someone willing to incorporate a universal history of architecture as its imaginative ground, Labrouste's library also had a site where it could readily be seen and judged against the very type of representation it called into question.[40]

The history of the Bibliothèque Sainte-Geneviève is bound up with that of Soufflot's neighboring church. The institution was founded in the early seventeenth century as the conventual library of the Abbey of Sainte-Geneviève, which was located just behind and to the east of the later church by Soufflot (see figs. 2.23 and 3.17). Placed on the top floor of the building in the late seventeenth century, it was enlarged early in the following one to consist of two long galleries crossing under a central dome.[41] When the abbey was turned into a municipally run lycée during the Revolution and the library in turn came under the jurisdiction of the national government, administrative difficulties soon arose, especially since the library, the third largest in Paris (and one of the largest in the world), now became the main study facility for the nearby Sorbonne and Law School. What finally made a move inevitable was the radical decision in 1838 by the minister of education to institute evening hours. This would require the installation of gas lighting in a completely isolated and fireproof structure of its own.[42]

Designed in 1838–39, shortly after Schinkel's project for the Berlin Library, and constructed from 1843 to 1850 on a narrow site diagonally across the Place du Panthéon from the existing facility, Labrouste's library closes the square to the north and forms a background for its focal neoclassical monument (fig. 4.14). Framed by Soufflot's Law School and Church of Sainte-Geneviève, the design was developed in critical reaction to the representational context they had established. Labrouste almost immediately hit upon the scheme he would adopt, which was a long, unrelieved, two-story structure with storage and special collections areas below, reading room above, staircase as a separate unit tacked on the rear, and a central spine of supports dividing the building lengthwise in half but stopping short of the ends to allow the longitudinal spaces to continue around in their full double-bay width (fig. 4.15).[43] One of the interesting things to note in the section of the preliminary sketch project, drawn sometime in late 1838 or early 1839, is that despite the relative thinness of the structure, stone rather than iron was originally proposed for the interior supports of the reading room (iron replaced stone in the reading room by the end of 1839).[44] In addition, and in contrast to the fairly simple decorative character of the rest of the surfaces, the entrance was highlighted by a columnar portico.

The historical sources for the initial design were numerous and varied, ranging from Roman and especially early Renaissance buildings the architect had studied in Italy (fig. 4.16) to Greek and Gothic examples primarily for the plan (see figs. 4.33–34). All the exterior and interior forms and decorative surfaces were eventually studied and

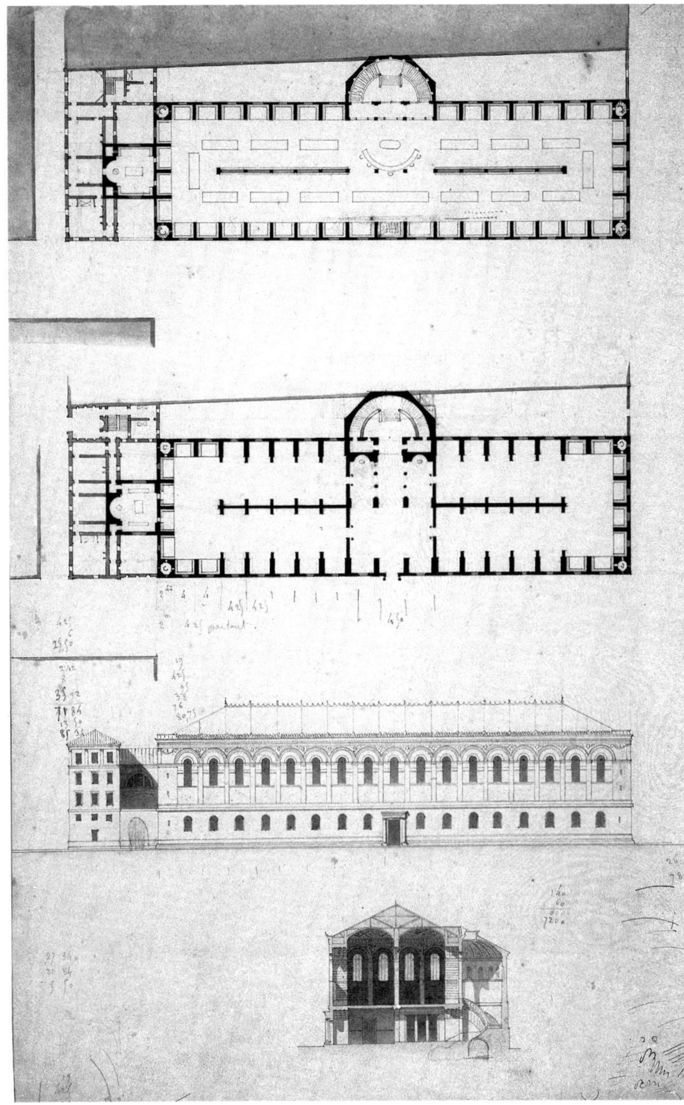

4.15 Bibliothèque Sainte-Geneviève. Preliminary sketch project, ca. 1838–39. Plans of first and second floors, facade elevation, and section (showing stone supports for vaults)

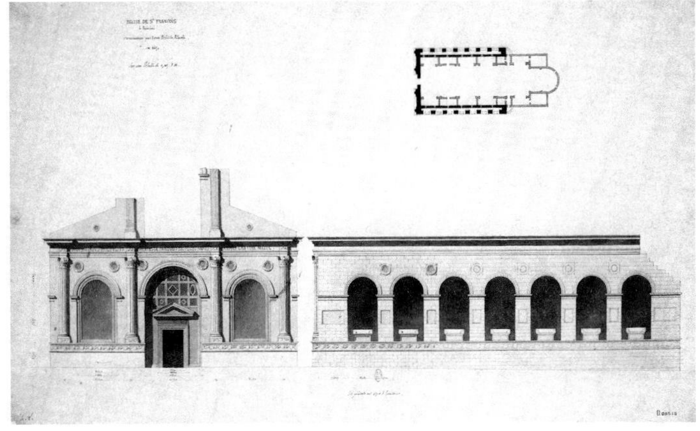

4.16 Henri Labrouste. San Francesco, Rimini, 1830. Elevation, side facade, and plan of additions by Leon Battista Alberti, ca. 1450

4.17 Bibliothèque Sainte-Geneviève. Exterior, from southeast

developed as the building was being constructed and in direct consequence of the materials and methods of construction employed, as well as the spatial disposition of the interior.[45] The ashlar exterior shell is dominated by a series of horizontal lines or ledges—at the base, midheight, and cornice levels—that establish a frontal plane along the street edge with no breaks, projections, or recessions (fig. 4.17). Round-arched windows above the base's deeper, lighter-colored blocks are the only openings in the plane of the ground floor aside from the arched entrance, from which the representational portico in the preliminary design was soon removed.

A thick, pendulous garland, supported alternately by black iron disks (paterae) and smaller stone knobs, defines the top of the ground floor beneath the ledgelike base from which the upper floor emerges (fig. 4.18). In contrast to the closed, planar character of the ground floor, the upper floor is thin, open, and skeletal. Piers support a continuous arcade containing large lunette windows in their upper thirds and gridded panels below. In the spandrels of the arches (in the same plane as the panels beneath the windows) are black iron knobs in circular depressions, from which stream curling stems terminating in flowers (fig. 4.19). A very small window is braced within the lower frame of the main panels. The panels themselves are divided vertically in thirds by inset uprights to create tables, on which were inscribed (and at first inpainted in red) the names of famous authors, 810 in all.[46]

Beginning at the northwest corner with that of Moses, the authors' names circumscribe the three normally visible faces of the building. Labrouste described this device as a "monumental catalogue" and likened the decorative

4.18 Bibliothèque Sainte-Geneviève. Detail of upper part of facade

4.19 Bibliothèque Sainte-Geneviève. Tie-rod fastener in spandrel of upper part of facade

effect of the upright letters to the spines of the books on the shelves of the reading room just behind them.[47] The last name in the sequence, in the lower right-hand corner of the final panel on the east flank of the building, is that of the Swedish chemist Jöns Jakob Berzelius, who died in 1848, the year the scheme for the exterior decoration was finalized. The panels on the rear of the building were left blank (fig. 4.20). The carving in the horizontal divisions was also eliminated, and that of the capitals and friezes much simplified. The garland stops as it drops over the first iron disk of the ground floor. But aside from these reductions in decorative detailing, most of the major elements that articulate the three other exterior surfaces remain intact on the rear—which leads one to think about the role of decoration and its relation to the actual construction.

In this regard, one can see how Labrouste worked from a conventional neoclassical form of representation to a more realistically expressive one in the design of the library's entrance. In both the preliminary sketch (see fig. 4.15) and the official project submitted for government approval in late 1839 (fig. 4.21), the door was framed by the

4.20 Bibliothèque Sainte-Geneviève. Side and rear facades, northeast corner (chimney removed, early 1990s)

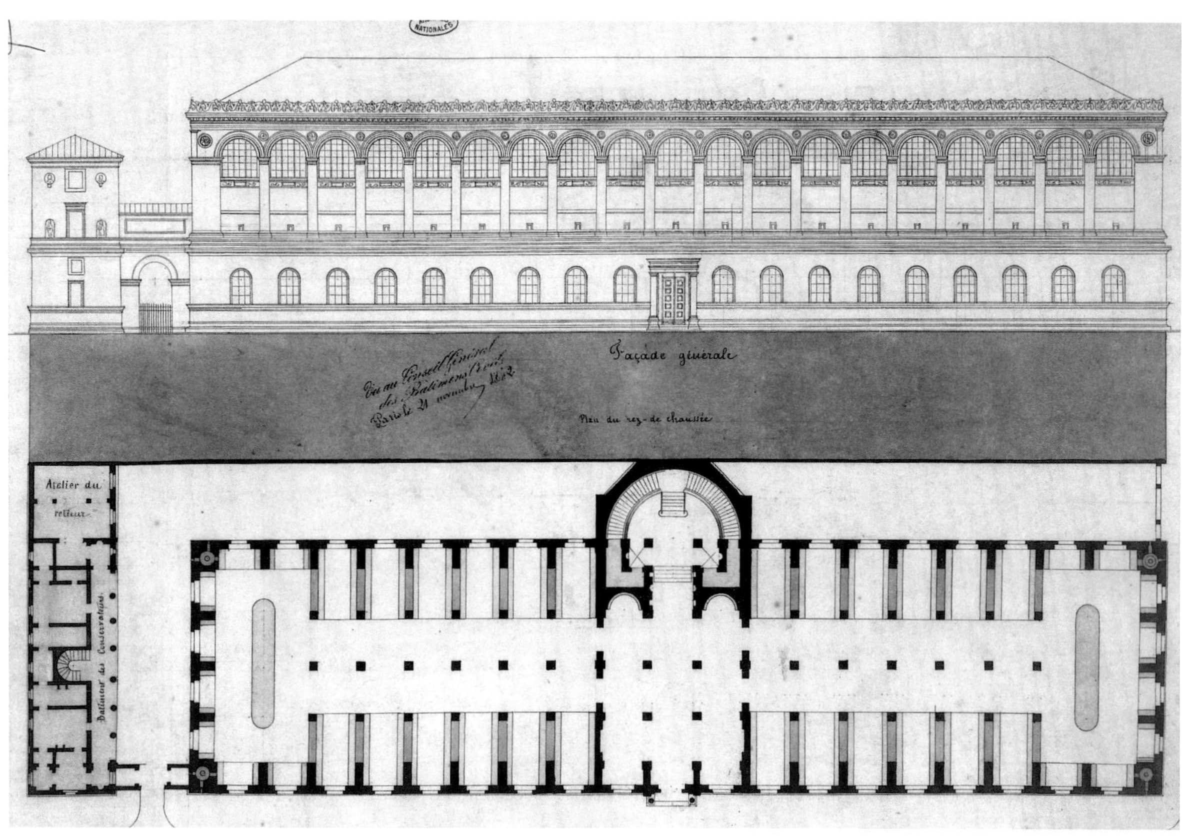

4.21 Bibliothèque Sainte-Geneviève. Project approved by government, December 1839. Elevation and first-floor plan

straightforward device of a pair of Doric columns supporting an entablature. This formulaic idea was soon dropped as extrinsic to the fabric and unrelated to the building's actual structure. Taking the stonework of the arch of the door jambs as the ground and considering the distinction between the lower courses of harder, lighter-colored stone and the softer, cream-colored limestone above, Labrouste sketched a number of possibilities (fig. 4.22). One, on the right jamb of the door, shows a female term looking across to what should have been her reflection, though, as an alternative, Labrouste also drew it as a tall candelabra. The term's base is appropriately carved out of the lower courses of denser stone. Entering the building between her and her companion would have been like passing through the beam of an electronic eye.

Most of the other schemes are for candelabra. One of these, on the bottom of the drawing, lying on its side, is carved within the thickness of the jamb. If chosen, it would have appeared to have been literally part of the wall. The most fascinating and most original of the group was designed on the principle of a telescope (fig. 4.23). The leaflike flame emerges from a base that directly corresponds to the coursing of the stone and thus makes this key decorative element at the entrance appear to grow out of the very foundations of the building. The relatively understated character of the design as executed might seem regressive by comparison (fig. 4.24). Still, the different parts of the lamps are strictly defined by the courses of stone; and the extreme shallowness of the relief makes the image read more like a sign than the real thing, thus subliminally reminding the user of the building's hours of opening and the purpose of enlightenment—and reminding the historian of the secondary and derivative role of decoration in a system based on the realities of construction. Nothing

4.22 Bibliothèque Sainte-Geneviève. Ideas for decoration of main entrance, 1847–48. Sketch

4.23 Bibliothèque Sainte-Geneviève. Ideas for entrance candelabra, 1847–48. Sketch

4.24 Bibliothèque Sainte-Geneviève. Entrance

could be further from the allegorical scenes surrounding the doors of Schinkel's Bauakademie or the statue columns rising from those of his Royal Library project (see figs. 3.47 and 3.54).

On the other hand, the entrance to the library, like those in both of Schinkel's later designs, fully submits to the building's structural grid (fig. 4.25). The plan of the ground floor shows the central spine of supports (which contain the heating ducts and registers) surrounded by a perimeter structure of finlike piers set perpendicular to the exterior facing. These piers act as internal buttresses and create carrel-like spaces within the arcade. In the front two corners, spiral stairs connect the lower floor to the upper one; in the rear two corners are the flues extending from the basement heating units to the roof, where they were designed to be encased in tall, tapering exposed brick chimneys, unabashedly factory-like in appearance (the western chimney still exists; the eastern one was removed in the 1990s). A central three-bay-wide vestibule occupying the entire depth of the ground floor leads to a shallow stairwell designed as a separate volume attached to the rear. Off the vestibule to the right is an area devoted to the library's extensive collection of prints, drawings, rare books, and manuscripts; to the left is general storage space for duplicates and less frequently consulted books.

The Space of Iron and Stone

If the outside entrance to the library is less imposing than what might have been expected, the vestibule, the first interior space that is encountered, takes one almost completely by surprise (fig. 4.26).[48] It is tall and cavernous, ungainly in its proportions and strange in its detailing. Six freestanding square piers create three equal-width passages leading to the stairwell. The piers terminate in tall impost blocks

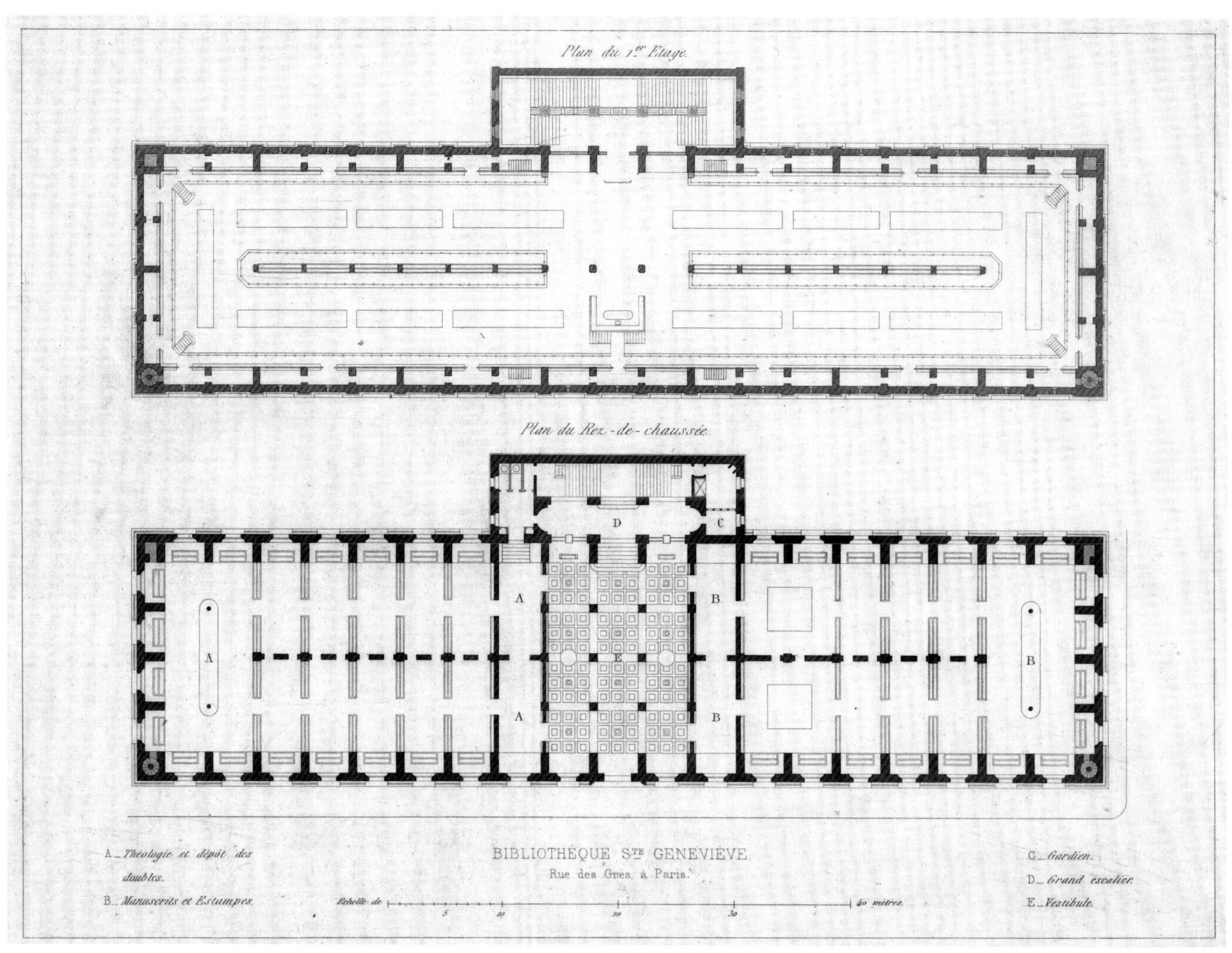

4.25 Bibliothèque Sainte-Geneviève. Plans, first and second floors. From *Encyclopédie d'architecture*, 1851

from which spring shallow cast-iron arches echoing the floor grid (fig. 4.27). The supporting iron structure is completely exposed. The arches are painted green to tie in with the images of trees in the upper part of the side walls, which are lined below with busts of well-known French writers and intellectuals. The illusionistic painting was based on ancient Roman wall paintings like those at Pompeii.[49] To complete the image of an enclosed arbor or garden, the ceiling was painted pale blue, like the sky.[50]

Labrouste described his design for the vestibule as a compensation for the "exiguity of the site," which did not allow for a "planted space" in front of the building "to distance it from the noise of the public way and instill in its users a state of contemplation." "My painted garden," he wrote in a rather modern, tongue-in-cheek way, "undoubtedly is not worth the same as a beautiful allée of chestnut or plane trees; but it does have the advantage of having green leaves and flowers all the time, even in the month of December; plus, without having to take into account the climate of Paris, I could, in this fertile ground of the imagination, plant trees from all countries, and place next to St. Bernard, Oriental palm trees, next to Racine, flowering

4.26 Bibliothèque Sainte-Geneviève. Interior. Vestibule, ca. 1900

orange trees, next to La Fontaine, an oak and a reed, and myrtles and laurel next to Poussin."[51]

The almost naive quality of the illusionistic painting throws into sharp relief the physicality of the structure and the mechanical character of its connections. A series of sketches for the impost blocks may provide the most acute evidence of Labrouste's struggle to find a form of expression—of materials, of structure, and of purpose—that would not rely on conventional means of representation and for which the hard facts of matter would be the determining factor (fig. 4.28). The problem he set himself was how to articulate the joining of a metal arch with a stone pier under a flat ceiling. This involved two fairly unusual conditions: the intimate connection between materials normally considered foreign to one another, namely iron and stone; and the accommodation of an essentially trabeated system, consistent with the grid of the plan, to the use of the arch, consistent with the structural expression of the building as a whole. The singular awkwardness of the result can be attributed to Labrouste's giving to each part of the equation the material emphasis it demanded.

4.27 Bibliothèque Sainte-Geneviève. Vestibule

4.28 Bibliothèque Sainte-Geneviève. Ideas for impost block and capital of vestibule piers, 1847. Sketch

The stone pier had to have a girth and height relative to the masonry structure in force throughout the rest of the building. An iron arch, functioning almost like a beam, would logically seem thin and skeletal by comparison, which it does. But the really knotty problem was how to join the two. Labrouste tried various ways. In the sheet of sketches shown in fig. 4.28, one can see that at first he was even unsure about making the horizontal iron member into an arch. As a beam, it would have been more consistent with its vertical support, though ultimately inconsistent with the rest of the building. In a few of the sketches, especially those on the left, diagonal braces are employed to soften the joint and allow the iron to collar the stone. The others, to the right, are more abrupt in letting the beam's point of insertion into the stone be perspicuous. The moment of penetration is only somewhat relieved by a short spur supporting the beam's lower edge.

Once Labrouste decided to detail the beam as an arch, albeit an inordinately flattened one, it no longer seemed reasonable to allow an element that was supposed to "spring" from its impost to appear to slice through the block. Nor could the springing be treated as an action plastically continuous with the block, due to the change in material. The result is a kind of visual standoff in which the arch appears simply to be shimmed into position, with the point of connection marked by flat painted lines (fig. 4.29). These describe the physical action of impact through a pictorial veil of energy rather than sculpturally embodying it in relief.

The relation between iron and stone adumbrated in the vestibule's gridded space discreetly prepares one for the experience of the reading room above it, which is reached by the stair cage at the rear. The large volume occupying the building's entire upper floor is ringed by a continuous stone arcade that buttresses and contains the diaphanous iron-and-plaster barrel vaults (fig. 4.30). These are carried on the edges of foliated cast-iron ribs, which are supported on

4.29 Bibliothèque Sainte-Geneviève. Vestibule. Impost block and capital of vestibule pier

thin iron columns that appear to be anchored to the floor by their tall stone pedestals (fig. 4.31). As originally furnished, the long tables for readers ran down the length of each nave. Bookshelves were set between the stone bases of the central columns. Others were built against the piers of the girding arcade, forming a mezzanine for a second level of shelves within the arcade just under the lunette windows. Beneath that gallery, and back-to-back with the lower bookshelves, is another layer of shelves lining the interior passage within the depth of the piers (fig. 4.32). This passage receives daylight from the little windows in the lower level of the facade panels.

Labrouste's decision to support the ceiling and roof by a single spine of columns was no doubt motivated in part by the size and shape of the site. But since such a solution

4.30 Bibliothèque Sainte-Geneviève. Interior. Reading room

4.31 Bibliothèque Sainte-Geneviève. Reading room, by Edouard-Antoine Renard. From *L'Illustration*, January 1851

4.32 Bibliothèque Sainte-Geneviève. Partial elevation and section, drawn for publication, 1850

4.33 Labrouste. Reconstruction of Temple of Hera I (as a *portique*, or stoa), Paestum, 1828–29. Cutaway interior perspective. From Labrouste, *Les Temples de Paestum: Restauration exécutée en 1829,* 1877.

4.34 Library (former refectory of Abbaye of Saint-Martin des Champs), Conservatoire des Arts et Métiers, Paris, 14th century; restored by Léon Vaudoyer, 1844–49. Interior

would have made surveillance difficult, it is quite clear that it was equally driven by other, expressive concerns.[52] A single, over-arching vault like the one Boullée had designed for his Royal Library project (see fig. 3.16) would have been too totalizing, a triple-nave solution too hierarchical for the type of space Labrouste deemed appropriate for the secular, individualized experience of reading in public. Double-galleried spaces had a history of secular applications of which Labrouste was fully aware. Perhaps to placate the government officials who had to pass on his project and were quite concerned about the thin iron structure that contravened the conventional rules of classical proportion, Labrouste noted in the legend on the drawing he submitted for approval that his design followed the plan of the sixteenth-century Vatican Library in Rome.[53]

A more significant point of reference for him, however, was the Greek Temple of Hera I at Paestum, which he had carefully studied and reconstructed in 1828–29 during his fellowship at the French Academy in Rome. Because of its single spine of interior columns, Labrouste determined

4.35 Bibliothèque Sainte-Geneviève. Reading room. Capital and springing of arches

4.36 Bibliothèque Sainte-Geneviève. Reading room. Detail of cast-iron capital

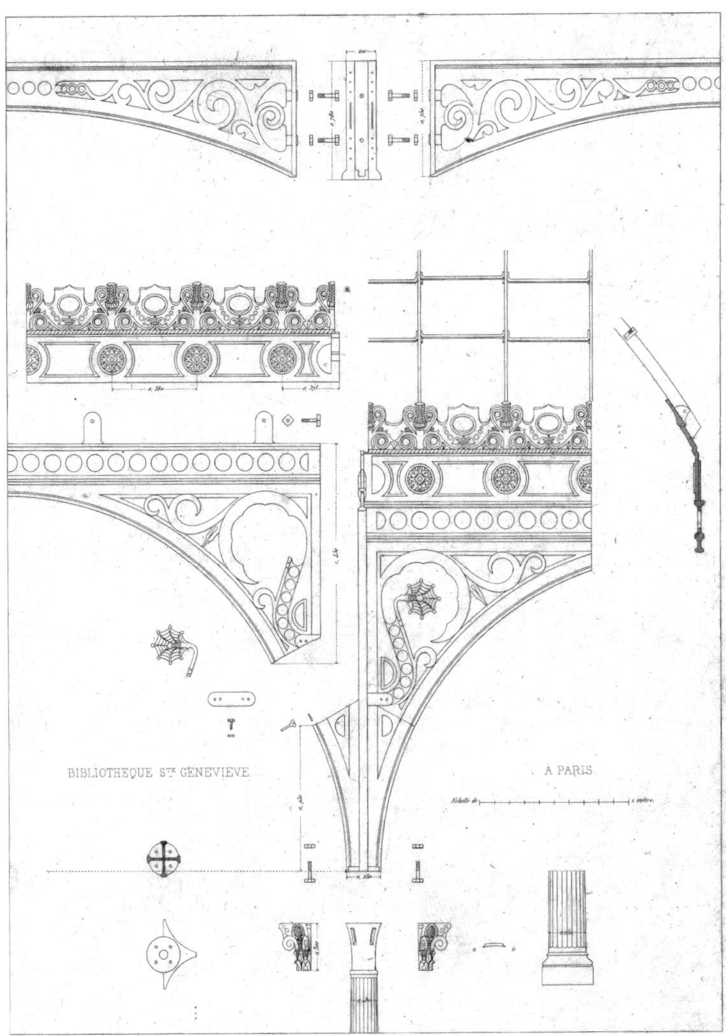

4.37 Bibliothèque Sainte-Geneviève. Reading room. Details of ironwork assembly. From *Encyclopédie d'architecture,* 1852

that the building was not a religious edifice but rather a stoa for public gatherings and notices (fig. 4.33).[54] The graffiti he drew on the walls were meant to drive the point home. Even closer to his conception of the Bibliothèque Sainte-Geneviève, however, was the Gothic refectory of the Abbey of Saint-Martin des Champs in Paris, which his friend Léon Vaudoyer (1803–1872) was about to restore for use as the library of the Conservatoire des Arts et Métiers (fig. 4.34).[55] The Gothic example, more than either of the other two, gave Labrouste a model for the special emphasis on the physical reality of structure that the presence of a central spine of columns would bring to bear on the space. The unprecedented use of exposed iron for a building of significant cultural purpose highlighted this new structural expressionism.

Following the Gothic model, Labrouste reduced the thickness of the members to a minimum. The skeletal character of the structure is foregrounded by the black paint that contrasts with the light cream color of the vaults. Although the Gothic detailing of the refectory is transformed into classical terms—the foliated capitals becoming composite and the banded columns fluted—a good deal of the Gothic structural diagram and logic are retained (fig. 4.35). Most revealing, perhaps, is the rotation of the cast-iron capitals at forty-five degrees: instead of turning their face to parallel the space, as a classical capital would, they are set diagonally, as in a Gothic rib vault (fig. 4.36).[56] They slice through the space in line with the edges of the exposed arches they support. The ductile forms of the capital express the molten material from which they were cast; and the physical process of bolting together its four faces is not only made visible but also becomes an integral element of the reconfigured classical volute (fig. 4.37).

One is gradually led to understand by the detailing of the decorative surfaces that nothing is hidden, not even the inner structure of the vaults. The radicality of such structural exposure can be immediately grasped by reminding oneself of what Schinkel had done at the Bauakademie and Soane at the Bank of England (see figs. 3.25–26, 3.46, and 3.50). The richly detailed cast-iron arches in the reading room of the Labrouste library are in fact the fully exposed ribs of the structure itself (fig. 4.38). They offer a kind of sectional view through the vault. Nor is the interior iron structure concealed on the exterior of the building, except for the roof trusses themselves. As can be seen in the detail to the right of the sectional study for the reading room ironwork, a tie-rod pierces the stone through the spandrel at the level of the painted rosettes. As the rod emerges through the wall, it is fastened to the exterior stone facing by a circular black iron knob, cast in a pointed conical form in the final detail (see fig. 4.19). A ridged washer is relieved by a concentric depression in the stone, and the action of turning and tightening the nut is reflected in the squiggly lines of stems and flowers that are seemingly forced out from the cushion beneath the iron. At the same time, the iron disks of the lower story, from which the garland hangs, bolt the iron floor trusses to the wall, though in a less energetic manner than above, consistent with the more static structural condition that obtains at that level (fig. 4.39).[57]

But it is not only the iron that is expressed—indeed, exposed—on the exterior. The other main structural and spatial elements are revealed as well, and it is this reflection on the exterior of the physical conditions of the interior structure and space that fundamentally informs the design. One of the large drawings Labrouste prepared for publication was specifically meant to show the intimate connection between one side of the wall and the other (see fig. 4.32). Let us focus our attention on the upper story. One can see on the left how the gallery-level floor projects onto the facade as the lower band of the panel between the piers of the arcade, and how the small window just beneath the band serves to light the internal passage. One can also see how the top frame of the bookshelves on the mezzanine level is projected into the upper decorative band just beneath the windows' sills. Finally, by comparing this drawing with the view of the interior in fig. 4.31, one can see how the vertical uprights of the shelves are transcribed onto the panels, and how the names of the authors reflect the spines of the books on the shelves just behind them.[58]

The Decoration of Construction and the Breach of the Neoclassical Facade

The reflexivity of interior and exterior in the Bibliothèque Sainte-Geneviève was based on a realism of expression that finds its correlate in the new concept of the decoration of construction, a deliberate inversion of the earlier classical principle of the construction of decoration. The working drawing for the stereotomy of the library's upper story (fig. 4.40) illustrates the degree to which the stone structure itself provided the framework on which and in which decorative details were inscribed to inform, elaborate, or otherwise embellish the specific structural or programmatic role each element had to play. Everything is tied to or derived from a real, functioning member of the construction.

Well before Pugin began his campaign for the decoration of construction as revealed in Gothic architecture—a campaign that barely predated the Berlin architect and historian Karl Bötticher's (1806–1899) analysis of Greek architecture in terms of a distinction between the structural mechanics of form (what he called the *kernform* or *werkform*) and the decorative dressing or elaboration of form (what he called the *kunstform*)—Labrouste had advanced this same idea, as early as 1830, as the basis for the teaching method he was pursuing in the atelier he had just opened in Paris.[59] The students, he wrote to his architect brother Théodore, "must

4.38 Bibliothèque Sainte-Geneviève. Reading room. Final study for ironwork, 1846. Sections, elevation, and sketches

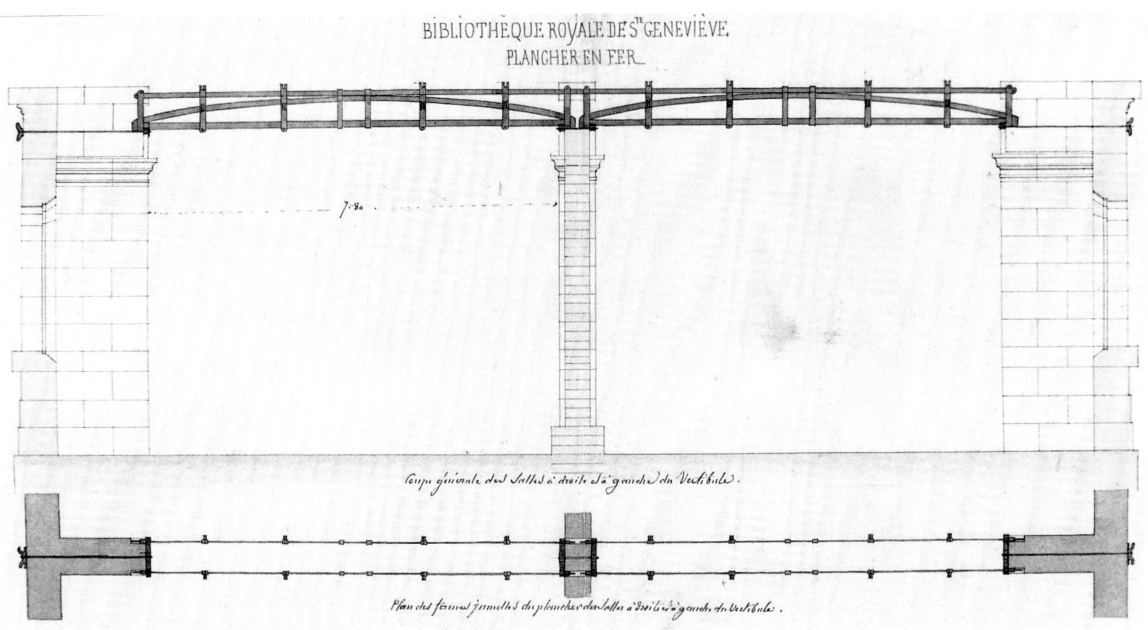

4.39 Bibliothèque Sainte-Geneviève. Preliminary study for iron floor trusses of first floor, 1846. Section and plan

first clearly see the purpose for which their building is intended and arrange the parts according to the importance it is reasonable to give them." "Once they know the first principles of construction," he continued, "I tell them that they must draw out from the construction itself a rational and expressive ornamentation. I repeat to them often that the arts have the power to embellish everything."[60]

Accounts of former students confirm the primacy Labrouste gave to construction in this new deductive logic of design. "Not allowing that one could conceive a work without considering the means for realizing it down to the smallest detail" and fully aware of the "minimal importance given to the teaching of construction at the Ecole des Beaux-Arts," Labrouste, according to Eugène Millet (1819–1879), "himself taught the art of building to his disciples." Significantly, this same architect, who was to go on to a major career in the restoration of medieval buildings, added that "arched construction furnished some fine lessons," with examples ranging from "the Etruscan Arch of Augustus at Perugia and the monuments of the early Roman Republic to ... the Colosseum and other much less ancient buildings."[61]

Those who were acquainted with Labrouste, or at least with what was happening in architecture in Paris, realized that when the Bibliothèque Sainte-Geneviève was completed and opened to the public in early 1851, not only did it represent something of major and fundamental importance; it also had to be seen as the built reflection of "approximately fifteen years" of the architect's teaching and thinking. César Daly (1811–1894), the editor of the *Revue générale de l'architecture et des travaux publics*, the leading architectural journal of the period, described the building as a "capital work" that is "without any doubt the complete realization in practice of all the thought of its author."[62] Achille Hermant (1823–1903), a young architect, called the building a "capital creation" that "continues the teaching of Mr. Labrouste and completes it: it is the best of his lessons."[63]

Not everyone agreed with Labrouste that jettisoning the neoclassical idea of decoration based on the construct of the orders was the proper or correct way to go. Many critics found the results puzzling and difficult to grasp. The critic for *The Builder* called the library "peculiar" and "original," noting that "it will not please everybody."[64] The one for the daily *Journal des débats* described it as "unconventional" and wrote that it would take some "getting used to."[65] The most serious critical review was by Hermant, published in the important journal *L'Artiste*. Despite his admission of its importance, Hermant found the building recalcitrant and ungiving. He was particularly displeased by Labrouste's refusal to employ the orders to impart the "grandiose character" demanded by the program and site. "The character of a building is not measured only by the use for which it is intended," he stated. "The idea that [the building] represents in the eyes of the public must have its place, and that place is primary." Almost echoing Boullée's words of over half a century before, Hermant wrote that, lacking the character that would have been achieved by the use of the orders, "the poetic idea of the work" remained unfulfilled.[66]

Hermant concluded that the main problem lay in Labrouste's conviction "that architecture is nothing but decorated construction." After explaining that construction is but a "means" and should never be allowed to "dominate" but always remain in the background, he issued his ultimate rebuke: "one should never forget that everything that is true is not always beautiful."[67] Clearly Hermant did not misunderstand what Labrouste was doing; he simply disagreed with him. And by opposing the idea of beauty to that of truth, he made it quite obvious that it was the fictive element of neoclassical representation and its controlling aesthetic of verisimilitude, with its basis in appearance as such, that Labrouste's work had called into question.

One can point to two aspects of the library that particularly distinguish its design from the inherited practices of architectural illusionism. Each involves a transgression of the rules of verisimilitude, and thus the ideal unity of neoclassical representation. The first is something that has often been remarked on and was, in fact, one of the serious criticisms of the design made by the Conseil des Bâtiments Civils in their 1840 review of the project. They objected that the two stories of the building were treated too unequally, and that the upper one did not look as if it formed part of the same composition as the lower one.[68] Since there is no indication that the piers of the upper story are brought down to the ground, one either has to assume that the entire ground floor is a giant base for the upper one (which is somewhat reasonable, given the high stylobate supporting it), or that the piers and arcade on which the upper story rests are simply masked by the continuous stone facing of the ground floor—in other words, that the ground-floor revetment is like a curtain wall slipped around the structure. This conclusion, which I think is the more logical and accurate one, would appear to be supported by the lack of any continuous vertical element such as a colossal order, and by the horizontal garland that runs uninterrupted around the corners and is attached to the structure by the iron disks that bolt the floor trusses to the wall.

The second point relates to the tie-rods and bolt heads themselves—not only those of the lower story, but especially the upper ones that tie the vaults of the reading room into the stone arcade. By puncturing the surface of the stone and allowing the interior structure to show through, the exposed iron denies the ideality of the facade plane in an even more radical way than does the discontinuity between the two stories. The iron bolt heads assert a sense of physical reality that disrupts the decorative fiction of a facade, much as the elements of a collage would later do to the illusionistic surface of a painted canvas.[69] The decision to expose the

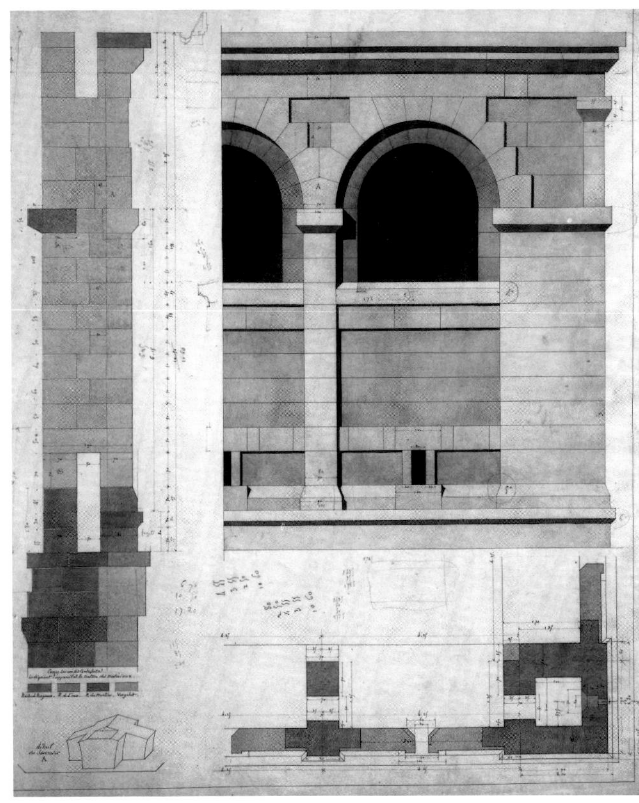

4.40 Bibliothèque Sainte-Geneviève. Working drawing of stereotomy of second floor, 1846. Elevation, section, and plan

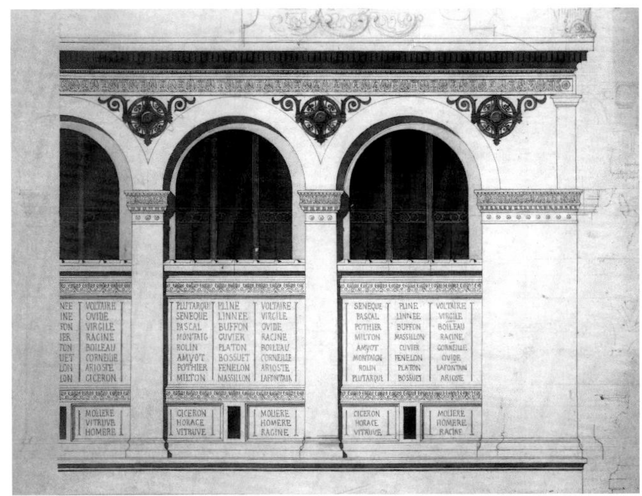

4.41 Bibliothèque Sainte-Geneviève. Study for tie-rod fasteners in spandrels of second-floor arcade, 1848. Elevation

iron on the exterior was hardly a minor one for Labrouste, a fact revealed by the number of his highly developed studies for the bolt heads (fig. 4.41). Some show a much more conspicuous and elaborate deployment of the material than was finally executed, including the circular plate around the bolt head as well as the tendrils or garland issuing from it. The exuberant decorative expression in these studies also suggests that a late Gothic model, rather than a classical one, likely lay behind the idea.[70]

In effect, the Bibliothèque Sainte-Geneviève reversed the historical evolution of Renaissance classicism that had reached a kind of culmination in Soufflot's neighboring church. There, iron had been employed to help construct the largest piece of neoclassical decoration, in the form of a freestanding portico, that had yet been built in France (see figs. 2.25–26). The iron was hidden in the stone to allow the stone to represent a type of construction it could not achieve on its own, just as the iron in Schinkel's Bauakademie did the same for brick (see figs. 3.44 and 3.50). By assigning a primary and visible role to each material of construction in his library, Labrouste made the fictive basis of neoclassical representation self-evident, while at the same time suggesting how this would affect the very idea of the facade as a matter of display.

As we have seen so far in this book, the relationship between appearance and reality in post-antique European classical architecture had fundamentally devolved from the subservience of construction to the demands of decoration. The inversion of the decoration/construction dyad in the Bibliothèque Sainte-Geneviève, and the expression of the real elements of structure and function on the exterior of the building, gave evidence of a new type of relationship between interior and exterior that entailed a new way of reading buildings.[71] The facades of the Rucellai Palace (see fig. I.7) or Schinkel's Bauakademie are read from bottom to top or top to bottom in the vertical dimension, and from one side to the other in the horizontal one. In some ways, it is no different from reading a painting. That is to say, the surface—which is what we take to be the building's reality—is scanned.

Much of the history of Renaissance and post-Renaissance classical architecture, like much of the history of Western painting, is about the production of an illusion of three-dimensional depth on a flat, two-dimensional surface. In Jacopo Sansovino's (1486–1570) Library of St. Mark in Venice, nearly a century after Alberti's Rucellai Palace, added depth or plasticity is supplied by increased surface relief and shadow (fig. 4.42). Modeling and chiaroscuro provided the architect with the means of giving "life" to the surface, so that the classical orders would appear to embody an internal sense of vitality. They support, they bulge, they rise up, and they finally reach a climax in the profusion and energy of the decorative cornice. One feels a depth of purpose and meaning, as one might feel gravity in an actor's performance or profundity in a painting or story; but one only interprets this from the surface indications. One never thinks about what is happening behind the surface, which is to say offstage, the very "reality" Hugo saw as the undoing of the verisimilar.

In the Labrouste library, the surfaces read as flat, diagrammatic, and lifeless. They are compacted and layered rather than modeled and relieved. The two stories are not plastically continuous in the vertical dimension, nor, in such an obviously repetitive design, does there seem to be much point in scanning the facade from side to side. Instead of scanning the surface and imagining a sense of depth within it, as in the Venice library, the Bauakademie, or the Schinkel library project (see fig. 3.52), one reads through the surface to the building's real depth. An active intellectual process of relating exterior to interior replaces the more submissive, empathic experience of sensorial pleasure and satisfaction.

4.42 Jacopo Sansovino. Library of St. Mark, Venice, begun 1536. Exterior

This increased emphasis on the active engagement of the viewer—a development I have traced back to Castle Howard—here assumes a reflexivity between interior and exterior that provides a new and radical sense of transparency. The reflexivity and the transparency can surely be attributed to the sectional basis of the composition (see fig. 4.32). As a vertical plan, the section enables us to see the actual disposition of interior spatial and structural elements along their edges, so that the exterior of the building is no longer perceived as a self-sufficient, representational facade—in the neoclassical definition of that term—but rather as a contingent expression of the realities on the other side of the wall. Though never seen as such, the section is where interior and exterior intersect and where the facts of construction are revealed. In forcing us to read the library in section, Labrouste brought to the surface, by means of decoration, those very elements of construction that had necessarily been masked or denied by the representational demands of verisimilitude.[72]

The Representational Realism of Pugin and Labrouste

In a celebrated comment made not long after the Bibliothèque Sainte-Geneviève opened to the public and Pugin was committed to Bethlehem Hospital, the French artist Gustave Courbet (1819–1877) declared that he did not and could not paint angels because he had never seen one.[73] This apparently simple statement defined his position as a Realist and thus a representational artist of a new sort. Transferred to the architecture of the period, this way of looking at the world allows us to make a distinction between the idealist form of representation that characterized the neoclassical position up to the 1830s and the new realist approach that we have seen emerge in this chapter. The structural rationalism and protofunctionalism of Pugin and Labrouste undermined the illusionism of the verisimilar that had been so carefully and rigorously argued by Laugier, Quatremère, Boullée, and others since the middle of the previous century to bolster a system of conventions and beliefs that until then had gone fundamentally unquestioned. The system of representation it left in place was a much diminished and delimited one, no longer equated with the imitation of nature and having history alone as its point of reference.

Pugin and Labrouste had substantially different ideas about what constituted a relevant history and how that historical reference should be used. For both, history had become an inescapable temporal phenomenon during which progress was neither necessarily continuous nor cumulative. For Pugin, this meant returning to a moment in time prior to what he considered to be the moral rupture in the evolutionary process, meaning the time when the integral employment of the arch in medieval Christian architecture was compromised by the return to the pagan system of the orders based, as they were, on the "primitive" post-and-lintel construction of the Greeks. Labrouste, by contrast, allowed himself a much wider range of historical references, since the meanings he attached to those forms were to be understood in a less literal, more analytic way.

Neither Pugin nor Labrouste thought it possible to work outside the historical framework and thus neither rejected the representational as such. The exclusivity of the one and the inclusivity of the other regarding historical style had nothing to do, however, with the idea of forging a new nineteenth-century style, an idea that would impassion much of the architectural discourse of the second half of the century, though rarely with fruitful results.[74] For both Pugin and Labrouste, the historical reference served as an agent of expression of the realities of structure, material, and program. If, as in the case of Pugin, the representation appeared so realistic and authentic as to allow one to forget for a moment that it was but a representation, in the case of Labrouste the specificity of each element of representation became so blurred and interwoven with others that one focused more on the physical realities expressed than the representational aspects themselves. In the long run, it was Labrouste's methodology that would gain greater currency.[75] In the short run, however, both approaches to representation revealed in their different ways the key issue that was to confront the next few generations of architects, which was how to manage and exploit the tension that had surfaced between representational means and material demands.

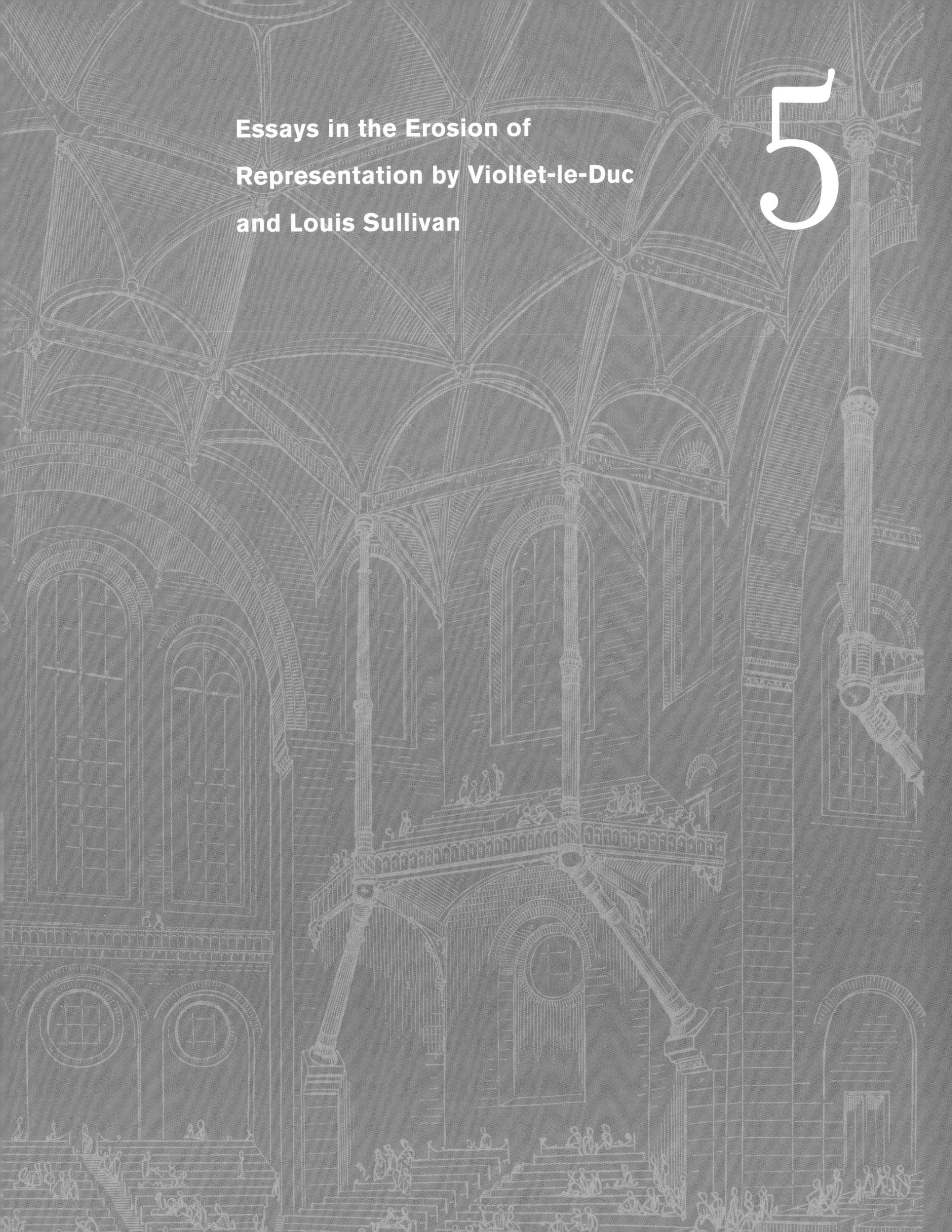

5

Essays in the Erosion of Representation by Viollet-le-Duc and Louis Sullivan

IT MAY HAVE SEEMED ARCH to bring Courbet's comment about angels into a discussion of architecture dealing in large part with Pugin, given the latter's devotion to re-creating an environment where angels might be thought to exist. Be that as it may, Courbet's more extended comments on what he meant by realism can justifiably serve to clarify crucial differences between pictorial and architectural representation in the mid- to later nineteenth century and the special challenge architecture faced in this regard.

The painter's most celebrated remarks on the subject of realism are contained in a letter he wrote in 1861 to a group of disgruntled students at the Ecole des Beaux-Arts who had asked him to open his own school. In refusing to accept the role of professor in the traditional sense of the word, Courbet set forth his idea of the artist as an independent, free-thinking individual whose work should grow out of a direct perception of nature and be manifest in unmediated material terms. He stated that "art in painting can only consist of the representation of objects that are visible and tangible to the artist." "Painting," he reiterated, "is an essentially CONCRETE art and can only consist of the representation of REAL AND EXISTING objects." "It is a completely physical language," he continued, "that has as words all visible objects." "An ABSTRACT object, invisible and non-existent is not part of painting's domain," he added. "Imagination in art consists in knowing how to find the most complete expression of an existing object, but never in imagining or in creating the object itself."[1]

The emphasis on the immediacy of experience inevitably entailed an affirmation of the importance of contemporaneity and put into question the allusion to a classical or medieval past. "No age can be depicted except by its own artists," Courbet declared. "I believe that the artists of one century are completely incompetent when it comes to depicting the objects of a preceding or future century, in other words, to paint either the past or the future." Courbet thereby linked the issue of realistic representation to that of historicism. "That which has been has been," he wrote. "It is the duty of the human spirit to always start anew, always in the present, taking as its point of departure that which has already been accomplished. We must never start something over again, but always march from synthesis to synthesis, from conclusion to conclusion."[2]

If painters could represent "real and existing objects" without recourse to myth, legend, or history, architects would have, at least in the nineteenth century, a nearly impossible task doing so. A vernacular or merely utilitarian structure, like a factory or warehouse, might have been the answer, but it would not have been considered architecture. Schinkel's Bauakademie and Labrouste's Bibliothèque Sainte-Geneviève came about as close to that model as might be imagined, but even they were far from ahistorical. Architecture's access to nature in the classical system was through history, but realism in architecture served to undermine and subvert the idealist connection between nature and history. This left the historical alone to carry the burden of material and functional expression. Divested of its metaphysical content as a work of imitation, architectural representation now was understood essentially as a matter of style, the concept of style itself having taken on by midcentury a purely analytic, classificatory meaning.

The critical study of the historical forms making up architecture's "physical language" that took place in the late 1820s, '30s, and '40s, following the demise of neoclassicism, was initially felt to offer a uniquely liberating opportunity. Whether it was someone like Pugin, who found the possibility of a new beginning in the arched construction of English Gothic buildings, or Labrouste, who envisaged a broader synthesis in the evolution of post-antique architecture in general, the freedom from the restraints imposed by the concept of verisimilitude inherent in the post-and-lintel system of the classical orders gave enormous hope that a modern style expressive of the age would soon emerge from whatever historical "point of departure" was chosen. But nature and history, as subject matter, could never be equated again. History, as it came to be studied and written about in the nineteenth century by such thinkers as Georg Wilhelm Friedrich Hegel (1770–1831), Leopold von Ranke (1795–1886), Jules Michelet (1798–1874), and Karl Marx (1818–1883), implied progress, evolution, change. Its forms carried on their surface an indelible and unforgettable imprint of the time in which they first appeared. Their reuse would inevitably seem anachronistic, no matter how much they were adjusted to contemporary needs and methodologies.

The major challenge for architects was therefore how to adapt a representational system based on the forms of historical styles to a modern, realistic, and materially driven conception of structure and purpose. Those who worked in a generically classical style were led to conceive of the decorative envelope of their buildings in terms of what Gottfried Semper (1803–1879) described as the "dressing" or cladding of the underlying structure.[3] The design of Labrouste's Bibliothèque Nationale (originally Impériale) in Paris, begun in 1857, focused almost entirely on issues of functional planning and interior spatial organization, leaving the bland and inert classical masonry of the exterior skin to operate almost purely as a contextual marker (fig. 5.1).[4] In contrast to his earlier library, where the representational was everywhere undercut by the physical exposure of the realities of structure and function, the existing seventeenth- and early eighteenth-century classical forms of the later building were re-created on the exterior in their superficial aspects so as to produce an overall effect of institutional and urban continuity, though drained of metaphoric force and reduced to the literal condition of the sign. In Charles Garnier's (1825–1898) nearly contemporary Paris Opera House (1861–75) as in Semper's own Hofburg Theater in Vienna (with Carl von Hasenauer, 1871–88), the exterior, by contrast, wraps the interior volumes in a rich and sculpturally active integument that is at once a revelation of programmatic purpose and an actor in the larger urban environment (figs. 5.2–3). On the other hand, architects working in the neo-Gothic and neo-Romanesque styles, such as William Butterfield (1814–1900) in England and Henry Hobson Richardson (1839–1886) in the United States, often placed greater emphasis on the structural composition and physical materiality of the exterior envelope than on its surface character as cladding (fig. 5.4).

The adjustment of the representational forms of history to contemporary structural and programmatic needs rarely, however, produced the kind of characteristically modern expression that many hoped would occur on a widespread basis. And so architects who, around midcentury, had mainly concerned themselves with the question of which style was most likely to provide the proper framework for development began to look beyond that issue to the bigger question of how to make the historical forms themselves into a truly "physical language" of expression. The French architect, theorist, historian, and archaeologist Eugène-Emmanuel Viollet-le-Duc (1814–1879) was the most outspoken, articulate, and influential of these. Having devoted himself in the late 1830s and 1840s to an intense study of French Gothic architecture in the belief that its strict revival would eventuate in an architecture appropriate to modern France, Viollet-le-Duc soon began to question whether such an approach would ever be fruitful and, if not, what might replace it.[5]

By the early 1860s Viollet-le-Duc expressed his anxiety in the final discourse of the first volume of his *Entretiens sur l'architecture*, the series of discourses or lectures published between 1858 and 1872 that remain his most cogent and significant contribution to modern architectural theory.[6] "Our public buildings appear to be bodies destitute of a soul, the relics of a lost civilization," he declared, "a language incomprehensible even to those who use it." "Is the nineteenth century destined to close without possessing an architecture of its own?" he asked. "Will this age, which

5.1 Henri Labrouste. Bibliothèque Nationale (originally Impériale), Paris, 1857–75. Exterior, southwest corner

is so fertile in discoveries, and which displays an energetic vitality, transmit to posterity only imitations or hybrid works, without character, and which it is impossible to classify?"[7]

What was lacking, in Viollet-le-Duc's view, was a "method" based on the idea of "truth." "Originality is impossible apart from truth," he wrote, and the pursuit of truth had gone by the wayside since the institution of classicism following the Renaissance, when "externals were made objects of imitation [and] our [French] architects ceased to make the alliance of the form with the requirements and the means of construction the chief consideration." There were, according to Viollet-le-Duc's method, just two essential criteria: "We must be true in respect of the program, and true in respect of the constructive processes. To be true in respect of the program is to fulfill exactly, scrupulously, the conditions imposed by the requirements of the case. To be true in respect of the constructive processes is to employ the materials according to their qualities and properties."[8]

In an extraordinary group of designs described and explained in the second volume of the *Entretiens*, Viollet-le-Duc illustrated how something new and valid might be achieved. They are comparable to Boullée's theoretical and highly abstracted projects of the 1780s and 1790s in terms of their didactic purpose as well as their erosion of representational form. Making ample use of iron, they combine the material expressiveness of Pugin with the structural rationalism of Labrouste in a method of projective analogy that suggests a way beyond the narrow limits of historical representation that would resonate throughout the rest of the century and into the next. This chapter will focus first on Viollet-le-Duc before turning to Louis Sullivan (1856–1924), whose work not only fulfilled many of the earlier architect's ambitions but also theorized, for the first time, the modern concept of the interdependence of form and function that was central to the critique of representation.

Viollet-le-Duc's Refutation of the Theory of the Hut

Viollet-le-Duc undertook the writing of the *Entretiens* in 1857, soon after embarking on his first teaching venture. Although only the initial four are thought to have been intended to be delivered as lectures to the students in his atelier, the discourses were clearly meant to serve a pedagogical purpose.[9] Between 1840, when he began the restoration of the medieval Church of the Madeleine at Vézelay, and 1857, when he was placed in sole charge of the restoration of the Cathedral of Notre-Dame in Paris following the death of his former collaborator and Labrouste student Jean-Baptiste-Antoine Lassus (1807–1857), Viollet-le-Duc had become France's leading figure in the Gothic Revival movement, as well as the most outspoken critic of the academic system in force at the Ecole des Beaux-Arts. It should therefore come as no surprise that when Labrouste decided to close his teaching atelier in late 1856, after many years of seeing his students denied prizes at the Ecole, a group of the most radical of those students asked Viollet-le-Duc to take them on. In this way, as in numerous others more theoretical, Viollet-le-Duc's teaching was a continuation of the Labrouste line of thought.

5.2 Charles Garnier. Opera House, Paris, 1860–75. Exterior

5.3 Gottfried Semper and Carl von Hasenauer. Hofburg Theater, Vienna, 1871–88. Exterior

5.4 Henry Hobson Richardson. Thomas Crane Public Library, Quincy, Mass., 1880–82. Exterior

Although it made a compelling case for the virtues of Gothic architecture and the supreme importance of studying it within the context of French building practices, the *Entretiens* was in no way a revivalist tract. Rather, Gothic architecture was shown to be the most available, visible, and recent historical exponent of the rational principles that should undergird any sound architectural system, and that did so almost equally in both fifth-century Greece and thirteenth-century France. From the beginning then, outward style was less the issue than underlying method. And critical to Viollet-le-Duc's elaboration of the differential evolution of rational form in Greek and Gothic architecture was the constancy of an anti-imitative use of materials. Indeed, unlike Gottfried Semper, who in the same years was espousing a similar material-based and technique-oriented approach to historical study, Viollet-le-Duc looked askance at formal explanations based on material transformation and refused to indulge in the search for archetypal patterns in primitive building that might be thought to inform later architectural production. Though propounded with a great deal of archaeological as well as anthropological evidence, Semper's theories of the textile origins for the wall as "dressing" and a metal plate–over-wood core source for the Egyptian and Greek column would have appeared to Viollet-le-Duc to be no more relevant—and surely no less credible—than Laugier's primitive hut.[10]

Viollet-le-Duc's history of architecture in the *Entretiens*, which is limited to the Western tradition, begins in the second discourse with developments in Greece. Significantly, more than half the text is devoted to a refutation of the wood origins of Greek architecture specifically and the neoclassical theory of imitation in general. The requirements of program and construction, rather than the desire for representation, are shown to have governed the foundational system of Western architecture and, by implication, to have defined the course of the "incessant progress" of architectural history up until the sixteenth century.[11] Viollet-le-Duc started by admitting that he had "only a slight respect for preconceived ideas" before stating his position outright: "Many authors and professors have asserted that the stone and marble temples of Greece exhibit in their structure the tradition of a wooden construction. This hypothesis may be ingenious, but it does not appear to me to be based on an attentive examination of these monuments. Those who originated it had no acquaintance, or at any rate a very superficial acquaintance, with the architecture of the Greeks, and, as always happens in such cases, the authors who afterwards treated the subject found it easier to repeat that hypothesis than to examine critically whether it should be accepted or questioned."[12]

Viollet-le-Duc then referred to Vitruvius to make the point that the Roman author's own description of the earliest huts as conical rather than square or rectangular should be taken almost as prima facie evidence against the wood origins of the Greek temple. As discussed in chapter 2, many others, such as William Chambers, had noted the same passage before but still argued for the derivation of the details of the orders from wood prototypes (see fig. I.9). Viollet-le-Duc, however, rejected any form of imitation whatsoever on the part of the Greeks, claiming that their rational and imaginative faculties would never have allowed

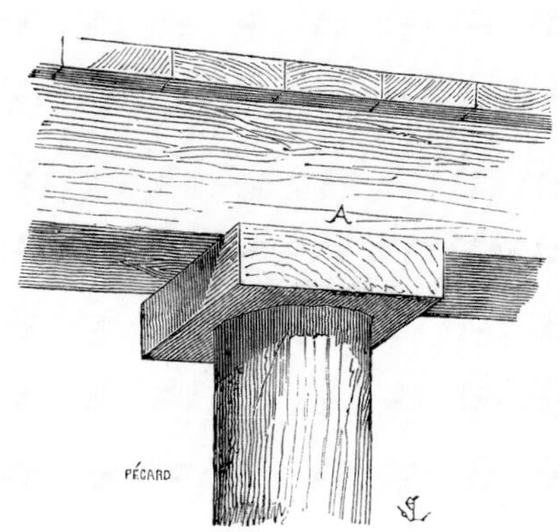

5.5 Eugène-Emmanuel Viollet-le-Duc. "Improbable primitive timber construction," *Entretiens sur l'architecture*, vol. 1, 1863

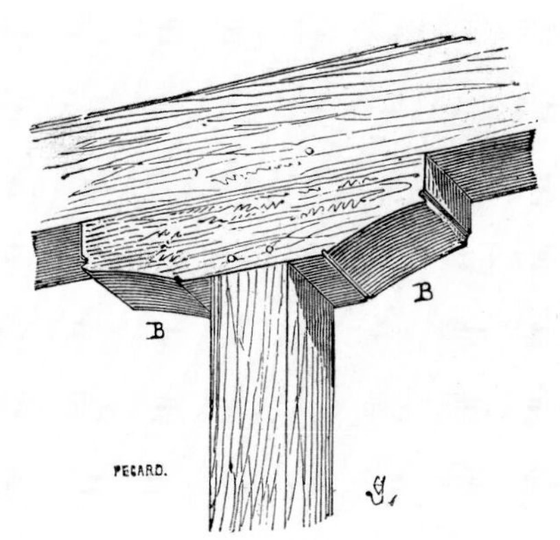

5.6 Viollet-le-Duc. "Probable primitive timber construction," *Entretiens sur l'architecture*, vol. 1

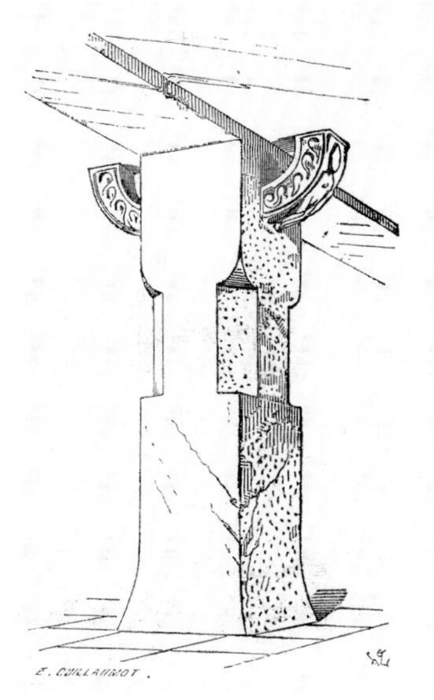

5.7 Viollet-le-Duc. "Stone pillar in imitation of timber construction, Cuttack, India," *Entretiens sur l'architecture*, vol. 1

for such an "essentially monstrous" thing. "The Greek temples are buildings in stone," he wrote. "Why not take them simply for what they are? Why contend that Greeks, the inventors of logic—men gifted with refined aesthetic sensibility—amused themselves with simulating in stone a construction in wood?"[13]

To prove the fundamentally lithic character of Greek architecture, Viollet-le-Duc did what he often did when it came to close-grained historical analysis. He put himself in the shoes of the Greek architect and reconstructed the building process as if he were there. And so, "to come to details," he wrote:

> Let us imagine that a man unacquainted with the resources of the art of building desires to place pieces of timber across the tops of wooden posts or uprights. Let us suppose that this man is intelligent, as the native tribes or aborigines of Greece were; and that he had already invented the axe at least, if not the saw and the mortising tool. The first idea that will occur to him with the view of getting the posts in line—which is essential if he means to connect them by a cross-piece—will be to square them; for it is not easy to place the trunks of trees in a straight line while in their natural form, which always presents some twist or inequality. Our intelligent workman then... has remarked that timbers bearing on their extremities, in a horizontal position, bend under their own weight, and still more if they are loaded; he therefore inserts between the top of his upright and the horizontal piece, the beam or lintel—an intermediate piece to lessen its bearing. Will he employ for this purpose a square parallelepiped of wood, such as shown at A in figure [5.5] ...? Certainly not; for in addition to other objections, this capital, this square parallelepiped, will give but very little aid in supporting the bearing of the beams.... [Instead], he will cut a piece of wood of some length, equal to the upright in width, and placing it between the head of the latter and the beam, he will succeed in effectually supporting the bearing of the beam, by means of the two considerable projections B, as indicated in figure [5.6].[14]

"This," Viollet-le-Duc concludes, "is veritably a timber construction" and a type one sees "imitated in stone in the ancient monuments of India, and even in those recently discovered at Nineveh," but never in classical Greece (fig. 5.7).[15]

5.8 Viollet-le-Duc. Doric order, *Entretiens sur l'architecture*, vol. 1, atlas. Cutaway aerial perspective

5.9 Viollet-le-Duc. "Greek mode of hoisting the lintel stones," *Entretiens sur l'architecture*, vol. 1

To demonstrate how all aspects of the Greek temple can be understood as having a lithic origin, Viollet-le-Duc goes through a virtual process of building one (fig. 5.8). He asks: "In the first place, what is the program?" After defining that, he inquires: "What, then, are the means of execution?" He begins his answer by following the architect to "a quarry in the immediate neighborhood." After watching him choose the proper stone for each part of the intended construction, he shows how pieces for the lintels and for the columns are shaped to allow for delivery and hoisting into place (fig. 5.9). Finally he describes how the stones are fitted in situ in relation to one another. Returning to the question of the abacus, he then explains procedurally why it had to be square if it was to be in stone. According to Viollet-le-Duc, the abacus had to be wider than the width of the lintel stones that were to sit on top of it, in order to allow for the proper placement of those "weighty blocks." The projections, he stated, "afforded means for placing balks of timber along the back and front, which kept the columns in line, and rendered them mutually supporting; they also enabled the stone-setters to stand on either side of the lintel, without need of other scaffolding, to guide the blocks and lower them gently on to the capitals without danger of mistake, because the two balks had left between them just the space of those lintels."[16]

In Viollet-le-Duc's estimation, the supposition that the Greek temple might have been a representation in stone of wood forms held implications extending well beyond Greek architecture itself. It was clearly for this reason that he spent so much time at the very beginning of the *Entretiens* refuting the idea. He concluded the discussion by expanding his critique to similar interpretations of Gothic architecture and calling for the kind of realistic, pragmatic approach to architectural history that he would elaborate in the remaining lectures:

It is by explanations such as these of the derivations of ancient and medieval architecture [from wood and other natural prototypes]—more ingenious than well-considered—that the course of architectural study has come to be misdirected, and consequently the mind of the architect perverted. In explaining buildings we think it a commendable principle to take them for what they really are, and not for that which we wish them to be. This supposition that the Greek temple is an imitation in stone of a wooden hut is of the same order as that which refers the architecture of our Gothic churches to the forest avenues of Gaul and Germany. Both are fictions well adapted to amuse the fancy of dreamers, but very hurtful, or at best useless, when we are called upon to explain the derivations of an art to those whose vocation it is to practice it.[17]

Viollet-le-Duc's Analogical Gothic

As discussed in previous chapters, Viollet-le-Duc was hardly the first to deny the wood origins of Greek architecture: Lodoli, Durand, and Hübsch are only the best known of those who took this position. But Viollet-le-Duc's method was different from theirs, and his purpose only superficially related to Hübsch's. For Lodoli and Durand, the primitive hut was a mythic construct that simply confused and overdetermined the case for the orders. The classical vocabulary, in their view, would have been much more acceptable and even more serviceable were it left unencumbered by the metaphoric content of imitation theory. Hübsch, on the other hand, came closer to Viollet-le-Duc's position and in fact predicted important aspects of it. For Hübsch, the realistic assessment of Greek architecture as a stone architecture allowed for a comparison of it with the arched construction of medieval architecture that highlighted the advanced state of the latter and thus its greater appropriateness as a direct model for the present.

As he would go on to demonstrate in the remaining discourses of the first volume of the *Entretiens*, Viollet-le-Duc fully agreed with Hübsch's conclusion regarding the progress that arched construction represented over its post-and-lintel predecessor, although he disagreed not only on the choice of Romanesque over Gothic as the exemplary form of arched construction but also on the degree of specificity and directness with which the historical model should be followed. His method of reconstructing historical events by transposing himself into the past had its parallel in his conception of the design process as one of projective analogy similar to Pugin's imaginary realm of the perfect conditional.[18] But unlike the self-effacing role the latter was willing to accept vis-à-vis the past, Viollet-le-Duc proposed, in the second volume of the *Entretiens*, an architecture ostensibly avoiding the representational language of either the Romanesque or the Gothic.

The idea of progress was essential to Viollet-le-Duc's way of thinking. In his view, there was an evolutionary sequence from Greek through Roman to Gothic architecture that remained unbroken until the full impact of Renaissance classicism was felt and decorative display went unregulated by the facts of construction. Progress was therefore not measured in purely aesthetic terms but rather involved, at every stage, a relationship between structural advance and formal language. Although Roman architecture fell short of Viollet-le-Duc's fullest admiration due to its "incongruous" combination of arched construction and an "adventitious decoration," purely "for show," that was borrowed from the Greek post-and-lintel system, its method of construction was of such significance for future developments that Viollet-le-Duc believed it necessary to "distinguish the construction of Roman monuments, which is excellent, from its borrowed envelope" (fig. 5.10).[19]

5.10 Viollet-le-Duc. Roman bath, partially restored, *Entretiens sur l'architecture*, vol. 1. Interior perspective

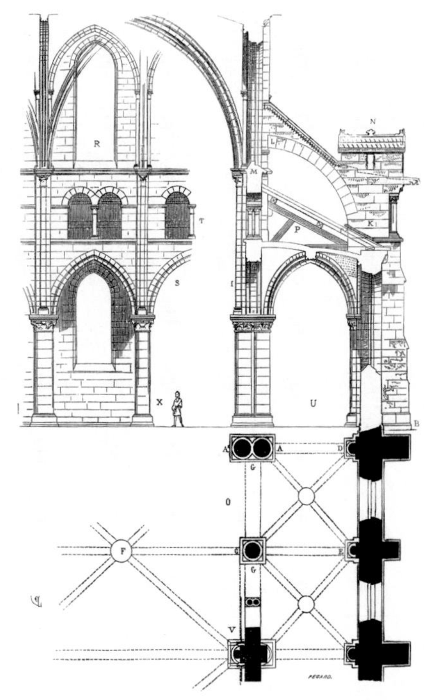

5.11 Viollet-le-Duc. Example of 12th-century construction, *Entretiens sur l'architecture*, vol. 1. Interior elevation, section, and partial plan

The Romans, in effect, were the first to span large spaces and thus create an architecture of interior enclosure. Their "concrete architecture" of hollowed-out, static masses presented a totally new type of structural system that replaced the "architecture of jointed stones, carried to perfection by the Greeks," and "led to vaulting and all its consequences." The apparent contradiction between the arcuated construction and trabeated decoration of Roman architecture set up a dialectic that would only be resolved in the medieval period, when the Gothic architects of the late twelfth and thirteenth centuries "succeeded in producing a composite art in which the influence of both [the Greek and the Roman] is simultaneously manifested" and the "two principles opposed, or at any rate very alien to each other," were reconciled "in a new principle ... of equilibrium .... more applicable than any former one to the various exigencies of our modern social condition."[20]

It was not just arched construction in general that provided a sound basis for contemporary design, in Viollet-le-Duc's view, but Gothic architecture in particular. This was due to its dynamic system of slender, interdependent, equilibrated forms rationally and logically developed in response to the particular social, economic, geological, and climatic conditions of northern Europe (fig. 5.11). The completely novel combination of rib vaults, pointed arches, and flying buttresses presented, according to Viollet-le-Duc's analysis, an "equilibrium in the constructive system by opposing active resistance to active pressure, the outward form resulting only from the structure and the requirements." Its governing idea was "the principle of elasticity," and its fundamental achievement "in less than a century [was to] reach the extreme limits imposed by the conditions of matter."[21] Perhaps the most remarkable sign of the inventiveness of this new system—and its radical departure from classical norms—was the visible employment of diagonal bracing and buttressing not only in a structural sense but in a decorative one as well (fig. 5.12). Viollet-le-Duc reserved special praise for this marshaling of "forces acting obliquely," noting that "substituting oblique for vertical resistance is a principle which... may assume a very high degree of importance and lead to novel combinations, now that the introduction of iron into buildings enables us to attempt undertakings of which former ages had only a vague presentiment."[22]

This brings us to Viollet-le-Duc's ultimate purpose in reviewing the history of Western architecture for his readers. He wanted to be able to extract principles for contemporary design and believed that it was necessary, as most others at the time would have agreed, to locate the moment in the past that could provide the most relevant and effective point of departure. He insisted that his interest was not in the representation of historical forms as such. "The study of the past is obligatory," he wrote, "in fact indispensable, but on condition of deducing therefrom principles rather than forms."[23] His methodology, as John Summerson explained in his pathbreaking essay on the architect's theory of design, was a twofold process, proceeding from an initial stage of historical analysis to a final one of rational synthesis.[24]

The two volumes of the *Entretiens* describe this trajectory. In the last discourse of the first volume, Viollet-le-Duc summarized the intentions and findings of his initial historical analysis, noting that, in studying past examples, "we must start from the ultimate result and ascertain successively the design and the program and means of execution; we must dissect the edifice, as it were, and verify the more or less complete relations that exist between that apparent result which first engages our attention and the hidden methods and reasons that have determined its form." "This," he continued, "is the best exercise we could engage in if we would learn to design, to create. To arrive at synthesis we must necessarily pass through analysis."[25]

The synthesis occurs in the second volume, where Viollet-le-Duc, as teacher by example, proposes numerous solutions to various modern design problems. He insists

5.12 Viollet-le-Duc. Basilica of Saint-Denis, *Dictionnaire raisonné de l'architecture française du XIe au XVIe siècle*, vol. 1, 1854. Cutaway perspective

that these proposals should not be taken as "models" but simply as indicating "a method of procedure for meeting special requirements by reverting to the principles previously explained" and making use of the new material "resources which our own age affords us."[26] Only by experimenting with new materials and becoming aware of the structural solutions they suggest could the young designer "invent that *architecture of our times* which is so loudly called for."[27] The critical new material was iron—cast, wrought, and rolled into plates—and, almost as if by predestination, it was the Gothic architects of the late twelfth and thirteenth

5.13 Viollet-le-Duc. Concert hall for three thousand people project, 1864, *Entretiens sur l'architecture*, vol. 2, 1872. Interior perspective

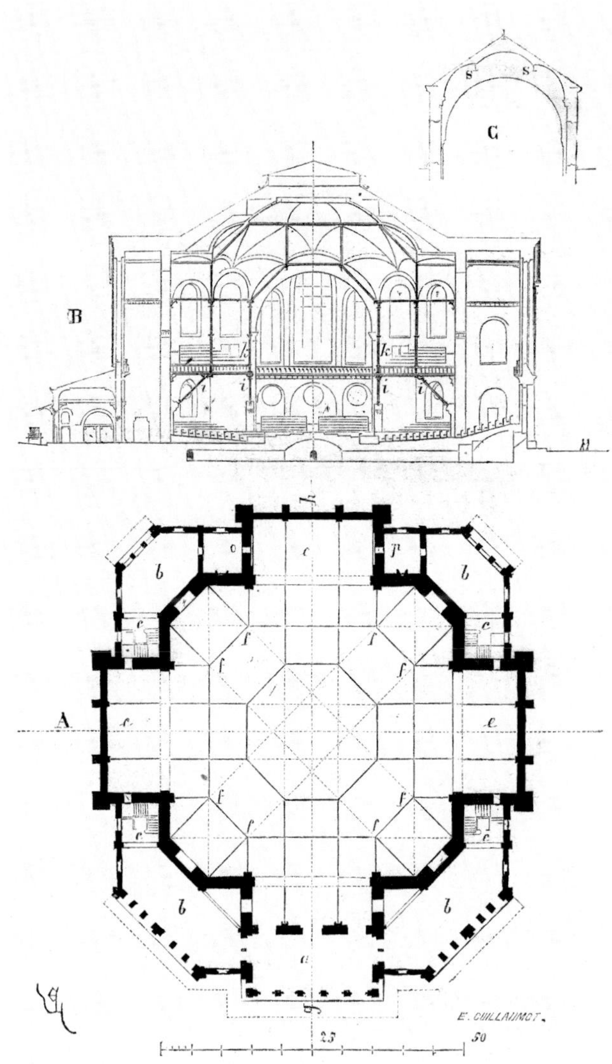

5.14 Concert hall project, *Entretiens sur l'architecture*, vol. 2. Sections and plan

centuries, with their "equilibrated structure," who most clearly predicted and pointed the way to its best use.[28] The synthesis thus became an analogical procedure.

As already noted, Viollet-le-Duc, like Pugin, set the stage for the procedure in the perfect conditional. But instead of seeking to re-create an authentic Gothic architecture in the present, he tried to imagine what the reborn Gothic architect would do if presented with modern materials and a list of modern requirements to fulfill. "It is plain" to see, he wrote, "that had the medieval builders possessed cast or rolled iron of considerable dimensions, they would not have employed such a material as they employed stone...; they would on the contrary have sought arrangements more in harmony with the nature of metal. It is likewise evident, however, that they would not have failed to take advantage of the principles of elasticity which they were already applying to buildings of stone, and that they would have rendered the different members of their structures still more independent." "By virtue of their logical and subtle intelligence," he added, "they would, for instance, have endeavored to reduce the great height of their vaulting—a height which was occasioned by the mode of structure adopted, much rather than by aesthetic considerations."[29]

Two projects for two different programs of contemporary significance can serve to illustrate Viollet-le-Duc's idea. The first was for a large concert hall to seat approximately three thousand people (figs. 5.13–14).[30] Cast and rolled iron are used to create an independent, internal framework supporting an octagonal dome composed of ribs that could be made either of molded brick or stone and webs of clay pottery or flat hollow bricks. All this was to be contained within a relatively thin masonry shell.[31] Open, unencumbered space, lightweight construction, good sight lines, ease of access and egress, fireproofing, and excellent acoustics were the desiderata; and all but the latter can be recognized as provided for in the design. The centralized plan, which can be described either as a chamfered square or an irregular octagon, is an extrusion of the shape of the dome, a shape that occurs nowhere in Gothic architecture and that had, for Viollet-le-Duc, a completely nonarchitectural source abstracted directly from nature (fig. 5.15). He stated that "solid bodies such as polyhedrons, consisting of plane surfaces, appear to suggest the elementary forms applicable to the structure of mingled iron and masonry where vaulting is in question," and that a study of "natural crystals" led him to this discovery, as well as the precise form it took in the covering of the concert hall.[32]

The dome's rib-vaulted structure is derived from Gothic precedent, as are the angled balcony supports set obliquely on forty-five-degree diagonals (see fig. 5.12). But to make the skeletal iron structure work with minimal masonry buttressing and without the external flying buttresses that would have been used in the Gothic period, Viollet-le-Duc took advantage of the tensile strength of the flat iron beams joining the columns and supporting the ribs of the dome to create a stayed, self-bracing "iron framework" that, he

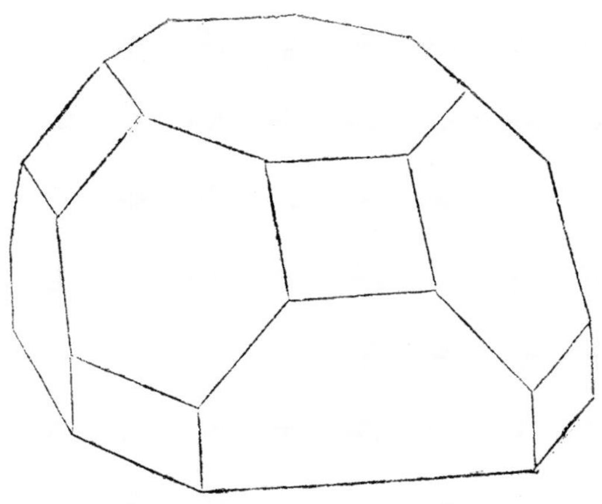

5.15 Concert hall project, *Entretiens sur l'architecture*, vol. 2. Concept drawing for dome

explained, "remains independent everywhere, and merely forms, as it were, the strings of bows in masonry." The connections between the iron and masonry were left loose "or slack so as not to hinder expansion" and allow "for some movement." Similarly, the vaults themselves were designed to be "independent of one another, like the webs of Gothic rib vaulting" and thus be able "to give with any movement without occasioning fractures or dislocations."[33] The independence of elements, the equilibration of parts, the use of oblique struts to help neutralize structural forces in a visually dynamic fashion, not to speak of the dematerialization of the whole—all these reflect the Gothic principles underlying the design. Yet the building does not look like any known or even typical Gothic structure, nor does it even use the pointed arch.[34] On the other hand, the dome's dependence on the "elementary" geometric form of crystals never succeeds in completely banishing its historicizing bearing. The best way to describe it is as an analogical Gothic.[35]

The second Viollet-le-Duc project I have chosen to illustrate is more radical in certain ways yet equally ambiguous on the strict question of representation. This is the design for a six-story apartment house with a shop on the ground floor (fig. 5.16).[36] The growing fashion for shop fronts with

5.16 Viollet-le-Duc. Apartment house with ground-floor shop project, 1871, *Entretiens sur l'architecture,* vol. 2. atlas. Exterior perspective

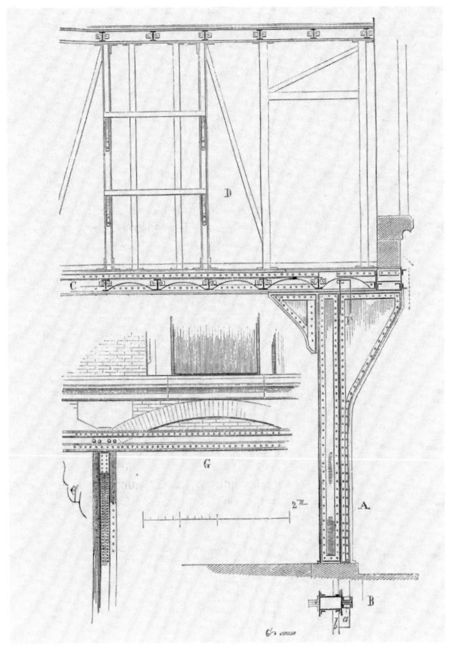

5.17 Apartment house project, *Entretiens sur l'architecture,* vol. 2. Section, partial elevation, and plan of variant design with brick and stone outer wall

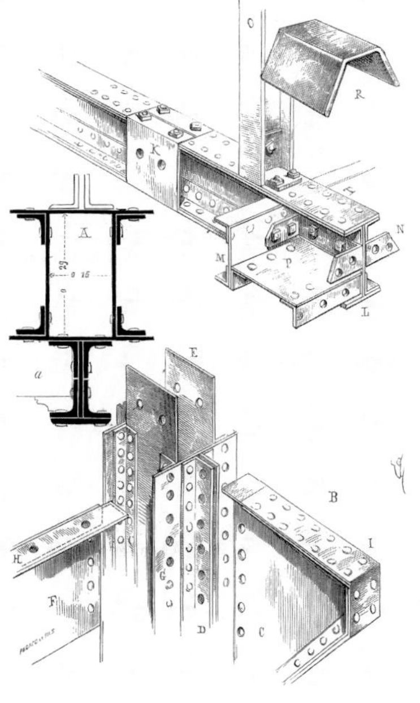

5.18 Apartment house project, *Entretiens sur l'architecture,* vol. 2. Details of iron frame. Plan and axonometrics

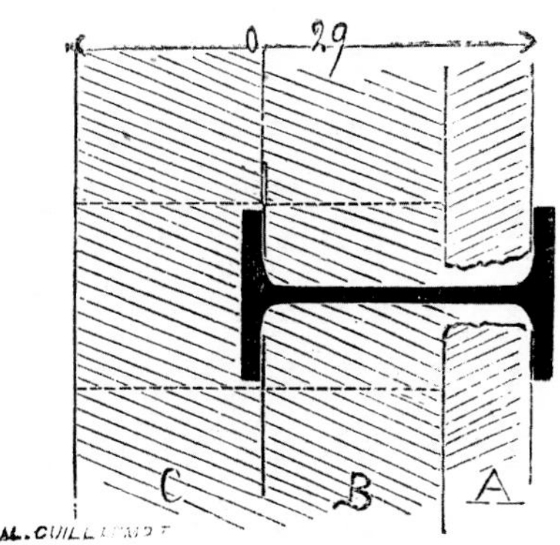

5.19 Apartment house project, *Entretiens sur l'architecture,* vol. 2. Section through outer wall of iron and brick with terra-cottta and brick facing

large areas of glazing seems to have been the catalyst for the idea of a building entirely constructed on an iron frame. Merely to open up the ground floor of a stone building and support the solid upper wall on thin cast-iron columns framing the shop windows, as was normally done, was criticized by Viollet-le-Duc as looking like an "after-thought," a "juxtaposition" of the two materials and structural systems "without any attempt to combine or unite them."[37] His integral solution was based on the adoption of a continuous iron frame forming both vertical supports and interior partition walls to create a three-dimensional lattice or spatial grid (fig. 5.17).[38] In addition to the structural integrity achieved, the use of an iron frame greatly decreased the amount of space taken up throughout the building by masonry supports and walls, while providing on the ground floor, in Viollet-le-Duc's words, "what business demands": "a surface entirely free, separated from the street only by glazed partitions admitting as much light as possible."[39]

Unlike the concert hall, where Viollet-le-Duc used cast-iron columns for the main supporting members and laminated plates of rolled iron for the connecting braces, here he used plate iron exclusively, in conjunction with angles, I-beams, and Ts, in order to maintain the rectangular sections needed for making the most efficient connections between columns, walls, window and door frames, fireplace cavities, and the like. Detailed axonometric drawings illustrate how the plates and angles would be bolted together to form the hollow structural columns and I-shaped floor girders (fig. 5.18). They also reveal the special fittings designed to allow the upper floors of the building to be corbeled out and to overhang the shop front, in effect placing the signs above the show windows in shadow.

One possibility for the facing of the upper floors was brick with stone trim, as was indicated in the drawing of the building's metal frame (see fig. 5.17). But Viollet-le-Duc thought better of this, stating that "there is no reason for not carrying out the [frame] principle to its ultimate consequences," meaning "to adopt the iron framing [of the interior] for the outer walls also." To provide insulation against cold, heat, and dampness, he embedded the rear flange of the exposed iron I-beams between two layers of brick, leaving space on the outer surface for a thin facing of colored, glazed terra-cotta tiles banded with courses of exposed brick (fig. 5.19). This solution allowed him not only to expose the iron frame on the exterior but also to integrate the structure with the infill.[40] Even the window frames form part of the structural composition. "Thus all holds together," Viollet-le-Duc wrote. "Each part contributes to the stability of the whole in this system of iron framing, and the window-cases participate in the structure." And because of this structural continuity and standardization of elements, the building could be prefabricated or, as Viollet-le-Duc put it, "completely executed in the workshop before being put up."[41]

The forward-looking, even radical aspects of the design should be obvious: a fully integrated and exposed three-dimensional metal structural frame; a lightweight exterior facing clearly treated as infill panels; a large, nearly fully glazed shop window; and a promise of prefabrication. All these might well have resulted in a form bearing no relation to historical prototypes and thus no representational resonance. Moreover, unlike the concert hall, which could be and in fact was compared by Viollet-le-Duc to earlier types of public gathering places such as medieval churches and palace halls, the "unpretentious habitation," as Viollet-le-Duc called his apartment house design, was a product of modern urban conditions alone.[42] He was himself convinced that the project for the apartment house, while not necessarily to be taken as a "model for ... the *architecture of the future*," should nevertheless be viewed as a deliberate effort to design outside the strict framework of historical representation. By virtue of the lack of significant historical precedent for such a program, the building was, in his view, "a study, without reminiscences to fall back upon, of the means which modern industries offer us for building so as to satisfy the requirements of our times." "I am quite aware," he added, "that it bears no resemblance to the palaces of Rome or Florence, or a mansion of the Renaissance or of the times of Louis XVI. But it will be allowed that here at any rate the use of iron is not dissembled—that it is frankly displayed."[43]

The iron may be "frankly displayed," as Viollet-le-Duc put it, and this serves to mask the vestigial historical references—but only just. While the architect discussed in detail the reasons for almost all aspects of the building's design, there are two that he never explained, one of which he never even mentioned. The one that he did not explain is why the upper floors of the building were designed to overhang the lower one and thus require the complex contrivance of iron brackets or corbels, not to speak of possibly obscuring the shop signs. The aspect he never even mentioned is the diagonal bracing of the facade's secondary iron members. What structural role they play and how necessary they are was not mooted. That they may be more decorative than functional becomes especially important when one considers the effect they have on the otherwise rational and clear-cut organization of the grid of glazed tiles.

Both the corbeling and the diagonal braces are, in effect, devices that characterize late Gothic half-timber houses, which Viollet-le-Duc knew extremely well. In fact, he referred to this type of domestic architecture, still in evidence in many French cities and towns at the time, earlier in the eighteenth discourse but never directly within the context of his own "unpretentious habitation."[44] Like the oblique struts and rib vaults of the concert hall, the diagonal braces and corbeled upper floors of the apartment house prevent one from reading the project completely abstractly in the nonobjective sense of the term. The "principles" of Gothic architecture are in neither case entirely disengaged from its "forms." But the blurring of the reference and the distance from the original short-circuit any interpretation based on verisimilitude and define the connection at the more abstract though not entirely nonrepresentational level of the analogue. One can therefore speak of an erosion of representation rather than its disappearance.

The Steel-Frame Tall Building in Chicago

Viollet-le-Duc's concert hall and apartment house designs can be taken as significant markers of change in architectural thought, although they were in no way typical of European production of the period or even of his own practice. The buildings he actually produced, like those of his contemporaries, were all explicitly representational, despite a strong emphasis on material and structure. The project he submitted for the Paris Opera House competition of 1860–61, for instance, was in a classical style with clear French Renaissance overtones (fig. 5.20); whereas the bulk of new churches he designed in the 1850s, '60s, and '70s followed medieval models (fig. 5.21). Program undoubtedly had much to do with this discrepancy between radical project and conservative production. For Viollet-le-Duc, as for Pugin, since the program of the church had not greatly changed since the Middle Ages, there was no real justification for its form to change. The same would go for an opera house, although here the reference was to a later time period. A modern concert hall for a large public audience could allow for more unconventional thinking, whereas an apartment house with a ground-floor store needing to advertise its wares had no relevant historical pedigree in Viollet-le-Duc's view.

5.20 Viollet-le-Duc. Paris Opera House project, 1860–61. Exterior perspective

5.21 Viollet-le-Duc. Church of Saint-Gimer, Carcassonne, 1852–59. Exterior

Still, Viollet-le-Duc's design for the apartment house only went so far. The three-dimensional lattice of the iron frame was not drawn or illustrated, nor does it seem that he truly visualized it as an entity with its own determining characteristics. He focused his attention on the traditional problem of a facade between two party walls, which ultimately led him to his compromise solution. Within less than twenty years, however, the truly revolutionary implications of the metal frame for architectural design began to be understood with the rapid development of tall building construction in the Midwest of the United States, where the availability of steel now allowed for much greater heights than had previously been possible in masonry, cast or rolled iron, or any combination thereof. Louis Sullivan, who had studied in Paris in the mid-1870s and knew Viollet-le-Duc's writings firsthand, was the architect who gave most consistent and expressive form to this new structural premise and articulated its theoretical implications for the issue of representation.

The steel frame was first applied to office building construction in Chicago in the mid-1880s by the engineer and

5.22 Burnham and Root. Masonic Temple, Chicago, 1890–92. Exterior

5.23 D. H. Burnham and Company. Reliance Building, Chicago, 1890–95. Under construction. From *Architectural Record,* 1895

architect William Le Baron Jenney (1832–1907), who, like Sullivan, whom he employed briefly in the 1870s, had also studied in Paris (he had received a degree from the Ecole Centrale des Arts et Manufactures in 1856). By the beginning of the following decade, the steel frame had become ubiquitous, and buildings were rising to heights three times that of the tallest commercial and residential structures in Europe. Chicago's Masonic Temple, by Burnham and Root (firm established 1873), which was begun in 1890 and completed in 1892, was twenty-two stories high, an entire block wide, and had a central, glass-covered atrium court and shopping arcade rising through its full height (fig. 5.22).[45] The steel-frame tall building was something "new under the sun," Sullivan wrote just a few years later, a product of the "most bald, most sinister, most forbidding conditions."[46] It presented a totally new structural and programmatic type that left architects with few, if any, relevant representational models or devices to rely on.

Four factors in particular stand out as uniquely characteristic of the steel-frame structural system as it rapidly evolved in the second half of the 1880s. First was the obvious and extremely powerful issue of scale. The new skyscrapers, as they were soon called, literally dwarfed the existing buildings around them (fig. 5.23). The only comparison some contemporaries could make was with the way a Gothic cathedral stood out from the town around it; but the Gothic cathedral was a singular urban event, having a special spiritual and civic meaning and expressing in its complex form the very hierarchies it embodied within its urban context. The new, tall steel-frame buildings were simply commercial extrusions of the gridiron plan of the city's streets, a stacking of one story upon another for reasons of economic profit alone.

The relation of the grid of the steel frame to the grid of the city's streets points to the second major new structural condition the steel frame brought to bear. This was the unequivocally abstract and nonhierarchical character of

5.24 Jenney and Mundie. Fair Store, Chicago, 1890–91. Under construction. From *Industrial Chicago: The Building Interests*, Chicago, 1891

the structural frame itself (fig. 5.24). Vertical piers rise uninflected at equal intervals to mark standard bay widths. Horizontal beams crisscross the vertical elements at constant ceiling heights. What happens across the outer surface is the same as what happens in depth. A reticulated three-dimensional lattice with no apparent focus and no apparent beginning or end is the lean physical result.[47]

One can hardly call the steel frame a skeleton, however, since that word implies a relation to a body, human or animal. There is no sense of the organic in the steel-frame structure—of the active force of pressure and resistance—which brings us to the third new characteristic of it as a system. By its abstract and nonhierarchical bearing, the steel frame makes no reference to traditional concepts of load and support, where what is below is usually heavier than what is above, or at least indicative of how the load is being carried (see fig. 3.44). In steel-frame construction, the cladding of the exterior is hung off the interior structure rather than constituting a load-bearing wall in itself. Early illustrations of steel-frame buildings under construction often made a dramatic point of this antigravitational character. The New York Life Building in Chicago, built in 1893–94 by Jenney and Mundie (partnership formed 1891), was shown with parts of its cladding completed and other parts not (fig. 5.25). The crucial point is that the masonry construction did not begin at ground level and work its way up, with each successive floor being carried by the ones beneath it. Instead, groups of floors appeared as if unsupported, hanging off the frame. Entirely new possibilities for scheduling were thus revealed, but, more important for us, the formal dissociation between structural frame and surface cladding was made explicit.[48]

The fourth characteristic of the steel frame that was critical to its modernity was its inherent distinction between

5.25 Jenney and Mundie. New York Life Building, Chicago, 1893–94. Perspective, under construction. From *American Architect and Building News*, 1894

structure and decoration. While architects earlier in the century had made such a distinction in a theoretical sense, the steel frame actualized the condition. For reasons of fireproofing, the metal structure, once erected, had to be encased in a material such as terra cotta, plaster, or cement. The fireproofed frame then needed to be clad in more finished and protective materials that would, at the same time, serve the purpose of filling in the void of the structural bays. The process of building a steel-frame skyscraper was thus, by necessity, one in which the construction was decorated. At the scale of the operation, this became both a liberating and a frightening prospect. It was the first time since Laugier had placed the issue of representation in the forefront of design theory that architects were impelled, by the very nature of the situation, to face the problem head-on. Still, most simply accepted the convention of representation as a matter of historical form and tried to adapt the new construction system to it. Sullivan was different, and this is where his significance lies. He not only approached the problem of the steel-frame tall building straightforwardly and fundamentally as one of decorated construction; he also understood the question of its design not in terms of individual solutions but in terms of the type they exemplified. He brilliantly theorized the larger issue in terms of the relation of form to function in such a way as to provide a new basis for understanding the role of representation in modern architecture.

Sullivan's Wainwright Building

A few years after returning to Chicago following his study at the Ecole des Beaux-Arts (1874–75), Sullivan went to work for Dankmar Adler (1844–1900) as his chief draftsman and designer, becoming a full partner in the new firm of Adler and Sullivan founded in 1883.[49] By the end of the decade, Adler and Sullivan had established itself as one of the city's leading firms and, because of Sullivan, its most artistically oriented. The young Frank Lloyd Wright (1867–1959) was inspired to apply for a position with them in early 1888, and did so well that he was promoted to chief draftsman by the middle of 1890. That was shortly before Sullivan designed the Wainwright Building in St. Louis, his first steel-frame high-rise, which established his conception of what the building type should be. Wright, who was profoundly affected by the design, later described it as "Louis Sullivan's greatest moment—his greatest effort. The 'skyscraper,' as a new thing, ... with ... [a] beauty all its own, was born." "The Wainwright," he wrote, "cleared the way, and to this day remains the master key to the skyscraper as a matter of Architecture in the work of the world."[50]

5.26 Louis Sullivan (with Dankmar Adler). Wainwright Building, St. Louis, 1890–91. Exterior

The ten-story Wainwright Building was designed in late 1890 and built in 1891 (fig. 5.26). It was the first of a group of steel-frame tall buildings that the firm designed before it broke up in 1895, shortly before the thirteen-story Guaranty (later Prudential) Building in Buffalo (1894–96) was completed.[51] In early 1896 Sullivan published "The Tall Building Artistically Considered," in which he described the thinking that lay behind the design of the Wainwright and its successors and articulated for the first time his theory of functionalism. Following in Viollet-le-Duc's footsteps, Sullivan characterized the design process as a rational synthesis in response to a prior analysis of needs, taking into account at every step the structural system brought into being by the "development of steel manufacture" (fig. 5.27).[52]

"The design of the tall building," Sullivan began, "must be recognized and confronted at the outset as a problem to be solved." The first step therefore was to "examine ... carefully the elements...of the problem."[53] These elements were then outlined, in an extraordinarily pragmatic and utilitarian tone, in the following order:

5.27 Wainwright Building. Under construction. From *Engineering Magazine,* 1892

> Wanted—1st, a story below-ground, containing...the plant for power, heating, lighting, etc. 2nd, a ground floor ... devoted to stores, banks, or other establishments requiring large area, ample spacing, ample light, and great freedom of access [fig. 5.28]. 3rd, a second story readily accessible by stairways...with corresponding liberality in structural spacing and expanse of glass and breadth of external openings. 4th, above this an indefinite number of stories of offices piled tier upon tier, one tier just like another tier, one office just like all the other offices—an office being similar to a cell in a honey-comb, merely a compartment, nothing more [fig. 5.29]. 5th, and last, ...is...the attic. In this the circulatory system completes itself and makes its grand turn, ascending and descending. The space is filled with tanks, pipes, valves, sheaves, and

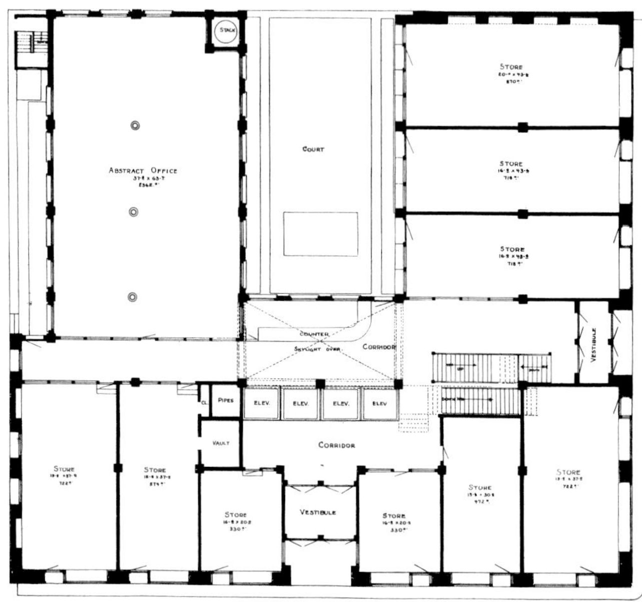

5.28 Wainwright Building. Plan, ground floor. From [Wainwright Real Estate Company], *The Wainwright Building,* [1891]

5.30 Wainwright Building. Main entrance

> mechanical equipment etcetera that supplement and complement the force-originating plant hidden below-ground in the cellar. Finally, or at the beginning rather, there must be on the ground floor a main aperture or entrance common to all the occupants or patrons of the building.[54]

The foursquare, reticulated block of the Wainwright Building was a direct consequence of these givens: its broad outlines were established by the width and height of the steel frame, its internal divisions by "the practical horizontal and vertical division" of "the individual cell."[55] The differentiation of major functional areas was achieved through distinctions in material and scale. The lowest two floors are faced with smooth reddish-brown sandstone. The relatively large size of these blocks correlates with the wide openings of the ground-floor spaces, meant for bank offices, shops, ticket agencies, and the like (fig. 5.30). The main entrance is just barely picked out by the band of terra-cotta decoration surrounding it. A rectilinear ledge, also decorated with flush terra-cotta panels, projects just above the second floor to define the lower edge of the "honey-comb" of offices, where the facing material of the steel frame changes from stone to brick. The ledge stops short of the corner piers to allow them to frame the facade as a single unit. The windows in the office tiers are separated by narrow vertical piers faced with brick and articulated at top and bottom with elongated decorative devices acting as bases and capitals (figs. 5.31–32). Horizontal decorative terra-cotta panels at the floor levels are inset behind the plane of the piers to allow them to read continuously in the vertical dimension. The top floor is treated as a continuous frieze, with round windows entwined in swirling foliage. Capping the composition is a deep, flat projecting cornice clearly related in scale to the structure as a whole.

The distinct divisions of the Wainwright Building derive from the "elements" of the tall office building Sullivan outlined. More than that, they highlight the differentiation of tasks by the specific scale and decorative treatment they are given. They also conform, in their insistent rectilinearity, to the abstract grid of the structural frame. But the correlation is not one-to-one, and it is here that Sullivan's larger artistic program comes into play, giving expression to what would otherwise be merely the practical solution

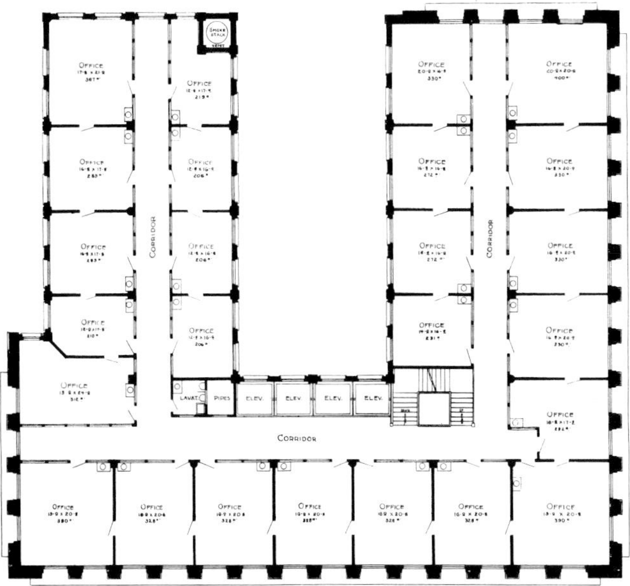

5.29 Wainwright Building. Plan, third through ninth floors. From [Wainwright Real Estate Company], *The Wainwright Building*, [1891]

5.31 Wainwright Building. Lower floors

5.32 Wainwright Building. Upper floors and cornice

to a problem. The ledge projecting above the second floor, for instance, not only indicates the beginning of the office tiers; it also serves as their base. But rather than providing a sense of firm footing, it appears more like a lower rail for the curtain wall that is drawn down from the frieze, whose circular forms express the "grand turn" of the "circulatory system," as Sullivan wrote, "ascending and descending." The nongravitational character of the steel frame is thus foregrounded as the central area of the grid, which reads as hanging in space. The elongated "bases" and "capitals" of the thin piers partake of this expression of stretch both upward and downward. Indeed, the place Sullivan gave in his list of requirements to the building's entrance is perhaps the best clue to his intentions. Mentioning it last in his progression from bottom to top, he placed it "finally, or at the beginning," thus leaving one to conclude, as one does in looking at the building itself, that there is a significant sense in which the structure is expressed as a self-reflexive loop rather than as a gravitational condition of load and support.

Sullivan explicitly addressed the nonhierarchical character of the steel frame in his treatment of the office block as a grid of standardized cells. But to achieve the desired image of a "honey-comb," he exaggerated the role of the underlying structural frame in its decorative elaboration. The actual width of the structural bay is only revealed on the ground floor (see figs. 5.27–29). As was typical of Chicago construction, the bay is horizontal rather than vertical (see fig. 5.24). To give the necessary density to the grid of offices, Sullivan added extra piers between the ones that face the actual vertical structural members. He did not differentiate the "fake" ones from the "real" ones and thus produced an image of condensation that is apparently so grounded in fact that one rarely stops to think about its illusoriness. This structurally unsanctioned move was so egregious in the context of architectural realism as established by the likes of Labrouste and Viollet-le-Duc that only some truly overriding expressive purpose could have occasioned it. For Sullivan, this had to do with the emotional and poetic dimension of architecture, which he felt was even more critical to the solution of the problem of the tall building than the "material satisfaction" of "considerations of literal planning, construction, and equipment"—and no less "a sound, logical, and coherent expression of the conditions."[56]

Sullivan's justification for the enhancement of the expression of structure through decorative overdetermination was based on the larger cultural meaning he attributed to the program of the modern high-rise steel-frame office building. For "our building" to be "that adequate solution of the problem I am attempting to define," he wrote,

> We must now heed the imperative voice of emotion. It demands of us, what is the chief characteristic of the

> tall office building? And at once we answer, it is lofty. This loftiness is to the artist-nature its thrilling aspect. It is the very open organ-tone in its appeal. It must be in turn the dominant chord in his expression of it, the true excitant of his imagination. It must be tall, every inch of it tall. The force and power of altitude must be in it, the glory and pride of exaltation must be in it. It must be every inch a proud and soaring thing, rising in sheer exultation that from bottom to top it is a unit without a single dissenting line—that is the new, the unexpected, the eloquent peroration of most bald, most sinister, most forbidding conditions.[57]

The acknowledgment of the program's emotive dimension in terms of a realistic understanding of its contemporary cultural meanings led Sullivan to a material expression of the building as an exemplar of a type, which resulted in his stretching the capacity of inherited conventions of architectural representation beyond anything we have examined so far. The division of the structure into its major functional units took the emphasis off associational references and replaced them with a synthetic expression of programmatic meaning. The startling new characteristic of tallness or loftiness was not represented through associations with medieval towers or pitched roofs, as was common at the time, but rather was revealed in the condensation and repetition of the vertical lines of the steel cage itself (see figs. 5.22 and 5.26). Thrown into relief by the deep-set, shadowy planes of decorative spandrels and windows and in contrast to their intermittent horizontal rhythm, the continuous vertical lines of the piers are powerfully emphasized, stretched taut between elongated bases and capitals, and florescently climaxed in the extended, crowning frieze and cornice. The constituent parts are thus synthesized into an image of aspiring, dominating commercial force, expressed through the emotional terms of rising and falling vertical lines.

The intention was abstract, and Sullivan knew it to be so; but the symbolic charge was so strong and so definite as to make it nearly impossible to realize the goal abstractly. Sullivan went back and forth on this issue in his explanation of how he proceeded. Toward the beginning of the "Tall Building" essay, he tried to assure the reader (and no doubt himself) that the "adequate solution" will result "inevitably, and in the simplest possible way, if we follow our natural instincts without thought of books, rules, precedents, or any such educational impedimenta." Any "quotation from this, that, or the other 'correct' building in some other land and some other time," he later reiterated, would make it impossible to arrive at the unity of conception demanded by the program.[58] Sullivan knew that the Wainwright Building hardly looked like any other historical type. But no matter how distant from the source it might have been in his eyes, he was bothered enough by the relationship between its tripartite division into base, shaft, and capital and the historical underpinnings of that idea in classical design that he developed the argument that "form ever follows function" to dispel any such connection and explain the nonrepresentational impetus of the design.

The Functionalization of Form and the Residue of Representation

Sullivan began the final section of "The Tall Office Building Artistically Considered" by stating that his search for a solution to the problem of designing the commercial high-rise was for a methodology so absolute and unconditional that it could be generalized into "a comprehensive, a final solution" that would "let the problem indeed dissolve."[59] From this statement of intention, he straightway launched into a criticism of those who "have advanced the theory that the true prototype of the tall office building is the classical column, consisting of base, shaft and capital," an approach typified by Bruce Price's (1845–1903) recent American Surety Building in New York (1894–95) (fig. 5.33). Yet he

5.33 Bruce Price. American Surety Building, New York, 1894–96. Exterior perspective. From *Architectural Record,* Great American Architects Series, 1899

acknowledged, in the same sentence, that his own design could easily be viewed in these terms, "the moulded base of the column [being] typical of the lower stories of our own building, the plain or fluted shaft suggesting the monotonous, uninterrupted stories of office-tiers, and the capital the completing power and luxuriance of the attic." Other justifications for a tripartite organization, he admitted, might include "a mystical symbolism" deriving from "the many trinities in nature and in art"; the "logical" argument that everything "should have a beginning, a middle, and an ending"; and the analogy with "organic" growth consisting of roots, trunk, and leaves. In opposition to all of these, Sullivan noted that there are some who place the idea of "the power of a unit" over "the grace of a trinity" and will "accept the notion of a triple division as permissible and welcome," as long as "the subdivision does not disturb the sense of singleness and repose."[60]

While not immediately taking sides or declaring his own position, Sullivan stated that "all of these critics and theorists" agree "that the tall office building should not, must not, be made a field for the display of architectural knowledge in the encyclopaedic sense," just as surely as they agree "that the sixteen-story building must not consist of sixteen separate, distinct and unrelated buildings piled one upon the other." Yet Sullivan did not come out in support of the unitarian position, which, he wrote, was only willing to accept "a triple division" if "the [primary] unit does not come from the alliance of the three."[61] His own analysis of the tall office building had led him to a five-part description of its requirements. One of these, however, was underground and therefore invisible, and two others formed a single unit, thus leaving three distinctly separate parts to be accounted for. And it was this straightforward programmatic analysis rather than any preconceived formal idea or representational strategy—be it historical, metaphysical, or otherwise—that Sullivan claimed led to his tripartite solution for the tall office building.

The justification was unimpeachable in Sullivan's view, since it was grounded in a law of nature—not an image of nature, but a "law." "Life seeks and takes on its forms in an accord perfectly responsive to its needs," he wrote. "Whether it be the sweeping eagle in his flight or the open apple-blossom, . . . form ever follows function, and this is the law. Where function does not change form does not change."[62] On this basis, and this basis alone, "the shape, form, outward expression, design or whatever we may choose [to call it], of the tall office building should in the very nature of things follow the functions of the building, and that where the function does not change, the form is not to change."[63] Sullivan then rested his case with the following rhetorical flourish:

> Does this not readily, clearly, and conclusively show that the lower one or two stories [of the building] will take on a special character suited to the special needs, that the tiers of typical offices, having the same unchanging function, shall continue in the same unchanging form, and that as to the attic, specific and conclusive as it is in its very nature, its function shall equally be so in force, in significance, in continuity, in conclusiveness of outward expression? From this results, naturally, spontaneously, unwittingly, a three-part division, not from any theory, symbol, or fancied logic.
>
> And thus the design of the tall office building takes its place with all other architectural types made when architecture ...was a living art. Witness the Greek temple, the Gothic cathedral, the medieval fortress.[64]

The references to "the Greek temple," "the Gothic cathedral," and especially "the medieval fortress" suggest that Sullivan had Viollet-le-Duc in mind when making the comparison between the tall office building and those earlier types.[65] Indeed, the very method of rational analysis Sullivan used to define and "solve" the problem stemmed directly from the kind of thinking Viollet-le-Duc had introduced into the world of architectural theory in the 1850s. But Sullivan's conclusions went further than Viollet-le-Duc's in removing the process of design from the grip of historical representation. Where Viollet-le-Duc relied on formal analogy to advance his proposals for dealing with modern materials and contemporary programs and acknowledged that he was intentionally doing what a Gothic architect would have done had the latter come back to practice in the nineteenth century, Sullivan proclaimed for himself a less "handcuffed" and ventriloquistic approach, one that would produce "results, naturally, spontaneously, unwittingly." Having simply complied with the law of nature that "form ever follows function," Sullivan could claim, as he did, that he was merely engaged in a "natural form of utterance"—the "physical language" of the type—in bringing a new species of architecture into the world.[66]

For most of the later history of modern architecture, the phrase "form follows function" (the "ever" is usually left out) has become almost a cliché, a neat formula for describing why anything might look "modern" and not historical or representational. Reyner Banham (1922–1988), in his revisionist (and Eurocentric) *Theory and Design in the First Machine Age* (1960), called it "Louis Sullivan's empty jingle," an outgrowth of "nineteenth-century determinism" that "may have a certain austere nobility, but ... is poverty-stricken symbolically."[67] The dismissal of the symbolic as an inherited set of historical-formal preconceptions was intentional on Sullivan's part. But the purpose, as well as the result, was hardly the elimination of the symbolic as such. If nothing else, it is precisely the symbolic, in the sense of contemporary Symbolist art and literature (in which Sullivan was well versed) that emerges in a building like the Wainwright as the major factor in its dissolution of a clear representational form.[68] As in Symbolist art in general, the emphasis is placed on the formal attributes of the medium, such as line and color, to underscore and carry the essentializing and totalizing cultural meaning of the image. In the Wainwright Building, it is not an image of Gothic pinnacles or rooflines that indicates the loftiness of the building's purpose but rather the emphatically expressed vertical lines overlying and, in effect, sublimating the brutal repetitiveness of the framed block of office windows.[69]

Still, it would be completely wrong to conclude that there is no residue of the representational in the Wainwright Building. At one level, the design is entirely representational, in the sense that its facade is quite simply just that—a facade. The foursquare appearance of the exterior belies the fact

5.34 Wainwright Building. Side and rear facades

that the building is designed on a U-shaped plan that provides for a light court opening onto the rear (see fig. 5.28). The two facades fronting on the intersecting streets are only carried partially around the sides (fig. 5.34). But unlike the Bibliothèque Sainte-Geneviève, where the decorative overlay of the most visible parts of the building is reduced to a minimum at the rear where the corner is turned and the essential underlying structure is maintained (see fig. 4.20), in the Wainwright Building the total decorative treatment is carried around four bays on both side facades before giving way to a completely simplified and basic brick structure, more like a vernacular loft building than an architect-designed one. Clearly, cost was a factor, but the maintenance of a semblance of the building as a continuous block in the observer's perceptual field causes appearances to override realities.

More significant, and more indicative of Sullivan's uneasy engagement with the matter of historical reference, is the explicit triple division of the Wainwright Building into something resembling the traditional base-shaft-capital idea that was seen at the time as an appropriate model for tall buildings.[70] Despite the architect's elaborate rationalization of it in his essay on "The Tall Building," the tripartite composition of the St. Louis design is classical in extremis. It connects the building to a long tradition reaching back from Schinkel and Boullée to Castle Howard and beyond. Indeed, the rationalization that "form ever follows function" should be recognized as a rationalization *as well as a* critique of the use of precedent by someone of a generation that was hardly able to think outside of precedent.

Even Montgomery Schuyler (1843–1914)—arguably the most acute architectural critic of the period and certainly one of Sullivan's most committed supporters—had to acknowledge that in treating "the base and the capital" of the Wainwright Building differently from "the intermediate division, the shaft"—the only unit of the three-part composition expressed "as a confessed [steel] cage coated with fireproof material"—the architect had resorted to a conventional classical concept of masonry construction, which held that the building "must be more solid at the bottom than at the top." In contrast to a true expression of "the steel cage that forms the skeleton of the skyscraper" that would make no visible differentiation "from the ground to the sky line," Sullivan's Wainwright Building, despite the "special stringency" with which it applied the classical formula, had to be judged "provisional and tentative" in its approach to the "new requirements," indeed, "rather an evasion than a solution" of the problem.[71]

Schuyler saw Sullivan's subsequent Guaranty Building in Buffalo (1894–96; fig. 5.35) and Bayard (later Condict) Building in New York (1897–99) (fig. 5.36) as advances in the direction of a more realistic, less representational articulation of the structural and programmatic conditions of the skyscraper type. Of the former building Schuyler wrote: "I know of no steel-framed building in which the metallic construction is more palpably felt through the envelope of baked clay [terra cotta]"; and of the latter: "It is an attempt, and a very serious attempt, to found the architecture of a tall building on the facts of the case. The actual structure is left or, rather, is helped, to tell its own story. This is the thing itself.... Neither the analogy of the column, nor any other tradition or convention, is allowed to interfere with the task of clothing the steel frame in as expressive forms as may be. There is no attempt to simulate the breadth and massiveness proper to masonry in a frame of metal that is merely wrapped in masonry for its own protection."[72]

But even in these two buildings, and despite their suggestion of a direct expression of "the thing itself," Schuyler pointed to the problematic nature of their arcuated terminal features, which "are not forms of metallic architecture [and] ... do not belong to metallic architecture."[73] One can, in fact, see the later buildings as recidivist rather than progressivist. While a direct and logical outcome of the Wainwright Building, the Guaranty turned its predecessor's structurally based grid of vertical and horizontal members into a rather stately, structurally unmotivated ten-story arcade that ends in an Egyptoid cavetto cornice.[74] Coming just slightly later in the sequence of the architect's application of the "pervading law...that form ever follows function," the Bayard Building is articulated by an even more ornate arcade that terminates in a row of early Renaissance–style biforate windows like those in the Rucellai Palace (see fig. I.7).[75] Moreover, this renewal of the representational in the architect's later work was in no way restricted to his tall buildings. In the group of small-town midwestern banks that the architect built in the first two decades of the twentieth century, the reliance on historical precedent became so strong that one can draw fairly close parallels between these works and the more standard productions of traditionalist designers.[76]

5.35 Sullivan, with Adler. Guaranty (later Prudential) Building, Buffalo, 1894–96. Exterior

5.36 Sullivan. Bayard (later Condict) Building, New York, 1897–99. Exterior perspective. From *Architectural Record,* 1899

Still, no matter how much certain aspects of the Bayard Building may resemble the Rucellai Palace or how much Sullivan's banks depended on classical forms for their imagery, there is, as in Viollet-le-Duc's work, an erosion of the descriptive specificity of the historical reference in its modern translation. This results in a kind of abstraction reminiscent of but not quite the same as in the works of Soane and Schinkel. Part of the difference has to do with the impact of the materials and structure on the forms. But it is also very much a matter of intention. Soane and Schinkel were attempting to create a formal synthesis by conscious reference to what certain historical traditions may have shared. Viollet-le-Duc and Sullivan, by contrast, were deliberately attempting to avoid any direct reference to historical forms and to claim that their solutions were simply a response to conditions imposed by the program and by the means and methods of construction. The abstraction in their case was less an epitomization than a deduction.

Both Viollet-le-Duc's notion of design as a form of projective analogy in the perfect conditional of the past and Sullivan's phrase "form ever follows function" suggest that the architect had little choice in the matter of design. However, the ellipsis in "form follows function," which is the way the phrase has most commonly been used since Sullivan, provided the opening for the modern architect to assume a more positive role in producing forms in direct response to materials and needs. The theoretical functionalization of architectural expression that Sullivan introduced thus offered, despite its author's own inability to follow through, a basis for generating and justifying forms without relying on representational forms and practices of the past.

6

Representation without History in the Architecture of Frank Lloyd Wright

FRANK LLOYD WRIGHT FELT strong intellectual and artistic links to both Viollet-le-Duc and Louis Sullivan. In his *Autobiography* (1932) he stated that he had read Viollet-le-Duc's *Dictionnaire raisonné de l'architecture française du XIe au XVIe siècle* (1854–68) while a student and that he considered it "the only really sensible book on architecture in the world." No doubt misremembering it for the *Entretiens* (*Discourses on Architecture*), which had just been published in English translation while he was in high school, Wright went on to say that he "got copies of it later for [his] sons." This was corroborated by John Lloyd Wright, who later recorded that his father gave him the "two volumes ... [of the] *Discourses on Architecture*" with the following advice: "In these two volumes you will find all the architectural schooling you will ever need."[1]

What Wright specifically got from Viollet-le-Duc is difficult to assess, but what he got from Sullivan is clear.[2] The latter was Wright's employer for almost five years, at the most impressionable point in Wright's career, and had a formative influence on him. Wright always referred to Sullivan as his "master," a word he found difficult if not impossible to use for anyone else. Wright began working for Adler and Sullivan in 1888, while the Auditorium Building in Chicago (1886–90) was under construction, and ended up being given major design responsibility for many of the residential projects that came into the office from late 1890 on, when he was appointed chief draftsman. In looking back over his time in the office, he pointed to four of the firm's designs as critical to their reputation. One was the Auditorium Building, which Wright credited in large part to Adler; a second was the Getty Tomb in Chicago's Graceland Cemetery (1890–91), which Wright praised as "a piece of sculpture, a statue, an elegiac poem"; the third was the "superb entertainment" of the temporary Transportation Building at the World's Columbian Exposition in Chicago (1891–93).[3] But it was the Wainwright Building (discussed in the previous chapter) that he considered the most important of all Sullivan's works, and it was the one that had the most profound effect on him during the first fifteen years of his independent practice. Its typological abstraction served him as a compositional model, while its decorated construction gave cause for reconceptualizing the relationship between surface and depth in architecture through the new medium of space.

Wright praised the Wainwright Building as "the master key to the skyscraper" (see fig. 5.26).[4] It defined the new tall building as a "type" through Sullivan's perception of how to make "its height triumphant" in a single "harmonious unit." That, for Wright, was a completely new and eye-opening experience: "When he [Sullivan] brought in the board with the motive of the Wainwright Building outlined in profile and in scheme on it, and threw it down on my table, I was perfectly aware of what had happened.... a new thing beneath the sun... was born."[5] Yet Wright also soon became aware of the design's shortcomings, which turned out to be as important for his own work as its virtues. He later remarked on the "eclecticisms" of the building "conceived ... as still a column," divided into "base, shaft, and capital... with no direct or apparent relation to actual construction." More important, he realized that "the picturesque verticality" of the facade, by means of which Sullivan "emphasize[d] its height, although appropriate, was still a mere facade."[6]

In reaction to the shortcomings he perceived in the Wainwright Building, Wright took upon himself "the task," as he later put it, "of making the countenance of building authentic of structure." Not satisfied with the exterior conceived "in two dimensions only," as in the Wainwright, he sought what he referred to as "the then still-mysterious third dimension." He characterized this rather abstract pursuit of spatial interpenetration in strikingly physical, down-to-earth terms. "I longed to see the thing go through and 'button at the back' [to] become genuinely unitarian," he wrote, "or to come through from within and button at the front would do as well."[7] How he managed this in the context of Sullivan's example and what implications it had for the lingering representationalism of his "master" will constitute the first section of this chapter.

Wright before and after the Wainwright Building, 1889–99

The first building Wright designed on his own and built in the Chicago area after entering Adler and Sullivan's office was a house for himself and his new wife, Catherine (fig. 6.1).[8] Located in the nearby suburb of Oak Park, it was begun in 1889, before the Wainwright Building was conceived, and finished in 1890. It is a small, two-story house, traditional in materials and massing. Both the ground floor, articulated by projecting bays, and the upper floor, composed of an enormous gable, are sheathed in wood shingles. The plan of the ground floor is relatively free, with the stair hall, living room, and dining room opening into one another around the brick mass of the fireplace (fig. 6.2). Placed within an inglenook, with a cautionary motto inscribed above its round-arched opening, this central element creates a symbolic as well as real inner sanctum for the family life revolving around it.

If the interior communicates a feeling of shelter to its inhabitants through the traditional device of the fireplace as hearth, the exterior projects that idea to the outside world through a conventional form of representational imagery. The overriding triangular shape of the gable is set like a classical pediment above a base of bay windows. Although one of the two bays serves as the entrance to the house and the other as a window for the living room, the two are equal in size and shape and support the overhanging gable with a symmetrical sense of gravity. The gable, which dominates the facade, contains a central Palladian window that brought natural light into Wright's original second-floor studio.[9]

Although unusual for its suburban Midwest context as well as rather stark in its interpretation of its sources, Wright's Oak Park house was in no way original from the point of view of formal imagery. As Vincent Scully (b. 1920)

6.1 Frank Lloyd Wright. Wright House (and Studio), Oak Park, Ill., initial construction, 1889–90. Exterior, ca. 1890

6.3 Bruce Price. Chandler House, Tuxedo Park, N.Y., 1885–86. Exterior. From *Architecture,* 1900

6.2 Wright House. Interior. Living room, with stair hall (to right) and original dining room (to left)

has shown, the design was clearly related to recent work in the Shingle Style mode by East Coast architects such as Bruce Price and McKim, Mead and White (firm founded 1879).[10] In moving away from their previous picturesqueness to a more classical discipline and order, these architects turned toward the vernacular Colonial tradition of New England, at times emphasizing the most atavistic aspects of it by bringing everything under a single, dominating gable (fig. 6.3). Wright indirectly acknowledged this source, commenting that neighbors used to ask whether his "funny little house" was "Seaside or Colonial."[11] His blunt, even primitivizing interpretation of the historicist convention not only reveals the representational impetus of his thought; it further suggests that he was well aware of the theory of the natural origin of the classical forms in the mythical primitive hut (see fig. 2.1).[12]

In his first major statement on his early work, the 1908 article "In the Cause of Architecture," published in *Architectural Record,* the leading professional architecture journal in America at the time, Wright made it clear that he understood the theory behind the myth as well as its historical effects. "Primarily," he wrote, "Nature furnished the materials for architectural motifs out of which the architectural forms as we know them to-day have been developed, and, although our practice for centuries has been for the most part to turn from her [nature], seeking inspiration in books and adhering slavishly to dead formulae, her [nature's] wealth of suggestion is inexhaustible." Acknowledging that he recognized "with what suspicion the man is regarded who refers matters of fine art back to Nature," he characterized his early work as "dedicated to a cause conservative" that maintained "a reverential recognition of the elements that made its ancient letter in its time vital and beautiful."[13]

During the years immediately following the completion of his Oak Park house, Wright sometimes took its representational intentions even further in the direction of a full-blown classical revivalism. The Blossom House in Chicago of 1892 and the competition project for the Milwaukee Public Library and Museum of the following year both employ the full gamut of classical elements to provide an imagery appropriate to their different programs, the former a large residence for an upper-middle-class client in the well-to-do Hyde Park neighborhood, the latter a monumental structure to house the major cultural institutions of its state's most populous city (fig. 6.4). In each of these designs, the conventional forms of representation are used without any attempt at dissimulation or abstraction.[14]

But in the first design he executed after leaving the Adler and Sullivan office and opening up his own, the Winslow House in River Forest, Illinois, of 1893–94, Wright set the stage and the parameters for the move away from conventional representation that he would pursue with unrelenting determination and rigor over the next fifteen years.[15] The catalyst for this new direction in his work was the Wainwright Building. Other examples of Wright's reliance on it, such as the All Souls Building (Abraham Lincoln Center) in Chicago of around 1896–1905 (fig. 6.5), designed in association with Dwight Perkins (1867–1941), and the later Larkin Building in Buffalo of 1902–6, are much more overt in terms of their debt to the Sullivan precedent, but the Winslow House is the critical one in the sequence.[16] This has less to do with its primacy than with its profound engagement of Sullivan's concept of typological abstraction and its translation from the commercial and urban context of the tall office building to the domestic and suburban realm of the single-family private house. In the first important publication of Wright's work, reviewing his production

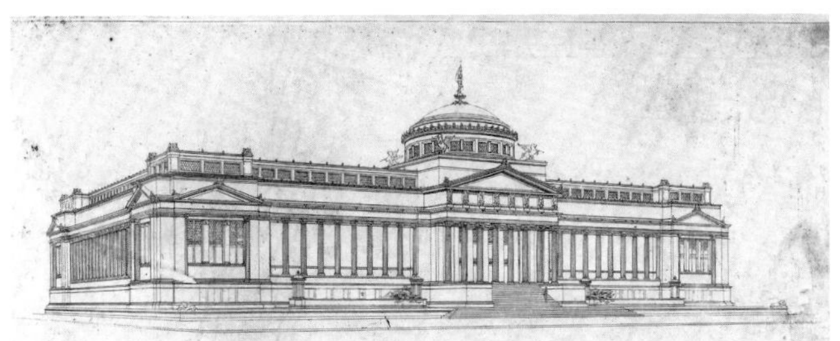

6.4 Wright. Public Library and Museum project, Milwaukee, 1893. Exterior perspective

6.5 Wright (in association with Dwight Perkins). All Souls Building (Abraham Lincoln Center) project, Chicago, ca. 1896–1905. Initial design, 1898–1900. Exterior perspective. From *Architectural Review* (Boston), 1900

6.6 Wright. Winslow House, River Forest, Ill., 1893–94. Entrance facade

up until 1900, the architect's friend and sometime collaborator Robert Spencer (1865–1953) featured the Winslow House, calling it "the broadest, the most characteristic, and the most completely satisfying thing that he [Wright] has done." After comparing the "daring…spirit" of the work to that evinced by Sullivan's tall buildings, Spencer remarked that, far from being coincidental, it had to be understood that the one followed from the other. "Wright," he wrote, "has been doing for the typical residence and apartment house what Sullivan has done for the theatre and office building."[17]

The Winslow House is in almost every way the polar opposite of Wright's own Oak Park house. Set off from the street by a formal terrace and reflecting pool, its central entrance is surrounded by a decorated stone frame that projects out from the main wall plane to highlight the facade's

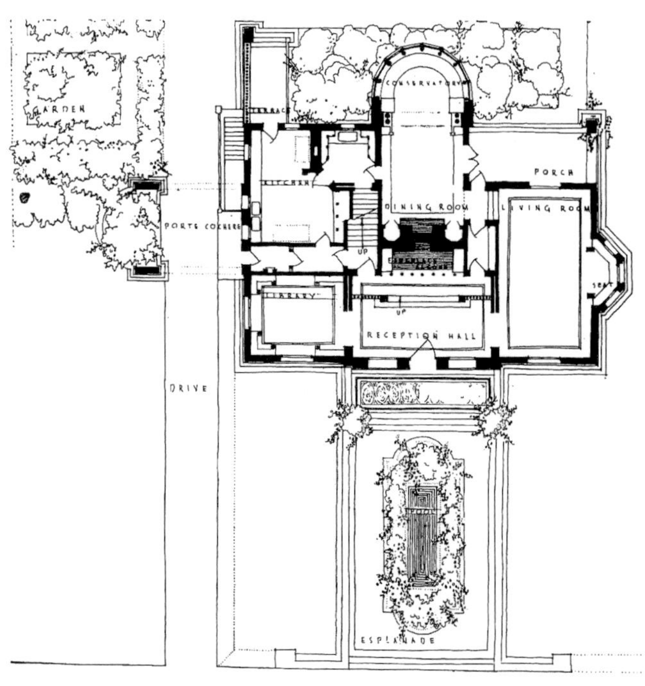

6.7 Winslow House. Plan, first floor (redrawn, ca. 1940)

symmetrical composition (see figs. 6.6–7). The pale, lightly etched surface of the frame contrasts with the tawny-colored Roman brick of the walls of the ground floor as well as with the (now) darker and more richly textured plaster frieze of the second floor. The frieze is thrown into shadow by the deep overhang of the hip roof, which is pinned low in its center by the broad mass of the stone-capped chimney situated directly behind the entrance. Originally planned to include an octagonal pavilion extending into the garden on the right, balancing the porte cochere on the left, the house gives the appearance from the street of a self-contained, freestanding block, classical in its bearing and outlines alone.[18]

Instead of relying on a single representational shape, as in the gable/pediment of the Oak Park house, to contain and carry the meaning of the design, Wright organized the exterior of the Winslow House into a series of horizontal divisions marked by changes in material and corresponding to differences in function. Each area is clearly outlined and related to the others in precisely modulated bands echoing the flat, level expanse of the surrounding prairie landscape. The house rests on a projecting stone water table—like "the stylobate" of an "ancient Greek temple," as Wright later explained—designed to make "the foundation itself visible as a low masonry platform" and thus give the impression that the house lies "comfortably and naturally flat with the ground."[19] Above the line of the water table, the ground floor—containing the more public spaces of the library, reception hall, and living room—is faced with brick that is relieved only in the center by the slightly projected stone frame of the entrance. The brick facing continues above the floor level of the second-story bedrooms to reach the height of the windowsills. There, a change in material, color, and texture occurs. A band of patterned plaster runs around the top of the wall, just under the eaves, to group all the smaller bedroom windows into a continuous frieze. The deep shadow line thus created enables the gently sloping hip roof to appear to float and thus provide, as Wright would later say, a sense of "broad shelter in the open, related to vista." The "quiet skyline" that he believed "natural" to the "quiet level" of the prairie is broken only by the single, massive chimney in the center, which projects an image of domestic warmth as it anchors the building firmly to the site.[20]

The division of the Winslow House into a series of horizontal layers marked by changes in material and expressing differences in function was a direct translation into domestic terms of Sullivan's crypto-classical design of the tall office building (see fig. 5.26). The high ground floor of the public or communal rooms, faced in Roman brick, corresponds to Sullivan's unification of the first and second stories of the Wainwright Building to provide "ample" space for functions of a public nature. Sullivan faced the two lower stories with sandstone ashlar and gave them a broader scale than those above in order to form a solid base for the upper grid of offices. The Winslow House's plaster frieze, integrating the bedroom windows into a single decorative pattern of light and shade, corresponds to the "honey-comb" of "typical offices" that Sullivan treated as an overall grid of interwoven lines of vertical brick piers and horizontal terra-cotta spandrels. Finally, the prominent hip roof of the house corresponds to the attic and projecting cornice of Sullivan's design, capping the structure, as Sullivan would say, with its "completing power and luxuriance."[21]

In the Winslow House, as in the Wainwright Building, the issue of expression is abstracted from the particular to the general to become one of type. As with Sullivan's use of the Wainwright to exemplify the type in his essay on "The Tall Building," Wright formulated a series of "propositions," based on the Winslow House, which he published in his article "In the Cause of Architecture" as the main principles for the design of the Prairie House type.[22] Indeed, Wright always considered the Winslow House to be the first of its type, that is to say, "the first 'prairie house.'"[23] In both Sullivan's and Wright's designs, the emphasis is

6.8 Winslow House. Entrance hall

taken off the associational references of conventional forms and replaced by a synthetic expression of programmatic meaning. Since that meaning differed from one type to the other, so too did its affective-expressive set. The emotional attributes of a suburban house are almost diametrically opposed to those of the urban high-rise, and Wright sought to express the special meaning of suburban domesticity in the Winslow House.

A suburban house, as Wright understood it, had to signify comfort, a sense of belonging, a feeling of privacy—in a word, the idea of shelter. "The horizontal line," he would assert, "is the line of domesticity."[24] On the flat prairie of the Midwest, breadth would be a sign of shelter as height was a sign of power and success in the city. Wright assumed "that *shelter* should be the essential look of any dwelling" because that idea is "probably rooted deep in racial instinct." In his view, only the low horizontal lines that "identify themselves with the ground" and "make the building belong to the ground" offered the sense of "comfort" and "repose" that satisfies the human need for a feeling of belonging.[25]

In the Wainwright Building, as discussed in the previous chapter, the emotional sense of loftiness and vigor of commercial enterprise deemed by Sullivan to be "the chief characteristic" of the tall building was projected through the ascending and descending vertical lines of the structure to make it look "tall, every inch of it tall."[26] In the Winslow House, by contrast, the distinctive and constituent elements of the residential program were synthesized into an image of domesticity expressed in horizontal lines that echo the earth and carry the sense of human warmth, comfort, and security—and thereby endow the house, in Wright's words, with "the sense of 'shelter' in the look of the building."[27] These two different expressive sets were thus achieved by the same means of programmatic abstraction in terms of type.

But there remains a fundamental difference between the two buildings, which has to do with Wright's criticism of the Wainwright Building as a "two-dimensional" solution, a "mere facade." Sullivan admitted that space was not a concern in his design and that the relation between exterior and interior was only metaphoric. "As to the necessary arrangements for light courts," he wrote, "these are not germane to the problem, and...need not be considered here." Nor need "such others as the arrangement of elevators, for example." "Only in rare instances," he concluded, "does the plan or floor arrangement of the tall office building take on an aesthetic value." He did not elaborate on what these might be, other than to speak of the possibility of making "the lighting court" either an external or internal "feature."[28]

From the outset, Wright considered the treatment of interior space crucial and its relation to the exterior an integral aspect of a house's expression of domesticity. The external sign of this link between outside and inside in the Winslow House is the massive, highly visible central chimney, Wright's first such use of the form. It literally and figuratively pins the structure to the earth and establishes the emotional core for the "sense of 'shelter'" as an "instinctual" relation between hearth and home. Where the fireplace in Wright's earlier Oak Park house is a self-contained unit not on any circulation axis (and the chimney is not visually part of the exterior composition), in the Winslow House it is seen directly upon entering and fills the entire field of vision (fig. 6.8). Raised three steps above floor level, on a podium separated from the main flow of space by low balustrades, it expands laterally behind an arcaded screen. Cushioned benches at both ends of this recess might lead one to think of it as an inglenook, but they are so far apart and the area is so open to view that it becomes more like a loggia, providing the interior of the house, at its core, with a space of familial representation and thus transforming the Renaissance prototype from an external to an internal device.[29] Part of the shock of the fireplace-loggia is the immediacy and scale of its presence; the other is its unexpected, even unprecedented representational bearing. There is nothing else so explicitly, or at least so prominently, historicizing in the rest of the house's design, or in the Wainwright Building for that matter.[30] For better or for worse, the device, which he never used again in the same way, served Wright's purpose of giving a significant spatial dimension and role to an element crucial to his formulation of the house type.

The fact that the fireplace is two-sided allows it to function as the central figure in the movement of space through the house and into the garden (see fig. 6.7). Situated in the exact center of the rectangular block, it becomes the design's internal focus and the pivot for its spatial composition. In dividing the front half of the house from the rear, it defines a counterclockwise path that moves through the enfilade of rooms along the front, around the living room on the side, and into the dining room that projects from the rear fireplace into the garden. As the space circles from front to rear, it increasingly becomes an independent force, pushing out from the core to open up the structure and ultimately erode its solidity. The side facade is peeled away from the block, first to contain the expanded space of the living room bay and then to make room for the open porch

6.9 Winslow House. Garden facade (porch later screened in)

in the corner cutout between the living and dining rooms. The garden facade reflects the spatially activated character of the plan at the rear (fig. 6.9). Unlike the closed, planar composition of the entrance facade, it presents an informal grouping of separate volumes that project and recede in depth: on the left, the void of the porch; in the center, the curved bay of the dining room; on the right, the octagonal stair tower cutting through the roof above the pantry; and finally, to the right of it, the freestanding screen wall masking the driveway from the view from the conservatory.

The contrast between the asymmetrical, informal, picturesquely composed garden facade and the symmetrical, strictly formal street facade reflects a real complexity in the domestic program that is not apparent in the schematic formulation of the type presented by the street facade alone. It also reveals the architect's understanding of the need to allow space for the unexpected, the casual, and the unrestrained in the three-dimensional realization of an idea. The two contrasting sides of the Winslow House in effect point to the two conflicting aspects of the reality of the suburban house.[31] The house had to address the street as part of a larger community. It had to be generous and open in this self-presentation, for the midwestern suburban community was by its very nature a coming together of neighborly and generally like-minded individuals. But one of the main purposes in leaving the city was to gain a certain amount of

6.10 Wright. Cheney House, Oak Park, 1903–4. Aerial perspective. From Wright, *Ausgeführte Bauten und Entwürfe von Frank Lloyd Wright,* 1910[–11]

space and privacy for the family, so the house had to clarify the line between the public space of the neighborhood and the private space of the house. And to enable the family to flourish as a group of individuals within its own private domain, the house had to provide for a freedom of movement and activity of various family members both inside the house and out into its garden.[32]

If the street facade of the Winslow House established Wright's modern Prairie House type categorically and unconditionally, it also implied through its implacable formality and irreducible frontality that it masked the many different and often conflicting conditions which the spaces of its interior would disclose. The garden facade was a reaction to these conditions and a reflection of their impact on the unified expression of the type. The disjunction between the front and the rear of the Winslow House thus expresses the complex duality of public and private, of community

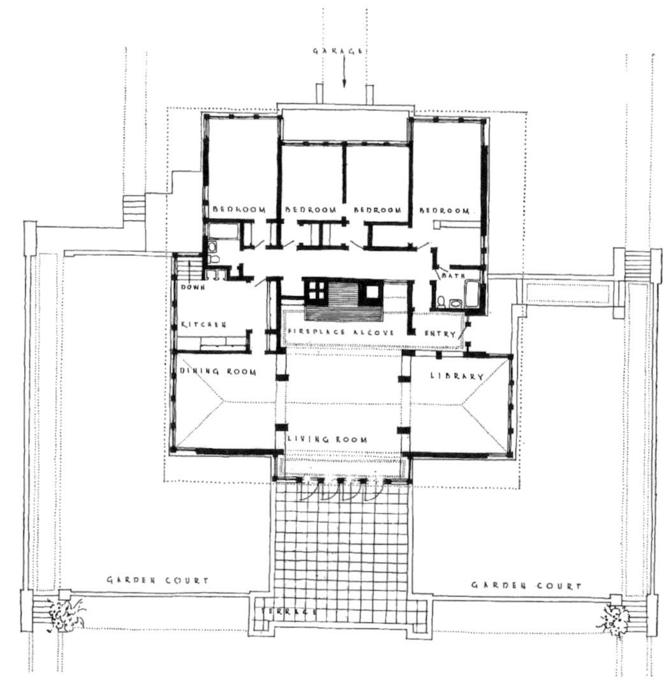

6.11. Cheney House. Plan (redrawn, ca. 1940).

and family, of the group and the individual inherent in the domestic program—but it does so by default, not by design. To achieve a truly unified expression of the type, Wright had to do precisely what he felt Sullivan had not been able to: to make "the thing go through and 'button at the back'" or "to come through from within and button at the front." Either way involved a radical restructuring of the relationship between exterior and interior, of surface and depth, that made three-dimensional space the new framework for architectural expression and the carrier of its meaning.

6.12 Cheney House. Living room, looking toward dining room

Wright on the Cusp of Pure Abstraction, 1900–1910

Wright's architecture remained under the strong influence of Sullivan throughout the decade of the 1890s, and this close reliance on his former employer's formal vocabulary and compositional method clearly constrained his own evolution toward a fully spatial conception of architecture. The retrospective publication in 1900 of Spencer's article "The Work of Frank Lloyd Wright" served as a way of putting a close to the first seven years of the architect's independent practice and ushering in the period during which he created some of his most original, inventive, and historically important work. Between 1900 and 1909, Wright replaced the quasi-classical, often highly decorative Sullivanesque forms with ones having a startling new simplicity and geometric clarity that verged on pure abstraction. This went hand in hand and was in large part the result of his efforts to rework the Prairie House type in terms of its spatial structure. Of the many houses built during the decade, two stand out as exemplary of the way he resolved the contradictory aspects of the Winslow House prototype. The first is the Cheney House in Oak Park of 1903–4, and the second the Robie House in Chicago of 1908–10.

The Cheney House is quite a bit smaller than the Winslow House (fig. 6.10). It is fundamentally a one-story structure set on a raised basement disguised across the front by a terraced embankment.[33] The main floor is divided crosswise by the line of the broad fireplace, which backs onto a corridor linking the four bedrooms and bathroom (fig. 6.11). The front part of the house is treated as a single space, symmetrically subdivided by pairs of open bookshelves into a central living room with dining room and library to either side. The reticulated wood and plaster structure of these freestanding partitions is integral with the visual framing of the walls, onto which the wood strips of the hipped ceiling are brought down (fig. 6.12).

The main volume of space is defined in its long direction by the continuous, tentlike ceiling. The central section of the living room broadens into another volume crossing it at right angles. Kept to the height of the freestanding screens, its decklike ceilings reinforce the intimate, human scale. On one side, this lower space burrows deep into the core of the house to incorporate the fireplace alcove; opposite the fireplace, it extends toward the street and into the light to open into a continuous screen of French doors leading onto a terrace surrounded by a low brick wall.

The Cheney House is thus an abstracted, exploded version of the Winslow House (see fig. 6.6). The stone frame of the central entrance of the earlier design is pulled out from the block to form the terrace's front wall; the planes of Roman brick to either side of the Winslow doorway become the walls of the garden courts; the plaster frieze under the eaves is fragmented into bands of windows alternating with recessed brick panels; and the heavyset hip roof of the Winslow House is reduced to a thin canopy, seemingly suspended from the thick mast of the central chimney projecting through it. What was once a solid wall combining the functions of support, enclosure, and penetration in the Winslow House has been separated into three different elements (and planes) discretely performing three different functions, while the earlier, homogeneous system of support has been dissected into a composite structure of piers and planes riven by space.

In the Cheney House, each of the conventional elements of the Winslow House—roof, wall, corner pier, chimney, door, window, frieze—has been separated from the others to allow it to stand on its own, without direct connection to the traditional mass of the building still evident in the earlier design. As the door frame of the Winslow House is pulled out to become the garden parapet wall at the Cheney House, and its roof plane is made to float above the continuous window band at the later house, the geometric shape and order of the elements come to dominate their inherent representational function and thus force a much more complex reading than before. It is not that the traditional representational character of those elements is entirely forsaken; it is just that the extent of their abstraction has resulted in a degree of openness and transparency so unprecedented that one focuses on the new sense of space rather than the structure that creates it. They neither represent, in Laugier's terms, the "parts which are essential to the composition of an architectural order," nor can they be read, as in the Winslow House, as "those which have been introduced by necessity."[34]

All this is most evident inside the Cheney House. The main volume, which constitutes the house's entire public area, is difficult if not impossible to perceive as three separate rooms. It is clearly one continuous space. Moreover, it is a space that appears to be unconfined, flowing through the structure and even expanding beyond its boundaries. The most obvious cause of this effect is the decorative trim of wood stripping that articulates the plaster ceiling and upper edge of the walls. These strips parallel the lines of the ceiling rafters and could thus be read as structurally rational and expressive. But unlike the Wainwright Building's design, where only half the brick piers reflect the underlying steel frame while the other half are there simply to reinforce the expression of structure, here the applied wood strips are more sparse than the rafters above them and laid out on a different system in order to emphasize the role of the ceiling as a spatial envelope.[35] In addition, and surely most important, is the fact that the strips are brought down onto the vertical plane of the wall without any molding marking the intervening horizontal joint. As a result, the ceiling appears to lift above the wall's lower plane, allowing the space to expand beyond the confines of the room. At the far corners, the impression of expanding space is magnified horizontally by the way in which the stripping creates the effect of an open corner (fig. 6.13). Needless to say, the ridgepole of the roof is not revealed nor is the structural ridge of the hip itself expressed.

Space takes precedence over structure in the Cheney House with two extremely significant consequences: the first has to do with Wright's resolution of the disjunctive aspect of the Winslow House and the second with the problem of representation in general. The creation of an interior space, active and positive in its own right rather than merely the result of structural conditions, gave Wright the means to open up the interior to the exterior and let it "come through from within and button at the front." In effect, the solid front of the Winslow House is invaded from within by the spaces that projected through its publicly invisible rear. The street facade of the Cheney House, with its protruding

6.13 Cheney House. Library, detail of corner

terrace and floating roof line, is at once open and closed, solid and void, plane and depth, formal and picturesque. It combines and integrates the two sides of its prototype in an integrated, three-dimensional expression of the public and the private. Both are brought out into the open at the same time, finding shelter and connection in the space the house shares with the street.

The new understanding of architecture as space, which the German architectural historian August Schmarsow had first theorized only ten years previously, had a corrosive effect on the representational forms of the building as well.[36] There are no traditional decorative details in the Cheney House as there are in the Winslow House—witness the earlier building's carved door frame, foliated window frieze, and especially the columns and capitals of the arcade that screen the fireplace. In the later house, the piers of the freestanding bookcases that support the deck running across the living space, for instance, are treated simply as banding frames, without capitals to indicate a structural function or juncture. Most important and obvious throughout is that all the stripping and banding are made up of pieces of flat, square stock trim, geometric in form and devoid of molded edges that might represent structural connections. At the basis of the neoclassical theory of representation that proposed the primitive hut as the model for the Greek temple lay the technique of carpentry, whose joints were translated into the masonry forms of the orders. In eliminating nearly all evidence of such transitional accommodations, the trim in the Cheney House makes it clear that an abstract geometry of line and plane is the logical result of the process of thinking in terms of space.

But if the case for such an argument can only be made inferentially in the Cheney House, Unity Temple, which Wright designed soon after the house was finished, offers positive proof of the corrosive impact of spatial thinking on traditional representational form. Designed in 1905–6 for the Unitarian Universalist congregation of Oak Park and completed in 1908, Unity Temple was, in Wright's own estimation, the building in which his conception of architecture as space found its most complete expression in the early years of his career (figs. 6.14–15).[37] In the main auditorium, a grid defined by the square pattern of skylights and made manifest in the clerestory windows, hanging light fixtures, and corner stair towers establishes an abstract, latticelike framework. The wood stripping on the cream-colored plaster dematerializes the surfaces and thus overrides any conceivable structural reference or reading.

The key is the treatment of the corner tower elements. In a preliminary sketch (fig. 6.16), these read like piers terminating in emphatic capitals, rigidly coursed in deep

6.14 Wright. Unity Temple, Oak Park, 1905–8. Interior. Auditorium

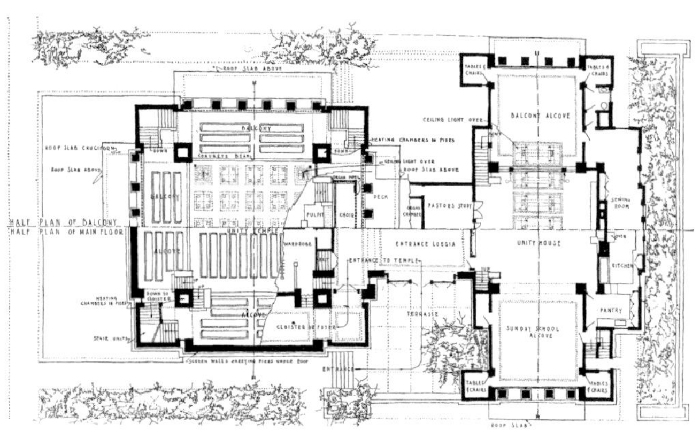

6.15 Unity Temple. Plan, multilevel (redrawn, ca. 1940)

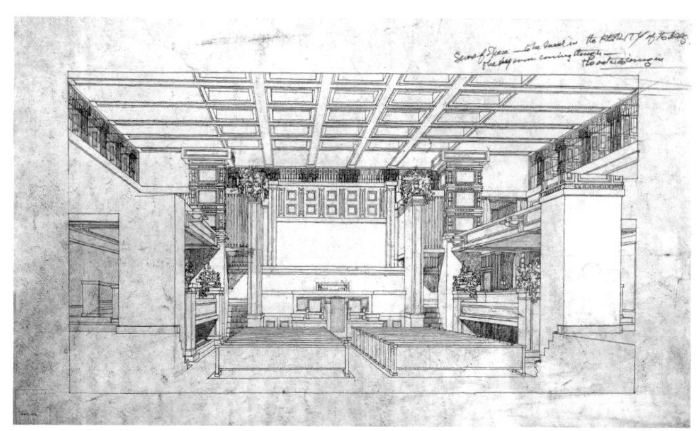

6.16 Unity Temple. Auditorium. Preliminary interior perspective

horizontal bands and topped by a wide echinus, similar to those used in the Larkin Building following the Sullivan model (fig. 6.17; see fig. 5.29). In the final version, however, Wright eliminated this reference to traditional tectonic imagery by suppressing the relation between load and support. The stair enclosure is simply articulated by a paneled frame that bends around the corner, denying a structural significance to that stiffening edge and turning the form into a weightless plane (fig. 6.18). At the juncture with the ceiling, the moldings on the vestigial echinus block spread apart before meeting at the corner, connecting the vertical element of the tower with the overhead plane of the skylights. From within the well of the corner skylight, thin vertical members drop down into the room's space to support lights, which in the earlier scheme had projected from the face of the upper balconies (fig. 6.19). The spatial grid itself is thus made palpable by the lines of force moving through it.

Nothing appears solid in the space of Unity Temple. The eye is never arrested by a structural joint or connection. The plastic lines of decorative stripping that articulate the space dominate and cause the overlapping planes to appear to float above and behind one another in a general expansion outward of space from within. Foreground and background interpenetrate. Space bends around corners. Verticals and horizontals intertwine. Most important for our discussion, distinctions between decoration and construction become moot. The applied decorative strips and bands clearly do not constitute a virtual and independent structural system and therefore can in no way be described as constructed decoration. On the other hand, they do not function as a form of decorated construction in the way Pugin, Labrouste, Viollet-le-Duc, or Sullivan would have understood. They neither reveal, emphasize, nor express the actual facts of construction. On the contrary, they create, with the surfaces to which they adhere, a unified nonrepresentational field where the very distinction between construction and decoration is canceled out.[38]

6.17 Wright. Larkin Building, Buffalo, 1902–6. Interior. From Wright, "In the Cause of Architecture," *Architectural Record,* 1908

6.18 Unity Temple. Auditorium. Corner stair tower

6.19 Unity Temple. Auditorium. View from upper balcony

6.20 Unity Temple. Exterior. Upper part of facade

As nonrepresentational as Unity Temple might seem when analyzed in terms of its radical spatial composition, the abstraction is in no way total. A critical tension exists in the work between the solvent action of space and an underlying memory of traditional forms and figures of representation. Unity Temple is in fact organized on a Greek cross plan deriving from the same Byzantine tradition as Soufflot's Church of Sainte-Geneviève (compare figs. 6.15 and 2.16). Wright himself stated that the building represented in this regard "a frank revival of the old temple form."[39] Perhaps the most prominent instance of representational imagery is the external pilastrade supporting the cantilevered roof over the clerestory windows in the arms of the Greek cross (fig. 6.20). Recalling in general terms the Sullivanesque piers the architect rejected for the interior, these tall capitals, based on a conventionalization of hanging ivy, perform a traditional structural role as elements in the church's public facade.[40]

The tension between abstraction and representation in Unity Temple pervades all of Wright's buildings of the period and is even more visible in his private houses than in buildings designed for institutional and commercial purposes. This is perhaps to be expected, given the fundamentally conventional idea of shelter Wright attributed to the domestic program, not to speak of the demands and expectations private clients would have had for their homes. Not only can the Robie House be considered the final outcome of the process of typological synthesis begun in the Winslow House and laid bare in the Cheney House; it also reveals through its powerful presence the full artistic import of the equation between abstraction and representation Wright had achieved by the end of the first decade of the twentieth century. Begun in 1908, at the time Unity Temple was being finished, it was completed in 1910 (fig. 6.21).[41]

The three-story brick and stone house is low to the ground yet deeply undercut with shadowed voids that cause it to appear buoyant, spacious, and open. The abstraction of parts into type elements and the extremely broad scale of their elaboration produce a highly generalized image of shelter-as-such, what Wright liked to think of as an "umbrageous architecture."[42] All is seemingly reduced to roofs suspended above volumes screened and faced by protective planes and kept in check by a massive chimney. No entrance is visible, no ground floor as such, nor anything much more than one long volume with a rooftop aerie clinging to the chimney.

In a significant sense the house is in effect a single space stretched out in both directions from a central hearth to form a continuous living and dining room above the plinth of a raised basement (fig. 6.22). The interior of this space opens onto the street in a balcony that runs along the entire southern exposure and becomes a porch at the corner

6.21 Wright. Robie House, Chicago, 1908–10. Exterior, from southwest

(fig. 6.23). These liminal spaces are girded by staggered brick parapets and bridges floating just below the overhanging cantilevered roofs. In the continuity of its living/dining space, the Robie House carries the Cheney House paradigm to an extreme. Instead of forming a solid wall from floor to ceiling, the two-sided fireplace in the Robie House is sunk into the floor to create a sense of vertical continuity and opened at the top to allow the space to flow through from one end of the house to the other (fig. 6.24). At each end, the space projects beyond in diagonally set bays articulated by pairs of staggered, inset piers (fig. 6.25). These define slots of space to either side of the prow and thereby increase the illusion of depth and sense of freedom of movement. Throughout, the wide bands and narrower strips of flat oak work to transform the actual structural components into floating, bending, and folded planes and panels.

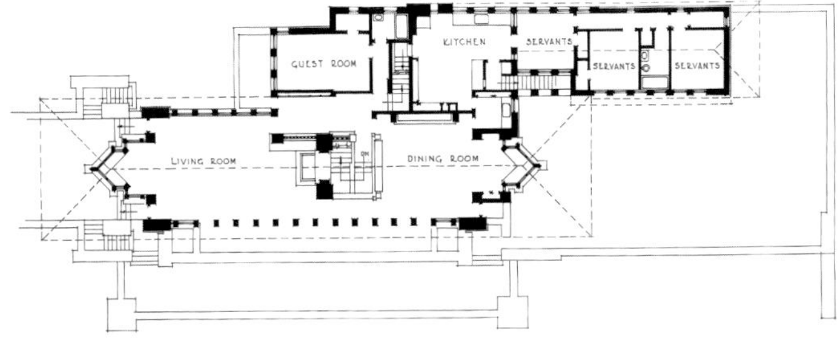

6.22 Robie House. Plan, second floor (redrawn, ca. 1940)

The only element in the house's main space that seems solid and anchored to the earth is the enormous, H-shaped central fireplace. Sunk into the floor and cut through at the top, it appears to rise uninterrupted from the ground through the ceiling and roof. On the interior, it provides an element of rootedness and permanency that underscores the openness and indeterminacy of the space. On the exterior, it provides the vertical axis of stability that counteracts the outspread, floating, and seemingly unsupported planes of the roof. As an isolated, autonomous source of strength and focus, the fireplace/chimney brings to the representational imagery of the Prairie House a compelling and nearly overwhelming aspect of abstraction. Yet it continues to read as a representational figure of the most meaningful sort, combining with the overhanging roofs to instantiate the "sense of 'shelter' in the look of the building."

The tension between abstraction and representation in Wright's work between 1900 and 1910 involved a radical restructuring of the language of architectural representation comparable to the invention of Cubism in painting at precisely the same time by Pablo Picasso (1881–1973) and Georges Braque (1882–1963).[43] Within the traditional framework of the house type, Wright dissected and pulled apart the planes, fracturing the image and opening it up to a freedom of space and ambiguity of relationships that was quintessentially modern. In the Robie and Cheney houses, as in Picasso's contemporaneous portraits, the conventional image of house or person is broken down into a series of intersecting, overlapping, and nearly autonomous planes (compare figs. 6.23 and 6.26). Where a molding would traditionally define the shape of a window or the boundary between wall and ceiling—just as the contour of a cheek or the brim of a hat might distinguish those forms from the background against which they are seen—planes now overlap in shallow depth to create ambiguous geometric shapes in constantly shifting patterns.[44] The elision of windows and walls creates "window walls," while the incorporation

6.23 Robie House. Exterior. Detail of west end

6.24 Robie House. Living room, looking east to fireplace, 1910

6.25 Robie House. Living room, looking west to porch, 1910

6.26 Pablo Picasso. *Portrait of Wilhelm Uhde,* 1910

of porches within the spatial framework of the house denies normal distinctions between figure and ground, thus turning the house inside out. Although the presence of such indices of representation as roof or chimney—like the eyes or mouth in a Cubist painting—continues to allow conventional readings, the oscillating relations of the parts sets up a tension between the poles of abstraction and representation that is more extreme and of a categorically different nature than had previously existed. The image, while rooted in memory, seems to exist in an autonomous space of its own—not quite an illusion, but not quite a denial of it either.

The reification of space in Wright's architecture of this period provided a solvent and unstable ground for representation. Later, the art critic Clement Greenberg (1901–1994) would coin the phrase "homeless representation" to describe the modern predicament, brought on by Cubism, of wanting to retain the figures of representation while no longer accepting the premodern conditions of illusionistic, perspectival space.[45] Similarly, Wright's space dissolved the structural ground of architectural representation in an ambiguous and shifting environment of lines and planes defining and delimiting space. In this nontraditional, nonperspectival space, a sense of shelter was produced by the abstract means of protective cover, envelopment, and rootedness, but these were given the conventional outlines of roof, window wall, and fireplace to prevent the image of shelter from becoming too diffuse. Like Picasso, Wright would have a long and varied career after this initial, revolutionary moment, but also like Picasso, he would never give up the tug of representation in favor of a purely geometric abstraction.

Taliesin and the Direct Imitation of Nature

By 1909 Wright concluded that his work had reached an impasse, a "dead wall" as he put it, and that he needed to take a break from the routine in which he found himself.[46] For both professional and personal reasons, he abandoned his Oak Park practice and spent a year in Europe. Not long after he returned, he made a life-changing decision to leave the Chicago area for good and move to the country. In the spring of 1911, he began building the house and studio in south central Wisconsin to which he gave the Welsh name Taliesin. He moved there permanently in late December as the house was nearing completion. This building marked a crucial shift in his thinking about architectural representation and became the foundation for his later career.[47]

Almost all the architect's work prior to this moment had been designed for urban or suburban lots generated by the abstract grid of Chicago. The orthogonal structure of that grid more often than not was reified in the buildings' plans and details. With Taliesin, Wright deliberately started from another base. Not only did he build deep in the countryside, in a river valley in a rolling landscape where his family had settled in the previous century; he also specifically chose a

6.27 Wright. Taliesin (Wright House and Studio), Hillside, Wis., begun 1911. Court, looking southeast, from stable bridge to living wing, ca. 1912

low hill overlooking the Wisconsin River that he had loved as a boy when visiting and working on his uncle's farm. In his *Autobiography*, he compared the liberating sense of space and vista the hill afforded to the experience of looking down to earth from an airplane: "When you are on its crown you are out in mid-air as though swinging in a plane, as the Valley and two others drop away leaving the tree-tops all about you."[48] In Wright's thinking, the hill came first and the house and studio had to accommodate to it.

Wright sited Taliesin to take advantage of the vista, without compromising the integrity of the hill by building on top of it. He wrapped the three wings of the complex around its sides, well below its crown, to make the house, as he later wrote, "a 'shining brow' for the hill" (the word Taliesin means "shining brow" in Welsh) (figs. 6.27–28).[49] Following the contours of the hill, the building forms an enclosed, loosely U-shaped court embracing it. The wing devoted to the living quarters is connected to the studio by a loggia and terrace, which provide access to both units while offering a view of the river between them. The longer studio wing extends into a stable and farm wing that terminates the complex with a bridge over the driveway and a belvedere tower tucked behind the hill crown (fig. 6.29).

The hill is a constant presence in the experience of the house. The belvedere tower indicates the deepest penetration of the house into the hill and can thus be read as an

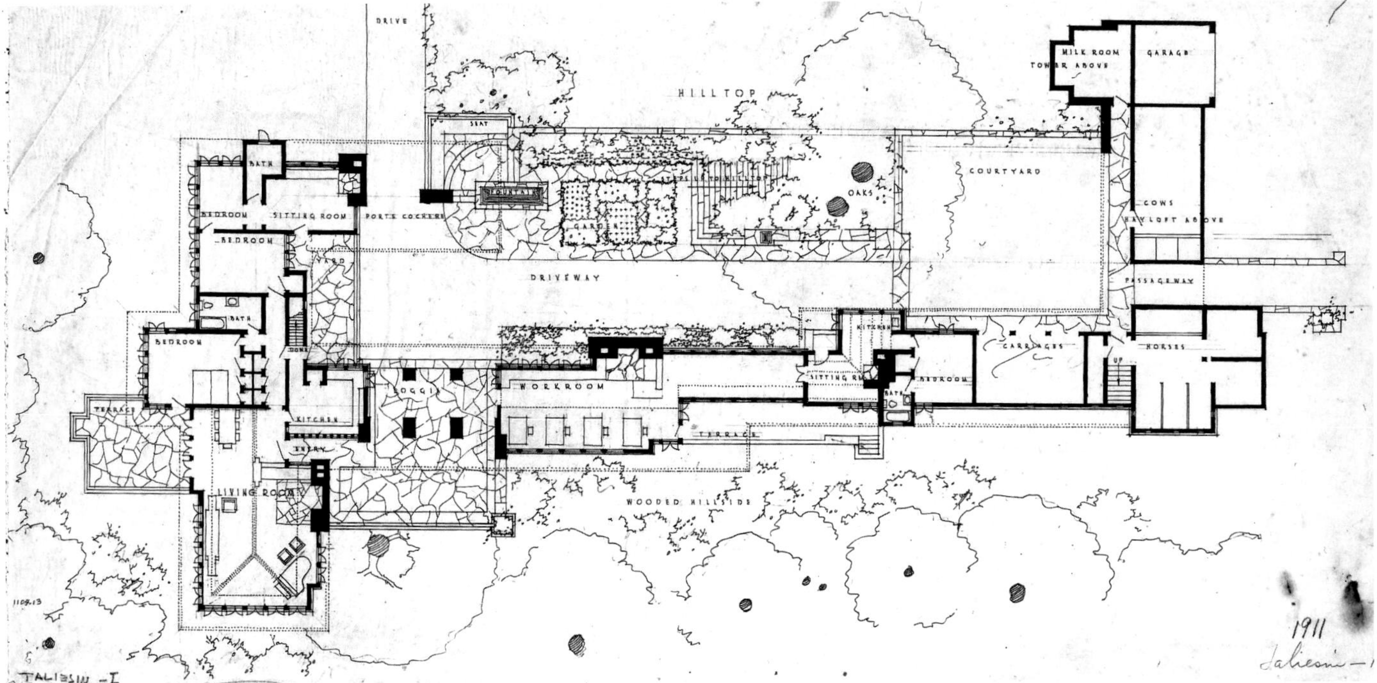

6.28 Taliesin. Plan, 1911 (redrawn, ca. 1940)

eccentric vertical axis staking the building to the site. From it, the house unwinds in a spiraling, clockwise direction around the hill and out to the porte cochere at the entrance. Instead of revolving around an internal and conventional element like the fireplace core of the earlier Prairie Houses, Taliesin takes its direction from an external, natural feature of the landscape. This intimate connection to the landscape determines all aspects of the plan and its material realization in three dimensions.

The plan has none of the self-reflexive, abstract formality of the Cheney and Robie houses. Nor does its disjointed, accidental appearance have anything to do with what occurs on the rear of the Winslow House. Taliesin's plan is not a reaction to the grid; rather, it is a contingency of the natural contours of the hill and of the hill's relationship to the river valley below. There is no obvious geometric order in the overall grouping of the parts, nor is there any symmetry in the individual parts themselves. Each wing is loosely organized in and of itself and joined to the next in a pattern meandering around the hill. Forsaking the rigid orthogonal plaiting and interweaving of rectilinear elements that characterized even the most open of his houses of the previous decade, Wright turned to diagonal axes as a way to approximate more closely nature's path and thus accommodate the building to its site.[50] Almost all the rooms are connected to one other and entered at their corners. The lines of sight thus carry diagonally from room to room to

6.29 Taliesin. Aerial perspective, ca. 1912

6.30 Taliesin. Interior. Living room, later 1930s

emphasize the sense of space. Above all, Wright used these diagonal axes to extend the views beyond the confines of the house, to relate interior to exterior in unexpected and unmediated ways.

The sense of oneness with the landscape is most fully expressed in the commanding diagonal view from the living room over the valley and river below (fig. 6.30). The rectangular living room, which is entered from the corner of the courtyard, occupies the angle between the loggia and the dining terrace.[51] Its diagonal axis is the resultant of their perpendicular spatial directions. From inside the loggia, there is a preliminary view of the valley and river just over the parapet of the terrace (fig. 6.31). But before coming out into the open, you turned ninety degrees to the right. Through the Dutch door leading into the living room, there was a second vista, across the dining table and terrace and up the valley toward the family chapel and hills behind it. A large fireplace and bookshelf seat block the view to the left. In forcing you to go around them before being able to look down the length of the living room, this corner element powerfully defines the implied diagonal axis of the space; at the same time, the inset, notched corner, and diagonally placed piano at the far end of the fireplace wall reinforce the spatial twist.

Once you come around the bookshelf and are positioned in front of the fireplace, the view opens into a 180-degree arc. It cuts across the room and over the hills in a single, effortless movement that seems to follow the curve of the earth, just as the stone fireplace to the rear, diagonally opposite the far corner window, anchors the vista in the hill behind. The catercornered placement of these two points of reference helps give the impression of shearing along the diagonal; and, with the planes of the hip ceiling spreading above and the floor sliding out toward the light, you have the boundless sense of being outside, in the center of things, in a space turned inside out. It is as if Wright had been able to re-create indoors that boyhood experience on the hill of feeling "out in mid-air as though swinging in a plane."

The living room's diagonal shear traces the axis from the hill to the bend in the river. The rough stone fireplace momentarily stands in for the hill crown as the center of an arch sweeping across the landscape. Taliesin is thus not to be "looked at" as much as it is to be "looked from." It is more akin to a natural outlook than a house. This feature, as much as anything else, differentiates it from Wright's previous houses. In those quintessentially suburban structures, he concentrated on the self-contained form of the house to create "a sense of 'shelter' in the look of the building." The Prairie Houses are all distinctly imageable. A single view can and does contain the meaning of the Robie House or Cheney House, and Wright believed it was possible to record this meaning in the perspectives he produced of these buildings (see fig. 6.10). There is no perspective of Taliesin, however, other than the one drawn from above and behind it, looking through it, so to speak, from the hill and over the valley (see fig. 6.29). There are no photographs of the building from the "outside"—that is, from the valley—that are either intelligible or truly memorable. The views of the "inside"—the court—are in essence views of or from the hill. What we remember about Taliesin is the way it embraces the hill to afford views of the natural world of which it is merely a part.

6.31 Taliesin. Loggia, with door to living room on right and studio to left, ca. 1912

6.32 Taliesin. Original entrance. From *Architectural Record,* 1915

Taliesin is thus an incident in the landscape, and its system of order is not independent of nature. In no previous building had Wright so utterly disconnected one section from another as he did at Taliesin by inserting the open loggia between the living and studio wings. It allows the hill literally to pass through the house. Taliesin only seems asymmetrical and disjunctive when it is considered out of context, for it is the hill that completes the house and makes the marriage of architecture and nature an affair of mutual interdependence. The typical Prairie House always asserts its own limits and edges so as to condense the image of the landscape in itself. In Taliesin, the line between building and landscape is deliberately blurred, so that it would not be "easy," as Wright said, "to tell where pavements and walls left off and ground began."[52]

Materials ultimately came to substantiate the new form of direct imitation of nature that Taliesin makes manifest. In contrast to the machinelike quality they took in Wright's houses prior to Taliesin and the recessive, generalizing role they assume in those designs, the materials in Taliesin have a primary part to play in representing the building's informality and intimacy with its site. Piers, chimneys, parapets, and lower walls are all built of limestone quarried just a mile away; intervening wall surfaces are roughly stuccoed with plaster made of the yellowish sand from the banks of the Wisconsin River; and the complex, multilevel roof is covered with weathered cedar shingles (fig. 6.32). Taliesin looks "homemade," as Wright wrote, "made out of the rocks and trees of the region" so as to be "part of the hill on which it stands."[53] The stonework in particular looks raw. It is quarry-faced and set in a pattern of randomly projecting blocks, producing a knobby, textured surface. By comparison with the earlier houses, the materials here display an undisguised naturalness.

Although the hip roofs, freestanding piers, and paneled planes remind one of his earlier work, these forms are so transfigured through their material realization that Wright could accurately claim that they imitate directly the appearance of nature. In one of the most significant passages describing Taliesin in his *Autobiography,* the architect stated that

> Taliesin was to be a combination of stone and wood as they met in the aspect of the hills around about. The lines of the hills were the lines of the roofs. The slopes of the hills their slopes, the plastered surfaces of the light wood-walls, set back into shade beneath broad eaves, were like the flat stretches of sand in the river

6.33 Taliesin. View from lake below, late 1950s

> below and the same in color, for that is where the material that covered them came from.
>
> The finished wood outside was the color of gray tree-trunks, in violet light.
>
> The shingles of the roof surfaces were left to weather, silver-gray like the tree branches spreading below them.[54]

Wright wanted the house literally to look like the hillside—to "belong to that hill, as trees and the rock ledges did."[55] Taliesin was to be an extrusion of its site, homologous with it in materials, structure, and surface. The horizontal lines and low-slung forms of the Prairie House paralleled the lines and forms of the prairie in an abstract way, but the representational elements of the house type predominated. Its image was bounded by the conventions of base, pier, chimney, and roof. The result was a house *on* the prairie, and the word "prairie" qualified the word "house." The building always remained a representational figure abstracted from its ground. In Taliesin, Wright worked to the opposite end. The house was to be "part" of the "countenance" of the landscape first, and a house second.[56] It was to be seen not as something added to the landscape but as continuous with it. Nature—the hill—came first, and was modified to become a house. The role of abstraction was not to counter but to reinforce that of representation.

A major difference between the Cheney House, for instance, and Taliesin lies in a change in the scale of representation. This was achieved through a completely new relation between material and image, which paralleled

Picasso's development of Synthetic Cubism around 1912. What had been limited to the scale of the part in the more literally naturalistic aspects of the Prairie Houses, such as the patterns of the leaded-glass windows, was now expanded to the shape of the whole. What had more often than not been a matter of decoration now became an aspect of construction. To ensure an illusion of continuity between figure and ground, Wright made the skin of the house look like the skin of the surrounding landscape. He wrote that he "scanned the hills of the region where the rock came cropping out in strata to suggest buildings" and took the structure and appearance of these "outcropping ledges in the facades of the hills" as the model for the house's stonework. He directed the masons to imitate the "pattern" of the rough ledges exposed in the quarry on the hill just to the northwest.[57] Banding the face of the hill in a series of horizontal layers, Taliesin thus became a "brow for the hill," in the image of a natural outcrop (fig. 6.33).

The illusion of equivalency with nature is only an illusion, however, and this must be kept in mind when assessing both the significance and the modernity of Taliesin. Taliesin does not in fact look like an actual rock outcrop, nor did Wright ever intend such a literal reading. Although one can trace the romantic naturalism of his thought back to John Ruskin (1819–1900), in whose writings he was well-versed, there is absolutely nothing descriptive or illustrative about the building. There are no naturalistic details, no sentimental concessions to local charm. Nor does Taliesin's naturalism have anything in common with late nineteenth-century tendencies toward primitivism, as expressed in the work of Henry Hobson Richardson, Antoni Gaudí (1852–1926), or Bernard Maybeck (1862–1957). In Richardson's Ames Gate Lodge at North Easton, Massachusetts (1880–81), to take just one example, small boulders and rocks are mounded to create a gigantic rubble construction resembling an antediluvian abode (fig. 6.34).

6.34 Henry Hobson Richardson. Ames Gate Lodge, North Easton, Mass., 1880–81. Exterior. From *Monographs of American Architecture*, vol. 3, *The Ames Memorial Building[s], North Easton, Mass., H. H. Richardson, Architect,* 1886

The texture, which overrides and contradicts the building's tectonic structure, produces a decorative surface that makes the design primitivistic in a Mannerist sense, going back at least to Giulio Romano (ca. 1499–1546), and thus understandable within the traditional category of the rustic mode.

The naturalism and primitivism of Taliesin are of another order, and a completely twentieth-century one at that. The relation between figure and ground that previously had been transmitted through conventional forms and signs is now conveyed directly through the abstract shapes of the materials themselves. This abstraction involves a progressive distinction between form and content, a disengagement of the shapes taken by materials from their traditional representational roles. In Richardson's work, as in Gaudí's, Maybeck's, and Wright's own prior to Taliesin, the materials are transparent as regards content and are subject to the general figure they are meant to form. In Taliesin, by contrast, the stone piers and parapets, the plaster wall planes, and the shingled roofs are primarily experienced as autonomous, physical presences, shapes disengaged from their normal figurative role (see fig. 6.32).

6.35 Picasso. *Student with a Newspaper*, 1913

They are, in that regard, much like the shapes Picasso employed in his contemporaneous collages and Synthetic Cubist paintings: shapes completely abstract in outline yet often either cut out of materials like wallpaper or oilcloth or painted to imitate their textures and designs in a most literal way (fig. 6.35). As these discrete shapes coalesce into the image of a person or thing on the plane of the supporting canvas, Picasso's revolutionary method of collage, especially as translated into Synthetic Cubism, confirmed the possibility for representation outside the limits of traditional illusionism. Similarly, in Taliesin the stone laid up in strata on the pattern of the surrounding outcrops, by virtue of its own material reality, forces us to read the building, as a whole, as a natural extension of the hillside. Paradoxically, the denial of the traditional transparency of material that was characteristic of Renaissance and post-Renaissance art and architecture makes the representation contiguous with its physical ground and therefore convincingly readable as a single gestalt.

Taliesin removed Wright's architecture from the functionalist concern for typological expression and showed the way in which the spatial implications of his previous work could be fulfilled in a more complex synthesis of architecture and nature. Wright wanted Taliesin to extend the representational possibilities for architecture from the individual building to its relation with the natural world. In expanding the role of representation from an almost exclusive concern with the part to a focus on the whole, and in switching the emphasis from the figure to the relation of figure to ground, Wright made Taliesin an outgrowth of its natural surroundings. As the outlines of the building became blurred with those of the landscape, the imitation of nature in Taliesin assumed a directness and immediacy of effect that could no longer be referenced to history. It thus brought into being a concept of representation without history—a century and a half after Laugier had made the link between nature and history the sine qua non of representation in architecture, and following a period of about half as long during which that link had dissolved in favor of a reliance on history alone.

Nature in Action at Fallingwater

Over the years, Wright made constant changes to Taliesin—for aesthetic as well as practical reasons—and rebuilt it twice after devastating fires. But it remained in a conceptual sense a static representation of nature. During the 1920s, however, Wright became interested in imitating the dynamic effects of nature as it evolves and changes over time. The project he proposed for a winter retreat for Albert M. Johnson in Death Valley in 1924–25 was the first example of this; it was followed at the end of the decade by the San Marcos in the Desert Hotel project of 1928–29 for the South Phoenix (formerly Salt River) Mountains.[58] Both attempted

6.36 Wright. Fallingwater (Kaufmann House), Mill Run, Pa., 1934–37. Exterior. View from below falls

to represent the effects of natural growth and erosion in built form. The most important of Wright's efforts in this regard, as well as the most significant from the point of view of modern architectural history, is the weekend house he built for the Kaufmann family in the middle of the following decade (1934–37). He named the house Fallingwater, after the site's most prominent natural feature and in recognition of the building's dynamic identification with it (fig. 6.36).[59]

The extensive property the Kaufmanns owned in the southwestern corner of Pennsylvania follows the winding and precipitous course of a mountain stream, Bear Run, which works its way down through the sandstone cliffs of an old glacial ravine, falling nearly 1,500 feet in four miles before emptying into the Youghiogheny River. About half a mile before it reaches the river, it drops in a series of dramatic falls over large boulders strewn in its bed. This is the place Edgar Kaufmann had in mind for the house, and it is where he took his architect in late 1934. According to reports, he had thought Wright would site the structure on the flat, lower bank of the stream facing the waterfalls. To his client's surprise, and later consternation, Wright decided to locate the house over the water by cantilevering it from

6.37 Fallingwater. Exterior. Entrance side

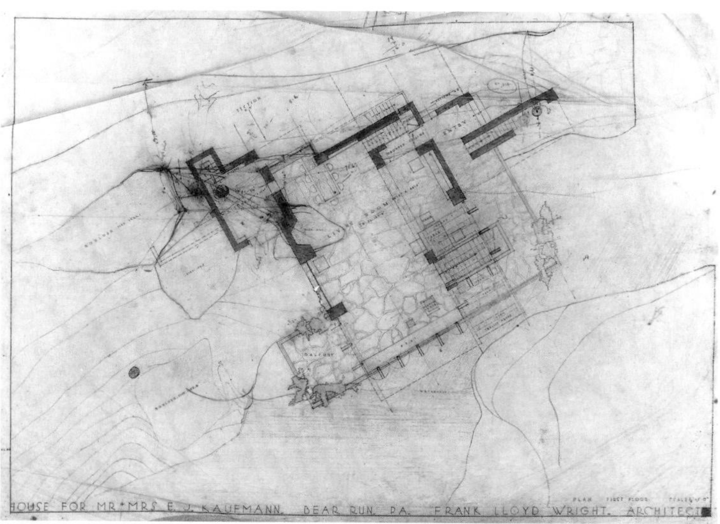

6.38 Fallingwater. Preliminary plan, first floor

the opposite cliff and balancing the structure on boulders in the streambed. Wright wrote to Kaufmann immediately upon his return to Taliesin that "the visit to the waterfall in the woods stays with me and a domicile has taken vague shape in my mind to the music of the stream." He later described his idea for the design as "an extension of the cliff beside a mountain stream."[60]

Though related to Taliesin in many important ways—not least of which is the similar manner in which the stone (here also from a nearby quarry) is laid—Fallingwater is much more explicitly abstract than the earlier building in its choice and delineation of architectural forms, a result no doubt of the influence of the European modern movement, the development of which is examined in the following chapter. There are no walls in the traditional sense, no windows as such, and no sheltering roofs. Instead, the elements of construction are configured into a pattern of verticals and horizontals suspended over the stream (fig. 6.37). A binary opposition of stone and concrete defines the pattern as it distinguishes those elements in compression from those in tension. The stone, quarried less than 500 feet from the house, was reserved for all vertical, load-bearing piers and walls; reinforced concrete was used to create the stack of horizontal balconies, or trays, cantilevered from the rock ledge over the stream. The trays, bounded by curved parapets, weave through the vertical stone structure to provide the living spaces. These are continuous inside and out. Where one tray overlaps another, doors and windows of plate glass in steel sash are inserted to mark the distinction between interior room and outdoor terrace. The lowest tray constitutes the main floor and contains a single space combining the functions of living, dining, reception, and library. The middle tray, with its main terrace forming the roof of the living room, contains the two main bedrooms plus a small guest room, each with its adjacent terrace. The top tray, roofing over the second-floor bedrooms and forming an aerie within the overarching branches of the tall oak trees, served as a separate bedroom suite.

The site on the north bank of Bear Run is a narrow shelf making an almost perfect thirty/sixty-degree triangle defined by a group of large boulders that follow the line of the ledge determining the upper of the two falls (fig. 6.38). The orthogonality of the plan contrasts with the triangularity of the shelf on which it is superposed. The interaction of the two geometries is reflected in the pivoting of the plan and the resulting diagonal axes that govern its spatial form. The east-west path of the existing road, along the top of the plan, served as the datum line from which Wright angled the house in a southeasterly direction so that the leading edge of the cantilevered trays would parallel the course of the stream beneath them and the diagonal axis defined by that line would become the axis of the main space of the house.[61] As "an extension of the cliff beside a mountain stream," the house swings with the glen to align with the stream, thus incorporating within its space the sense of direction and motion of the body of water it overhangs. The dynamic quality of this representation is perceived kinesthetically as an experience of virtual movement.

Fallingwater is approached from a bridge that crosses the stream just above the two falls. From it one can hear the sound of the falls but cannot see them. One senses a drop-off beyond the house, but only the height of the trees and the depth of the sky suggest that. The bridge's abutments, which are constructed of the same thin ledges of quarried stone as the house, blend into the stratified, natural stone walls of the stream. Joining the house's lower walls on the downstream side, they form a seamless transition between architecture and nature. The concrete span of the bridge, on the other hand, is like the cantilevered trays of the house. Its softly rounded parapets effect a fluid connection between the stone piers of the banks, suggesting an allusion to moving water. This dual reference was pointed out by the architectural critic and social theorist Lewis Mumford (1895–1990) shortly after the house was completed. "The stones represent, as it were, the earth theme," he wrote, "the concrete slabs are the water theme."[62]

Beyond the bridge, the drive bends around the rear of the house and cuts between it and the cliff. The horizontal lines of the building's stone walls, which are extended left and right into space by concrete beams and slabs, echo the strata of stone ledges in the walls of the glen, while the rippling effect of the cliff is picked up by the staggered vertical slots in the house's rear wall. The passageway underneath the transverse beams that tie the house back into the cliff gives the impression of a natural cut shaded by an arbor-like trellis. Water can be seen seeping out of the cliff face on the right. It also streams from a spout in the pier next to the entrance into a small basin that functioned as a footbath. As you pass between the stone walls of the loggia into the deep recess of the entry area, you hear the water and feel its moisture. The transition from outside to inside is so orchestrated as to seem like a gradual change in atmosphere and light rather than a change of place.

The gray-blue flagstone paving of the bridge and loggia continues into the house to become the living room floor. The only difference is that the flagstones inside are waxed and polished to give them a shiny, reflective appearance (fig. 6.39). This causes the eye to skim the surface quickly, following the line of the diagonal axis across the room toward the light at the far side, which comes through the band of windows and doors opening onto a terrace projecting over the ravine. One is reminded of the arching vista in the living room at Taliesin; but where that room roots you solidly to the earth, the shiny surface of the flagstone floor in Fallingwater has a slippery look and feel that suggest the instability of the moving water underfoot.

The reference to the stream below the living room floor is not merely metaphorical. One of the boulders of the rock

6.39 Fallingwater. Living room. View from entrance to southwest terrace

6.40 Fallingwater. Living room. Hatch

6.41 Fallingwater. Living room. View from entrance to fireplace

ledge supporting the house projects through the floor plane as the fireplace hearth; and, at the opposite corner of the room, a glass-enclosed hatch opens to reveal a view of the stream as well as a suspended stairway leading down to it (figs. 6.40, 6.41). Located under a skylit trellis of concrete beams, the twelve-foot-long hatch opening brings directly into the room the view, sound, smell, and moisture of the water rushing over the stream's stone bed. Its reflective surface appears to be continuous in color, texture, and substance with the waxed flagstone floor. The cool, damp air coming off it is funneled through the hatch, while the steady burble resonates in the rear concrete wall of the chamber, which echoes, in its curve, the semicylindrical hollow of the fireplace. United by a geometry that reflects their shared connection to the streambed, the fireplace and hatch combine to define a secondary diagonal axis that crosses the main one leading from the entry to the far terrace at approximately the center of the room.

The stream itself is brought into direct apposition with the living room floor along the main diagonal axis that parallels the ledge of the falls (see fig. 6.38). The polished flagstones reconstitute its rocky bed. Their uneven surface reflects the constantly changing light that filters into the room through the trees. The irregular outline of their raised joints re-creates the stream's swirling movement as it rounds the bend before meeting the ledge. The connection to the stream is not a disembodied, optical one. It is felt underfoot, through the body, and through all the senses. The waxed floor imparts a sense of fluid motion to the body and suggests the suspended animation of the drop of the waterfall from one level to the next. Walking across the imaginary line between the projection of the stone through the hearth and the opening of the floor at the hatch, one is made aware of the changes in level that determine the direction and flow of the water, and is thus subliminally induced to project one's thoughts beyond the space of the

6.42 Fallingwater. Southwest terrace of living room

room. As the floor continues through the plate-glass doors onto the southwest terrace, the dark flagstone plane turns up into a rounded concrete parapet. In its light, airborne mass, this shape echoes the color, texture, and trajectory of the cascade of white foam spilling over the rock ledge just below it (fig. 6.42). One is left to imagine that the virtual pressure of water welling up in the terrace is released in the overflow of the cantilever.

This returns us to Mumford's perception of the concrete slabs and parapets as representing the "water theme," a perception that should be taken all the more seriously given his acute understanding of Wright's work and close personal relationship with him at the time. All the stone in the house, except for the thin, waxed flagstones of the living room floor, is treated, as it is in Taliesin, as an inert, static material, acting in compression—the "earth theme," as Mumford noted. In vivid contrast, the concrete is treated as fluid and dynamic, acting in tension. While the deeply raked and randomly laid stone literally reproduces the eroded appearance of the cliff face, the two terraces cantilevered over the falls, being broader in scale and smoother in treatment than the stone walls, at first appear to echo the large boulders in the streambed. But that is only an initial and partial impression. Their rounded, fluid contours and light, insubstantial surfaces relate more to water than to stone—not to a thin film of water as in the waxed flagstones, but to water aerated and become foam. The different directions in which these two main cantilevered terraces point correspond almost exactly to the relative disposition of the two falls beneath them (see fig. 6.36). Appearing to spill out from the stone masses to either side of them like the actual falls between the banks of the stream, the two seemingly airborne trays effect changes in level that echo those in the stream. In its representation of the falling water, the house itself becomes a natural step in the descent of Bear Run to the river.

The perspective Wright produced of his conception for the house shows it as one part of the larger environment—not merely the physical one as at Taliesin but the phenomenal one as well (fig. 6.43). As the water rushing down the glen passes beneath the living room floor, the cantilevered terraces hover weightlessly above, appearing as if suspended in the air. Rising through the dense cover of trees, the billowing forms turn into cloudlike bands that seem to condense the mist and spray coming off the falls. Soft, ethereal, intangible, almost vaporous in substance, the terraces open into trellises and filter through the trees to join with the clouds and sky, thus completing a cycle of transformation of nature that is activated by the replenishing, vitalizing element of water.

Wright meant Fallingwater to represent nature in flux, to suggest the phenomenon of change over time. The sound of Fallingwater and the references to hearing and listening that abound in Wright's descriptions of the building are not merely coincidental. Sound and hearing are functions of time and necessarily introduce that element into the visual field, as pure opticality does not. The sound of Fallingwater fills the space of the glen and immerses the house and its occupants in nature. The movement of the stream continues throughout the year; the seasonal variations in intensity of the white water are registered, amplified, and reverberated by the house. The question one constantly asks is not *where* this or that begins or ends, as at Taliesin, but *when*. And the answer is never. In earlier architectural uses of moving water, as in late Renaissance and Baroque fountains, the tradition was fundamentally a theatrical one: when the play was over, the fountains were turned off.[63] What is so extraordinary about Fallingwater is that it never stops. When one leaves, one expects it to be turned off—but it, like the water it represents, can never be. Verisimilitude is beyond the point, as reality and illusion here literally coincide.

The representation of nature as an active, changing phenomenon necessarily implies a temporal dimension, and Fallingwater clearly owes much of its uniqueness to its ability to evoke a perception of duration without transgressing the limits of the material present. But representation, almost by definition, and at least from Laugier on, meant re-presenting nature through history. Representation without history is a purely twentieth-century conception, which both Taliesin and Fallingwater exemplify. Ironically though, when nature itself was given full scope to include its temporal as well as spatial reality, the problem of history almost immediately reemerged. To suggest a sense of time through the static forms of art was almost exclusively the prerogative of poets and painters. A figurative artist such as Nicolas Poussin might depict the change of seasons in the sequential imagery of multiple canvases (for example, *The Four*

6.43 Fallingwater. Perspective from below first falls, 1936

6.44 Wright. Marin County Civic Center, San Rafael, Calif., 1957–70

Seasons, 1660–64) by relying on the beholder's willingness to accept the narrative continuity of virtual time. But architects have usually felt constrained by the physical realities of their medium. Boullée, as in his project for the Newton Cenotaph, thought it possible to suggest the evolution from night to day within the same virtual space (see figs. 3.11–12). But he could only do that by using the techniques of pictorial or theatrical representation. The desire to involve time in the perception of actual buildings, as discussed in the earlier chapters in this book, usually relied on the appeal to history, where a reuse of earlier forms might bring to mind a train of associations transporting the beholder into a world distant in time (see fig. 1.20). Re-created ruins were especially efficacious in this regard, as they carried on their surface the very imprint of nature's relentless activity.

And so, despite Wright's aversion to anything that smacked of "eclecticism," but given his commitment to an architecture of representation, it is not all that surprising that not long after Fallingwater was completed he started to make use of historical imagery as a way of producing the effects of the temporal. In Taliesin West, the winter headquarters for the Taliesin Fellowship (founded 1932) that he began building outside Phoenix in 1938, he incorporated ancient Native American petroglyph boulders found on the site to link the complex with its earlier history. In the Guggenheim Museum in New York, conceived in 1943–45 and built from 1956 to 1959, he transformed the ancient Mesopotamian ziggurat into a space of continuous movement. And in northern California's Marin County Civic Center, designed in 1957–59, he appropriated the Roman Pont du Gard near Nîmes, France, to re-create an image of regional administration and public works (fig. 6.44).[64] But all this later work of Wright's is part of a larger story of the return to history that will be discussed in this book's final chapter. The unusual and lasting significance of Taliesin and Fallingwater, on the other hand, lies in their exhibition of the power of architecture to employ the devices of representation without recourse to history and through forms both purely abstract and entirely dependent on their material presence.

7

The Reemergence of Representation out of Abstraction in Mies van der Rohe

THREE YEARS AFTER FALLINGWATER was completed and two years after it was the subject of a one-building exhibition at New York's Museum of Modern Art (1938), the German architect Ludwig Mies van der Rohe (1886–1969), who emigrated to the United States in the same year as the exhibition, wrote "A Tribute to Frank Lloyd Wright," in which he acknowledged the great debt he believed modern architecture owed to the American architect.[1] Recalling "the situation [in Europe] in 1910," when the "potential vitality" of architecture had "been lost" and "the attempt to revive architecture from the standpoint of form was apparently doomed," Mies singled out the "extensive publication" and "comprehensive display" of Wright's work in Berlin that year as having

> revealed an architectural world of unexpected force and clarity of language, and also a disconcerting richness of form. Here finally was a master-builder drawing upon the veritable fountainhead of architecture, who with true originality lifted his architectural creations into the light. Here, again, at last, genuine organic architecture flowered.
>
> The more deeply we studied Wright's creations, the greater became our admiration for his incomparable talent, for the boldness of his conceptions, and for his independence in thought and action. The dynamic impulse emanating from his work invigorated a whole generation. His influence was strongly felt even when it was not actually visible.
>
> After this first encounter, we followed the development of this rare man with eager hearts. We watched with astonishment the exuberant unfolding of the gifts of one who had been endowed by nature with the most splendid talents. In his undiminishing power he resembles a giant tree in a wide landscape, which, year after year, ever attains a more noble crown.[2]

While Mies's "tribute" to Wright is exceedingly complimentary, it is not unqualifiedly so. His reference to the older architect's "disconcerting richness of form" should raise eyebrows. The important caveat that Wright's "influence," though "strongly felt" often "was not actually visible," makes it clear that the historical relationship being described is not a simple filial one, like that, say, between Sullivan and Wright, but a more complex give and take between participants who may agree in principle on what is desirable but not necessarily on how to achieve it. The uneasy, even combative relationship between Wright and the younger Europeans who were grouped together in 1932 under the rubric of the International Style has become a commonplace of modern architectural history.[3] It is a subject worth revisiting within the context of this book, however, because the issue that fundamentally separated the two camps in the 1920s and '30s was the matter of abstraction versus representation, just as the return to a new form of representation in Mies's work after 1938 can be more fully understood in terms of his continued appreciation for "the exuberant unfolding of [Wright's] gifts," as manifest in such works as Fallingwater.

Henry-Russell Hitchcock (1903–1987), who was to curate with Philip Johnson (1906–2005) the Museum of Modern Art's 1932 exhibition of recent architecture and to coauthor with him *The International Style* (1932), wrote a groundbreaking account of the evolution of modern architecture in a two-part article in 1928 that became the basis for the exhibition as well as for his book *Modern Architecture: Romanticism and Reintegration,* published in 1929. Hitchcock used the two parts of the article to divide the evolution of modern architecture into two successive phases. The first he called "The New Tradition" and the second "The New Pioneers." The first was characterized by a new attitude toward history, "eclectic in its reminiscences and free in its adaptation of traditional features." Frank Lloyd Wright, "the full New Traditionalist" in Hitchcock's estimation, was identified as "one of the founders of [the] New Tradition" in America and "one of the first great masters of the New Tradition," which included, most notably in Hitchcock's view, Hendrik Petrus Berlage (1856–1934), Auguste Perret (1874–1954), and Josef Hoffmann (1870–1956).[4]

The architecture of the New Pioneers, by contrast, called for a "purification of the earlier manner from extraneous elements not demanded by engineering," along with "the ascetic avoidance of ornament...and representational or reminiscent detail." Their buildings were to be seen purely as "the disposition of masses, volumes, and surfaces in geometrically significant forms" (fig. 7.1).[5] Mies van der Rohe, Le Corbusier (1887–1965), Walter Gropius (1883–1969), and Jacobus Johannes Pieter Oud (1890–1963), whose recent Housing Estate at the Hook of Holland (1924–27) received two illustrations, were singled out as the most prominent "New Pioneers."

Hitchcock described the New Tradition as rejecting the strict adherence to historical styles practiced by the "Old Traditionalists" but fully accepting their basic concept of historical representation (one must keep in mind that he was writing about Wright before Fallingwater). "Like the Old Traditionalists," Hitchcock said, "the New Traditionalists are retrospective in their tendency to borrow freely from the past, but they are also modern in that they feel free to use and combine without regard for archaeological properties the elements thus borrowed. The essential principle which governs both their retrospection and their modernity is the belief that not any one period of the past but the works of the past as a whole offer the surest guide."[6]

The role of representation in the work of the New Tradition, as Hitchcock saw it, was to mediate between "contemporary conditions" expressed in the simplification of the New Tradition's forms and "the desire on the part of

7.1 J. J. P. Oud. Housing Block, Hook of Holland, 1924–27. Exterior detail. From Henry-Russell Hitchcock, "Modern Architecture. II: The New Pioneers," *Architectural Record,* 1928

7.3 Richard Neutra. Steel-frame construction of Chicago's Palmer House, *Wie baut Amerika?* 1927

7.2 Le Corbusier. "Grain Silo," *Vers une Architecture,* 1923

the average man for the sentimental comfort of representation." The "New Traditionalists," he asserted, "make no impossible demands on the public to appreciate architecture as other than a representative art—decorative detail, and that inherited particularly, being more or less equivalent to the recognizable elements in painting and sculpture."[7] Although Wright, as Hitchcock noted in his book of 1929, came close to producing "some of the effects of the New Pioneers," "his approach to a pure [meaning abstract] architecture is complicated with the Nature worship" he inherited from Whitman and Sullivan.[8]

Hitchcock did not use the word "abstract" in his characterization of the work of the New Pioneers in 1928. That only came a bit later, when he was able to see the work in perspective and, it should be added, with greater knowledge of the development of abstract art out of Cubism in the period from the later teens through the twenties and thirties.[9] Instead, the functionally straightforward forms of engineering, as they were presented in such texts as Le

Corbusier's *Vers une architecture* (1923) and Richard Neutra's (1892–1970) *Wie baut Amerika?* (1927), were seen as replacing those of the historical styles and thereby offering architects a nonreferential, nonrepresentational vocabulary (figs. 7.2–3).[10] "The New Pioneers," Hitchcock wrote, "insist that tradition must not restrain architecture from taking advantage of the latest engineering possibilities" that "permit far greater freedom and boldness in design than do traditional materials and do not distract by their texture or craftsmanship from the surfaces and volumes as integral wholes." Rendered with a "simplicity that makes surfaces and volume forcefully intelligible as wholes," and thereby expressing "the most purely and essentially architectural values," the buildings of the New Pioneers, in following the model of engineering, demonstrated that their architects were "unwilling to obscure the matter by trifling and incidental pandering to the bourgeois taste for representational prettiness, and for reminiscent trophies of culture."[11]

In his description of the New Pioneers, however, Hitchcock noted that their "theory owes something to the cubism of the years after 1910," which for Hitchcock and others writing about architecture at the time essentially meant the Dutch abstract movement known as De Stijl and the various forms of Purism that were related to it (fig. 7.4). Hitchcock referred to the leader of De Stijl, Theo van Doesburg (1883–1931), as a "cubist painter" and described what Piet Mondrian (1872–1944) called Neo-Plasticism as "the specific name for the Cubist painting of Mondriaan and van Doesburg."[12] But Hitchcock, like many of the New Pioneers themselves, focused at first on engineering as the source and explanation for the geometric abstractness of the architectural forms. The "New Pioneers," he wrote, "find in machines something of the purity, something of the austere beauty, they demand in architecture."[13] Ahistorical, nonnaturalistic, the forms produced by engineers were the epitome of the nonrepresentational. "The engineers of to-day," Le Corbusier wrote, "show us the way and create plastic facts, clear and limpid, giving...to the mind the pleasure of geometric forms." The "purely abstract point of view" of the "engineer's aesthetic," according to Le Corbusier, enabled one to see that fundamentally, and behind all representational appearances, "Egyptian, Greek or Roman architecture is an architecture of prisms, cubes and cylinders, pyramids or spheres" (fig. 7.5).[14]

The advances made toward abstraction in painting and sculpture were soon acknowledged to have opened the eyes of architects to engineering itself. In 1927 Oud wrote that "the new architecture needed the constructive force of cubism [i.e., De Stijl]" to see the way beyond traditional approaches. Two years later, Hitchcock wrote that the "abstract painting which began to appear from about 1910...suggested strongly the architectural values in the elemental volumes and planes of machinery and engineering."[15] And two years after that, Sigfried Giedion (1888–1968) quoted Oud's statement about the instrumental role of De Stijl painting to preface his own claim that, "without the push forward of painting, architecture, despite the methods of modern construction, would have remained formal and servile" in relation to the past. Rejecting the "effects of the associations of ideas that represented objects would provoke in the mind of the spectator," as Giedion put it, "Doesburg and Mondrian wanted a 'pure art,' an art that did not allow itself to be distracted by exterior motifs" and that would achieve the desired sense of "harmony" entirely from "the juxtaposition of absolute colors." In the field of architecture, the effect would be purely one "of surface and of volumes."[16]

By the 1940s this interpretation of the abstraction of the architecture of the modern movement in Europe had become standard fare. In his influential *Space, Time and Architecture: The Growth of a New Tradition* (1941), Giedion declared that "the discovery of a new space conception"

7.4 Theo van Doesburg. *Rhythm of a Russian Dance*, 1918

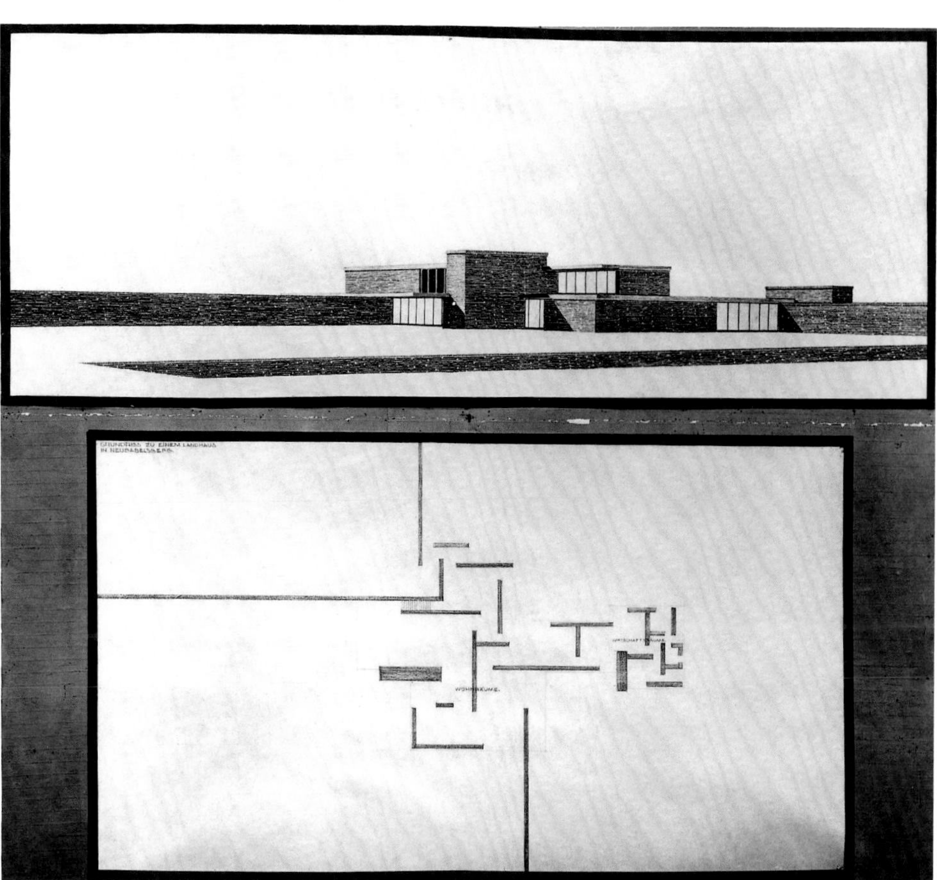

7.6 Ludwig Mies van der Rohe. Brick Country House project, (possibly) Potsdam-Neubabelsberg, 1924. Perspective and plan

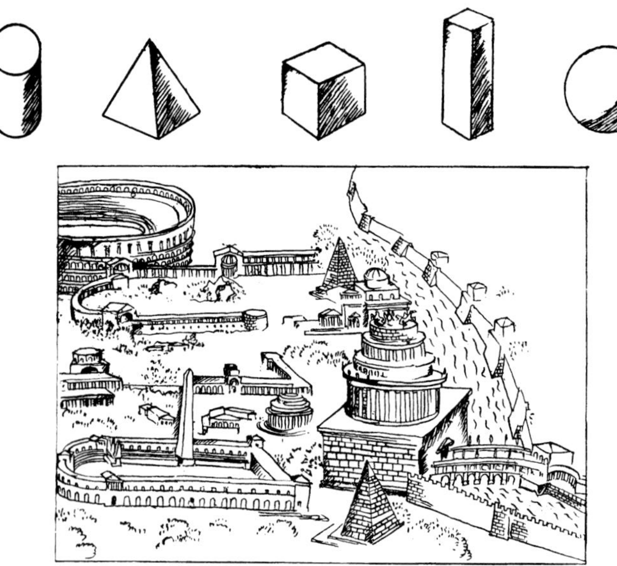

7.5 Le Corbusier. "Everything Is Spheres and Cylinders" (1920), *Vers une architecture*, 1923

by Cubist painters and sculptors, here referring more specifically to the work of Picasso and Braque circa 1908–10, was the single most important factor in providing "architecture [with] the objective means of organizing space" and thus giving architects "the hints they needed to master reality in their particular sphere."[17] And before the end of the postwar decade, Hitchcock would summarize the issue in stating that the leading exponents of the movement he had previously called the New Pioneers had "sought and found the architectural equivalent of abstract painting."[18] Although the equation with abstraction was not always later made, the historiography of modern architecture from the 1950s on has assumed the fundamental influence of painting on architecture in the development of what soon came to be called the "machine aesthetic."[19]

Mies's Embrace of Abstraction: The German Years

Of all the so-called New Pioneers, none achieved a greater degree of abstraction nor a more striking expression of the affinity with its pictorial precedent than Mies van der Rohe. Philip Johnson, one of his earliest admirers and critics, went so far as to describe Mies's plan for the 1924 Brick Country House project as looking "less like a diagram of a house than an abstract drawing" (fig. 7.6).[20] And the comparison between such a Mies plan as this or the later one for his German Pavilion at the International Exhibition in Barcelona (1928–29) with Theo van Doesburg's 1918 painting *Rhythm of a Russian Dance* has become a cliché of modern architectural history (compare figs. 7.4 and 7.11).[21] To trace Mies's conversion from historicist representation to abstraction and his subsequent search for another kind of representation is thus to highlight a pattern that characterized the development of modern architecture in general.

Like most of the other New Pioneers, Mies began his career as a New Traditionalist. An early house such as that for the Urbig family in Potsdam-Neubabelsberg of 1915–17 is quite typical of his "half-modern" or premodern work, with its symmetrical main facade, arched entrance, rendered stucco surface, classically framed windows and French doors, and hip roof with dormer windows (fig. 7.7). What is rather unusual about Mies's early career vis-à-vis his peers in the modern movement, however, is that he continued to employ historical models well into the mid-1920s, coincident with some of his most radical experiments in abstraction. His house for the Mosler family, also in Potsdam-Neubabelsberg, was built between 1924 and 1926, shortly after the design for the Brick Country House, the plan of which Johnson later likened to an abstract drawing (fig. 7.8).

7.7 Mies. Urbig House, Potsdam-Neubabelsberg, 1915–17. Exterior

7.8 Mies. Mosler House, Potsdam-Neubabelsberg, 1924–26. Exterior

Like the Urbig House, the one for the Moslers continues safely within the representational framework of eighteenth-century vernacular classicism. The symmetrical masonry block, contained under a high pitched roof punctuated by dormer windows, clearly expresses the conservative, *bürgerlich* ethos Hitchcock scorned in the New Tradition's "pandering to the bourgeois taste for representational prettiness and... reminiscent trophies of culture." The synchronicity of the Mosler and Brick Country House designs makes it clear that for Mies the move to abstraction was a deliberate and categorical one. It also makes it clear that the move from representation to abstraction in architecture in the 1920s was without precedent and without predictable consequences.

The comparison of the Urbig and Mosler houses to the Brick Country House should also help to clarify the very word "abstraction" and thus distinguish its use here from its previous uses in this book. The two houses in Potsdam-Neubabelsberg are "abstract" in the sense the term was used to describe the work of Schinkel, Soane, and Boullée (see figs. 3.32 and 3.38). Indeed, the simplified, stylized detailing of the houses and their overall stripped-down quality are part and parcel of the "free...adaptation of traditional features" that Hitchcock considered characteristic of the modernity of the New Tradition and which, he explained, had "a root" in the eighteenth century "in the person of Sir John Soane" and a continuous history through Schinkel and Labrouste to Sullivan and Wright.[22] Abstraction in this pre-twentieth-century sense of the word is a transitive concept, a process of simplifying, clarifying, and reducing to its essentials a preexisting model or subject. In Soane's later interiors for the Bank of England (see fig. 3.27), Schinkel's Berlin Royal Library (see fig. 3.51), or Boullée's projects for a cemetery entrances (see fig. 3.20), the historical or natural models are distilled to their geometric structures in order to render the representational image or illusion more powerful. In the work of Viollet-le-Duc, Sullivan, and Wright (at least up to the early 1930s), the abstraction of historical models could be read as a response to the pressure put upon them for the expression of material form and programmatic content (see figs. 5.16, 5.26, and 6.21).

Abstraction as it came to be practiced in the twentieth century, first in painting and sculpture and then in architecture, must be understood as an intransitive rather than transitive concept. The work started from the manipulation of nonrepresentational forms themselves, meaning ones that did not refer to existing natural or historical images or models. Generally these would be purely geometric—lines, planes, or solids—but they could also be more free-form, as in the work of Wassily Kandinsky (1866–1944), František Kupka (1871–1957), and Jean Arp (1887–1966). Because of the possible confusion over the use of the word "abstract," which could have ambiguous meanings related to the history outlined above, many modern artists and critics in the first half of the twentieth century tried to come up with a new term that would be uniquely descriptive of what they believed to be a uniquely modern form of artistic expression. Van Doesburg offered the name "Elementarism," Mondrian that of "Neo-Plasticism" or "Pure Plastic Art," Kazimir Malevich (1878–1935) that of "Suprematism," and Hilla Rebay that of "Non-Objectivity." They all stressed that the nonrepresentational was such a new phenomenon in the history of art that it needed a completely new term to describe it. In the end, however, even the most doctrinaire and narrowly focused of these artists, such as Van Doesburg and Mondrian, used the adjective "abstract" or the noun "abstraction" when referring to the type of forms they had chosen to work with as the only proper means for achieving an expression of modernity liberated from the constraints of the past and of nature and issuing directly from the spiritual and technological possibilities opened up by the machine age. As Van Doesburg wrote, "architecture had to free its characteristic elements from the art jungle of the past, and in so doing become 'abstract.'"[23]

The nonrepresentational abstraction of Mies's Brick Country House project can be read, on one level, as a translation into the three dimensions of built form of the aesthetic of dynamic, interlocking lines and sliding planes that Van Doesburg had introduced in his painting *Rhythm of a Russian Dance* (see figs. 7.6 and 7.4). Mies had known the painter since 1920 or 1921, and few have ever doubted the influence Van Doesburg exerted on him, as well as on the Bauhaus in general, where the Dutch artist was based for two years beginning in 1921. But the abstraction of the Brick Country House is more complex than a mere translation of a pictorial idea into an architectural one, a fact signaled by

Mies's naming the project after the primary material that was to be used in its construction. In effect, the design also involves an abstraction, in the transitive sense, of the New Traditionalist work of Wright (see figs. 6.22–23). Oud had written in 1918 that Wright's work offered "a new 'plastic' architecture" using the "primary means" of the "movement of planes" to "open up entirely new aesthetic possibilities for architecture."[24] Through the purifying lens of De Stijl abstraction, Mies saw through the referential shapes of the Robie House to their elementary expression of disaggregated volumes and interweaving lines that "revealed," as he later said, "an architectural world of unexpected force and clarity of language." This secondary level of abstraction turned the Cubist fragmentation of referential figures into a construction of purely geometric elements unified through the fluid agent of space.

For Van Doesburg, abstraction meant much more than a way of picture making. It was a release from the subjective, individualistic, fragmented, and illusory "art jungle of the past" that characterized nineteenth-century bourgeois society. The untrammeled new world of space it opened up spoke directly of transcendent spiritual values through its universally understandable, rationally ordered, and reproducible system of forms. Such a utopian vision neatly dovetailed with the social and political aims of modern architecture, which called for mass housing of a prefabricated, standardized sort grounded in a functional and hygienic rigor. Architects such as Le Corbusier, Oud, and Gropius exploited this reduction of architectural form to elemental volumes to create new types of superblock configurations specifically responsive to the need for adequate sunlight, air, and greenery (fig. 7.9; also see fig. 7.1).

Although Mies did participate in some of the socially driven programs of early modernism, most notably in his direction of the Weissenhofsiedlung housing exhibition at Stuttgart in 1927, his interest in abstraction focused mainly

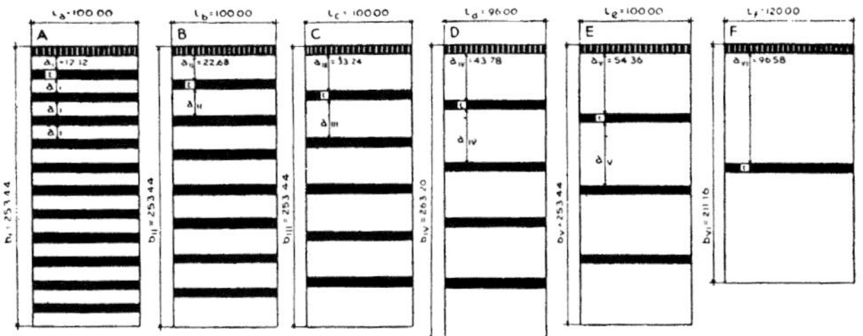

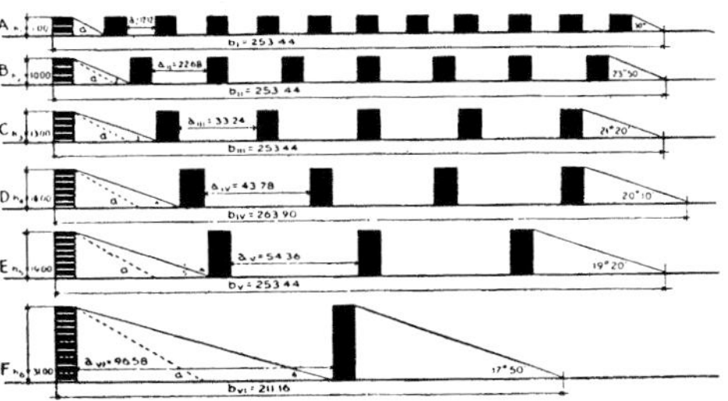

7.9 Walter Gropius. "Diagram Illustrating the Development of a Rectangular Building-Site with Parallel Rows of Tenement Blocks of Different Heights," ca. 1928. From Gropius, *The New Architecture and the Bauhaus,* 1935

on artistic issues. His major achievements in the later 1920s were in the area of exhibition design and domestic architecture of a particularly refined and elegant sort. The two most remarkable and well-known examples of this are the German Pavilion for the Barcelona International Exhibition and the Tugendhat House in Brno, Czech Republic, both designed and built between 1928 and 1930. The so-called Barcelona Pavilion was intended to show off products of German industry. Set on one end of a plinth whose other end is occupied by a shallow reflecting pool, the structure is composed of a grid of chrome-encased steel columns supporting a thin, flat slab roof (figs. 7.10–11). Freestanding planes of glass, polished marble, and onyx slide between roof and floor to partition the space and direct its flow. The transparent and reflective surfaces deny a sense of physical exertion to the structure and thereby dematerialize it. Lacking any explicit reference to preexisting natural or historical models, the structure is read as a three-dimensional spatial network of flat planes and thin lines of a completely abstract order. The chrome-encased cruciform columns foreground

7.10 Mies. German (Barcelona) Pavilion, International Exhibition, Barcelona, 1928–29; reconstructed 1981–86. Exterior

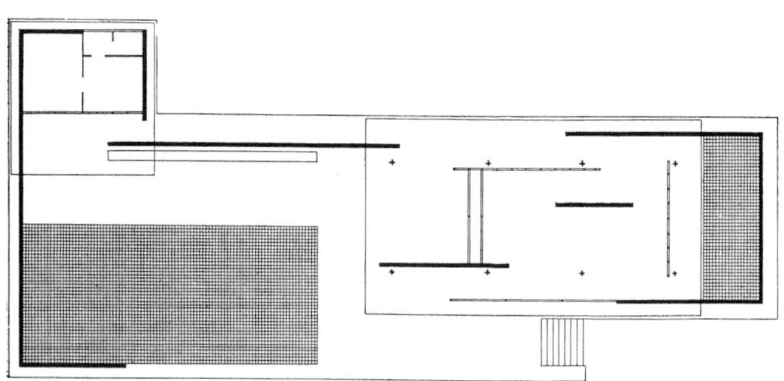

7.11 Barcelona Pavilion. Plan

7.12 Barcelona Pavilion. Column base

this denial of classical representation and become the design's most telling feature (fig. 7.12). Having neither base nor capital, they appear to have been extruded from a purely rational idea of point support, punctuating the space as they delineate its underlying grid.[25]

Mies remained in Germany throughout most of the 1930s, during which time he continued to produce an architecture committed to the ideals of abstraction, the only significant change being an increased emphasis on monumentality, achieved in large part through the use of symmetry he had avoided in the previous decade. A competition project for the Reichsbank in Berlin of 1933 was designed just prior to Hitler's putsch and assumption of the title of Führer, whereas the project for a Pavilion of the Third Reich for the Brussels International Exhibition of 1935 was produced after that event and in full cognizance of the need to create an architecture to symbolize the new Nazi regime. A sketch of the exterior shows an enormous Imperial eagle over the main entrance, flanked by tall poles flying the flags of the German state and the National Socialist party (fig. 7.13). The grand interior Court of Honor features a second Imperial eagle directly opposite the entrance (fig. 7.14). It is flanked by a partition wall to the left inscribed with the words "Deutscher Reich" and one on the right inscribed with a gigantic swastika. Each of these side walls is preceded by an "altarlike" table, the one on the left being supported by svelte, Ionic-looking capitals, the one on the right possibly intended as a base for sculpture.[26]

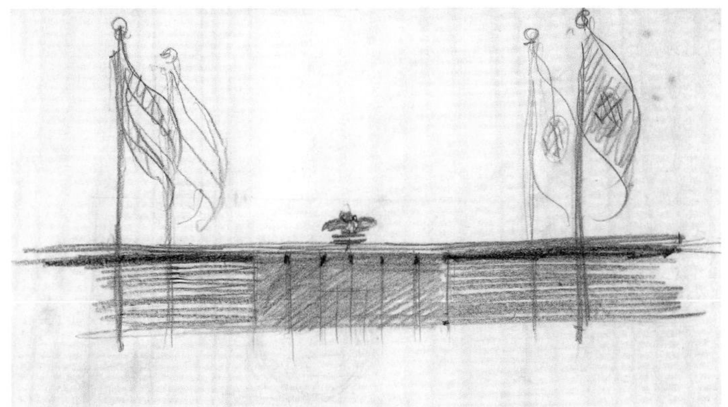

7.13 Mies. German Pavilion project, International Exhibition, Brussels, 1934. Exterior perspective

7.14 German Pavilion project, Brussels. Court of Honor. Interior perspective

Aside from the explicit use of classical and political symbols, the building remains starkly modern and can thus be interpreted as part of Mies's continuing effort, even in the face of the aggressive return to classical representation favored by Hitler, to promote an architecture of geometric abstraction as an appropriate way to express the collective ideals and technological prowess of the new Nazi state. This effort would last through at least the first half of 1937—well beyond the time when most, if not all, of the avant-garde circle with whom he was previously associated had left Germany to go into exile. By contrast, Mies joined a number of National Socialist organizations and even signed a petition in support of Hitler, all of which has raised certain questions and even suspicions about his politics.[27]

Although Sibyl Moholy-Nagy, the wife of László, Mies's former colleague at the Bauhaus, called Mies a "traitor" and others have described him as an "opportunist," serious scholarly opinion is almost undivided in maintaining that Mies's attempts to work with Hitler's regime merely illustrate a dogged belief in the possibility of convincing the Nazis of the value of modern architecture for their cause, as well as his complete naïveté and disinterest in matters political.[28] Whatever the case, Mies decided by 1937 that it was time to cut ties and leave. After a preliminary trip to the United States in the late summer of that year, in the fall of 1938 he settled permanently in Chicago, where he was appointed director of the Department of Architecture at the Armour Institute of Technology (AIT, which became the Illinois Institute of Technology [IIT] in early 1940) and embarked on a second career that took his architecture in a substantially different direction than it had followed in Germany.

Mies in Exile

In the turbulent years between 1938—when he arrived in America as an enemy alien—and 1942—when the first component of his master plan for IIT was nearing completion—Mies produced three designs for projects that remain, in the form of the collages by which they are best known, among the most significant works of his entire career and absolutely crucial for understanding its postwar evolution. Rarely viewed or studied as a group, the Resor House (1937–39), the Concert Hall (1941–42), and the Museum for a Small City (1943) share a particularly powerful set of formal and expressive concerns that force us to think about how one should read their imagery and content, both in terms of their immediate wartime context and as a basis for the reengagement with representation—and the consequent movement away from abstraction—that Mies's architecture came to manifest after the war. Fundamental aspects to this development were that Mies now chose the pictorial medium of collage as the one best suited to his expressive purposes and that the ready-made images he incorporated were by no means neutral in political and cultural terms. The method of appropriation and application implicit in the collage technique soon informed the system of structural expression he developed in his actual buildings at IIT and ultimately became his way of characterizing—and representing—what he liked to call "the will of the epoch" and what the American President Dwight D. Eisenhower was to describe in early 1961 as the growing danger of America's "military-industrial complex."

Although it is axiomatic to any analysis of Mies's architecture that his career can be neatly divided into two halves—the earlier German period and the later American phase—with each having its own particular structural and spatial characteristics, a rigorous continuity of philosophical purpose is generally held to underlie and unify the two halves in a seamless and almost timeless fashion.[29] The interregnum of emigration and war are deemed to have had no significant effect on his pursuit of an architecture of pure structure and pure space, a world of form whose meaning lies in the abstraction of expression devolving from those two absolutes. Certainly Mies's own silence on matters such as government policy, ideology, or leadership lends support to the commonly held view that he was a totally apolitical individual, disengaged from the social problems of his time and their mundane, quotidian aspects.

It is therefore hardly surprising that the abstractionist reading of the Mies of the 1920s and '30s has carried over into the wartime and postwar work. Despite their rather blatant political references, the first projects he designed in America, like the one for the Concert Hall (see fig. 7.25), have invariably been described as simply predicting the focus on the purely formal aspects of structure and space of his subsequent steel and glass buildings of the later 1940s, '50s, and '60s (see fig. 7.40). In fact, the disinclination to acknowledge representational imagery initially forced critics into a position of almost consciously having to avoid accurate description. When first Philip Johnson and then Arthur Drexler, both close acquaintances of Mies, described the Concert Hall collage that the architect had created by pasting pieces of colored paper and a reproduction of a Maillol sculpture over a photograph of the interior of a wartime American assembly plant that was then being used to manufacture planes for bombing Germany, they both refused to admit the project's ready-made aspect, leaving the reader to assume that Mies had been responsible for designing the structure rather than merely retrofitting it.

In the text of his monograph on Mies accompanying the architect's exhibition at the Museum of Modern Art in 1947, Johnson simply noted how, in the Concert Hall, "walls and ceilings are pulled apart and disposed within a trussed steel and glass cage" so that "space eddies in all directions among interior planes of subaqueous weightlessness."[30] According to Drexler's more disingenuous account thirteen years later, "here [in the Concert Hall project] interior columns have

7.15 Mies. House with Three Courts project, ca. 1934–35. Model

been eliminated. They are replaced by a vast steel truss *of the sort* used in airplane hangars or factories [italics added]. In the entirely free space this roof makes possible, Mies suspends completely separate wall and ceiling planes," thus fulfilling, in the author's view, the architect's exclusively formal program.[31] Although later commentators have noted the identity of the preexisting photograph, the meaning a bomber plant might have had as the basis for a concert hall designed soon after the United States entered World War II has continued to remain undiscussed, thus preserving the abstract, formalist interpretation of the project.[32]

It would be wrong, however, to argue that all of Mies's work has evaded sociopolitical interpretation. Indeed, there is one important and highly relevant group of projects, the so-called court houses proposed just before he left Germany, that provide a basis for such an alternative point of view (fig. 7.15). While using the same formal language and compositional system of the Barcelona Pavilion, these consistently inward-turning designs have often been described as registering a sense of withdrawal from the hostile world of Berlin of the mid-1930s and thus expressing a mood of isolation, even escapism. It is therefore important to note that the court house became one of Mies's prime building types after leaving Germany, especially in his teaching curriculum for IIT, although it underwent a significant change in being rendered through collage.[33]

This collage technique was prominently used by Mies for the Resor House project that first brought him to the United States in 1937 (see figs. 7.20–21). While these drawings clearly evince a sense of alienation and estrangement that can be related to the previous Berlin designs, there is something radically different in them. In response to the social and political environment of Berlin in the mid-thirties, the court houses reflected a subtle shift in expression through a realignment of forms. The American collages, with their physical imprint of elements from the real world, register a more profound change that speaks not merely of isolation or escape but of the search to construct a new practice and a new identity in a world where things could no longer be considered natural and transparent but had to be reviewed in all their opacity as objects of representation. The three projects we shall now turn to can be seen as responses to the profound dislocation of exile and the consequent trauma of living and working as an enemy alien in time of war.[34]

Resor House

The commission that initially brought Mies to America was a vacation house for Helen and Stanley Resor, vice president and president, respectively, of the J. Walter Thompson Advertising Agency, the biggest in the world at the time. The Resors, who were important collectors of modern painting with strong ties to the Museum of Modern Art in New York, owned a large ranch along the Snake River in the Grand Teton Mountains near Jackson Hole, Wyoming.[35] A creek branching off from the river and running through the property defined the eastern edge of the flat area where the log cabins they lived in were located (fig. 7.16). Just north of a dam in the creek was a group of farm buildings. These unassuming structures were dwarfed by the snow-capped mountains looming behind them.

Having decided to build a guest cottage as well as a new

7.16 Snake River Ranch (Resor House), Wilson (near Jackson Hole), Wyo. Creek with farm buildings, looking north from new house site, ca. 1937

7.17 Philip Goodwin and Marc Peter. Resor House, 1935–37. Under construction. Service wing and piers in creek, ca. 1937

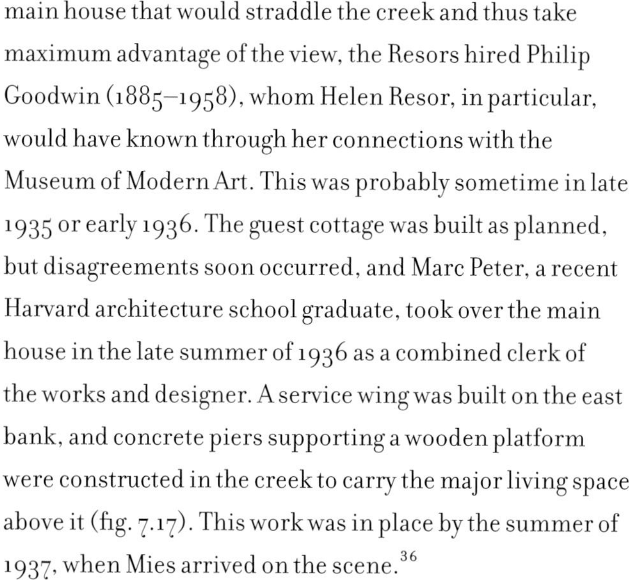

main house that would straddle the creek and thus take maximum advantage of the view, the Resors hired Philip Goodwin (1885–1958), whom Helen Resor, in particular, would have known through her connections with the Museum of Modern Art. This was probably sometime in late 1935 or early 1936. The guest cottage was built as planned, but disagreements soon occurred, and Marc Peter, a recent Harvard architecture school graduate, took over the main house in the late summer of 1936 as a combined clerk of the works and designer. A service wing was built on the east bank, and concrete piers supporting a wooden platform were constructed in the creek to carry the major living space above it (fig. 7.17). This work was in place by the summer of 1937, when Mies arrived on the scene.[36]

Looking for a way to get Mies out of Germany and into the United States, Alfred Barr, who was director of the Museum of Modern Art and particularly close to Helen Resor, supported the Resors in their decision to turn the job over to Mies. Helen Resor asked Barr to contact the architect on her behalf in early February 1937, and in July she interviewed Mies in Paris and offered him the job. He visited the Wyoming site in August and spent two weeks there studying it. After stopping in Chicago, where he met with the advisory committee of AIT to discuss the possibility of directing the school's architecture program, Mies spent the fall and winter of 1937–38 in New York, completing the design of the Resor House in the office of two of his former Bauhaus students, John Barney Rodgers and William Priestley. He returned to Germany in early April to settle his affairs prior to taking up the directorship he had been offered, in the meantime, at AIT.[37]

The contract drawings for the Resor House, dated March 21, 1938, were produced by Rodgers and Priestley under Mies's close supervision (figs. 7.18–19). The design preserved the already built structure (which appears to the right on the upper elevation, and to the left on the lower one) and more or less doubled it on the other side of the stream, creating an open-plan, glass-walled space between the two blocks on the existing platform, which Mies hoped eventually to be able to lower somewhat. The steel-frame and wood structure was to be sheathed in cypress panels and to incorporate large areas of plate glass and fieldstone masonry. The plan shows the eccentrically shaped block on the east reused as a service wing, the new block on the west bank housing the bedrooms, and the central, open living/dining space articulated by cruciform-shaped columns supporting the flat roof, which is cantilevered well beyond the edge of the floor-to-ceiling "Picture windows," the term Rodgers used to describe the expansive window walls.[38]

The house proceeded in fits and starts over the next few years: it was postponed indefinitely (by Stanley Resor), mainly for financial reasons, as Mies was leaving for

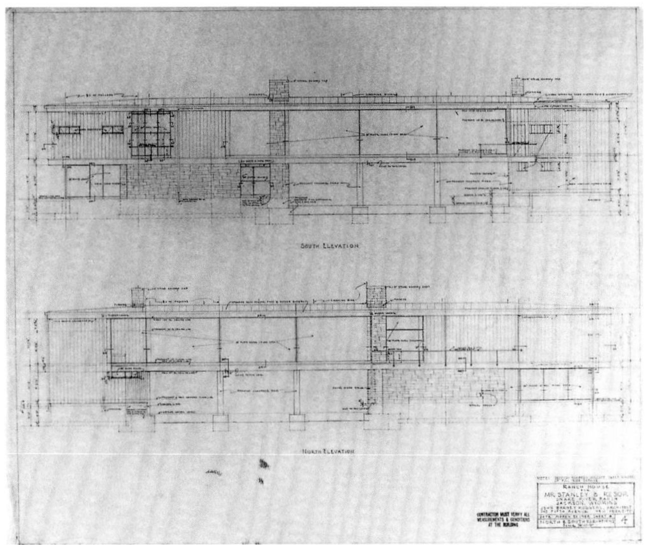

7.18 Mies. Resor House project, 1937–39. Elevations. Contract drawing, by John B. Rodgers, 1938

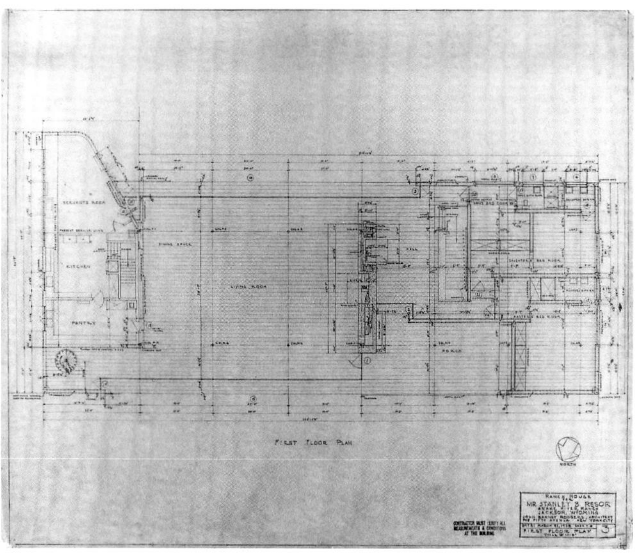

7.19 Resor House project. Plan, second (main) floor. Contract drawing, by John B. Rodgers, 1938

Germany in early April 1938; it was revived the following November and redesigned at a reduced scale and cost by March 1939; discussions continued through 1941, but all thought of building ceased in 1943 after a spring flood washed away the existing piers and service building. Most interesting for us, however, is the way in which Mies developed the design in the form of two extraordinary collages: one looking south and the other north, the latter in the direction of the existing farm buildings seen in the photograph (see fig. 7.16) supplied to him by the Resors (see figs. 7.20–21).[39]

The collages are in fact perspectives seen from the living room that bridges the stream. But instead of extending the space into depth, as the foreshortened lines of internal columns and window mullions would imply, the compositions of cut-and-pasted photographs sandwich the room and compress the space into a strange, depthless void. Foreground becomes background, and vice versa. Architecture, as construction, disappears in this photographic tabula rasa. The blank vertical lines of the cruciform-shaped columns and window mullions, and the horizontal planes of floor and ceiling, are treated as reserved, negative spaces, cutting, surrounding, and providing the neutral two-dimensional ground for the freestanding objects in the room and the photographic images of the landscape hermetically sealing it and pressing in from the outside.

The view to the south shows the mountains in forced perspective, with a greatly enlarged color reproduction of the Paul Klee (1879–1940) painting *The Colorful Meal*, bought by the Resors in December 1937, acting as a floor-to-ceiling room divider behind a wood veneer service bar (fig. 7.20).[40] The sense of disorientation and displacement is physically reinforced by the deliberate play on distance and perspective.[41] The view in the other direction, to the snow-capped Tetons, provides even fewer spatial indices, foregrounding the image of the mountains as a matter of topographic location rather than a continuous field of human occupation (fig. 7.21). Indeed, a preliminary version of the collage looking north offers many more indications of local culture, such as the rustic bridge in the foreground and the nearby barn and ranch buildings (fig. 7.22). As they were cropped out, the singular drama of the scene now made it seem as if nothing else were there but the mountains.

The spatial discontinuity and sense of alienation conveyed by the collages contrasts palpably with many of the country house designs Mies had produced in Germany in the earlier part of the decade. In the project for the Hubbe House at Magdeburg (1935), for instance, a delicate perspectival drawing weaves interior and exterior together in a composition where space, structure, and landscape are seen and felt as transparent to and integral with one another

7.20 Resor House project. Interior perspective (collage), looking south, ca. 1939

7.21 Resor House project. Interior perspective (collage), looking north, ca. 1939

7.22 Resor House project. Preliminary interior perspective (collage), looking north, ca. 1939

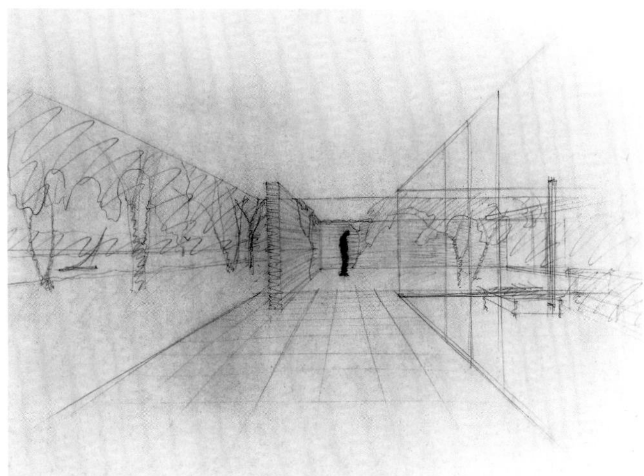

7.23 Mies. Hubbe House project, Magdeburg, 1935. Interior perspective

7.24 Mies. Alexanderplatz project, Berlin, 1928. Aerial view (photomontage)

7.25 Mies. Concert Hall project, 1941–42. Interior perspective (collage) (later altered)

(fig. 7.23).[42] The sense of being at home in the world contrasts with the *unheimlich* quality of the Resor House. In large part, this has to do with the difference between the seamless continuity of the drawing and the abrupt transitions and dislocations of the collage. This leads one to consider the Resor House in relation to Mies's earlier photomontages, the technique he favored in the twenties.

In his project of 1928 for the redevelopment of Berlin's Alexanderplatz (fig. 7.24), there is a similar opposition of light and dark—of new construction and existing environment. But in the earlier photomontage, the new is highlighted in contrast to the old. The modern buildings are foregrounded with an auratic glow, while the surrounding environment is seen in dreary relief. In the Resor House, the priorities are reversed. The building's modern structure is dematerialized, almost to the point of self-denial, while the surrounding environment is made the positive visual presence. One can almost speak here of an absence of volition, a submission to forces beyond one's control. The continuous surface and hierarchically gradated design for the Alexanderplatz show the architect in control, manipulating the existing urban fabric and asserting a new presence in the center. In the Resor House, modern technology is reduced to a mere frame—and a negative one at that—for editing a distant, alien, and unfamiliar nature. The photographic representation of the landscape preserves and asserts its exteriority to the perceiving subject, as a perspectival rendering would not. The architecture registers the mountain's existence as a fact, outside and beyond, yet constantly in view. The collage maintains the environment's otherness, "for only in this way," as Wolf Tegethoff noted, "can the interior maintain its identity and integrity, provide shelter and security, and nevertheless convey a feeling of freedom."[43]

These signs of alienation and displacement read as powerful expressions of the experience of exile in a personal and general, rather than a specifically political, sense. Between the Resor House and the new campus for AIT/IIT, which he began planning in 1939 and where he completed the Minerals and Metals Research Building in 1942–43, his first building in the United States (see fig. I.2), Mies designed two hypothetical large public structures that gave expression to the political dimension through explicit references to the war in Europe. The first was the Concert Hall and the second the Museum for a Small City. Designed between 1941 and 1943, both were developed in connection with masters' theses at IIT that Mies had been supervising.[44]

Concert Hall and Museum for a Small City

The Concert Hall, which is generally dated 1941–42, was described by Mies's biographer Franz Schulze as arguably "the pivotal work of his career" (fig. 7.25).[45] Philip Johnson highlighted the project in the retrospective of the architect's work he organized at New York's Museum of Modern Art in 1947 and described it in the monograph that accompanied

7.26 Albert Kahn. Martin Assembly Building, Glenn L. Martin Aircraft Plant, Middle River, Md., 1937. Interior, ca. 1938

the exhibition as Mies's "most astounding new creation."[46] Surely as an indication of the personal significance Mies himself attached to the design, he offered the collage as a present to his lover, the sculptor Mary Callery, whom he met around the time of the exhibition and who eventually donated the drawing to the Museum of Modern Art to form a centerpiece of their collection of Mies's works.

Both in its formal and its political implications, the collage represents one of the most provocative moves in the history of twentieth-century architecture. As Mies scholars have consistently asserted, it is the first example of the type of "universal space" that would characterize many of the architect's most unusual and influential designs in the postwar period.[47] But as a collage pure and simple, meaning an autonomous object of art—and it was nothing other than that, since it was accompanied by no plans, elevations, or sections—it had much more radical implications. Instead of designing the building himself, Mies used a photograph of one that had recently been published and then merely inserted his spatial arrangement and iconographic treatment by means of collage. The Mies building thus became a kind of "assisted readymade," to use Marcel Duchamp's

7.27 Martin Assembly Building. Exterior, with Martin Mars airplane, ca. 1941–42. From *Martin Star*, 1942

7.28 Concert Hall project. Preliminary interior perspective (collage)

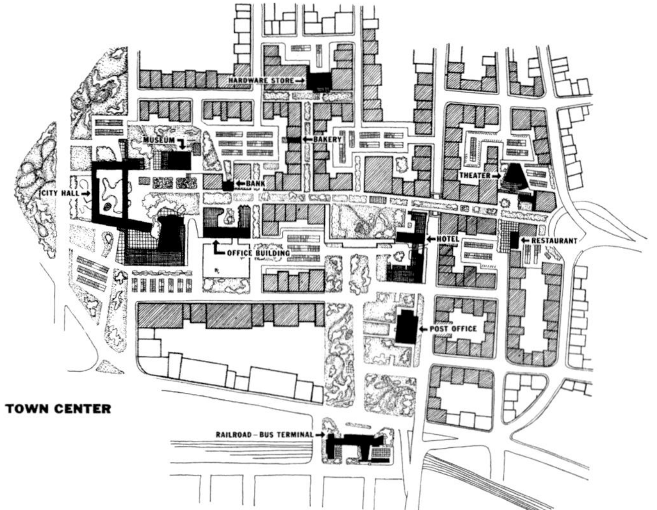

7.29 Town Center, "New Buildings for 194X." Plan. From *Architectural Forum*, 1943

(1887–1968) term. The photograph was of Albert Kahn's (1869–1942) Assembly Building for the Glenn Martin Aircraft Plant at Middle River, Maryland, built in 1937 and published by George Nelson in a monograph on Kahn two years later (fig. 7.26).[48]

The Kahn building was a landmark in the history of engineering. With its 300-foot-long, 30-foot-deep trusses, it was the largest flat span ever constructed. But this was not merely technology for technology's sake. The structure's purpose was to provide a large enough column-free space for the manufacture of the Martin Mars airplane (fig. 7.27). Designed to serve the Navy as a "flying battleship," with a range of 5,000 miles and a payload of 35,000 pounds, this major investment in America's accelerating preparations for war had a 200-foot wingspan, the largest of any plane at the time.[49] The Kahn building was also used to manufacture the B-26 bomber (called the Marauder), the A-30 Maryland fighter plane (already being used by France and Britain against Germany, beginning in 1939), and the PBM-1 Mariner, designed to destroy German submarines. In the photograph published by Nelson, there is a China Clipper (the prototype of the Mars), a Maryland, and B-26 Marauder behind it, as well as a PBM-1 Mariner to the far right, in front of the dark partition. By the time Mies fixed upon the photograph of the Martin Assembly Building, the United States had entered the war, and the Mariners and Marauders being manufactured in it had begun to attack German positions. For a German living in America, to call this image highly charged can hardly be an overstatement.[50]

Unlike the collages for the Resor House, which were constructed, in effect, of planes of paper, here Mies worked by a gradual and deliberate process of negation: erasing, defacing, and masking evidence of the actual airplanes. After having the photograph enlarged into a photostat, he apparently first blacked out the small Mariner on the right, along with the high wing and propellers of the China Clipper in the center, by inking in the spaces between the Benday dots. The next step was to overlay the perspectivally adjusted pieces of white, gray, and yellow paper forming the floor, ceiling, and walls of the auditorium proper, leaving visible only a group of men just to the right of center, in front of the B-26 (fig. 7.28). They were then obliterated, and along

7.30 Mies. Museum for a Small City project, "New Buildings for 194X," 1943. Elevation

with them almost any suggestion of an airplane behind, by a final overlay consisting of a reproduction of French sculptor Aristide Maillol's (1861–1944) figure of *The Mediterranean* (1902–5) (see fig. 7.25).[51]

Originally called *La Pensée* or *Thought*, the Maillol sculpture diverts attention from the background by confronting the viewer head-on with its inwardly directed expression of contemplation. Insulated from the surrounding factory by the panels of the auditorium shell, this image of self-absorption defines a zone of silence within what would otherwise be an indescribable din of machine tools, motors, and metalworking. The silencing of the noise of airplane manufacture becomes the aural metaphor for the visual masking of its production.[52] Why, one might ask, make this Sisyphean effort to fabricate concert hall conditions out of an acoustic nightmare, if not to foreground the very process of denial and negation underlying the act of introspection? Support for this conjecture is offered by the collage of the Museum for a Small City that Mies produced the following year, for which he chose as the focal image the most celebrated antiwar and most explicit anti-German work of art of the time.

The Museum for a Small City was the response to a commission by *Architectural Forum* in early February 1943 for an issue to be published in May devoted to the creation of an ideal American small city for the postwar period (fig. 7.29). Mies was asked to design a church, but he chose a museum, no doubt influenced by the fact that his student George Danforth had been working since 1940 on a master's thesis on the subject, in which Mies had become increasingly involved over the previous year.[53] The site, at the heart of the hypothetical town center, forms one side of the main plaza, adjoining Charles Eames's (1907–1978) City Hall and facing the concert hall and civic auditorium. A sketchy perspective of the pavilion-like building, however, shows it in an idealized setting, more reminiscent of the Teton Mountains than of the urban site it was supposed to occupy (fig. 7.30).

The collages of the museum's interior are in fact clearly dependent on the earlier Resor House, evincing the same type of planar composition, akin to Picasso's most classical papiers collés of 1912 or so, and completely different not only from that of the Concert Hall but also from the German and Soviet types of dynamic, diagonally based compositions—such as those of El Lissitzky (1890–1941) or Kurt

7.31 Museum for a Small City project. Interior perspective (collage)

Schwitters (1887–1948)—that Mies would have known. Among the collages of the museum, there is one in particular that illustrates what Mies stated was the driving idea of the design (fig. 7.31). That was, as he wrote, to create a space for Picasso's *Guernica* (1937) so that "it can be shown to greatest advantage," becoming "an element in space against a changing background."[54] While this description has led later critics and historians to assume that Mies approached the project as a purely formal problem in abstract design, the images themselves tell another story of a more representational order.[55]

Guernica is placed in the middle ground, slightly off-center. It is framed by two figures by Maillol: *Night* (1902) on the right and the *Monument to Cézanne* (1912–25) on the left. Behind are photographs of foliage (on the right) and water (on the left). Nature thus becomes the calm and serene background for culture. But unlike the Resor House (though similar to the Concert Hall), the flat cutouts here describe a perspectival space in which Picasso's painting—the only scene of activity—is isolated in space and time, like an event still unfolding. Maillol's *Night,* which turns its back on the painting, acts as a *repoussoir* figure, situating the image of war in the deep recesses of the mind—in sleep—somewhere between dream and reality. Based on such a reading, it is difficult not to see, in this premonition of André Malraux's (1901–1976) photograph-inspired *musée imaginaire* (museum without walls), a reaction to the terror of a new form of technological warfare that the photographs of Guernica's bombing had broadcast to the world just a few years before.

The incorporation of the Picasso painting, depicting the German Luftwaffe's brutal destruction of the Basque town of Guernica in late April 1937, could hardly have been taken by Mies simply as a formal problem. The painting's continual public display as the most powerful representation of antiwar, anti-Nazi propaganda began in the early summer of 1937 when it was exhibited in José-Luis Sert's (1902–1983) Spanish Pavilion at the Paris World's Fair as an act of protest against the Franco regime (fig. 7.32).[56] Mies visited Paris in early July that year to meet Helen Resor, just a few weeks after the much celebrated and highly controversial installation of Picasso's painting (Mies also went through Paris on his way to Wyoming in mid-August).[57] Throughout 1938 and early 1939, *Guernica* toured Scandinavia and Great Britain. In May 1939 it was brought to the United States by the Spanish Refugee Relief Campaign for a series of stops in different cities. Between the spring of 1939 and the fall of 1941, it was exhibited twice in Chicago (where Mies was living): first in the fall of 1939 at the Chicago Arts Club, and then in early 1940 as part of the large Picasso exhibition at the Chicago Art Institute that had been organized by Alfred Barr and first seen at New York's Museum of Modern Art.[58]

Wherever it was displayed, the painting evoked powerful feelings about the horrors of war and the dehumanizing effects of the technology driving it, symbolized by Picasso in the central lightbulb. Mies's construction of a "museum without walls" to show *Guernica* "to greatest advantage" leaves little doubt that he was aware of the painting's message. Like the painting itself, Mies's collage is black, white, and gray. Water, foliage, and bronze are drained of natural color. The modern nightmare depicted by Picasso is framed in a discourse of sleep, dream, and nature's timeless rhythms. In the face of the event, the human is reduced to a state of inaction, personified by what the French writer André Gide (1869–1951) described as the "muteness" of Maillol's figures. Before the war, Wilhelm Lehmbruck (1881–1919) and Georg Kolbe (1877–1947) were Mies's favorite sculptors; now the French neoclassicist Maillol took the place of the German Expressionists as his figural interlocutor.[59] The ambiguity of Maillol's figures may well have been the attraction. Does *Night* refuse to look at what is going on behind her back? Is she ashamed of what she has seen? Is her posture an expression of sorrow, or of despair? All these questions and more are inevitably brought to mind by the narrative of the museum-as-collage.

7.32 José-Luis Sert. Spanish Pavilion, International Exhibition, Paris, 1937. Interior, with Picasso's *Guernica*. From *Cahiers d'art*, 1937

Considered together, as pendants, the Concert Hall and the Museum reinforce one another's political and

7.33 El Lissitzky. *"Make More Tanks,"* 1941

representational content. Maillol's enigmatic role as mediator links the two projects while magnifying the questions they leave unresolved. The political message of the Concert Hall is clearly not as straightforward as, say, Lissitzky's contemporaneous work for the Stalin regime (fig. 7.33), although it is not for that reason any less political or representational. In his 1941 poster entitled *"Make More Tanks,"* Lissitzky used all the avant-garde conventions of the twenties to dramatize the collective Soviet wartime effort. The white halos around the tank and plane reify the thoughts in the minds of the workers, leading them toward a positive goal. The elements of collage in Mies's project have the opposite effect, erasing and wiping from the mind almost all evidence of war. Which necessarily brings up the question of how to read the design in relation to the war.

The combined meaning of the Concert Hall and the Museum is surely a complex one, to which we may never really be able to give a definitive answer. I should like, however, to offer some suggestions, placing special emphasis on the evidence of the works rather than the conscious or unconscious intentions of the author. Let me begin with the matter of program. In their devotion to music on one hand and fine arts on the other, these two civic projects can be seen as instituting a kind of aesthetic defense against the war. Yet the replacement of destructive war machinery by constructive cultural activity in the Concert Hall, along with the primacy of place given to Picasso's *Guernica* in the Museum, could lead one to interpret the projects as a profession of antiwar sentiment. But the character of the painting's installation, combined with the Concert Hall's silence on the subject, raises certain doubts.

In the Museum, the painting of the Nazi bombing is framed by two works of art and situated against a background of water and foliage; in the Concert Hall, the evidence of war is obliterated by the very act of sublimation the building performs to come into being. War, in effect, is naturalized and aestheticized by the act of collage. And so, one might then ask, is it not also neutralized? Here too we find we must defer, although Mies's collages can be seen as going that one step further and becoming a denial of the very condition of war itself, an attempt to turn one's back to the evidence and refuse to look it in the eye. This, of course, would fit with Mies's apolitical image. But if that were the case, why would he go to the trouble of producing such politically charged images in the first place? A reasonable response might be that, no matter how much an intellectual and artist like Mies tried to distance himself from everyday affairs, the war, if only because of his own enemy alien status, surely weighed heavily on his mind and raised certain issues about the interrelationship of architecture, politics, and culture that demanded to be acknowledged and ultimately represented in built form.

During the war, while Mies's activities were essentially limited to the drawing board, collage became a crucial means for such investigation. The inherent ambiguities of collage, as opposed to the more unified and totalizing character of the photomontage technique he had explored in the twenties, became the architectural correlative of his evolving political thought. Following the adoption of this new method in the Resor House, where it registered the condition of alienation and exile by the distancing of subject from object, Mies pressed the medium in the Concert Hall into a unique form of construction by occlusion that internalized the effects of war and represented, through figures of denial and silence—and against the powerful background of American industry—the sense of limbo one might have experienced as a German émigré at the time. And finally, in the Museum for a Small City, Mies manipulated the shifting, multilayered possibilities of the collage technique to project a more direct (though no less ambiguous) and even more complex statement about the war in Europe.

Postwar I-Beam

After the war, Mies's architecture underwent a decisive revision, based in large measure on ideas adumbrated in the collages of the three wartime projects discussed above. Franz Schulze, Fritz Neumeyer, and others have stressed the formal precedent they variously provide for the prismatic shape, static composition, large-scale clear-span space, and structural expression of Mies's later works.[60] In the concluding section of this chapter, however, I will focus on a more substantive issue deriving from the conception of figurative imagery and representational means the collages *as collages* display, in order to show how that underwrote the changes Mies effected in his system of design and ultimately determined the later architecture's content. Central to this

7.34 Mies. Navy Building (later Alumni Memorial Hall), Illinois Institute of Technology, Chicago, 1945–46. Exterior

discussion will be Mies's adoption of the standard American rolled steel I-beam as the "ready-made" signifier of a new structural order of representation.

Mies first used exposed steel I-beams or, more precisely, wide-flange beams in the Minerals and Metals Research Building, completed during the war as part of America's wartime effort, approximately four years after planning was begun for the new campus of what was soon to be IIT (see fig. I.2).[61] But it was only in 1946–47, with the completion of the buildings at the formal center of the campus, namely the Navy Building (later Alumni Memorial Hall), the Metallurgy and Chemical Engineering Building (later Perlstein Hall), and the Chemistry Building (later Wishnick Hall), that the question of representation came to the surface (fig. 7.34). In these, for the first time, Mies externalized the steel structure of the buildings as an essentially decorative and representational construct, acknowledging the applied, indeed collaged, character of the elements by stopping them just short of the ground (figs. 7.35–36). For reasons of fireproofing, he had to encase the I-shaped steel columns in concrete. But unlike earlier Chicago architects such as Louis

7.35 Navy Building. Exterior. Corner detail

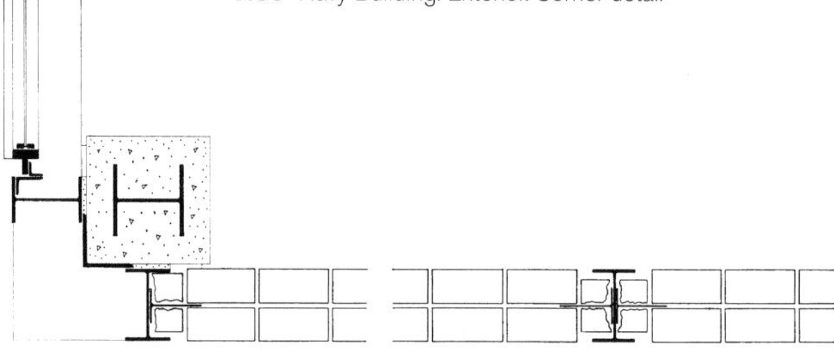

7.36 Navy Building. Partial plan

Sullivan who had faced the same problem, Mies believed that to give the structure visible expression he had to represent or replicate it in the same material on the building's surface (see fig. 5.26). As Mies later commented, there was what might be called a "good reason" for such a solution, and then there was the "real reason."[62] The "good reason," in this case, was that the channels of the exposed I-beams could act as receptacles for the aluminum window mullions and brick infill panels. But the "real reason," as is made evident again, even more clearly, in the plan of 860–880 North Lake Shore Drive (1948–51), was an aesthetic one (figs. 7.37–38). There, the attached I-beams, which do serve to stiffen the frame, set up an insistent and overall rhythm of vertical elements that represent the concealed structure for expressive purposes.[63]

Now let us consider how the three wartime collages provided the basis for this development. The first thing to note is that the I-beam was new to Mies's vocabulary and contrasted in almost every way with the typical cruciform-shaped support he had favored since the 1920s. Where the I-beam asserts a strong figural presence, with a face, a back, and a solid vertical spine, the cruciform-shaped column is a negative, inward-turning form. It is perceived as the linear abstraction of a point support (fig. 7.39; compare fig. 7.12). This was further emphasized by the reflective chrome casing that Mies had often used to sheathe the four steel angles bolted together to form the column's cross-section. The plan of the columns for the Barcelona Pavilion reveals another interesting fact, which is that the center of the construct is hollow, reinforcing our reading of the column not as a figure of support but as an abstract marker of space. It defines the internal edges of the floor's square grid and manifests in purely spatial terms the point of intersection of the planes. As a delineation of conjunction and crossing, the shimmering, chrome-sheathed column becomes as abstract as the Cartesian grid it defines.

Mies continued to employ this type of support in the Resor House (where it was to have been encased in bronze) and in the Museum for a Small City, but now the abstraction of the form came into conflict with the objective "reality" of the photographic image.[64] The contrast with the ready-made, sheer physical presence of the photograph in the Resor House threw into bold relief the column's dematerialized, nonobjective character—and this to such an extent that the cruciform-shaped support no longer appeared as a positive point of intersecting planes but rather as a negative cut or gap in the picture of reality presented in the view of the landscape. The cruciform column thus became a void

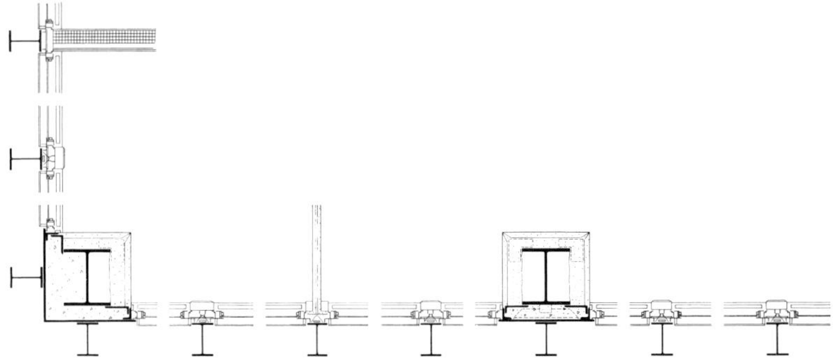

7.37 Mies. 860–880 North Lake Shore Drive Apartment Buildings, Chicago, 1948–51. Partial plan

7.38 860–880 North Lake Shore Drive Apartment Buildings. Under construction

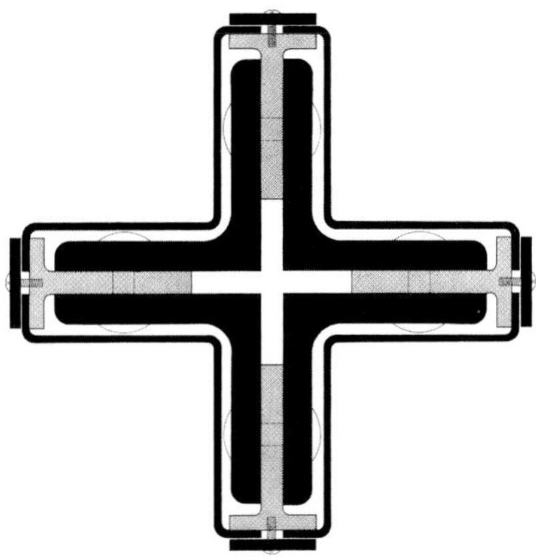

7.39 Barcelona Pavilion. Plan of column

7.40 Mies. Farnsworth House, Plano, Ill., 1945–51. Exterior

that had to be and soon would be filled, as in the Farnsworth House (conceived 1945–46; built 1949–51), by the ready-made, structural reality of the more assertive wide-flange I-shaped column (fig. 7.40).

In the Farnsworth House, the physical reality of the steel structure in the background of the Concert Hall is literally brought into the foreground as the building's declarative image. Though not strictly representational in Laugier's terms, since the exposed columns do not portray anything otherwise hidden, the whiteness of their painted surface nevertheless transforms the standard steel members into something other than a mere structural apparatus. Like actors onstage, the members seem to be playing a special role in an architectural drama and thus are, in effect, idealized. More important for us, however, is the way in which the photographic reality of the figure of the landscape in the Resor House seems to have imploded in on the structural voids of its architectural ground to reemerge, on the exterior plane of the window walls of the Farnsworth House, with a physical presence that now gives the structure a figural role of its own. As the embodiment of a new technological order, the I-shaped columnar figure positively defines—as it frames—the surrounding landscape.

We can see how the figure-ground reversal may have occurred by revisiting the Concert Hall, the project that lay on the cusp of Mies's changeover from the cruciform to the I-shaped column.[65] At the same time, we will be able to see more clearly what this reversal implies about the question of concealment and expression of meaning. From the point of view of representation, the Concert Hall can be read as an inversion of the Resor House (see figs. 7.21 and 7.25). In the house, the physical reality of the ready-made imagery is given over to the nonarchitectural elements; in the Concert Hall, by contrast, it is the architectural structure that is made physically present through the photograph. And where the structure is kept in reserve in the house, obstructing a continuous view of the landscape, in the Concert Hall it is the applied planes of paper that mask the structure and its graphic contents. Thus, when the reality of the ready-made imagery finally takes on the positive form of the steel structure of Albert Kahn's airplane factory, its connotations and supplementary meanings relating to the military-industrial complex are concealed from the observer's aesthetic attentions.

Because of its idealizing whiteness and bucolic setting, the Farnsworth House appears to exemplify the process of transformation and sublimation that lies at the core of artistic representation. But it is Mies's more typical buildings, like the Navy Building (Alumni Memorial Hall) at IIT and the double apartment block on North Lake Shore Drive, that prove more instructive and enlightening for the very fact that they had to accommodate those realities of construction such as fireproofing that forced the architect to make the distinction between the real and the ideal—or truth and verisimilitude—and thus give us the evidence of deception, which is to say the fiction that is a fundamental aspect of the process of representation.

The "Homeless Representation" of Mies in America

Mies's system of representation, while grounded in a theory of fiction no less absolute than that of Alberti or Laugier, was different from the earlier conceptions in an important way. Where classical and neoclassical architects placed little artistic value on the real physical substrate of a building and invested the process of transformation from one material to another with transcendental meaning, Mies refused to disregard the facts of construction in the representational operation. Nor did he see the need, as had Sullivan and the other early skyscraper architects, to give the outward expression of the inner construction a substantially different shape or even material form of existence. Mies thus both came to terms with the reliance on the "thing-in-itself" that lay at the core of modern abstraction while at the same time restoring to representation some of its historical force.

The attached I-beams in Mies's postwar buildings are neither the structure itself nor merely a heterogeneous "expression" of it. Rather, they are, as Robert Venturi noted, "rhetorical."[66] Those who have dealt with this matter in any great detail have tended to describe the Miesian solution, especially as it evolved at North Lake Shore Drive, either as a form of "symbolic" substitution or as a matter of "metaphor." In what remains the most interesting and extensive treatment of the subject, William Jordy (1917–1997) called the applied I-beams a "surrogate of the actual structure" and characterized Mies's rhythmic grouping of them as "the symbolic pilasters of his builded-art."[67] In employing these I-beams "to articulate the walls... much as pilasters articulated a classical or Renaissance wall," Mies, in Jordy's view, "reinvigorate[d] the whole of the classicizing tradition for present use."[68] Thomas Beeby, in a general discussion of the idea of ornament in modern architecture, spoke of the "very sophisticated ornamental device" of the attached I-beams "as a visual metaphor for the structure behind," acutely noting that the steel mullions are merely a "reiteration" and not a transformation of what lies underneath.[69]

In idealizing the actual structure rather than imitating an ideal one, Mies's collaged I-beams do not represent something other than what they are. They function as signs of what is not there to be seen otherwise. In sidestepping the issue of illusionism by short-circuiting the question of credibility, the reiterated I-beams redefine the process and meaning of representation in quintessentially modern terms, that is to say as a matter of signification rather than one of figuration. The form "I-beam" is neither "invented" nor "reinvented"; it is, as Jordy noted, just "the utterly commonplace, banal stock item of the steel mill."[70] Such is what Mies had in mind, I think, when he would paraphrase Thomas Aquinas, saying "truth is the significance of facts."[71] Mies's represented structure signifies the factual conditions on which its being depends and from which it draws its meaning. As an idealization of these conditions, it gives new meaning to the modern myth of the "thing-in-itself" and thereby collapses the idea of abstraction into a new and credible form of representation.[72]

The history of modern art and architecture has been written mainly from the point of view of abstraction, so it is often difficult to comprehend fully the significance and changing character of the representational impulse that has been equally at work within it. It is no doubt for this reason that Clement Greenberg referred to Jasper Johns's (b. 1930) work of the mid- to late 1950s as a prime example of the "homeless representation" he traced back to the influence of Cubism (fig. 7.41). Though lacking any true ground in a traditional sense of the word, Johns's literalist form of "reproduction" was, in the critic's view, alien to modern abstract practices, his "'sculptures' amount[ing] to nothing more than what they really are." "Everything that usually serves representation and illusion is left to serve nothing but itself, that is, abstraction; while everything that usually serves the abstract," Greenberg wrote, "... is put to the service of representation."[73]

7.41 Jasper Johns. *Light Bulb*, 1960

Thinking of Mies in terms of Johns's nearly contemporary cast bronze sculptures of commonplace objects might therefore be of some use in understanding the broader implications of what occurred worldwide, though perhaps first and most trenchantly in American art and architecture of the postwar period. Like Mies's I-beam, Johns's *Light Bulb* or *Painted Bronze* (ale cans) of 1960 redefine representation in the mechanical terms of replication and reproduction. Literality, even more than metaphor, is the issue. Muteness and silence are the operative terms of expression. The material presence of a common object—the "thing-in-itself"—becomes a means for questioning the loss of subjectivity and the increasing abstraction and anonymity of modern life.[74]

Seriality—and the attendant flattening out of experience—is one result of mechanical reproduction, as Andy Warhol (1928–1987) showed in his multiple representations of silk-screened photographs ranging from dollar bills and Campbell soup cans to electric chairs and fatal car crashes (fig. 7.42). His 1965 painting of an atom bomb blast drives home the power of modernist representation to disclose, in unexpected ways, things that otherwise might be allowed to slip back into the recesses of the mind. Yet, no matter how literal and seemingly self-evident the image appears, there is always a blur. By definition, representation entails the concealing of something else, something that is both suggested by its replacement, as well as something we are dissuaded from thinking about by that very act

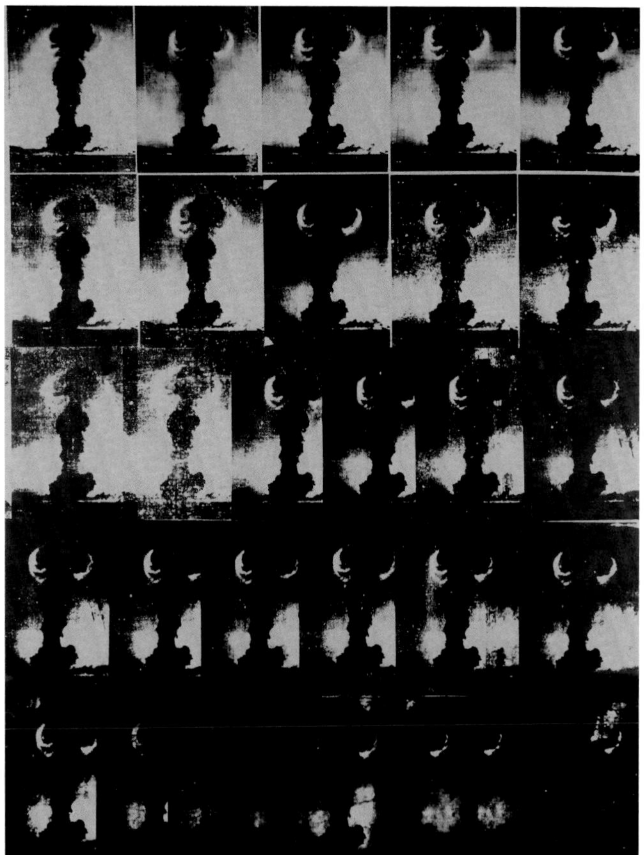

7.42 Andy Warhol. *Atomic Bomb*, 1965

of replacement. To begin to correlate in our mind's eye the seen and the unseen, the known and the unknown, we first have to identify the signs.

If we are eventually to understand what Mies's architecture represents in terms of modern culture and its history, we must, at the outset, try to determine what value and meaning to assign to the I-beam, the sign par excellence of the architect's representational vocabulary. There can be little doubt that steel, especially for the European looking to America for a vision of modernity in the 1920s and '30s, was not a neutral, value-free material. Both Richard Neutra, in his book *Wie baut Amerika?* (1927), and Erich Mendelsohn (1887–1953), in his *Amerika* of one year earlier, depicted the application of the products of the steel industry to architecture in a quasi-utopian light (see fig. 7.3). Steel and later aluminum represented, as perhaps no other materials did, the power and force of modern industry, initially embodied in the railroad, then in the ocean liner and automobile, and finally in the manufacture of airplanes. It was a force both for good and for ill. Mies clearly pondered the meaning of all this long and hard, as was his wont. "Technology is far more than a method," he wrote in 1950, "it is a world in itself."[75] In Mies's view, it was technology that distinguished the modern age from all previous periods in history and defined, in "objective" and "expressive" terms, as he noted, "the inner structure of the epoch out of which [a true architecture] arises."[76] But technology, he also said, "promises both power and grandeur, a dangerous promise for man who has been created neither for one nor the other."[77]

Although Mies often presented himself as merely an instrument of this power—"serving" it rather than "ruling" it, as he would say[78]—he surely saw, in its unalloyed expression in the Martin Assembly Building, something that needed editing and even commentary. However we wish to interpret it, the process of editing involved concealment and sublimation. That editing and that sublimation took a different course once the war was over. At that point, the power of technology came to the surface. It was represented, and made into an order, with all the authority the classical orders once had, though without their metaphorical transparency. Mies openly celebrated and gave ideal form to the industrial machinery that had brought Allied victory in World War II and his adopted country of the United States to its position of international power.[79] His new technological order encoded those "facts" and gave modern architecture, for nearly a quarter of a century, a lingua franca rigorously commensurate with them. In this light, Mies's wartime experience, as viewed through the collages for the Resor House, the Concert Hall, and the Museum for a Small City, seems less like an interregnum in his career than a time of profound and substantive reorientation for modern architecture as a whole. Key to this rethinking was his transformation into purely material terms of the fictive language of representation. In the process, the previously hard and fast distinction between the abstract and the representational was suspended.

8

The Aesthetic of the Unfinished and the Example of Louis Kahn

IN ONE OF THE MOST celebrated and oft-quoted statements defining the romantic condition of early modern art and thought, Friedrich Schlegel (1772–1829) noted in his *Athenaeum Fragments* (1798) that, whereas "many works of the ancients have become fragments" and are known only in the form of ruins, "many works of the moderns are fragments at the time of their origin."[1] For Schlegel, as for numerous writers and artists since, the fragmentary nature of ancient and medieval ruins was of contemporary import precisely because it reflected and thereby expressed the sense of incompleteness, openness, ambiguity, and potentiality that has been at the core of the modern achievement and dilemma in the production of art and architecture.[2]

Throughout the ongoing architectural debate in the later eighteenth, nineteenth, and twentieth centuries over questions of structure, function, ornament, and representation, the ruin generally served as the avatar of the unfinished in a dynamic, dialectical relationship with its double. Almost by default, the peculiarly modern aesthetic of the unfinished was invariably represented by the more obvious historical image of the ruin. Nowhere is this subtle interchange more evident than in the work of Louis Kahn (1901–1974). Commenting on his design for the Library at Phillips Exeter Academy (1965–72) in an interview that was published the year after the building's opening, Kahn responded to the question of whether "the architect ever build[s] just for needs" in the following way:

> No. Never build for needs! ... I think a space evokes its use. It transcends need. If it doesn't do that then it has failed .... When a building is being built, there is an impatience to bring it into being. Not a blade of grass can grow near this activity. Look at the building after it is built. Each part that was built with so much activity and joy and willingness to proceed tries to say when you're using the building, "Let me tell you about how

I was made." Nobody is listening because the building is now satisfying need. The desire in its making is not evident. As time passes, when it is a ruin, the spirit of its making comes back. It welcomes the foliage that entwines and conceals. Everyone who passes can hear the story it wants to tell about its making. It is no longer in servitude; the spirit is back.[3]

Kahn had previously described the unglazed, freestanding, arcaded screen walls he designed to provide protection from the sun for the interiors of some of his structures as "wrapping ruins around buildings" (fig. 8.1), so it is not surprising that most historians and critics have focused on the end result of the story he told of the intercourse of "need" and "desire."[4] But for Kahn, the "breakthrough," the "wonder," was always found in "beginnings," the "Volume 0, ...which has not yet been written."[5] It is also not surprising to note that earlier iterations of his unfinished/ruin narrative downplay the role of the ruin to give proper weight to the conceptually more significant state of incompleteness. In an essay entitled "Architecture: Silence and Light," published in 1970, Kahn remarked that "I note that when a building is being made, free of servitude, its spirit to be is high—no blade of grass can grow in its wake. When the building stands complete and in use, it seems to want to tell you about the adventure of its making. But all the parts locked in servitude make this story of little interest. When its use is spent and it becomes a ruin, the wonder of its beginning appears again."[6]

In Kahn's little tale, the ruin simply perpetuates and reflects the suggestive potentiality of the unfinished. As for Schlegel, the sense of incompleteness in a building was perceived by Kahn as a fundamental reality of modern artistic thought and thus had to be embodied in the completed work itself. But more important for us, in its dyadic relation to the ruin, the projection of a sense of the unfinished became for

8.1 Louis Kahn. Salk Institute for Biological Studies, La Jolla, Calif., 1959–65. Meeting House project, 1960–62. Partial model

Kahn a fundamental means for reengaging modern architecture with certain representational practices of the previous two centuries that had come to seem irrelevant over the course of the first half of the twentieth century. In returning modern architectural thinking about representation to its origins, Kahn's work from the mid-1950s through the mid-1970s serves both to close the era that has been the subject of this book and to provide a basis for the postmodern one that would follow.[7]

The Aesthetic of the Unfinished

The aesthetic of the unfinished first emerged with the Renaissance, at the very beginning of the postmedieval era.[8] Both Leonardo and Michelangelo were plagued at various points in their careers by an inability or lack of will to bring certain of their paintings and sculpture to completion. Of the two, it was Michelangelo who is responsible for having made an aesthetic of the idea, if not entirely self-consciously, then at least in the eyes of history. The very term *non finito* was in fact coined during the period to describe works like the "*Slave*" or "*Captives*" (1513–16) and the *Rondanini Pietà* (ca. 1555–74) (fig. 8.2).[9] Giorgio Vasari, a colleague and friend of the sculptor and author of the first work of modern art history, explained the lack of finish in part as an index of the artist's "grandiose and awesome conceptions" that could never be given complete physical expression.[10]

Michelangelo's case was unusual, and it was not until the early nineteenth century that his *non finito* was taken as a prescription for practice and appropriated to serve as a sign of modern ideas of suggestiveness, ambiguity, and subjectivity. These romantic readings of Michelangelo stressed the aspects of intentionality, of self-consciousness, and of the Neoplatonic distinction between conception and realization, between idea and form.[11] Finish, in this modern understanding of the Renaissance sculptor, implied superficiality, mere virtuosity, and most of all an academic conventionality devoid of individual expression and divorced from the complexities of contemporary life.[12] The unfinished, by contrast, revealed the difficult transaction that takes place in art between the unknown and the known, between the abstraction of thought and the material demands of brute matter.

The most immediate and direct indicator of an artist's original idea, and therefore of his or her imaginative faculty, was thought to be the sketch, an idea that can be traced back to the seventeenth century. But, by the nineteenth century, with John Constable (1776–1837) and J. M. W. Turner (1775–1851) in England and Eugène Delacroix (1798–1863) in France, the vitality and spontaneity of the initial sketch were incorporated into the final work, which now rejected the tight contour drawing and smooth shading of the academic manner in favor of a looseness and roughness in the handling of the pictorial surface.[13] It is perhaps no coincidence that Delacroix was one of the first artists to reread Michelangelo in modern terms and to appreciate the artistic effect of his *non finito*.

By the third quarter of the nineteenth century, with Manet and the Impressionists, lack of conventional finish

8.2 Michelangelo. "*Young Slave*" (for Tomb of Julius II), 1513–16

8.3 Willem de Kooning. *Two Women's Torsos*, 1952

became a defining feature of modern art.[14] In seeking to create the image of an immediate and direct transcription of a person, object, or event, these artists emphasized as never before the essential character of the medium of paint as perceived in natural light and at a specific moment in time. While there were deviations from the purely painterly effects of sketchiness in certain types of modern art in the following century, a refusal to adopt the broader idea of conventional finish either in terms of form or of subject matter characterized the advanced art of the period. From Fauvism and Cubism through Abstract Expressionism, the effects of the unfinished were employed to manifest a range of meanings—from the expression of spontaneity and creative vitality to the insistence on the nature of the medium, to the porousness and openness of the image to interpretation, to the very ambiguity and occlusion of meaning the last might imply (fig. 8.3). Indeed, by the 1950s, when Kahn began designing his first mature buildings, the aesthetic of the unfinished had come to be taken for granted as a fundamental determinant of modern art.[15]

8.4 Giulio Romano. Palazzo del Te, outside Mantua, 1526–31. Entrance

The aesthetic of the unfinished has played a much less obvious role in the evolution of modern architecture than in that of the other arts—or so it would seem. It also took a more varied course, involving a broad range of motivations producing often quite disparate effects. Despite the fact that the very first building recorded in the Western literary tradition, the Tower of Babel, was unfinished—and gained its meaning thereby—the deliberately unfinished as an architectural concept would appear to be an oxymoron. Buildings, by definition, have to be finished if they are to be used. Alberti's Palazzo Rucellai and the Church of San Francesco at Rimini are both unfinished (see figs. I.7 and 4.16), but we generally either read that aspect out of our consideration or use it as a basis for reconstructing the artist's intention. For buildings to function, it would seem, they must be finished. Visibly unfinished buildings such as the Guggenheim Foundation in Venice, where only the ground floor of the former eighteenth-century Palazzo Venier dei Leoni that it occupies was ever constructed, strike us as bizarre, not simply because they are unfinished but because we use them and think of them as if they were finished. On the other hand, a work like Antoni Gaudí's church of the Sagrada Familia in Barcelona (begun 1880s) is understood less as unfinished than as being continually in the process of construction—and thus akin to the medieval cathedrals on which it was modeled.

Although Michelangelo never translated his *non finito* into the realm of architecture, other architects of the period played with the idea in a way that suggests how it would ultimately be understood in later romantic and modern thought. Giulio Romano's Palazzo del Te outside Mantua (1526–31) is a perfect example. The entrance to the central court is through a passage covered by an elaborately decorated barrel vault composed of alternating octagonal and square coffers, delicately outlined by raised moldings (fig. 8.4). However, the flat-arched lintels, themselves finely

8.5 John Soane, *Bank of England,* 1788–1833. Cutaway aerial perspective, by Joseph Gandy, 1830

detailed with running moldings and intermittent vermiculated keystones, are supported by crude Tuscan Doric columns designed to look unfinished. Instead of sporting smooth shafts from base to capital, they are left in the rough. Hollows at the tops and bottoms of the shafts, just above the base moldings and below those of the capitals, indicate that the process of carving was stopped midway. Though understandable as part of a Mannerist game, the unfinished shafts make the more significant point that finish in architecture, especially in classical architecture, is a matter of superficial decorative or ornamental elaboration—and that a lack of finish is therefore a lack of appropriate dressing.

In the second half of the eighteenth century, Laugier's postulation of the primitive hut as the origin of the classical temple as well as the guarantor of its rational form placed the image of the unfinished at the center of advanced thinking in the field. By its celebration of the supposed rude wooden structures of early humans, the concern with origins increased the self-consciousness of the distinction between mere construction and the decorative development of the orders. At the same time, the relationship between finish and decoration became more explicit and more problematic as the interest in ruins—those "fragments" of the ancient world, as Schlegel referred to them—excited architects' imaginations as well as archaeological study. A ruin represents part of what once existed, the remains of a past having been acted upon by the forces of nature and time. The eroded surfaces of a ruin present an appearance of incompleteness that only archaeological reconstruction can undo. In this theoretical sense, then, the ruin is the double of the unfinished. Both provide a similar basis for the imaginary to operate, and both, figured in the mind as fragments, came to share the same ontological status. The late eighteenth-century Temple of Modern Philosophy at the Château of Ermenonville, discussed in chapter 2, makes that identity manifest (see figs. 2.4–5).

René de Girardin's unfinished temple even today forces the observer to do a double take. No matter how much we are prepared for it, the realization that the building is unfinished (and not a ruin) is difficult to internalize. Indeed, the attraction of such architectural indeterminacy led to a fascinating type of didactic representation in the nineteenth century that links John Soane and Joseph Gandy to Viollet-le-Duc and Auguste Choisy (1841–1909). At the beginning of this chain lies Gandy's watercolor of Soane's Bank of England, exhibited at London's Royal Academy in 1830 (fig. 8.5). It shows the entire block Soane began working on in 1788, in a cutaway aerial perspective taken from the southeast. A storm has just passed over the building, appearing to leave in its wake a path of destruction brought to light in the ensuing calm. But on closer inspection, what seemed at first to be a ruin is verisimilarly a projection of the site under construction. Only the image's southwest corner, which represents a small percentage of the whole, is completed. Still under the storm cloud, it reveals the undercroft of foundations while at the same time offering a fairly realistic view of how the architect would employ the decorative orders of the classical system to enclose and finish the structure.[16]

Like Gandy's other drawings of various interiors of the bank, showing them both before and after completion—meaning decoration (see figs. 3.25–26)—the final aerial perspective told the nineteenth-century audience a story about the representational capacities of contemporary classical architecture through the relation between construction and decoration. The narrative relied on the image of the unfinished to make its point, namely that building only becomes architecture—and thus takes on meaning—when it receives the finish of decoration, or rather, as in the neoclassical context, when the decoration is constructed. Just about twenty-five years later, but with a different perspective on the value of the classical tradition, Viollet-le-Duc employed the same time-lapse technique to produce a more ambiguous message. Beginning with the first volumes of his *Dictionnaire raisonné de l'architecture française du XIe au XVIe siècle* (1854–68) and including, most notably, the historical survey of architecture from ancient times to the present recounted in the first volume of his *Entretiens sur l'architecture* (1863), he made considerable use of the cutaway perspectival section to illustrate, in a single drawing, the multiple stages in a building's construction (see fig. 5.10). But it was in two large-scale color drawings that he prepared in 1867 for the new curriculum at Emile Trélat's (1821–1907) Ecole Centrale (later Spéciale) d'Architecture that the power of the idea became fully manifest.[17]

One of the drawings is a cutaway aerial perspective of a Greek Doric temple, the other of a Roman bath (based on the Baths of Caracalla) (figs. 8.6–7). The Greek temple is the less ambiguous of the two. Aside from the roof, which has yet to be completed, only two columns and the upper parts of the order are shown unfinished. The unfluted drums of the columns recall Giulio Romano's conceit at the Palazzo del Te. But here the purpose is the more straightforward one of showing the student how the temple's main structural elements received an integral decorative finish, as well as how nonarchitectural objects such as shields or war spoils were employed for ornamental purposes. Each material—be it stone, wood, terra cotta, bronze, or leather—is given its own specific color and treatment.

The analysis of the Roman bath is more complex. The view into the interior visualizes the process of construction in greater detail, so that we are made fully aware of what the concept of finish in this case means. The walls in the foreground are cut away and revealed in plan. The left half of the structure is stripped back to its brick and concrete piers, arches, and vaults, with a few marble elements just beginning to appear. The wall in the alcove in the center is broken open into a rough, gaping hole that, like the dome behind it and the haunches of the vaults above it, gives the partial impression of a structure in ruins. The building's right half,

8.6 Eugène-Emmanuel Viollet-le-Duc. *Analysis of the Structure of a Doric Temple,* prepared for the Ecole Centrale d'Architecture, 1867. Cutaway aerial perspective and plan

on the other hand, has received its enclosing vaults and much of its stucco and marble decoration. In its reliance on traditions of trabeation, that decoration contrasts markedly with the underlying arcuated construction in brick and concrete.

Unlike the finish in the Greek temple, which makes the building come alive, here the effect is almost the opposite. The disintegral character of the decorative system renders us skeptical of and ultimately hostile to its effects. The time-lapse drawing thus allows us to "see through" the missteps of the past, which the present, according to Viollet-le-Duc, had too often blindly followed.[18] With such historical hindsight, we therefore not only can read the drawing from left to right to see how the structure was brought to completion by the layering of representational decoration; we just as readily can read it the opposite way to understand what lies behind the surface and thus gain a more fundamental and "truthful" level of information. This act of disassembly throws into relief the dissembling appearance of the finished product. The unfinished thus serves as a critique of the finished and becomes a model for how the contemporary architect might proceed in rethinking the past.

Few nineteenth-century buildings achieved anything like the structural nakedness of the ruin or its counterpart, the unfinished. Only when iron was substituted for masonry in certain interiors did that begin to occur. Starting with Labrouste's Bibliothèque Sainte-Geneviève, the introduction of a metal structural system produced such enormous shifts in the perception of the relationship of mass to support that one has the impression of looking through a virtual surface to its internal skeleton (see fig. 4.30). In the vestibule, especially, the realization that the ceiling has been removed to allow a view of its internal beams almost immediately translates into a sense of a lack of conventional finish (fig. 4.27). The thin metal structure of the Produce Exchange at Berlage's Beurs in Amsterdam (1898–1903) is even less tied to traditional ornamental motifs than Labrouste's library and, partly as a result, causes

8.7 Viollet-le-Duc. *Analysis of the Structure of Roman Baths*, prepared for the Ecole Centrale d'Architecture, 1867. Cutaway aerial perspective

the observer to assume that a vaulted ceiling was never contemplated and that what is visible is the rather utilitarian roof structure that would otherwise have been hidden by it (fig. 8.8).

The complete elimination of the decorative cladding of a building's exterior envelope rarely occurred before the beginning of the twentieth century. In the Bibliothèque Sainte-Geneviève Administration Building, Labrouste repeated the decorative masonry detailing of the library located across the street—but only sparingly (fig. 8.9). While the corners received the full treatment, the rest was left comparatively unfinished, thus giving the smaller building an appropriate character of subservience. The exterior of Berlage's Exchange is even more plain. Except for some sculptural panels and the structural articulation of windows and arcades, the relatively flat and expansive surface of brick reminds one of the unfinished side of Viollet-le-Duc's Roman bath. It is therefore little wonder that Berlage was one of the first Europeans to be impressed with the radical bluntness and directness of expression that Frank Lloyd Wright's early work demonstrated to him when he visited the United States in 1911.[19]

Buildings such as Wright's Larkin Building, Unity Temple, and Robie House, all of which Berlage saw, revealed a new understanding of the relationship between construction and decoration (see figs. 6.17, 6.19, and 6.24). Writing in 1912, the American critic Montgomery Schuyler described such work as "rude, incomplete, unfinished," claiming that its "stark unmodelled" character made "the buildings seem 'blocked out,' and awaiting completion rather than completed."[20] Wright's search for an "integrity" of structure and form led him to eliminate the very idea of applied decoration in order to make material and shape, or volume, read as one. Wright also self-consciously accompanied his built work with texts that adopted a discourse of negation and elimination ("Decoration is dangerous..., for the present you are usually better off without it"; "Strip the wood of varnish and let it alone").[21]

8.8 Hendrik Petrus Berlage. Exchange, Amsterdam, 1898–1902. Interior. Produce Exchange

8.9 Henri Labrouste. Bibliothèque Sainte-Geneviève. Administration Building, 1845–50. Exterior

In the essay he wrote in 1911 for the smaller Wasmuth edition of Wright's early work, which may in fact have inspired Schuyler's thoughts on the subject, the British architect Charles Robert Ashbee (1863–1942) concluded that, although a lack of finish in the traditional understanding of the term was what gave Wright's architecture an undeniable power and modernity, it was something so unaccustomed and even crude that he thought the work ultimately failed on this score. "On the Romanesque churches of the old world," Ashbee wrote, "later generations set the mosaic, the tracery, the refinement and the culture that came with more leisure and sympathy; another century may

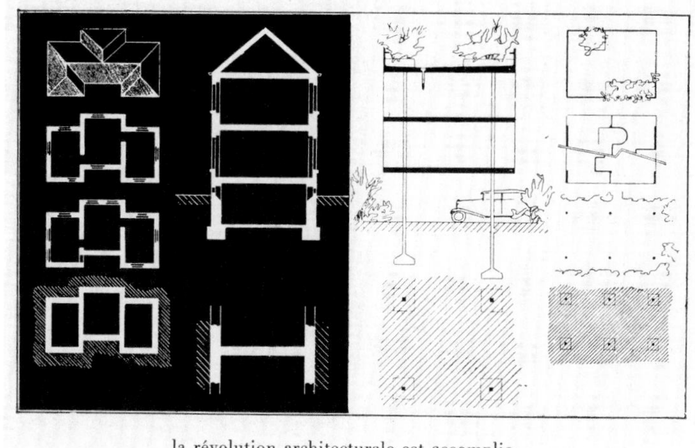

8.10 Le Corbusier. "The architectural revolution is complete . . .," ca. 1930. From Le Corbusier, *La Ville radieuse,* 1935

8.11 Le Corbusier, with Pierre Jeanneret. Museum of Living Artists project, Paris, 1930. Aerial perspective. From *Cahiers d'art,* 1931

do the same with the great experiments in architecture that America is putting forth. I have seen buildings of Frank Lloyd Wright's that I would like to touch with the enchanted wand; not to alter their structure in plan or form, but to clothe them with a more living and tender detail. I do not know how, and the time is not yet—nor would I like to see Wright do it himself, because I do not believe he could."[22] A leading figure in the Arts and Crafts movement, Ashbee believed that nothing would change until the resources of modern craftsmanship rose to the task of reviving the earlier idea of finish. Wright, on the other hand, was convinced that the machine had altered things forever.[23]

Ashbee's vision, of course, was never to come to fruition, but the thrust of his criticism, rephrased in terms of the larger social and economic conditions advanced by Wright in his advocacy of the machine, soon gave modern architecture an opening that it turned to its own advantage. In the buildings of the modern movement produced between the two world wars, the very idea of finish was reconceptualized in terms of modern industrial materials and methods of construction. Finish no longer implied an elaboration and disguising of the underlying structure through the addition of moldings, string courses, columns, cornices, and the like (see fig. 7.1). Rather, it was entirely redefined in the abstract terms of precision of detailing, clarity of natural surface, and purity of geometric forms (see fig. 7.10).[24] This had nothing to do with the traditional notion of finish and could, indeed, be interpreted as its opposite. At the same time, more positive aspects of the unfinished gave new directions to certain aspects of design, as they did in the allied arts. In terms of composition, for instance, Mies's celebrated Brick Country House project makes use of a centrifugal form of openness and lack of delimitation that ran counter to the idea of finish in the containment of classical composition (see fig. 7.6). Similarly, his Berlin projects for glass skyscrapers in the same period depend on the idea of the unfinished not only for their radical transparency and reflectivity but also for their refusal of any terminating devices that might delineate where the building meets the sky.

In his work of the 1920s and early '30s, Le Corbusier made the aesthetic of the unfinished an intrinsic part of his conception of modern architecture through the substitution of *pilotis* for the ground floor and a *toit-jardin* for the roof (fig. 8.10). The most radical extension of his programmatic embrace of the unfinished was his 1930 project for a Museum of Living Artists (fig. 8.11). The proposed building takes the form of a square spiral that starts from a small central core, expanding outward over time to accommodate future needs for additional exhibition space. The building thus has no facade. As at a construction site, a large stack of *pilotis* in front of the work in progress lies ready for use, not unlike the columns on the ground next to the Temple of Modern Philosophy at Ermenonville. This scheme became the model for his 1939 project for a Museum of Unlimited Growth for Philippeville (now Skikda), Algeria, and for the museums the architect ultimately built in Tokyo, Ahmedabad, and Chandigarh in the 1950s and '60s. But it was only in the post–World War II period, starting with the Unité d'Habitation at Marseille (1946–52), that the unfinished became the overriding and critical design element in Le Corbusier's work through his reliance on exposed reinforced concrete as a mono-material integrating structure and surface (fig. 8.12).[25] Le Corbusier referred to the material as *béton brut*, thus emphasizing its unfinished character. *Brut* can mean "brute" in the sense of "brute force"; but in its more typical reference to materials and their fabrication, it means "raw," "unpolished," "undressed," "crude," or, most important for us, "unfinished."

8.12 Le Corbusier. Unité d'Habitation, Marseille, 1946–52. Exterior. End with exposed stairway

Reacting to the Marseille Unité, the critic Reyner Banham spoke of the "crudities" and "rugged grandeur" of its unfinished concrete and described the result as "a kind of modern equivalent for rustication." Although he, like many others, ultimately equated the building with a "well-weathered," even "magnificent ruin," it was the unfinished, *brut* aspect of its *béton* that resonated most with the larger artistic discourse of the period and that came to have the greatest relevance for Louis Kahn.[26] Living for a time, as he said, "in a beautiful city called Le Corbusier," Kahn soon found a powerful new design methodology that combined the Corbusian material/structural technique and the open-ended modularity of the Miesian grid with a renewed interest in history, transforming the aesthetic of the unfinished into a thoroughgoing renewal of the concept of representation.[27]

Yale University Art Gallery and the Appearance of the Unfinished

Kahn's career as a mature architect is usually considered to have begun in 1951 with his rather Miesian design for the Yale University Art Gallery in New Haven, Connecticut, but only to have achieved his own characteristic voice with the more historicizing and overtly representational work produced from the early 1960s on. If his later return to Roman precedent signals a clear break with the abstraction of modern architecture of the interwar years as well as with the representational strategy offered by Mies's postwar example, Kahn's abiding interest in the idea of the unfinished links the two apparently distinct phases of his architectural production.

Despite the fairly considerable literature that is now devoted to Kahn's architecture, there are precious few references to the unfinished quality of his buildings. Vincent Scully, who had been a friend of Kahn's since 1947 and wrote the first book-length study of his work, once commented in passing that "in a curious way, the Yale [University] Art Gallery is an unfinished building" but then, without elaborating, quickly went on to note that it was eventually "completed by Rudolph's Art and Architecture Building" when the latter was built just beyond it on Chapel Street.[28] Scully also remarked that in his later work at Phillips Exeter Academy, Kahn "won't allow [the Library] to come together at the corners as a completed building" (see fig. 8.45). But there the architect's reason, according to Scully, was not to give an appearance of the unfinished; rather, it was to have "us see the building as a brick and concrete ruin."[29] Indeed, as early as his extremely influential 1962 monograph on the architect, Scully related the major changes in Kahn's work around 1960 to his interest in Roman ruins. The idea that Kahn envisaged his buildings as resembling ruins has been a dominant theme in scholarship ever since.[30]

In her book on the architect, Sarah Williams Goldhagen points out that the paintings and drawings Kahn produced between 1948 and 1950 while he was teaching at Yale "suggest that he...absorbed [the artist Willem] de Kooning's [1904–1997] interest in the unfinished and in the expression of the artistic process, first directly and then later from de Kooning himself" (see fig. 8.3).[31] But she does not explore how this interest might have affected Kahn's architectural design thinking as a whole other than to note, without reference back to de Kooning, the Corbusian use of *béton brut* and a general directness and frankness in revealing the materials and methods of construction of the first significant building he was commissioned to design following his exposure to the Abstract Expressionist painter's thought. Scully's perception of the unfinished character of the Yale University Art Gallery, which was built in 1951–53, is thus the logical starting point for an analysis of the initial impact of the idea on Kahn's architecture, especially since it predates by nearly a decade the introduction of the metaphor of the ruin into his vocabulary.

The Yale Art Gallery has almost always been perceived as an indecisive work, its dissembling tetrahedral ceiling being the compromise most often noted in the criticism of the time. The building's prismatic volume reads as if extruded from the 1920s Art Gallery by Egerton Swartwout, of which it was to be an extension (figs. 8.13–14). The link between the two structures is provided by a shallow unit set back from the two main facades to either side, revealing what, in the Kahn addition, looks like an exposed interior bay protected from the elements by an infill steel-and-glass wall. The same steel-and-glass elements reoccur at the new building's west (High Street) end, and it is here that they truly make Kahn's addition look cropped—and incomplete (fig. 8.15). The open end wall is contained between the building's two long facades, each different in articulation from the other as well as from the end wall itself. The rectangularity and modular clarity of the design has led most observers to read the building in terms of Mies, especially the Mies of the early years of the Illinois Institute of Technology (IIT) (see figs. 7.34–36). But, in comparison to Mies's work there, Kahn's Art Gallery looks decidedly unfinished.

To begin, it must be observed that, unlike the typically Miesian square bay, the one at Yale is not only rectangular; its defining concrete piers are rectangular as well. This means that Kahn's bays have a directionality, which here runs east-west, paralleling the front and rear facades. Thus, instead of the bay being equal in both directions, as it is in Mies's Navy Building at IIT, and the facade being able to wrap around the structure, in the Yale Art Gallery only the front and rear facades maintain the status of facade in the sense of enclosure and containment (see fig. 8.13). The front (Chapel Street) facade is indeed attached to and so masks the concrete piers behind it; the rear facade is composed of units of glass-and-steel curtain walling that

8.13 Kahn. Yale University Art Gallery, New Haven, Conn., 1951–53. Exterior, from southeast (along Chapel Street)

project from the concrete piers to create another, different kind of additive surface treatment. Both solutions seem completely rational, since the piers themselves present their flat faces to the facades. The end wall offers the opposite condition, however, for the supporting concrete piers there present themselves in profile. In acknowledgment of that, Kahn allowed the piers to come to the surface and butted the window panels into them. The result creates the impression that, like the glass void of the entrance, the end wall is not truly a facade but merely a kind of sectional view of where the building was stopped to make way for the sidewalk and street. Eschewing the sense of closure and finish provided by Mies's continuous representational surface of attached I-beams, Kahn's open-ended solution appears inconclusive and indefinite, but not indecisive.[32]

Trenton Jewish Community Center: Kahn's Move to Representation

Representation, whether in the Miesian sense or not, plays little obvious part in the design of the Yale Art Gallery. The concrete structure is either simply revealed through the glass curtain wall or concealed behind the masonry plane of the Chapel Street facade. No transformation or translation occurs at any point. Yet there is one element that seems to stand out in a different way. The brick surface of the main facade is relieved by a series of thin, horizontal bands of lighter color stone that project as shallow ledges. One can read these either in the Labroustian sense as simply the exposed edges of the interior floor levels or in a more allusive sense as string courses referring to traditions of late medieval and early Renaissance Italian palace architecture.

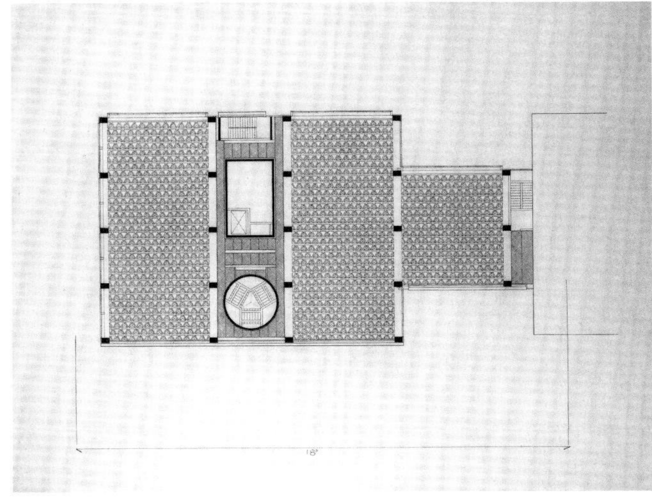

8.14 Yale University Art Gallery. Reflected ceiling plan, first floor

It is tempting to accept the latter, representational reading of the string courses, given that Kahn began work on the Yale project shortly after returning from Italy, where he had been resident architect at the American Academy in Rome from November 1950 through February 1951.[33] During that four-month period, he visited Greece and Egypt as well. In postcards sent to his office staff, he described the sites in Greece as "magnificent" and the monuments of Egypt as "really Terrific," both "wonderful and instructing." His descriptions of Rome were equally enthusiastic, though modulated by a more pragmatic tone. "There is so much to

8.15 Yale University Art Gallery. Exterior, west (High Street) end

8.16 Kahn. Trenton Jewish Community Center, Ewing Township, N.J., 1954–59. Preliminary site plan, February 1955

see and feel here [in Rome] which can influence the work of any architect," he wrote in one note. "Not so much the modern but the old original source." "I firmly realize," he wrote in another, "that the architecture in Italy will remain as the inspirational source of the works of the future. Those who don't see it that way ought to look again. Our stuff looks tinny compared to it and all the pure forms have been tried in all the variations. What is necessary is the interpretation of the architecture of Italy as it relates to our knowledge of building and needs."[34]

If one takes Kahn at his word, the architecture of "the future," as he saw it from the perspective of Rome in 1951, did not lie in one of the many "variations" of the "pure forms" of modernism; the solidity and monumentality of Roman architecture made those look "tinny" by comparison. The problem, however, as it had been for architecture since the eighteenth century, was one of "interpretation": how to translate "the old original source" into forms appropriate to contemporary "knowledge of building and needs." Perhaps because Kahn had not yet had enough time to digest his Roman experience, the Yale Art Gallery did not go very far in this process of adaptation and "interpretation." The site where this investigation was carried out and where Kahn translated his interest in the unfinished into the realm of the representational was the Jewish Community Center near Trenton, New Jersey (1954–59), a commission that came to him the year after the Yale Gallery was completed. The four-year period during which he worked on the Trenton project can be seen as a continual process of meditation and projection; the result, a narrative or schema of interpretive possibilities. The successive designs for the different parts of the center built upon, illuminated, and consolidated the previous ones, providing a specific and appropriate representational character to each individual element. The result was such that Kahn would later say that in the Trenton project "I discovered myself."[35]

The commission for the Trenton Jewish Community Center came to Kahn in July 1954, when he was fifty-two

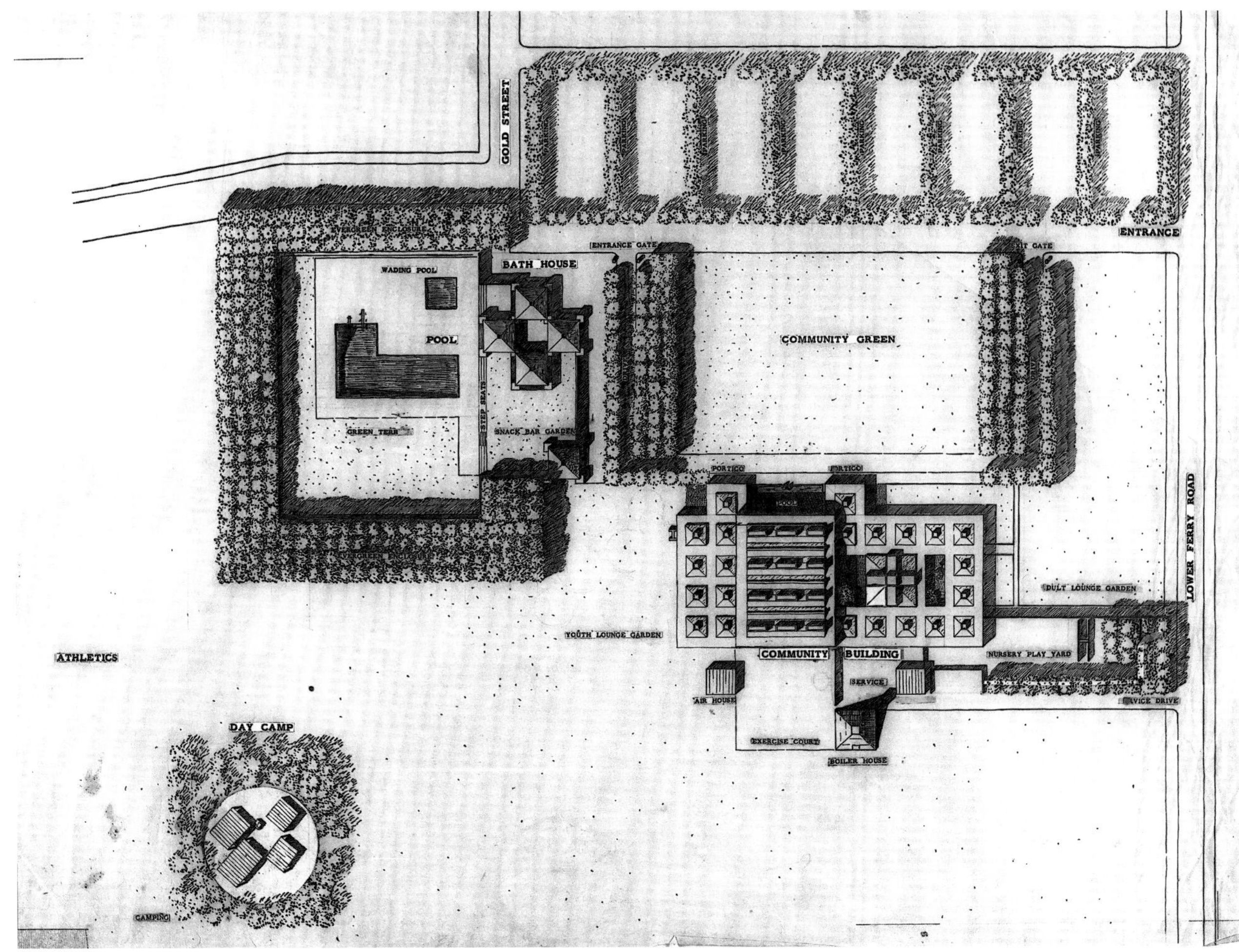

8.17 Trenton Jewish Community Center. Site plan, July 1957

years old, twenty years after he had established an independent practice. Nothing he had done prior to it predicted its departure from the norms of postwar modern design established by Mies and Le Corbusier. The project involved three main components: a Bath House, a Day Camp, and the Community Center building itself. Only the first two of these were built. All three were derived in part from ancient classical or early medieval prototypes. This was the first time Kahn consciously turned to the use of historical sources in this manner, and this direct referencing led him to a process of abstraction that gave the idea of the unfinished a new inflection, as well as the possibility for new meanings.[36]

The forty-seven-acre site is located in Ewing Township, New Jersey, about five miles northwest of downtown Trenton, in a suburban development that follows the course of the Delaware River. Although a plan for a community center building at a nearby location had been prepared by a local firm in the fall of 1951, nothing was done until three years later, when a new and larger site was acquired.[37] Kahn's initial plans, which can be dated to February 1955, called for a Community Building, closely following the footprint of the one projected for the previous site, plus a pool and Bath House complex to the north (fig. 8.16). Over the next year and a half, the grounds were developed to include playing fields, gardens, and, most significantly for us, a Day Camp, located on the western edge of the site (fig. 8.17).

The Bath House was the first of the three structures to be studied in detail. Intended to serve as a place for changing

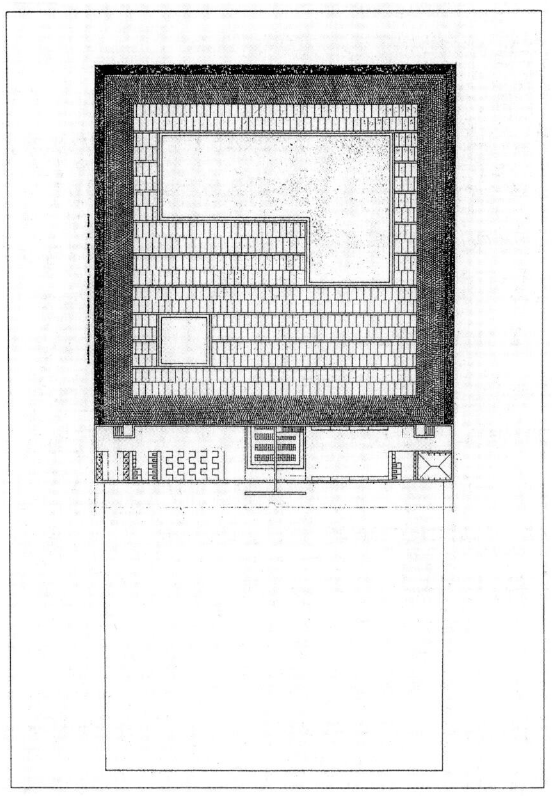

8.18 Trenton Jewish Community Center. Bath House, 1955. Preliminary plan, February 1955

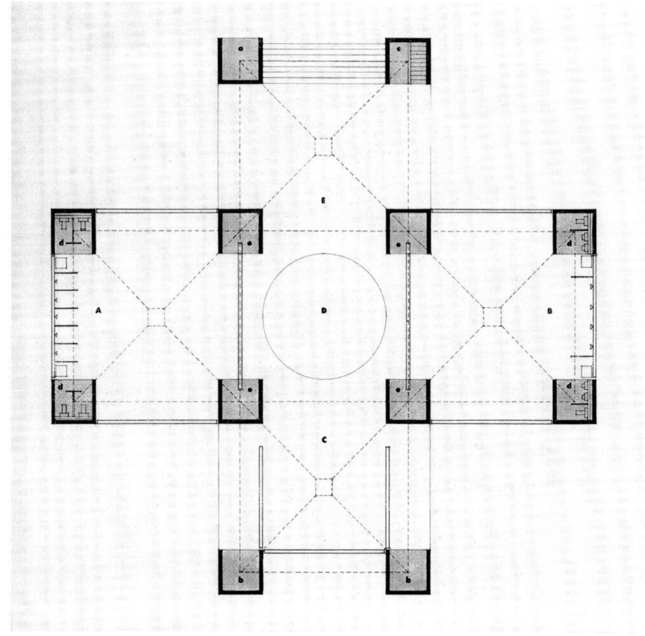

8.19 Trenton Jewish Community Center. Bath House. Plan. From *Perspecta: The Yale Architectural Journal,* 1957

rooms, showers, and toilets, it was originally designed as a modest oblong enclosure attached to the southeast side of the square swimming pool area (fig. 8.18). Discreetly wedged between the pool and a grove of trees, the structure was divided in half by a bafflelike entrance providing separate access to the women's and men's changing rooms. After moving this simple walled enclosure to the pool's northeast side and reconfiguring it as an open-air square surrounding a central roofed section containing the toilets and checkroom, Kahn restudied the design completely. In the process, he came to abandon any semblance of the spatial openness typical of the modern free plan. By mid-April 1955, the building had been returned to its original location but was now composed of four individual pavilions laid out on a biaxially symmetrical Greek cross plan (fig. 8.19).[38] Each of the units was square in plan, the central, unroofed one marked by a circular impluvium. The lower square was the "basket room," through which users were to enter and then leave their clothes after undressing and showering in the women's and men's dressing rooms to the left and right. The open-sided pavilion at the top of the plan leads up a few steps to the pool. Built of inexpensive concrete blocks, the structure was based on an eight-foot-square hollow pier that defines the corners of each pavilion, provides space for services and circulation, and supports the four wood-frame, asphalt-shingled hip roofs (fig. 8.20). These pyramidal elements are lifted slightly above the tops of the walls to provide slots for clerestory lighting, while square-shaped oculi admit light from above (fig. 8.21).

Final plans were completed by late April and revised the following month, when the small structure and pool were shifted slightly to the northwest. Construction began in late May and the building, though still unfinished, was opened for use by the end of July. What remained to be done, and would only be done in the following fall, were the roofs, one of the building's most characteristic and telling features. During the course of construction, there was a significant design change—the first of those contextual

8.20 Trenton Jewish Community Center. Bath House. Interior. Central atrium, ca. 1956

8.21 Trenton Jewish Community Center. Bath House. Interior. Men's dressing room

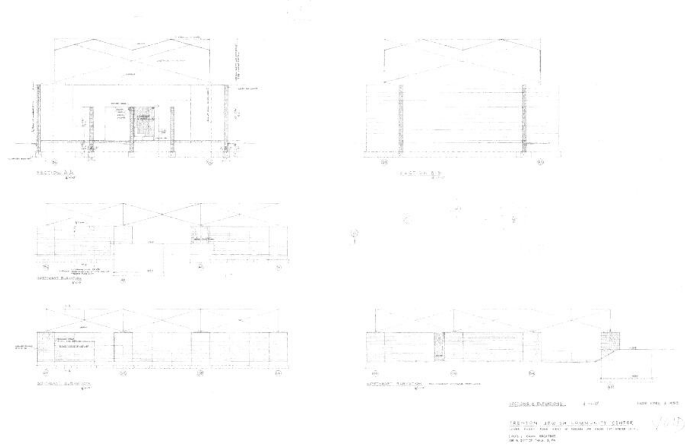

8.22 Trenton Jewish Community Center. Bath House. Contract drawing for proposed metal roof, April 1955. Sections

reconsiderations that reveal Kahn's process of "discovery" of how to interpret the past. According to the contract drawings, the roofs were to have been constructed of corrugated galvanized steel plates, folded into triangular webs and welded to a steel-pipe frame (fig. 8.22). With its flat upper profile and geometric metallic surfaces, the floating space-frame would have contrasted with the solidity of the concrete-block piers and given a radically different appearance to the building as a whole. The concept and materials remind one of Le Corbusier's metal "parasol" for the 1950 Porte Maillot Synthèse des Arts Majeurs project (similar to that finally built in Zurich in the early sixties as the Centre Le Corbusier).

It is not known why Kahn abandoned this design and so completely changed the roof's final form. There may have been financial reasons, but there can be no doubt that other concerns of a more representational nature took hold once he saw the masonry Greek cross structure in place. A metal roof would have given the building a hybrid character, with two different structural systems, each implying divergent spatial conceptions—one open and continuous, the other closed and compartmented. The more traditional wood hip roofs, while preserving some of the diagonal geometry of the earlier high-tech scheme, define the individual bays of the plan in section, thus accentuating each room's sense of self-containment and enclosure (fig. 8.23). Instead of appearing as a single floating plane, the roofs now read as a grouping of primitive-looking domes, reflecting in their materials and structure the theory (most recently enunciated by E. Baldwin Smith, a professor of architectural history at Princeton, where Kahn had been invited for reviews the previous spring) that the origin of masonry domes lay in wooden prototypes.[39] Kahn's square domes with their unglazed oculi thus reversed the evolutionary transformation from wood to stone that had formed the basis of eighteenth-century theories of representation. Top-lit, with additional daylight from the clerestories washing the walls, the enclosed rooms took on the inward-focused, upward-directed character of a Roman or Byzantine space.[40]

The change in the roof structure helps to clarify the historical source of Kahn's Greek cross plan. Both Susan Solomon and Sarah Williams Goldhagen have noted that, in the trend toward modular design of the period, such a configuration was not unheard of, pointing, among other examples, to a prototype elementary school with a similar plan by The Architects' Collaborative published the previous October in *Progressive Architecture*.[41] The addition of the square domes in the Bath House had the effect of emphasizing the separate volumes of space and in turn of making the corner piers, both as structural supports and as *poché*, more perspicuous. The result called clearly to mind the series of late antique and Byzantine domed basilicas built on a Greek cross plan, beginning with Justinian's sixth-century Church of the Holy Apostles in Constantinople and including, most notably, the eleventh-century Basilica of St. Mark's in Venice and the twelfth-century Cathedral of Saint-Front at Périgueux in southwestern France (figs. 8.24–25).[42] Both of the latter, which were well known to Kahn, have corner piers hollowed out to create spaces for circulation, prefiguring the architect's conception of the piers of the Trenton Bath House as "servant spaces," his initial development of an idea that was to be crucial to his later approach to design.[43] The use of masonry and wood rather than more modern materials such as steel, glass, and concrete underlined the representation of Byzantine and medieval models.

The willful symmetry and overriding static order of the Bath House thus appear to derive neither from strictly functional considerations nor from the use of modern materials and methods of construction, but rather from an investigation of the historical bases of certain architectural types and forms. This distances it from the characteristically modern free plan, whose functional distinction and differentiation of parts generally resulted in an asymmetrical, dynamic, centrifugal composition. The photographs chosen to illustrate the building when it was first published in the 1957 issue of *Perspecta* emphasized its massiveness, opaqueness, and archaizing references (see figs. 8.20 and 8.23). Whatever residue there might have been of a modern sense of transparency, freedom, and openness disappeared when the galvanized metal roof was changed to the square wooden domes. At that point also, the building lost the abstractness of "pure form" and took on an almost aggressive representational cast. The full implications of that representational meaning, however, can only be appreciated when one considers the Bath House within the context of the designs for the two other buildings Kahn designed for the Trenton site.

The larger Community Building, as noted previously, was originally laid out on an irregular pattern, expressing the different spaces for gymnasium, health club, auditorium, and offices and classrooms through its asymmetrical disposition of modular elements (see fig. 8.16). Although we have

8.23 Trenton Jewish Community Center. Bath House. Exterior, ca. 1956

8.24 Basilica of St. Mark's, Venice, 1063–96. Interior

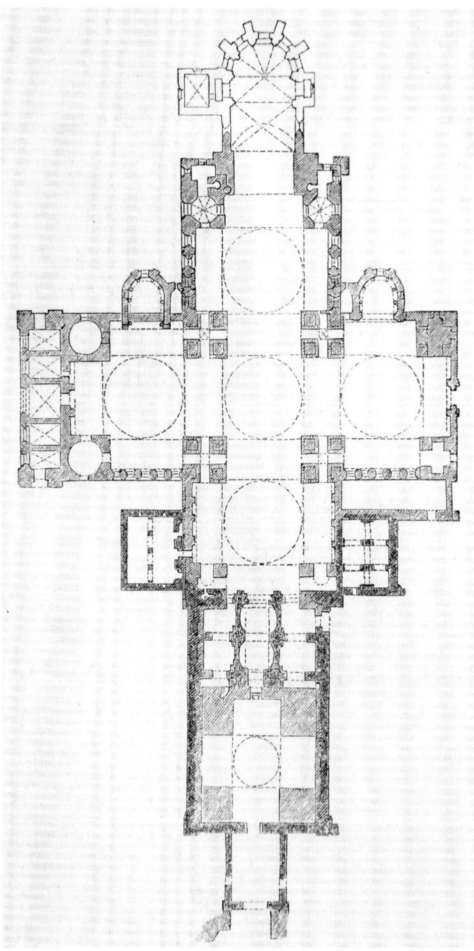

8.25 Cathedral of Saint-Front, Périgueux, 11th–12th centuries. Plan

no evidence other than the outlines of the original architect's plan, it appears that Kahn did little more at first than adapt it to his own module and site plan. A separate contract for the structure was signed at the time the Bath House went into construction, and it was only then that Kahn began to do further work on it. Three things remained fairly consistent during this initial stage of design, which extended from the early summer of 1955 through the early spring of 1956. One was the adoption of an octagonal modular unit interconnected by square "servant spaces"; a second was the use of a space-frame-like structure to group the various

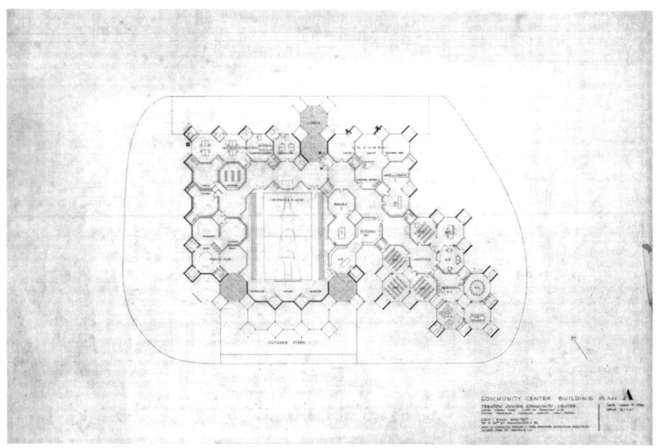

8.26 Trenton Jewish Community Center. Community Building project. Plan, March 1956

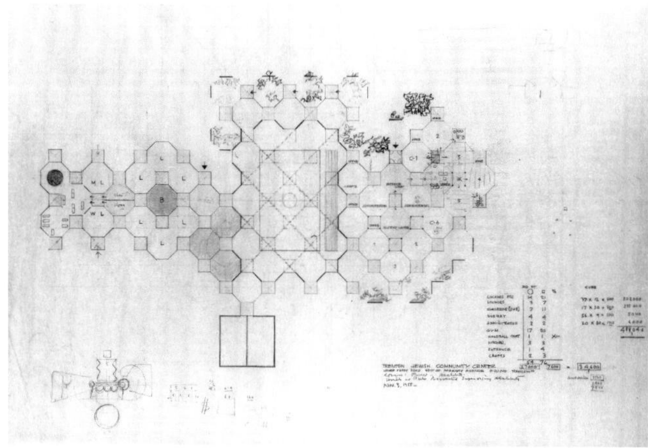

8.27 Trenton Jewish Community Center. Community Building project. Plan, November 1955

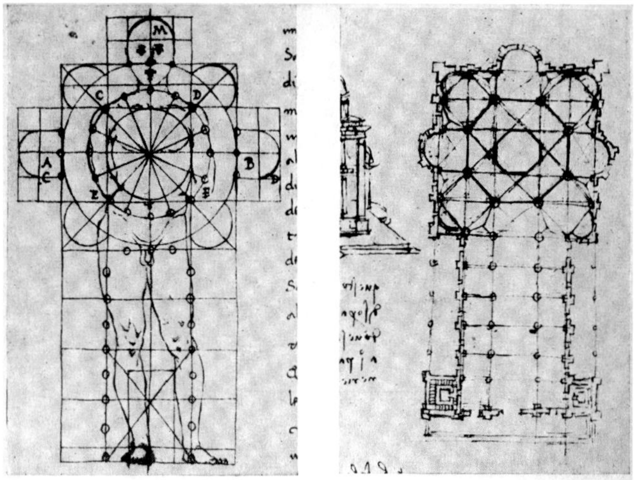

8.28 Plans for Latin cross churches by Franceso di Giorgio and Leonardo da Vinci, late 15th century. From Rudolf Wittkower, *Architectural Principles in the Age of Humanism*, 1949

programmatic elements in a rather organic fashion; and the third was the ninety-degree rotation of the structure so that it no longer blocked the view of the Bath House from Lower Ferry Road. Its long flank, now paralleling the access road, defined a broad entrance court closed by the Bath House at its upper end.

Of the three major elements of the program, the gymnasium tended to dominate. In one project, the auditorium became an outdoor theater. The main facade, facing away from the Bath House, functioned as the *episcenium*, and the nursery area, trailing off on a diagonal to the south, shielded the arena from the street (fig. 8.26). One of the first of this group of designs, and perhaps the most interesting, took the form of a basilica-type, Latin cross church (fig. 8.27). The narrow nave contained lounges and other spaces for social gatherings; the gymnasium filled the crossing under what would have been the dome; and the administrative offices and nursery were incorporated in the choir and surrounding ambulatory. The west transept extended to the entrance court in the form of a three-bay loggia or porte cochere. In its modular configuration and distinct hierarchical organization, this plan specifically recalled the ideal church designs by Francesco di Giorgio and Leonardo that were published in 1949 as the first two illustrations in Rudolf Wittkower's (1901–1971) influential *Architectural Principles in the Age of Humanism* (fig. 8.28).[44] As it mounted from the lower nave toward the crossing, the elevation, as can be visualized from a related design, would have described *in abstracto* the silhouette of the two great domed churches of Renaissance Italy: the Cathedral of Florence and the Basilica of St. Peter in Rome (fig. 8.29).[45]

The fundamental incongruity on the level of form between this preliminary series of schemes for the Community Building and the Bath House must have raised questions in Kahn's mind regarding issues of typology, historical reference, and the coherence of the project as a whole. All this neared resolution in the early part of 1957, when the

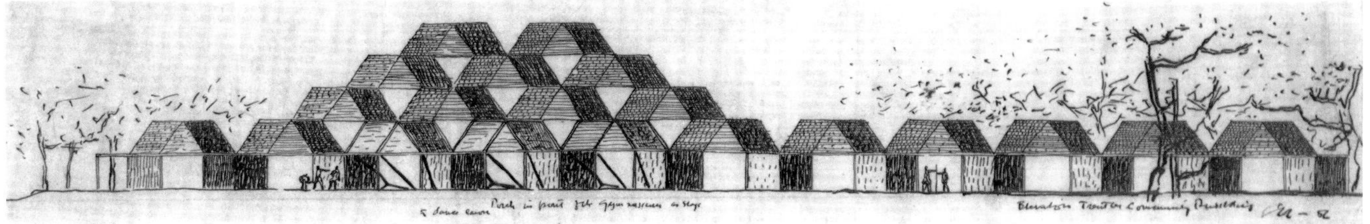

8.29 Trenton Jewish Community Center. Community Building project. Elevation, March 1956

architect abandoned the octagonal module space-frame idea for an entirely different geometric and structural solution based on a different historical model—one no longer relating to "modern" Italy but now going back to ancient Rome. At the same time, Kahn began work on the design of the site's third building, the Day Camp, which surely helped to clarify his thinking on the role each structure would play in the representational schema of the whole.

Planning of the Day Camp began in a general way sometime in 1956, although the architect's ideas changed rapidly once construction became imminent. The final design and realization took place in a very short space of time, the spontaneity perhaps being an important factor for Kahn.[46] Conceived as a play area for young children, the Day Camp was set off on its own in a grove of trees at the site's western edge (see fig. 8.17). After briefly experimenting with a latticelike space-frame consistent with the diagonal geometry of the ongoing Community Building scheme, Kahn quickly came up with an idea that at first glance seems totally anomalous and eccentric (fig. 8.30). The plan is composed of four rectangular pavilions surrounding an open central space, all contained within a large circle. The central space is dominated by an outdoor fireplace. But what is most unusual about the plan is the seemingly anarchic relationship of one pavilion to another, with no clear geometric order at work.

8.30 Trenton Jewish Community Center. Day Camp, 1956–57. Plan

8.31 Trenton Jewish Community Center. Day Camp. Exterior

8.32 Trenton Jewish Community Center. Day Camp. Interior

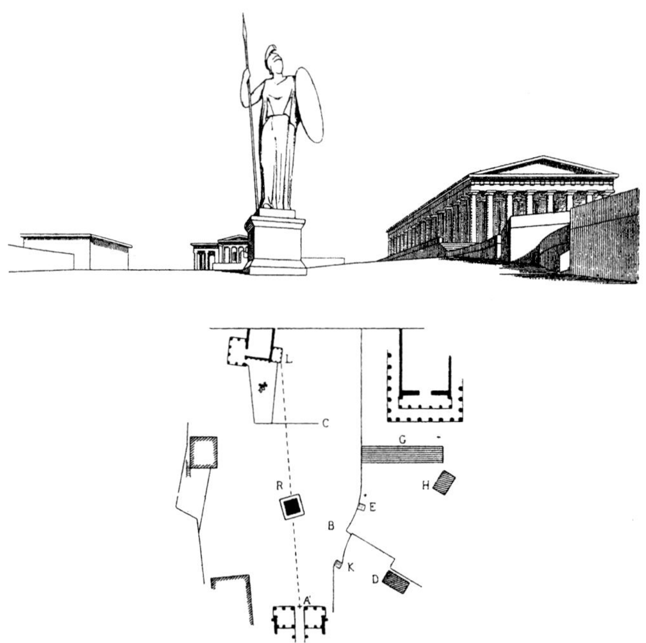

8.33 Auguste Choisy, Acropolis, Athens. *Histoire de l'architecture,* vol. 1, 1899. Plan and perspective

8.34 Viollet-le-Duc. Imaginary Roman construction in Gaul, *Entretiens sur l'architecture,* vol. 1, 1863. Cutaway aerial perspective

The pavilions themselves are simple open frames (figs. 8.31–32). Piers of terra-cotta flue tiles filled with concrete and spaced at eight-foot intervals rest on slabs at ground level and carry elemental lintels supporting precast concrete roof slabs. The structures are really more like temples than pavilions. The two larger ones are unobstructed inside, while the two smaller ones are partially enclosed to accommodate areas for an office, storage, and toilets. The wide, low proportions and deep pronaos of the main "temple" facing the fireplace remind one of Vitruvius's description of the Etruscan temple, models of which Kahn could easily have seen when he was at the American Academy in Rome.[47] Consistent with this pre-Roman reference, the overall plan recalls the siting of buildings in Etruria and Greece, where temples and other structures were often related to one another at odd angles for reasons of orientation or topography, rather than being forced to conform to strictly orthogonal axial conventions. Choisy's plan and description of the Athenian Acropolis, made famous by Le Corbusier in his *Vers une architecture* (1923), became the image of such nonaxial planning for modern architects (fig. 8.33). Certainly well aware of the connection, Kahn referred to the Day Camp as "a little acropolis."[48]

Kahn's use of an informal, pregeometric means of organization gives the Day Camp a casual air, a childlike atmosphere, and a "natural" appearance that are entirely appropriate for its purpose.[49] At the same time, in referencing a pre-Roman, though nonetheless Italic, model, the Day Camp distinguishes itself from the Bath House (and, as we shall see, the Community Building) by locating its source at the earliest point in the historical horizon the Community Center as a whole was to describe. There can be little doubt that the Day Camp was intended to be read in a reciprocal relationship to the Bath House: the one is almost literally an inversion of the other. Each is based on an eight-foot module and has four units surrounding a central open space (see figs. 8.19 and 8.30). In one, those units are all equal in size and symmetrically organized in relation to one another.

In the other, they are unequal and apparently randomly disposed. In the Bath House, the circle is in the center surrounded by a square; in the Day Camp, the circle surrounds the whole.[50] The Day Camp is an open, centrifugal composition; the Bath House is closed and centripetal. The Day Camp is trabeated, the Bath House pseudo-arcuated or domical (see figs. 8.32 and 8.20). The former describes a moment in historical time preceding the Roman development of axial planning and monumental concrete-vaulted spaces; in its large scale and biaxially symmetrical plan, ultimately derived from Justinian's Church of the Holy Apostles, the latter makes one think of late antique, Romano-Byzantine constructions, such as the one Viollet-le-Duc imagined in his *Entretiens* to illustrate how provincial builders in France and Germany had adapted grandiose Imperial Roman ideas to programs of a more plebeian nature (fig. 8.34). Here, in an uncanny premonition of Kahn's Bath House, four square hollow piers containing corner rooms surround a central communal space covered by a groin vault and lit by large clerestory windows.

The Day Camp thus established one extreme of a temporal continuum stretching from the pre-Roman to the post-Imperial, of which the Bath House represented the other. Small and on the periphery of the site, both structures were given a rather "provincial" treatment. That left an obvious historical space at the center for the main Community Building to fill. And it was precisely the model of the Roman Imperial bath that Kahn adapted to its program. Conceived either just prior to or at the same time as the Day Camp and developed through the first half of 1957, this scheme took the Bath House's rectilinear system of hollow pier and square bay and magnified it into a monumental composition in which the main space of the gymnasium was now covered by square concrete domes supported on tall brick arches (figs. 8.35–36).[51] Following the disposition of the earlier basilican scheme, the interior volumes were organized along a longitudinal north-south axis that now built up from the four-bay social hall protruding between two open courts to the much higher gymnasium, raised on exposed brick piers and arches at the site's upper end. The longitudinal directionality of the plan, however, contradicted the axis of approach to the building and thereby undercut any sense of processional movement or hierarchy of space the historical model might have suggested. This first of Kahn's two Roman bath schemes for the Community Building bears a closer relationship to McKim, Mead and White's Pennsylvania Railroad Station in New York (1902–10) than it does to the actual source of that building in the Baths of Caracalla in Rome (fig. 8.37).[52]

Although it is usually maintained that the Latin cross/Roman bath compromise most fully represents Kahn's ideal for the Community Building in terms of structural clarity and spatial dynamics, questions related to program, cost, and access led the architect to redesign the project in a way that much more closely approximates the Baths of Caracalla itself (figs. 8.38–40).[53] In the late spring and early summer of 1958, Kahn reworked the previous scheme to include a large auditorium that had been subsumed within the gymnasium in earlier schemes. To provide a single main entrance and lobby demanded by the client, he gave the plan a new laterality that asserted the importance of the long facade fronting the entrance court. A lobby at the south end of the projecting loggia leads into an open court surrounded by lounges, club rooms, and offices. Corridors running the full length of the building along the front and rear lead to multistory spaces at the extremities, containing the gymnasium on the right and the auditorium on the left.

Never presented in as elaborate a form as the previous scheme, this final design for the Trenton site would have been a grand composition emphasizing the organizational breadth and balance of parts characteristic of Roman Imperial architecture. As in the Baths of Caracalla, space moves out laterally from the center, here devoted to the health club

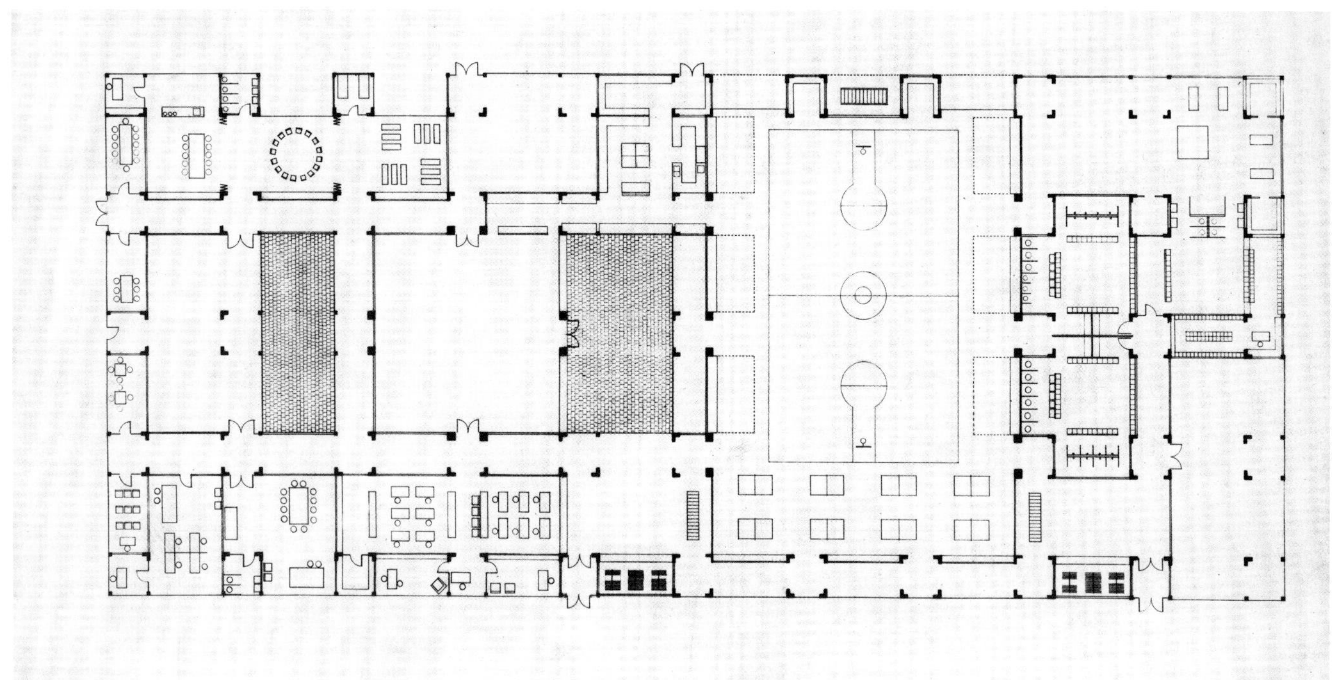

8.35 Trenton Jewish Community Center. Community Building project. Plan, spring 1957

8.36 Trenton Jewish Community Center. Community Building project. Model, spring 1957

8.37 McKim, Mead and White. Pennsylvania Railroad Station, New York, 1902–10. Aerial view, 1910

and given the shape of an embedded Greek cross. The tall, top-lit gymnasium and auditorium in the Trenton design replace the palaestrae that terminate the sequence in Rome. Building directly upon the antique structure that Kahn often referred to as his favorite, the Community Building in its final iteration would have established itself as the main focus and directive force of the Trenton Jewish Community Center, while clarifying and unifying the historical narrative underlying the project's full development.[54]

Form and Design: A Theory of Representation for the Unfinished

Though separated from Castle Howard by more than two centuries and vastly different in purpose as well as appearance, the representational organization of the Trenton

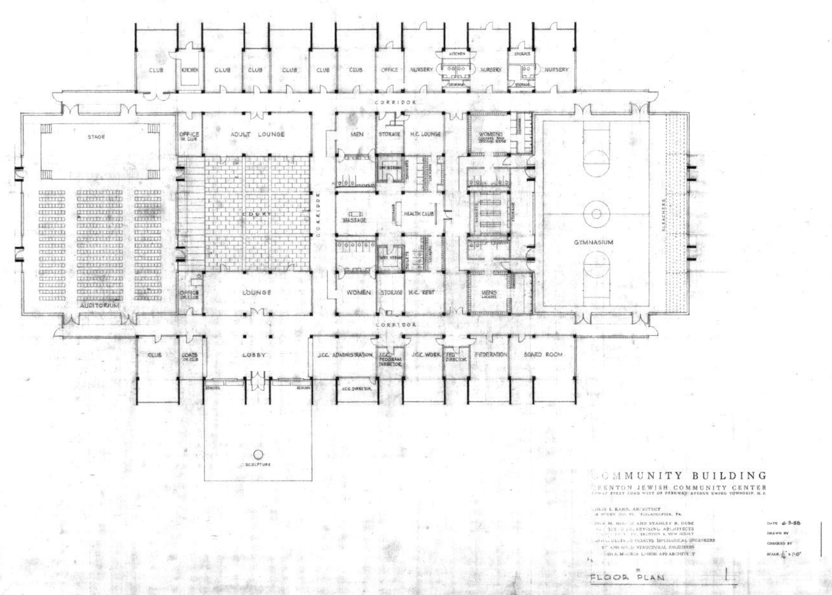

8.38 Trenton Jewish Community Center. Community Building project. Plan, June 1958

8.39 Trenton Jewish Community Center. Community Building project. Longitudinal section, summer 1958

Jewish Community Center site calls to mind the earlier landscape garden in its narrative structure, its differentiated forms, and the interpretive demands it makes on the observing subject. All this is not to say that Kahn's project took shape in a historical void. Indeed, quite the contrary is true. The architect's initial application for a fellowship to the American Academy in Rome in 1947 (which was unsuccessful) coincided with the ongoing debate in the immediate postwar years over what Sigfried Giedion described as the "need for a new monumentality."[55] The reaction against the light, seemingly impermanent planar forms and dematerialized volumes of prewar modern architecture ushered in a return to classical models of symmetrical, formal, and hierarchically ordered planning, as in Mies's IIT campus

8.40 Baths of Caracalla, Rome, 212–16. Aerial view

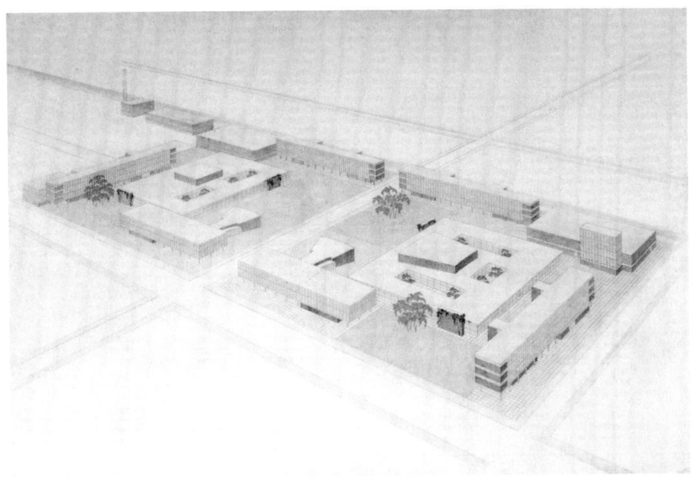

8.41 Ludwig Mies van der Rohe. Illinois Institute of Technology, Chicago, begun 1939. Preliminary aerial perspective, 1939–40

(fig. 8.41). This was accompanied, as discussed in the case of Mies, by a renewal of the concept of classical representation, which led many writers to describe the phenomenon variously as an updated neoclassicism, a new formalism, and even a new historicism.[56] Philip Johnson's earliest allusions to the work of John Soane occurred by the mid-1950s.[57] Even "form givers" as committed to the ideals of modern architecture as Wright, Gropius, and Le Corbusier turned to classical models, especially Roman ones, to create public images of a monumental order (see fig. 6.44).

Most of these moves toward formality and a sense of permanence relied on overtly decorative devices of vaguely classical derivation or abstractly conceived structural and compositional patterns. Kahn's use of ancient Roman precedent was different. It was more profoundly historicizing at the same time as it was more fully integrated at both the structural and conceptual levels. Perhaps most telling was his eschewal of modern materials such as steel and glass in favor of older and simpler ones such as masonry and wood. Unlike Mies, Kahn did not seek to recalibrate the classical idea of representation in terms of materialist or functionalist criteria. Rather, his effort was directed at rethinking how functionalist theory itself would have to be reevaluated in light of the traditional demands of representation. This is where the relationship between the ruin and the unfinished came most clearly into play.

Despite its analogies with classical procedures, Mies's postwar work achieved its representational goals without direct reference to the past and entirely in terms of the modern credo of truth to materials and reliance on advanced methods of construction. Kahn's designs for Trenton, by contrast, sought a more integral relationship between ancient prototypes and their original means of production. The massive, opaque, and static image of the Trenton Bath House refuses comparison with the light, dynamic, and transparent character of modern designs typical of the period, even those aspiring to a "new monumentality" (compare figs. 7.30, 7.40, and 8.23). One is compelled by the building's archaic-looking form to read it against the grain of its historical prototypes. And here is where its uniqueness and interest become movingly, even painfully, clear. Compared to the glittering mosaics and richly decorated domes of St. Mark's in Venice or to the enormous cut stone piers and annular domes of Saint-Front at Périgueux, the commonplace concrete-block masonry at Trenton, with its asphalt-shingled hip roofs acting as poor substitutes for domes, makes Kahn's design seem denuded, ascetic, even cheap. The Bath House, not to speak of the absolutely minimal Day Camp, expresses *lack.*

By forcing the comparison with much grander historical models rather than doing the most he could with modern forms and materials, Kahn allowed his representations to appear to fall short—to lack something that once was possible and no longer is. The effect is subversive. The Trenton Bath House, Day Camp, and Community Building bring to mind the Neoplatonic distinction between idea and its realization, the very duality to which Michelangelo's *non finito* has often been attributed. Kahn described this distinction as a tension between desire and need and would soon refer to that tension as one between Form and Design.[58] Form, the pure historical absolute, precedes Design and is, of necessity, eroded and diminished to accommodate need. Desire is revealed in the gulf, or perception of lack. The perception of lack thus transformed the aesthetic of the unfinished into a metaphor of desire, which provided the basis for a new methodology of design ultimately committed to the concept of representation as an act of the historical imagination.

Kahn worked out the binary process of Form and Design in 1959–60, the year following his final studies for Trenton, while elaborating the project for the First Unitarian Church of Rochester, New York (1959–63).[59] It was a process, as he explained, that took into account the very fact of lack or loss in the evolution of an architectural idea from its initial proposition to its final resolution. Offering an alternative to the modern functionalist approach, where form was considered to be an organic response to programmatic needs and constructional demands outside the economy of representation, Kahn's Form/Design process established an a priori representational construct based on historical models and typologies that he believed embodied the proposed building's generative institutional idea—its "existence-will" or what it "wants to be," as he would often put it.[60]

Through a sequence of sketches he drew to illustrate the stages in the process, Kahn revealed how the church's representational core image was defined and then ultimately distorted and undone (fig. 8.42). The sketches read from top to bottom. The concentric circles enclosing a question mark in a central square, seen at the top left, illustrate the initial, geometric diagram of the Form. This was given an ideal, representational shape in the centralized plan seen just beneath it. Placing the school rooms and offices in a ring around the square sanctuary, Kahn closely followed Pedro Machuca's (1485–1550) plan for the Palace of Charles V at the Alhambra (begun 1527; fig. 8.43), which itself was based on Bramante's ideal courtyard scheme for the Church of San Pietro in Montorio in Rome.[61]

Kahn reported that when he showed the central-plan

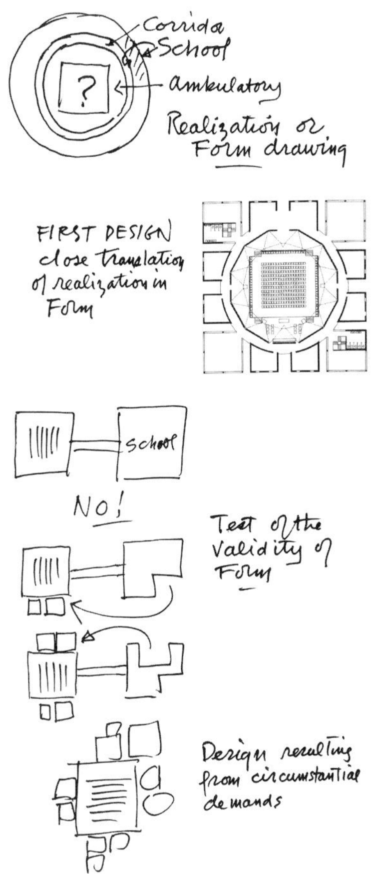

8.42 Kahn. First Unitarian Church, Rochester, N.Y., 1959–63. Form/Design drawing. From *Progressive Architecture,* 1961

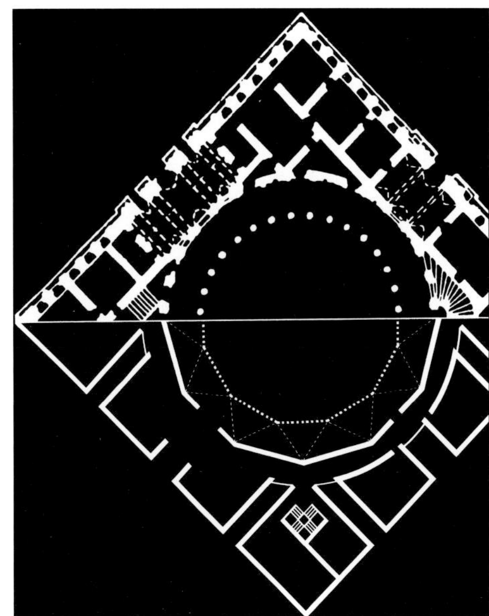

8.43 Collage of plan of First Unitarian Church and Palace of Charles V, Alhambra, Granada, by Pedro Machuca, 1526–68. From *Perspecta: The Yale Architectural Journal,* 1965 (front and back covers)

8.44 First Unitarian Church. Exterior

Renaissance scheme to the members of the building committee, he was asked, among other things, to explain what purpose the corner spaces served. When he responded that those on the top left and bottom right were for bathrooms but that the other two had no specific function and were merely included for the sake of symmetry, he was advised to rethink the project in more realistic terms.[62] At this point, questions of need and use prompted by client concerns entered the picture, and Kahn peremptorily separated the school and office components from the church proper. The result, shown in the sketch in the middle of the sheet, looks much like a typical bubble diagram of the period, although it also has an obvious precedent in Wright's separation of the auditorium from the school building in Unity Temple (see fig. 6.15). However, instead of forming the functional basis for the planning process at its most preliminary stage, as would normally be the case, here the bubble diagram was used midway through the operation as a way of inflecting the ideal toward the real. The final phase of accommodation is illustrated in the last three sketches at the bottom. In these, Kahn recombined the school rooms and administrative offices with the church auditorium so as to preserve as best he could the original idea of centrality and concentricity, while at the same time taking into account the specifics of the program. This compromise with the circumstantial was what he called Design. Its distortions revealed how an expression of the needs of the client worked to erode the representational ideal first mooted in the Form.

Kahn in the 1960s and '70s: Exeter Library and Kimbell Art Museum

In the Rochester church, Kahn's first deliberate application of his theory of Form and Design, the result was a functionally articulated exterior and plan of a rather Brutalist character in which the initial expression of desire seems to have been almost completely sacrificed to that of need (fig. 8.44). Kahn was clearly unhappy with this and sought to relocate the effect of erosion at the stage of Form itself, so that the element of lack or loss would be built into the representational "existence-will" from the beginning. One way to achieve such an image of the erosive effects of the circumstantial from the outset, which came to him at just this moment, was the idea of "wrapping ruins around buildings." But freestanding, unglazed screen walls, such as those he proposed in 1960 for the chancellery building of the U.S. consulate in Luanda, Angola, and the meeting house for the Salk Institute in La Jolla, California, could easily be likened to the "useless" corner spaces at Rochester and thus raise eyebrows about cost (see fig. 8.1). The transformation of the ruin into an avatar of the unfinished was a more efficient and integral way to proceed, and it became Kahn's preferred method. This endowed the Form itself with a built-in capacity for the containment of temporal and circumstantial effects that eventually enabled the representational image to retain its coherence throughout the process of adaptation to need.

Among the buildings of the 1960s and early '70s following this discovery, two stand out for the clarity with which they differentially demonstrate the architect's use of the aesthetic of the unfinished to make need align with desire

8.45 Kahn. Library, Phillips Exeter Academy, Exeter, N.H., 1965–72. Exterior

in the process of representation. The first is the library built at Phillips Exeter Academy in 1965–72, and the second is the Kimbell Art Museum in Fort Worth, Texas, of 1966–72.[63] Like a number of Kahn's buildings of the period, the library is faced with load-bearing brick walls using true arch construction in the ancient Roman manner, which the architect had earlier studied at places such as Ostia (figs. 8.45–46). The four elevations of the library form a thick square ring, one bay deep, around an inner reinforced-concrete frame that opens into a tall, central clerestoried space of no determined purpose but of extremely grand proportions (figs. 8.47–48).

8.46 "House of Diana," Ostia, Italy, mid-2nd century

The naked brick walls are perforated by closely spaced, flat-arched windows that turn the walls into screens. This effect of insubstantiality is further increased by the way the corners are treated. As Vincent Scully noted, the two planes never quite meet. Nor is there any visible terminal element

8.47 Library, Exeter Academy. Interior. Central hall

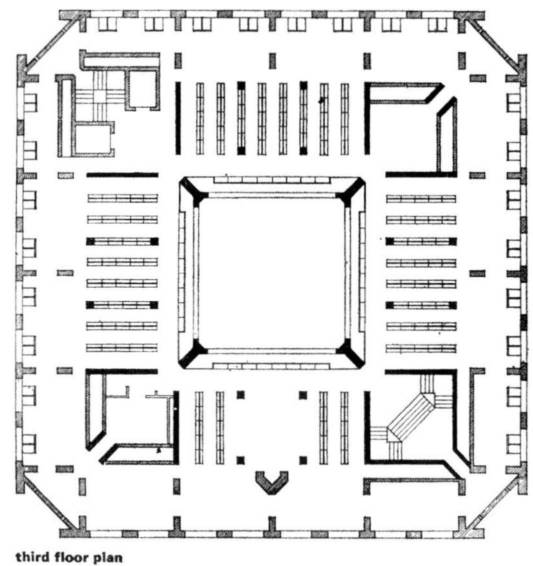

8.48 Library, Exeter Academy. Plan, third floor

8.49 McKim, Mead and White. Low Library, Columbia University, New York, 1894–98. Exterior. From *A Monograph of the Work of McKim, Mead & White, 1879–1915*, 1915–20

such as a roof or, more to the point, a vault or dome, which one might expect from this type of Roman arched construction (see fig. 8.7). The library seems to be caught in a state of arrested development, as if it were still in the process of being built—"free of servitude," as Kahn would say—like Viollet-le-Duc's drawing of the Roman bath under construction. In other words, we are seeing a Roman construction in brick and concrete without its decorative stucco and stone finish and lacking its space-enclosing, silhouette-defining roofs—therefore not a ruin but something still in the making.

The sense of the unfinished resonates even deeper when we consider the design in relation to McKim, Mead and White's late nineteenth-century Low Library at Columbia University in New York, a building whose plan and general organization are remarkably similar to the Exeter Library and may well have served as a model for it (figs. 8.49–50). In both, a symmetrical, centralized, and concentrically organized plan based on a square rotated forty-five degrees around another creates a diagonal structural and circulation system. But whereas Charles Follen McKim (1847–1909) devoted his central space to the reading room, to which he gave a fitting Roman grandeur by covering it with a large dome and encasing it in a richly detailed classical framework, Kahn voided the center of his structure, acknowl-

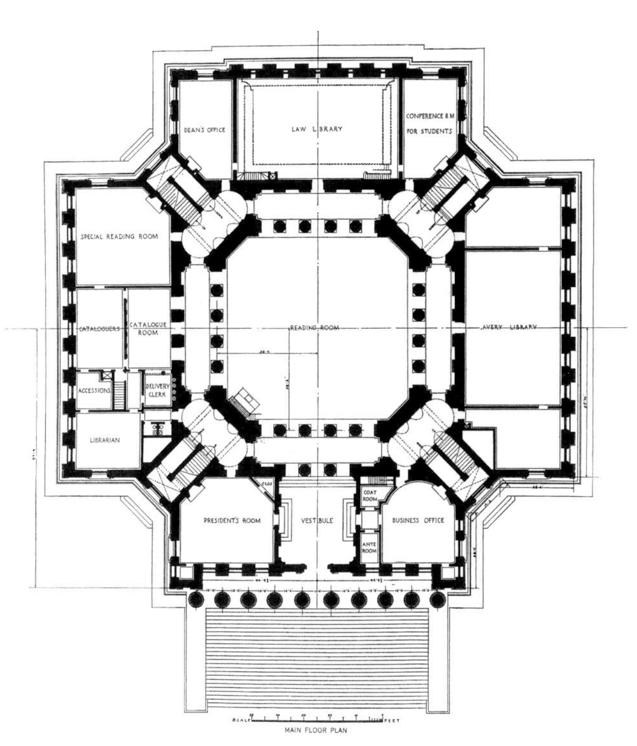

8.50 Low Library. Plan. From *A Monograph of the Work of McKim, Mead & White,* 1915–20

8.51 Library, Exeter Academy. Roof pergola

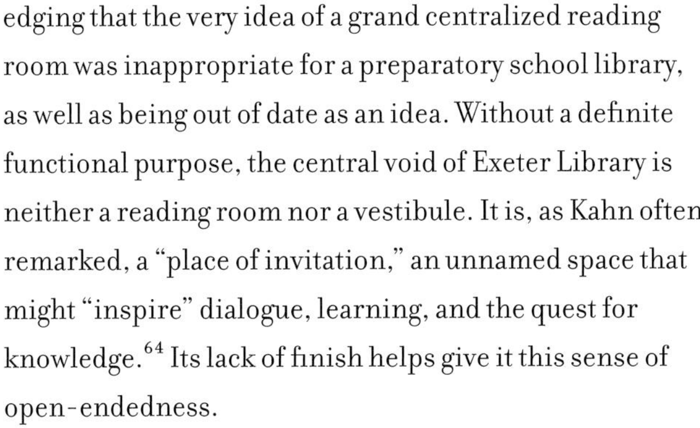

edging that the very idea of a grand centralized reading room was inappropriate for a preparatory school library, as well as being out of date as an idea. Without a definite functional purpose, the central void of Exeter Library is neither a reading room nor a vestibule. It is, as Kahn often remarked, a "place of invitation," an unnamed space that might "inspire" dialogue, learning, and the quest for knowledge.[64] Its lack of finish helps give it this sense of open-endedness.

In like fashion, the conventionally classical exterior of Low Library is disassembled in the Exeter Library and represented as if by X-ray. Looking through the surface becomes like looking back in time, as in Gandy's and Viollet-le-Duc's retrospective drawings. But where Kahn's library most strikingly appears incomplete is at the roofline, where the four seemingly disconnected brick facades rise above the enclosed interior space to reveal views of the sky through the top level of rectangular openings. Only after a trip to the abbreviated *toit-jardin* does one discover that these openings form a raised pergola around the building's perimeter, an arcaded stoa in the sky (fig. 8.51). Here, as in the central void of the interior, the unfinished provides a place for the mind to wander and the body to be refreshed.

The unfinished, as a strategy of representation, thus became the key to Kahn's conception of architecture as an "offering" or gift, something transcending need and, by its visible evidence of lack, eliciting desire.[65] In none of his buildings is this made more physically present and available to the visitor than in the Kimbell Art Museum, designed shortly after the Exeter Library (fig. 8.52). The low,

8.52 Kahn. Kimbell Art Museum, Fort Worth, Tex., 1966–72. Exterior

spread-out structure is composed of contiguous concrete barrel vaults calling to mind Roman basilicas, warehouses, and baths. Acknowledging the antique source of the forms, Kahn said in his talk at the museum's dedication that his "mind [was] full of Roman greatness" while developing the idea of the building.[66]

The museum's plan is organized around a classical-type central court, planted like a sacred grove and approached from either side through open porticos that look out across reflecting pools to the park beyond. Nothing could be more serene. Each individual concrete vault is supported at its ends by piers to form an elongated bay. Where the vaults join together to create the interior space, the piers are doubled to give each unit its independence, as well as to provide a "servant" space in the interstices, echoing the hollow piers in the Trenton Bath House. The building's two lateral facades are treated like the High Street end of the Yale Art Gallery, simply cropped or sliced off (see fig. 8.15). Between the concrete piers of the vaults are butted panels of travertine, leaving a sliver of space near the top for light to penetrate. The travertine panels between the vault bays themselves resemble temporary partitions.

The unfinished appearance of the Kimbell's side facades is magnified by the open porticos in front of each wing leading to the main entrance (fig. 8.53). Their unenclosed vaults repeat, or rather predict, the spatial module of the interior. But by contrast with those inside, the exterior vaults have no apparent motivation other than to provide a purely representational (in both the rhetorical and referential senses) outdoor gallery in which to welcome the visitor and to offer a place of respite and reflection. In an interview soon after the building was opened to the public, Kahn explained that each portico was "like a presentation, like a piece of sculpture outside," with no particular function and "without any

8.53 Kimbell Art Museum. Entrance portico

obligation of paintings on its walls." The unneeded porticos were not "the solution of a problem but a presentation of its spirit…an offering to architecture itself."[67] By their naked presence, the porticos reveal the underlying structural system of the building prior to its conversion to use.

The porticos are a "gift" in Kahn's terms. As pure representations, historical in derivation though reduced nearly to the point of abstraction, they introduce the user to the higher purposes of the art of architecture through a narrative of the unfinished. It is almost as if Kahn's words quoted at the beginning of this chapter were meant to describe the experience of passing through one of these barely articulated voids: "Everyone who passes can hear the story it wants to tell about its making. It is no longer in servitude; the spirit is back." That spirit is only truly perceptible, as Kahn wrote, when "a building is being built"—or once it becomes a ruin, which was in effect the same thing for him.

Making History Modern: Representation without Ornament

Kahn's architecture is thoroughly modern in its reliance on the aesthetic of the unfinished. It is also critical to the history of modern architecture in its elaboration of the representational potentiality of the unfinished and the multiple meanings that could bring to buildings. Beginning with the Yale University Art Gallery, Kahn created an expression of open-endedness and indeterminacy consistent with the modularity of the plan and apposite to the deliberately unembellished materials and exposed construction. Links can be drawn to contemporary Abstract Expressionism, to postwar Mies and Le Corbusier, and back to the material-based innovations that gave rise to the directness and immediacy of Impressionist painting. Kahn's increased interest in using historical models in a representational way both for construction and for planning soon began to complicate the issue. His adoption of Roman arched and vaulted structural techniques as well as medieval and classical plan types brought with it a need to deal with the problem of finish in the traditional sense, which is to say the problem of decoration.

To be modern meant to avoid any surface ornamentation or decoration that masked the underlying structure. This was something already affirmed by Viollet-le-Duc and others in the nineteenth century and made doctrinal by the early part of the twentieth. Kahn's reliance on the concept of the unfinished gave him access to a framework of history that allowed him to reimagine the concept of representation without transgressing the modern injunction against what Adolf Loos (1870–1933) described as the "crime of ornament."[68] Kahn's uncanny combination of representation and abstraction led to an extraordinary degree of ambiguity and ambivalence in the reading of forms hardly predicted by Mies's own conflation of the two artistic modalities in his symbolic I-beams. Is the exterior of Exeter Library merely an expression of the rational use of brick? Or is it an adaptation of Roman construction to modern purposes? Or is it rather a translation, more or less direct, of the ruined state of such Roman buildings as those in Ostia? Are the open porticos fronting the Kimbell Museum to be read as vaulted Roman galleries or minimalist sculpture? A rigorous sense of abstraction and a profound analysis of history combined to create this polyvalence. Abstraction, the prime means of modern art, was used by Kahn not to transcend history but to make history modern.

As it was for Schlegel, the ruin as fragment became the perfect metaphor at one level for Kahn. It presented history as an already abstracted phenomenon, an architecture denuded of its original finish and reduced to its bare construction. The ruin thus brought the architecture of the past into alignment with the modern proscription of ornament. But the ruin was fundamentally just another manifestation of the aesthetic of the unfinished. And that aesthetic had a greater potentiality and a broader meaning in the development of modern architecture than the ultimately sentimental concept of the ruin. As Kahn himself described the narrative of a building's life span from unfinished back to unfinished-as-ruin, he acknowledged an important temporal aspect in the perception of a building's meaning.

Perhaps more than anything else, this temporality provided a basis for the expression of the philosophical and psychological dimensions of loss and lack that ultimately underpinned the concept of the unfinished, be it the biblical story of Babel, the *non finito* of Michelangelo, or the Temple of Modern Philosophy at the Château of Ermenonville. In its willingness to entertain the presence of a denuded past, Kahn's architecture transformed the artistic opposition of idea and material realization into an affective tension between desire and need that could be physically expressed and perceived in the abstraction of the unfinished. The methodology of the unfinished enabled Kahn to resolve the problem of representation in quintessentially modern terms. Taking the issue well beyond the self-reflexive system proposed by Mies, Kahn's work would thus serve as a critical basis for the postmodern architecture that was to follow.[69]

Conclusion

When Louis Kahn began his career in the 1930s, modern architecture, in the sense of what we would now call "modernist" architecture, was still a battle being waged by a small, avant-garde elite against an entrenched, tradition-minded establishment. Kahn himself was educated at the University of Pennsylvania in the 1920s in the French classical Beaux-Arts system of design that claimed its origins in the late seventeenth-century Academy of Fine Arts established by Jean-Baptiste Colbert under Louis XIV. Kahn, like the modern architects of the two generations before him, had to deny a significant part of his training and almost all of what he saw being produced in order to make himself modern. His was the last generation to have to do that.

To make oneself modern was, almost by definition, a process of reduction and negation. This book has attempted to show how that reduction and that negation, when viewed as a response to the problem of representation, can be seen to describe a continuous historical sequence going back to the eighteenth century. Representation was not a new phenomenon in architecture when designers such as Vanbrugh and Hawksmoor replaced the conventional methodology of hierarchical distinction with one based on typological, geometric, and historical differentiation. Nor was the myth of the origins of Greek architecture in the primitive hut something invented in the mid-eighteenth century by the Abbé Laugier. What was new was the way these ideas were subjected to individual interpretation and rational, critical inquiry.

The eclecticism evident at Castle Howard, though by no means as subversive and corrosive as the later historical relativism of Soane and Schinkel, served to undermine the existence of a universally valid and meaningful order in the manipulation of the elements of classical architecture according to traditional rules of representation and display. It is doubtful, however, that this was a deliberate act of negation on the part of the architects of Castle Howard. In the case of Laugier, however, there can be no doubt about intentionality. This is the crucial reason for giving his *Essai sur l'architecture* such an important place in the study of the beginnings of modern architecture.

Laugier's description of the putative transformation of primitive wood prototypes into the sophisticated masonry forms of the Greek temple was based upon a long tradition of classical writing on the subject. But such texts, which generally focused exclusively on the parts of the entablature discussed by Vitruvius, invariably emphasized the sophistication of the end result rather than the virtues of the primitive source. Laugier not only inverted that value system; he instituted something much more radical in the process. The almost incalculable distance between model and imitation (be it of the hut or the human body) in earlier discussions lent a certain vagueness and indeterminacy to the representational construct. It was something implied and accepted on face value but never formally analyzed. Laugier laid bare the concept of verisimilitude that subtended the theory of imitation and thereby gave the problem of representation a critical role to play in the ensuing architectural discourse. In effect, Laugier did nothing more and nothing less than make architects self-conscious about an issue that had for centuries been taken for granted.

Nor was representation just any issue. It was the issue on which the transcendent value of the classical system ultimately rested and thus the issue against which modern architecture would have to define itself. It is therefore not surprising that almost as soon as the representational paradigm was clarified, it came under attack, was defended as a matter of doctrinal truth, and then gradually but ultimately laid to rest. In its first half century of existence it was disputed, most notably by Lodoli and Durand, only to be even more forcefully upheld as an article of faith by Quatremère de Quincy, the leading theorist of the first third of the nineteenth century. The most important architects of the period, including Boullée, Soane, and Schinkel, all paid at least lip service to the principle of the natural origin for man-made forms that it embodied. For nearly a century, Laugier's text established the structural sign of the hut as the intermediary between nature and history.

Although one might think that Laugier's introduction of the material implications of structure would have upset the equation of truth and appearance in the classical concept of verisimilitude sooner than it did, it took the ever expanding and ever more serious study of history to serve as the lever for opening up the discussion of the generation of architectural form to a full consideration of the physical realities of construction, materials, and program. When this occurred, first in the writings, teaching, and practice of architects such as Pugin and Labrouste before being elaborated on an international scale by Viollet-le-Duc, it became clear that history divorced from nature did not completely eliminate the issue of representation; it simply displaced and devalued it. Without the justification of nature that previously gave it an exclusive hold on meaning, the classical idea of constructed decoration was turned inside out. Freed from the constraint of a single hegemonic model, decoration was placed in the ambiguous role of expressing structure by means of forms derived from a representational vocabulary based on historical example.

When understood in this context, Louis Sullivan's phrase "form ever follows function" regains the radical meaning it originally had. Viewed against the backdrop of Viollet-le-Duc and in relation to the architecture of his own contemporaries in America and Europe, Sullivan's effort to derive forms solely from the requirements of the program and in terms of the new materials and structural system he and others employed was unprecedented in the distance it claimed to place between itself and history. Disengaged from explicit reference to conventional formal models, a highly personalized and naturalistic decoration exploded across the surface to carry the full implications of the underlying material and programmatic conditions.

Sullivan's protégé Frank Lloyd Wright translated the methodology from the tall office building to the single-family house, where he was able to expand and develop Sullivan's ideas by reconceptualizing the medium of architecture as one of space. No longer bound by the material conditions of the structure, the fluid and dynamic space acted as a solvent, reducing the role of decoration to lines of force and eliminating any reference to history other than that of the most generic and abstract sort.

Wright's work in the first decade of the twentieth century predicted many of the changes that took place in the interwar years, although Wright himself never accepted the rigor of geometric abstraction that characterized the architecture of the following generation of the European avant-garde. Like Picasso, he rejected the idea of abstraction in the nonobjective sense of the word. During the 1920s and '30s, Wright worked toward a modern type of representation that reestablished the link between architecture and nature, but without the intermediary of history. The direct expression of materials and structure evident in his work of these years was, by contrast, given a more autonomous, less referential form in the buildings produced contemporaneously by Mies, Oud, Le Corbusier, and others under the influence of the preceding decade's abstract painting and sculpture.

Despite the fact that the International Style, as understood by Hitchcock and Johnson, was conceived in opposition to the hard-line functionalism of architects such as Hannes Meyer (1889–1954), which the two curators of the 1932 Museum of Modern Art exhibition considered far too reductive, the term "functionalism" soon came to be applied to the work of the European modern movement in general as a description of the unadorned, nonrepresentational machine aesthetic of its forms. Following World War II, modern architects searched for a way out of the perceived impasse of functionalist abstraction. Mies's work in America offered one of the most compelling arguments for a renewal of representation. Its obdurate and apparently unflinching realism provided a credibly modern basis for the reintegration of classical ideas of composition, form, order, and metaphor that would characterize much of the architecture of the later 1950s, '60s, and '70s that preceded the advent of postmodernism. The most significant exponent of this was Louis Kahn. Filtered through the abstracting lens of the unfinished, his structurally rational, materially grounded historicism returned to modern architecture a sense of connectedness to its earliest beginnings at the same time that it foreshadowed a new era.

The final years of Kahn's career coincided with the first inklings of the sea change in architectural thinking that would soon be known as postmodernism. In 1966 New York's Museum of Modern Art published *Complexity and Contradiction in Architecture,* the "gentle manifesto" by Kahn's former employee, Robert Venturi (b. 1925), that has often been seen as the first sign of the more thoroughgoing revisionism to follow. In the two years preceding Kahn's death, *Learning from Las Vegas* (1972), the book Venturi coauthored with Denise Scott Brown and Steven Izenour, and the first volume of the journal *Oppositions: A Journal for Ideas and Criticism in Architecture* (1973), published by the Institute for Architecture and Urban Studies under the editorship of Peter Eisenman, Kenneth Frampton, and Mario Gandelsonas, both appeared, with enormous ramifications for the direction contemporary architecture was to take.[1]

The year after Kahn died, the Museum of Modern Art (MoMA), which had served as the locus classicus for the presentation and interpretation of modern art in the United States as well as much of the world, and which had first opened the eyes of the American public to what it labeled the International Style in architecture, seemed to turn its back on this legacy by mounting an exhibition of the "The Architecture of the Ecole des Beaux-Arts" (1975–76), the very institution the museum's ideology and programming had opposed up until then.[2] In 1977 Arthur Drexler, the director of the Department of Architecture and Design at

MoMA and the curator of the exhibition, published *The Architecture of the Ecole des Beaux-Arts*, and the critic Charles Jencks brought out *The Language of Post-Modern Architecture*, the book that helped to establish the name for the recent developments. The same year also saw the second editions of *Complexity and Contradiction in Architecture* and *Learning from Las Vegas*, the latter now accompanied by the subtitle *The Forgotten Symbolism of Architectural Form*. The following year, Rem Koolhaas's *Delirious New York: A Retroactive Manifesto for Manhattan* and Colin Rowe and Fred Koetter's *Collage City* appeared. Drexler's *Transformations in Modern Architecture* (1979, accompanying the MoMA exhibition of the same year); *Architecture 1980: The Presence of the Past: Venice Biennale* (1980); and Paolo Portoghesi's *After Modern Architecture* (1980) all related to exhibitions documenting the transitional state of affairs.[3]

Louis Kahn—or better, "circa 1975"—can thus be taken as a terminus ad quem for the gradual, progressive, and continuous evolution of modern architecture outlined in this book. Postmodernism, however one defines the term (which would be the subject of another study), can be understood at a most basic and essential level as marking a division between an era called modern and one called something else. That something else had already surfaced by the late 1970s and become common parlance in the following decade. It was "modernism," and the architecture produced in its name was "modernist." Before the mid-1970s, one spoke of Mies or Kahn as modern architects and what they created as modern architecture. By the 1980s that architecture came, anachronistically, to be called modernist, while the earlier designation "modern movement," which proved recalcitrant to being updated in this way, would continue to serve as the preservationist term for historical modernism.[4]

The changeover from the word "modern" to that of "modernist" involved a major shift in ideas and values, not to speak of political, social, and cultural conditions. Modernism had been the term used to describe the avant-garde movement in literature that took hold in the second quarter of the twentieth century. Writers such as James Joyce, Ernest Hemingway, Gertrude Stein, and Wallace Stevens, for instance, were called modernists. The term, however, was never applied to artists or architects at that time in the same way. *Modernismo* was a circumscribed phenomenon of turn-of-the-century Spain and Latin America having little to do with what we today mean by modernism. If an architect or building prior to 1975 was called modernist, it was usually derogatory and meant to imply something less than modern. In his book *Modern Architecture* (1929), Henry-Russell Hitchcock noted that the term "'Modernist'" was fundamentally one that described a diluted, compromised form of the modern. It was, he said, "frequently" applied to the works of the New Tradition but never to that of the New Pioneers. For Lewis Mumford, writing in 1931, "to be modern [wa]s in fact to be at the opposite pole from being 'modernist,'" which he described as "the esthetic collywobble of the pusher, the advertiser, the booster" and "an even lower and deader stage of architecture than the archaism of the past generation."[5]

Sometime around 1960, the situation changed drastically in contemporary art criticism. Whether or not Clement Greenberg was the first to adopt the term "modernist" to describe advanced painting and sculpture, he was certainly the one responsible for giving it currency.[6] And it was his take on the subject that ultimately crept into architectural parlance and dominated its theoretical discourse. "The essence of modernism," Greenberg explained in his celebrated article of 1960 entitled "Modernist Painting," "lies in the use of characteristic methods of a discipline to criticize the discipline itself, not in order to subvert it but in order to entrench it more firmly in its area of competence." "The self-criticism of Modernism," he continued, "grows out of, but is not the same thing as, the criticism of the Enlightenment. The Enlightenment criticized from the outside, the way criticism in its accepted sense does; Modernism criticizes from the inside, through the procedures themselves of that which is being criticized."[7]

Each artistic medium under the directive of modernism had to limit its expression to "all that was unique in the nature of its medium." In this way, Greenberg, claimed, "the task of self-criticism became to eliminate from the specific effects of each art any and every effect that might conceivably be borrowed from or by the medium of any other art. Thus would each art be rendered 'pure.'" For painting that meant "the stressing of the ineluctable flatness of the surface," since "flatness was the only condition painting shared with no other art."[8] It also inevitably meant an adherence to abstraction, since the representational, were it not to become "homeless," depended on some form of spatial illusionism.

Modernism for Greenberg was thus ultimately a question of art making itself "more conscious of itself" and thus autonomous in a disciplinary sense. Despite the obvious potential for retrospection and institutionalization this implied, Greenberg refused to consider the process, which in his view began with Manet, as anything other than a pragmatically progressive one. The move toward self-awareness, at least up until 1960, "has never been carried on in any but a spontaneous and largely subliminal way," he maintained. "It has been altogether a question of practice, immanent to practice, and never a topic of theory."[9] When, however, the concept of modernism was removed from the historical to the contemporary scene, and especially when it was transferred from painting and sculpture to architecture (a discipline Greenberg hardly ever referred to), it took on a decidedly theoretical, retrospective, and deliberate cast. Adding an "ist" or "ism" to the name of an artistic movement, as many modern artists and architects had often pointed out, was invariably an indication that the movement had become formularized and set in its ways and thus lost the drive toward the uncharted and unknown that originally gave it force. When modern architecture became modernist, the indication was that it had become a historically delimited phenomenon.

Beginning in the 1970s, theory took over as a dominant factor in contemporary architecture, and historical retrospection assumed an important role in its evolution. Robert Venturi's eclectic referencing of a wide range of sources as compositional models in *Complexity and Contradiction in Architecture* set the example. For him, the modern period was only the latest to be considered. For others, most notably Peter Eisenman (b. 1932), it was the most important and generally the only one that needed to be taken into account. In his important 1976 editorial in *Oppositions* entitled "Post-Functionalism," Eisenman, like Venturi, pictured what he still called "the early Modern Movement" as a finite historical phenomenon whose governing idea of "functionalism is really no more than a late phase of humanism, rather than an alternative to it." While acknowledging Greenberg's contention that "sometime in the nineteenth century, there was...a crucial shift within Western consciousness...from humanism to modernism," Eisenman maintained that, "for the most part, architecture, in its dogged adherence to the principles of function, did not participate in or understand the fundamental aspects of that change." And he surmised that "it is probably for this reason that modernism has not up to now been elaborated in architecture." Only by discarding the outmoded, "oversimplified form-follows-function formula," he concluded, could "a new consciousness in architecture" arise that recognizes "modernism as a new and distinct sensibility."[10]

"Modern architecture," Eisenman contended over the next several years, "was not a rupture with history, but simply a moment in the same continuum." It was merely "classical architecture...[in] its modernist aspect." The "'fiction' of representation" was one of its most damaging holdovers from the past. "The late twentieth century, with its retrospective knowledge that modernism has become history," the architect declared, "has inherited nothing less than the recognition of the end of the ability of a classical or referential architecture to express its own time as timeless." To overcome that historical obstacle and discard the baggage of representation required finding "an alternative model." A truly modernist architecture, in this sense, would be for Eisenman "the realization of *architecture as an independent discourse,*" offering nothing more than "a representation of itself, of its own values and internal experience." Such an architecture, "having no a priori origins—whether functional, divine, or natural," would only result from a study of "architectural form," whose goal "is to allow architecture to be a cause" rather than the "subservient representation of another architecture."[11]

Eisenman's intention was to rid architecture of reference and representation "in order to entrench it," as Greenberg might say, "more firmly in its area of competence."[12] Venturi's, by contrast, was to increase architecture's dependence on "symbolic and representational elements [that] may often be contradictory to the form, structure, and program" of the building. In *Learning from Las Vegas,* Venturi and Scott Brown argued for "an architecture of meaning" over and against "an architecture of expression," "symbolism" over "abstraction," an "evocative architecture" over an "innovative architecture," in short, a "representational art" over "'abstract expressionism.'" "When it cast out eclecticism," they claimed, "Modern architecture submerged symbolism. Instead it promoted expressionism, concentrating on the expression of architectural elements themselves: on the expression of structure and function."[13]

Despite their opposed positions on the role and value of representation in the generation of architectural form, Venturi and Eisenman agreed on a number of fundamental issues, all of which point to the postmodern condition they differentially helped to establish and underwrite.[14] First was the sense of separation of the present from a modern architecture now seen as history. Second was the importance of the concept of representation, either as something to be absolutely rejected or wholeheartedly embraced. Third was the denial of a material, structural, or programmatic basis for the generation of form (Eisenman proposed the "idea of architecture as 'writing'"; Venturi and Scott Brown called for "decoration by the attaching of superficial elements" rather than the "articulation of integral elements").[15] And fourth was the felt need to set forth a new historical framework based on which architecture might retain its significance and relevance in the later twentieth century. The combined effect of their theoretical writings during the 1970s and '80s was to move the architectural discourse toward a postmodern definition of architecture. In the course of their review of the past—especially the modern past—for the purpose of locating and articulating usable strategies and formal processes, historical modern architecture gradually and almost imperceptibly became assimilated to the recently articulated modernist paradigm.

We should, however, be wary of such a collapse of historical categories. Modernism in architecture, as I have briefly tried to indicate, was a postmodern construct created upon different premises and with different aims from those of modern architecture as it existed through the mid-1970s and as it has been understood in this book. The postmodern, either as conceived by Venturi or by Eisenman, proposed a reading of form—be it representational or abstract—essentially independent of material and structural considerations and fundamentally textual in nature. At the same time, the representational and the abstract were disjoined from one another in such a categorical way as to deny and eliminate the kind of tension that had existed between those two modes of expression during the previous two and a half centuries.

Modern architecture, in its evolution from the eighteenth through the later twentieth centuries, was intimately and profoundly tied to the problem of expression of structure, materials, function, and program as seen against the background of history and of nature. The tension that developed between the impulse toward abstraction and the rhetorical purposes and conventions of representation became, as I hope to have shown, one of the main ways in which the architectural advances of the period were achieved and made manifest. The reevaluation of the interrelationship of structure, materials, function, and program within the context both of history and of nature was, in effect, one of the crucial ways in which modern architecture differentiated itself from the classical architecture of the preceding Renaissance and Baroque periods.

The garden buildings at Castle Howard, Laugier's hut, Labrouste's Bibliothèque Sainte-Geneviève, Sullivan's tall buildings, Mies's I-beams, Kahn's "unfinished"—each in their own way attests to a transaction with function, material, or structure that gives a certain historical thickness and expressive meaning to the resulting architectural form. Representation was never independent of these a priori conditions once the previous classical system of hierarchical distinctions was abandoned. Nor was architectural form ever, in the modernist sense described by Eisenman, the sole "cause" of form. The drive toward the clarification of the purposes, means, and methods of representation, on one hand, and later the disintegration of those same conditions, on the other, reveal an evolutionary history that would not otherwise be so complete, so complex, or so interesting. Modern architecture's continuing search for more rational, more credible, and more relevant means of representation gave new meaning to the concept of verisimilitude. Its engagement with representation sheds important light on the impact of new materials and new technologies on architectural form and the critical role architectural space played in the devaluation of the historicist project. And finally, by its necessary link to the other pictorial arts, the issue of representation provides a critical tool for evaluating the interactions between architecture and painting, in particular, and how modern architecture sought, during the course of its nearly three-century-long development, to find its own means and methods of expression in the face of reality.

Notes

Introduction

1 Among the texts of modern architectural history that were most influential in establishing and institutionalizing the views described above are Sigfried Giedion, *Building in France: Building in Iron, Building in Ferroconcrete*, orig. pub. 1928; trans. J. Duncan Berry, Texts & Documents (Santa Monica, Calif.: Getty Center for the History of Art and the Humanities, 1995); Emil Kaufmann, *Von Ledoux bis Le Corbusier: Ursprung und Entwicklung der Autonomen Architektur* (Vienna: Rolf Passer, 1933); Nikolaus Pevsner, *Pioneers of the Modern Movement, from William Morris to Walter Gropius* (London: Faber and Faber, 1936); Giedion, *Space, Time, and Architecture: The Growth of a New Tradition* (Cambridge, Mass.: Harvard University Press, 1941); Kaufmann, *Three Revolutionary Architects: Boullée, Ledoux, and Lequeu* (Philadelphia: American Philosophical Society, 1952); and Kaufmann, *Architecture in the Age of Reason: Baroque and Post-Baroque in England, Italy, and France* (Cambridge, Mass.: Harvard University Press, 1955). The continuing influence of these works can be seen in Leonardo Benevolo, *History of Modern Architecture*, 2 vols., orig. pub. 1960; trans. H. J. Landry (London: Routledge and Kegan Paul, 1971); Kenneth Frampton, *Modern Architecture: A Critical History* (New York: Oxford University Press, 1980); Anthony Vidler, *Claude-Nicolas Ledoux: Architecture and Social Reform at the End of the Ancien Régime* (Cambridge, Mass.: MIT Press, 1990); and Alan Colquhoun, *Modern Architecture*, Oxford History of Art (Oxford: Oxford University Press, 2002).

To be sure, not all histories of modern architecture have followed this line. Beginning with Henry-Russell Hitchcock Jr., *Modern Architecture: Romanticism and Reintegration* (1929; repr., New York: Hacker Art Books, 1970), a number of accounts have tried to see the entire period from the eighteenth to the twentieth century as a continuous though complexly interwoven evolution. Among these can be cited Hitchcock's own later *Architecture: Nineteenth and Twentieth Centuries*, Pelican History of Art (Harmondsworth, Middlesex, England: Penguin, 1958); Vincent Scully, *Modern Architecture: The Architecture of Democracy*, Great Ages of World Architecture (New York: George Braziller, 1961); and Peter Collins, *Changing Ideals in Modern Architecture, 1750–1950* (London: Faber and Faber, 1965). Since the 1970s, however, the tendency has been to avoid the problems of seeing the period as a whole and to split the history of modern architecture into two separate accounts, one focusing on the eighteenth and nineteenth centuries and the other exclusively on the twentieth.

2 On the subject of representation in this sense, which became of great significance in architectural history in the later 1970s, '80s, and '90s, see Eve Blau and Edward Kaufman, eds., *Architecture and Its Image: Four Centuries of Architectural Representation: Works from the Collection of the Canadian Centre for Architecture* (Montreal: Centre Canadien d'Architecture / Canadian Centre for Architecture, 1989); and James S. Ackerman, *Origins, Imitation, Conventions: Representation in the Visual Arts* (Cambridge, Mass.: MIT Press, 2002).

3 Kaufmann, *Architecture in the Age of Reason*, 130, 165, and passim.

4 Brenda Preyer, "The Rucellai Palace," in *A Florentine Patrician and His Palace*, vol. 2 of *Giovanni Rucellai ed Il Suo Zibaldone*, Studies of the Warburg Institute 24 (London: Warburg Institute, University of London, 1981), 155–78. Preyer further posits that the palace facade was built in two stages (179–207). The first five bays, beginning at the west, or left, shown in fig. I.7, were supposedly constructed between 1455 and 1458; the final two bays were added in 1465–70. Originally intended to have an eighth bay, this addition was left unfinished. On the other hand, Rucellai had begun to think about the enlargement as early as 1456, and thus a ragged edge was left to the east or right of the sixth pilaster, giving even the first phase of construction an appearance of being unfinished. In Preyer's estimation, Alberti was involved only in the original five-bay construction.

5 As explained by Jan Bialostocki, "The Renaissance Concept of Nature and Antiquity," in *The Message of Images: Studies in the*

History of Art (Vienna: IRSA, 1988), 64, the concepts of "nature as the reality which the senses have access to" and of nature as "the general, cosmic law of the world" were, since the Middle Ages, understood in terms of the distinction between *natura naturata,* that is, "created nature," and *natura naturans,* that is, "creative nature." Beginning with Alberti, according to Bialostocki, architecture, unlike painting or sculpture, was thought to imitate nature mainly in the sense of *natura naturans,* although he notes how certain later writers claimed that "the origin of Gothic architecture is derived from the imitation of trees" and that the classical column of the Greeks and Romans was based on the imitation of the human form (246 n. 16). Finally, he points out how, in the sixteenth century, the works of antiquity came to be viewed as an "ideal" or "second nature," "created according to the general mathematical laws, reasons, and proportions in nature" (67). As a mediating term between *natura naturata* and *natura naturans,* these canonical works became the basis for the academic classical theory of imitation that held sway during the following centuries. While Bialostocki does not expand on the role this third concept played in relation to architecture, it is precisely this that I will show to lie at the core of architectural representation as it evolved in the eighteenth and nineteenth centuries.

6 Henry-Russell Hitchcock Jr., "Modern Architecture. I: The Traditionalists and the New Tradition," *Architectural Record* 63 (April 1928): 349, 348.

7 Henry-Russell Hitchcock, *Painting toward Architecture: The Miller Company Collection of Abstract Art* (New York: Duell, Sloan and Pearce, 1948), 11.

8 Richard Krautheimer, "Introduction to an 'Iconography of Medieval Architecture,'" *Journal of the Warburg and Courtauld Institutes* 5 (1942); repr. in *Studies in Early Christian, Medieval, and Renaissance Art* (New York: New York University Press, 1969), 115–50. This article was followed by a number of investigations of the theme of the central plan's representation, the best known of which is probably the first chapter in Rudolf Wittkower, *Architectural Principles in the Age of Humanism* (1949; 2nd ed., New York: Random House, 1962), 1–32. It should be pointed out that although Krautheimer uses the terms represent and representational, he more often than not relies on the terms copy/imitation and reproduce/reproduction.

9 There can be little doubt that the antimodern embrace of a reactionary form of representational art and architecture by the totalitarian regimes of Europe in the 1930s and 1940s played a significant role in coloring the immediate postwar attitude toward what was often then called the "return to the figure" or a "new humanism."

10 Richard Meier, interview with Charles Jencks, in *Richard Meier* (London: Academy Editions; New York: St. Martin's Press, 1990), 31.

11 Mitchell Schwarzer, "Ontology and Representation in Karl Bötticher's Theory of Tectonics," *Journal of the Society of Architectural Historians* 52 (September 1993): 267–80. See also his *German Architectural Theory and the Search for Modern Identity* (Cambridge: Cambridge University Press, 1995).

12 Kenneth Frampton, *Studies in Tectonic Culture: The Poetics of Construction in Nineteenth and Twentieth Century Architecture,* ed. John Cava (Cambridge, Mass.: MIT Press, 1995).

13 William Chambers, *A Treatise on the Decorative Part of Civil Architecture,* orig. pub. 1759; 3rd ed., enl. (London: Joseph Smeeton, 1791), 23.

14 See chap. 4, esp. note 59.

15 See note 8 above.

16 An example of the type of historical prolepsis I avoid is the relationship Fritz Neumeyer, in *The Artless Word: Mies van der Rohe on the Building Art,* orig. pub. 1986; trans. Mark Jarzombek (Cambridge, Mass.: MIT Press, 1991), 129–31, draws between his subject's structural rationalism and Laugier's proposition regarding the paradigmatic meaning of the primitive wood hut for classical architecture.

17 The signal text here is Emil Kaufmann's *Von Ledoux bis Le Corbusier* (1933), although the author's later *Three Revolutionary Architects* (1952) and *Architecture in the Age of Reason* (1955), all cited in note 1 above, were probably more widely read. The impact of Kaufmann's belief in the protomodernism of the Age of Enlightenment and the disintegration that occurred in the nineteenth century suffuses the writings of Manfredo Tafuri, surely one of the most, if not the most, important historian of modern architecture of the later twentieth century. Prime texts of his are *Architecture and Utopia: Design and Capitalist Development,* orig. pub. 1973; trans. Barbara Luigia La Penta (Cambridge, Mass.: MIT Press, 1976); *Theories and History of Architecture,* orig. pub. 1976; trans. Giorgio Verrecchia (Cambridge, Mass.: MIT Press, 1980); and *The Sphere and the Labyrinth: Avant-Gardes and Architecture from Piranesi to the 1970s,* orig. pub. 1980; trans. Pellegrino d'Acierno and Robert Connolly (Cambridge, Mass.: MIT Press, 1990).

A good example of Kaufmann's enduring influence can be seen in Vidler, *Ledoux,* xv, where the author introduces his subject in the following way:

> In tracing the historical Ledoux, I have at the same time remained conscious of his formal inventiveness as an architect and have tried to bring more than an account of sources and styles to the interpretation of his compositional techniques. This is where I remain convinced by Kaufmann's formal insights, as he sensed a Ledoux whose approach anticipated the elementarism of a later period. And while it may be historically risky to compare Ledoux to Le Corbusier once again, it is nevertheless true that both architects, relying on the firm precedent of Palladian classicism, developed their formal systems out of the interplay of narrative and structure, movement and volume, as they, in different ways, transgressed their model.

The term elementarism comes from the Dutch abstractionist Theo van Doesburg, who coined it to define his specific version of De Stijl, in contrast to Piet Mondrian's Neo-Plasticism (see chapter 7). Vidler characterized Ledoux's approach to history as "entirely absorbed in a universal aesthetic of abstract allusions" and his designs as "stripped, almost ahistorical" (383, 386).

Combining the Kaufmann thesis with

Sigfried Giedion's argument that the problem with the period ca. 1800–1920 was the schizophrenic separation of the "realms of thought and feeling, science and art," with the result that "for a hundred years architecture lay smothered in a dead, eclectic atmosphere" (*Space, Time, and Architecture*, 14, 24), Antoine Picon, in *French Architects and Engineers in the Age of Enlightenment*, orig. pub. 1988; trans. Martin Thom, Cambridge Studies in the History of Architecture (Cambridge: Cambridge University Press, 1992), wrote that "the end of the Enlightenment saw a definite breach in the domain of architecture and planning" that was characterized by a "tension...between the certainties of the science of building and a history of the art...[creating] a widespread malaise at the start which was gradually to spread" (335, 339). "The 1800s were a watershed," he argued. "In disconnecting itself from" the scientific "interrogation of nature," "architecture went into a long-term crisis. If neo-classicism cannot be readily related to that of architectural modernity, its related uncertainties prefigure it" (333–34).

A number of recent studies offer an increasingly nuanced view of the eighteenth-century/twentieth-century pairing. One of the most interesting of these is Sylvia Lavin, *Quatremère de Quincy and the Invention of a Modern Language of Architecture* (Cambridge, Mass.: MIT Press, 1992). For a discussion of the interrelationship between the Giedion and Kaufmann positions, see Detlef Mertins, "System and Freedom: Sigfried Giedion, Emil Kaufmann, and the Constitution of Architectural Modernity," in *Autonomy and Ideology: Positioning an Avant-Garde in America*, ed. R. E. Somol (New York: Monacelli Press, 1997), 213–31.

18 Giedion, *Building in France*, 85.

19 An early perception of the overlapping of strategies of representation and abstraction in Pop Art is Robert Rosenblum, "Pop Art and Non-Pop Art," *Art and Literature* 5 (Summer 1964); repr. in John Russell and Suzi Gablik, *Pop Art Redefined* (New York: Praeger, 1969), 53–56.

Chapter 1. Castle Howard and the Subject Matter of History

1 Emil Kaufmann, *Architecture in the Age of Reason: Baroque and Post-Baroque in England, Italy, and France* (Cambridge, Mass.: Harvard University Press, 1955), 75–88 and passim.

2 In a number of essays published in the 1940s on the subject of the eighteenth-century English garden, mainly in the *Architectural Review*, Nikolaus Pevsner provided essential documentation for the argument. "The Genesis of the Picturesque" (1944), "A Note on Sharawaggi" (1949), "Richard Payne Knight" (1949), "Uvedale Price" (1944), and "Humphrey Repton" (1948) were republished in his *Studies in Art, Architecture, and Design*, vol. 1, *From Mannerism to Romanticism* (London: Thames & Hudson, 1968), 78–155. A primary source for the subject was Christopher Hussey, *The Picturesque: Studies in a Point of View* (London: G. P. Putnam's Sons, 1927). Among the many recent studies of the subject are John Dixon Hunt and Peter Willis, eds., *The Genius of the Place: The English Landscape Garden, 1620–1820* (London: Elek, 1975); Ann Bermingham, *Landscape and Ideology: The English Rustic Tradition, 1740–1860* (Berkeley: University of California Press, 1986); J. D. Hunt, *Gardens and the Picturesque: Studies in the History of Landscape Architecture* (Cambridge, Mass.: MIT Press, 1992); Tom Williamson, *Polite Landscapes: Gardens and Society in Eighteenth-Century England* (Baltimore: Johns Hopkins University Press, 1995); and J. D. Hunt, *The Picturesque Garden in Europe* (London: Thames & Hudson, 2002).

3 The main credit for considering Castle Howard as coeval with, if not necessarily prior to, Stowe is due to Christopher Hussey's important study *English Gardens and Landscapes, 1700–1750* (London: Country Life, 1967). Although his chapter on Stowe precedes that on Castle Howard, its first paragraph reads (and equivocates) as follows: "Landscape design can be said to have originated at Stowe and Castle Howard simultaneously, in the second decade of the 18th century. Indeed landscape in the sense of scenic values was appreciated earlier at Castle Howard and shaped subsequent developments more consistently. But the progress of garden design from the point we have reached can be traced more certainly and consecutively if we give precedence to Stowe, where not only each stage in the transition, but also the antecedents have left their mark, or can be deduced. Moreover it is there that the development of specifically pictorial garden design, as distinct from broadly scenic landscape-making, can be watched step by step, although a parallel stride was taken at Castle Howard a little sooner" (89).

4 Hussey, *English Gardens and Landscapes*, 89–113.

5 Ibid., 101.

6 Aside from Hussey's *English Gardens and Landscapes*, 114–31, the key publications are Kerry Downes, *Hawksmoor* (1959; 2nd ed., London: A. Zwemmer, 1979), 217–31; K. Downes, *Vanbrugh*, Studies in Architecture 16 (London: A. Zwemmer, 1977), 26–39, 108–10; K. Downes, *Sir John Vanbrugh: A Biography* (London: Sidgwick & Jackson, 1987), 193–221, 284–85, 464–70; Charles Saumarez Smith, *The Building of Castle Howard* (1990; new ed., London: Pimlico, 1997); Hunt, *Gardens and the Picturesque*, 18–46 ("Castle Howard Revisited"); and Christopher Ridgway and Robert Williams, eds., *Sir John Vanbrugh and Landscape Architecture in Baroque England, 1690–1730* (Phoenix Mill, Thrupp, Stroud, England: Sutton Publishing, 2000).

7 Other relevant works on Castle Howard not already cited include H[enry] T[ipping], "The Outworks of Castle Howard," *Country Life* 112 (August 6–13, 1927): 200–208; H. A. Tipping and Christopher Hussey, *English Homes, Period IV*, vol. 2, *Sir John Vanbrugh and His School, 1699–1736* (London: Country Life, 1928); Laurence Whistler, "The Evolution of Castle Howard," *Country Life* 113 (January 30, 1953): 276–79; James Lees-Milne, *English Country House: Baroque, 1685–1715* (1970; repr., Woodbridge, Suffolk, England: Antique Collectors' Club, 1986); Wolfgang Kaiser, *Castle Howard, ein englischer Landsitz des frühen 18. Jahrhunderts: Studien zu Architektur und Landschaftspark* (Freiburg

im Breisgau, Germany: Gaggstatter, 1984); and Venetia Murray, *Castle Howard: The Life and Times of a Stately Home* (London: Viking, 1994). For the architects, see also Bonamy Dobrée and Geoffrey Webb, *The Complete Works of Sir John Vanbrugh*, vol. 4, *The Letters*, ed. G. Webb (London: Nonesuch Press, 1928); and L. Whistler, *The Imagination of Vanbrugh and His Fellow Artists* (London: Art and Technics, B. T. Batsford, 1954).

8 Downes, *Vanbrugh* (1977), 32, and Hunt, *Gardens and the Picturesque*, 24, both describe the plan as Palladian. The unusual use of a dome on a domestic building further points to Palladio.

9 Kerry Downes, "Vanbrugh over Fifty Years," in Ridgway and Williams, *Vanbrugh and Landscape Architecture*, 4–7. Saumarez Smith, *Castle Howard*, 60, claims that construction began only in 1701.

10 Saumarez Smith, *Castle Howard*, 42, states that the drawing in fig. 1.7 is by George London and illustrates the footprint of Talman's design for the house. Hunt, *Gardens and the Picturesque*, 33, merely comments that "the design (if not the drawing) is probably by William Talman," making no mention of any input from London. There is a second garden plan by London, including the footprint of Vanbrugh's design for the house. See Downes, *Vanbrugh* (1977), 28–31.

11 "The History of Vanbrug's House" (1706), in Harold Williams, ed., *The Poems of Jonathan Swift*, 2nd ed., 3 vols. (Oxford: Clarendon Press, 1958), 1:86. For Vanbrugh's activity as a playwright, see Frank McCormick, *Sir John Vanbrugh: The Playwright as Architect* (University Park: Pennsylvania State University Press, 1991).

12 Stephen Switzer, *Ichnographia Rustica, or, The Nobleman, Gentleman, and Gardener's Recreation*, 3 vols. (1718; repr., New York: Garland, 1982), 1:87.

13 Hussey, *English Gardens*, 123–25, was the first to point out the importance of Ray Wood, but both Saumarez Smith, *Castle Howard*. 124–30, and Hunt, *Gardens and the Picturesque*, 36–37, caution against interpreting its design in overly naturalistic terms and instead emphasize its conventional use of mythological, ornamental, and other traditional devices and artifices. Although Lord Burlington had done work on his garden at Chiswick starting in 1716, it was only after the house was finished in the mid-1720s that a development comparable to Castle Howard occurred. The same is true at Rousham, where once again Charles Bridgeman took over in the mid-1720s. Alexander Pope began redesigning the garden at his villa at Twickenham around 1719–20.

14 The plan published in Colen Campbell, *Vitruvius Britannicus; or the British Architect*, vol. 1 (London: by the author, 1715), refers to the apartments in the east and west wings as "the two principall Apartments." In a letter to Carlisle of 1706, Hawksmoor called the east wing "the App of State"; and, according to Saumarez Smith, *Castle Howard*, 90, the bedroom in that wing was referred to as the "second state bedchamber" in the probate inventory of the fourth Earl of Carlisle. However, Saumarez Smith describes the suite in the east wing as "Lord Carlisle's private apartments" (61).

15 The Villa Trissino connection is pointed out in Hunt, *Gardens and the Picturesque*, 30. The west wing was redesigned and completed by the fourth Earl of Carlisle's brother-in-law, Thomas Robinson, in 1753–59. The garden facade was lengthened to accommodate the change in design. A completely separate stable building was constructed to the west of the house by John Carr in 1781.

16 The order in a preliminary scheme was Corinthian rather than Doric, which would have matched that of the garden facade.

17 Saumarez Smith, *Castle Howard*, esp. 1–32.

18 Anne, Viscountess Irwin, *Castle Howard* (1732), in Downes, *Vanbrugh* (1977), 264. The poem was used in the literature on Castle Howard for the first time by Hussey in *English Gardens and Landscapes*.

19 Tom Williamson, "Estate Management and Landscape Design," in Ridgway and Williams, *Vanbrugh and Landscape Architecture*, 23.

20 A few years before the Carrmire Gate, Hawksmoor had proposed Porsenna's tomb as a possible model for the Mausoleum. Nicholas Hawksmoor to the Earl of Carlisle, September 3, 1726, in Geoffrey Webb, "The Letters and Drawings of Nicholas Hawksmoor Relating to the Building of the Mausoleum at Castle Howard, 1726–1742," *Walpole Society* 19 (1930–31): 117.

21 Robert Williams, "Fortified Gardens," in Ridgway and Williams, *Vanbrugh and Landscape Architecture*, 49–60. Among the examples Williams cites is Vanbrugh's own design for Seaton Delaval, built in 1719–26.

22 Horace Walpole to George Selwyn, August 12, 1772, in Hussey, *English Gardens and Landscapes*, 114. A detailed description of his visit is contained in Paget Toynbee, ed., "Horace Walpole's Journals of Visits to Country Seats, &c.," *Walpole Society* 16 (1927–28): 72–73.

23 Wings were added to both sides of the Pyramid Gate in 1756 to provide space for lodging visitors. The architect was Thomas Robinson.

24 As Williams, "Fortified Gardens," 59, shows, the line of mock fortifications continued around to the north side to tie in with the wall surrounding the "Wilderness" and from there to link eventually with the fortified wall enclosing Ray Wood. The latter, the first such wall to be constructed on the estate, was begun in 1706.

25 A number of other less significant garden structures were built by Vanbrugh and Hawksmoor, as well as by others after their deaths. These include the so-called Temple of Venus at the northeast corner of Ray Wood (Hawksmoor, 1731–35); the Pyramid and Four Faces monument in Pretty Wood (Hawksmoor, probably 1730s); and the Bridge over the serpentine river (Daniel Garrett, early 1740s).

26 In correspondence with the Earl of Carlisle, Vanbrugh referred to it as "the Temple with the four Porticos." Vanbrugh to Carlisle, February 18, 1724, in Webb, *Letters*, 157. Hawksmoor invariably referred to it as simply "the Temple," although he did call it the "Temple of Belvidera" in Hawksmoor to Carlisle, October 26, 1729, in Webb, "Letters and Drawings," 124. In her poem of 1732, Lady Irwin refers to it both as the "Temple" and the "Belvidere." In the account of his visit to the site, John Tracy Atkyns, *Iter Boreale*, 1732, MS, Yale Center for British Art, Yale University, New Haven, Conn., 22, describes

it as "a temple of the Ionic order." And in the account of his visit in 1772, Walpole calls it "the Temple"; "Walpole's Journals," 72. Hawksmoor was responsible for completing the building after Vanbrugh's death. I am grateful to Christopher Ridgway for supplying me with a copy of the Atkyns text.

27 Hawksmoor to Carlisle, January 7, 1724, in Downes, *Hawksmoor,* 243. Hawksmoor later used the same term to describe his design for the octagonal rustic Temple of Venus. Webb, "Letters and Drawings," 129, 131.

28 Vanbrugh to Carlisle, February 11 and April 11, 1724, in Webb, *Letters,* 156, 160. Hawksmoor also completed an Italianate design for a "Belvidera" that was probably conceived of as an alternative to his "Turret" project. Dated 1723 by the inscription panel on the building itself, it is a square, domed structure with a Serlian window articulating the front entrance and rear loggia facades. In his letter to Carlisle of January 7, 1724, Hawksmoor describes the design as based on Vignola.

29 James S. Ackerman, *The Villa: Form and Ideology of Country Houses* (London: Thames & Hudson, 1990), 106. Describing the Villa Rotonda in his earlier *Palladio* (Baltimore: Penguin, 1966), 70, Ackerman remarked that "it is not, then, a villa at all, in the sense that the others are, but a *belvedere.*" Vanbrugh was quite advanced in his use of the Palladian model in such an explicit manner. Although one usually associates neo-Palladianism in England with the circle of Lord Burlington, the latter's villa at Chiswick was designed in 1725, at least a year and a half after the Castle Howard Temple, and built in 1727–29. Only Colen Campbell's villa at Mereworth for John Fane was earlier, having been designed in 1722.

30 Williamson, "Estate Management," 28, notes how the "enclosed, improved farmland" of "this working landscape...was observed from the Temple...as a picture at one remove from the habitation of gentility," with no attempt "to emphasize the practical involvement of the landowner in agrarian production."

31 Hawksmoor to Carlisle, February 16, 1730/31, December 4, 1732, June 2, 1733, January 14 and July 3, 1735, in Webb, "Letters and Drawings," 125, 140, 143, 155. At least as often, if not more, however, Hawksmoor used the term "Temple" to describe the building's combined religious and memorial functions. In his will, drawn up before the building was designed, Carlisle specified that "this Burial place should be built in ye form of a little chapple." Saumarez Smith, *Castle Howard,* 169.

32 Hawksmoor to Carlisle, September 3, 1726, in Webb, "Letters and Drawings," 117.

33 Saumarez Smith, *Castle Howard,* 172, maintains that the idea for the colonnade was Viscount Morpeth's, something one can certainly deduce from a literal reading of the correspondence. Hawksmoor refers to Bramante's Tempietto in letters to Carlisle of May 6, 1729, and October 3, 1732. In the latter, he also refers to Palladio as his source. Webb, "Letters and Drawings," 121, 137.

34 Robert Williams, "Vanbrugh's India and His Mausolea for India," in Ridgway and Williams, *Vanbrugh and Landscape Architecture,* 128, suggests that the decision to place a mausoleum such as this in an open landscape setting may possibly be related to Vanbrugh's experience living in Surat in 1683–85.

35 Giles Worsley, "'After ye Antique': Vanbrugh, Hawksmoor and Kent," in Ridgway and Williams, *Vanbrugh and Landscape Architecture,* 147, similarly describes the Howard bust, noting that "had [it] been dug up in York and declared to date from the time of Constantine, no one would have been surprised."

36 In 1731 Hawksmoor suggested to Carlisle that if William Etty, the clerk of works at Castle Howard, were to "send him a rough scetch of the park," he would have it engraved. Hawksmoor to Carlisle, October 4, 1731, in Webb, "Letters and Drawings," 127. Clearly, nothing was done about this, leaving the anachronistic aerial perspective of the house published in *Vitruvius Britannicus* in 1725 as the only contemporary view of the landscape garden.

37 The redrawing of Ralph Fowler's estate map of 1727 in Saumarez Smith, *Castle Howard,* 118–19, incorrectly places the Pyramid to the west of the house's north-south axis.

38 The only designed place from which one can see all three monuments in panorama is the Bridge, which was built after Vanbrugh and Hawksmoor had died. There is no evidence to suggest, however, that affording such a view was part of its purpose. A well-known example of an English garden planned as a continuous narrative circuit is the one at Stourhead, designed by Henry Hoare and Henry Flitcroft and executed from the mid-1740s through the 1770s. Downes, *Vanbrugh* (1977), 109, compared the strangeness of the experience at Castle Howard to the typical English garden in the following way: "At one moment seen and at the next hidden by another hill," the garden structures "give the traveller that feeling of being silently observed which is stronger and deeper than the conventional sense of the *genius loci* of many an eighteenth-century garden peopled with classical statues and summer houses."

39 Vanbrugh to Carlisle, March 26, 1724, in Webb, *Letters,* 159.

40 When Hawksmoor was called upon to add the so-called Temple of Venus to the northeastern edge of Ray Wood after the design of the Mausoleum was set, he chose an octagonal geometry as a way of differentiating the rustic structure from the three main outbuildings and apparently never wavered in this decision. He also always referred to it simply by its geometric form (e.g., "the Octogon") or by that as a qualifier of its typological form (e.g., "our octogonall Turret," "ye octogon Tower," "the Octogon turret"). Webb, "Letters and Drawings," 129, 131, 153–55. Also, he invariably referred to it as a Turret or Tower, as he had previously described his rustic design for the Temple.

41 In this regard, Hawksmoor was adamant, as with no other structure at Castle Howard, in emphasizing (and reiterating) how the design of the Mausoleum was "Authentic and what is According to the practice of ye antients" (Hawksmoor to Carlisle, November 10, 1727), how it "will answer all the Beautys of ye Antique" (Hawksmoor to Carlisle, May 6, 1729), and how it was made "in ye imitation of ye Antique" (Hawksmoor to Carlisle, July 20, 1734); Webb, "Letters and Drawings," 118, 124, 148.

42 In his 1724 description of Stowe, for instance, where Vanbrugh had recently built a pyramid, Lord Perceval described the inordinately acute structure as "a copy in miniature of the most famous one in Egypt"; Hussey, *English Gardens*, 96. Hunt, *Gardens and the Picturesque*, 44–45, however, speaks of the Pyramid at Castle Howard as "a strikingly Roman form" and characterizes it as "antique."

43 Saumarez Smith, *Castle Howard*, 1–32 and passim; and Hunt, *Gardens and the Picturesque*, 44–46.

44 Saumarez Smith, *Castle Howard*, 159–60, points out that Vanbrugh had written to Carlisle in July 1722, in reference to Blenheim, of the idea of a monumental mausoleum as representing "a Show, and a Noble one, to many future Ages." This would have been at about the same time discussions apparently started regarding Carlisle's own burial place.

45 Downes, *Vanbrugh* (1977), 109–10, lays great stress, by contrast, on the "practical" value of the structures, seeing this as a significant aspect of their uniqueness in garden design of the period.

46 Viscountess Irwin, *Castle Howard*, in Downes, *Vanbrugh* (1977), 264–65.

47 Saumarez Smith, *Castle Howard*, 116–55; and Hunt, *Gardens and the Picturesque*, passim.

48 The idea for the Mausoleum dated back to 1722 and thus may even have preceded the discussions of the Temple. Vanbrugh accompanied Carlisle to Stowe in the summer of 1725, where the latter would have seen, and no doubt discussed with the architect, his recently completed and quite unprecedented Pyramid. On that visit, see Vanbrugh to Jacob Tonson, August 12, 1725, in Webb, *Letters*, 166–67.

49 When the model of King Porsenna's tomb was rejected for the Mausoleum, it was transferred by Hawksmoor to the Carrmire Gate, and after the turret idea for the Temple was rejected, it was revived for the octagonal tower known as the Temple of Venus. All of this suggests a kind of lexicon of historical types and forms and geometric equivalents that, when used singly or in juxtaposition with one another, take on specific contextual meanings.

50 The source for this progression is Marcus Vitruvius Pollio, *De architectura (On Architecture)*, 2 vols., ed. and trans. Frank Granger, Loeb Classical Library (Cambridge, Mass.: Harvard University Press, , 1945), 1.2.5, 4.1.1–12. For recent discussions of the orders, see John Onians, *Bearers of Meaning: The Classical Orders in Antiquity, the Middle Ages, and the Renaissance* (Princeton, N.J.: Princeton University Press, 1988); and Alina A. Payne, *The Architectural Treatise in the Italian Renaissance: Architectural Invention, Ornament, and Literary Culture* (Cambridge: Cambridge University Press, 1999).

51 In his well-known series of illustrations for stage sets in the second book of his architectural treatise, *Tutte l'opere d'architettura et prospettiva*, published in 1545, Sebastiano Serlio gave literal expression to the theatrical model of Aristotle by showing how a rustic mode would be the appropriate setting for the lowlife characters in a satire, and an eclectic mixture of quasi-Gothic elements the proper one for the middle-class citizens in a comedy, whereas a scene for a tragedy, with its noble characters of the highest rank, demanded a consistently classical framework.

52 As noted above, the entrance facade in Vanbrugh's original scheme was also Corinthian, leading one to believe that the distinction between the facades ultimately achieved by the difference in the orders was an entirely calculated and deliberate one. In response to criticism, Hawksmoor later defended the use of the different orders to Carlisle by arguing that "the South side, and the North front...cannot be seen together at the same Time, nor at any time upon the Diagonall (or angular view)"; Hawksmoor to Carlisle, July 13,1734, in Downes, *Hawksmoor*, 254. Downes, *Vanbrugh* (1977), 37–38, also points out the gradation in status of the different facades.

53 Henry Wotton, however, believed that the Composite order was more a bastardization of the Ionic and Corinthian than a synthesis of the two. In *The Elements of Architecture* (1624; repr. of 2nd ed.[1651], Springfield, Mass.: F. A. Bassette, n.d.), 233, he described it as "nothing in effect, but a *Medlie*, or an *Amasse* of all the precedent *Ornaments*, making a new kinde, by stealth; and though the most richly tricked, yet the poorest in this, that he is a borrower of all his Beauty." William Chambers later agreed with Wotton on this point.

54 The nascent historicism in Vanbrugh's and Hawksmoor's thinking during the 1720s and '30s coincides precisely with the publication of Johann Fischer von Erlach's *Entwurff einer historischen Architektur*, which appeared first in 1721, followed by new editions in 1725, 1730, and 1737.

55 Joshua Reynolds, *Discourses*, ed. Pat Rogers (1797; repr., New York: Penguin, 1992), 298 (13th discourse, 1786); and John Vanbrugh, "Reasons Offer'd for Preserving Some Part of the Old Manor," June 11, 1709, in Christopher Ridgway, "Rethinking the Picturesque," in Ridgway and Williams, *Vanbrugh and Landscape Architecture*, 191. Vanbrugh's "Reasons" were sent as a memorandum to the Duchess of Marlborough in defense of his idea of retaining the old manor in Woodstock Park, where Blenheim Palace was being constructed.

56 Viscountess Irwin, *Castle Howard*, in Downes, *Vanbrugh* (1977), 264.

57 The classic statement of the *paragone* by Leonardo da Vinci is in Martin Kemp, ed., *Leonardo on Painting: An Anthology of Writings by Leonardo da Vinci with a Selection of Documents Relating to His Career as an Artist* (New Haven, Conn.: Yale University Press, 1989), 20–46 ("The Works of the Eye and Ear Compared"). An early nineteenth-century revisiting of the idea is in Antoine-Chrysostôme Quatremère de Quincy, *Essai sur la nature, le but et les moyens de l'imitation dans les beaux-arts* (1823; repr. as *De l'imitation, 1823*, ed. Leon Krier and Demetri Porphyrios [Brussels: Archives d'Architecture Moderne, 1980]), 143–50.

58 See Introduction, note 1, above.

59 Hussey, in *English Gardens and Landscapes*, 115, wrote: "The aim was to embody, in the actual substance of architecture and scenery, the poetic reality itself, not to reproduce at third hand painters' interpretations of it.

The forms employed might be shared with painters...but these extracts show the aim to have been to recreate the imagined scenery and atmosphere of the 'Golden Age': a conception to be regarded as parallel to the composition of an epic poem or to the landscape paintings of Claude, rather than imitative of either." This Hussey contrasted with William Kent's approach, which he described as intentionally imitating the work of painters.

60 Ernst Gombrich, *Art and Illusion: A Study in the Psychology of Pictorial Representation*, A. W. Mellon Lectures in the Fine Arts, 1956, Bollingen Series 35, no. 5 (1960; 2nd ed., New York: Pantheon Books, 1961), 93–115.

61 Yve-Alain Bois, "A Picturesque Stroll around *Clara-Clara*," *October* 29 (Summer 1984): 32–62, presents a compelling analysis of some of these issues, relating eighteenth-century picturesque theory to twentieth-century practices.

Chapter 2. The Appearance of Truth and the Truth of Appearance in Laugier's Primitive Hut

1 The definitive study of Laugier is Wolfgang Herrmann, *Laugier and Eighteenth-Century French Theory* (London: A. Zwemmer, 1962). The second edition of the *Essai*, originally published in 1755, was reprinted by Gregg Press (Farnborough, England) in 1966 and by Pierre Mardaga (Brussels and Liège) in 1979. An English translation by Wolfgang and Anni Herrmann was published as Marc-Antoine Laugier, *An Essay on Architecture*, Documents and Sources in Architecture 1 (Los Angeles: Hennessey & Ingalls, 1977).

The pirated English edition of 1755, which made no mention of the author's name, is entitled *An Essay on Architecture; In Which Its True Principles are explained, And Invariable Rules proposed, For Directing the Judgment and Forming the Taste of the Gentleman and the Architect, With regard to the Different Kinds of Buildings, the Embellishment of Cities, And the Planning of Gardens*. It was published by T. Osborn and Shipton, London. The 1756 English edition, entitled *An Essay on the Study and Practice of Architecture. Explaining The true Principles of the Science; and Directing the Gentleman and Builder to design and finish in every Article, with Judgment and Taste*, was published by Stanley Crowder and Henry Woodgate, London. The first German translation, entitled *Versuch über die Baukunst*, was published in Frankfurt and Leipzig in 1756. It was followed by editions of 1758, 1768, and 1771. On the publishing history of the *Essai*, see Wolfgang Herrmann's introduction to Laugier, *An Essay on Architecture* (1977), xx–xxii; Herrmann, *Laugier*, 173–90; Eileen Harris with Nicholas Savage, *British Architectural Books and Writers, 1556–1785* (Cambridge: Cambridge University Press, 1990), 280–83; and *British Architectural Library, Royal Institute of British Architects, Early Printed Books 1478–1840: Catalogue of the British Architectural Library Early Imprints Collection*, vol. 2, *E–L*, comp. Nicholas Savage et al. (London: Bowker-Saur, 1995), 938–39.

2 John Summerson, in *Sir John Soane, 1753–1837*, Architectural Biographies 4 (London: Art and Technics, 1952), 21 n. 2, maintained that the number was eleven, including four copies of different French editions, five of the 1755 English translation, and two of a later (1756) English edition. David Watkin, in *Sir John Soane: Enlightenment Thought and the Royal Academy Lectures*, Cambridge Studies in the History of Architecture (Cambridge: Cambridge University Press, 1996), 117 n. 84, states, however, that the number was ten, which included one copy of the 1753 French edition and two of the 1755 edition, five of the 1755 English translation, and two of the 1756 English translation. For Durand, see chapter 3; for Quatremère, see the end of this chapter.

3 See, for example, Kenneth Frampton, *Studies in Tectonic Culture: The Poetics of Construction in Nineteenth and Twentieth Century Architecture*, ed. John Cava (Cambridge, Mass.: MIT Press, 1995); and Fritz Neumeyer, *The Artless Word: Mies van der Rohe on the Building Art*, orig. pub. 1986; trans. Mark Jarzombek (Cambridge, Mass.: MIT Press, 1991). The broadest historical treatment of the primitive hut is Joseph Rykwert, *On Adam's House in Paradise: The Idea of the Primitive Hut in Architectural History*, Museum of Modern Art Papers on Architecture (New York: Museum of Modern Art, 1972).

4 [Jacques-François] Blondel [with Jean-Francois de Bastide], *L'Homme du monde éclairé par les arts*, 2 vols. (Amsterdam, 1774), 2:13. The translation of the second phrase comes from Emil Kaufmann, *Architecture in the Age of Reason: Baroque and Post-Baroque in England, Italy, and France* (Cambridge, Mass.: Harvard University Press, 1955), 253 n. 127.

5 William Chambers, *A Treatise on Civil Architecture, in Which the Principles of that Art are Laid Down and Illustrated by a Great Number of Plates* (London: by the author, 1759), 31–32, 58. In the expanded third edition of 1791, Chambers maintained the critique of Laugier despite the fact that he used Laugier's definition of architecture (preceding that of Vitruvius's) to open the new introduction (*A Treatise on the Decorative Part of Civil Architecture*, 3rd ed. [London: Joseph Smeeton, 1791], 7).

6 Johann Wolfgang von Goethe's *Von deutscher Baukunst: D. M. Ervini a Steinbach* was first published anonymously in 1772 in the *Züricher Gedenkausgabe* 13:16ff.; in the following year it was reprinted under his own name in Johann Gottfried Herder's *Von deutscher Art und Kunst: Einige fliegende Blätter* (Hamburg: bey Bode, 1773). The English translations here are based on those by Geoffrey Grigson, in "The Architectural Review Gothic Number. Act 2: Romantic Gothic. Scene 1: Goethe and Strassburg," *Architectural Review* 98 (December 1945): 156–59; and Elizabeth G. Holt, ed., *A Documentary History of Art*, vol. 2, *Michelangelo and the Mannerists: The Baroque and the Eighteenth Century* (1947; repr., Garden City, N.Y.: Doubleday, 1958), 361–69.

7 See, for example, Louis Hautecoeur, *Histoire de l'architecture classique en France*, vol. 4, *Seconde Moitié du XVIII siècle: Le Style Louis XVI, 1750–1792* (Paris: A. et J. Picard, 1952), 28–36; Robin Middleton, "French Eighteenth-Century Opinion on Wren," in *Concerning Architecture: Essays on Architectural Writers and Writing Presented to Nikolaus*

Pevsner, ed. John Summerson (London: Allen Lane, 1968), 40–57; Dora Wiebenson, *The Picturesque Garden in France* (Princeton, N.J.: Princeton University Press, 1978); Allan Braham, *The Architecture of the French Enlightenment* (Berkeley: University of California Press, 1980), 12–17, 33–35; and John Dixon Hunt, *The Picturesque Garden in Europe* (London: Thames & Hudson, 2002), 90–139.

8 Josephine Grieder, *Anglomania in France, 1740–1789: Fact, Fiction, and Political Discourse*, Histoire des Idées et Critique Littéraire 230 (Geneva: Librairie Droz, 1985), treats English influence on all aspects of French culture and society of the second half of the eighteenth century.

9 On Stourhead, see Kenneth Woodbridge, "Henry Hoare's Paradise," *Art Bulletin* 47 (March 1965): 85–116; and K. Woodbridge, *Landscape and Antiquity: Aspects of English Culture at Stourhead, 1718 to 1838* (Oxford: Clarendon Press, 1970).

10 Girardin's book *De la composition des paysages, ou des moyens d'embellir la nature autour des habitations, en joignant l'agréable à l'utile* was published in Geneva in 1777 and translated into English by D. Malthus in 1783 as *An Essay on Landscape; or, on the means of improving and embellishing the country round our habitations*. An anonymously published guide to the gardens, *Promenade, ou Itinéraire des jardins d'Ermenonville*, which has sometimes been attributed to Girardin's son Stanislas, appeared in 1788. The 1777 and 1788 publications are now both available in René-Louis de Girardin, *De la composition des paysages, suivi de Promenade ou itinéraire des jardins d'Ermenonville*, ed. Michel H. Conan (Seyssel, France: Champ Vallon, 1992). On Ermenonville, see also J.-H. Volbertal, *Aux environs de Paris, un domaine célèbre. Ermenonville: Ses sites, ses curiosités, son histoire* (Senlis, France: Imprimeries réunies de Senlis, 1923); J. H. Ernest de Ganay, "Le Jardin d'Ermenonville," *Gazette illustré des amateurs de jardins* (1925): 1–18; Wiebenson, *Picturesque Garden*, esp. 81–88; and Denis Lambin, "Ermenonville Today," *Journal of Garden History* 8 (January–March 1988): 42–59.

11 Inscribed below the name of each person is a Latin word or phrase that Girardin believed best characterized his thought. For Newton, it is "lucem"; for Descartes, "nil in rebus inane"; for Voltaire, "ridiculum"; for Rousseau, "naturam"; for Penn, "humanitatem"; and for Montesquieu, "justitiam." The monument as a whole was dedicated to Montaigne, "who," according to an inscription on the interior, "said everything." Volbertal, *Aux environs de Paris*, 57, states that a local historian whom he knew well told him that Girardin had planned at one point to erect two other columns, one in honor of Joseph Priestley, carrying the inscription "aerum," and the other in honor of Benjamin Franklin, with the inscription "fulmen."

12 Wiebenson, *Picturesque Garden*, 84, notes that "the Rustic Temple and the Monuments of Old Loves were both intended to recall specific locations in Clarence, the estate described in Rousseau's *Héloise*." In the 1788 guide, *Promenade, ou Itinéraire des jardins d'Ermenonville*, repr. in Girardin, *De la composition*, 147, it is noted that the following quotation from Virgil was inscribed on the temple's pediment:

> Fortunatus et ille Deos qui novit agrestes!
> Illum, non populi fasces, non purpura Regum,
> Flexit, et infidos agitans discordia fratres.

13 Marc-Antoine Laugier, *Essai sur l'architecture*, 2nd ed., rev. and enl. (1755; repr., Farnborough, England: Gregg Press, 1966), 13–28 and passim.

14 Ibid., 11. My translations from the French generally follow Wolfgang and Anni Herrmann's (see note 1 above). But since I make certain modifications, I will provide all the references to the original 1755 French edition.

15 Ibid., 17–25. For Laugier's criticism of the pediment over the central pavilion of the Louvre colonnade, see chapter 3, note 8, below.

16 Ibid., 10–12.

17 Ibid., 8–9.

18 Ibid., 9–10.

19 In the second edition of 1755, Laugier added a final paragraph, which was, in effect, a response to the (unsigned) critical review of the first edition by La Font de Saint-Yenne and Charles-Etienne Briseux, published in 1754 as *Examen d'un Essai sur l'architecture*.

20 Herrmann, *Laugier*, 47, notes that "during the second half of the seventeenth century the view gained ground that in the same way as the column had been modelled after the shape of trees and the members of the Doric Order after the carpentry of wooden buildings, architecture as a whole [and here Herrmann quotes from Pierre Bullet's *Architecture pratique* of 1691] 'was formed on the idea of its first models' and that in effect the hut, 'the simplest and most natural of all (buildings), had been taken by the ancient Greek architects as a model to be imitated in their most beautiful buildings.'" For other readings of the subject, see Rykwert, *On Adam's House;* and Anthony Vidler, *The Writing of the Walls: Architectural Theory in the Late Enlightenment* (Princeton, N.J.: Princeton Architectural Press, 1987), 7–21 ("Rebuilding the Primitive Hut: The Return to Origins from Lafitau to Laugier").

21 Marcus Vitruvius Pollio, *De architectura (On Architecture)*, ed. and trans. Frank Granger, 2 vols., Loeb Classical Library (Cambridge, Mass.: Harvard University Press, 1945), 2.1.1–2.

22 Ibid., 2.1.8, 6, 2.

23 Ibid, 2.1.3.

24 Ibid., 2.1.4.

25 Ibid., 2.1.6–7.

26 Ibid., 2.1.8.

27 Ibid., 4.2.3, 5.

28 Chambers, *Treatise on Civil Architecture*, 1–2. Cf. Robin Middleton, "Chambers, W. 'A Treatise on Civil Architecture,' London 1759," in *Sir William Chambers: Architect to George III*, ed. John Harris and Michael Snodin (New Haven, Conn.: Yale University Press, 1996), 68–72. Eileen Harris, "The *Treatise on Civil Architecture*," in John Harris, *Sir William Chambers: Knight of the Polar Star* (London: A. Zwemmer, 1970), 128–43, makes no mention of the dispute with Laugier, nor does she use the first edition of the text for her analysis.

29 Chambers, *Treatise on Civil Architecture*, 31. As E. Harris, "*Treatise on Civil Architecture*,"

139–41, points out, the third edition of 1791 was even more explicitly pro-Roman and "progressive" than the earlier two editions.

30 Vidler, *Writing of the Walls*, 20, notes that Charles Eisen, who drew the frontispiece for the second edition of Laugier's *Essai*, also drew the frontispiece for Rousseau's *Discourse on the Origins of Inequality*. He compares the images from the two books to make the point that, whereas "the site of Rousseau's natural society might…be envisaged as somewhere between the savage forest and the civilized town," "Laugier, in contradistinction to Rousseau, had chosen to eliminate altogether the *social* roots of dwelling, preferring architectural criteria derived from the internal logic of architecture to the external influences of customs or mores" (16, 20).

31 Laugier, *Essai*, 10–11.

32 E. Harris, *British Architectural Books*, 281, notes that the first English edition became available on April 15, 1755. The second French edition passed the censor on November 22, 1754, and was published by sometime in April 1755, when the first review of it appeared.

33 In addition to the frontispiece by Eisen, there are eight other plates, all drawn by Quirijn Fonbonne. Placed at the end of the volume on foldout sheets, they comprise the following: Doric order; Ionic order; Corinthian order; Composite order; four pediments; arcade with detached Corinthian columns supporting balustrade; arcade with engaged Doric columns supporting triangular pediment; and arcade with Ionic pilasters supporting segmental pediment. In his "Avertissement" to the second edition, Laugier, *Essai*, xxxi, noted that he included the additional plates to "facilitate the understanding" of a "dictionary of [architectural] terms" he also had added. Although he made no reference to the frontispiece, it is clear that he intended the second edition to appeal to a broader audience and, as he wrote, "either to resolve difficulties that have been pointed out to me or to make points clearer that had seemed to be a bit obscure" (ibid., xxxii). Unfortunately, we have no information so far regarding the degree to which Laugier instructed Eisen in the production of the image of the hut.

Charles Eisen (1720–1778) was one of the most important French book illustrators of the second half of the eighteenth century, serving for a time as the drawing master to Madame de Pompadour. See Vera Salomons, *Charles Eisen, 18th Century French Book Illustrator and Engraver* (1914; repr., Amsterdam: G. W. Hissink, 1972); Claire Lemoine-Isabeau, "François et Charles Eisen, ou les tribulations d'un peintre belge et de son fils vignettiste entre la France et les Pays-Bas méridionaux," *Cahiers de Mariemont* 24, no. 25 (1993): 68–75; and Antony Griffiths, "Publishers and Authors," in *Prints for Books: Book Illustration in France, 1760–1800*, Panizzi Lectures 2003 (London: British Library, 2004), 1–56. I am indebted to Cammie McAtee for this information.

34 Laugier, *Essai*, 12. Giusta Nicco Fasola, in *Ragionamenti sulla architettura* ([Bari]: Macrì, 1949), 177, wrote that "the hut is the image around which the eighteenth century developed its architectural aesthetic.…Art is imitation, and all arts have their model; this happens naturally because every kind of knowing or human operation is based on nature…[and thus] the hut, a work of primitive man in his innocence, retains the near-sanctity of natural things."

35 Laugier, *Essai*, 3.

36 This was the point, already referred to in the Introduction, that Chambers reiterated in the third edition of his treatise: "Nature is the supreme and true model of the imitative arts upon which every great artist must form his idea of the profession, in which he means to excel; and the antique is to the architect, what nature is to the painter or sculptor; the source from which his chief knowledge must be collected; the model upon which his taste must be formed." But in contradistinction to Laugier, Chambers urged a discerning eclecticism rather than a puristic "primitivism" in deciding what models to follow. "But as in nature few things are faultless," he continued, "so neither must it be imagined that every ancient production in architecture, even among the Romans, was perfect; or a fit model for imitation.…On the contrary, their remains are so extremely unequal, that it requires the greatest circumspection, and effort of judgement, to make a proper choice." Chambers, *Treatise on the Decorative Part of Civil Architecture* (1791), 23.

37 Laugier, *Essai*, xvii.

38 The distinction, which can be traced back to Vitruvius, was embedded in students' minds by the very organization of the teaching of classical architecture as revealed in the period's major texts. The most significant for the mid- to late eighteenth century was Jacques-François Blondel's *Cours d'architecture, ou, Traité de la décoration, distribution & construction des bâtiments*, 6 vols. (1771–77; repr., Paris: Monum, Editions du Patrimoine; Ivry-sur-Seine: Phénix Editions, 2002), wherein the Vitruvian triad of *venustas, commoditas,* and *firmitas*, translated as *décoration, distribution,* and *construction,* governed the organization and sequence of the lessons. Volumes 1–3 were exclusively devoted to *décoration*, meaning the application of the orders and other elements of the classical vocabulary to the physical design of both exterior and interior wall surfaces; volume 4 to *distribution*, or planning; and part of volume 5 and all of volume 6 to *construction* (the other part of volume 5 returned to the matter of the *décoration* of interiors).

39 Laugier, *Essai*, 39–60.

40 Ibid., 27, 25, 16–17, 24. In this argument against representational redundancy and disavowal of verisimilitude, Laugier echoes the logic of Vitruvius, *De architectura*, 4.2.5: "In the Doric order, the detail of the triglyphs and mutules was invented with a purpose. Similarly in Ionic buildings, the placing of the dentils, has its appropriate intention. And just as in the Doric order the mutules have been the representation of the projecting principal rafters, so, in the case of Ionic dentils, they also imitate the projection of the ordinary rafters. Therefore in Greek architecture no one puts dentils under a mutule. For ordinary rafters cannot be put beneath principals. For if what ought to be placed above principals and purlins in

reality is placed below them in the imitation, the treatment of the work will be faulty. Further, as to the ancients neither approving nor arranging that in the pediments there should be either mutules or dentils, but plain cornices, this was because neither principals nor rafters are fixed to project on the front of gables, but are placed sloping down to the eaves. Thus what cannot happen in reality cannot (they thought) be correctly treated in the imitation."

41 In his *Nouveau traité de toute l'architecture; ou, l'art de bastir; utile aux entrepreneurs et aux ouvriers* (Paris: Jean-Baptiste Coignard, 1706), Jean-Louis de Cordemoy expressed a sympathy for the lightness and elegance of Gothic construction and proposed a trabeated columnar architecture owing much to it. Laugier openly acknowledged the influence of Cordemoy, stating in the preface to the first edition of the *Essai:* "All modern authors, with the exception of M. de Cordemoy, give no more than commentaries on Vitruvius, following him uncritically in all his errors.... This author, being more profound than most of the others, saw the truth that was hidden from them. His treatise on architecture... contains excellent principles and well-considered notions" (xxvi–xxvii).

42 Laugier, *Essai,* 3, 173–74.

43 Robin Middleton, "The Abbé de Cordemoy and the Graeco-Gothic Ideal: A Prelude to Romantic Classicism," *Journal of the Warburg and Courtauld Institutes* 25 (1962): 278–320; 26 (1963): 90–123. This article has had an enormous and fully justified influence on later scholarship. Among the most significant recent examples are Frampton, *Studies in Tectonic Culture,* esp. 29–59; and Antoine Picon, "The Freestanding Column in Eighteenth-Century Religious Architecture," *Things That Talk: Object Lessons from Art and Science,* ed. Lorraine Daston (New York: Zone Books, 2004), 67–99. A different, wider-ranging take on the Laugier-Soufflot connection was developed by Picon in his "Architettura ed espressione costruttiva: Il problema del razionalismo costruttivo / Architecture and Constructive Expression: The Problem of Structural Rationalism," *Lotus International: Rivista trimestrale di architettura / Quarterly Architectural Review* 47, no. 3 (1985): 6–18.

44 Marc-Antoine Laugier, "Discours sur le rétablissement de l'architecture antique," 1761, in Herrmann, *Laugier,* 129. Laugier repeated this encomium in his *Observations sur l'architecture* (The Hague and Paris: Desaint, 1765), 182, describing the church as "a work whose effects will be singular, majestic, sublime, a work that will be unique in Europe, and that will mark its epoch in the History of Architecture, where it will be referred to as the first and most beautiful of monuments since the renaissance of the Arts."

45 On the Church of Sainte-Geneviève, see Michael Petzet, *Soufflots Sainte-Geneviève und der franzözische Kirchenbau des 18. Jahrhunderts* (Berlin: De Gruyter, 1961); and *Le Panthéon, symbole des révolutions: De l'église de la nation au temple des grands hommes* (Paris: Picard, 1989). On Soufflot, see Jean Monval, *Soufflot: Sa vie, son oeuvre, son esthétique (1713–1780)* (Paris: A. Lemerre, 1918); *Soufflot et l'architecture des lumières* (Paris: Ministère de l'Environnement et du Cadre de Vie, Direction de l'Architecture; Centre National de la Recherche Scientifique, 1980); and Jean-Marie Pérouse de Montclos, *Jacques-Germain Soufflot* (Paris: Monum, Editions du Patrimoine, 2004).

46 Soufflot's drawings were used by Gabriel-Pierre-Martin Dumont in his *Suitte de plans, coupes, profils, élévations géométrales et perspectives, tels qu'ils existoient en mil sept cent cinquante, dans la bourgade de Poesto qui est la ville Poestum de Pline* (Paris: by the author, 1764) and his *Les Ruines de Paestum, autrement Posidonia, ville de l'ancienne Grande Grèce, au Royaume de Naples* (London and Paris: by the author, 1769), the latter being based on a translation of John Berkenhout's anonymously published *The Ruins of Poestum or Posidonia, a City of Magna Graecia in the Kingdom of Naples* (London, 1767). On the "discovery" of Paestum, see S. Lang, "The Early Publications of the Temples at Paestum," *Journal of the Warburg and Courtauld Institutes* 13 (1950): 48–64; and Joselita Raspi Serra, ed., *Paestum and the Doric Revival, 1750–1830: Essential Outlines of an Approach* (Florence: Centro Di, 1986).

47 Daniel Rabreau, "La Basilique Sainte-Geneviève de Soufflot," in *Le Panthéon,* 37–96. Soufflot's 1741 lecture to the Lyon Academy, entitled "Mémoire sur l'architecture gothique," was reprinted in Petzet, *Soufflots Sainte-Geneviève,* 135–42, and in *Le Panthéon,* 305–8. According to Pérouse de Montclos, *Soufflot,* 43, the architect presented the same "Mémoire" at the Royal Academy in Paris in December 1761 and again in December 1762.

48 Braham, *Architecture of the French Enlightenment,* 13–15. Hawksmoor's St. George, Bloomsbury, was built in 1716–27 and Gibbs's St. Martin-in-the-Fields in 1721–26. Both have single-story temple porticos as facades. They were preceded by nearly a century by the even more archaeologically inspired temple portico of Inigo Jones's St. Paul's, Covent Garden (1630–31). According to Herrmann, *Laugier,* 116, Pierre Patte proposed a design in 1754 for the facade of the Parisian Church of Saint-Eustache, based on the temple portico model.

49 Julien-David Le Roy, *Histoire de la disposition et des formes différentes que les Chrétiens ont données à leurs temples depuis le règne de Constantin le Grand jusqu'à nous* (Paris: Desaint and Saillant, 1764), offers a contemporaneous history and comparative analysis of the development of church types, the basilical Latin cross culminating in Pierre Contant d'Ivry's first design for the Madeleine in Paris (1763) and the centralized Greek cross in that of Sainte-Geneviève.

50 Although Bramante's project for St. Peter's had much thinner piers than those later designed by Michelangelo, the earlier architect still did not employ freestanding columns in the arms of the church, nor were his piers at the crossing articulated like Soufflot's to give the appearance of being composed of essentially freestanding supports.

51 Maximilien Brébion, "Mémoire à Monsieur le Comte de la Billarderie Angiviller, Directeur et Ordonnateur Général des

Batimens," 1780, in Petzet, *Soufflots Sainte-Geneviève,* 147. Mitchell Schwarzer, "Ontology and Representation in Karl Bötticher's Theory of Tectonics," *Journal of the Society of Architectural Historians* 52 (September 1993): 267–80, traces this idea as informing the German theorist Karl Bötticher's writings as late as the 1840s.

52 [Charles-Nicolas Cochin], *Doutes raisonnables d'un marguillier de la paroisse de S. Etienne-du-Mont sur le problême proposé par M. Patte, architecte, concernant la construction de la coupole de l'Eglise de Sainte-Geneviève* (Amsterdam and Paris: Jombert fils, 1770), 11 ("Lettre de M. C***** à M. D*****, ancien Commissaire des Pauvres de la Paroisse de la Magdeleine"). Although the pamphlet was issued anonymously, Cochin almost immediately took credit for it in a letter published in the *Mercure de France* the same year.

53 Laugier, *Essai,* 182, 198. Laugier, *Observations,* 297–98, repeated this advice, stating that the buttressing of vaults "must be disguised and hidden from view as much as possible. The building should be constructed so that nothing appears to exert thrust or to buttress," this in contradistinction to "gothic buildings" where a " forest of flying buttresses and abutments surround their exterior perimeter...giving the appearance of a building propped up and threatening to collapse." "The vaults of the new Church of Sainte Geneviève," by contrast, "will be perfectly buttressed, but no one will perceive how they are. Nothing on the exterior will announce the effort and the resistance.... Free of any anxiety in this regard, one will only be concerned with the beauty of the work."

54 Laugier, *Essai,* 127–29.

55 Blondel, *Cours d'architecture,* 1:189, titled the first part of his first book "Treatise on the Exterior Decoration of Buildings" and gave as the heading to its first chapter "Origin of the Orders. Source from which one must draw the precepts of the exterior decoration of Buildings." Following this, he noted that "of all the parts of Architecture, none more than the orders that decorate buildings more fully herald the magnificence of the Art" (1:191). Farther along in the first book, Blondel asserted the near synonymity of decoration and architecture in the following passage: "In order to acquire the art of decorating our buildings with precision and with taste, let us begin with the study of the proportions of the five Orders, as being the basis of the principles that concern the decoration of our buildings, the part of architecture that must be regarded, if not as the most essential, then at least as the one that creates the greatest honor for the Architect, and that contributes the most to herald the opulence of our Cities" (1:214). For the relation of this passage to the overall organization of Blondel's text, see note 38 above.

56 Soufflot gained significant experience in using iron to reinforce stone construction while restoring the colonnade of the Louvre's west facade (begun 1756). The colonnade, dating from the later 1660s, was considered to be the earliest and most prominent example of such a structural system. See Robin Middleton, "Architects as Engineers: The Iron Reinforcement of Entablatures in Eighteenth-Century France," *AA Files: Annals of the Architectural Association School of Architecture* 9 (Summer 1985), 54 et seq.; Antoine Picon, *Claude Perrault, 1613–1688; ou, La Curiosité d'un classique* (Paris: Picard, 1988), 184–96; and Picon, "Freestanding Column," esp. 72–81.

The generation following Soufflot's began to question such use of iron reinforcement, although initially on purely technical grounds. In an unpublished "Note sur l'Employ du Fer en Bâtimens" written in 1804 and revised in 1842, Antoine-Laurent-Thomas Vaudoyer (1756–1846), secretary-archivist of the Ecole des Beaux-Arts from 1807 on, noted that although "it has become proverbial to say that iron is the soul of a building," it "is often one of the causes that accelerates the ruin of buildings" through "rusting." Vaudoyer pointed out that Soufflot had learned from his experience at the Louvre to "take the precaution of giving two coats of paint to all the internal pieces of iron" in the Church of Sainte-Geneviève. While "none of the iron so far has caused any rupture [of the stone]," Vaudoyer wondered whether Soufflot's solution was "durable enough to conserve" the building in the long run. Vaudoyer concluded that one should use iron only "with prudence" and when "forced" to do so and "not to place an absolute confidence" in this method of construction. Carton 32 architectes, dossier A.-L.-T. Vaudoyer, Bibliothèque d'Art et d'Architecture Jacques Doucet, Institut Nationale d'Histoire de l'Art, Paris.

57 Laugier, in *Observations,* 298–99, praised the way the flat lintels of the Louvre colonnade "disguised any idea of thrust and buttressing" without, however, mentioning the role the internal iron bars and cramps played.

58 Laugier, *Essai,* xvii.

59 Ibid., xviii. This argument differs from that of most historians and critics, who have preferred to see Laugier as predicting a more modern form of structural rationalism in which the distinction between truth and appearance is less the issue than what Picon, in "Freestanding Column," 94, speaks of as "the emergence of modern structural thought." In somewhat parallel fashion, Vidler, in *Writing of the Walls,* 17–21, sees Laugier as the source of a modernist "autonomous architecture": "Laugier had eliminated all reference to the traditional symbolic and allegorical meanings of architecture, religious and secular.... The elements of building [in his theory] were first and foremost constructional and logical; their assembly followed a law of geometry; architecture was not a language but a construct." Alan Colquhoun, in *Modern Architecture,* Oxford History of Art (Oxford: Oxford University Press, 2002), 37–38, writes that Laugier "argued for...the expression of a skeleton construction" that had its ultimate outcome in the steel-frame system adopted in Chicago in the 1880s.

60 Laugier did not use the term *vraisemblance* in the *Essai.* By contrast, Jacques-François Blondel, in his *Cours d'architecture,* 1:286, considered a respect for verisimilitude, along with a sense of decorum and good judgment, critical to the creation of good

architecture. Most of his references to the concept, however, do not extend beyond the surface of illusion. More often than not, they point to the lack of verisimilitude in the use of such elements as caryatids, trophies, consoles, and corbels or brackets, where the sculptural or ornamental object does not appear to be capable of doing the job it would do were the situation a real rather than a virtual one (1:339, 346, 348, 349, 361; 3:448). On the other hand, Blondel noted the risk of a lack of verisimilitude when using the colossal order due to the resultant incompatibility between exterior expression and interior arrangement (3:49); the potential lack of verisimilitude when the vaults or domes of a church are painted rather than decorated with ribs or coffers, which would be more in keeping with the actual construction (3:419); and the lack of verisimilitude when inexperienced architects substituted bombast and complexity for simplicity by "introduc[ing] many elements of Architecture and Sculptural ornaments in the decoration of facades and the interior of Appartments" (4:lvi).

In the important chapter on the "Analysis of the Art [of Architecture]" in the first volume of the *Cours*, Blondel devoted an entire section to "Verisimilitude in Architecture" ["De la vraissemblance en Architecture"], although here he used the term in a different and more restricted way than throughout the rest of the text. His main purpose in this section was to distinguish the *vraissemblable* from the *vrai* in terms of the idea of architectural style (1:391–93). The "style vrai en Architecture," the definition of which immediately precedes the discussion of *vraissemblance*, "presents a resolute character, which puts each element in its place, [and] which uses ornaments that are only necessary to embellish it"; it "is devoid of any equivocation, reveals itself beautiful in its ordonnance, commodious in its distribution, and solid in its construction." "This character of truth alone can produce unity, which must be seen as the highest quality of art." "The verisimilar [*vraissemblable*]," by contrast, must be understood as something that "substitutes" and "compensates for the true style" when the architect finds himself under financial, material, or programmatic constraints. Through such devices as the optical correction of proportions and increased appearance of support, it reveals the architect's ability to overcome difficulties and achieve a sense of "beauty." Whereas "a true architecture pleases all eyes, a verisimilar architecture pleases only the enlightened mind," Blondel states. It "is more the fruit of reasoning and of the meditation on the part of the architect than the strict application of precepts, verisimilitude therefore being sometimes preferable to a truth that rebuffs often more than it pleases."

Although Blondel never subjects the concept of verisimilitude to a reading in terms of structural truth along the lines opened up by Laugier, Antoine-Chrysostôme Quatremère de Quincy's *Architecture*, 3 vols., in *Encyclopédie méthodique, ou par ordre de matières, par une société de gens de lettres, de savans et d'artistes*, ed. C[harles] J[oseph] Panckoucke (Paris: Panckoucke, 1788; Henri Agasse, 1801; Mme la veuve Agasse, 1825), 1:114 (s.v. "Architecture") and I:385 (s.v. "Cabane"), uses the term *vraisemblance* in precisely the way I have done.

61 Aristotle, *Poetics*, 9.2–4.

62 Alina Payne, "*Ut Poesis Architectura:* Tectonics and Poetics in Architectural Criticism circa 1570," in *Antiquity and Its Interpreters*, ed. Alina Payne, Ann Kuttner, and Rebekah Smick (Cambridge: Cambridge University Press, 2000), 147–48, refers to the Aristotelian concept of verisimilitude in her discussion of Palladio's explanation of the ornamental aspect of volutes. She notes that his "departure point is clearly Vitruvius' origin story of the *ornamenta* above the columns (4.2.1–5 [see note 38 above]), where the temple's entablature and pediment are described as stone *simulacra* of wooden structure." Laugier, however, extends the domain of verisimilitude from the ornamental detail to the entirety of the building.

63 The association of reality with appearance permeates discussions of Alberti's work and clearly derives from the architect's own sometimes ambiguous writing on the subject. In his *On the Art of Building in Ten Books*, orig. pub. as *De re aedificatoria*, 1486; trans. Joseph Rykwert, Neil Leach, and Robert Tavernor (Cambridge, Mass.: MIT Press, 1988), Alberti states that "the column is the principal ornament, without any doubt...to adorn a portico, wall, or other form of opening" (6.13), earlier on defining "ornament, rather than being inherent [as having] the character of something attached or additional" (6.2). On the other hand, while stating that "columns may either be added to the wall or inserted into an opening" (7.11), Alberti also describes the "piers, columns, and anything else that acts as a column and supports the trusses and roof arches" as composing the "bones" of the structure (3.6), such "bones" being "the solid part of the wall" (7.4). The "wall," he describes in another part of the text, as comprising "skin, infill, bonding, and bones" (9.8).

64 In his *Observations sur l'architecture* of 1765, however, Laugier came back to the subject with a vengeance, devoting the entire first part of the book to it—71 out of the book's overall 314 pages.

65 Laugier, *Essai*, 56.

66 Antoine-Chrysostôme Quatremère de Quincy, *De l'architecture égyptienne considérée dans son origine, ses principes et son goût, et comparée sous les mêmes rapports à l'architecture grecque*, dissertation qui a remporté, en 1785, le prix proposé par l'Académie des Inscriptions et Belles-Lettres (Paris: Barrois l'aîné et fils, 1803); Quatremère de Quincy, *Architecture;* and Quatremère de Quincy, *Dictionnaire historique d'architecture, comprenant dans son plan les notions historiques, descriptives, archéologiques, biographiques, théoriques, didactiques et pratiques de cet art*, 2 vols. (Paris: A. Le Clere, 1832). The entries on "Architecture," "Character," "Idea," and "Imitation" from *Architecture* were translated by Tanis Hinchcliffe and published (with some editing) in "Extracts from the *Encyclopédie méthodique d'architecture:* Antoine-Chrysostome Quatremère de Quincy, 1755–1849," *9H*, no. 7 (1985), 25–39. Selections from the *Dictionnaire historique* were translated into English in Samir Younés, ed., *The True, the Fictive, and the Real: The "Historical Dictionary of Architecture" of Quatremère*

de Quincy (London: Andreas Papadakis, 1999). On Quatremère, see R[ené] Schneider, *Quatremère de Quincy et son intervention dans les arts (1788–1850)* (Paris: Hachette, 1910); Schneider, *L'Esthétique classique chez Quatremère de Quincy (1805–23)* (Paris: Hachette, 1910); and Sylvia Lavin, *Quatremère de Quincy and the Invention of a Modern Language of Architecture* (Cambridge, Mass.: MIT Press, 1992).

Quatremère's adoption of a stricter, more doctrinaire, and reductive neoclassicism can be seen clearly in his critique of Soufflot's design of the Church of Sainte-Geneviève. While praising the church for being the most responsible for "bringing the style of antiquity back into favor," Quatremère nevertheless criticized Soufflot in his *Histoire de la vie et des ouvrages des plus célèbres architectes du XIe siècle jusqu'à la fin du XVIIIe*, 2 vols. (Paris: J. Renouard, 1830), 2:344, 341, for failing to endow the church with "the great simplicity of line and detail, the severity of forms, the density of intercolumniations, [and] the economy of ornaments" appropriate to such a building, and instead giving it "a style of elegance and variety...that, in the language of his art, become the marked expression of gaiety and pleasure." In addition, Quatremère condemned the mixing of unrelated elements, such as "naves with freestanding columns" supporting "cut-stone vaults" or a "triple-shell stone dome surrounded on the outside by a freestanding colonnade" (341). More than anything else, the dome contradicted Quatremère's neoclassicism. In his *Dictionnaire historique*, 2:100–101, he called the form an expensive and wasteful "superfetation" or "pleonasm," the "mania for the erection of [which] is a vestige of the Gothic legacy."

67 Quatremère de Quincy, *De l'architecture égyptienne*, esp. 239–41.

68 Ibid., 207.

69 Ibid., 242–43. These thoughts were repeated almost word for word in Quatremère de Quincy, *Architecture*, 1:114–15 (s.v. "Architecture").

70 Quatremère de Quincy, *Architecture*, 1:114.

71 Ibid., 111.

72 Ibid., 115.

73 Quatremère more fully developed the concepts of fiction and verisimilitude in the context of the imitation of nature in painting and sculpture in his *Essai sur la nature, le but et les moyens de l'imitation dans les beaux-arts* (Paris: Treuttel et Würtz, 1823).

74 Quatremère de Quincy, *Architecture*, 1:118–20 (s.v. "Architecture").

75 Ibid., 115, 123; and 500, 505 (s.v. "Caractère"). In his *Essai sur la nature, le but et les moyens de l'imitation dans les beaux-arts* (1823; repr. as *De l'imitation, 1823*, ed. Leon Krier and Demetri Porphyrios [Brussels: Archives d'Architecture Moderne, 1980]), 147, however, Quatremère wrote that "architecture, which imitates nothing that is real or positive, nevertheless takes its place on this imitative ladder [of the arts of imitation] due to the fact that its characteristic feature is to employ matter, its forms, and the relationships of their proportions to express moral qualities, or at least those that nature makes visible in its works, and by which is produced in us the ideas and the sensations correlative to order, harmony, grandeur, richness, unity, variety, duration, eternity."

76 Quatremère de Quincy, *Architecture*, 1:382 (s.v. "Cabane"). In ibid., 115 (s.v. "Architecture"), Quatremère resorted to an argument similar to the one maintaining that "if God did not exist, he would have to be invented," observing that "Even if one succeeded in proving to us that this imitation [of the hut] did not exist at all, that it was nothing but a system created after the fact, and the result of a later comparison of ideas subsequently fabricated, one could only conclude that what might not have existed should have existed, and that it would be a new obligation for us to the art to create voluntarily for it a model the imitation of which is for us an added pleasure."

77 Ibid., 115. In his entry on "Décoration" in the second volume of *Architecture* (1801), 178, Quatremère reiterated his argument for the hut as a "constructed" model of imitation in Greek architecture:

> It is in the creations of nature, or the manner in which nature creates, that this art [of architecture] finds its models and its rules...[,] drawing the primitive types and characters of its constitution from the analogy with the first constructions made by the instinct of need. . . .
> . . . There is no architecture more than that of Greece...where the imitative and *decorative* system is visibly written in the nature of things.
>
> The Greeks did two things that rendered their combinations the most excellent of all; they gave themselves a positive model, which preserved them from the deviations of any fantasies; they then demanded that the ornaments proper to embellishing this model also be drawn from the same source; so that for want of a model of building in the works of nature, which creates no houses, they chose the work of art closest to the inspirations of need, of instinct and of the habits of nature....They demanded that everything that announced the crude framework and anatomy of the undeveloped model that they took as a type should become the principle of the ornament in the copy.

78 Quatremère de Quincy, *Architecture*, 1:115 (s.v. "Architecture"). Quatremère de Quincy, *De l'architecture égyptienne*, 230, noted that "such a model [as the hut] acquires, relative to the imitative art [of architecture] the force and the authority of nature." Vidler, *Writing of the Walls*, 147–64 ("From the Hut to the Temple: Quatremère de Quincy and the Idea of Type"); and Lavin, *Quatremère de Quincy*, esp. 102–13, offer quite different readings of Quatremère's understanding of the imitative basis of architecture in the hut.

79 Quatremère de Quincy, *Architecture*, 1:116 (s.v. "Architecture").

80 Ibid., 114.

81 For an example of Quatremère's hard-line conservatism, see his critique of Soufflot referred to in note 66 above.

82 Quatremère de Quincy, *Architecture*, 1:500 (s.v. "Caractère").

Chapter 3. From Imitation to Abstraction in the Neoclassicism of Boullée, Soane, and Schinkel

1 Antoine-Chrysostôme Quatremère de Quincy, *Architecture*, 3 vols., in *Encyclopédie méthodique, ou par ordre de matières, par une société de gens de lettres, de savans et d'artistes*, ed. C[harles] J[oseph] Panckoucke (Paris:

Panckoucke, 1788; Henri Agasse, 1801; Mme la veuve Agasse, 1825), 1:114 (s.v. "Architecture").

2 Fifteen years later, however, in his *De l'architecture égyptienne considérée dans son origine, ses principes et son goût, et comparée sous les mêmes rapports à l'architecture grecque*, dissertation qui a remporté, en 1785, le prix proposé par l'Académie des Inscriptions et Belles-Lettres (Paris: Barrois l'aîné et fils, 1803), 239–42, Quatremère did identify Lodoli as the person responsible for this point of view in a footnote. After stating that "the transposition from wood to stone is...the principal cause of the pleasure Greek architecture procures for us, and this pleasure is of the nature of that which we eagerly seek in the other arts of imitation," Quatremère wrote of certain "detractors of this metamorphosis." "There are critics," he continued, "who blame the system by virtue of which Architecture is constrained to imitate primitive wood constructions," referring the reader to "Il Padre fra Carlo Lodoli" in a note to the text (242 n. 1). "They disapprove [of the idea] that stone might become representative of another material; they pity in a way the marbles for being degraded by this subordinate role, subjected as they are to reproduce the appearance of poor and undeveloped huts. They want each material to draw out of itself and its own constitution its forms and its taste." According to Quatremère, this type of thinking would never have led to the architecture invented by the Greeks; rather, "it is what happened in the generation of Egyptian Architecture."

3 See Emil Kaufmann, "At an Eighteenth Century Crossroads: Algarotti vs. Lodoli," *Journal of the Society of Architectural Historians* 4 (April 1944): 23–29; Edgar Kaufmann Jr., "Memmo's Lodoli," *Art Bulletin* 46 (June 1964): 159–75; Joseph Rykwert, "Lodoli on Function and Representation," *Architectural Review* 160 (July 1976): 21–26; and J. Rykwert, *The First Moderns: The Architects of the Eighteenth Century* (Cambridge, Mass.: MIT Press, 1980), 288–337. The following texts are generally used to reconstruct Lodoli's thought: Francesco Algarotti, *Saggio sopra l'architettura*, vol. 2 of *Opere* (Leghorn: M. Coltellini, 1764), 51ff.; Andrea Memmo, *Elementi dell'architettura Lodoliana o sia L'arte del fabbricare con solidità e con eleganza no cappriciosa* (Rome: Pagliarini, 1786); and Francesco Milizia, *Principij di architettura civile* (1781; repr., Milan: Sapere, 2000).

4 Jean-Nicolas-Louis Durand, *Précis of the Lectures on Architecture; with Graphic Portion of the Lectures on Architecture*, orig. pub. 1802–5/1821; trans. David Britt, Texts & Documents (Los Angeles: Getty Research Institute, 2000), 133, 84, 82, 83. The terms "fitness and economy," which are translations of *convenance et économie*, should not be confused with modern, that is to say twentieth-century, ideas of functionalism. The basic work on Durand is Werner Szambien, *Jean-Nicolas-Louis Durand, 1760–1834: De l'imitation à la norme* (Paris: Picard, 1984). See also Sergio Villari, *J. N. L. Durand (1760–1834): Art and Science of Architecture* (1984; New York: Rizzoli, 1990); and Antoine Picon, introduction to Durand, *Précis*, 1–68.

5 Durand, *Précis*, 136. Durand states that this idea comes from David Le Roy. In his matter-of-fact manner, Durand "distinguished those antique details that are to be adopted from those that are to be rejected...[from] those that may be tolerated" (ibid., 137).

6 Ibid., 192.

7 Ibid., 139. Albert Rosengarten, in his widely read history of architecture, *Die architektonischen Stylarten: Eine kurze, allgemeinfassliche Darstellung der charakterischen Verschiedenheiten der architektonischen Stylarten*, orig. pub. 1859; trans. W. Collett-Sandars (New York: D. Appleton, 1876), 461, stated that "the French school of Durand...endeavoured to lead architecture back again to the Italian Renaissance, and the study of ancient Roman monuments, which were employed as models, were its foundation. A certain rational treatment," he added, "is peculiar to this school: its tendency is rather to work out new designs and to form systems than to promote the expression of the imagination and aesthetic conceptions." Rosengarten studied in Paris with Henri Labrouste in the late 1830s and subsequently made his career in Hamburg.

8 Durand, *Précis*, 155. In criticizing the pediment, Durand was strictly following Laugier, who declared it an error "to construct a Pediment on the long facade of a building. Since the Pediment is but the representation of the gable of the roof," Laugier explained, "it must be placed in conformity with the object it represents." "I always note with regret," he continued, "that the great man who designed the Colonnade of the Louvre, forgot himself to the point of erecting a great Pediment in the middle [of it]." Marc-Antoine Laugier, *Essai sur l'architecture*, 2nd ed., rev. and enl. (Paris: Duchesne, 1755; repr., Farnborough, England: Gregg Press, 1966), 35–36.

9 Durand, *Précis*, 86–87.

10 For the French text of Boullée's manuscript, along with other unpublished writings of his, now in the collection of the Bibliothèque nationale de France, Paris, see Etienne-Louis Boullée, *Architecture: Essai sur l'art*, ed. Jean-Marie Pérouse de Montclos (Paris: Hermann, 1968). For an English translation followed by the original French, see E.-L. Boullée, "Architecture, an Essay on Art" and "Architecture, Essai sur l'art," in Helen Rosenau, *Boullée & Visionary Architecture, including Boullée's 'Architecture, Essay on Art'* (London: Academy Editions, 1976), 81–143. The translation, which I find not always reliable and therefore depart from at times, is by Sheila de Vallée. I shall, however, use this edition for references to the French text. In his introduction to the 1968 publication, Pérouse de Montclos notes that although the text "is written all in one spurt," it incorporates material from at least as early as 1785. He gives a terminus ad quem of 1793, based on the inventory of the architect's last will and testament of that year (12–14).

11 Boullée, "Architecture," in Rosenau, *Boullée*, 136.

12 The term "nonobjective" was used by artists like Malevich and popularized by the curator and critic Hilla Rebay to distinguish a kind of modern art making no reference to the forms of external reality (such as Mondrian's mature paintings) from an art that simplifies and "abstracts" shapes given by the natural world. In the latter category would fall most Cubist and Cubist-derived art. For further discussion, see chapter 7.

13 Boullée, "Architecture," 120. For a broad treatment of the subject of architecture and the imitation of nature in the eighteenth century, see Dorothea Lehner-Löhr, *Architektur und Natur: Zur Problematik des "Imitatio-Naturae-Ideals" in der französischen Architekturtheorie des 18. Jahrhunderts* (Munich: Mäander, 1987).

14 The basic work on Boullée is Jean-Marie Pérouse de Montclos, *Etienne-Louis Boullée* (Paris: Flammarion, 1994). This is a revised edition of his *Etienne-Louis Boullée (1728–1799): De l'architecture classique à l'architecture révolutionnaire* (Paris: Arts et Métiers Graphiques, 1969). See also Philippe Madec, *Boullée* (Paris: F. Hazan, 1986).

15 Boullée, "Architecture," 118. See also 123–24.

16 Ibid., 141.

17 Pérouse de Montclos, *Boullée* (1994), relates the design to the 1781 program for a cathedral for the Grand Prix at the Ecole des Beaux-Arts, which, he writes, "may have been given by Boullée."

18 Boullée, "Architecture," 124–26.

19 Ibid.

20 Ibid., 126.

21 Ibid. Entirely associating the use of the orders with the act of decoration, Boullée wrote that "the temples of the Greeks were decorated, outside as well as inside, by colonnades that envelopped the whole building" (125).

22 Ibid.

23 Ibid.

24 Ibid., 127.

25 Ibid.

26 Ibid. Rosenau, *Boullée*, 94, rather lamely translates the phrase as "avail ourselves of nature."

27 Boullée, "Architecture," 119.

28 Ibid.

29 Ibid., 143.

30 See Wolfgang Herrmann, *The Theory of Claude Perrault*, Studies in Architecture 12 (London: A. Zwemmer, 1973); and Antoine Picon, *Claude Perrault, 1613–1688; ou, La Curiosité d'un classique* (Paris: Picard, 1988), esp. 115–96. Boullée specifically referred to Perrault as "Vitruvius's commentator" ("Architecture," 119), referring to the earlier architect's translation and edition of *Les Dix livres d'architecture de Vitruve*, published in 1673.

31 Boullée, "Architecture," 119–22.

32 Vitruvius, it should be noted, did not relate the two arts in terms of proportions.

33 Boullée, "Architecture," 122.

34 Ibid., 121–22.

35 Ibid. In the English translation by Sheila de Vallée that precedes the French text, the word *corps* is consistently, and in my view quite erroneously, rendered as "volume."

36 Ibid., 121, 118.

37 Ibid., 143.

38 Ibid., 123.

39 Ibid., 138.

40 Boullée, *Architecture* (1968), 45. Although there is a footnote reference to it, the epigraph does not appear in either the French text or English translation in Rosenau, *Boullée*.

41 Boullée, "Architecture," 120; and E.-L. Boullée, "Considérations sur l'importance et l'utilité de l'architecture, suivies de vues tendant aux progrès des beaux-arts," in Boullée, *Architecture* (1968), 34–35.

42 Pérouse de Montclos, *Boullée* (1994), 151–55, 254–55. See also Adolf Max Vogt, *Boullées Newton-Denkmal: Sakralbau und Kugelidee*, Geschichte und Theorie der Architektur 3 (Basel: Birkhäuser, 1969); and Barbara Maria Stafford, "Science as Fine Art: Another Look at Boullée's Cenotaph for Newton," *Studies in Eighteenth-Century Culture* 11 (1982): 241–78. Pérouse de Montclos also includes reference to Adolf Max Vogt, *Die französische Revolutionarchitektur und der Newtonismus: Epochen europäischer Kunst* (Berlin, 1967), which I have not seen.

43 Boullée, "Architecture," 136.

44 Ibid.

45 Ibid., 137.

46 Ibid., 136.

47 Ibid., 137.

48 Ibid., 135.

49 Ibid., 134.

50 Ibid.

51 Ibid., 135. Pérouse de Montclos, *Boullée* (1994), 264, dates the funerary monuments mainly to 1782–84. On eighteenth-century Parisian cemeteries, see Richard A. Etlin, *The Architecture of Death: The Transformation of the Cemetery in Eighteenth-Century Paris* (Cambridge, Mass.: MIT Press, 1984).

52 Boullée, "Architecture," 135, 140.

53 Ibid., 135.

54 Ibid.

55 Ibid., 124, 135–36.

56 Ibid., 136.

57 Robert Rosenblum, "The Origin of Painting: A Problem in the Iconography of Romantic Classicism," *Art Bulletin* 39 (December 1957): 279–90.

58 Boullée, "Architecture," 136.

59 See chapter 2, note 2 above. Although David Watkin's *Sir John Soane: Enlightenment Thought and the Royal Academy Lectures*, Cambridge Studies in the History of Architecture (Cambridge: Cambridge University Press, 1996), esp. 115–29, makes a strong case for Soane's indebtedness to Laugier, the fact is that Soane in no way followed Laugier's argument about the significance of the primitive hut in the early development of Greek architecture as set forth in his first lecture at the Royal Academy (490–500). Instead, after revisiting the Quatremère division of early types of structures into the cave, the hut, and the tent, Soane followed a typically Vitruvian/William Chambers version of the origins story.

For Soane's architecture in general, see Arthur T. Bolton, *The Works of Sir John Soane* (London: Sir John Soane's Museum, 1924); John Summerson, *Sir John Soane, 1753–1837*, Architectural Biographies 4 (London: Art and Technics, 1952); Dorothy Stroud, *Sir John Soane, Architect* (London: Faber and Faber, 1984); *John Soane*, Architectural Monographs (London: Academy Editions; New York: St. Martin's Press, 1983); Pierre de la Ruffinière Du Prey, *Sir John Soane* (London: Victoria and Albert Museum, 1985); and Margaret Richardson and Mary-Anne Stevens, eds., *John Soane, Architect: Master of Space and Light* (London: Royal Academy of Arts, 1999).

60 See Daniel M. Abramson, *Building the Bank of England: Money, Architecture, Society, 1694–1942* (New Haven, Conn.: Yale University Press, 2005), esp. 93–196.

61 Summerson, *Sir John Soane*, esp. 25–28; and John Summerson, "The Evolution of Soane's Bank Stock Office in the Bank of England," *Architectural History*, vol. 27, *Design and Practice in British Architecture: Studies in Architectural History Presented to Howard Colvin* (1984); repr. in *The Unromantic Castle* (London: Thames & Hudson, 1990), 143–56, provide seminal readings of this space. Summerson's *Architecture in Britain, 1530 to 1830*, Pelican History of Art (1953; 4th ed., rev. and enl., Harmondsworth, Middlesex, England: Penguin, 1963), 301, describes Soane's "unique mode of abstraction from Neo-classicism," evidenced in such interiors as the Bank Stock Office, while also pointing out that the architect "never wholly relinquished the fully articulated classicism" of his early works. Henry-Russell Hitchcock Jr., in *Modern Architecture: Romanticism and Reintegration* (1929; repr., New York: Hacker Art Books, 1970), 20, may have been the first to remark on Soane's abstraction: "Primarily Soane was working with space, and even with light, for effects of abstract form." "Although clearly reminiscent of the Pantheon," the Bank's "central rotunda," he continued, "provides the ideal climax of the scheme merely as regards abstract form," while "in the loggia of the Governor's Court Soane... [achieved] a reduction of Classical elements almost to their geometrical base in original creation" (21).

62 Watkin, *Soane*, 122–23, notes that Soane translated the description of Soufflot's vaults that Laugier gave in his *Observations sur l'architecture* (The Hague and Paris: Desaint, 1765).

63 Following Summerson, *Soane*, 21, 27, Watkin, *Soane*, 121–22, notes that Soane justified the elimination of certain details and the simplification of others in Laugier's chapter on the "Inconveniences of the Architectural orders in the interior of buildings," in his *Observations sur l'architecture*, 110–18.

64 This and other construction details are pointed out in Abramson, *Building the Bank*, 107.

65 The stable block that Soane built at Chelsea Hospital in London in 1814 is another example of such use of round arches, although here the utilitarian program can be read as the reason for the choice of an astylar mode. For more on the international *rundbogenstil*, see chapter 4.

66 The one at the top right with the pedimented portico appears to have a circular plan, perhaps covered by a dome. While the medievalizing designs surely have arches supporting interior galleries, they are undoubtedly not vaulted and rather have open or flat timber ceilings like the classical ones. A separate drawing for a church with a trabeated exterior and an arched interior that is related to this group (Soane Museum, Drawer xv, 4, 6) supports such a hypothesis.

67 Watkin, *Soane*, 287–309, 490–514. He did, however, refer to Quatremère's theory of the three different models of the cave, the hut, and the tent as preceding the development of more sophisticated timber-frame constructions. For Chambers, see chapter 2.

68 In his second lecture, included in Watkin, *Soane*, 502–3, Soane spoke of the "parts [of the orders] which are essential and have an immediate analogy with the primitive objects of imitation" as being "the pedestal, column, and the entablature." However, he then went on to say that although "some suppose the idea of columns to have been taken from the trunks of large trees," the fact is that "in Grecian works the column owed its origin to the rudely shaped timbers which were placed as supports to the roofs of the early habitations," just as their "bases and capitals owe their origin to early constructions in timber." Despite his rejection of the Laugier model, Soane never doubted the imitative basis of classical form. One of his earliest designs, in fact, was for a Dairy at Hammels Park, Hertfordshire, for Philip Yorke (1783), in which he used real tree trunks, with the bark still on, for the columns of the portico. And it was over the issue of imitation that he took violent disagreement with Durand. Watkin, *Soane*, 179, publishes the following excerpt from a note Soane wrote while translating the *Précis* in 1815. After the statement by Durand claiming that "architecture owes its origin to necessity alone and its only object is public and private utility," Soane retorted: "Yes, in its origin, but it afterwards went further and became a pleasing art. Hence the origin of the orders; man is by nature a child of imitation. He therefore naturally imitates in stone what he had seen in wood." Unwilling to leave it there, Soane ascribed a natural origin to Gothic architecture, something even Laugier did not venture: "In like manner our Gothic ancestors, when they ceased to worship in groves and erected churches, they imitated those groves in which they had worshipped the divinity."

69 Goerd Peschken, *Karl Friedrich Schinkel: Das architektonische Lehrbuch*, in *Karl Friedrich Schinkel: Lebenswerk*, ed. Margarete Kühn (Munich: Deutscher Kunstverlag, 1979), 150. This was probably written in the 1830s. For more on this moment in Schinkel's career, see the discussion of the Bauakademie and Royal Library project below. The basic resource on Schinkel is the multivolume *Karl Friedrich Schinkel: Lebenswerk*, begun in 1939 under the editorship of Paul Ortwin Rave and continued under Margarete Kühn after 1962. See also Nikolaus Pevsner, "Karl Friedrich Schinkel," *Journal of the Royal Institute of British Architects* 59 (January 1951); repr. in *Studies in Art, Architecture, and Design*, vol. 1, *From Mannerism to Romanticism* (London: Thames & Hudson, 1968), 175–95; Julius Posener, *From Schinkel to the Bauhaus* (New York: Wittenborn, 1972); Hermann G. Pundt, *Schinkel's Berlin: A Study in Environmental Planning* (Cambridge, Mass.: Harvard University Press, 1972); Mario Zadow, *Karl Friedrich Schinkel* (Berlin: Rembrandt Verlag, 1980); Erik Forsmann, *Karl Friedrich Schinkel: Bauwerke und Baugedanken* (Munich: Schnell und Steiner, 1981); Werner Szambien, *Schinkel* (Paris: Hazan, 1989); Michael Snodin, ed., *Karl Friedrich Schinkel: A Universal Man* (New Haven, Conn.: Yale University Press, 1991); Barry Bergdoll, *Karl Friedrich Schinkel: An Architecture for Prussia* (New York: Rizzoli, 1994); John Zukowsky, ed. *Karl Friedrich Schinkel, 1781–1841: The Drama of Architecture* (Chicago: Art Institute of Chicago; Tübingen: Wasmuth, 1994); and Andreas Haus, *Karl Friedrich Schinkel als Künstler: Annäherung und Kommentar* (Munich: Deutscher Kunstverlag, 2001).

70 Karl Friedrich Schinkel, *Collection of Architectural Designs, Including Designs Which Have Been Executed and Objects Whose Execution Was Intended,* orig. pub. 1819–40 as *Sammlung architektonischer Entwürfe, enthaltendtheils Werke welche ausgeführt sind, theils Gegenstände, deren Ausführung, beabsichtigt wurde* (New York: Princeton Architectural Press, 1989), 40, explains that the choice of Gothic style enabled him to deal best with the problem of designing an adequately sized steeple for the exiguous site: "It was required to make the steeple, located at the end of a very long street, an important and effective piece of architecture. Since the size of the church was predetermined by the site, we could achieve this feat only by making the steeple effective through its height, a device better suited to the style of the Middle Ages than to that of the Classical period."

71 Bergdoll, *Schinkel,* offers a similar understanding of the architect's development. For a more philosophically and socially based reading of Schinkel's historicism, see John Edward Toews, *Becoming Historical: Cultural Reformation and Public Memory in Early Nineteenth-Century Berlin* (Cambridge: Cambridge University Press, 2004), 117–206 ("Building Historical Identities in Space and Stone: Schinkel's Search for the Shape of Ethical Community").

72 Paul Ortwin Rave, *Berlin,* vol. 1, *Bauten für die Kunst, Kirchen, Denkmalpflege,* in *Karl Friedrich Schinkel: Lebenswerk* (1941; new ed., Berlin: Deutscher Kunstverlag, 1981), 25–78; Sabine Spiero, "Schinkels Altes Museum in Berlin: Seine Baugeschichte von den Anfängen bis zur Eröffnung," *Jahrbuch der preuszischen Kunstsammlungen* 55 (1934): suppl., 41–81; and Pundt, *Schinkel's Berlin,* 138–58. The Altes Museum was called simply the Museum until the Neues (New) Museum by Schinkel's student August Stüler, was built behind it in 1841–55, at which point it became known as the Altes (Old) Museum.

73 Quoted in Rave, *Berlin,* 1:34. These comments were made by Schinkel in early February 1823 in response to the opinions expressed by Aloys Ludwig Hirt, one of the key players on the Museum Building Commission.

74 Martin Goalen, "Schinkel and Durand: The Case of the Altes Museum," in Snodin, *Karl Friedrich Schinkel,* 26–35, notes that it was Sigfried Giedion who first made the case for this connection in his *Spätbarocker und romantischer Klassizismus* (Munich: F. Brückmann, 1922), 73–74, 144–47. Goalen, like many recent scholars, questions the closeness of the Durand connection. Haus, *Schinkel,* 235–36, notes the link to Durand but also compares the Schinkel facade to Boullée's library project.

75 Kurt W. Forster, "Schinkel's Panoramic Planning of Central Berlin," *Modulus* 16 (1983): 62–77, describes the importance of the relationship of building to cityscape as revealed by the view from the upper floor of the open-air vestibule.

76 The capital derives its characteristic feature of the lotus-and-palmette anthemion, or necking band, from the Erechtheum but, unlike the architect's earlier Theater (Schauspielhaus) in Berlin (1818–21), where the Erechtheum model is quite closely imitated, the capital of the Altes Museum has a deep egg-and-dart echinus similar to those on the Ionic capitals of the Propylaea and Temple of Athena Nike in Athens as well as the Temple of Athena Polias in Priene. Furthermore, Schinkel himself noted that instead of using the Attic base that "was normally used with this order," he substituted "the base of the Monuments in ancient Ionia" because of "their more delicate character…and their finer correspondence with the ionic Order." Schinkel, *Collection of Architectural Designs,* p. 5 of German text. Aloys Hirt, *Die Baukunst nach den Grundsätzen der Alten* (Berlin, 1809), vol. 2, 105–6, and pl. XX, fig. 1, performed a similar, though inverse, operation, combining the capital of the Temple of Athena Polias (Minerva) at Priene with the base of the Ionic order at the Erechtheum.

77 The comparison between the rear corner of the Altes Museum and later modern buildings such as Peter Behrens's AEG Turbine Factory and Mies van der Rohe's early buildings at the Armour (later Illinois) Institute of Technology (IIT) has become a standard trope of modern architectural criticism and history. Stanford Anderson, in "Schinkel, Behrens, an Elemental Tectonic, and a New Classicism," in *Karl Friedrich Schinkel: Aspects of His Work / Aspekte seines Werks,* ed. Susan M. Peik (Stuttgart: Axel Menges, 2001), 121–22, traced the Behrens connection back to the architect's 1927 Schinkel-Festrede lecture, in which he acknowledged the reference, which was published in Julius Posener, ed., *Festreden: Schinkel zu Ehren, 1846–1980* (Berlin: Architekten-und Ingenieur-Verein zu Berlin, 1981), 281–90. The connection to Mies's buildings at IIT was pointed out by Henry-Russell Hitchcock in his *Architecture: Nineteenth and Twentieth Centuries,* Pelican History of Art (Harmondsworth, Middlesex, England: Penguin, 1958), 32.

One element of the museum's construction, however, is allowed to appear in its strictly utilitarian aspect. This is the downspout in the gap between the pier and wall panels at the corners. The pipe slides behind the molding between the basement and the first floor before it disappears through the stylobate into the ground. It is a highly unusual feature that may owe something to the architect's study of ancient architecture, although specifically to what is unclear. In any event, the device of articulating the corner by means of the functional element of a downspout became a leitmotif in Schinkel's work, appearing in all sorts of later designs irrespective of material or style.

78 In his role as Geheimer Oberbaurat, Schinkel was called in 1821 to give his opinion on designs that had been suggested for the church, at which time he offered one of his own, based on the idea of a peripteral Roman temple. The design process that eventuated in the building constructed between 1825 and 1830 occurred in 1823–24. See Rave, *Berlin,* 1:254–300; and Martina Abri, *Die Friedrich-Werdersche Kirche zu Berlin: Technik und Ästhetik in der Backstein-Architektur K. F. Schinkels,* Die Bauwerke und Kunstdenkmäler von Berlin 22 (Berlin: Gebr. Mann, 1992).

79 Peschken, *Schinkel: Architektonische Lehrbuch,* esp. 127ff. Cf. Julius Posener, "Schinkel's Eclecticism and the 'Architectural,'" *Architectural Design* 53, nos. 11–12 (1983), 32–39; and Haus, *Schinkel,* 339–72. Haus's

final chapter argues for the architect's evolution toward a "synthetic architecture" (367–72). The same theme is developed throughout Bergdoll, *Schinkel.*

80 Schinkel, *Collection of Architectural Designs,* 46–47, plates 85–90. Schinkel described the floor plans of the two designs as "similar." In discussing the choice of the double-towered solution over the single-towered one (see fig. 3.41), he explained that the latter would have been too expensive and taken up too much interior space as compared to the former. This was because a single tower had to be thought of as a "steeple" and designed to be "quite high in correct relation to [the] width [of the church]." The two-towered solution could result in a more classical and thus synthetic design in his view, since these projections could be thought of as "two small campaniles" that could be given "a fine and delicate appearance...without making them too high." Most authors agree that Schinkel made the Gothic designs under the influence of Crown Prince Friedrich Wilhelm IV and in deference to King Friedrich Wilhelm III's wishes. This does not explain, however, Schinkel's many other ventures in medieval design, both predating and postdating this commission. Bergdoll, *Schinkel,* 90, states correctly in my view that the architect's willingness to contemplate more than one style for the Friedrich-Werdersche Church should neither be seen "as evidence of Schinkel's growing eclecticism, [nor] as evidence that he was constrained by his royal patrons to make certain stylistic choices."

81 Bergdoll, *Schinkel,* 92.

82 See Emil Flaminius, "Ueber den Bau des Hauses für die allgemeine Bauschule in Berlin," *Allgemeine Bauzeitung mit Abbildungen* no. 1 (1836): 3–5; no. 2 (1836): 9–13; no. 3 (1836): 18–24; and pls. 1–8; Rave, *Berlin,* vol. 3, *Bauten für Wissenschaft, Verwaltung, Heer, Wohnbau, und Denkmäler,* in *Karl Friedrich Schinkel: Lebenswerk* (Berlin: Deutsche Kunstverlag, 1962), 38–60; Goerd Peschken, *Schinkels Bauakademie in Berlin: Ein Auftrag zu ihrer Rettung,* orig. pub. 1961; repr. in *Mythos Bauakademie: Die Schinkelsche Bauakademie und ihre Bedeutung für die Mitte Berlins,* ed. Frank Augustin (Berlin: Verlag für Bauwesen, 1997), 217–32; Jan Fiebelkorn, "Bauakademie und Martin-Gropius Bau," in *Karl Friedrich Schinkel: Werke und Wirkungen,* ed. J. Fiebelkorn (Berlin: Senat von Berlin, 1981), 107–21; Jonas Geist, *Karl Friedrich Schinkel, die Bauakademie: Eine Vergegenwärtigung* (Frankfurt: Fischer Taschenbuch, 1993); Elke Blauwelt, ed., *Karl Friedrich Schinkels Berliner Bauakademie: In Kunst und Architektur, in Vergangenheit und Gegenwart* (Berlin: Kunstbibliothek Staatliche Museen zu Berlin, Preußischer Kulturbesitz, Nicolai, 1996); Harald Bodenschatz, *"Der Rote Kasten": Zu Bedeutung, Wirkung und Zukunft von Schinkels Bauakademie* (Berlin: Transit, 1996); Augustin, *Mythos Bauakademie;* Doris Fouquet-Plümacher, ed., *Mythos Bauakademie: Die Schinkelsche Bauakademie und ihre Bedeutung für die Mitte Berlins: Ausstellungskatalog* (Berlin: Verlag für Bauwesen, 1998); and Nany Wiegand-Hoffmann, ed. *Karl Friedrich Schinkel, Bauakademie: Essays 2003* (Berlin: Berliner Wissenschafts-Verlag, 2003).

83 Schinkel, *Collection of Architectural Designs,* 49, merely said of "the interior courtyard" that it "will accept drainage from the roofs." The bay module was 18 German feet (approximately 18.5 U.S. feet) square.

84 Much of the interior was altered in 1874–75, and there is little photographic record of what preceded that moment in time.

85 Schinkel, *Collection of Architectural Designs,* 49, noted that "all" the terra-cotta ornaments "were added to the building only after the building structure was finished and secure, so as to avoid any damage due to construction."

86 Ibid.

87 Quoted in Bergdoll, *Schinkel,* 216; from Peschken, *Schinkel: Architektonische Lehrbuch,* 115 (Peschken dates the statement to around 1830).

88 For example, Pevsner, "Karl Friedrich Schinkel," 191, wrote that "the pilasters, if one may call them that, which articulate the elevation, are so elongated that they are really like mediaeval lesenes"; and Rand Carter, "Karl Friedrich Schinkel, 'The Last Great Architect,'" in Schinkel, *Collection of Architectural Designs,* 32, commented that "the buttresses which articulate the elevation resemble the colossal pilasters of the Schauspielhaus in some respects and the medieval lesenes of the Friedrich-Werdersche Kirche in others."

89 Karl Friedrich Schinkel, *The English Journey: Journal of a Visit to France and Britain in 1826,* ed. David Bindman and Gottfried Riemann (New Haven, Conn.: Yale University Press, 1993). Leopold D. Ettlinger, "A German Architect's Visit to England," *Architectural Review* 97 (May 1945): 131–34, first brought the importance of this trip to the attention of the scholarly community. Between May 24 and June 14, 1826, Schinkel visited, in addition to the British Museum, Wren's church of St. Stephen, Walbrook, Soane's Bank of England, London churches, and house at Lincoln's Inn Fields, as well as the famous docks by Thomas Telford and others. For the influence of the industrial aesthetic on the Bauakademie, see Goerd Peschken, "Technologische Ästhetik in Schinkels Architektur," *Zeitschrift des deutschen Vereins für Kunstwissenschaft* 22, nos. 1–2 (1968): 45–81.

90 Geist, *Schinkel, Bauakademie,* 31.

91 Almost nothing has been written about this project. For the basic documentation, see Rave, *Berlin,* 3:24–37; and Haus, *Schinkel,* 260–65. Rave dates the drawings for the second project "around 1835" in the captions and "around 1837" in the list of illustrations at the end of the chapter. Haus, *Schinkel,* dates both projects to 1835.

92 Rave, *Berlin,* 3:31; and Comte [Léon] de Laborde, *De l'organisation des bibliothèques dans Paris,* 8th letter, *Etude sur la construction des bibliothèques* (Paris: A. Franck, April 1845), 37. The comments to Laborde were made in a letter of April 10, 1840, in response to a request by the author for information about the building.

93 This second project uncannily recalls Boullée's 1792 design for a Municipal Palace, which also, and unusually for him, was designed on a grid using round arches that were expressed on the facade.

94 As Bergdoll, *Schinkel,* 40, 87, noted, Schinkel's project for the reconstruction of the Petrikirche in Berlin (1810) already laid the

groundwork for the adoption of the round-arched style as an appropriate form for German Protestant architecture.

Chapter 4. Pugin, Labrouste, and the New Realism of Decorated Construction

1 Victor Hugo, *Cromwell* (1827; Paris: Garnier-Flammarion, 1968), 81. Hugo here was specifically describing the convention of the three "unities" of classical theater: the unities of space, time, and action.

2 Victor Hugo, *Notre-Dame de Paris, 1482* (1831–32; Paris: Garnier-Flammarion, 1967), 198–211 (bk. 5, chap. 2, "Ceci tuera cela"). For a broader discussion of Hugo's ideas in relation to the architecture of his time, see Neil Levine, "The Book and the Building: Hugo's Theory of Architecture and Labrouste's Bibliothèque Ste-Geneviève," in *The Beaux-Arts and Nineteenth-Century French Architecture*, ed. Robin Middleton (London: Thames & Hudson, 1982), 138–73.

3 The conservative Louis-Pierre Baltard (1764–1846), who was educated in the late eighteenth century and served as professor of theory at the Ecole des Beaux-Arts from 1819 to 1846, still referred to Quatremère as the sole modern authority worth quoting in his lectures at the Ecole in the late 1830s and early 1840s. See, for example, his *Introduction au cours de théorie d'architecture de l'année 1839* (Paris: Ecole Royale des Beaux-Arts, 1839), 29–31. Quatremère's waning influence can be seen in the rearguard battle he launched and eventually lost over Henri Labrouste's fourth-year restoration project at the French Academy in Rome of the temples at Paestum (1828–30). See Neil Levine, "The Romantic Idea of Architectural Legibility: Henri Labrouste and the *Néo-Grec*," in *The Architecture of the Ecole des Beaux-Arts*, ed. Arthur Drexler (New York: Museum of Modern Art, 1977), 357–93.

4 One of the first and still one of the most moving accounts of Pugin's life and career is in Kenneth Clark, *The Gothic Revival: An Essay in the History of Taste* (1928; 3rd ed., Harmondsworth, Middlesex, England: Penguin, 1964), 106–33. For later studies, see Phoebe Stanton, *Pugin* (London: Thames & Hudson, 1971); Paul Atterbury and Clive Wainwright, eds., *Pugin: A Gothic Passion* (New Haven, Conn.: Yale University Press, 1994); and Paul Atterbury, ed., *A. W. N. Pugin: Master of Gothic Revival* (New Haven, Conn.: Yale University Press, 1995).

5 For Labrouste's career at the Ecole and the Academy in Rome, see Neil Levine, "The Competition for the Grand Prix in 1824," in *The Beaux-Arts and Nineteenth-Century French Architecture*, ed. Robin Middleton (London: Thames & Hudson, 1982), 66–123; Barry Bergdoll, "La formazione presso l'atelier Vaudoyer e Lebas," in *Henri Labrouste, 1801–1875*, ed. Renzo Dubbini (Milan: Electa, 2002), 26–49; and Marco Gaiani, "Il viaggio in Italia, 1824–30," in ibid., 50–80. For his career in general, see Renée Plouin, "Henri Labrouste: Sa vie, son oeuvre (1801–1875)," 3rd cycle thesis, University of Paris, 1966; "Henri Labrouste," *Les Monuments historiques de la France* 6 (1975): 3–37; Pierre Saddy, *Henri Labrouste, architecte, 1801–1875* (Paris: Caisse Nationale des Monuments Historiques, 1977); Robin Middleton, "Henri Labrouste," *International Architect* 1, no. 3 (1980): 40–46; David Van Zanten, *Designing Paris: The Architecture of Duban, Labrouste, Duc and Vaudoyer* (Cambridge, Mass.: MIT Press, 1987), esp. 83–98; D. Van Zanten, *Building Paris: Architectural Institutions and the Transformation of the French Capital, 1830–1870* (Cambridge: Cambridge University Press, 1994), 143–47; Dubbini, *Labrouste;* and Jean-Michel Leniaud, ed., *Des palais pour les livres: Labrouste, Sainte-Geneviève et les bibliothèques* (Paris: Maisonneuve & Larose, Bibliothèque Sainte-Geneviève, 2002).

6 Pugin's initial designs may date to the fall of 1839. According to Michael Fisher, *Pugin-Land: A. W. N. Pugin, Lord Shrewsbury, and the Gothic Revival in Staffordshire* (Stafford, England: by the author, 2002), 95, "Pugin's diary records a visit to Cheadle in October 1839, probably to inspect the site of the new church."

7 The organization was officially established in 1843. The following year it was decided to create a medal to be given to each new member of the société and a smaller *jeton de présence* to be offered as an honorarium to directors for attendance at board meetings. Members were invited to submit designs and, following an initial call that was unsuccessful, those by Labrouste for the *jeton* and Simon-Claude Constant-Dufeux for the medal were selected in the late spring of 1846. The first examples of the two coins were fabricated by the end of 1847.

8 Labrouste, in "Jeton et médaille de la Société centrale des Architectes," *Revue générale de l'architecture et des travaux publics* 8 (1849–50): 151, describes his design as "representing, on one side, Architecture. Monuments of all periods crown her head and seem to emerge from her brain. . . . On the reverse are written these words, Société Centrale des Architectes and are engraved two attributes, a *compass* and a *flower*, emblems of *science* and of *art*, of *precision* and of *liberty*."

9 Antoine-Chrysostôme Quatremère de Quincy, *De l'architecture égyptienne considérée dans son origine, ses principes et son goût, et comparée sous les mêmes rapports à l'architecture grecque*, dissertation qui a remporté, en 1785, le prix proposé par l'Académie des Inscriptions et Belles-Lettres (Paris: Barrois l'aîné et fils, 1803), 230; and A.-C. Quatremère de Quincy, *Architecture*, 3 vols., in *Encyclopédie méthodique, ou par ordre de matières, par une société de gens de lettres, de savans et d'artistes*, ed. C[harles] J[oseph] Panckoucke (Paris: Panckoucke, 1788; Henri Agasse, 1801; Mme la veuve Agasse, 1825), 1:115–16 (s.v. "Architecture").

10 Both Sigfried Giedion, in *Building in France: Building in Iron, Building in Ferro-Concrete*, orig. pub. 1928; trans. J. Duncan Berry, Texts & Documents (Santa Monica, Calif.: Getty Center for the History of Art and the Humanities, 1995), 103–9, and Nikolaus Pevsner, in "A Short Pugin Florilegium," *Architectural Review* 94 (August 1943): 31–34, early on stressed the protofunctionalism of the two architects while underplaying the historicist decorativeness of their buildings.

11 The London church is that of St. Mary the Virgin, Eversholt Street, which was built in 1824–27; the Yorkshire one is Bishop Skirlaw's Chapel at Skirlaw. The plate of "Contrasted House Fronts" was the only

one published in the 1836 edition that was eliminated in the second edition of 1841. The title of the second edition was changed to *Contrasts: or, a Parallel between the Noble Edifices of the Middle Ages, and Corresponding Buildings of the Present Day, Shewing the Present Decay of Taste.*

12 A[ugustus] Welby [Northmore] Pugin, *Contrasts: or, a Parallel between the Noble Edifices of the Middle Ages, and Corresponding Buildings of the Present Day, Shewing the Present Decay of Taste,* Victorian Library, 2nd ed., rev. and enl. (1841; repr., New York: Humanities Press; Leicester: Leicester University Press, 1969), 10.

13 Henri Delaborde, *Notice sur la vie et les ouvrages de M. Henri Labrouste* (Paris: Institut de France, Académie des Beaux-Arts, 1878), 18.

14 The full title of the publication is *The True Principles of Pointed or Christian Architecture: Set forth in Two Lectures Delivered at St. Marie's, Oscott.* Pugin was appointed professor of ecclesiastical architecture and antiquities at the college in 1837 and began lecturing there on a regular basis the following year.

15 See Denis Gwynn, *Lord Shrewsbury, Pugin, and the Catholic Revival* (London: Hollis and Carter, 1946); and Fisher, *Pugin-Land,* esp. 92–122.

16 A[ugustus] Welby [Northmore] Pugin, *The True Principles of Pointed or Christian Architecture: Set forth in Two Lectures Delivered at St. Marie's, Oscott* (1841; repr. of 1853 ed., Oxford: St. Barnabas Press, 1969), 1. Italics in this and all future quotes are Pugin's except where otherwise noted.

17 Pugin, *True Principles,* 1. Pugin returned to this criticism of classical architecture as a matter of display in *An Apology for the Revival of Christian Architecture in England* (1843; repr., Oxford: St. Barnabas Press, 1969), 10–11, where he accused such architects of "*showing off what they could do,* instead of *carrying out what was required.*"

18 [Charles-Nicolas Cochin], *Doutes raisonnables d'un marguillier de la paroisse de S.-Etienne-du-Mont sur le problême proposé par M. Patte, architecte, concernant la construction de la coupole de l'Eglise de Sainte-Geneviève* (Amsterdam and Paris: Jombert fils, 1770), 11 ("Lettre de M. C***** à M. D*****, ancien Commissaire des Pauvres de la Paroisse de la Magdeleine"); and Etienne-Louis Boullée, "Architecture: Essai sur l'art," in Helen Rosenau, *Boullée & Visionary Architecture, including Boullée's 'Architecture, Essay on Art'* (London: Academy Editions, 1976), 126.

19 As noted in chapter 2, note 63, Alberti, in *On the Art of Building in Ten Books,* orig. pub. 1486 as *De re aedificatoria;* trans. Joseph Rykwert, Neil Leach, and Robert Tavernor (Cambridge, Mass.: MIT Press, 1988), 6.13, wrote that "in the whole art of building the column is the principal ornament without any doubt." He continued that "it may be set in combination, to adorn a portico, wall, or other form of opening, nor is it unbecoming when standing alone. It may embellish crossroads, theaters, squares; it may support a trophy; or it may act as a monument. It has grace, and it confers dignity." Andrea Palladio, in *The Four Books of Architecture,* orig. pub. 1579 as *I quattro libri dell'architettura;* trans. Isaac Ware, 1738 (repr., New York: Dover Publications, 1965), 25, described "the ornaments of architecture, that is, the five orders," much as Alberti did. For a nuanced reading of the Renaissance understanding of the relation between construction and ornament or decoration, see Alina A. Payne, *The Architectural Treatise in the Italian Renaissance: Architectural Invention, Ornament, and Literary Culture* (Cambridge: Cambridge University Press, 1999).

20 Boullée, "Architecture," 125. See also chapter 3, note 21.

21 Jean-Nicolas-Louis Durand, *Précis of the Lectures on Architecture; with Graphic Portion of the Lectures on Architecture,* orig. pub. 1802–5/1821; trans. David Britt, Texts & Documents (Los Angeles: Getty Research Institute, 2000), 153–54. Britt unfortunately translates the unusual phrase "*décoration architectonique*" as simply "architectural decoration."

22 Eileen Harris, "The *Treatise on Civil Architecture,*" in John Harris, *Sir William Chambers: Knight of the Polar Star* (London: A. Zwemmer, 1970), 129, notes that Chambers remarked in 1759 that, if the first edition was "well received, it would be followed by a second volume on the construction and economics of architecture." But even though it was successful, that never happened, and the second edition of 1768 bore the same title as the first. Harris offers no explanation for the change of title in the third edition. In line with his general dependence on Chambers for the theory he offered in his lectures at the Royal Academy in the early nineteenth century, John Soane stated in the second lecture: "To the orders of architecture all buildings are indebted for the highest magnificence of decoration." Quoted in David Watkin, *Sir John Soane: Enlightenment Thought and the Royal Academy Lectures,* Cambridge Studies in the History of Architecture (Cambridge: Cambridge University Press, 1996), 502.

For a recent discussion of the construction-decoration issue, see Anne-Marie Sankovitch, "Structure/Ornament and the Modern Figuration of Architecture," *Art Bulletin* 80 (December 1998): 687–717.

23 Pugin, *True Principles,* 4, 19, 6.

24 Ibid., 1–2.

25 Ibid., 3–4.

26 Ibid., 2–3.

27 Although some writers had proposed a natural model for the vaulted naves of Gothic cathedrals in the forests of northern Europe, this idea never received wide currency among architects and historians although, as noted in chapter 3, note 67, Soane did profess the idea in his Royal Academy lectures.

28 Heinrich Hübsch's *Über griechische Architectur* (Heidelberg: J. C. B. Mohr, 1822) was specifically directed against Aloys Ludwig Hirt's *Die Baukunst nach den Grundsätzen der Alten* (Berlin, 1809), in which the leading German theorist and historian of Greek and Roman architecture, following Quatremère and others, marshaled the theory of the wood origin of Greek forms as the basis for his discussion of the universal value of the classical tradition. Hirt counterattacked with his *Vertheidigung der griechischen Architectur gegen H. Hübsch* (Berlin, 1823) to which Hübsch in turn responded with his *Vertheidigung der griechischen Architectur gegen A. Hirt,* published as an appendix to the second edition of *Über griechische Architectur* (Heidelberg: J. C. B. Mohr, 1824). Barry

Bergdoll, "Archaeology vs. History: Heinrich Hübsch's Critique of Neoclassicism and the Beginnings of Historicism in German Architectural Theory," *Oxford Art Journal* 5, no. 2 (1983): 3–12, offers an in-depth analysis of this debate and its relation to Hübsch's contribution to nineteenth-century architectural theory.

29 Heinrich Hübsch, "In What Style Should We Build?" orig. pub. 1828; trans. Wolfgang Herrman, in *In What Style Should We Build? The German Debate on Architectural Style*, ed. W. Herrman, Texts & Documents (Santa Monica, Calif.: Getty Center for the History of Art and the Humanities, 1992), 63–101 (the quotation is from p. 71). Hübsch did, however, accept the timber derivation of certain Greek forms, noting that the "strong projection" of the cornice in the Greek gable as compared with Roman ones "is probably a reminiscence of the timber construction" that preceded it (94). See also Bergdoll, "Archaeology vs. History," 8–12. A similar position was articulated slightly later in France in Léon Vaudoyer and Albert Lenoir, "Etudes d'architecture en France," *Magasin pittoresque*, vols. 7–21 (1839–53), esp. 2:122; and L. Vaudoyer, "Histoire de l'architecture en France," in J. Aicard et al., *Patria: La France ancienne et moderne, morale et matérielle, ou, Collection encyclopédique et statistique de tous les faits relatifs à l'histoire physique et intellectuelle de la France et de ses colonies*, 2 vols. (Paris: J.-J. Dubochet, Lechevalier, 1847), esp. 2:2138. On the Rundbogenstil and the revival of Romanesque architecture in general, see Kathleen Curran, *The Romanesque Revival: Religion, Politics, and Transnational Exchange*, Buildings, Landscapes, and Societies 2 (University Park: Pennsylvania State University Press, 2003).

30 Hübsch, "In What Style Should We Build?" 98, 79, 96.

31 Ibid., 70, 93, 95, 90.

32 Barry Bergdoll, in "The Ideal of the Gothic Cathedral in 1852," in Atterbury, *Pugin*, 120–28, discusses Hübsch within the context of German neomedievalism but does not connect him in any way with Pugin.

33 Pugin, *True Principles*, 2.

34 Ibid., 2–3; Pugin, *Apology*, 8.

35 For the history of the Gothic Revival and Pugin's place in it, see esp. Georg Germann, *Gothic Revival in Europe and Britain: Sources, Influences, and Ideas*, orig. pub. 1972; trans. Gerald Onn (Cambridge, Mass.: MIT Press, 1973); James Macaulay, *The Gothic Revival, 1745–1845* (Glasgow: Blackie, 1975); Michael J. F. McCarthy, *The Origins of the Gothic Revival* (New Haven, Conn.: Yale University Press, 1987); and Michael J. Lewis, *The Gothic Revival* (New York: Thames & Hudson, 2002).

36 Pugin worked with his father, Augustus Charles Pugin, on *Examples of Gothic Architecture, selected from various antient edifices in England* (London: H. G. Bohn, 1838–40), 3 vols., completing the final volume on his own. He also published *Details of antient timber houses of the 15th & 16th centuries, selected from those existing at Rouen, Caen, Beauvais, Gisors, Abbeville, Strasbourg, etc.* (London: Ackermann, 1836); *Glossary of Ecclesiastical Ornament and Costume, compiled and illustrated from antient authorities with Extracts from the Works of Durandus, Georgius, Bona, Catalani, Gerbert, Martene, Molanus, Thiers, Mabillon, Ducange, etc.* (London: H. G. Bohn, 1844–68); and *A Treatise on Chancel Screens and Rood Lofts, their antiquity, use, and symbolic signification* (London: C. Dolman, 1851). Pugin's personal investigation of Gothic remains took place against a background of work that had begun in the 1810s and included books and articles by the likes of John Britton, Pugin's own father, J. S. Cotman, and Arcisse de Caumont. The major preserved "treatise" by a medieval architect was not published until 1858. This was the *Album de Villard de Honnecourt, architecte de XIIIe siècle*, ed. Jean-Baptiste-Antoine Lassus and Alfred Darcel (Paris: Imprimerie Impériale, 1858).

37 A. W. Pugin to John Rouse Bloxam, January 10, 1841, in Margaret Belcher, ed., *The Collected Letters of A. W. N. Pugin*, vol. 1, *1830–1842* (Oxford: Oxford University Press, 2001), 191. Stanton, *Pugin*, 104, transcribes the letter as saying "an English parish church restored with scrupulous fidelity." In *The Present State of Ecclesiastical Architecture in England* (1843; repr., Oxford: St Barnabas Press, 1969), 30, Pugin described the church, then under construction, as "a perfect revival of an English parish church of the time of Edward I; decidedly the best period of pointed architecture."

38 Pugin, *Contrasts*, v.

39 Pugin, *Apology*, 22.

40 For Labrouste and the Bibliothèque Sainte-Geneviève, see Levine, "Romantic Idea," 324–57; Levine, "Book and the Building," 138–73; and Neil Levine, "Il rovesciamento del sistema della rappresentazione nelle biblioteche di Labrouste," in Dubbini, *Labrouste*, 166–90. See also Van Zanten, *Designing Paris*, 83–98, 225–46; Robin Middleton, "La struttura in ferro della Bibliothèque Sainte-Geneviève come base di un decoro civico," in Dubbini, *Labrouste*, 121–42; Roberto Gargiani, "Ornamento e costruzione in Sainte-Geneviève," in ibid., 143–65; *Visions: Bibliothèque Sainte-Geneviève*, ed. Christine Vendredi-Auzanneau and Alain Colas (Paris: Bibliothèque Sainte-Geneviève, 2002); and Leniaud, *Des palais*. Martin Bressani and Marc Grignon, "Henri Labrouste and the Lure of the Real: Romanticism, Rationalism and the Bibliothèque Sainte-Geneviève," *Art History* 28 (November 2005): 712–51, appeared too late to have been of use in this study.

41 Nicolas Petit, "La Bibliothèque de l'Abbaye Sainte-Geneviève aux xviie et xviiie siècles, une grande bibliothèque monastique," in Leniaud, *Des palais*, 25–35.

42 For documentation of the commission and construction of the Bibliothèque Sainte-Geneviève, see F^{13}1066; F^{17}3497; F^{21}14, 678, 751, 1362–64, 2535–37, Archives Nationales, Paris; and MSS 3910–39, Bibliothèque Sainte-Geneviève, Paris.

43 Among the early sketches, there are a few showing a single span without a central spine of columns. However, a sketch plan on the envelope of a letter postmarked November 28, 1838, would seem to indicate that the double-nave idea came to the fore at the very inception of the project (MS 3911, Bibliothèque Sainte-Geneviève). It should also be noted that the small structure connected to the left end of the library was intended to serve as the administrative offices and

residences of the staff. These were moved by the mid-1840s to an entirely separate building located across the rue de la Montagne Sainte-Geneviève to the east (see figs. 8.9 and 2.23). The main public collections of Labrouste's drawings for the Bibliothèque Sainte-Geneviève are N III Seine 1135, Album 45, Versement de la Direction de l'Architecture, and F^{21} 3507, Archives Nationales, Paris; Rés. Suppl. W Fol. 19, and MS 4273, Bibliothèque Sainte-Geneviève, Paris; RF 4141, Cabinet des Dessins, Musée du Louvre, Paris; and F 18000 ser., Cabinet des Estampes, Bibliothèque nationale de France, Paris.

44 The exposed iron in the vestibule did not appear until a few years later.

45 Cf. Gargiani, "Ornamento e costruzione."

46 According to certain sources, the letters in some if not all the arcades were originally inpainted in red as indicated in the elevation in fig. 4.32. In the daily workbook that he maintained during the library's construction, Labrouste noted that the inpainting began on October 14, 1848, and that by October 19 the "letters of the inscriptions" of "the three arcades at the west corner [of the facade]...were completely engraved and painted." Nothing further was mentioned until November 15, when Labrouste noted that "the letters were being engraved on the short western facade" and that "the rest is finished." There was no mention this time, however, of any inpainting. On November 21 a final reference to the subject states that "the engraving of the inscriptions is finished," again with no mention of inpainting. (The note in Leniaud, *Des palais*, 148, that on July 8, 1850, "the inscriptions on the busts of the vestibule receive[d] the same red painting as the engraved letters of the facade" is incorrect.) Henri Labrouste, "Bibliothèque Ste. Geneviève: Journal des travaux," 1843–1850, MS 3910, Bibliothèque Sainte-Geneviève, Paris.

Of all the published accounts of the building, including Labrouste's own (see note 47 below), there are only two that refer to the color, and one of these appeared well before the building was finished. A notice in *Le Corsaire*, December 27, 1848, in the article "Beaux-Arts: Le Panthéon—La Bibliothèque Sainte-Geneviève," reported that "the letters [of the authors' names] are engraved and colored in red," giving the impression that this was true for all twenty-seven arcade panels. In his discussion of the library written in 1851, Gustave Planche, "Le Musée du Louvre," in *Portraits d'artistes: Peintres et sculpteurs*, 2 vols. (Paris: Michel Lévy frères, 1853), 2:268, noted, disapprovingly, that the authors' "names [were] inscribed in vermilion on the walls of the library." I thank Hélène de La Mure for the reference to *Le Corsaire*. Although one might be led to question, based on this evidence, whether the inpainting was ever fully carried out, the chief curator of the library and head of the department of buildings and materiel informed me that, when the four bays of the east facade were restored with the red inpainting in 2001, the references to the original color in Labrouste's workbook were "confirmed...[by] the traces of painting still visible after cleaning." Monique Refouil to Cammie McAtee, September 1, 2006.

47 Henri Labrouste, "A M. le Directeur de la Revue d'ARCHITECTURE," *Revue générale de l'architecture et des travaux publics* 10 (1852): 384.

48 Achille Hermant, "La Bibliothèque Sainte-Geneviève," *L'Artiste*, 5th ser., 7 (December 1, 1851): 130, used the word "*choquant*" to describe the space's structural expressionism.

49 The panels of trees were painted by Alexandre Desgoffe, a student of Ingres, to whom Labrouste gave, as he noted in his "Journal des travaux," April 1, 1850, MS 3910, Bibliothèque Sainte-Geneviève, "two small studies of ancient [Roman] paintings" to serve as models.

50 It is not known whether Labrouste may also have had in mind Leonardo da Vinci's painting of the Sala delle Asse in the Sforza Castle in Milan.

51 Labrouste, "A M. le Directeur," 382. Labrouste continued, still in a tongue-in-cheek way: "The vestibule is a bit somber; but the readers in passing through it will believe, perhaps for an instant, that this obscurity is nothing but the shade of the trees that strikes their gaze, and they will pardon me, I hope." Labrouste's almost congenital dislike for allegorical decoration and painting and his preference for landscape images are revealed early in his career in a letter written to the architect Louis Duc toward the end of 1831. "If I were to design a hospital," Labrouste wrote, "I would like to put paintings in the rooms; I believe that painting, due to the diversity of its colors and above all by the subjects that can be portrayed, would be of some aid in the healing of the sick. But do not think...that I would choose to represent Sappho called back to life by the songs of her companions; rather, I would place large realistic [*vrais*] landscapes, views of Normandy and Brittany that could perhaps lift the spirits of the poor Norman workers who come [to live] in Paris." He added that "events [*faits*] of our military history would give back strength to the old soldiers who have not died of their wounds and who come to die in our hospitals." Ch[arles] L[ucas], "Causerie. Henri Labrouste: Lettres inédites sur l'enseignement de l'architecture (Paris, 1830–1831)," part 2, *La Construction moderne* 10 (March 9, 1895): 268.

52 Comte [Léon] de Laborde, *De l'organisation des bibliothèques dans Paris*, 8th letter, *Etude sur la construction des bibliothèques* (Paris: A. Franck, April 1845), 28, criticized the plan for this very reason.

53 Henri Labrouste, "Plan Général du Panthéon et de Ses Abords Actuels ou Projetés. Projet d'un Bâtiment à Eriger sur l'Emplacement de l'Ancien Prison Montaigu Destiné à Recevoir la Bibliothèque Sainte-Geneviève," December 15, 1839, N III Seine 1135/2, Archives Nationales, Paris. The relevant part of the legend reads: "The first [upper] floor would form a single and large reading room divided, like the Vatican Library in Rome, into a double nave by a row of cast-iron columns set on the axis of the building and serving to support the roof which would be entirely in metal."

54 See Henri Labrouste, *Les Temples de Paestum: Restauration exécutée en 1829*, Restaurations des monuments antiques par les architectes pensionnaires de l'Académie de France à Rome depuis 1788 jusqu'à nos jours (Paris: Firmin-Didot, 1877), 12–14; and Levine, "Romantic Idea," 357–93.

55 See Barry Bergdoll, *Léon Vaudoyer: Historicism in the Age of Industry* (New York: Architectural History Foundation; Cambridge, Mass.: MIT Press, 1994), 164–67.

56 Henry Trianon, who was a librarian at the Bibliothèque Sainte-Geneviève and thus must have discussed the issue with Labrouste, noted in his review of the building, "Nouvelle Bibliothèque Sainte Geneviève," *Illustration* 17 (January 10–17, 1851): 30, that this unusual solution was a direct "function" of the structural condition. The iron arches of the barrel vault supported on their outer edge by the "consoles" of the piers of the stone arcade, he wrote, "come down to rest on the listel of the capital of the central columns, to which this function imposes the structural law of presenting itself in the direction of their volutes." The Trianon article provided the basis for "Die Bibliothek St. Geneviève in Paris," *Allgemeine Bauzeitung mit Abbildung* 17th year (1852): 139–42.

57 Unlike the upper floor, however, not all the iron on the lower floor is exposed. In fact, except for a pair of simple, completely undecorated cast-iron columns in the rooms at each end of the building, only the iron in the public area of the vestibule is revealed. Undoubtedly for reasons of economy, the standard floor trusses in the collections and storage areas to either side of the vestibule are encased in plaster. To expose the structural elements meant to give them a decorative treatment that involved expensive custom casting and assembly procedures. The partial elevation in fig. 4.32 shows the letters "SG" on the iron disks of the ground floor to be picked out in gold paint. According to Labrouste, "Journal des travaux," October 12, 1848, the same artist who did the red inpainting of the authors' names was to do the gilding of the disks. On November 25, 1848, the workbook notes that "several of the cast-iron plates with the gilded initials S. G." were put in place and that Labrouste directed the job of "attaching and painting these plates" to proceed with alacrity. The gilding of the disks of the four bays of the library's east facade was "restored" in 2001, at the same time as the inpainting of the authors' names.

58 In his review of the building, "Die Bibliothek St. Geneviève in Paris," *Allgemeine Bauzeitung mit Abbildungen*, 16th yr. (1851): 68, the former Labrouste student and Hamburg architect Albert Rosengarten made many of these same points. "There is in the facade," he wrote, "a complete correspondence with the interior arrangement and the expression of the purpose of the building; one recognizes that the ground floor, in its usage, plays a subordinate role; that the upper wall under the large windows, which provide ample light, is divided into panels that correspond to the interior divisions; on these panels are written the names of the authors from earliest to most recent times, in chronological order, forming, so to speak, a table of contents of the works that are arranged on the inner side of the same wall; the small windows in between let you guess where the cabinets are located."

59 Bötticher, who studied architecture at Berlin's Allgemeine Bauschule in the late 1820s and eventually taught there in the 1840s, first adumbrated this theory in his "Entwickelung der Formen der hellenischen Tektonik," *Allgemeine Bauzeitung mit Abbildungen*, 5th yr. (1840): 316–30. It was fully developed in his *Die Tektonik der Hellenen*, 2 vols. (Potsdam: Ferdinand Riegel, 1844–52). It was through the use of iron that Bötticher thought a new nineteenth-century style would arise, essentially because of the new structural form it introduced, which demanded a new decorative approach and vocabulary. He expressed this view in "The Principles of Hellenic and Germanic Ways of Building, with Regard to Their Application to Our Present Way of Building," orig. pub. 1846; trans. Wolfgang Herrman, in *In What Style Should We Build?* 147–67. On Bötticher, see esp. Mitchell Schwarzer, "Ontology and Representation in Karl Bötticher's Theory of Tectonics," *Journal of the Society of Architectural Historians* 52 (September 1993): 267–80; M. Schwarzer, *German Architectural Theory and the Search for Modern Identity* (Cambridge: Cambridge University Press, 1995), esp. 182–92; and Harry Francis Mallgrave, *Modern Architectural Theory: A Historical Survey, 1673–1968* (Cambridge: Cambridge University Press, 2005), 110–13.

60 Henri Labrouste to Théodore Labrouste, November 20, 1830, in Léon Dassy [Laure Labrouste], *Souvenirs d'Henri Labrouste, architecte, membre de l'Institut: Notes recueillies et classées par ses enfants* (Fontainebleau: by the author, 1928), 24. The word "ornamentation" was interchangeable with "decoration" in French discourse of the period. In his entry on "Décoration" in *Architecture*, vol. 2 (1802), esp. 173–74, Quatremère de Quincy spoke of "ornament or decoration" as if they were one and the same thing. In his description of the Bibliothèque Sainte-Geneviève, "A M. le Directeur," 384, Labrouste described the inscription of the names of the authors on the exterior of the building as "the principal decoration of the facade, just as the books themselves are the most beautiful ornament of the interior."

Despite his different conception of the construction/decoration dyad, Labrouste's comments to his brother are not so different on the surface from Quatremère's definition of the relationship in his article on "Décoration" in the *Encyclopédie méthodique*. There Quatremère wrote: "In effect, the art of architecture is nothing other than the art of embellishing constructions that are given birth to by need. . . . Architectural *decoration* consists in the application to the forms resulting from need objects that can embellish these forms" (*Architecture*, 2:176).

In his discussion of Greek and Gothic architecture, especially in opposition to Roman architecture, Heinrich Hübsch, "In What Style Should We Build?" 70, described the positive virtue of "embellishment" as "that of adorning (not overloading) the essential forms or elements" of construction. In Greek buildings of the classic period, "once the elements had been consistently arranged, the decoration was spread over them, not in order to conceal one or another of the elements but to adorn them" (78). Similarly in the Gothic period "sculptural decoration, when not excessive, is almost exclusively an adornment of the essential parts" (98). Whether one chooses to read these remarks as closer to Labrouste than to Quatremère is less important in my view than the fact that they remain a matter of historical analysis rather than a proposal for a theory of practice.

61 Eugène Millet, "Notice sur la vie et les travaux de Pierre-François-Henry Labrouste, Membre de l'Institut, Président de la Société centrale des Architectes," *Bulletin mensuel de la Société centrale des Architectes*, 5th ser., 3 (1880), *Supplément au Bulletin de l'exercise 1879–80: Congrès annuel des Architectes*, 7th and 8th sessions, 210. This was also published separately as *Henry Labrouste, Architecte, Membre de l'Institut, Président de la Société centrale des Architectes: Sa vie, ses oeuvres (1801–1875). Notice biographique* (Paris: C. Marpon et E. Flammarion, 1881), 10.

62 César Daly, "Bibliothèque Sainte-Geneviève," *Revue générale de l'architecture et des travaux publics* 10 (1852): 380.

63 Hermant, "Bibliothèque Sainte-Geneviève," 129, 131.

64 Anon., "Promenades in Paris," *The Builder* 8 (March 9, 1850): 111.

65 F[rançois] Barrière, "Embellissemens de Paris," *Journal des débats*, December 31, 1850, 2.

66 Hermant, "Bibliothèque Sainte-Geneviève," 130.

67 Ibid.

68 "Conseil des Bâtiments civils. Rapport fait au Conseil par Mr. Caristie, Inspecteur général," January 23 and 25, 1840, 9, fasc. 1, F[21] 1362, Archives Nationales, Paris.

69 Trianon, "Nouvelle Bibliothèque Sainte-Geneviève," 30, noted how Labrouste "frankly revealed the materials that had been so useful to him. Beginning on the exterior, the iron announces itself in the form of large paterae resembling nuts. Above the windows of the ground floor, it is by their head that these nuts present themselves. Above the windows of the upper floor, it is by the tip."

70 Rosengarten, "Bibliothek," 68, specifically remarked on this innovation, noting that "the iron vaults of the library along with the iron beams of the ground floor are held together by the anchors that are shown on the exterior as iron disks."

71 The critic François Barrière, in "Embellissemens," 2, who admitted that the building would take some "getting used to," specifically referred to the problem of having to read the facade in nonconventional ways. "The appearance of the exterior," he wrote, "is unusual; [but] a moment of reflection explains it. Since finally a library for books has been built, it had to be done for their use. The books are not at all placed in the windows; instead they lean and line up comfortably against the long walls. From that results the fact that a fairly large space prevails between the windows of the ground floor and the forty round-arched openings by which the interior [of the reading room] is lit. What has been put in that space? The names of philosophers, poets, historians, and learned men of all the centuries. Inside, their works, outside, their names, just as one places the title of a good book on the spine of the volume."

72 The importance of the section in thinking through a design must have featured in Labrouste's teaching, as evidenced by the commentary of his former student Antoine Couchaud on one of the buildings he illustrated in his *Choix d'églises bysantines en Grèce* (Paris: Lenoir, 1842), 12, which he described as "offer[ing] an example of that principle, so true in architecture, which demands that the exterior facade of a building be nothing but the representation of its interior conformation, or to put it better, the section translated into the facade."

73 This is based on a conversation recorded in Victor Fournel, *Les Artistes français contemporains: Peintres–sculpteurs* (Tours: Alfred Mame et fils, 1884), 356. What Courbet actually said is the following: "Angels! Madonnas! Who has ever seen one? Auguste, come here. Have you ever seen an angel?" When Auguste said no, Courbet continued: "Well, neither have I. As soon as one appears, don't forget to tell me."

74 See, for example, Peter Collins, *Changing Ideals of Modern Architecture, 1750–1950* (London: Faber and Faber, 1965), 128–46. As noted above (note 59), as early as 1846, Bötticher, in "Principles of Hellenic and Germanic Ways of Building," 157–58, proposed that it would be possible to develop a "new style...one specific to our generation" through the new structural means of iron. "Iron will become the basis for the covering system of the future and...structurally it will in times come to be as superior to the Hellenic and medieval systems as the arcuated medieval system was to the monolithic trabeated system of antiquity." In France, the self-taught Louis-Auguste Boileau (1812–1896) proposed a similar idea, to little avail, in his *Le Fer, principal élément constructif de la nouvelle architecture* (Paris: by the author, 1871); and *Histoire critique de l'invention en architecture: Classification méthodique des oeuvres de l'art monumental au point de vue du progrès et de son application à la composition de nouveaux types architectoniques dérivant de l'usage de fer* (Paris: Ch. Dunod, 1886). Viollet-le-Duc's entry into this arena, much more positive in my view, is discussed in chapter 5.

75 The opposition of a single, unified historical source as in Pugin to the multifarious approach of Labrouste served as the basis for Henry-Russell Hitchcock's distinction between the "eclecticism of taste" and the "eclecticism of style" that underwrote his pathbreaking *Modern Architecture: Romanticism and Reintegration* (1929; repr., New York: Hacker Art Books, 1970). For Hitchcock, the "eclecticism of style," where "features of different styles [were] used together on one building" (6) was the foundation for the "New Tradition," the early modern architecture of Frank Lloyd Wright, Peter Behrens, Auguste Perret, and others.

Chapter 5. Essays in the Erosion of Representation by Viollet-le-Duc and Louis Sullivan

1 Gustave Courbet to a Group of Students, December 25, 1861, in *From the Classicists to the Impressionists: A Documentary History of Art and Architecture in the Nineteenth Century*, ed. Elizabeth Gilmore Holt (Garden City, N.Y.: Anchor Books, 1966), 351–52. On Courbet and the issue of realism in general, see Linda Nochlin, *Realism* (Harmondsworth, Middlesex, England: Penguin, 1971).

2 Courbet to Students, 351–52.

3 Semper's *bekleidungstheorie* was first articulated in the early 1850s and fully developed

in *Der Stil in den technischen und tektonischen Künsten; oder, Praktische Aesthetik: Ein Handbuch für Techniker, Künstler und Kunstfreunde*, orig. pub. 1860–63; trans. Harry Francis Mallgrave and Michael Robinson as *Style: Style in the Technical and Tectonic Arts: or, Practical Aesthetics*, Texts & Documents (Los Angeles: Getty Research Institute, 2004), esp. 237–429. On Semper's architecture and career, see Wolfgang Herrmann, *Gottfried Semper: In Search of Architecture* (Cambridge, Mass.: MIT Press, 1984); and Harry Francis Mallgrave, *Gottfried Semper: Architect of the Nineteenth Century* (New Haven, Conn.: Yale University Press, 1996).

4 See Neil Levine, "Il rovesciamento del sistema della rappresentazione nelle biblioteche di Labrouste," in *Henri Labrouste, 1801–1875*, ed. Renzo Dubbini (Milan: Electa, 2002), 180–88, for an analysis of the architect's transference of the critique of neoclassical representation and display in the forms of the earlier Bibliothèque Sainte-Geneviève to the programmatic level in the later library, mainly through the adoption and foregrounding of the stack system recently developed for the British Museum Library in London by Antonio Panizzi (1852–54).

5 Viollet-le-Duc's polemical call for the revival of French Gothic architecture was most powerfully set forth in his "Le Style gothique au XIXe siècle," *Annales Archéologiques* 4 (1846): 325–53; and in the preface to his *Dictionnaire raisonné de l'architecture française du XIe au XVIe siècle*, 10 vols. (Paris: B. Bance, 1854–63; A. Morel, 1864–68), 1:v–xx. For Viollet-le-Duc's architecture and career, see Paul Gout, *Viollet-le-Duc: Sa vie, son oeuvre, sa doctrine* (Paris: E. Champion, 1914); *Viollet-le-Duc* (Paris: Editions de la Réunion des musées nationaux, Ministère de la Culture et de la Communication, 1980); Jean-Michel Leniaud, *Viollet-le-Duc, ou les délires du système* (Paris: Mengès, 1994); and Laurent Baridon, *L'Imaginaire scientifique de Viollet-le-Duc* (Paris: Harmattan, 1996).

6 The twenty discourses or lectures forming the *Entretiens sur l'architecture* were published separately, beginning with the first four in 1858. Discourses 1–10 were published as the first volume of the *Entretiens* in 1863, and Discourses 11–20 were published as the second volume in 1872. An atlas accompanying volume 1 appeared in 1863; the atlas accompanying volume 2 is dated 1864, although Bertrand Lemoine, in "Viollet-le-Duc et l'architecture métallique," *Viollet-le-Duc* (1980), 254 n. 1, believes that this date must be a typographical error and should read 1874. The publication history of the *Entretiens* is summarized in Robin Middleton, "Viollet-le-Duc's Academic Ventures and the *Entretiens sur l'Architecture*," in *Gottfried Semper und die Mitte des 19. Jahrhunderts: Symposium vom 2–6 Dezember 1974*, ed. Eva Börsch-Supan et al., Institut für Geschichte und Theorie der Architektur, Eidgenössische Technischen Hochschule, Zürich (Basel: Birkhäuser, 1976), 239–54. See also Françoise Boudon, "Le Réel et l'imaginaire chez Viollet-le-Duc: Les figures du *Dictionnaire de l'architecture*," *Revue de l'art* 58–59 (1983): 95–114; and Barry Bergdoll, introduction to Eugène-Emmanuel Viollet-le-Duc, *The Foundations of Architecture: Selections from the "Dictionnaire Raisonné*," trans. Kenneth D. Whitehead (New York: George Braziller, 1990), 1–30.

7 Eugène-Emmanuel Viollet-le-Duc, *Lectures on Architecture*, 2 vols., trans. Benjamin Bucknall (1877–81; repr., New York: Dover Publications, 1987), 1:446. A second English translation of the first volume only, by the American architect Henry Van Brunt, was published in Boston in 1875. This chapter will use Bucknall's translation with certain minor changes and adjustments. Where significant, such changes will be noted.

8 Ibid., 1:447–48.

9 Middleton, "Viollet-le-Duc's Academic Ventures," 246–47.

10 I say "would have" because, according to Middleton, "Viollet-le-Duc's Academic Ventures," 242–44, Viollet-le-Duc read little, if anything, of Semper's writings. For his theory of a metal casing "tubular tectonics," see Semper, *Style*, 362–94.

11 Viollet-le-Duc, *Lectures on Architecture*, 1:34.

12 Ibid., 1:35.

13 Ibid., 1:52.

14 Ibid., 1:37–38.

15 Ibid., 1:38. Viollet-le-Duc's information on India, he noted, came from the first volume of James Fergusson, *The Illustrated Handbook of Architecture: Being a Concise and Popular Account of the Different Styles of Architecture Prevailing in All Ages and All Countries*, 2 vols. (London: J. Murray, 1855).

16 Viollet-le-Duc, *Lectures on Architecture*, 1:44–49.

17 Ibid., 1:52–53.

18 In ibid., 1:456, Viollet-le-Duc asked: "What would these [Gothic artists of twelfth century] have done if they had had the materials and the means which we possess? And what could we not do if, instead of playing the dilettante with all the arts without examining their principles, we determined simply to start from the point at which they arrived, and the principles they recognized?"

19 Ibid., 1:72, 116, 108, 94. "The Roman," Viollet-le-Duc wrote, "separates the construction from the decoration—regarding the latter as a mere luxury—a dress whose use or origin is of slight concern to him" (ibid., 93). I have changed Bucknall's translation of *enveloppe* from "wrapping" to "envelope."

20 Ibid., 1:454.

21 Ibid., 1:263–64, 286, 455.

22 Ibid., 2:66, 61. I have changed Bucknall's translation of *combinaisons* from "contrivances" to "combinations."

23 Ibid., 2:61.

24 John Summerson, "Viollet-le-Duc and the Rational Point of View," *Heavenly Mansions and Other Essays on Architecture* (1949; repr., New York: W. W. Norton, 1963), 135–58. It was Summerson, in this essay, who suggested the idea of Viollet-le-Duc's use of "analogy" as a design tool (154). Cf. Hubert Damisch, introduction to Viollet-le-Duc, *L'Architecture raisonnée: Extraits du "Dictionnaire de l'architecture française"* (Paris: Hermann, 1964), 9–26; Philippe Boudon and Philippe Deshayes, *Viollet-le-Duc: Le Dictionnaire d'architecture: Relevés et observations*, Architecture + Recherches (Brussels: Pierre Madarga, 1979), 7–10, 348–81; and Martin Bressani, "Notes on Viollet-le-Duc's Philosophy of History: Dialectics and Technology," *Journal of the Society of Architectural Historians* 48 (December 1989): 327–50.

25 Viollet-le-Duc, *Lectures on Architecture,* 1:460.

26 Ibid., 2:38. I have changed Bucknall's translation of *ressources* from "appliances" to "resources."

27 Ibid., 2:59.

28 Ibid., 2:44.

29 Ibid., 2:58, 68. I have changed Bucknall's translation of *dispositions* from "contrivances" to "arrangements."

30 The design is dated 1864 on the woodcut published in the second volume of the *Entretiens* (1872). According to Middleton, "Viollet-le-Duc's Academic Ventures," 248 n. 19, the twelfth discourse, in which it was included, was separately published sometime between "the beginning of 1866 and the middle of 1868." For Viollet-le-Duc's projects in the *Entretiens,* see Lemoine, "Viollet-le-Duc et l'architecture métallique," 248–59.

31 Viollet-le-Duc specifically set out to solve the problem of building in iron *and* masonry rather than iron alone, the latter being in his view a much less complicated problem and one with fewer applications. He felt that no truly successful combinations of the two materials had yet been achieved. Labrouste's Bibliothèque Sainte-Geneviève was the most obvious example, and Viollet-le-Duc referred to it a number of times, generally characterizing it as "timid" in its reliance on classical geometry and structural forms (Viollet-le-Duc, *Lectures on Architecture,* 1:462, 468; 2:44, 58).

32 Ibid., 2:89, 93. The reference to natural sources for the geometry of the dome leads one to think of Buckminster Fuller's geodesic domes. It is interesting that Viollet-le-Duc, like Fuller, made a point about the lightweight nature of his structure, describing in detail how much the concert hall would actually weigh (ibid., 2:94–95).

33 Ibid., 2:94. I have changed Bucknall's translation of *voûtains* from "surfaces" to "webs" and of *voûtes d'arêtes Gothiques* from "Gothic groined vaulting" to "Gothic rib vaulting."

34 The dome's shape calls to mind some of Pierre Bossan's contemporaneous churches in the Lyon area and may ultimately derive from very late Gothic structures in Spain. A more obviously historicizing, though no less easily classifiable, version of the octagonal dome appears in Viollet-le-Duc's 1867 project for a Funeral Chapel for the Duchess of Alba.

35 Approaching the issue from a modernist position concerned with the idea of style in the qualitative and vitalist sense of the word, Summerson summed up the design in the following way: "It is all marvellously clever, but . . . not very moving. It does lack style. It is rather like a language invented *ad hoc;* a sort of esperanto evolved from the salient characteristics of other languages lacking the vital unity which any one language possesses" ("Viollet-le-Duc and the Rational Point of View," 156–58).

36 This design is difficult to date precisely. It was included in the eighteenth discourse, which Middleton, "Viollet-le-Duc's Academic Ventures," 248 n. 19, does not date. According to him, the seventeenth discourse was begun in the second half of 1870 but only finished in the following year. Since the twentieth discourse was written in March 1872, just prior to the publication of the second volume, it must be assumed that the eighteenth dates from mid- to late 1871. The perspective drawing for the plate published in the atlas (and here as fig. 5.16) is dated 1871, which surely confirms that, as Lemoine, "Viollet-le-Duc et l'architecture métallique," 254 n. 1, suggests, the second part of the atlas was only published in 1874 and not 1864, as the title page states.

37 Viollet-le-Duc, *Lectures on Architecture,* 2:320.

38 In a footnote earlier in the discourse, Viollet-le-Duc cites the architect François Liger's *Pans de bois et pans de fer* of 1867 for its discussion of iron framing for walls (2:304).

39 Viollet-le-Duc, *Lectures on Architecture,* 2:320.

40 Viollet-le-Duc referred to Jules Saulnier's recently completed factory for the Menier chocolate company at Noisiel-sur-Marne (1869–73) as an example of how an exposed iron structure could be integrated with glazed brick (ibid., 2:327 n. 1).

41 Ibid., 2:326, 330.

42 Ibid., 2:45, 329.

43 Ibid., 2:329. I have changed Bucknall's translation of the words *moyens* from "appliances" to "means" and *industries* from "manufactures" to "industries."

44 Ibid., 2:317, 319.

45 Studies of the Chicago development of the skyscraper are legion. Among the early formative ones are Sigfried Giedion, *Space, Time, and Architecture: The Growth of a New Tradition* (Cambridge, Mass.: Harvard University Press, 1941), 291–315; Carl W. Condit, *The Rise of the Skyscraper* (Chicago: University of Chicago Press, 1952); C. Condit, *The Chicago School of Architecture* (Chicago: University of Chicago Press, 1964); and William H. Jordy, *American Buildings and Their Architects,* vol. 3, *Progressive and Academic Ideals at the Turn of the Twentieth Century* (Garden City, N.Y.: Doubleday, 1972), 1–179. Significant additions, emendations, and qualifications to these classic works are contained in Manfredo Tafuri, "The Disenchanted Mountain: The Skyscraper and the City," in *The American City: From the Civil War to the New Deal,* by Giorgio Ciucci et al. (Cambridge, Mass.: MIT Press, 1979), 389–528; John Zukowsky, ed., *Chicago and New York: Architectural Interactions* (Chicago: Art Institute of Chicago, 1984); J. Zukowsky, ed., *Chicago Architecture, 1872–1922: Birth of a Metropolis* (Chicago: Art Institute of Chicago; Munich: Prestel-Verlag, 1987); Rosemarie Bletter, "The Invention of the Skyscraper: Notes on Its Diverse Histories," *Assemblage* (February 1987): 110–17; Daniel Bluestone, *Constructing Chicago* (New Haven, Conn.: Yale University Press, 1991), 104–51; Carol Willis, *Form Follows Finance: Skyscrapers and Skylines in New York and Chicago* (New York: Princeton Architectural Press, 1995); Robert Bruegmann, *The Architects and the City: Holabird & Root of Chicago, 1880–1918* (Chicago: University of Chicago Press, 1997), esp. chaps. 5–7 and 12; and Roberta Moudry, ed., *The American Skyscraper: Cultural Histories* (Cambridge: Cambridge University Press, 2005).

46 Louis Sullivan, "The Tall Building Artistically Considered," *Lippincott's Monthly Magazine* 57 (March 1896); repr. in *Inland Architect and News Record* 27 (May 1896) and in *Louis Sullivan: The Public Papers,* ed.

Robert Twombly (Chicago: University of Chicago Press, 1988), 104, 108. The architectural critic and historian Barr Ferree similarly stated in his article "Structure and Material in High Design," *Brickbuilder* 3 (March 1894): 43, that "first of all, ... it is necessary to premise that the high building is something entirely new under the sun. It corresponds to needs essentially modern, the conditions that call it into existence are modern.... Viewed from every standpoint, the high building is wholly new." Ferree was an early admirer of Sullivan's work and no doubt discussed things with the architect on his trips to see new buildings in Chicago. As editor of *Engineering Magazine*, he published Sullivan's article "Ornament in Architecture" in August 1892. It may be just a coincidence that he and Sullivan used the phrase "new under the sun" just two years apart, or it may not be. As David Van Zanten pointed out in *Sullivan's City: The Meaning of Ornament for Louis Sullivan* (New York: W. W. Norton, 2000), 61–64, Ferree's and Sullivan's writings shared much in common at this moment in time.

47 Colin Rowe, "Chicago Frame," *Architectural Review* 120 (November 1956): 285–89; repr. in *The Mathematics of the Ideal Villa and Other Essays* (Cambridge, Mass.: MIT Press, 1976), 89–117, eloquently emphasizes these points.

48 In a note on "The Constructive Methods Used in the New York Life Building, Chicago," *American Architect and Building News* 43 (10 February 1894): 72, Jenney and Mundie explained that "The view of the building... taken while in the process of construction [fig. 5.25] shows the granite first and second stories set, but as the granite is invariably slow and the third-story granite was not at hand, the terra-cotta was set from the fifth story up, the granite of the third story and terra-cotta of the fourth to be filled in later." Ferree, who wrote in "Structure and Material," 43, that because the tall building was "entirely new" the architect "must begin his task [of design] by ridding his mind of all preconceived notions," noted in "The High Building and Its Art," *Scribner's* 15 (March 1894): 298, "that it is perfectly feasible, were such a thing necessary, to begin filling in the stone- or brick-work of a building at the top floor, and so on down to the ground, instead of following the ancient, and really old-fashioned style, of beginning with the lowest floor and building upward." He repeated this point in "The Modern Office Building," part 1, *Journal of the Franklin Institute* 141 (January 1896): 55; repr. in *Inland Architect and News Record* 27 (February 1896): 5.

49 For Sullivan, see esp. Hugh Morrison, *Louis Sullivan: Prophet of Modern Architecture* (1935; rev. ed., New York: W. W. Norton, 1998); Narciso Menocal, *Architecture as Nature: The Transcendentalist Idea of Louis Sullivan* (Madison: University of Wisconsin Press, 1981); Robert Twombly, *Louis Sullivan: His Life and Work* (New York: Viking, 1986); Wim de Wit, ed., *Louis Sullivan: The Function of Ornament* (New York: W. W. Norton, 1986); Mario Manieri-Elia, *Louis Henry Sullivan*, orig. pub. 1995; trans. Antony Shugaar with Caroline Green (New York: Princeton Architectural Press, 1996); R. Twombly and N. Menocal, *Louis Sullivan: The Poetry of Architecture* (New York: W. W. Norton, 2000); and David Van Zanten, *Sullivan's City: The Meaning of Ornament for Louis Sullivan* (New York: W. W. Norton, 2000).

50 Frank Lloyd Wright, "Louis H. Sullivan, His Work," *Architectural Record* 56 (July 1924): 28–32; repr. in *Frank Lloyd Wright: Collected Writings*, ed. Bruce Brooks Pfeiffer, 5 vols. (New York: Rizzoli, 1992–95), vol. 1, *1894–1930* (1992): 198.

51 See Donald Hoffmann, *Frank Lloyd Wright, Louis Sullivan, and the Skyscraper* (Mineola, N.Y.: Dover Publications, 1998), 20–36.

52 Sullivan, "Tall Building," in *Sullivan: Public Papers*, 104. The reprint of the article in *Inland Architect and News Record* 27 (May 1896): 32–34, appeared in the same issue as the fourth and penultimate installment of Ferree's "Modern Office Building," to which it has many similarities in thought as well as language. Sullivan's text was preceded by a number of articles that laid out the issue of the design of the tall office building as a problem to be analyzed and solved rationally and innovatively. Among these are John W[ellborn] Root, "A Great Architectural Problem," *Inland Architect and News Record* 15 (June 1890): 67–71; Montgomery Schuyler, "The Romanesque Revival in America," *Architectural Record* 1 (October–December 1891): 151–98; Ferree, "Structure and Material"; Thomas Hastings, "High Buildings and Good Architecture: What Principles Should Govern Their Design," *American Architect and Building News* 46 (November 17, 1894): 67–68; F. C. Gordon, "The 'Sky-Scraper,'" *American Architect and Building News* 46 (December 8, 1894): 100–101; Ferree, "Modern Office Building"; Ferree, "High Building and Its Art"; M. Schuyler, "A Critique (with Illustrations) of the Works of Adler & Sullivan, D. H. Burnham & Co., Henry Ives Cobb," Great American Architects Series, no. 2, 3 parts, *Architectural Record* (February 1896): esp. parts 1–2, 3–71 (part 1, devoted to the work of Adler and Sullivan, has a date of December 1895 on its title page).

53 Sullivan, "Tall Building," in *Sullivan: Public Papers*, 104–5.

54 Ibid., 105–6. The New York Beaux-Arts architect Thomas Hastings, in "High Buildings and Good Architecture," 67, offered a somewhat similar analysis, arguing that "the utilitarian problem which confronts us is a bee-hive, or manifold collection of similar cells, with equal divisions, both lateral and perpendicular. As in all architectural study, our facades should, as much as possible, interpret this interior condition of things." To solve "this exceptional problem," he advised that "we must demand... perfect freedom in composition, and above all, avoid copying or adapting entire *motifs* or parts of other buildings we have seen." On the other hand, he asserted in no uncertain terms that this could only be done "while holding to precedents and traditions as much as possible."

55 Sullivan, "Tall Building," in *Sullivan: Public Papers*, 106–7.

56 Ibid., 108, 107. Although Sullivan repeated the device of doubling the number of piers with ones of the same size in the Guaranty Building (see fig. 5.35), for instance, he more often than not later made the added piers thinner to indicate their nonstructural role. Examples of this include the Bayard

(Condict) Building in New York (1897–99; see fig. 5.36). He also sometimes allowed the exterior to express the horizontality of the bay, as in the Carson Pirie Scott (originally Schlesinger & Mayer) Department Store in Chicago (1899–1904).

57 Ibid., 108. Of all Sullivan's contemporaries who focused on the problem of the skyscraper, it was Barr Ferree who most consistently stressed the need to emphasize the vertical as opposed to the horizontal or gridlike dimension of the building type. In his "Structure and Material," 43, he wrote that "the vertical treatment is the only rational system to design a high building,—a system, by the way, that Messrs. Adler & Sullivan entirely understand, and which they have applied with enormous success to their... Wainwright and Union Trust Buildings in St. Louis." "Verticality, in truth, is not only the natural and rational method of high design," he added, "it is the only way in which the structure can appear in it" (44). In "High Building and Its Art," 316, he wrote that "the chief element of a vertical design... is the vertical line"; and in "Art of High Building," 463, he reiterated that "the most impressive element in the high building is its height; that is the single feature that distinguishes it from all other structures," adding that "Louis H. Sullivan... has alone frankly expressed the vertical element and given the high building logical, as well as genuinely artistic expression."

58 Sullivan, "Tall Building," in *Sullivan: Public Papers,* 106–7, 110. One can find evidence of all these arguments and analogies in the critical writing of the period, although many, like that of the classical column, were only fully developed in the years after the publication of Sullivan's text. The idea that a tall building should exhibit a tripartite division into base, middle section, and crowning element was the most commonly expressed notion preceding Sullivan's discussion. Schuyler, in "Romanesque Revival," 189–90, broached the idea of "a general triple division" and its efficacy in his discussion of Shepley, Rutan, and Coolidge's fourteen-story Ames Building in Boston (1889). He contrasted the "central and chief division, the shaft of the tower,... to its supporting and to its crowning member." While Ferree, in "Chicago Architecture," *Lippincott's Monthly Magazine* 52 (July 1893): 82, described the triple division of "a basement, superstructure, and frieze" as "meaningless and absurd when stretched over a height of two hundred feet," the following year, in "High Building," 311, he stated unequivocally that "the front of the high building is naturally divided into three parts. Every structure must have a beginning and an end, and quite as naturally what comes between must be the middle." In reference to Sullivan's Wainwright Building, he added that "vertical designing being the natural system to be followed in high facade design,... the superstructure naturally grows out of the basement, and, in turn, forms itself the natural base of the crowning frieze" (314).

The interpretation of the tripartite division as a classical column was less common prior the appearance of Sullivan's article than the more general assumption of a triple division. Just prior to the publication of "The Tall Building Artistically Considered," an unsigned article entitled "A Picturesque Sky-Scraper," *Architectural Record* 5 (January–March 1896): 299, 301, noted that "the precept that every work must have a beginning, a middle and an end" has become a "settled" convention for tall building design and that "reflection upon this... has led thinking architects to the analogy, more and more closely followed as experience accumulates, of the column as prototype of the tall building. It must have a base, a shaft, and a capital." In his discussion of Adler and Sullivan's work in "A Critique," 27, Schuyler noted that Sullivan's "purpose is uniformly evident to give as much importance as may be to the basement and the upper division, the base and the capital, to confine the enrichment to these and to leave the intermediate division, the shaft, as a confessed cage coated with fire-proof material." But it was only in the years following the publication of Sullivan's text that Schuyler specifically referred to the columnar analogy as the archetypal tripartite division. In "The 'Sky-Scraper' up to Date," *Architectural Record* 8 (January–March 1899): 234, he remarked that often the "triple division" of the tall building "is founded on the analogy of a column, with its division into base, shaft and capital, and even conforms, as far as may be, to the proportions of the classical column." Four years later, in "The Skyscraper Problem," *Scribner's Magazine* 34 (September 1903): 253, he explained that "the Aristotelian requirement in every work of art of a beginning, a middle, and an end" becomes, when "speaking the language of architecture,... a division into base, shaft, and capital."

An example of the "organic" analogy of the tree referred to by Sullivan is Gordon, "The 'Sky-Scraper,'" 101, in which the author states that although "a good building is always divided into three main divisions," "the whole facade should be an integrated whole, a unit, having a head, body and feet. It should grow up organically from the ground to the top stone, as a tree in the forest, and not be, as is often seen, a number of parts, each complete in itself, piled one on top of the other." I thank Erica Allen-Kim for her research and analysis of these issues.

59 Sullivan, "Tall Building," in *Sullivan: Public Papers,* 109.

60 Ibid., 109–10.

61 Ibid., 110. Ferree similarly noted in his "Modern Office Building," part 3, *Journal of the Franklin Institute* 141 (February 1896): 133, 131, that the "three great divisions in a high design," which is to say, the "base, superstructure and frieze," relate to the fact of "each having a function of its own to express, and each having a logical meaning." Schuyler, "'Sky-Scraper' up to Date," 251, restated the functional argument for the three-part division.

62 Sullivan, "Tall Building," in *Sullivan: Public Papers,* 111. For Schuyler's critique of the crypto-classicism of this statement, see note 71 below.

63 Ibid., 111–12.

64 Ibid., 112.

65 Menocal, *Architecture as Nature,* 24, 46, 187 n. 25, notes that Sullivan owned copies of a number of Viollet-le-Duc's books and was influenced by him in both general and

specific ways. Robin Middleton, "Viollet-le-Duc et sa posterité architecturale," *Viollet-le-Duc* (1980), 369, states that "Louis Sullivan... recommended the writings of Viollet-le-Duc to his students" and "disciples," among them Frank Lloyd Wright.

66 Sullivan, "Tall Building," in *Sullivan: Public Papers*, 112.

67 Reyner Banham, *Theory and Design in the First Machine Age* (New York: Praeger, 1960), 320.

68 Menocal, *Architecture as Nature*, 128, makes this point, noting the strong influence in particular of the playwright Maurice Maeterlinck on Sullivan. See also Lauren S. Weingarden, "Louis H. Sullivan's Metaphysics of Architecture (1885–1901): Sources and Correspondences with Symbolist Art Theories," Ph.D. diss., University of Chicago, 1981.

69 It is interesting to note how Sullivan's former partner, Dankmar Adler, reacted to "The Tall Building Artistically Considered" when it first appeared. In "The Influence of Steel Construction and Plate-Glass upon Style," published in the *American Architect and Building News* 54 (October 31, 1896): 37–39, Adler wrote that Sullivan's phrase "'form follows function'" should be read in opposition to the idea that "*form follows historic precedent*" and thus as offering "a scientific and vastly more practical" definition of the subject. Although he amended Sullivan's phrase to read "'function and environment determine form,'" he allowed that "if it was necessary to state in a three-worded aphorism the entire law of architectural design and composition, nothing could have been better suited to the purpose than the words" used by Sullivan. Adler's remarks were originally read at the annual convention of the American Institute of Architects on October 21, 1896. They were reprinted in "Influence of Steel Construction and of Plate Glass upon the Development of Modern Style," *Inland Architect and News Record* 28 (November 1896): 34–36.

70 C[larence] H[oward] Blackall, "The Legitimate Design of the Architectural Casing for Steel Skeleton Structures," *American Architect and Building News* 66 (December 2, 1899): 78, wrote that despite the great "differences from point-of-view" that separate the "impressionist" work of Sullivan and the "Classic" approach of Bruce Price and others, there was in both "practically a similar treatment of design for tall buildings" in terms of what can be called "the columnar form of design."

71 Schuyler, "A Critique," 27, 25. He particularly remarked on the "solecism" of the "pilaster-capital," which he described as "irrelevant and unmeaning" in relation to "a frame of uprights and cross beams that are riveted together" (29).

72 Ibid., 33; and Schuyler, "'Sky-Scraper' up to Date," 255. Schuyler specifically referred to the fact that in the Bayard Building, following a suggestion he made to the architect, Sullivan reduced the expression of the "base" from "the lower two (or possibly three) stories" to simply the "ground floor."

73 Schuyler, "'Sky-Scraper' up to Date," 257. In the case of the Bayard Building, the critic justified "the arches and the rudimentary tracery" on the basis that there was a change in structural material at that point and that "the arches are in fact of brick-work, faced with terra-cotta, and the thrust of them is visibly, as well as actually, taken up by the tie-rods at the springing."

74 A similar device for terminating the composition was used by Burnham and Root in their Monadnock Building, Chicago, of 1889–91. Shortly after the Wainwright was finished, Sullivan proposed a design for the thirty-six-story Fraternity Temple in Chicago (1891) that had a slender, stepped-back central tower ringed on its upper floors with an arcaded balcony and capped by an eight-sided pyramidal roof similar to the one over the crossing of Richardson's Trinity Church, Boston (1873–77), which was based on the Romanesque Cathedral of Salamanca. On the Guaranty Building, see Joseph Siry, "Adler and Sullivan's Guaranty Building in Buffalo," *Journal of the Society of Architectural Historians* 55 (March 1996): 6–37.

75 According to Twombly, *Sullivan*, 339, the commission for the Bayard Building was Sullivan's first after the breakup of his partnership with Adler. According to Frank Lloyd Wright, "Form and Function," *Saturday Review of Literature* 13 (December 14, 1935): 6, the building was Sullivan's favorite.

76 Wim de Wit, "The Banks and the Image of Progressive Banking," in his *Sullivan: The Function of Ornament*, 175–77, illustrates many such connections, although he concludes that Sullivan designed "without resorting to historical references."

Chapter 6. Representation without History in the Architecture of Frank Lloyd Wright

1 Frank Lloyd Wright, *An Autobiography*, orig. pub. 1932; repr. in *Frank Lloyd Wright: Collected Writings*, ed. Bruce Brooks Pfeiffer, 5 vols. (New York: Rizzoli, 1992–95), vol. 2, *1930–1932, Including "An Autobiography"* (1992): 154; John Lloyd Wright, *My Father Who Is on Earth* (1946; new ed., Carbondale: Southern Illinois University Press, 1994), 69. After the statement that I have quoted, Frank Lloyd Wright added: "What you cannot learn from them [the *Discourses*], you can learn from me."

2 On Wright and Viollet-le-Duc, see Donald Hoffmann, "Frank Lloyd Wright and Viollet-le-Duc," *Journal of the Society of Architectural Historians* 28 (October 1969): 173–83. On Wright and Sullivan, see D. Hoffmann, *Frank Lloyd Wright, Louis Sullivan, and the Skyscraper* (Mineola, N.Y.: Dover Publications, 1998).

3 Frank Lloyd Wright, "Louis H. Sullivan, His Work," *Architectural Record* 56 (July 1924); repr. in *Wright: Collected Writings*, vol. 1, *1894–1930* (1992): 198.

4 Ibid. On the Wainwright Building, see chapter 5.

5 Ibid.

6 Frank Lloyd Wright, *Genius and the Mobocracy*, orig. pub. 1949; repr. in *Wright: Collected Writings*, vol. 4, *1939–1949* (1994): 360.

7 *Wright: Collected Writings*, vol. 4, *1939–1949* (1994): 361. There was a lag between Wright's architectural understanding and articulation of space and his verbal definition of it. It was only in the 1920s that he began to talk about the "third dimension" as that of "depth" and of architectural "space" as such. For the critical texts on these matters, see Frank Lloyd Wright, "In the Cause of

Architecture: The Third Dimension," February 9, 1923, MS III/2, John Lloyd Wright Collection, Avery Library, Columbia University, New York; published in *The Life-Work of the American Architect Frank Lloyd Wright*, ed. H[endrikus] Th[eodorus] Wijdeveld (Santpoort, Holland: C. A. Mees, 1925), 48–65; repr. in *Wright: Collected Writings*, 1:209–14; F. L. Wright, "In the Cause of Architecture, II: What 'Styles' Mean to the Architect," *Architectural Record* 63 (February 1928); repr. in *Wright: Collected Writings*, 1:263–68; and F. L. Wright, "In the Cause of Architecture, IX: The Terms," *Architectural Record* 64 (December 1928); repr. in *Wright: Collected Writings*, 1:310–16.

8 The literature on Wright is vast. Among the most important art historical studies of his work relevant to this chapter are Henry-Russell Hitchcock, *In the Nature of Materials: The Buildings of Frank Lloyd Wright, 1887–1941* (1942; repr., with a new foreword and bibliography, New York: Da Capo Press, 1975); Grant Carpenter Manson, *Frank Lloyd Wright to 1910: The First Golden Age* (New York: Reinhold, 1958); Vincent Scully Jr., *Frank Lloyd Wright*, Masters of World Architecture (New York: George Braziller, 1960); Norris Kelly Smith, *Frank Lloyd Wright: A Study in Architectural Content* (1966; repr., Watkins Glen, N.Y.: American Life Foundation & Study Institute, 1979); Neil Levine, *The Architecture of Frank Lloyd Wright* (Princeton, N.J.: Princeton University Press, 1996); and Robert McCarter, *Frank Lloyd Wright* (London: Phaidon Press, 1997). For Wright's Oak Park House, see Ann Abernathy with John G. Thorpe, eds., *The Oak Park Home and Studio of Frank Lloyd Wright* (Oak Park, Ill.: Frank Lloyd Wright Home and Studio Foundation, 1988); and Elaine Harrington, *Frank Lloyd Wright Home and Studio, Oak Park*, Opus 35 (Stuttgart: Axel Menges, 1996).

9 In time, as his family increased in size, Wright turned the upper-floor room into a dormitory for his children and built a separate studio and office on the north (Chicago Avenue) side of the house (1897–98).

10 Vincent J. Scully Jr., *The Shingle Style and the Stick Style: Architectural Theory and Design from Downing to the Origins of Wright* (orig. pub. 1955 as *The Shingle Style: Architectural Theory and Design from Richardson to the Origins of Wright*; rev. ed., New Haven, Conn.: Yale University Press, 1971), 159. Scully points to George William Sheldon, *Artistic Country-Seats: Types of Recent American Villas and Cottage Architecture, with Instances of Country Club-Houses*, 2 vols. in 5 parts (New York: D. Appleton, 1886–87) and to the journal *Building*, which published Price's Chandler House in September 1886, as the most likely sources for Wright's knowledge.

11 Wright, *Genius and the Mobocracy*, in *Wright: Collected Writings*, 4:352.

12 In his most important theoretical text of the period prior to 1910, Wright wrote in "In the Cause of Architecture," *Architectural Record* 23 (March 1908); repr. in *Wright: Collected Writings*, 1:94:

> I have observed that Nature usually perfects her forms; the individuality of the attribute is seldom sacrificed; that is deformed or mutilated by co-operative parts. She rarely says a thing and tries to take it back at the same time. She would not sanction the "classic" proceeding of, say, establishing an "order," a colonnade, then building walls between the columns of the order reducing them to pilasters, thereafter cutting holes in the wall and pasting on cornices with more pilasters around them, with the result that every form is outraged, the whole an abominable mutilation, as is most of the architecture of the Renaissance wherein style corrodes style and all the forms are stultified.

Wright's most explicit discussion of the theory of the wood origins of the Greek temple is in *Modern Architecture: Being the Kahn Lectures for 1930*, Princeton Monographs in Art and Archaeology, orig. pub. 1931; repr. in *Wright: Collected Writings*, 2:19–79. A more wide-ranging discussion of the origins of architecture in various early forms of natural dwellings occurs in the chapter "Some Aspects of the Past and Present of Architecture," in Baker Brownell and Frank Lloyd Wright, *Architecture and Modern Life*, orig. pub. 1937; repr. in *Wright: Collected Writings*, vol. 3, *1931–1939* (1993): 222–25. On the issue of representation in Wright's work in general, see Neil Levine, "Abstraction and Representation in Modern Architecture: The International Style and Frank Lloyd Wright," *AA Files: Annals of the Architectural Association School of Architecture* 11 (Spring 1986): 3–21; and N. Levine, "Frank Lloyd Wright's Own Houses and His Changing Concept of Representation," in *The Nature of Frank Lloyd Wright*, ed. Carol R. Bolon, Robert S. Nelson, and Linda Seidel (Chicago: University of Chicago Press, 1988), 20–69.

13 Wright, "In the Cause," in *Wright: Collected Writings*, 1:86.

14 Henry-Russell Hitchcock, in "Frank Lloyd Wright and the 'Academic Tradition' of the Early Eighteen-Nineties," *Journal of the Warburg and Courtauld Institutes* 7 (January–June 1944), 46–63, was the first to discuss this moment in Wright's work and point to its significance. See, more recently, Patrick Pinnell, "Academic Tradition and the Individual Talent: Similarity and Difference in Wright's Formation," *On and by Frank Lloyd Wright: A Primer of Architectural Principles*, ed. Robert McCarter (London: Phaidon Press, 2005), 22–55.

15 According to Paul Sprague, "Who Designed the Charnley House, Louis Henry Sullivan or Frank Lloyd Wright?" *The Charnley House: Louis Sullivan, Frank Lloyd Wright, and the Making of Chicago's Gold Coast*, ed. Richard Longstreth (Chicago: University of Chicago Press, 2004), 235 n. 41, the Winslow House was incorrectly dated by Wright and others to 1893 and was only designed and built in 1894. He claims that "building notices confirm" this later date but supplies no documentation nor any description of what he means by "building notices."

16 Joseph M. Siry, *Unity Temple: Frank Lloyd Wright and Architecture for Liberal Religion* (Cambridge: Cambridge University Press, 1996), 36–50, attributes the early design of the All Souls Building to Wright and Perkins equally and notes that Manson, *Wright to 1910*, 156, stated that Wright first began work on the project in 1897 (based on a statement by Perkins); whereas Eric Emmett Davis, "Dwight Heald Perkins: Social Consciousness and Prairie School Architecture," in *Dwight Heald Perkins: Social Consciousness*

and Prairie School Architecture (Chicago: Gallery 400, University of Illinois at Chicago, 1989), 7, gives the date of the commission as 1896, based on a historical survey by Paul Sprague. On the Larkin Building, see Jack Quinan, *Frank Lloyd Wright's Larkin Building: Myth and Fact* (New York: Architectural History Foundation; Cambridge, Mass.: MIT Press, 1987).

17 Robert Spencer Jr., "The Work of Frank Lloyd Wright," *Architectural Review* (Boston) 7 (June 1900): 65–66. Wright, "In the Cause," in *Wright: Collected Writings*, 1:86, reiterated the idea that he had essentially translated Sullivan's thinking about the tall building into the domain of the domestic: "Adler and Sullivan had little time to design residences.... So largely, it remained for me to carry into the field of domestic architecture the battle they had begun in commercial building."

18 In "In the Cause," in *Wright: Collected Writings*, 1:94, Wright described the "sweet reasonableness of form and outline naturally dignified" that he sought in the Prairie House type as "an expression pure and simple, even classic in atmosphere."

19 In ibid., 93; Wright, *Autobiography*, in *Wright: Collected Writings*, 2:203; and Frank Lloyd Wright, *An Autobiography*, 2nd ed. (New York: Duell, Sloan and Pearce, 1943), 139. In the first edition the word "flat" was written "flatwise."

20 Frank Lloyd Wright, "Recollections: United States, 1893–1920," part 1, *Architects' Journal* 84 (July 16, 1936): 77; and Wright, "In the Cause," in *Wright: Collected Writings*, 1:87. The word "skyline" is actually plural in the text and is spelled "sky lines" in the original 1908 version.

21 Louis Sullivan, "The Tall Building Artistically Considered," *Lippincott's Monthly Magazine* 57 (March 1896); repr. in *Inland Architect and News Record* 27 (May 1896); and in *Louis Sullivan: The Public Papers*, ed. Robert Twombly (Chicago: University of Chicago Press, 1988), 109.

22 Wright, "In the Cause," in *Wright: Collected Writings*, 1:87, states that these "'propositions'" were "formulated" in 1894 and "set... down here much as they were written then." Key for the concept of the Prairie House is the third, which reads:

> A building should appear to grow easily from its site and be shaped to harmonize with its surroundings....
>
> We of the Middle West are living on the prairie. The prairie has a beauty of its own and we should recognize and accentuate this natural beauty, its quiet level. Hence, gently sloping roofs, low proportions, quiet sky lines, suppressed heavy-set chimneys and sheltering overhangs, low terraces and out-reaching walls sequestering private gardens.

The other principles dealt with reducing the number of rooms and combining all the social functions of the ground floor into "but one room, the living room"; making all windows "occur as integral features of the structure and form"; eliminating excessive and extrinsic decoration and designing "appliances or fixtures" as part "of the structure"; considering the furniture as an "integral" part of "the whole"; choosing colors that blend with the surrounding landscape; and leaving the materials as much as possible in their natural state (ibid., 87).

23 Wright, "Recollections," 78. The perspective of the Winslow House was the first plate in the so-called Wasmuth Portfolio, Wright's *Ausgeführte Bauten und Entwürfe von Frank Lloyd Wright (Studies and Executed Buildings by Frank Lloyd Wright)* (1910[–11]; repr., Palos Park, Ill.: Prairie School Press, 1975). In the caption to the plate, Wright wrote the following:

> Many of the features which have since characterized this work originated in this house. The setting of the basement outside the main walls of the house to form a preparation for the sill courses; the division of the exterior wall surfaces into body and frieze, changing the material above the second story sill line; the wide level eaves, with low sloping roofs; the one massive chimney; and the feeling for contrast between plain wall surface and richly decorated and contrasted masses; the use of the window as a decorative feature in itself; the lines of the building extending into the grounds, the low walls and parterre utilized to associate it with its site.

24 Wright, *Ausgeführte Bauten*, in *Wright: Collected Writings*, 1:113.

25 Wright, "Recollections," 77.

26 Sullivan, "Tall Building," in *Sullivan: Public Papers*, 108.

27 Wright, *Autobiography*, in *Wright: Collected Writings*, 2:200.

28 Sullivan, "Tall Building," in *Sullivan: Public Papers*, 106. David Van Zanten, *Sullivan's City: The Meaning of Ornament for Louis Sullivan* (New York: W. W. Norton, 2000), 93–119, however, makes a strong case for reconsidering the spatial implications of Sullivan's planning, an idea picked up by Richard Longstreth in his *Charnley House*, 1–35.

29 I owe this interpretation of the screened-off fireplace area as a loggia to Tim Love. Smith, *Wright*, 85, by contrast, characterized the space in religious terms, describing the "delicate wooden arcade" as carrying "something of the sense or flavor of a rood screen before an altar."

30 The other historicizing features are the colonnaded semicircular bay of the conservatory extension of the dining room, the arched porte cochere, and the medievalizing stair tower that is only visible on the exterior from the rear and on the interior at the northeast corner of the second floor (see fig. 6.9).

31 This was first pointed out in 1900 by Robert Spencer, "Wright," 65. "The street facade," he wrote, "is simple with a breadth of treatment that carries the exquisite refinement of its detail with perfect dignity. Within the grounds to the rear we are afforded a more intimate knowledge of the conditions of life within and the scheme becomes less reticent and is more picturesque without sacrificing the quiet formality of the whole." Hitchcock, *Nature of Materials*, 24; Scully, *Wright*, 16; and Smith, *Wright*, 86–87, all noted the importance of the distinction between front and rear in the house.

32 The problem of resolving the tension between the desire for privacy and the importance of community remained a critical issue for Wright throughout this part of his career. It was most clearly formulated in 1900–1901 in his project for the Quadruple Block Plan, which he published in "A Home in a Prairie Town," *Ladies' Home Journal* 17

(February 1901); repr. in *Wright: Collected Writings*, 1:73–79, where he explained that the main idea of the grouping was to create "an arrangement of the four houses that secures breadth and prospect to the community as a whole, and absolute privacy both as regards each to the community, and each to each of the four." For a fuller discussion, see Neil Levine, "The Quadruple Block Plan: L'obsession de Frank Lloyd Wright pour la grille / The Quadruple Block Plan and Frank Lloyd Wright's Obsession with the Grid," *EaV: La Revue de l'école nationale supérieure de l'architecture de Versailles / Versailles Architecture School Journal* 11 (2005/2006), esp. 62–76.

33 The basement was originally reserved for the servants' quarters, heating, storage, and a garage. The latter, which would have been accessed through the rear alley, was deemed illegal, and in its place was built an apartment for a relative.

34 Marc-Antoine Laugier, *Essai sur l'architecture*, 2nd ed., rev. and enl. (Paris: Duchesne, 1755; repr., Farnborough, England: Gregg Press, 1966), 10.

35 I am grateful to John Thorpe for his technical expertise on this issue.

36 August Schmarsow, "The Essence of Architectural Creation," orig. pub. 1894; trans. and ed. Harry Francis Mallgrave and Eleftherios Ikonomou, *Empathy, Form, and Space: Problems in German Aesthetics, 1873–1893*, Texts & Documents (Santa Monica, Calif.: Getty Center for the History of Art and the Humanities, 1994), 281–97. See also Mitchell Schwarzer, "The Emergence of Architectural Space: August Schmarsow's Theory of *Raumgestaltung*," *Assemblage* 15 (Fall 1991): 50–61; and Paul Zucker, "The Paradox of Architectural Theories at the Beginning of the 'Modern Movement,'" *Journal of the Society of Architectural Historians* 10 (September 1951): 8–14.

37 Wright, *Autobiography*, in *Wright: Collected Writings*, 2:211–18. On the church, see Siry, *Unity Temple*, 51–246; Rodney F. Johonnot, *The New Edifice of Unity Church, Oak Park, Illinois: Frank Lloyd Wright, Architect* (1906; repr., Oak Park, Ill.: Unitarian Universalist Church, 1961); Robert McCarter, *Unity Temple: Frank Lloyd Wright*, Architecture in Detail (London: Phaidon Press, 1997); and David M. Sokol, *The Noble Room: The Inspired Conception and Tumultuous Creation of Frank Lloyd Wright's Unity Temple* (Oak Park, Ill.: Top Five Books, 2008). The Sokol book appeared too late to have been of use in this study.

38 J[acobus] J[ohannes] P[ieter] Oud, in "Architectural Observations Concerning Wright and the Robie House (1918)," *De Stijl* 4, no. 1 (1918); repr. in *Writings on Wright: Selected Comment on Frank Lloyd Wright*, ed. H. Allen Brooks (Cambridge, Mass.: MIT Press, 1981), 135–26, early on noted how "the embellishment" of Wright's buildings was "achieved by primary means: the effect of the masses themselves," rather than "by the secondary means of detail—ornament" that was characteristic of contemporary Dutch architecture. For a somewhat different reading of this issue specifically in relation to Unity Temple, see Thomas Beeby, "The Grammar of Ornament / Ornament as Grammar," *Via: The Journal of the Graduate School of Fine Arts, University of Pennsylvania* 3 (1977): 10–29.

39 Frank Lloyd Wright, "In the Cause of Architecture," *Architectural Record* 23 (March 1908): 212. Rodney Johonnot, who was the minister of the church at the time it was built and whose description of the building in his 1906 brochure was clearly based on discussions with Wright, claimed that the name "temple" rather than "church" was more fitting for the building "because the building has the feeling and to some extent the form of an ancient temple." He then elaborated: "The religious feeling...has been reached in this structure not by the adoption of...the Gothic style of the Middle Ages, but by a frank return to the simpler and more ancient forms of religious architecture" (*New Edifice*, n.p.).

40 H[endrik] P[etrus] Berlage, in "Neuere amerikanische Architektur," *Schweizerische Bauzeitung* 60 (September 21, 1912), 165; trans. in *The Literature of Architecture: The Evolution of Architectural Theory and Practice in Nineteenth-Century America*, ed. Don Gifford (New York: E. P. Dutton, 1966), 614, compared the building to "an Egyptian temple."

41 See Donald Hoffmann, *Frank Lloyd Wright's Robie House: The Illustrated Story of an Architectural Masterpiece* (New York: Dover Publications, 1984); and Joseph Connors, *The Robie House of Frank Lloyd Wright* (Chicago: University of Chicago Press, 1984).

42 Wright, *Ausgeführte Bauten*, in *Wright: Collected Writings*, 1:112.

43 See Levine, "Abstraction and Representation," 3–21. Analogies of this sort can be tricky yet revealing. Already by the early 1930s, Sigfried Giedion, in "Les Problèmes actuels de l'architecture: A l'occasion d'un manifeste de Frank Lloyd Wright aux architectes et critiques d'Europe," *Cahiers d'art* 7, nos. 1–2 (1932): 72, saw Le Corbusier rather than Wright as understanding and putting to use the "revolutionary transformation of the visual image of which cubism was the initiator." Since World War II, Le Corbusier's architecture of the 1920s has usually been proffered as the architectural analogue of Cubist painting, despite the nearly fifteen-year lag between the two phenomena. See, for example, John Summerson, "Architecture, Painting and Le Corbusier," in *Heavenly Mansions and Other Essays on Architecture* (1949; repr., New York: W. W. Norton, 1963), 177–94; Colin Rowe and Robert Slutzky, "Transparency: Literal and Phenomenal," *Perspecta: The Yale Architectural Journal* 8 (1963); repr. in Colin Rowe, *The Mathematics of the Ideal Villa and Other Essays* (Cambridge, Mass.: MIT Press, 1976), 159–83; and Eve Blau and Nancy J. Troy, eds., *Architecture and Cubism* (Montreal: Centre Canadien d'Architecture / Canadian Center for Architecture; Cambridge, Mass.: MIT Press, 1997).

As early as 1918, on the other hand, the Dutch modernist Oud, in "Architectural Observations Concerning Wright," 136, described Wright's formal inventions as paralleling those of Cubist and Futurist painting. "Instead of a stable and rigid compactness of the various parts," he wrote, "Wright *detaches the masses from the whole* and rearranges their composition," adding that "there is a direct relation here with the way the futurists have overcome rigidity in painting...by achieving movement of the planes." "In this way," Oud concluded, "Wright has created a new 'plastic' architecture" that "opens up entirely new aesthetic possibilities for architecture." By the mid-1920s, however, in "The Influence of Frank Lloyd Wright on the Architecture of Europe," in Wijdeveld, *Life-Work of Wright*, 87–88, Oud differentiated between Wright and the recent European development of what he called "Cubism in architecture," while continuing to assert the parallelism between Wright's work and the formal characteristics of earlier Cubist painting. "Wright's work smoothed...the way for cubism [in architecture]," Oud wrote, while "cubism paved the way for the more actual execution of that which was his [Wright's] theory too." Both Cubism and Wright, he noted, "seem to agree in the preference for the right angle, in the three-dimensional tendency, in the breaking up of bodies and again combining their parts...into a whole which in its appearance still betrays the elements of the original dissection."

At the same time, Oud criticized (the later) Wright for not taking these ideas to their logical conclusion in the form of "abstraction," as many in Europe and especially Holland had done. The "plastic exuberance" and "sensuous abundance" of his work was in sharp contrast to the "puritanic asceticism" and "mental abstinence" of the recent European architecture and thus, despite the "inner affinity" between them, Oud was forced to conclude that "in reality the two were wholly different, nay rather opposed to one another" (ibid., 88). Ed Taverne, Cor Wagenaar, and Martien de Vletter, in *J. J. P. Oud, Poetic Functionalist, 1893–1963: The Complete Works* (Rotterdam: NAi, 2001), 154–56, shed light on Theo van Doesburg's role in Oud's reappraisal of Wright vis-à-vis an independent European development of Cubism, meaning De Stijl Neo-Plasticism. Oud's critique of Wright was similar to, although not quite the same as, that which Le Corbusier and his collaborator at the time, the painter Amédée Ozenfant, made of Picasso and Braque's Cubism. Their manifesto, *Après le cubisme* (Paris: Editions des Commentaires, 1918) was a diatribe against Cubist painting and an attempt to establish Purism as its successor through a complete inversion of everything Cubism stood for.

44 Frank Lloyd Wright, "In the Cause of Architecture, V: The Meaning of Materials—The Kiln," *Architectural Record* 63 (June 1928); repr. in *Wright: Collected Writings*, 1:286–88, later commented that Sullivan's ornament led toward the kind of "flattening" out of space that became characteristic of Cubism: "Into the living intricacy of his loving modulations of surface, 'background'—the curse of all stupid ornament—ceased to exist. None might see where terra-cotta left off and ornamentation came to life." Wright added: "Background disappeared but surface was preserved. There was no sense of background, as such, anywhere. All was of the surface, out of the material."

45. Clement Greenberg, "After Abstract Expressionism," *Art International* (October 25, 1962); repr. in *Clement Greenberg: The Collected Essays and Criticism*, ed. John O'Brian, 4 vols. (Chicago: University of Chicago Press, 1986–93), vol. 4, *Modernism with a Vengeance, 1957–1964*, 124–28.

46 Wright, *Autobiography*, in *Wright: Collected Writings*, 2:219.

47 A full account of his trip to Europe and the building of Taliesin is given in Levine, *Architecture of Frank Lloyd Wright*, 58–111; and in Anthony Alofsin, *Frank Lloyd Wright: The Lost Years, 1910–1922: A Study of Influence* (Chicago: University of Chicago Press, 1993), 29–100.

On Taliesin, see "The Studio-Home of Frank Lloyd Wright," *Architectural Record* 33 (January 1913): 45–54; C[harles] R[obert] Ashbee, "Taliesin, the Home of Frank Lloyd Wright, and a Study of the Owner," *Western Architect* 19 (February 1913): 16–19; Thomas Beeby, "The Song of Taliesin," *Modulus: University of Virginia School of Architecture Review* (1980–81): 2–11; Walter L. Creese, *The Crowning of the American Landscape: Eight Great Spaces and Their Buildings* (Princeton, N.J.: Princeton University Press, 1985), 241–78; and "Taliesin: 1911–1914," *Wright Studies* 1 (1992), ed. Narciso Menocal (Carbondale: Southern Illinois University Press, 1992).

48 Wright, *Autobiography*, in *Wright: Collected Writings*, 2:223.

49 Ibid., 2:226.

50 For a fuller treatment of this planning development within the context of Wright's career as a whole, see Neil Levine, "Frank Lloyd Wright's Diagonal Planning Revisited," in McCarter, *On and by Wright*, 232–63.

51 This description follows as much as possible the plan laid out in 1911.

52 Wright, *Autobiography*, in *Wright: Collected Writings*, 2:226.

53 Frank Lloyd Wright, "Taliesin III," June 8, 1926, MS XXI/4, J. L. Wright Collection.

54 Wright, *Autobiography*, in *Wright: Collected Writings*, 2:227. The curious punctuation in the third sentence of the first paragraph may have occurred during revisions for publication. In the original manuscript there were dashes between the second and third sentences, as well as between the first clause of the third sentence and the rest of that sentence. Frank Lloyd Wright, "Taliesin," 4, MS 1201.028 A, Frank Lloyd Wright Foundation, Taliesin West, Scottsdale, Ariz.

55 Wright, *Autobiography*, in *Wright: Collected Writings*, 2:224.

56 Ibid. According to a reporter who was shown the house by the architect soon after it was finished, the stone was "laid in close imitation of the cliff" where the stone was quarried. "Spend Christmas Making 'Defense' of 'Spirit Hegira,'" *Chicago Tribune*, December 26, 1911, 2. Although one might think that Wright would never use the word "imitation," it is also an unlikely one for a reporter to have used in this context.

57 Wright, *Autobiography*, in *Wright: Collected Writings*, 2:224, 226–27.

58 For a discussion of these projects, see Levine, *Architecture of Frank Lloyd Wright*, 148–215.

59 On Fallingwater, see Bruno Zevi and Edgar Kaufmann Jr., *La casa sulla cascata di F. L. Wright: F. Lloyd Wright's Fallingwater* (Milan: ETAS/Kompass, 1963); Edgar Kaufmann Jr., *Fallingwater: A Frank Lloyd Wright Country House* (New York: Abbeville Press, 1986); Donald Hoffmann, *Frank Lloyd Wright's Fallingwater: The House and Its History*, 2nd ed. rev. (New York: Dover Publications, 1993);

Robert McCarter, *Fallingwater: Frank Lloyd Wright*, Architecture in Detail (London: Phaidon Press, 1994); Richard L. Cleary, *Merchant Prince and Master Builder: Edgar J. Kaufmann and Frank Lloyd Wright* (Pittsburgh: Heinz Architectural Center, 1999); Ezra Stoller, with text by Neil Levine, *Frank Lloyd Wright's Fallingwater*, Building Blocks (New York: Princeton Architectural Press, 1999); and Franklin Toker, *Fallingwater Rising: Frank Lloyd Wright, E. J. Kaufmann, and America's Most Extraordinary House* (New York: Alfred A. Knopf, 2003).

60 Frank Lloyd Wright to Edgar Kaufmann, December 26, 1934, in Bruce Brooks Pfeiffer, ed., *Frank Lloyd Wright: Letters to Clients* (Fresno: Press at California State University, 1986), 82; and F. L. Wright, "Frank Lloyd Wright," *Architectural Forum* 68 (January 1938); repr. in *Wright: Collected Writings*, 3:280.

61 Hoffmann, *Fallingwater*, 19, provides an excellent description of Wright's use of the thirty/sixty-degree triangle to accomplish this.

62 Lewis Mumford, "The Sky Line—at Home, Indoors and Out," *New Yorker* 13 (February 12, 1938): 31. There is also a tree/leaf imagery in Fallingwater that works in parallel with the stone/water imagery and equally involves the theme of movement and change.

63 John Fabian Kienitz, in "The Romanticism of Frank Lloyd Wright," *Art in America* 32 (April 1944): 99, early on related Fallingwater to Claude-Nicolas Ledoux's project for a House of the Directors of the Loue River (1790s), where the river water is channeled through an open oval occupying the center of the structure. But here the idea was to symbolize the function of the house as a kind of sluice gate, whose very purpose was to turn the water on and off.

64 On these three later buildings, see Levine, *Architecture of Frank Lloyd Wright*, 254–363, 404–17.

Chapter 7. The Reemergence of Representation out of Abstraction in Mies van der Rohe

1 "A Tribute to Frank Lloyd Wright" was written in 1940 for the unpublished catalogue that was planned to accompany the retrospective exhibition of Wright's work held at the Museum of Modern Art in the fall and early winter of 1940–41. It was first published in the *College Art Journal* in 1946 and most recently reprinted in Peter Reed and William Kaizen, eds., *The Show to End All Shows: Frank Lloyd Wright and the Museum of Modern Art*, Studies in Modern Art 8 (New York: Museum of Modern Art, 2004), 169–70. Mies's initial trip to the United States took place in August 1937–April 1938. When he was in Chicago in September, he made it a point of contacting Wright. According to Cammie McAtee, "Alien #5044325: Mies's First Trip to America," in *Mies in America*, ed. Phyllis Lambert (Montreal: Canadian Centre for Architecture; New York: Whitney Museum of American Art, 2001), 161, Mies first went to Taliesin, intending to spend just a day. In the end, he spent four days with Wright, three at Taliesin and the final one visiting Unity Temple, the Robie and Coonley houses, and the Johnson Wax Headquarters construction site. It is not known whether Mies saw the Fallingwater exhibition when he was in New York, although it is hard to believe he did not. Mies was there from mid-September 1937 until the beginning of April 1938. The Fallingwater exhibition opened on January 24 and closed on March 1, 1938.

2 Mies, "Tribute to Wright," 169–70. Questioning the fact that there was an exhibition of Wright's work in Berlin in 1910, Anthony Alofsin, in *Frank Lloyd Wright—The Lost Years, 1910–1922: A Study of Influence* (Chicago: University of Chicago Press, 1993), 33–34, downplays the importance of these remarks, noting, as many others have, that they were written thirty years after the event. Alofsin backs up this position by maintaining that there was no formal exhibition of Wright's work in Berlin at the time Mies references. However, it seems difficult to believe that Mies did not accurately remember, after only thirty years, how Wright's architecture first came to his attention.

3 See, for example, Alfred H. Barr et al., *Modern Architecture: International Exhibition* (New York: Museum of Modern Art, 1932), esp. 12–17, 29–37; and Vincent J. Scully Jr., "Wright vs. the International Style," *Art News* 53 (March 1954); repr. in *Modern Architecture and Other Essays*, ed. Neil Levine (Princeton, N.J.: Princeton University Press, 2003), 54–63.

4 Henry-Russell Hitchcock Jr., "Modern Architecture. I: The Traditionalists and the New Tradition," *Architectural Record* 63 (April 1928): 344, 346, 340, 341. By 1932, Hitchcock had dropped the term "New Traditionalist" in favor of "half-modern." H.-R. Hitchcock and Philip Johnson, *The International Style*, orig. pub. 1932; 2nd ed. (New York: W. W. Norton, 1966), 24. As Hitchcock acknowledged in the bibliographical note to *Modern Architecture: Romanticism and Reintegration* (1929; repr., New York: Hacker Art Books, 1970), 240, Gustav Adolf Platz's *Die Baukunst der neuesten Zeit*, Propyläen-Kunstgeschichte series (Berlin: Propyläen-Verlag, 1927) was important to him as a source for information and ideas.

5 Henry-Russell Hitchcock Jr., "Modern Architecture. II: The New Pioneers," *Architectural Record* 63 (May 1928): 455.

6 Hitchcock, "Modern Architecture: New Tradition," 340. Douglas Haskell, "Organic Architecture: Frank Lloyd Wright," *Creative Art* 3 (November 1928): lvi–lvii, echoed Hitchcock in stating that Wright's "imagination belongs, after all, to the eclectic period. McKim, Mead & White took 'Italian Renaissance' and modelled it; Frank Lloyd Wright ranged over the entire world's architecture and digested it. Not for nothing are some of his constructions related to Japanese, some to Maya, some to Egyptian art."

7 Hitchcock, "Modern Architecture: New Tradition," 349, 348.

8 Hitchcock, *Modern Architecture*, 114, 117. In his treatment of Wright in the book, Hitchcock indicated a certain ambiguity about whether Wright's work really was exclusively of the New Tradition, indicating at numerous points how closely he thought Wright approached the position of the New Pioneers. In the Robie House's "three dimensional organization of planes that is absolutely unprecedented," he wrote, "Wright seems almost to have pushed

beyond the New Tradition and foreseen thus early some of the effects of the New Pioneers" (114). "His house interiors," though "dark, uncomfortable and generally at once cluttered and monotonous," "were at times very close indeed, but for the failure of some spark to give them real life, to the interiors of the New Pioneers to whose principles, not for many years to be fully articulated in Europe, they largely conform" (115). In this regard, Hitchcock was probably influenced by Oud's reading of Wright in "The Influence of Frank Lloyd Wright on the Architecture of Europe," in *The Life-Work of the American Architect Frank Lloyd Wright*, ed. H[endrikus] Th[eodorus] Wijdeveld (Santpoort, Holland: C. A. Mees, 1925), 85–89.

9 For this, his friendship with Alfred Barr, the founding director of New York's Museum of Modern Art, was crucial. See Alfred H. Barr, *Cubism and Abstract Art* (New York: Museum of Modern Art, 1936). Already in 1925, Oud's "Influence of Frank Lloyd Wright," 88, spoke of the "humble level of an abstraction" that European modernism had reached in contrast to the "luxurious growth" represented by Wright's architecture. And in 1932, Sigfried Giedion, in "Les Problèmes actuels de l'architecture: A l'occasion d'un manifeste de Frank Lloyd Wright aux architectes et critiques d'Europe," *Cahiers d'art* 7, nos. 1–2 (1932), 70, stated categorically: "In its form, the mode of expression of the 20th century will remain abstract. It will aim solely at fulfilling a function."

10 Le Corbusier, *Vers une architecture* (Paris: G. Crès, 1923); and Richard J. Neutra, *Wie baut Amerika?* (Stuttgart: J. Hoffmann, 1927). Le Corbusier first published an image of a grain elevator in the article he wrote with Amédée Ozenfant, "Trois rappels à MM. les architectes. Premier rappel: Le Volume," *L'Esprit nouveau* 1 (October 1920): 95. That image had previously been published in Walter Gropius, "Die Entwicklung moderner Industrie-baukunst," *Jahrbuch des deutschen Werkbundes* (Jena, Germany: Eugen Diederichs, 1913), opp. p. 16. The plates in Platz's *Baukunst der neuesten Zeit* open with sixty-one pages of works of engineering, including bridges, factories, dams, and so on. This constitutes nearly one-fifth of all the reproductions, exclusive of plans and line drawings.

11 Hitchcock, "Modern Architecture: New Pioneers," 455–56.

12 Ibid., 454, 458; and Hitchcock, *Modern Architecture*, 178. Oud, "Influence of Frank Lloyd Wright," 87–89, stated that "cubism [meaning De Stijl] was born" when "the adoration of Wright's work by his colleagues on this side of the Atlantic had reached its culminating point [i.e., ca. 1915–17] and characterized "cubism in architecture" as a "puritanic asceticism," a "mental abstinence," and a form of "abstraction" producing an expression "of number and measure, of purity and order, of completeness and finish." In a letter to Gustav Adolf Platz of July 1926, quoted in Mariëtte van Stralen, "Kindred Spirits: Holland, Wright, and Wijdeveld," in *Frank Lloyd Wright: Europe and Beyond*, ed. Anthony Alofsin (Berkeley: University of California Press, 1999), Oud wrote that "Cubism in architecture goes back to Mondrian." Hitchcock and Johnson, in *International Style*, 29–30, state that "during the war years, Oud...came into contact with the group of Dutch cubist painters led by Mondriaan and Van Doesburg, who called themselves Neoplasticists." Reyner Banham, in *Theory and Design in the First Machine Age* (New York: Praeger, 1960),153–57, remarks on this elision of Cubism and De Stijl, especially in Oud's thinking. This historically significant definition of Cubism, however, never surfaces in Blau and Troy, *Architecture and Cubism*.

13 Hitchcock, "Modern Architecture: New Pioneers," 457.

14 Le Corbusier, *Vers une architecture*, trans. Frederick Etchells as *Towards a New Architecture*, 1927 (London: Architectural Press, 1965), 41, 19, 31.

15 Hitchcock, *Modern Architecture*, 158. In the book's introduction, he described modern architecture, in the broadest sense of the term, as having "more or less conscious intellectual interests in abstract form" (xvi). Already in 1928, Haskell, in "Organic Architecture," lvii, wrote that "the 'cubes, spheres and cylinders' of this new art [of architecture] derive from the lessons learned by painting...rather than the old traditions of architecture."

16 S[igfried] Giedion, "Theo van Doesburg," *Cahiers d'art* 6, no. 4 (1931): 228. The statement by Oud is from the tenth anniversary issue of *De Stijl*. Painters such as Van Doesburg and Mondrian were quick to emphasize their own leadership roles. In an article published in *De Stijl* in 1923, Van Doesburg declared: "Only in our time has the leading art form, painting, shown the way which architecture must take in order that it may...realize in material form what is already present [in painting] in imaginary (aesthetic) form" (repr. in Hans L. C. Jaffé, *De Stijl* [New York: Harry N. Abrams, 1967], 181). In the same volume of the journal, in an article entitled "Is Painting Secondary to Architecture?" Mondrian noted that, since painting had shown the way toward abstraction, it naturally followed that "the new aesthetic for architecture is that of the new painting" (Jaffé, *De Stijl*, 184).

17 Sigfried Giedion, *Space, Time, and Architecture: The Growth of a New Tradition* (Cambridge, Mass.: Harvard University Press, 1941), 26; see also 355–57. Walter Curt Behrendt, whose *Der Sieg des neuen Baustils* (trans. as *Victory of the New Building Style*, 2000), originally published in 1927, was one of the first narratives of modern architecture's history, stressed in his later *Modern Building: Its Nature, Problems, and Forms* (New York: Harcourt, Brace, 1937), 148–52, that "cubism created in architecture a new form-type which...gained an almost international validity." "Containing the principles of abstract painting divorced from a mere imitation of reality," "this style of cubism," he added, brought a "new spirit of building [which then] entered a new phase which up to now [1937] is also its latest one."

18 Henry-Russell Hitchcock, *Painting toward Architecture* (New York: Duell, Sloan and Pearce, 1948), 32. This statement by Hitchcock was made specifically in reference to Oud, his Dutch colleagues, and Le Corbusier, but Hitchcock later noted that the "Dutch abstract artists were, in the 20s, very influential in Germany as well as Holland.

Indeed their work...seems to have been the particular catalyst which crystallized what has sometimes been miscalled the 'Bauhaus Style'" (34). As noted in chap. 6, n. 43, John Summerson, in "Architecture, Painting and Le Corbusier," in *Heavenly Mansions and Other Essays on Architecture* (1949; repr., New York: W. W. Norton, 1963), 177–94, 191–92, linked Le Corbusier to Cubism, going so far as to state that "no doubt Picasso has influenced Le Corbusier" but then pulling back to observe that " the question of the *influence* of modern painting on modern architecture is not so important as the historical truth that Le Corbusier, the architect, has shared the same vision as some of the cubist and abstract painters." Throughout the essay, the author confuses Cubism of the Picasso-Braque sort with abstraction.

19 Vincent Scully, "Modern Architecture: Toward a Redefinition of Style," *Perspecta: The Yale Architectural Journal* 4 (1957); repr. in Scully, *Modern Architecture*, 74–87, directly followed Hitchcock and Giedion in crediting "the researches into continuity and its interruptions which had been carried on by such De Stijl artists as van Doesburg" along with Wright's "fragmentation of building mass" as the basis for the International Style's "sharply defined boxes which are at once machined and Neoclassic." Reyner Banham, in *Theory and Design in the First Machine Age* (New York: Praeger, 1960), 87, wrote that the "aesthetic discipline" of modern architecture "was to come from the realm of painting and sculpture, from that development towards purely Abstract art that had already been launched by the Cubists and Futurists... [before] the War." Peter Collins, in *Changing Ideals of Modern Architecture, 1750–1950* (London: Faber and Faber, 1965), 271 ff., echoed Banham in stating that "the dominant influence on architectural design during the second quarter of the twentieth century has undoubtedly been that of painting and sculpture." Manfredo Tafuri and Francesco Dal Co, in *Modern Architecture*, orig. pub. 1976; trans. Robert Erich Wolf (New York: Harry N. Abrams, 1980), 120, prefaced their chapter on "The Role of the Masters" (Le Corbusier, Gropius, Mies, and Wright) with one entitled "Architecture and the Avant-Garde from Cubism to the Bauhaus: 1906–1923," in which they discussed how Cubism, later followed by Italian and Russian Futurism, "launched a new phase of modern art."

20 Philip Johnson, "Ludwig Miës van der Rohe," in Barr, *Modern Architecture*, 114.

21 The comparison between the Brick Country House and the Van Doesburg painting made what may be its first appearance in Barr, *Cubism and Abstract Art*, 156–57.

22 Hitchcock, "Modern Architecture: New Tradition," 140; and Hitchcock, *Modern Architecture*, 102–18.

23 Theo van Doesburg, "Painting and Sculpture," *De Stijl* 7, nos. 75–76 (1926); repr. in Jaffé, *De Stijl*, 208.

24 J. J. P. Oud, "Architectural Observations Concerning Wright and the Robie House," *De Stijl* 1, no. 4 (1918); repr. in H. Allen Brooks, ed., *Writings on Wright: Selected Comment on Frank Lloyd Wright* (Cambridge, Mass.: MIT Press, 1981), 135–36.

25 Because of the elegant materials, the placement on a podium, and the trabeated system of load and support, the building has often been interpreted as a modern form of classicism. While this may be true, it in no way contradicts the nonrepresentational reading of the forms as purely abstract.

26 The word "altarlike" was used by Richard Pommer in his excellent description of the project in his "Mies van der Rohe and the Political Ideology of the Modern Movement in Architecture," in *Mies van der Rohe: Critical Essays*, ed. Franz Schulze (New York: Museum of Modern Art, 1989), 126.

27 These questions were first raised in print by Sibyl Moholy-Nagy in "The Diaspora" and in her comments in "Sunday Session," *Journal of the Society of Architectural Historians* 25 (March 1965): 24–25, 83–84. See also "Letters," *Journal of the Society of Architectural Historians* 25 (October 1965): 254–56. For the most well-researched and balanced account of the issue, see Richard Pommer, "Mies van der Rohe and the Political Ideology of the Modern Movement in Architecture," in *Mies van der Rohe: Critical Essays*, ed. Franz Schulze (New York: Museum of Modern Art, 1989), 96–145. For a more contentious view of Mies's attitude toward Nazi Germany, see Elaine S. Hochman, "The Politics of Mies van der Rohe," *Sites* 15 (1986): 44–49; E. Hochman, "Confrontation: 1933—Mies van der Rohe and the Third Reich," *Oppositions* 18 (Fall 1979): 49–59; and E. Hochman, *Architects of Fortune: Mies van der Rohe and the Third Reich* (New York: Fromm International, 1990). For more recent discussions, see Jean-Louis Cohen, *Mies van der Rohe* (Paris: Hazan, 1994), 70–73; Peter Hahn, "Bauhaus and Exile: Bauhaus Architects and Designers between the Old World and New," and Franz Schulze, "The Bauhaus Architects and the Rise of Modernism in the United States," in Stephanie Barron with Sabine Eckmann, eds., *Exiles + Emigrés: The Flight of European Artists from Hitler* (Los Angeles: Los Angeles County Museum of Art; New York: Harry N. Abrams, 1997), 210–23, 224–34; and Margret Kentgens-Craig, *The Bauhaus and America: First Contacts, 1919–1936* (Cambridge, Mass.: MIT Press, 1999), 92–103, 128–39.

28 Moholy-Nagy, "Sunday Session," 84; and Hahn, "Bauhaus and Exile," 220. For the most consistent expression of Mies as apolitical, see Franz Schulze, *Mies van der Rohe: A Critical Biography* (Chicago: University of Chicago Press, 1985), esp. 185–204. George Nelson, in "Architects of Europe Today, 7: Van Der Rohe, Germany," *Pencil Points* 16 (September 1935): 453–60, presents an early view of Mies's political inclinations.

29 A demonstrative example in the recent literature is Fritz Neumeyer, *The Artless Word: Mies van der Rohe on the Building Art*, orig. pub. 1986; trans. Mark Jarzombek (Cambridge, Mass.: MIT Press, 1991).

30 Philip Johnson, *Mies van der Rohe* (New York: Museum of Modern Art, 1947), 164.

31 Arthur Drexler, *Ludwig Mies van der Rohe*, Masters of World Architecture (New York: George Braziller, 1960), 25.

32 Werner Blaser, in *After Mies: Mies van der Rohe—Teaching and Principles* (New York: Van Nostrand Reinhold, 1977), 188, noted the identity of the preexisting photograph but glossed over its subject in commenting only that it provided Mies with a neutral ground to "investigate...the various possibilities

of enclosing the auditorium with [space-defining] screens," adding that the "rounded forms [of the Maillol sculpture] were intended [merely] as a foil to the angular architecture." Neumeyer, in *Artless Word*, 228, repeats this formalist interpretation in stating that "now the building withdrew to give way to space, reduced to the naked, engineered construction of a neutral frame that could be filled with changing contents." He concludes that the work should be read as a "demonstration" of "the possibilities of a new spatial freedom." Most recently, and despite its being part of a collection of essays specifically examining the impact of the war on American architecture, Peter S. Reed's "Enlisting Modernism," in *World War II and the American Dream*, ed. Donald Albrecht (Washington, D.C.: National Building Museum; Cambridge, Mass.: MIT Press, 1995), 4, 8, states that, "awed by the impressive size of the overarching steel structure, Mies chose a photograph of the Martin plant with planes in the background as the setting for his 1942 Concert Hall proposal, which elevated Kahn's factory aesthetics to the realm of pure Miesian universal space."

Reference to the specific Kahn photograph as the basis for Mies's design occurred first, as far as I have been able to determine, in A. James Speyer, *Mies van der Rohe* (Chicago: Art Institute of Chicago, 1968), 60; and Ludwig Glaeser, *Ludwig Mies van der Rohe: Drawings in the Collection of the Museum of Modern Art* (New York: Museum of Modern Art, 1969), note to pl. 29. The photograph was published side by side with the Mies project in Oswald W. Grube, *Industrial Buildings and Factories* (New York: Praeger, 1971), 24. While the caption correctly identifies the project as the Concert Hall, the Grube text instead refers to Mies's "famous study for a Chicago Convention Hall" (26). The first architectural historian to publish the photograph of the Kahn building and discuss the building's original purpose was William H. Jordy, in *American Buildings and Their Architects*, vol. 4, *The Impact of European Modernism in the Mid-Twentieth Century* (Garden City, N.Y.: Doubleday, 1972), 223–25.

33 Glaeser, *Mies: Drawings*, note to pls. 22–25; and Wolf Tegethoff, *Mies van der Rohe: The Villas and Country Houses*, orig. pub. 1981; trans. Russell M. Stockman (New York: Museum of Modern Art, 1985), 124–25. It is now generally accepted that, aside from the early Bismarck Monument project of 1910, where collage is used in a precubist manner, Mies did not use the technique again until coming to the United States.

34 For a survey of the subject of exile and emigration, with specific reference to Nazi Germany, see Barron with Eckmann, *Exiles + Emigrés*. For the particular context of Chicago, see Perry R. Duis and Scott La France, *We've Got a Job To Do: Chicagoans and World War II* (Chicago: Chicago Historical Society, 1992). Mies's collages are treated as a group in Penelope Curtis, *Patio and Pavilion: The Place of Sculpture in Modern Architecture* (London: Ridinghouse; Los Angeles: J. Paul Getty Museum, 2008), 59–75. Unfortunately, this appeared too late to have been of use to me.

35 On the Resor House, see Franz Schulze, ed., with George E. Danforth, consulting ed., *The Mies van der Rohe Archive: An Illustrated Catalogue of the Mies van der Rohe Drawings in the Museum of Modern Art*, part 2, *1938–1967: The American Work* (New York: Garland Publishing, 1992), vol. 7, *Resor House*; Tegethoff, *Mies*, 127–29; and McAtee, "Alien #5044325," 153–80.

36 It was Helen Resor who was the more involved with art and who was apparently the real client for the Mies project. She was a member of the board of trustees of the Museum of Modern Art and was very much a protégée of its director, Alfred H. Barr. See Nina Bremer, "The Resor House Project," January 19, 1976, Resor House Research File, Mies van der Rohe Archive, Museum of Modern Art, New York; and Marc Peter to [Nina] Bremer, November 30, 1975, Resor Ranch House—Correspondence with Marc Peter, Mies Archive, MoMA. According to Peter, Helen Resor "often told the story of horse riding near the future site and seeing a view of the mountains (Tetons, Grosventre, etc.) which could not be had from the window of an earth level house. So then and there she decided to have a living room on 'pilotis'" (Peter to Bremer, November 30, 1975). Stressing Helen Resor's role in the project, Peter went on to write:

> There also was some difference of approach between Mrs. and Mr. Resor. She was moved and interested by the architecture side of the problem, the opportunity of building a ranch in the modern vocabulary developed and exemplified by Wright, Corbusier, Mies. She was well informed, had studied and knew a good deal about current solutions, schools, individual styles and details. She told the story of sitting on the backstairs of her house in Greenwich while her german [*sic*] laundress translated texts and articles on or by Mies.
>
> I know she saw in the new building an opportunity to obtain maybe not a landmark but certainly a noteworthy example of modern architecture. . . .
>
> Mr. Resor, on the other hand[,] was quite candid about the necessity of being economical and seldom commented about the architectural aspect of the project. Moreover the existing ranch facilities were very comfortable, in fact luxurious, and so why change.

Marc Peter was known to the Resors through a family friend. He worked at the Wyoming site from mid-August through October 31, 1936. He continued working on the project until early January 1937.

37 McAtee, "Alien #5044325," 156–62. AIT had initiated contact with Mies as early as March 1936, but when Harvard showed interest soon thereafter, Mies declined the AIT offer. When the Harvard job went to Gropius the following year and AIT persisted, Mies finally accepted the AIT offer and took up his position in the fall of 1938.

38 [John Barney Rodgers], "Notes on House for Wyoming—Ogden," October 21, 1937, Resor House folder 3, Professional Papers, Mies Archive, MoMA.

39 No definitive date has yet been assigned to the collages, although 1939 seems the most likely. George Danforth, who worked on them in Mies's office in Chicago, told me they were done sometime between 1939 and 1941, suggesting that it was probably closer to the earlier date since they relate to the model produced in 1939 (in conversation, May 12, 1994). McAtee, "Alien #5044325,"

190 n. 112, reports that Danforth told her in May 2000 that they were made "in the late summer or fall of 1939." The 1939 date is further supported by events. The Resors met with Rodgers in New York on November 28, 1938, to clarify what had to be done to cut costs. The list of desiderata was translated into German and sent to Mies (Resor House folder 6, Professional Papers, Mies Archive, MoMA). Mies worked on the revisions from December 1938 to late March 1939, when he wrote to Stanley Resor, reporting that the "ranch house" was "completely refigured," and included a new set of specifications (Mies van der Rohe to Stanley Resor, March 25, 1939, Resor House folder 7, Professional Papers, Mies Archive, MoMA). It is this design that was presented in the collages.

40 Cohen, *Mies,* 79, interprets the use of the Klee detail as an expression of "nostalgia for a friend left behind in Europe" without, however, noting the painting's ownership by the Resors. The close-up view of the mountain with the couple on horseback makes one wonder whether Mies, like Marc Peter, was "told the story [by Helen Resor] of horse riding near the future site and seeing a view of the mountains...which could not be had from the window of an earth level house [and which]...then and there...decided [her] to have a living room on 'pilotis'" (Peter to Bremer, November 30, 1975).

41 Tegethoff, *Mies,* 128, describes the "distinctly pictorial quality" in terms of an "almost stagelike character."

42 Mies did produce a number of interior perspectives of the Resor House that show how the interior space would relate to the exterior. However, most of these are orthogonal views of the living/dining room that focus on the fireplace and only show the exterior mountain ranges peripherally.

43 Tegethoff, *Mies,* 129.

44 The relative chronology of these two projects has never been precisely determined. In the 1940s the Mies van der Rohe office gave the Museum for a Small City the project number 4201 and the Concert Hall the project number 4202. In the 1947 Mies exhibition organized by Philip Johnson at New York's Museum of Modern Art, both projects were dated 1942. In the book accompanying the exhibition, Johnson (*Mies,* 164) followed the office chronology in stating that "one of the museum's original features is the auditorium composed of free-standing partitions and an acoustical dropped ceiling" and "from this Mies has developed his most astounding new creation, the project for a concert hall." Schulze, in *Mies Archive,* part 2, vol. 13, *Cantor Drive-In Restaurant, Farnsworth House, and Other Buildings and Projects,* 76, simply remarks that the two projects were designed "in the same year"; but in his *Mies: Critical Biography,* 231, he follows Johnson in implying that the Concert Hall design grew out of the Museum's auditorium and thus is the later of the two. George Danforth, one of the two graduate students involved in the projects, told me that the Concert Hall was "probably a year after the Museum [for a Small City]" (in conversation, May 12, 1994). The most solidly based argument for placing the Museum after the Concert Hall rather than before it is given in Cammie McAtee, "Le 'Musée pour une petite ville' de Mies van der Rohe: Avant-texte ou avant-textes?" *Genesis: Manuscrits-Recherche-Invention* 14 (2000): 219–47.

George Danforth began studying ideas for his master's thesis on a museum in the spring of 1940 and continued to develop the project up through January 1943. According to McAtee, "'Le 'Musée,'" 233–40, Mies only became directly involved in the design process in 1942, when the idea of incorporating an auditorium surfaced. Paul Campagna, a classmate of Danforth's in the master's class of 1940–41, designed a concert hall for his thesis project based on a suggestion by Mies. His thesis was completed by the spring of that school year. Whereas Danforth has never taken any credit for the design of the published Museum for a Small City other than to claim a part in the execution of the collages, Campagna has suggested an important role for himself in the conceptualization and realization of the Concert Hall (see note 48 below). That being said, it is worth quoting from Franz Schulze's analysis of Mies's interaction with graduate students: "Mies very early established a habit of refining his own ideas through projects assigned to his students. To some extent he had done this with his charges at the German Bauhaus, but in Chicago the process accelerated and grew more varied....Thus it was that the Library and Administration Building developed out of a master's thesis by Daniel Brenner and the Museum for a Small City from a similar project by George Danforth. Mies oversaw all these activities, pointing the way to each of his students rather than following paths they had plotted. There is no doubt who the master was" (*Mies: Critical Biography,* 230).

45 Schulze, *Mies: Critical Biography,* 231–32.

46 Johnson, *Mies,* 164. For an exhibition in Chicago just prior to the MoMA show, Mies chose the Concert Hall as one of only sixteen projects to represent his work. See *An Exhibition of Architecture by Mies van der Rohe,* May 16–June 7, 1947 (Chicago: Renaissance Society at the University of Chicago, 1947), n.p.

47 As pointed out in note 32 above, the formalist interpretation of the project has predominated. Schulze, *Mies: Critical Biography,* 231–32, for instance, states: "One can imagine easily enough what Mies found to admire in [the Kahn Assembly Building]. It was an exercise in raw structure...clearly indicative of the unique capacity of modern engineering in steel to enclose a stupendous space....Using his familiar collage-montage technique, [Mies] proposed...to define a space within the larger space, where groups of people could attend musical performances....The...yawning hall in which all this took place prefigured the vast emptiness and spatial stasis that characterized his later American works." More recently, however, Cohen, *Mies,* 84, has suggested that Mies's use of the Kahn photograph "might be read as an adherence to the American war effort," but then demurred: "It reveals rather, in my view, the impact of the great works of engineers, much as the publications of the Werkbund had made them available before 1914 and the importance of which—real as well as metaphoric—Mies discovered along with its potential for his own production."

48 George Nelson, *Industrial Architecture of Albert Kahn, Inc.* (New York: Architectural Book Publishing, 1939), 38. Much of the

material in this book was published the previous year in "Albert Kahn," *Architectural Forum* 69 (August 1938): 87–142, although the photograph of the interior in question was not included. Mies owned a copy of the Nelson monograph, which is now in the Mies van der Rohe Collection, #240656, Special Collections, University of Illinois at Chicago. I am grateful to Tom Beeby for bringing to my attention the existence of the Nelson book in Mies's personal library and to Patricia Bakunas for providing me with access to it. Based on the amount of space visible on the right of the Mies collage, however, it appears that Mies used an original photograph rather than a copy made from the Nelson book.

Jordy, in *American Buildings,* 4:223–25, reports that Myron Goldsmith, a former student of Mies, told him "that Mies was much interested in a publication in 1939 of the factories of the Detroit architect-engineer Albert Kahn. A photograph of the Glenn Martin bomber plant from this volume provided the background on which Mies pasted planes (geometrical rather than aeronautical in this instance) to create a project for a concert hall." Paul Campagna, on the other hand, whom many credit with bringing the photograph to Mies's attention while he was working on an auditorium project for his master's thesis in 1941 (see note 44 above), told me that he found the image in *Architectural Forum* (in conversation, May 16, 1994). Since the image Mies used did not appear in the *Forum,* either Campagna used a different one in his project or he misremembered the source. A few years after my conversation with him, he told Cammie McAtee that he found it in a recently published book on Albert Kahn (telephone conversation, March 31, 1999). I am grateful to McAtee for providing me with her notes from that conversation.

Paul Campagna entered the graduate program at IIT in the fall of 1940 and received his master's degree at the end of the academic year. Mies apparently first suggested to him that he design a house for his thesis project, and Campagna began work on that (this and most of the following information was provided to me by Campagna in conversation, May 16, 1994). Soon thereafter, Mies said he thought Campagna should do a "big job...a concert hall or a theater." Campagna came up with three *partis,* one of which was a large "undifferentiated space" (Campagna told McAtee, March 31, 1999, that it was Mies who suggested the three different approaches). Although he had not thought of an industrial building as a model, Campagna said Mies told him to "look in magazines for big industrial spaces, like an airplane hangar." The one that Campagna said "looked the best to me was [the] Glenn Martin plant." (Campagna, whose parents lived in Washington, D.C., said he immediately recognized the building because he had visited it and knew a lot about Kahn's work.) Mies liked the choice and told his student to have it blown up to six feet across. According to McAtee, Mies then told him "to cut paper to make a room" (ibid). For the rear of the stage, Mies advised the use of gold foil, which Campagna recouped from a Japanese screen (he told McAtee the two of them decided against using the gold since the screen was very old). Campagna remembers that his rear stage wall was flat, not curved, as it was in Mies's Concert Hall (where it was gray in color). Finally, Campagna's project had no sculpture. In trying to recall the original Kahn photograph, Campagna maintained that the space "was devoid of airplanes." On the other hand, he claimed that when he saw the reproduction of the Concert Hall for the first time in Johnson's Mies book of 1947, he thought the collage "was his own"; yet he admitted that Mies "added to his" in certain ways. McAtee reports that, in any event, Campagna felt "Mies was really doing the project" all along (ibid.).

It is clear that Campagna's design was not simply appropriated by Mies. And since the Campagna design was never published and apparently no longer exists, we will never be able to compare it with Mies's. It is also pure speculation as to whether Campagna independently hit upon the Kahn photograph or Mies planted the idea in Campagna's mind in telling him to look for something like "an airplane hangar." Finally, even in the unlikely event that Mies had learned of the Kahn image from Campagna, we can hardly assume that Mies also saw in the photograph, as Campagna did, simply a large industrial space "devoid of airplanes."

It should also be noted that the name of the Kahn building in question is the Glenn Martin Assembly Building and not the Glenn Martin Bomber Plant, as it so often appears in the literature.

49 "Month of the Mars...Colossus Nearly Ready," *Martin Star* 1 (April 1942): 4. The in-house *Martin Star,* which began publication in February 1942, provides valuable information on the company's products and activities. See also *Box Kites to Bombers: The Story of the Glenn L. Martin Company, Baltimore, U.S.A.* (Baltimore: Martin Company, n.d.).

50 In one of the rare references we have to any direct comments by Mies about the war, and particularly the bombing of Germany by Allied aircraft, former student Edward Duckett remembered the following:

> During World War II the Allies were pattern bombing Germany....Ed Olencki and I were going into the school office one morning and Mies's secretary, Marta Moeller, was...crying. Mies had just arrived and she had not gotten to tell us why she was crying so we asked her what was wrong. Anyway, it turned out her parents were still in Germany, in Dresden I believe....She was looking at the newspaper and...the headlines said "Hundreds of Bombers Destroy Dresden." So she told Mies, "They are destroying my country and I'm worried about my parents," and I remember Mies looked at her and he said, "That has to be done. Society cannot tolerate such a leader as Hitler." And he repeated it. He said, "You can't have an animal like Hitler loose in the world and if it means annihilating Germany in order to accomplish that; then that's what has to be done." That was a dramatic thing to me and to Ed because here he was talking about his own country. (*Impressions of Mies: An Interview on Mies van der Rohe, His Early Years, 1938–1958,* ed. William S. Shell, with former students and associates Edward A. Duckett and Joseph Y. Fujikawa [n.p., 1988])

The relationship between Albert Kahn's work and the American war effort was clearly drawn, at the very time Mies was working on the collage, in "Albert Kahn, Architect: Producer of Production Lines" and "Architecture for War Production," *Architectural Record* 91 (June 1942): 39–52.

51 The Concert Hall collage no longer exists in the state Mies left it. Mary Callery, to whom he gave it as a gift around 1947, later replaced the image of the Maillol sculpture with one of an Old Kingdom *Egyptian Scribe*. Mies's early employer Peter Behrens used the same Maillol sculpture in the room he designed for the Mannheim International Art Exhibition of 1907.

52 Following his purely formalist interpretation of the Concert Hall as a study of "the possibilities of an auditorium defined by various independent [geometric] planes within a much larger space," Speyer (*Mies*, 60) states that "the superimposed Maillol sculpture shows the effect of a rounded form set within the space," a remark repeated in Blaser, *After Mies*, 188 (see note 32 above). Schulze, in *Mies: Critical Biography*, 232–33, does not mention the sculpture, but in *Mies Archive*, part 2, 13:76, he states, without noting the identity of the Maillol, that "a photograph of *a* sculpture was added in the foreground to indicate scale" [italics added].

53 McAtee, "Le 'Musée'"; and "New Buildings for 194X," *Architectural Forum* 78 (May 1943): 84–85 (includes project description by Mies). The published collages were prepared with the assistance of George Danforth. The project was chosen by Mies, along with the Concert Hall, for the 1947 Renaissance Society exhibition in Chicago referred to in note 46 above.

54 "New Buildings for 194X," 84. Mies prefaced this by commenting that "a work such as Picasso's *Guernica* has been difficult to place in the usual museum gallery."

55 Typical of such formalist interpretations are the following:

> The exhibiting of Pablo Picasso's "Guernica" has always presented a problem. . . . Mies van der Rohe, however, proposed a simple and most effective solution. In his study for the Museum for a small city, . . . he made of Picasso's painting a free-standing wall. As such, the painting is isolated from its surroundings to its own benefit, but at the same time it is strongly united with the building as a legitimate architectural element (Ludwig Hilberseimer, *Mies van der Rohe* [Chicago: Paul Theobold, 1956], 46).
>
> This project for an exhibition hall [*sic*] was the upshot of studies concerned with concrete art [i.e., painting and sculpture] and of reflections on the problems of integrating it in space. (Werner Blaser, *Mies van der Rohe: Less Is More* [Zurich: Waser, 1986], 180)

Neither in Schulze, *Mies Archive*, part 2, 13:68, nor in Schulze, *Mies: Critical Biography*, 230–31, where the Museum is discussed, is there a mention of the Picasso painting. Neumeyer, *Artless Word*, 228, also avoids mentioning the painting by name. Two conspicuous exceptions to this purely formalist reading are Tegethoff, *Mies*, 128, where it is noted that, as a result of the effects of the collage technique, "the dramatic events in Picasso's *Guernica* appear to be incomparably intensified"; and Cohen, *Mies*, 84, where it is noted that "the most striking part [of the Museum] is a reproduction of Picasso's *Guernica*, an evocation of the savagery of the Nazi war." I thank Andrew Phillips for stressing the importance of the subject matter of Picasso's painting of *Guernica* in a seminar he took with me at Harvard.

56 On the history and reception of the painting, see Ellen C. Oppler, ed., *Picasso's Guernica: Illustrations, Introductory Essay, Documents, Poetry, Criticism, Analysis*, Norton Critical Studies in Art History (New York: W. W. Norton, 1988); Herschel B. Chipp, *Guernica: History, Transformations, Meanings* (Berkeley: University of California Press, 1988); and Meyer Schapiro, "Guernica: Sources, Changes," *The Unity of Picasso's Art* (New York; George Braziller, 2000), 150–93.

57 Mies was in Paris from at least July 8 through July 12, 1937. He returned again on August 12, coming from Aachen on his way to New York, where he landed on August 20. The 1937 World's Fair in Paris was supposed to open on May 1 but was delayed until May 24. Picasso began the painting of *Guernica* two days after hearing the news of the bombing and completed the work by the end of the first week of June. Although the painting was installed shortly thereafter, the Spanish Pavilion did not officially open to the public until July 12.

58 The exhibition at the Arts Club of Chicago, in the Wrigley Tower, opened on October 3, 1939. On this occasion, the critic C. J. Bulliet wrote in the *Chicago Herald-American*, October 4, 1939: "Here, instead of being a lofty adventure in pure and cold form, as is his custom [Picasso] was frankly a 'propagandist' doing his level best to express all the indignities of his soul against the rape of Guernica and the horrors of war generally." The exhibition at the Museum of Modern Art, entitled "Picasso—40 Years of His Art," opened less than two months after the outbreak of war in Europe and ran from November 15, 1939, through January 17, 1940. Its Chicago stay at the Art Institute lasted from February 1 through March 3, 1940. See Frederick A. Sweet, "Picasso—Forty Years of His Art," *Bulletin of the Art Institute of Chicago* 34 (February 1940): 22–24.

59 For an analysis of Maillol's activities during World War II, see Michèle C. Cone, *Artists under Vichy: A Case of Prejudice and Persecution* (Princeton, N.J.: Princeton University Press, 1992).

60 Schulze, *Mies Archive*, part 2, 7:2, and 13:68, 76; and Neumeyer, *Artless Word*, 227–28. On a more mundane level, one could point to the similarity between the factory designs of Albert Kahn, such as his General Motors Diesel Engine Division Plant in Redford, Michigan (1937), and Mies's earliest structures at IIT, such as the Minerals and Metals Research Building (1941–43; see fig. I.2). Grube, in *Industrial Buildings*, 34, notes, with specific reference to illustrations of works by Albert Kahn, that "the first buildings erected by Mies van der Rohe in the United States . . . reflect the expression of the industrial complexes built in America in the preceding decade . . . and opened the eyes to the importance of that previously anonymous architecture."

61 As Jordy, in *American Buildings*, 4:240–41, points out, there are two types of standard steel beams with an I-shaped section. The type most generally used in building construction has wide flanges, producing nearly an H section, and is correctly called a wide-flange beam. The type with narrow flanges is the only one, technically speaking, that should be called an I-beam. Jordy decided, as is the case with most of the literature on Mies, not to make this distinction and to call all the I-shaped beams "I-beams." I shall follow suit wherever the distinction seems unnecessarily technical.

62 "Mies van der Rohe," *Architectural Forum* 97 (May 1952): 99.

63 Mies explained, in ibid., that the "good reason" for the attached I-beams in the Lake Shore Drive towers was "to stiffen the plate which covers the corner column so this plate would not ripple, and also we needed it for strength when the sections [of horizontal plates and attached vertical mullions] were hoisted into place." The "real reason," however, was "to preserve and extend the rhythm which the mullions set up on the rest of the building."

64 In the original Resor House project, the cruciform-shaped steel columns were to have been encased in sheet bronze. For reasons of economy, the 1939 version eliminated the bronze and substituted paint.

65 Mies's move from the cruciform-shaped column to the I-shaped section occurred in early 1942, while he was developing the working drawings for the Minerals and Metals Research Building (see fig. I.2). According to Phyllis Lambert, "Mies Immersion," in *Mies in America*, 287–89, the original design for the first building to be constructed at IIT had cruciform-shaped columns, and these were only changed to those with I-sections sometime in early 1942, which coincides with Mies's design for the Concert Hall.

66 Robert Venturi, *Complexity and Contradiction in Architecture*, Museum of Modern Art Papers on Architecture 1 (New York: Museum of Modern Art, 1966), 45. This comment was made as part of a general discussion of "the ['rhetorical'] function of ornament." After remarking on the "use of Baroque pilasters for rhythm," Venturi noted that "Mies used the rhetorical I-beam with an assurance that would make Bernini envious" (ibid.).

67 Jordy, *American Buildings*, 4:247, 262. See also his "Seagram Assessed," *Architectural Review* 124 (December 1958); repr. in W. H. Jordy, *"Symbolic Essence" and Other Writings on Modern Architecture and American Culture*, ed. Mardges Bacon (New Haven, Conn.: Yale University Press, 2005), esp. 231–34. The article on Mies in the *Architectural Forum* of May 1952 cited in note 62 above already remarked that the attached I-beams "have been called pilasters, usually by people who do not like pilasters" (99).

68 Jordy, *American Buildings*, 4:243. In emphasizing the classical reference, Jordy was following an interpretation of Mies that others such as Philip Johnson, Vincent Scully, and Colin Rowe had helped establish by the late 1950s. According to Bernard Goodman, a student at IIT, Frank Lloyd Wright said the following to Mies on seeing the plans for the IIT Library and Administration Building in 1944: "You know what you've done? You have invented a new classicism." David A. Spaeth, *Mies van der Rohe* (New York: Rizzoli, 1985), 132). Schulze, in *Mies: Critical Biography*, 226, 243, writes that "the attached I-beam," which, already at Alumni Memorial Hall at IIT, "is not fact but symbol of fact," "had become [at North Lake Shore Drive] a prime symbol for the transcendence of technology into architecture, prose into poetry. The I-beam, that is to say, took on decorative significance." George Danforth, in Schulze, *Mies Archive*, part 2, vol. 10, *IIT*, vol. 3, *Alumni Memorial Hall, Field House Building, Gymnasium, Natatorium, and Other Buildings*, 2, acknowledged that "the curtain wall" of Alumni Memorial Hall "became a secondary structure, one that nonetheless symbolized the building's structural frame."

69 Thomas Beeby, "The Grammar of Ornament / Ornament as Grammar," *Via: The Journal of the Graduate School of Fine Arts, University of Pennsylvania* 3 (1977): 26. Kenneth Frampton, *Studies in Tectonic Culture: The Poetics of Construction in Nineteenth and Twentieth Century Architecture*, ed. John Cava (Cambridge, Mass.: MIT Press, 1995), 191, on the other hand, takes a more narrowly focused position that views the mullion/curtain wall separately from the steel plate to which it is attached. He mentions the "representative steel profiles...of the fireproofed steel within" at the IIT buildings but maintains that only "the steel facing and angles [at the corners]" should be considered as "representing the [hidden] column." The attached "I-sections that formed the receiving frame for the...brick...infill walls spanning between the uprights of the framework" should not be thought of as part of the representational construct. Similarly, in the North Lake Shore Drive Apartments, "the columns and beams [of the fireproofed steel frame] are represented by plated surfaces implanted on the outside of the fireproofed structure," whereas "the secondary framing system of the mullions, carrying the fenestration, is mounted on these steel plates, thereby rendering the overall assembly as a continuous curtain wall."

70 Jordy, *American Buildings*, 4:243–44.

71 Mies used the phrase "Truth is the significance of facts," paraphrasing Thomas Aquinas, in his acceptance speech on receiving the Gold Medal of the American Institute of Architects in 1960 (quoted in ibid., 4:221).

72 While describing the attached I-beams of his buildings as an aspect of "structure," Mies, in "Mies van der Rohe," 94, felt compelled to point out to the editors of *Architectural Forum* that "we are not decorating."

73 Clement Greenberg, "After Abstract Expressionism," *Art International*, October 25, 1962; repr. in *Clement Greenberg: The Collected Essays and Criticism*, ed. John O'Brian, vol. 4, *Modernism with a Vengeance, 1957–69* (Chicago: University of Chicago Press, 1993), 127. See chapter 6 for Wright and Analytic Cubism, which Greenberg saw as the origin of "homeless representation" in its "way of depicting objects in planar segments kept parallel to the picture plane that ended up by effacing the objects themselves."

74 Interestingly, Tafuri and Dal Co, in *Modern Architecture*, 342, compared Mies's later Federal Court Building in Chicago to "a Pop Art sculpture that obliges the American metropolis to look at itself reflected . . . in the neutral mirror that breaks the city web." One might trace this Pop interpretation to Robert Venturi, who in *Complexity and Contradiction*, 50, described "latter-day Mies [as] employ[ing] the structural elements of vernacular American industrial architecture . . . with unconscious irony." For a different reading of Mies's later work, yet one that similarly sets up a relation to Pop Art, see K. Michael Hays, "Odysseus and the Oarsmen, or, Mies's Abstraction Once Again," in *The Presence of Mies*, ed. Detlef Mertins (New York: Princeton Architectural Press, 1994), 234–48; and K. M. Hays, "Abstraction's Appearance (Seagram Building)," in *Autonomy and Ideology: Positioning an Avant-Garde in America*, ed. R. E. Somol (New York: Monacelli Press, 1997), 278–91.

75 Mies van der Rohe, "Architecture and Technology," *Arts and Architecture* 67, no. 10 (1950); repr. in Neumeyer, *Artless Word*, 324.

76 Mies van der Rohe, "Building Art of Our Time (My Professional Career)," orig. pub. with slightly different wording in Werner Blaser, *Mies van der Rohe: The Art of Structure*, trans. D. Q. Stephenson (New York: Praeger, 1965), 6; repr. in Neumeyer, *Artless Word*, 336.

77 Mies van der Rohe, undated lecture, in Neumeyer, *Artless Word*, 325. For another reading of Mies's view of the relation between architecture and technology, see Fritz Neumeyer, "A World in Itself: Architecture and Technology," in Mertins, *Presence of Mies*, 71–83.

78 Mies van der Rohe, undated lecture, in Neumeyer, *Artless Word*, 325.

79 Without referring specifically to the war and its effect on the growth of American industrial prowess, Jordy, in *American Buildings*, 4:243, wrote: "Symbolically, finally, the I-beams not only record the technology, but celebrate it. . . . As specifically 'modern' objects, bluntly accepted for what they are, the I-beams intensify our awareness that the building belongs to our time." Cohen, in *Mies*, 87, describes IIT at the time Mies began teaching and building there as "an institution dominated by research centers financed by industry and the military establishment." Although he adds that it "became extremely prosperous due to the abundantly subsidized industrial and military research," he does not relate this context to the expressive meaning or significance of the architecture Mies developed in it.

Chapter 8. The Aesthetic of the Unfinished and the Example of Louis Kahn

1 Friedrich Schlegel, *Dialogue on Poetry and Literary Aphorisms*, orig. pub. 1798; trans. and ed. Ernst Behler and Roman Struc (University Park: Pennsylvania State University Press, 1968), 134.

2 Thomas McFarland, *Romanticism and the Forms of Ruin: Wordsworth, Coleridge, and Modalities of Fragmentation* (Princeton, N.J.: Princeton University Press, 1981), esp. 3–55. See also Christoph Meckel, *Über das Fragmentarische* (Mainz: Akademie der Wissenschaften und der Literatur, F. Steiner, 1978); Musée d'Orsay, Paris, and Schirn Kunsthalle, Frankfurt, *Le Corps en morceaux* (Paris: Ministère de la Culture, de la Communication, des Grands Travaux et du Bicentenaire; Réunion des Musées Nationaux, 1990); Elizabeth Wanning Harries, *The Unfinished Manner: Essays on the Fragment in the Later Eighteenth Century* (Charlottesville: University Press of Virginia, 1994); and Barry Bergdoll and Werner Oechslin, eds., *Fragments: Architecture and the Unfinished: Essays Presented to Robin Middleton* (London: Thames & Hudson, 2006).

3 John W. Cook and Heinrich Klotz, eds., *Conversations with Architects* (New York: Praeger, 1973), 183.

4 Kahn first described the light-diffusing screen walls of his project for the American Consulate at Luanda, Angola (1959–62), in this way in "Kahn," a recording of a discussion in Kahn's office in February 1961, *Perspecta: The Yale Architectural Journal* 7 (1961); repr. in *Louis I. Kahn: Writings, Lectures, Interviews*, ed. Alessandra Latour (New York: Rizzoli, 1991), 123. In the first monograph on the architect, Vincent Scully, *Louis I. Kahn*, Makers of Contemporary Architecture (New York: George Braziller, 1962), 36, quoted this statement and established the precedent for interpreting Kahn's work in terms of the ruin.

5 Louis Kahn, "Architecture and Human Agreement," lecture, University of Virginia, Charlottesville, April 1972; repr. in *What Will Be Has Always Been: The Words of Louis I. Kahn*, ed. Richard Saul Wurman (New York: Access, Rizzoli, 1986), 138; and Louis Kahn, "I Love Beginnings," speech, International Design Conference, Aspen, Colo., 1972; in *Kahn: Writings*, 286.

6 Louis Kahn, "Architecture: Silence and Light," orig. pub. in Arnold Toynbee et al., *On the Future of Art*, 1970; repr. in *Kahn: Writings*, 248. Another iteration appears in Louis Kahn, "The Room, the Street, and Human Agreement," *AIA Journal* 56 (September 1971); repr. in *Kahn: Writings*, 268.

7 In a number of early interviews, Frank Gehry reiterated Kahn's idea regarding the value of the unfinished. In Barbaralee Diamonstein, *American Architecture Now* (New York: Rizzoli, 1980), 36, he is quoted as saying: "We all like buildings in construction better than we do finished. . . . The structure is always so much more poetic than the finished thing." And in Peter Arnell and Ted Bickford, eds., *Frank Gehry: Buildings and Projects* (New York: Rizzoli, 1985), xii, he remarked: "Buildings under construction look nicer than buildings finished. . . . Buildings that are just done by ordinary people—they look like hell when they're finished—but when they're under construction they look great."

8 On the general issue of the unfinished, see Claude Lorin, *L'Inachevé: Peinture, sculpture, littérature* (Paris: B. Grasset, 1984); and Annie Rivara and Guy Lavorel, eds., *L'Oeuvre inachevée: Actes du colloque international (11 et 12 décembre 1998)* (Lyon: Aprime, 1999). Neither has anything significant to say about architecture, however.

9 David Summers, *Michelangelo and the Language of Art* (Princeton, N.J.: Princeton University Press, 1981), esp. chap. 13; and Maria Teresa Fiorio, "Broken Sculpture:

Michelangelo and the Aesthetic of the Fragment," in *The Genius of the Sculptor in Michelangelo's Work*, ed. Pierre Théberge (Montreal: Montreal Museum of Fine Arts, 1992), 75.

10 Giorgio Vasari, *The Lives of the Artists*, orig. pub. 1550–68 as *Le vite de' più eccellenti architetti, pittori, et scultori italiani, da Cimabue insino a' tempi nostri;* trans. Julia Conaway Bondanella and Peter Bondanella (Oxford: Oxford University Press, 1991), 472. Vasari comments at one point that the sculptor refused to go on with a work once he noticed any sort of imperfection in the marble he was carving. At another, he writes that Michelangelo's perfectionism had more to do with a "distinctive and perfect imagination" that "envisioned" works "of such a nature" as to make it "impossible to express such grandiose and awesome conceptions with his hands" (ibid.). And at yet another, he declares that even when "various parts" of a sculpture "were unfinished, what is left roughed out and full of chisel marks reveals, in its incomplete state, the perfection of the work" (ibid., 455). Cf. Leonard Barkan, *Unearthing the Past: Archaeology and Aesthetics in the Making of Renaissance Culture* (New Haven, Conn.: Yale University Press, 1999), 207.

11 Paola Barocchi, "Finito e non-finito nella critica vasariana," *Arte Antica e Moderna: Rivista degli Istituti di Archeologia e di Storia dell'arte dell'Università di Bologna e dei Musei del Commune di Bologna* 3 (July–September 1958): 221–35. Cf. Renato Bonelli, "Michelangelo e il non-finito," in *Atti del Convegno di studi michelangioleschi* (Rome: Edizioni dell'Ateneo, 1966), 403–16; Teddy Brunius, "Michelangelo's non finito," *Figura (Contributions to the History and Theory of Art)*, n.s., 6 (1967): 29–67; Juergen Schulz, "Michelangelo's Unfinished Works," *Art Bulletin* 57 (September 1975): 366–73; and Barkan, *Unearthing the Past*, 204–7.

12 See Charles Rosen and Henri Zerner, *Romanticism and Realism: The Mythology of Nineteenth-Century Art* (New York: Viking, 1984), 205–32.

13 Ibid., 226–27; and Wendelin A. Guenter, "British Aesthetic Discourse, 1780–1830: The Sketch, the *Non Finito*, and the Imagination," *Art Journal* (Summer 1993): 40–47. Delacroix wrote that "one cannot finish a painting without spoiling it a little. The final touches, which are supposed to put different parts in harmony with each other, take away some of the work's freshness." Quoted in Françoise Viatte, "Weaving a Rope of Sand," *Drafters: Yale French Studies* 89 (1996): 85–102. For earlier interest in the sketch, see Philip L[indsay] Sohm, *Pittoresco: Marco Boschini, His Critics, and Their Critique of Painterly Brushwork in Seventeenth- and Eighteenth-Century Italy* (New York: Cambridge University Press, 1991). I owe the last reference to Alina Payne.

14 See Felix Baumann, ed., *Cézanne: Finished, Unfinished* (Ostfildern-Ruit, Germany: Hatje Cantz, 2000).

15 In a three-day panel discussion of radical New York artists held in Greenwich Village in 1950 for the purpose of defining what they were doing and what ideas and methodologies they held in common, almost the entire first day was devoted to the subject of finish, or the lack thereof, and the impossibility of determining what it might be in contemporary art. Willem de Kooning said that he "refrain[ed] from 'finishing'" his paintings, while Ad Reinhardt noted that "'finishing' paintings" was always "a problem for [him]" and that, anyway, "among modern artists there is a value placed upon 'unfinished' work." Barnett Newman said he thought that "the idea of a 'finished' picture is a fiction." Robert Goodnough, ed., "Artists' Sessions at Studio 35 (1950)," *Modern Artists in America*, Robert Motherwell and Ad Reinhardt, gen. eds., 1st ser. (New York: Wittenborn Schultz, 1949–50), 11–13. I thank my former colleague Yve-Alain Bois for reminding me of this event and its publication. Umberto Eco's *Opera aperta* (*The Open Work*), published in 1962, can be read as both summarizing this moment and predicting certain aspects of later art that would develop from its premises.

16 For a discussion of the drawing in the context of the bank as a whole, see Daniel Abramson, "The Bank of England," in *John Soane, Architect: Master of Space and Light*, ed. Margaret Richardson and MaryAnne Stevens (London: Royal Academy of Arts, 1999), 208–51; and D. M. Abramson, *Building the Bank of England: Money, Architecture, Society, 1694–1942* (New Haven, Conn.: Yale University Press, 2005), 193–96. Abramson, *Building the Bank*, 265 n. 93, points out that John Summerson, in *The Architecture of the Eighteenth Century* (London: Thames & Hudson, 1986), 146–47, was the first to suggest that the Gandy drawing shows the building in construction rather than as a ruin.

17 One of these drawings (fig. 8.7) appears on the cover of Frédéric Seitz, *L'Ecole spéciale d'architecture, 1865–1930: Une entreprise d'idée* (Paris: Picard, 1995). Lithographs of the drawings exist in the library of the Ecole Spéciale d'Architecture and in the Médiatheque de l'Architecture et du Patrimoine, Paris. They were published in black and white in Eugène-Emmanuel Viollet-le-Duc, *Compositions et dessins de Viollet-le-Duc* (Paris: Librairie centrale d'architecture, 1884).

18 Eugène-Emmanuel Viollet-le-Duc, in *Lectures on Architecture*, 2 vols., trans. Benjamin Bucknall (1877–81; repr., New York: Dover Publications, 1987), 1:271, stated that Roman buildings are much better seen in their ruined state than as finished and decorated. For Viollet-le-Duc's comments on the incongruous decoration of Roman buildings, see chapter 5.

19 See H[endrik] P[etrus] Berlage, "Neuere amerikanische Architektur," *Schweizerische Bauzeitung* 60 (September 14, 21, and 28, 1912), 148–150, 165–66, 178; trans. in *The Literature of Architecture: The Evolution of Architectural Theory and Practice in Nineteenth-Century America*, ed. Don Gifford (New York: E. P. Dutton, 1966), 611–15; and H. P. Berlage, *Amerikaanische Reisherinneringen* (Rotterdam: W. L. & J. Brusse, 1913), 35–48.

20 Montgomery Schuyler, "An Architectural Pioneer: Review of the Portfolios Containing the Works of Frank Lloyd Wright," *Architectural Record* 31 (April 1912); repr. in Montgomery Schuyler, *American Architecture*

and Other Writings, ed. William H. Jordy and Ralph Coe, 2 vols. (Cambridge, Mass.: Harvard University Press, Belknap Press, 1961), 2:640.

21 Frank Lloyd Wright, "In the Cause of Architecture," *Architectural Record* 23 (March 1908); repr. in *Frank Lloyd Wright: Collected Writings*, ed. Bruce Brooks Pfeiffer, 5 vols. (New York: Rizzoli, 1992–95), vol. 1: *1894–1930* (1992): 87.

22 C[harles] R[obert] Ashbee, "Frank Lloyd Wright: A Study and an Appreciation," orig. pub. 1911 (in German) in *Frank Lloyd Wright: Ausgeführte Bauten;* repr. (in English) in *Frank Lloyd Wright: The Early Work* (New York: Horizon Press, 1968), 8.

23 See, for example, Frank Lloyd Wright, "The Art and Craft of the Machine," *Catalogue of the Fourteenth Annual Exhibition of the Chicago Architectural Club*, 1901; repr. in *Wright: Collected Writings*, 1:58–69.

24 Alfred H. Barr et al., *Modern Architecture: International Exhibition*, February 10–March 23, 1932 (New York: Museum of Modern Art, 1932), 15. Walter Curt Behrendt, in *Modern Building: Its Nature, Problems, and Forms* (New York: Harcourt, Brace, 1937), 174, repeated this idea, stating that "modern building, since it relies on the work of machine and industrial technique rather than on the work of craftsmen, cannot have ornament. But what it loses in this respect, it regains many fold by the charm and expressiveness inherent in its refined materials, the exactitude of its technique, and the precision of its forms."

A story related in Valerie Fraser, *Building the New World: Studies in the Modern Architecture of Latin America, 1930–1960* (London: Verso, 2000), 166, points up the relationship perceived at the time between modern abstraction and the lack of finish. When Gregori Warchavchik, a Russian émigré, built the first modern house in Brazil, in Vila Mariana in São Paulo in 1927–28, he had to resort to a ruse to circumvent local regulations: "From the street the house has the appearance of a very symmetrical cubic design with flat white walls and simple, metal-framed windows. In order to get the plans accepted by the São Paulo city authorities the drawings Warchavchik submitted included traditional architectural mouldings around the door and windows, and a cornice across the top of the façade. When he built the house he included none of these, on the grounds that he had run out of money, leaving the house officially unfinished but in fact strikingly modern in appearance."

25 Le Corbusier had used exposed reinforced concrete prior to World War II for the supporting structure of the main slab of the Swiss Pavilion at the Cité Universitaire in Paris (1930–32).

26 Reyner Banham, *The New Brutalism: Ethic or Aesthetic?* Documents of Modern Architecture (New York: Reinhold, 1966), 16.

27 Quotation in Scully, *Kahn*, 15.

28 Vincent Scully, "Works of Louis Kahn and His Method," in *Louis I. Kahn: Sono zenbo*, ed. Toshio Nakamura, special issue of *A+U: Architecture and Urbanism* (Tokyo, 1975), 290.

29 Vincent Scully, "Louis I. Kahn and the Ruins of Rome," *MoMA: The Members Quarterly of the Museum of Modern Art* 12 (Summer 1992); repr. in *Modern Architecture and Other Essays*, ed. Neil Levine (Princeton, N. J.: Princeton University Press, 2003), 298–319.

30 Scully, *Kahn*, 36.

31 Sarah Williams Goldhagen, *Louis Kahn's Situated Modernism* (New Haven, Conn.: Yale University Press, 2001), 52.

32 A similar comparison could also be made to Le Corbusier's Swiss Pavilion at the Cité Universitaire in Paris, where the cast-stone panels of the ends of the dormitory slab provide a sense of closure and completeness.

33 According to Patricia Cummings Loud, *The Art Museums of Louis I. Kahn* (Durham, N.C.: Duke University Press, 1989), 54, Kahn received word of the Yale commission while in Rome. Knowing the New Haven site well, he no doubt began thinking about the project before returning to the United States. Kahn had applied to become a fellow of the Academy as early as the spring of 1947 but was rejected at that time. The appointment as resident was to have started in October. In his 1947 letter of application, Kahn gave the following reasons for wanting to spend time in Rome:

> I should consider work in Rome…as the opportunity I have looked for to develope [*sic*] thoughts I have on architecture of to-day. These thoughts are about the frames and enclosures of new architectural spaces, their effect and relation to painting, sculpture and the crafts, their significance to the people and their place in the continuing evolution of traditional forms.
>
> I believe that living in the environment of the great planning and building works of the past should stimulate better judgement in maturing these thoughts. (Kahn to American Academy in Rome, April 25, 1947, Box LIK 61, Louis I. Kahn Collection, University of Pennsylvania and Pennsylvania Historical and Museum Commission [hereafter cited as Kahn Collection])

34 Kahn to office staff, n.d. [February 1951]; Kahn to office staff, n.d. [January 1951]; Kahn to office staff, n.d. [ca. January 1, 1951], Box LIK 60; and Kahn to Dave [Wisdom], Anne [Tyng], and others, December 6, 1960, "Rome 1951," Boxes LIK 60–61, Kahn Collection.

35 Susan Braudy, "The Architectural Metaphysic of Louis Kahn," *New York Times Magazine*, November 15, 1970, 86. In recounting this moment of self-discovery, Kahn was specifically referring to the Bath House, the first of the two parts of the project that were built. For an account of Kahn's relationship with the Jewish community in the Philadelphia–New Jersey area and of the commission for the Trenton Community Center, see Susan G. Solomon, *Louis Kahn's Trenton Jewish Community Center*, Building Studies 6 (New York: Princeton Architectural Press, 2000). My own analysis of the Trenton project derives from a site visit in February 1982, the findings of which were first presented in a lecture, "Postmodern History Volume Zero: Louis Kahn's Trenton Bath House and Day Camp," at the University of North Carolina, Charlotte, later that spring.

36 Denise Scott-Brown, in "A Worm's Eye View of Recent Architectural History," *Architectural Record* 172 (February 1984):

71–72, states that "When I reached Penn in late 1958,...Kahn was deeply involved in historical architecture. His students would sit around him in the library looking at Roman plans from the rare book collection." Scott-Brown gives much of the credit for this involvement to Robert Venturi: "On his return [from Rome] in 1956, Bob [Venturi] worked for Kahn for nine months. At the same time he was Lou's teaching assistant at Penn. In 1957 Bob left Kahn's office to start his own practice. He and Kahn were on the faculty at Penn and maintained the friendship that was cemented when Bob returned from Rome. They talked a great deal. Bob was often in Lou's office to give crits. He shared his recent experience in Rome with the older architect and it is probably from these talks that Lou's real interest in history as source material dates. . . ." (73).

37 The 1951 design was by Louis S. Kaplan (1897–1964), who later served for a time as Kahn's associated architect. Solomon, *Kahn's Jewish Community Center,* 47–65.

38 Anne Tyng, who worked in Kahn's office and had returned from a year in Rome in late January 1955, takes credit for the final design of the Bath House. In her *Louis Kahn to Anne Tyng: The Rome Letters, 1953–1954* (New York: Rizzoli, 1997), 192, she relates: "The first job I worked on when I returned was the Trenton Bathhouse. Lou had started work with Tim Vreeland on a roofless rectangular scheme, but almost immediately I came up with the proposal of four symmetrically arranged squares with hipped roofs...supported on 8-foot square occupiable hollow columns. The idea of using hollow columns as baffled entrances came from my memory of the bathhouses in China made of woven bamboo matting with only a system of baffles for privacy. It was a simple, straightforward concept, combining archetypal and innovative aspects, and Lou went for it."

It is extremely important to note, however, that the hip roofs were not part of the initial Greek cross pavilion plan and were only designed after the building was finished. Sarah Williams Ksiazek [Goldhagen], "Changing Symbols of Public Life: Louis Kahn's Civic and Religious Architecture," Ph.D. diss., Columbia University, 1995, 202–3 , supports Tyng's claim, reporting the following conversation with Tim Vreeland, another of Kahn's employees: "Anne, Lou, and I were working late in the office one night, and it was around midnight. Lou was over with me, working on my [square] scheme for the bathhouse, which he just hated. Suddenly, Anne said, 'Lou, come here.' We went over to her drawing board, and there on it was the plan for the Trenton Bathhouse, the scheme that subsequently dictated the ideas for the Community Center as a whole."

39 E[arl] Baldwin Smith, *The Dome: A Study in the History of Ideas,* Princeton Monographs in Art and Archaeology 25 (Princeton, N.J.: Princeton University Press, 1950), esp. 3–44. Antoine-Chrysostôme Quatremère de Quincy, in *De l'architecture égyptienne considérée dans son origine, ses principes et son goût, et comparée sous les mêmes rapports à l'architecture grecque,* dissertation qui a remporté, en 1785, le prix proposé par l'Académie des Inscriptions et Belles-Lettres (Paris: Barrois l'aîné et fils, 1803), 28–29, traced the origin of stone vaulting (and, by extension, domes) to earlier systems of construction in wood: "The use of roofs and the timber work of which roofs are formed undoubtedly produced in Greece the crowning element of the building that is called the pediment. But I think that the use of vaults also resulted from this. Whoever looks closely into the true source of the origin of their principal forms of architecture will easily perceive that every vault is a replacement for the roof and that, based on this simple connection, it [the vault] must have been suggested by this type of [timber work] covering." Kahn referred to the similarly shaped concrete pyramids planned to cover the social hall of the Community Center as "high coffers or triangular domes." Solomon, *Kahn's Jewish Community Center,* 116. Vincent Scully, in his introduction to *The Travel Sketches of Louis I. Kahn,* ed. Richard J. Boylen (Philadelphia: Pennsylvania Academy of the Fine Arts, 1978), 20; and "Ruins of Rome," in Scully, *Modern Architecture,* 305–6, on the other hand, has consistently maintained that the pyramidal shape rather than the space-enclosing form is the issue and has thus related the design to Kahn's drawings of the Egyptian pyramids at Giza.

40 Solomon, in *Kahn's Jewish Community Center,* 87, compares the Bath House to "a Roman house."

41 "Prototype Elementary School," *Progressive Architecture* 35 (October 1954): 127–32. Solomon, *Kahn's Jewish Community Center,* 99–100, and Goldhagen, *Kahn's Situated Modernism,* 109–10, also refer to Gilboy, Bellante & Clauss's design for a "Home for the Indigent," published in "PA Awards: Public Buildings," *Progressive Architecture* 36 (January 1955): 90–91.

42 Goldhagen, in *Kahn's Situated Modernism,* 111, curiously calls the plan a "Renaissance Greek cross" and makes no reference to its Romano-Byzantine origins. She does, however, note that Robert Venturi illustrated the early Byzantine Tomb of Galla Placidia in his thesis project, which Kahn reviewed (126). She also refers to the "bay system" as Palladian, despite its clear origins in late Roman and medieval architecture.

43 Soon after the building was finished, Kahn wrote that the "Trenton Bath House is derived from a concept of space order in which the hollow columns supporting the pyramidal roofs distinguish the spaces that serve from those being served." Louis Kahn, "Order in Architecture," *Perspecta: The Yale Architectural Journal* 4 (1957); repr. in *Kahn: Writings,* 72. Kahn drew a sketch for the Adler House (1954–55) based on a Greek cross plan, either at the same time as the Bath House or slightly before. It is on the back of a letter dated September 27, 1954. See David B. Brownlee and David B. DeLong, eds., *Louis I. Kahn: In the Realm of Architecture* (New York: Rizzoli; Los Angeles: Museum of Contemporary Art, 1991), 58–59. One should also relate the Bath House's modular plan to Le Corbusier's so-called Weekend House (Villa Henfel/Félix) at La Celle-Saint-Cloud of 1935, and the idea of the pavilion in the park to Mies's 50 × 50 House project

of 1951–52. To appreciate the difference between a "pure" geometry evoking no historical associations and that of the Bath House, one could cite Kahn's earlier Fruchter House project of 1952–53, where the sides of three squares form a central triangular court.

44 After meeting with Kahn in December 1955, Colin Rowe sent him a copy of Wittkower's book on February 2. Brownlee and DeLong, *Kahn*, 59, however, note that Kahn "had earlier been familiar with the book" and that this was merely a "new copy."

45 Ksiazek [Goldhagen], in "Changing Symbols," 223, points out that Kahn described the main axis of the Philadelphia Civic Center project on Market Street East that he had begun work on at this time as being similar to that extending from the apse of St. Peter's Basilica to the end of Bernini's colonnade. He also related the design to the Roman Forum.

46 The story of the historical reception of the Day Camp is fascinating. Though discussed at length in Solomon, *Kahn's Jewish Community Center*, 123–28, it was never, to my knowledge, even referred to in passing in the literature on Kahn before Brownlee and DeLong, *Kahn* (1991), despite the fact that drawings and photographs of it were published in Heinz Ronner, Sharad Jhaveri, and Alessandro Vasella, *Louis I. Kahn: Complete Work, 1935–74* (Basel and Stuttgart: Birkhäuser; Boulder, Colo.: Westview Press, 1977), 96. When I visited the Trenton site in 1982, I was shocked to discover the existence of the Day Camp. I was so impressed by it that when I got back I called Anne Tyng to find out more about it. She said it was never built. I told her that I just saw it and, furthermore, that she could check for herself in the *Complete Work*. She looked it up but claimed it was not there. She said she had the first edition and that I might be looking at the second (I was not). She added that she was going to her daughter's for dinner and would check her copy, which was the second edition. She called back that evening to say that the Day Camp was in the book and indeed was built, all of which puts into grave doubt her supposed role in the design of the final project (Goldhagen credits her with the final design). Tyng finally said that she had no real memory of Kahn's designing the Day Camp and then, significantly, added that she dimly recalled his designing it very quickly, all by himself one evening, and giving the sketches to Jack MacAllister to draw up. She ended by saying that it was a very inexpensive little thing and not very important. Her vagueness on the whole question makes one wonder about how involved she really was in the Trenton project. Goldhagen, in *Kahn's Situated Modernism*, 151, does not refer to the Day Camp within the context of the Trenton project but only later, in the chapter on the Rochester Unitarian Church, where she mentions it simply as the product of circumstantial "design" rather than the evidence of a determined conception of "form."

47 There are models of the fifth-century temples from Veii in the Institute of Etruscology and Italian Antiquity in Rome. The archaeologist Frank Brown, a friend of Kahn, published one in his book *Roman Architecture* (New York: George Braziller, 1965), fig. 4, and may have taken Kahn to see them.

48 According to Ksiazek [Goldhagen], "Changing Symbols," 254, this was said to MacAllister while they were working on the project. Robin Middleton has suggested that the nonorthogonal plan of the Day Camp may be related to the Iron Age huts of Romulus, reconstructed in the Palatine Museum. Solomon, in *Kahn's Jewish Community Center*, 125, describes the pavilions as "four classical temples," "open peristylar buildings [that] were obvious descendants of Greek temples." Goldhagen, in *Kahn's Situated Modernism*, 195, notes that Kahn later referred to this nonorthogonal organization of space as "dichotomous space."

49 Solomon, in *Kahn's Jewish Community Center*, 126, remarks on the nonaxiality of the plan "recalling the siting and form of Greek temples" as relating to "children's play."

50 Prior to the design of the Day Camp, Kahn had proposed enclosing the Bath House and pool in a circular precinct.

51 It was these elements in particular that Kahn was referring to when he spoke of the individual roof covers as "high coffers or triangular domes." See note 39 above.

52 This was a building Kahn knew well, not only as an architect but as a commuter, having passed through it for many years on his way from Philadelphia to New Haven.

53 Goldhagen, in *Kahn's Situated Modernism*, 175, refers to Kahn's speaking in 1960 of how one would have bathed in grandeur in the Baths of Caracalla. Marcello Angrisani, on the other hand, in "Louis Kahn e la storia," *Edilizia moderna* 86 (1965): 83–93, relates the architect's historical references almost exclusively to the "revolutionary" neoclassical projects of Boullée and Ledoux. Cf. Francesco Tentori, "Il passato come un amico," *Casabella* 275 (May 1963): esp. 26–28; and Manfredo Tafuri, "Storicità di Louis Kahn," *Comunità* 117 (February 1964): 38–49.

54 Kahn's association with the Trenton project ended by late 1959. In January 1960 Kelly and Gruzen were offered the Community Building job, which they designed and built over the following two years.

55 For Kahn's correspondence with the Academy in 1947, see note 33 above. For the "monumentality" debate, see esp. Sigfried Giedion, "The Need for a New Monumentality," *New Architecture and City Planning*, ed. Paul Zucker (New York: Philosophical Library, 1944), 549–68; and "In Search of a New Monumentality," a symposium by Gregor Paulsson, Henry-Russell Hitchcock Jr., William Holford, S. Giedion, Walter Gropius, Lucio Costa, and Alfred Roth, *Architectural Review* 104 (September 1948): 117–28. Kahn contributed an essay to the Zucker volume entitled "Monumentality" (577–88). There is little in this essay resembling his post–Rome Academy work, which speaks for the importance of the time he spent in Rome.

56 See Vincent Scully, "Archetype and Order in Recent American Architecture," *Art in America* 42 (December 1954); repr. in *Modern Architecture*, 64–73; William H. Jordy, "The Formal Image: USA," *Architectural Review* 157 (March 1960): 157–65; Nikolaus Pevsner, "The Return of Historicism," *Journal of the Royal Institute of British Architects*, 3rd ser., 68 (1961); repr. in N. Pevsner, *Studies in Art*,

Architecture, and Design, vol. 2, *Victorian and After* (London: Thames & Hudson, 1968), 242–59; and Colin Rowe, "Neo-'Classicism' and Modern Architecture I" and "Neo-'Classicism' and Modern Architecture II," *Oppositions* 1 (September 1973); repr. in *The Mathematics of the Ideal Villa and Other Essays* (Cambridge, Mass.: MIT Press, 1976), 119–58. Emil Kaufmann's *Three Revolutionary Architects: Boullée, Ledoux, and Lequeu* (Philadelphia: American Philosophical Society, 1952) and his *Architecture in the Age of Reason: Baroque and Post-Baroque in England, Italy, and France* (Cambridge, Mass.: Harvard University Press, 1955) inspired an interest in the protomodern aspects of eighteenth-century neoclassicism in which Kahn participated. See Louis Kahn, "Twelve Lines," preface to *Visionary Architects: Boullée, Ledoux, Lequeu*, ed. Jean-Claude Lemagny (Houston: University of St. Thomas, 1968), 9.

57 The most explicit were the redecoration of the Guest House bedroom at his New Canaan, Conn., estate, done in 1952–53, and the Kneses Tifereth Israel Synagogue at Port Chester, N.Y., built in 1954–56.

58 Kahn spoke of the difference between "the desires and the needs" of human beings as expressed in their architecture as early as 1953, in his remarks in "On the Responsibility of the Architect," *Perspecta: The Yale Architectural Journal* 2 (1953); repr. in *Kahn: Writings*, 53. Goldhagen, in *Kahn's Situated Modernism*, 148, relates the pairings "desires/needs" and "Form/Design" and dates that relation to 1960.

59 Louis Kahn, "On Form and Design," *Journal of Architectural Education* 15 (Fall 1960); repr. in *Kahn: Writings*, 102–8; and Louis Kahn, "Form and Design," lecture, 1960; in *Kahn: Writings*, 112–20.

60 *Kahn: Writings*, 113, 115.

61 The model and drawings of the exterior accompanying this scheme bear a strong resemblance to some of the ideal, central-plan church designs of Leonardo that Wittkower published in his *Architectural Principles in the Age of Humanism* (1949; repr., New York: Random House, 1962). Goldhagen, in *Kahn's Situated Modernism*, 146–47, notes that Kahn made a direct reference to Leonardo on one of the Rochester drawings. Robert Venturi, in *Complexity and Contradiction in Architecture*, Museum of Modern Art Papers on Architecture 1 (New York: Museum of Modern Art, 1966), 82–83, compared the Kahn and Machuca plans and illustrated them side by side across the centerfold of the pages. As shown in fig. 8.43, half plans of the Palace of Charles V and the first Rochester design were collaged together on the cover of *Perspecta: The Yale Architectural Journal* 9/10 (1965), ed. Robert A. M. Stern.

62 Kahn, "Form and Design," in *Kahn: Writings*, 115–16; and "Kahn," discussion in Kahn's office, February 1961, *Perspecta: The Yale Architectural Journal* 7 (1961); repr. in ibid., 132–40.

63 For the evolution of the Exeter Library's design, see Jay Wickersham, "The Making of Exeter Library," *Harvard Architecture Review* 7 (1989): 138–49. For the application of the form/design paradigm to the library's design, see Libero Andreotti, "Conceptual and Artifactual Research Programmes in Louis I. Kahn's Design of the Phillips Exeter Academy Library (1966–72)," *Design Studies* 5 (July 1984): 159–65. For the Kimbell Museum, see Patricia Cummings Loud, "History of the Kimbell Art Museum," in *In Pursuit of Quality: The Kimbell Art Museum, An Illustrated History of the Art and Architecture* (Fort Worth: Kimbell Art Museum, 1987), 1–95; and Loud, *Art Museums of Louis I. Kahn*, 100–169.

64 Louis Kahn, comments on the Library, 1972; repr. in Wurman, *What Will Be*, 178–83.

65 See, for example, Kahn, "The Room, the Street," in *Kahn: Writings*, 263–69.

66 Wurman, *What Will Be*, 177.

67 Louis Kahn, interview with William Marlin, 1972, in Loud, *Art Museums of Louis I. Kahn*, 156. Kenneth Frampton, in *Studies in Tectonic Culture: The Poetics of Construction in Nineteenth and Twentieth Century Architecture*, ed. John Cava (Cambridge, Mass.: MIT Press, 1995), 246, also characterizes the entrance porticos as "purely representational," although he does not develop the idea of representation in any greater depth. He describes the "tension between modernization and monumentality" in Kahn's architecture but does not relate this to Kahn's historicism (222).

68 Adolf Loos's "Ornement et crime," *Les Cahiers d'aujourd'hui* 5 (June 1913): 247–56, was republished by Le Corbusier in *L'Esprit nouveau* 2 (1920): 159–68. Despite the self-assurance displayed by the buildings themselves, one has a sense that Kahn felt a certain degree of modern guilt about the architectural tightrope he was walking in his historicism. In a conversation with students at Rice University in 1964, he stated: "I have used brick arches, and I have used the same old stuff" and that "because it's absolutely magnificent." Then, on second thought, he exclaimed: "*Why shouldn't I use it…the old stuff?*" Finally, as if to justify himself, he added: "What I am using here is just an order which is completely clear. It's not phony, and it costs less. I could make the same [building], if I wanted to, in the damnedest beautiful concrete…, but I have no fascination for it." Louis I. Kahn, *Talks with Students*, orig. pub. 1969; repr. in *Kahn: Writings*, 188.

69 Examples of the trope of the unfinished abound in the architecture of the postmodern period. Some owe their origin to the same sources that Kahn referenced; others are directly or indirectly based on Kahn's work itself. Some of the most prominent are Robert Venturi and Denise Scott-Brown's Franklin Court, Philadelphia, 1972–76, and Sainsbury Wing, National Gallery, London, 1985–91; Frank Gehry's own house in Santa Monica, Calif., begun 1977–78; Philip Johnson's Gehry Ghost House, New Canaan, Conn., 1984–85; and Peter Eisenman's Wexner Center for the Visual Arts, Ohio State University, Columbus, 1984–90. Gehry, as noted above (see note 7), followed Kahn rather closely in his thinking about the "poetic" value of the unfinished. Regarding his own Malibu house, he stated in "Suburban Changes: Architect's House, Santa Monica, 1978," *International Architect* no. 2 (1979): 34: "I was concerned with

maintaining a 'freshness' in the house. Often this freshness is lost—in over-working details, in over finishing them, their vitality is lost. I wanted to avoid this by emphasizing the feeling that the details are still in the process, that the 'building' hasn't stopped." On a more general level, Gehry explained in Diamonstein, *American Architecture*, 36, that he "was interested in the unfinished—or the quality that you find in paintings by Jackson Pollock, for instance, or de Kooning, or Cézanne, that look like the paint was just applied. The very finished, polished, every-detail-perfect kind of architecture seemed to me not to have that quality. I wanted to try that out in a building. The obvious way to go about it was the wood studs," which led him, in his Malibu house, to "working with the studs exposed."

Conclusion

1 Robert Venturi, *Complexity and Contradiction in Architecture*, Museum of Modern Art Papers on Architecture 1 (New York: Museum of Modern Art, 1966); R. Venturi, Denise Scott Brown, and Steven Izenour, *Learning from Las Vegas* (Cambridge, Mass.: MIT Press, 1972); rev. ed., with subtitle *The Forgotten Symbolism of Architectural Form* (Cambridge, Mass.: MIT Press, 1977); and *Oppositions: A Journal for Ideas and Criticism in Architecture* 1 (September 1973).

2 For a contemporaneous account of the turn in MoMA's direction, see Russell Lynes, *Good Old Modern: An Intimate Portrait of the Museum of Modern Art* (New York: Atheneum, 1973).

3 Arthur Drexler, ed., *The Architecture of the Ecole des Beaux-Arts* (New York: Museum of Modern Art, 1977); Charles A. Jencks, *The Language of Post-Modern Architecture*, rev. enl. ed. (New York: Rizzoli, 1977); Rem Koolhaas, *Delirious New York: A Retroactive Manifesto for Manhattan* (New York: Oxford University Press, 1978); Colin Rowe and Fred Koetter, *Collage City* (Cambridge, Mass.: MIT Press, 1978); A. Drexler, *Transformations in Modern Architecture* (New York: Museum of Modern Art, 1979); *Architecture 1980: The Presence of the Past: Venice Biennale* (New York: Rizzoli, 1980); and Paolo Portoghesi, *After Modern Architecture*, orig. pub. 1980, trans. Meg Shore (New York: Rizzoli, 1982).

4 No study that I know of has documented the changeover in usage in architectural writing from the term "modern" to those of "modernist" and "modernism." A cursory review of Peter Eisenman's writings in *Eisenman Inside Out: Selected Writings, 1963–1988* (New Haven, Conn.: Yale University Press, 2004), reveals that the *ist* and *ism* versions only appear around 1977 and do not entirely displace the conventional descriptors for a couple of years. Kenneth Frampton, in *Modern Architecture: A Critical History* (New York: Oxford University Press, 1980), uses the term "modernist" exceedingly rarely, and essentially to refer to general cultural conditions such as the "modernist tendency to reduce all form to abstraction" (210) and the "evolution of modernist culture" (288–89). Unusually for its time, Reyner Banham's *Theory and Design in the First Machine Age* (New York: Praeger, 1960), occasionally used the term "Modernists" or "Modernist" to characterize people (e.g., 275, 308, 312) but never "modernist" or "modernism" to describe their work. Christopher Wilk, ed., in *Modernism: Designing a New World, 1914–1939* (London: V&A Publications, 2006), 12–14, offers a cursory and, at times, misleading review of the history of the use of the terms before proceeding to a wholesale adoption of them to define what was once called modern or the modern movement. In an essay intended to review and analyze the history of the reception of modern architecture, Sarah Williams Goldhagen, in "Coda: Reconceptualizing the Modern," in *Anxious Modernisms: Experimentation in Postwar Architectural Culture*, ed. S. W. Goldhagen and Réjean Legault (Montreal: Canadian Centre for Architecture; Cambridge, Mass.: MIT Press, 2000), 301–23, uses the terms "modern," "modern movement," "modernist," and "modernism" interchangeably and without differentiation.

5 Lewis Mumford, "Notes on Modern Architecture," *New Republic* 66 (March 18, 1931): 122. Henry-Russell Hitchcock Jr., *Modern Architecture: Romanticism and Reintegration* (1929; repr., New York: Hacker Art Books, 1970), 92. Hitchcock used the term "'modernism,'" always in quotes, in other places to describe the simplified "eclecticism of taste," as he called it, of the New Tradition (see 103, 116). In his discussion of Oud's background and early years, he remarked on the architect's being "hampered by an already academicized 'modernism,' that of the New Tradition [of Berlage]" (176). Less informed and less critical writers such as Sheldon Cheney, in *The New World Architecture* (1930; repr., New York: Tudor Publishing, 1935), used the terms "modernism," "modernist," "modernistic," and "modern" indiscriminately and often interchangeably in describing works that could be either.

6 See esp. Clement Greenberg, "Modernist Painting," *Forum Lectures* (Washington, D.C.: Voice of America, 1960) and *Arts Yearbook* 4 (1961); repr. in *Clement Greenberg: The Collected Essays and Criticism*, vol. 4, *Modernism with a Vengeance*, ed. John O'Brian (Chicago: University of Chicago Press, 1993), 85–93. The term was still so unusual by the mid-1960s that Michael Fried, in "Modernist Painting and Formalist Criticism," *American Scholar* 33 (Autumn 1964): 642, could refer to "the development [of modern painting] over the past hundred years" as "what Mr. Greenberg calls 'modernist' painting." Even eight years later, Rosalind Krauss, in "A View of Modernism," *Artforum* 11 (September 1972): 48–51, described "modernism" and the "'modernist' critical position" as a new "doctrine" characterized by an astringent self-reflexiveness and historicism that was adumbrated by Greenberg and only recently elaborated by a small group of followers. The words "modernism" and "modernist" were set within quotation marks in the first two pages of the article and then, without explanation, printed without them in the last two.

7 Greenberg, "Modernist Painting," *Collected Essays*, 4:85.

8 Ibid., 4:86–87.

9 Ibid., 4:88–89, 86.

10 Peter Eisenman, "Post-Functionalism," *Oppositions* 6 (Fall 1976); repr. in *Eisenman Inside Out*, 85–86.

11 Peter Eisenman, "The End of the Classical: The End of the Beginning, the End of the End," *Perspecta: The Yale Architectural Journal* 21 (Summer 1984); repr. in *Eisenman Inside Out*, 158, 161, 153, 160, 163.

12 Eisenman's discussion of modernism, which played a dominant role in the translation of Greenbergian art criticism into architecture, was clearly dependent upon Greenberg's writings. In "In My Father's House Are Many Mansions," in *Institute for Architecture and Urban Studies Catalogue 12: John Hejduk: Seven Houses*, 1980; repr. in *Eisenman Inside Out*, 122, the architect clearly distinguishes what "Modernism (as opposed to modern architecture)" means in disciplinary terms related to Greenberg's concept of self-criticism and medium specificity. Eisenman begins the article by stating that "the structure of any discipline may be defined at two levels; first, those aspects of it that distinguish it from other disciplines; second, those which reveal it, in itself, to be the discipline and no other" (122).

13 Venturi, Scott Brown, and Izenour, *Learning from Las Vegas* (1977), 87, 101–3.

14 See Robert A. M. Stern, "The Doubles of Post-Modern," *Harvard Architecture Review* 1 (Spring 1980): 75–87.

15 Eisenman, "End of the Classical," in *Eisenman Inside Out*, 163; and Venturi, Scott Brown, and Izenour, *Learning from Las Vegas* (1977), 87, 102.

Bibliography

Publications Cited in Text and Notes

ABERNATHY, ANN, WITH JOHN G. THORPE, EDS. *The Oak Park Home and Studio of Frank Lloyd Wright.* Oak Park, Ill.: Frank Lloyd Wright Home and Studio Foundation, 1988.

ABRAMSON, DANIEL M. *Building the Bank of England: Money, Architecture, Society, 1694–1942.* New Haven, Conn.: Yale University Press, 2005.

ABRI, MARTINA. *Die Friedrich-Werdersche Kirche zu Berlin: Technik und Ästhetik in der Backstein-Architektur K. F. Schinkels.* Die Bauwerke und Kunstdenkmäler von Berlin 22. Berlin: Gebr. Mann, 1992.

ACKERMAN, JAMES S. *Origins, Imitation, Conventions: Representation in the Visual Arts.* Cambridge, Mass.: MIT Press, 2002.

———. *Palladio.* Baltimore: Penguin, 1966.

———. *The Villa: Form and Ideology of Country Houses.* London: Thames & Hudson, 1990.

ADLER, DANKMAR. "The Influence of Steel Construction and Plate-Glass upon Style." *The American Architect and Building News* 54 (October 31, 1896): 37–39. Reprinted as "Influence of Steel Construction and of Plate Glass upon the Development of Modern Style." *Inland Architect and News Record* 28 (November 1896): 34–36.

ALBERTI, LEON BATTISTA. *On the Art of Building in Ten Books.* Translated by Joseph Rykwert, Neil Leach, and Robert Tavernor. Cambridge, Mass.: MIT Press, 1988. Originally published as *De re aedificatoria,* 1486.

ALBRECHT, DONALD, ed. *World War II and the American Dream.* Washington, D.C.: National Building Museum; Cambridge, Mass.: MIT Press, 1995.

ALGAROTTI, FRANCESCO. *Saggio sopra l'architettura.* Vol. 2 of *Opere.* Leghorn: M. Coltellini, 1764.

ALOFSIN, ANTHONY. *Frank Lloyd Wright: The Lost Years, 1910–1922: A Study of Influence.* Chicago: University of Chicago Press, 1993.

ANDREOTTI, LIBERO. "Conceptual and Artifactual Research Programmes in Louis I. Kahn's Design of the Phillips Exeter Academy Library (1966–72)." *Design Studies* 5 (July 1984): 159–65.

ANGRISANI, MARCELLO. "Louis Kahn et l'histoire." *Architecture, mouvement, continuité* 6 (June 1968): 4–11.

"The Architectural Review Gothic Number. Act 2: Romantic Gothic. Scene 1: Goethe and Strassburg." *Architectural Review* 98 (December 1945): 156–59.

Architecture 1980: The Presence of the Past: Venice Biennale. New York: Rizzoli, 1980.

ARNELL, PETER, AND TED BICKFORD. *Frank Gehry: Buildings and Projects.* New York: Rizzoli, 1985.

ASHBEE, C[HARLES] R[OBERT]. "Frank Lloyd Wright: A Study and an Appreciation." In *Frank Lloyd Wright: The Early Work,* 3–8. New York: Horizon Press, 1968. Originally published 1911 as "Frank Lloyd Wright: Eine Studie zu seine Würdigung" in *Frank Lloyd Wright: Ausgeführte Bauten.*

———. "Taliesin, the Home of Frank Lloyd Wright, and a Study of the Owner." *Western Architect* 19 (February 1913): 16–19.

ATTERBURY, PAUL, ED. *A. W. N. Pugin: Master of Gothic Revival.* New Haven, Conn.: Yale University Press, 1995.

———, AND CLIVE WAINWRIGHT, EDS. *Pugin: A Gothic Passion.* New Haven, Conn.: Yale University Press, 1994.

AUGUSTIN, FRANK, ED. *Mythos Bauakademie: Die Schinkelsche Bauakademie und ihre Bedeutung für die Mitte Berlins.* Berlin: Verlag für Bauwesen, 1997.

BANHAM, REYNER. *Theory and Design in the First Machine Age.* New York: Praeger, 1960.

———. *The New Brutalism: Ethic or Aesthetic?* Documents of Modern Architecture. New York: Reinhold, 1966.

BARIDON, LAURENT. *L'Imaginaire scientifique de Viollet-le-Duc.* Paris: Harmattan, 1996.

BAROCCHI, PAOLA. "Finito e non-finito nella critica vasariana." *Arte Antica e Moderna: Rivista degli Istituti di Archeologia e di Storia dell'arte dell'Università di Bologna e dei Musei del Commune di Bologna* 3 (July–September 1958): 221–35.

BARR, ALFRED H., *Cubism and Abstract Art.* New York: Museum of Modern Art, 1936.

——, et al. *Modern Architecture: International Exhibition.* New York: Museum of Modern Art, 1932.

BARRIÈRE, F[RANÇOIS]. "Embellissemens de Paris." *Journal des débats,* December 31, 1850, 1–2.

BARRON, STEPHANIE, WITH SABINE ECKMANN, EDS. *Exiles + Emigrés: The Flight of European Artists from Hitler.* Los Angeles: Los Angeles County Museum of Art; New York: Harry N. Abrams, 1997.

BAUMANN, FELIX, ED. *Cézanne: Finished, Unfinished.* Ostfildern-Ruit, Germany: Hatje Cantz, 2000.

BEEBY, THOMAS. "The Grammar of Ornament / Ornament as Grammar." *Via: The Journal of the Graduate School of Fine Arts, University of Pennsylvania* 3 (1977): 10–29.

——. "The Song of Taliesin." *Modulus: The University of Virginia School of Architecture Review* (1980–81): 2–11.

BEHRENDT, WALTER CURT. *Modern Building: Its Nature, Problems, and Forms.* New York: Harcourt, Brace, 1937.

——. *Victory of the New Building Style.* Translated by Harry Francis Mallgrave. Texts & Documents. Los Angeles: Getty Research Institute, 2000. Originally published as *Der Sieg des neuen Baustils* (Stuttgart: Akademischer Verlag Dr. Fr. Wedekind, 1927).

BELCHER, MARGARET, ED. *The Collected Letters of A. W. N. Pugin.* 2 vols. Oxford: Oxford University Press, 2001.

BERGDOLL, BARRY. "Archaeology vs. History: Heinrich Hübsch's Critique of Neoclassicism and the Beginnings of Historicism in German Architectural Theory." *Oxford Art Journal* 5, no. 2 (1983): 3–12.

——. Introduction to *The Foundations of Architecture: Selections from the "Dictionnaire Raisonné,"* by Eugène-Emmanuel Viollet-le-Duc, translated by Kenneth D. Whitehead. New York: George Braziller, 1990.

——. *Karl Friedrich Schinkel: An Architecture for Prussia.* New York: Rizzoli, 1994.

——. *Léon Vaudoyer: Historicism in the Age of Industry.* New York: Architectural History Foundation; Cambridge, Mass.: MIT Press, 1994.

——, AND WERNER OECHSLIN, EDS. *Fragments: Architecture and the Unfinished: Essays Presented to Robin Middleton.* London: Thames & Hudson, 2006.

BERLAGE, H[ENDRIK] P[ETRUS]. *Amerikaanische Reisherinneringen.* Rotterdam: W. L. & J. Brusse, 1913.

——. "Neuere amerikanische Architektur." Originally published 1912. Translated in *The Literature of Architecture: The Evolution of Architectural Theory and Practice in Nineteenth-Century America,* edited by Don Gifford. New York: E. P. Dutton, 1966.

BERMINGHAM, ANN. *Landscape and Ideology: The English Rustic Tradition, 1740–1860.* Berkeley: University of California Press, 1986.

BIALOSTOCKI, JAN. "The Renaissance Concept of Nature and Antiquity." In *The Message of Images: Studies in the History of Art,* 64–68. Vienna: IRSA, 1988.

"Die Bibliothek St. Geneviève in Paris." *Allgemeine Bauzeitung mit Abbildungen* 17th yr. (1852): 139–42.

BLACKALL, C[LARENCE] H[OWARD]. "The Legitimate Design of the Architectural Casing for Steel Skeleton Structures." *American Architect and Building News* 66 (December 2, 1899): 78–80.

BLASER, WERNER. *After Mies: Mies van der Rohe—Teaching and Principles.* New York: Van Nostrand Reinhold, 1977.

——. *Mies van der Rohe: Less Is More.* Zurich: Waser, 1986.

——. *Mies van der Rohe: The Art of Structure.* Translated by D. Q. Stephenson. New York: Praeger, 1965.

BLAU, EVE, AND EDWARD KAUFMAN, EDS. *Architecture and Its Image: Four Centuries of Architectural Representation: Works from the Collection of the Canadian Centre for Architecture.* Montreal: Centre Canadien d'Architecture / Canadian Centre for Architecture, 1989.

BLAU, EVE, AND NANCY J. TROY, EDS. *Architecture and Cubism.* Montreal: Centre Canadien d'Architecture / Canadian Center for Architecture; Cambridge, Mass.: MIT Press, 1997.

BLAUWELT, ELKE, ED. *Karl Friedrich Schinkels Berliner Bauakademie: In Kunst und Architektur, in Vergangenheit und Gegenwart.* Berlin: Kunstbibliothek Staatliche Museen zu Berlin, Preußischer Kulturbesitz, Nicolai, 1996.

BLETTER, ROSEMARIE. "The Invention of the Skyscraper: Notes on Its Diverse Histories." *Assemblage* (February 1987): 110–17.

BLONDEL, JACQUES-FRANÇOIS [WITH PIERRE PATTE]. *Cours d'architecture, ou Traité de la décoration, distribution & construction des bâtiments.* 1771–77. 6 vols. Reprint, Paris: Monum, Editions du Patrimoine; Ivry-sur-Seine: Phénix Editions, 2002.

—— [WITH JEAN-FRANÇOIS DE BASTIDE]. *L'Homme du monde éclairé par les arts.* 2 vols. Amsterdam, 1774.

BLUESTONE, DANIEL. *Constructing Chicago.* New Haven, Conn.: Yale University Press, 1991.

BODENSCHATZ, HARALD. *"Der Rote Kasten": Zu Bedeutung, Wirkung und Zukunft von Schinkels Bauakademie.* Berlin: Transit, 1996.

BOIS, YVE-ALAIN. "A Picturesque Stroll around *Clara-Clara.*" *October* 29 (Summer 1984): 32–62.

BOLTON, ARTHUR T. *The Works of Sir John Soane.* London: Sir John Soane's Museum, 1924.

BONELLI, RENATO. "Michelangelo e il non-finito." In *Atti del Convegno di studi michelangioleschi,* 403–16. Rome: Edizioni dell'Ateneo, 1966.

BÖTTICHER, KARL. "Entwickelung der Formen der hellenischen Tektonik." *Allgemeine Bauzeitung mit Abbildungen* 5th year (1840): 316–30.

——. *Die Tektonik der Hellenen.* 2 vols. Potsdam: Ferdinand Riegel, 1844–52.

BOUDON, FRANÇOISE. "Le Réel et l'imaginaire chez Viollet-le-Duc: Les figures du *Dictionnaire de l'architecture.*" *Revue de l'art* 58–59 (1983): 95–114.

BOUDON, PHILIPPE, AND PHILIPPE DESHAYES. *Viollet-le-Duc: Le Dictionnaire d'architecture: Relevés et observations.* Architecture + Recherches. Brussels: Pierre Madarga, 1979.

BOULLÉE, ETIENNE-LOUIS. *Architecture: Essai sur l'art.* Edited by Jean-Marie Pérouse de Montclos. Paris: Hermann, 1968.

——. "Architecture, an Essay on Art" and "Architecture, Essai sur l'art." Translated by Sheila de Vallée. In Helen Rosenau, *Boullée & Visionary Architecture, including Boullée's 'Architecture, Essay on Art.'* London: Academy Editions, 1976.

BRAHAM, ALLAN. *The Architecture of the French Enlightenment.* Berkeley: University of California Press, 1980.

BRESSANI, MARTIN. "Notes on Viollet-le-Duc's Philosophy of History: Dialectics and Technology." *Journal of the Society of Architectural Historians* 48 (December 1989): 327–50.

——, AND MARC GRIGNON. "Henri Labrouste and the Lure of the Real: Romanticism, Rationalism and the Bibliothèque Sainte-Geneviève." *Art History* 28 (November 2005): 712–51.

BROWNLEE, DAVID B., AND DAVID B. DELONG, EDS. *Louis I. Kahn: In the Realm of Architecture.* New York: Rizzoli; Los Angeles, Museum of Contemporary Art, 1991.

BRUNIUS, TEDDY. "Michelangelo's non finito." *Figura (Contributions to the History and Theory of Art),* n.s., 6 (1967): 29–67.

CAMPBELL, COLEN. *Vitruvius Britannicus; or the British Architect.* 3 vols. London: by the author, 1715–25.

CHAMBERS, WILLIAM. *A Treatise on Civil Architecture, in Which the Principles of that Art are Laid Down and Illustrated by a Great Number of Plates.* London: by the author, 1759.

——. *A Treatise on the Decorative Part of Civil Architecture.* 3rd ed., enl., of *A Treatise on Civil Architecture.* London: Joseph Smeeton, 1791.

CHENEY, SHELDON. *The New World Architecture.* Originally published 1930. Reprint, New York: Tudor Publishing Company, 1935.

CHIPP, HERSCHEL B. *Guernica: History, Transformations, Meanings.* Berkeley: University of California Press, 1988.

CLARK, KENNETH. *The Gothic Revival: An Essay in the History of Taste.* Originally published 1928. 3rd ed. Harmondsworth, Middlesex, England: Penguin, 1964.

CLEARY, RICHARD L. *Merchant Prince and Master Builder: Edgar J. Kaufmann and Frank Lloyd Wright.* Pittsburgh: Heinz Architectural Center, 1999.

[COCHIN, CHARLES-NICOLAS]. *Doutes raisonnables d'un marguillier de la paroisse de S. Etienne-du-Mont sur le problême proposé par M. Patte, architecte, concernant la construction de la coupole de l'Eglise de Sainte-Geneviève.* Amsterdam and Paris: Jombert Fils, 1770.

COHEN, JEAN-LOUIS. *Mies van der Rohe.* Paris: Hazan, 1994.

COLLINS, PETER. *Changing Ideals in Modern Architecture, 1750–1950.* London: Faber and Faber, 1965.

CONDIT, CARL W. *The Chicago School of Architecture.* Chicago: University of Chicago Press, 1964.

——. *The Rise of the Skyscraper.* Chicago: University of Chicago Press, 1952.

CONE, MICHÈLE C. *Artists under Vichy: A Case of Prejudice and Persecution.* Princeton, N.J.: Princeton University Press, 1992.

CONNORS, JOSEPH. *The Robie House of Frank Lloyd Wright.* Chicago: University of Chicago Press, 1984.

COOK, JOHN W., AND HEINRICH KLOTZ, EDS. *Conversations with Architects.* New York: Praeger, 1973.

COUCHAUD, A[NTOINE]. *Choix d'églises bysantines en Grèce.* Paris: Lenoir, 1842.

CREESE, WALTER L. *The Crowning of the American Landscape: Eight Great Spaces and Their Buildings.* Princeton, N.J.: Princeton University Press, 1985.

CURRAN, KATHLEEN. *The Romanesque Revival: Religion, Politics, and Transnational Exchange.* Buildings, Landscapes, and Societies 2. University Park: Pennsylvania State University Press, 2003.

DALY, CÉSAR. "Bibliothèque Sainte-Geneviève." *Revue générale de l'architecture et des travaux publics* 10 (1852): 380–81.

DAMISCH, HUBERT. Introduction to *L'Architecture raisonnée: Extraits du "Dictionnaire de l'architecture française,"* by [Eugène-Emmanuel] Viollet-le-Duc. Paris: Hermann, 1964.

DASSY, LÉON [LAURE LABROUSTE]. *Souvenirs d'Henri Labrouste, architecte, membre de l'Institut: Notes recueillies et classées par ses enfants.* Fontainebleau: by the author, 1928.

DELABORDE, HENRI. *Notice sur la vie et les ouvrages de M. Henri Labrouste.* Paris: Institut de France, Académie des Beaux-Arts, 1878.

DE WIT, WIM, ED. *Louis Sullivan: The Function of Ornament.* New York: W. W. Norton, 1986.

DIAMONSTEIN, BARBARALEE. *American Architecture Now.* New York: Rizzoli, 1980.

DOBRÉE, BONAMY, AND GEOFFREY WEBB. *The Complete Works of Sir John Vanbrugh.* 4 vols. London: Nonesuch Press, 1927–28.

DOWNES, KERRY. *Hawksmoor.* Originally published 1959. 2nd ed. London: A. Zwemmer, 1979.

——. *Sir John Vanbrugh: A Biography.* London: Sidgwick & Jackson, 1987.

——. *Vanbrugh.* Studies in Architecture 16. London: A. Zwemmer, 1977.

DREXLER, ARTHUR, ED. *The Architecture of the Ecole des Beaux-Arts.* New York: Museum of Modern Art, 1977.

——. *Ludwig Mies van der Rohe.* Masters of World Architecture. New York: George Braziller, 1960.

——. *Transformations in Modern Architecture.* New York: Museum of Modern Art, 1979.

DUBBINI, RENZO, ED. *Henri Labrouste, 1801–1875.* Milan: Electa, 2002.

DUMONT, GABRIEL-PIERRE-MARTIN. *Les Ruines de Paestum, autrement Posidonia, ville de l'ancienne Grande Grèce, au Royaume de Naples.* London and Paris: by the author, 1769.

——. *Suitte de plans, coupes, profils, élévations géométrales et perspectives, tels qu'ils existoient en mil sept cent cinquante, dans la bourgade de Poesto qui est la ville Poestum de Pline.* Paris: by the author, 1764.

DU PREY, PIERRE DE LA RUFFINIÈRE. *Sir John Soane.* London: Victoria and Albert Museum, 1985.

DURAND, JEAN-NICOLAS-LOUIS. *Précis of the Lectures on Architecture; with Graphic Portion of the Lectures on Architecture.* Originally published 1802–5/1821. Translated by David Britt, with an introduction by Antoine Picon. Texts &

Documents. Los Angeles: Getty Research Institute, 2000.

ECO, UMBERTO. *The Open Work.* Originally published 1962. Translated by Anna Cancogni. Cambridge, Mass.: Harvard University Press, 1989.

EISENMAN, PETER. *Eisenman Inside Out: Selected Writings, 1963–1988.* Theoretical Perspectives in Architectural History and Criticism. New Haven, Conn.: Yale University Press, 2004.

ETLIN, RICHARD A. *The Architecture of Death: The Transformation of the Cemetery in Eighteenth-Century Paris.* Cambridge, Mass.: MIT Press, 1984.

ETTLINGER, LEOPOLD D. "A German Architect's Visit to England." *Architectural Review* 97 (May 1945): 131–34.

FERREE, BARR. "The Art of the High Building." *Architectural Record* 15 (May 1904): 445–66.

——. "Chicago Architecture." *Lippincott's Monthly Magazine* 52 (July 1893): 80–94.

——. "The High Building and Its Art." *Scribner's* 15 (March 1894): 297–318.

——. "The Modern Office Building," parts 1–3. *Journal of the Franklin Institute* 141 (January 1896): 47–71; (February 1896): 115–33. Reprinted in *Inland Architect and News Record* 27 (February 1896): 4–5; (March 1896): 12–14; (April 1896): 23–25; (May 1896): 34–35; (June 1896): 45–47.

——. "Structure and Material in High Design." *The Brickbuilder* 3 (March 1894): 43–45.

FIEBELKORN, JAN, ED. *Karl Friedrich Schinkel: Werke und Wirkungen.* Berlin: Senat von Berlin, 1981.

FIORIO, MARIA TERESA. "Broken Sculpture: Michelangelo and the Aesthetic of the Fragment." In *The Genius of the Sculptor in Michelangelo's Work,* edited by Pierre Théberge, 68–84. Montreal: Montreal Museum of Fine Arts, 1992.

FISHER, MICHAEL. *Pugin-Land: A. W. N. Pugin, Lord Shrewsbury, and the Gothic Revival in Staffordshire.* Stafford, England: by the author, 2002.

FLAMINIUS, EMIL. "Ueber den Bau des Hauses für die allgemeine Bauschule in Berlin." *Allgemeine Bauzeitung mit Abbildungen* no. 1 (1836): 3–5; no. 2 (1836): 9–13; no. 3 (1836): 18–24; and pls. 1–8.

FORSMANN, ERIK. *Karl Friedrich Schinkel: Bauwerke und Baugedanken.* Munich: Schnell und Steiner, 1981.

FORSTER, KURT W. "Schinkel's Panoramic Planning of Central Berlin." *Modulus* 16 (1983): 62–77.

FOUQUET-PLÜMACHER, DORIS, ED. *Mythos Bauakademie: Die Schinkelsche Bauakademie und ihre Bedeutung für die Mitte Berlins: Ausstellungskatalog.* Berlin: Verlag für Bauwesen, 1998.

FRAMPTON, KENNETH. *Modern Architecture: A Critical History.* New York: Oxford University Press, 1980.

——. *Studies in Tectonic Culture: The Poetics of Construction in Nineteenth and Twentieth Century Architecture.* Edited by John Cava. Cambridge, Mass.: MIT Press, 1995.

FRIED, MICHAEL. "Modernist Painting and Formalist Criticism." *American Scholar* 33 (Autumn 1964): 642–48.

GANAY, J. H. ERNEST DE. "Le Jardin d'Ermenonville." *Gazette illustré des amateurs de jardins* (1925): 1–18.

GARGIANI, ROBERTO. "Ornamento e costruzione in Sainte-Geneviève." In *Henri Labrouste, 1801–1875,* edited by Renzo Dubbini, 143–65. Milan: Electa, 2002.

GEHRY, FRANK. "Suburban Changes: Architect's House, Santa Monica, 1978." *International Architect* no. 2 (1979): 33–46.

GEIST, JONAS. *Karl Friedrich Schinkel, die Bauakademie: Eine Vergegenwärtigung.* Frankfurt: Fischer Taschenbuch, 1993.

GERMANN, GEORG. *Gothic Revival in Europe and Britain: Sources, Influences, and Ideas.* Originally published 1972. Translated by Gerald Onn. Cambridge, Mass.: MIT Press, 1973.

GIEDION, SIGFRIED. *Building in France: Building in Iron, Building in Ferroconcrete.* Originally published 1928. Translated by J. Duncan Berry. Texts & Documents. Santa Monica, Calif.: Getty Center for the History of Art and the Humanities, 1995.

——. "The Need for a New Monumentality." In *New Architecture and City Planning,* edited by Paul Zucker, 549–68. New York: Philosophical Library, 1944.

——. "Les Problèmes actuels de l'architecture: A l'occasion d'un manifeste de Frank Lloyd Wright aux architectes et critiques d'Europe." *Cahiers d'art* 7, nos. 1–2 (1932): 69–73.

——. *Space, Time, and Architecture: The Growth of a New Tradition.* Cambridge, Mass.: Harvard University Press, 1941.

——. *Spätbarocker und romantischer Klassizismus.* Munich: F. Brückmann A.-G., 1922.

——. "Theo van Doesburg." *Cahiers d'art* 6, no. 4 (1931): 228.

GIRARDIN, RENÉ-LOUIS DE. *De la composition des paysages, suivi de Promenade ou itinéraire des jardins d'Ermenonville.* Originally published 1777 and 1788. Edited by Michel H. Conan. Seyssel, France: Champ Vallon, 1992.

GLAESER, LUDWIG. *Ludwig Mies van der Rohe: Drawings in the Collection of the Museum of Modern Art.* New York: Museum of Modern Art, 1969.

GOETHE, JOHANN WOLFGANG VON. *Von deutscher Baukunst: D. M. Ervini a Steinbach.* Originally published anonymously in *Züricher Gedenkausgabe* 13 (1772): 16ff. Translated by Geoffrey Grigson in "The Architectural Review Gothic Number. Act 2: Romantic Gothic. Scene 1: Goethe and Strassburg." *Architectural Review* 98 (December 1945): 156–59. Also translated by Elizabeth G. Holt in *A Documentary History of Art.* Vol. 2, *Michelangelo and the Mannerists: The Baroque and the Eighteenth Century.* Originally published 1947. Reprint, Garden City, N.Y.: Doubleday, 1958.

[GOLDHAGEN], SARAH WILLIAMS KSIAZEK. "Changing Symbols of Public Life: Louis Kahn's Civic and Religious Architecture." Ph.D. diss., Columbia University, 1995.

——. *Louis Kahn's Situated Modernism.* New Haven,, Conn.: Yale University Press, 2001.

——, AND RÉJEAN LEGAULT, EDS. *Anxious Modernisms: Experimentation in Postwar Architectural Culture.* Montreal, Canadian Centre for Architecture; Cambridge, Mass.: MIT Press, 2000.

GOMBRICH, ERNST. *Art and Illusion: A Study in the Psychology of Pictorial Representation.* A. W. Mellon Lectures in the Fine Arts, 1956. Bollingen

Series 35, no. 5. Originally published 1960. 2nd ed. rev. New York: Pantheon Books, 1961.

GORDON, F. C. "The 'Sky-Scraper.'" *American Architect and Building News* 46 (December 8, 1894): 100–101.

GOUT, PAUL. *Viollet-le-Duc: Sa vie, son oeuvre, sa doctrine.* Paris: E. Champion, 1914.

GREENBERG, CLEMENT. *Clement Greenberg: The Collected Essays and Criticism.* Edited by John O'Brian. 4 vols. Chicago: University of Chicago Press, 1986–93.

GROPIUS, WALTER. "Die Entwicklung moderner Industrie-baukunst." In *Jahrbuch des deutschen Werkbundes,* 17–22. Jena, Germany: Eugen Diederichs, 1913.

GUENTER, WENDELIN A. "British Aesthetic Discourse, 1780–1830: The Sketch, the *Non Finito,* and the Imagination." *Art Journal* (Summer 1993): 40–47.

HARRIES, ELIZABETH WANNING. *The Unfinished Manner: Essays on the Fragment in the Later Eighteenth Century.* Charlottesville: University Press of Virginia, 1994.

HARRINGTON, ELAINE. *Frank Lloyd Wright Home and Studio, Oak Park.* Opus 35. Stuttgart: Axel Menges, 1996.

HARRIS, JOHN. *Sir William Chambers: Knight of the Polar Star.* London: A. Zwemmer, 1970.

——, AND MICHAEL SNODIN, EDS. *Sir William Chambers: Architect to George III.* New Haven, Conn.: Yale University Press, 1996.

HASKELL, DOUGLAS. "Organic Architecture: Frank Lloyd Wright." *Creative Art* 3 (November 1928): li–lvii.

HASTINGS, THOMAS. "High Buildings and Good Architecture: What Principles Should Govern Their Design." *American Architect and Building News* 46 (November 17, 1894): 67–68.

HAUS, ANDREAS. *Karl Friedrich Schinkel als Künstler: Annäherung und Kommentar.* Munich: Deutscher Kunstverlag, 2001.

HAUTECOEUR, LOUIS. *Histoire de l'architecture classique en France.* Vol. 4, *Seconde Moitié du XVIIIe siècle : Le Style Louis XVI, 1750–1792.* Paris: A. et J. Picard, 1952.

HAYS, K. MICHAEL. "Abstraction's Appearance (Seagram Building)." In *Autonomy and Ideology: Positioning an Avant-Garde in America,* edited by R. E. Somol, 278–91. New York: Monacelli Press, 1997.

——. "Odysseus and the Oarsmen, or, Mies's Abstraction Once Again." In *The Presence of Mies,* edited by Detlef Mertins, 234–48. New York: Princeton Architectural Press, 1994.

"Henri Labrouste." *Les Monuments historiques de la France* 6 (1975): 3–37.

HERMANT, ACHILLE. "La Bibliothèque Sainte-Geneviève." *L'Artiste,* 5th ser., 7 (December 1, 1851): 129–31.

HERRMANN, WOLFGANG. *Gottfried Semper: In Search of Architecture.* Cambridge, Mass.: MIT Press, 1984.

——, ED. *In What Style Should We Build? The German Debate on Architectural Style.* Texts & Documents. Santa Monica, Calif.: Getty Center for the History of Art and the Humanities, 1992. (Includes Heinrich Hübsch, "In What Style Should We Build?" Originally published 1828.)

——. *Laugier and Eighteenth-Century French Theory.* London: A. Zwemmer, 1962.

——. *The Theory of Claude Perrault.* Studies in Architecture 12. London: A. Zwemmer, 1973.

HILBERSEIMER, LUDWIG. *Mies van der Rohe.* Chicago: Paul Theobold, 1956.

HIRT, ALOYS LUDWIG. *Die Baukunst nach den Grundsätzen der Alten.* Berlin, 1809.

HITCHCOCK, HENRY-RUSSELL. *Architecture: Nineteenth and Twentieth Centuries.* Pelican History of Art. Harmondsworth, Middlesex, England: Penguin, 1958.

——. "Frank Lloyd Wright and the 'Academic Tradition' of the Early Eighteen-Nineties." *Journal of the Warburg and Courtauld Institutes* 7 (January–June 1944): 46–63.

——. *In the Nature of Materials: The Buildings of Frank Lloyd Wright, 1887–1941.* Originally published 1942. Reprint, with a new foreword and bibliography by the author, New York: Da Capo Press, 1975.

——. "Modern Architecture. I: The Traditionalists and the New Tradition." *Architectural Record* 63 (April 1928): 337–49; "Modern Architecture. II: The New Pioneers." *Architectural Record* 63 (May 1928): 453–60.

——. *Modern Architecture: Romanticism and Reintegration.* Originally published 1929. Reprint, New York: Hacker Art Books, 1970.

——. *Painting toward Architecture: The Miller Company Collection of Abstract Art.* New York: Duell, Sloan and Pearce, 1948.

——, AND PHILIP JOHNSON. *The International Style.* Originally published 1932. 2nd ed. New York: W. W. Norton, 1966.

HOCHMAN, ELAINE S. *Architects of Fortune: Mies van der Rohe and the Third Reich.* New York: Fromm International, 1990.

——. "Confrontation: 1933—Mies van der Rohe and the Third Reich." *Oppositions* 18 (Fall 1979): 49–59.

——. "The Politics of Mies van der Rohe." *Sites* 15 (1986): 44–49.

HOFFMANN, DONALD. "Frank Lloyd Wright and Viollet-le-Duc." *Journal of the Society of Architectural Historians* 28 (October 1969): 173–83.

——. *Frank Lloyd Wright, Louis Sullivan, and the Skyscraper.* Mineola, N.Y.: Dover Publications, 1998.

——. *Frank Lloyd Wright's Fallingwater: The House and Its History.* 2nd ed. rev. New York: Dover Publications, 1993.

——. *Frank Lloyd Wright's Robie House: The Illustrated Story of an Architectural Masterpiece.* New York: Dover Publications, 1984.

HÜBSCH, HEINRICH. *Über griechische Architectur.* Heidelberg: J. C. B. Mohr, 1822.

HUGO, VICTOR. *Cromwell.* Originally published 1827. Paris: Garnier-Flammarion, 1968.

——. *Notre-Dame de Paris, 1482.* Originally published 1831–32. Paris: Garnier-Flammarion, 1967.

HUNT, JOHN DIXON. *Gardens and the Picturesque: Studies in the History of Landscape Architecture.* Cambridge, Mass.: MIT Press, 1992.

——. *The Picturesque Garden in Europe.* London: Thames & Hudson, 2002.

——, AND PETER WILLIS, EDS. *The Genius of the Place: The English Landscape Garden, 1620–1820.* London: Elek, 1975.

HUSSEY, CHRISTOPHER. *English Gardens and Landscapes, 1700–1750.* London: Country Life, 1967.

——. *The Picturesque: Studies in a Point of View.* London: G. P. Putnam's Sons, 1927.

"In Search of a New Monumentality." A symposium by Gregor Paulsson, Henry-Russell Hitchcock, William Holford, Sigfried Giedion, Walter Gropius, Lucio Costa, and Alfred Roth. *Architectural Review* 104 (September 1948): 117–28.

JAFFÉ, HANS L. C. *De Stijl.* New York: Harry N. Abrams, 1967.

JENCKS, CHARLES A. *The Language of Post-Modern Architecture.* Rev. enl. ed. New York: Rizzoli, 1977.

"Jeton et médaille de la Société centrale des Architectes." *Revue générale de l'architecture et des travaux publics* 8 (1849–50): 151.

John Soane. Architectural Monographs. London: Academy Editions; New York: St. Martin's Press, 1983.

JOHNSON, PHILIP. *Mies van der Rohe.* New York: Museum of Modern Art, 1947.

JOHONNOT, RODNEY F. *The New Edifice of Unity Church, Oak Park, Illinois: Frank Lloyd Wright, Architect.* Originally published 1906. Reprint, Oak Park, Ill.: Unitarian Universalist Church, 1961.

JORDY, WILLIAM H. *American Buildings and Their Architects.* Vol. 3, *Progressive and Academic Ideals at the Turn of the Twentieth Century;* and vol. 4, *The Impact of European Modernism in the Mid-Twentieth Century.* Garden City, N.Y.: Doubleday, 1972.

——. "The Formal Image: USA." *Architectural Review* 157 (March 1960): 157–65.

——. *"Symbolic Essence" and Other Writings on Modern Architecture and American Culture,* edited by Mardges Bacon. New Haven, Conn.: Yale University Press, 2005.

KAHN, LOUIS I. *Louis I. Kahn: Writings, Lectures, Interviews,* edited by Alessandra Latour. New York: Rizzoli, 1991.

——. *What Will Be Has Always Been: The Words of Louis I. Kahn,* edited by Richard Saul Wurman. New York: Access, Rizzoli, 1986.

KAISER, WOLFGANG. *Castle Howard, ein englischer Landsitz des frühen 18. Jahrhunderts: Studien zu Architektur und Landschaftspark.* Freiburg im Breisgau, Germany: Gaggstatter, 1984.

KAUFMANN, EDGAR, JR. *Fallingwater: A Frank Lloyd Wright Country House.* New York: Abbeville Press, 1986.

——. "Memmo's Lodoli." *Art Bulletin* 46 (June 1964): 159–75.

KAUFMANN, EMIL. *Architecture in the Age of Reason: Baroque and Post-Baroque in England, Italy, and France.* Cambridge, Mass.: Harvard University Press, 1955.

——. "At an Eighteenth Century Crossroads: Algarotti vs. Lodoli." *Journal of the Society of Architectural Historians* 4 (April 1944): 23–29.

——. *Three Revolutionary Architects: Boullée, Ledoux, and Lequeu.* Philadelphia: American Philosophical Society, 1952.

——. *Von Ledoux bis Le Corbusier: Ursprung und Entwicklung der Autonomen Architektur.* Vienna: Rolf Passer, 1933.

KENTGENS-CRAIG, MARGRET. *The Bauhaus and America: First Contacts, 1919–1936.* Cambridge, Mass.: MIT Press, 1999

KIENITZ, JOHN FABIAN. "The Romanticism of Frank Lloyd Wright." *Art in America* 32 (April 1944): 91–101.

KOOLHAAS, REM. *Delirious New York: A Retroactive Manifesto for Manhattan.* New York: Oxford University Press, 1978.

KRAUSS, ROSALIND. "A View of Modernism." *Artforum* 11 (September 1972): 48–51.

KRAUTHEIMER, RICHARD. *Studies in Early Christian, Medieval, and Renaissance Art.* New York: New York University Press, 1969.

LABORDE, COMTE [LÉON] DE. *De l'organisation des bibliothèques dans Paris.* 8th letter, *Etude sur la construction des bibliothèques.* Paris: A. Franck, April 1845.

LABROUSTE, HENRI. "A M. le Directeur de la Revue d'Architecture." *Revue générale de l'architecture et des travaux publics* 10 (1852): 382–84.

——. *Les Temples de Paestum: Restauration exécutée en 1829.* Restaurations des monuments antiques par les architectes pensionnaires de l'Académie de France à Rome depuis 1788 jusqu'à nos jours. Paris: Firmin-Didot, 1877.

LAMBERT, PHYLLIS, ED. *Mies in America.* Montreal: Canadian Centre for Architecture; New York: Whitney Museum of American Art, 2001.

LANG, S. "The Early Publications of the Temples at Paestum." *Journal of the Warburg and Courtauld Institutes* 13 (1950): 48–64.

LASSUS, JEAN-BAPTISTE-ANTOINE, AND ALFRED DARCEL, EDS. *Album de Villard de Honnecourt, architecte de XIIIe siècle.* Paris: Imprimerie Impériale, 1858.

LAUGIER, MARC-ANTOINE. *Essai sur l'architecture.* Originally published 1753. 2nd ed., rev. and enl., originally published 1755. Reprint, Farnborough, England: Gregg Press, 1966.

——. *Essai sur l'architecture / Observations sur l'architecture.* Originally published 1755 (2nd ed.) / 1765. Reprint, with an introduction by Geert Bekaert. Brussels: Pierre Madarga, 1979.

——. *An Essay on Architecture.* Translated by Wolfgang and Anni Herrmann. Documents and Sources in Architecture 1. Los Angeles: Hennessey & Ingalls, 1977.

[——]. *An Essay on Architecture; In Which Its True Principles are explained, And Invariable Rules proposed, For Directing the Judgment and Forming the Taste of the Gentleman and the Architect, With regard to the Different Kinds of Buildings, the Embellishment of Cities, And the Planning of Gardens.* Anon. translation. London: T. Osborn and Shipton, 1755.

LAVIN, SYLVIA. *Quatremère de Quincy and the Invention of a Modern Language of Architecture.* Cambridge, Mass.: MIT Press, 1992.

LE CORBUSIER. *Towards a New Architecture,* 1927. Translated by Frederick Etchells. London: Architectural Press, 1965. Originally published 1923 as *Vers une architecture.*

——, WITH SAUGNIER [AMÉDÉE OZENFANT]. "Trois rappels à MM. les architectes. Premier rappel: Le Volume." *L'Esprit nouveau* 1 (October 1920): 91–95.

LEHNER-LÖHR, DOROTHEA. *Architektur und Natur: Zur Problematik des "Imitatio-Naturae-Ideals" in der französischen Architekturtheorie des 18. Jahrhunderts.* Munich: Mäander, 1987.

LEMAGNY, JEAN-CLAUDE, ED. *Visionary Architects: Boullée, Ledoux, Lequeu.* Houston: University of St. Thomas, 1968.

LENIAUD, JEAN-MICHEL, ED. *Des palais pour les livres: Labrouste, Sainte-Geneviève et les bibliothèques.* Paris: Maisonneuve & Larose, Bibliothèque Sainte-Geneviève, 2002.

——. *Viollet-le-Duc, ou les délires du système.* Paris: Mengès, 1994.

LE ROY, JULIEN-DAVID. *Histoire de la disposition et des formes différentes que les Chrétiens ont données à leurs temples depuis le règne de Constantin le Grand jusqu'à nous.* Paris: Desaint and Saillant, 1764.

LEVINE, NEIL. "Abstraction and Representation in Modern Architecture: The International Style and Frank Lloyd Wright." *AA Files: Annals of the Architectural Association School of Architecture* 11 (Spring 1986): 3–21.

——. *The Architecture of Frank Lloyd Wright.* Princeton, N.J.: Princeton University Press, 1996.

——. "The Book and the Building: Hugo's Theory of Architecture and Labrouste's Bibliothèque Ste-Geneviève." In *The Beaux-Arts and Nineteenth-Century French Architecture,* edited by Robin Middleton, 138–73. London: Thames & Hudson, 1982.

——. "The Competition for the Grand Prix in 1824." In *The Beaux-Arts and Nineteenth-Century French Architecture,* edited by Robin Middleton, 66–123. London: Thames & Hudson, 1982.

——. "Frank Lloyd Wright's Diagonal Planning Revisited." In *On and by Frank Lloyd Wright: A Primer of Architectural Principles,* edited by Robert McCarter, 232–63. London: Phaidon Press, 2005. Earlier version published as "Frank Lloyd Wright's Diagonal Planning." *In In Search of Modern Architecture: A Tribute to Henry-Russell Hitchcock,* edited by Helen Searing, 245–77. New York, Cambridge, Mass., and London: Architectural History Foundation and MIT Press, 1982.

——. "Frank Lloyd Wright's Own Houses and His Changing Concept of Representation." In *The Nature of Frank Lloyd Wright,* edited by Carol R. Bolon, Robert S. Nelson, and Linda Seidel, 20–69. Chicago: University of Chicago Press, 1988.

——. Introduction to *Frank Lloyd Wright's Fallingwater.* Photographs by Ezra Stoller. Building Blocks. New York: Princeton Architectural Press, 1999.

——. "The Quadruple Block Plan: L'obsession de Frank Lloyd Wright pour la grille / The Quadruple Block Plan and Frank Lloyd Wright's Obsession with the Grid." *EaV: La Revue de l'école nationale supérieure de l'architecture de Versailles / Versailles Architecture School Journal* 11 (2005/2006): 62–84.

——. "The Romantic Idea of Architectural Legibility: Henri Labrouste and the *Néo-Grec.*" In *The Architecture of the Ecole des Beaux-Arts,* edited by Arthur Drexler, 324–416. New York: Museum of Modern Art, 1977.

——. "Il rovesciamento del sistema della rappresentazione nelle biblioteche di Labrouste." In *Henri Labrouste, 1801–1875,* edited by Renzo Dubbini, 166–90. Milan: Electa, 2002.

LEWIS, MICHAEL J. *The Gothic Revival.* New York: Thames & Hudson, 2002.

LOOS, ADOLF. "Ornement et crime." *Les Cahiers d'aujourd'hui* 5 (June 1913): 247–56. Reprinted in *L'Esprit nouveau* 2 (1920): 159–68.

LORIN, CLAUDE. *L'Inachevé: Peinture, sculpture, littérature.* Paris: B. Grasset, 1984.

LOUD, PATRICIA CUMMINGS. *The Art Museums of Louis I. Kahn.* Durham, N.C.: Duke University Press, 1989.

——. "History of the Kimbell Art Museum." In *In Pursuit of Quality: The Kimbell Art Museum, An Illustrated History of the Art and Architecture.* 1–95. Forth Worth: Kimbell Art Museum, 1987

L[UCAS], CH[ARLES]. "Causerie. Henri Labrouste: Lettres inédites sur l'enseignement de l'architecture. (Paris, 1830–1831)." Parts 1 and 2. *La Construction moderne* 10 (March 2, 1895): 253–55; (March 9, 1895): 268–69.

LYNES, RUSSELL. *Good Old Modern: An Intimate Portrait of the Museum of Modern Art.* New York: Atheneum, 1973.

MACAULAY, JAMES. *The Gothic Revival, 1745–1845.* Glasgow: Blackie, 1975.

MADEC, PHILIPPE. *Boullée.* Paris: F. Hazan, 1986.

MALLGRAVE, HARRY FRANCIS. *Gottfried Semper: Architect of the Nineteenth Century.* New Haven, Conn.: Yale University Press, 1996.

——. *Modern Architectural Theory: A Historical Survey, 1673–1968.* Cambridge: Cambridge University Press, 2005.

MANIERI-ELIA, MARIO. *Louis Henry Sullivan.* Translated by Antony Shugaar with Caroline Green. New York: Princeton Architectural Press, 1996.

MANSON, GRANT CARPENTER. *Frank Lloyd Wright to 1910: The First Golden Age.* New York: Reinhold, 1958.

MCATEE, CAMMIE. "Alien #5044325: Mies's First Trip to America." In *Mies in America,* edited by Phyllis Lambert, 132–91. Montreal: Canadian Centre for Architecture; New York: Whitney Museum of American Art, 2001.

——. "Le 'Musée pour une petite ville' de Mies van der Rohe: Avant-texte ou avant-textes?" *Genesis: Manuscrits-Recherche-Invention* 14 (2000): 219–47.

MCCARTER, ROBERT. *Fallingwater, Frank Lloyd Wright.* Architecture in Detail. London: Phaidon Press, 1994.

——. *Frank Lloyd Wright.* London: Phaidon Press, 1997.

——. *Unity Temple: Frank Lloyd Wright.* Architecture in Detail. London: Phaidon Press, 1997.

MCCARTHY, MICHAEL J. F. *The Origins of the Gothic Revival.* New Haven, Conn.: Yale University Press, 1987.

MCFARLAND, THOMAS. *Romanticism and the Forms of Ruin: Wordsworth, Coleridge, and Modalities of Fragmentation.* Princeton, N.J.: Princeton University Press, 1981.

MECKEL, CHRISTOPH. *Über das Fragmentarische.* Mainz: Akademie der Wissenschaften und der Literatur, F. Steiner, 1978.

MEMMO, ANDREA. *Elementi dell'architettura Lodoliana o sia L'arte del fabbricare con solidità e con eleganza no cappriciosa.* Rome: Pagliarini, 1786.

MENOCAL, NARCISO. *Architecture as Nature: The Transcendentalist Idea of Louis Sullivan.* Madison: University of Wisconsin Press, 1981.

MERTINS, DETLEF. "System and Freedom: Sigfried Giedion, Emil Kaufmann, and the Constitution of Architectural Modernity." In *Autonomy and Ideology: Positioning an Avant-Garde in America*, edited by R. E. Somol, 213–31. New York: Monacelli Press, 1997.

MIDDLETON, ROBIN. "The Abbé de Cordemoy and the Graeco-Gothic Ideal: A Prelude to Romantic Classicism." *Journal of the Warburg and Courtauld Institutes* 25 (1962): 278–320; 26 (1963): 90–123.

———. "Architects as Engineers: The Iron Reinforcement of Entablatures in Eighteenth-Century France." *AA Files: Annals of the Architectural Association School of Architecture* 9 (Summer 1985): 54–64.

———. "Henri Labrouste." *International Architect* 1, no. 3 (1980): 40–46.

———. "La struttura in ferro della Bibliothèque Sainte-Geneviève come base di un decoro civico." In *Henri Labrouste, 1801–1875*, edited by Renzo Dubbini, 121–42. Milan: Electa, 2002.

———. "Viollet-le-Duc's Academic Ventures and the *Entretiens sur l'Architecture.*" In *Gottfried Semper und die Mitte des 19. Jahrhunderts: Symposium vom 2–6 Dezember 1974*, edited by Eva Börsch-Supan et al., 239–54. Institut für Geschichte und Theorie der Architektur, Eidgenössische Technischen Hochschule, Zürich. Basel: Birkhäuser, 1976.

"Mies van der Rohe." *Architectural Forum* 97 (May 1952): 93–111.

MIES VAN DER ROHE, LUDWIG. "A Tribute to Frank Lloyd Wright." Originally published 1946. Reprinted in *The Show to End All Shows: Frank Lloyd Wright and the Museum of Modern Art*, edited by Peter Reed and William Kaizen, 169–70. Studies in Modern Art 8. New York: Museum of Modern Art, 2004.

MILIZIA, FRANCESCO. *Principij di architettura civile.* Originally published 1781. Edited by Angelo Ruggieri. Milan: Sapere, 2000.

MILLET, EUGÈNE. "Notice sur la vie et les travaux de Pierre-François-Henry Labrouste, Membre de l'Institut, Président de la Société centrale des Architectes." *Bulletin mensuel de la Société centrale des Architectes*, 5th ser., 3 (1880). *Supplément au Bulletin de l'exercise 1879–80: Congrès annuel des Architectes*, 7th and 8th sessions, 203–19.

MOHOLY-NAGY, SIBYL. Comments in "Sunday Session." *Journal of the Society of Architectural Historians* 25 (March 1965): 83–84.

———. "The Diaspora." *Journal of the Society of Architectural Historians* 25 (March 1965): 24–25.

MONVAL, JEAN. *Soufflot: Sa vie, son oeuvre, son esthétique (1713–1780).* Paris: A. Lemerre, 1918.

MORRISON, HUGH. *Louis Sullivan: Prophet of Modern Architecture.* Originally published 1935. Rev. ed. New York: W. W. Norton, 1998.

MOUDRY, ROBERTA, ED. *The American Skyscraper: Cultural Histories.* Cambridge: Cambridge University Press, 2005.

MUMFORD, LEWIS. "Notes on Modern Architecture." *New Republic* 66 (March 18, 1931): 119–22.

———. "The Sky Line—at Home, Indoors and Out." *New Yorker* 13 (February 12, 1938): 31.

NELSON, GEORGE. "Architects of Europe Today, 7: Van Der Rohe, Germany." *Pencil Points* 16 (September 1935): 453–60.

———. *Industrial Architecture of Albert Kahn, Inc.* New York: Architectural Book Publishing, 1939.

NEUMEYER, FRITZ. *The Artless Word: Mies van der Rohe on the Building Art.* Originally published 1986. Translated by Mark Jarzombek. Cambridge, Mass.: MIT Press, 1991.

———. "A World in Itself: Architecture and Technology." In *The Presence of Mies*, edited by Detlef Mertins, 71–83. New York: Princeton Architectural Press, 1994.

NEUTRA, RICHARD J. *Wie baut Amerika?* Stuttgart: J. Hoffmann, 1927.

"New Buildings for 194X." *Architectural Forum* 78 (May 1943): 68–152, 189.

NICCO FASOLA, GIUSTA. *Ragionamenti sulla architettura.* [Bari]: Macrì, 1949.

ONIANS, JOHN. *Bearers of Meaning: The Classical Orders in Antiquity, the Middle Ages, and the Renaissance.* Princeton, N.J.: Princeton University Press, 1988.

OPPLER, ELLEN C. *Picasso's Guernica: Illustrations, Introductory Essay, Documents, Poetry, Criticism, Analysis.* Norton Critical Studies in Art History. New York: W. W. Norton, 1988.

OUD, J[OHANNES] J[ACOBUS] P[IETER]. "Architectural Observations Concerning Wright and the Robie House." Originally published 1918. In *Writings on Wright: Selected Comment on Frank Lloyd Wright*, edited by H. Allen Brooks, 135–37. Cambridge, Mass.: MIT Press, 1981.

———. "The Influence of Frank Lloyd Wright on the Architecture of Europe." In *The Life-Work of the American Architect Frank Lloyd Wright*, edited by H[endrikus] Th[eodorus] Wijdeveld, 85–89. Santpoort, Holland: C. A. Mees, 1925. Originally published in *Wendingen* 7 (1925): 85–91.

OZENFANT, [AMÉDÉE], AND [CHARLES-EDOUARD] JEANNERET [LE CORBUSIER]. *Après le cubisme.* Paris: Editions des Commentaires, 1918.

Le Panthéon, symbole des révolutions: De l'église de la nation au temple des grands hommes. Paris: Picard, 1989.

PAYNE, ALINA A. *The Architectural Treatise in the Italian Renaissance: Architectural Invention, Ornament, and Literary Culture.* Cambridge: Cambridge University Press, 1999.

———. "Ut Poesis Architectura: Tectonics and Poetics in Architectural Criticism circa 1570." In *Antiquity and Its Interpreters*, edited by A. A. Payne, Ann Kuttner, and Rebekah Smick, 145–58. Cambridge: Cambridge University Press, 2000.

PEIK, SUSAN M., ED. *Karl Friedrich Schinkel: Aspects of His Work / Aspekte seines Werks.* Stuttgart: Axel Menges, 2001.

PÉROUSE DE MONTCLOS, JEAN-MARIE. *Etienne-Louis Boullée.* Paris: Flammarion, 1994. Rev. ed. of *Etienne-Louis Boullée (1728–1799): De l'architecture classique à l'architecture révolutionnaire.* Paris: Arts et Métiers Graphiques, 1969.

———. *Jacques-Germain Soufflot.* Paris: Monum, Editions du Patrimoine, 2004.

PESCHKEN, GOERD. *Karl Friedrich Schinkel: Das architektonische Lehrbuch.* In *Karl Friedrich Schinkel: Lebenswerk*, edited by Margarete Kühn. Munich: Deutscher Kunstverlag, 1979.

——. "Technologische Ästhetik in Schinkels Architektur." *Zeitschrift des deutschen Vereins für Kunstwissenschaft* 22, nos. 1–2 (1968): 45–81.

PETZET, MICHAEL. *Soufflots Sainte-Geneviève und der französische Kirchenbau des 18. Jahrhunderts.* Berlin: De Gruyter, 1961.

PEVSNER, NIKOLAUS. *Pioneers of the Modern Movement, from William Morris to Walter Gropius.* London: Faber and Faber, 1936.

——. "A Short Pugin Florilegium." *Architectural Review* 94 (August 1943): 31–34.

——. *Studies in Art, Architecture, and Design.* 2 vols. London: Thames & Hudson, 1968.

PFEIFFER, BRUCE BROOKS, ED. *Frank Lloyd Wright: Letters to Clients.* Fresno: Press at California State University, 1986.

PICON, ANTOINE. "Architettura ed espressione costruttiva: Il problema del razionalismo costruttivo / Architecture and Constructive Expression: The Problem of Structural Rationalism." *Lotus International: Rivista trimestrale di architettura / Quarterly Architectural Review* 47, no. 3 (1985): 6–18.

——. *Claude Perrault, 1613–1688; ou, La Curiosité d'un classique.* Paris: Picard, 1988.

——. "The Freestanding Column in Eighteenth-Century Religious Architecture." In *Things That Talk: Object Lessons from Art and Science,* edited by Lorraine Daston, 66–99. New York: Zone Books, 2004.

——. *French Architects and Engineers in the Age of Enlightenment.* Originally published 1988. Translated by Martin Thom. Cambridge Studies in the History of Architecture. Cambridge: Cambridge University Press, 1992.

"A Picturesque Sky-Scraper." *Architectural Record* 5 (January–March 1896): 299–302.

PLANCHE, GUSTAVE. "Le Musée du Louvre." In *Portraits d'artistes: Peintres et sculpteurs,* vol. 2, 241–75. Paris: Michel Lévy frères, 1853.

PLOUIN, RENÉE. "Henri Labrouste: Sa vie, son oeuvre (1801–1875)." 3rd cycle thesis. University of Paris, 1966.

PORTOGHESI, PAOLO. *After Modern Architecture.* Originally published 1980. Translated by Meg Shore. New York: Rizzoli, 1982.

POSENER, JULIUS. *From Schinkel to the Bauhaus.* New York: Wittenborn, 1972.

——. "Schinkel's Eclecticism and the 'Architectural.'" *Architectural Design* 53, nos. 11–12 (1983): 32–39.

"Promenades in Paris." *The Builder* 8 (March 9, 1850): 110–11.

PUGIN, A[UGUSTUS] WELBY [NORTHMORE]. *An Apology for the Revival of Christian Architecture in England.* Originally published 1843. Reprint, Oxford: St. Barnabas Press, 1969.

——. *Contrasts: or, a Parallel between the Noble Edifices of the Middle Ages, and Corresponding Buildings of the Present Day, Shewing the Present Decay of Taste.* 2nd ed., rev. and enl. Originally published 1841. Reprint, Victorian Library. New York: Humanities Press; Leicester: Leicester University Press, 1969. 1st ed. published 1836 as *Contrasts, or a Parallel between the Noble Edifices of the Fourteenth and Fifteenth Centuries, and Similar Buildings of the Present Day, Shewing the Present Decay of Taste.*

——. *The Present State of Ecclesiastical Architecture in England.* Originally published 1843. Reprint, Oxford: St Barnabas Press, 1969.

——. *The True Principles of Pointed or Christian Architecture: Set forth in Two Lectures Delivered at St. Marie's, Oscott.* Originally published 1841. Reprint of 1853 ed., Oxford: St. Barnabas Press, 1969.

PUNDT, HERMANN G. *Schinkel's Berlin: A Study in Environmental Planning.* Cambridge, Mass.: Harvard University Press, 1972.

QUATREMÈRE DE QUINCY, ANTOINE-CHRYSOSTÔME. *Architecture.* 3 vols. In *Encyclopédie méthodique, ou par ordre de matières, par une société de gens de lettres, de savans et d'artistes,* edited by C[harles] J[oseph] Panckoucke. Paris: Panckoucke, 1788; Henri Agasse, 1801; Mme la veuve Agasse, 1825.

——. *De l'architecture égyptienne considérée dans son origine, ses principes et son goût, et comparée sous les mêmes rapports à l'architecture grecque.* Dissertation qui a remporté, en 1785, le prix proposé par l'Académie des Inscriptions et Belles-Lettres. Paris: Barrois l'aîné et fils, 1803.

——. *Dictionnaire historique d'architecture, comprenant dans son plan les notions historiques, descriptives, archéologiques, biographiques, théoriques, didactiques et pratiques de cet art.* 2 vols. Paris: A. Le Clere, 1832.

——. *Essai sur la nature, le but et les moyens de l'imitation dans les beaux-arts.* Originally published 1823. Reprint as *De l'imitation, 1823,* edited by Leon Krier and Demetri Porphyrios. Brussels: Archives d'Architecture Moderne, 1980.

——. *Histoire de la vie et des ouvrages des plus célèbres architectes du XIe siècle jusqu'à la fin du XVIIIe.* 2 vols. Paris: J. Renouard, 1830.

QUINAN, JACK. *Frank Lloyd Wright's Larkin Building: Myth and Fact.* New York: ;Cambridge, Mass.: MIT Press, 1987.

RAVE, PAUL ORTWIN. *Berlin.* Vol. 1, *Bauten für die Kunst, Kirchen, Denkmalpflege.* In *Karl Friedrich Schinkel: Lebenswerk.* Originally published 1941. New ed., edited by Margarete Kühn. Berlin: Deutscher Kunstverlag, 1981.

——. *Berlin.* Vol. 3, *Bauten für Wissenschaft, Verwaltung, Heer, Wohnbau, und Denkmäler.* In *Karl Friedrich Schinkel: Lebenswerk,* edited by P. O. Rave. Berlin: Deutsche Kunstverlag, 1962.

RICHARDSON, MARGARET, AND MARYANNE STEVENS, EDS. *John Soane, Architect: Master of Space and Light.* London: Royal Academy of Arts, 1999.

RIDGWAY CHRISTOPHER, AND ROBERT WILLIAMS, EDS. *Sir John Vanbrugh and Landscape Architecture in Baroque England, 1690–1730.* Phoenix Mill, Thrupp, Stroud, England: Sutton Publishing, 2000.

RIVARA, ANNIE, AND GUY LAVOREL, EDS. *L'Oeuvre inachevée: Actes du colloque international (11 et 12 décembre 1998).* Lyon: Aprime, 1999.

RONNER, HEINZ, SHARAD JHAVERI, AND ALESSANDRO VASELLA. *Louis I. Kahn: Complete Work, 1935–74.* Basel and Stuttgart: Birkhäuser; Boulder, Colo.: Westview Press, 1977.

ROOT, JOHN W[ELLBORN]. "A Great Architectural Problem." *The Inland Architect and News Record* 15 (June 1890): 67–71.

ROSEN, CHARLES, AND HENRI ZERNER. *Romanticism and Realism: The Mythology of Nineteenth-Century Art.* New York: Viking, 1984.

ROSENBLUM, ROBERT. "The Origin of Painting: A Problem in the Iconography of Romantic Classicism." *Art Bulletin* 39 (December 1957): 279–90.

——. "Pop Art and Non-Pop Art." Originally published 1964. In John Russell and Suzi Gablik, *Pop Art Redefined*, 53–56. New York: Praeger, 1969.

——. *Transformations in Late Eighteenth-Century Art*. Princeton, N.J.: Princeton University Press, 1967.

ROSENGARTEN, ALBERT. *Die architektonischen Stylarten: Eine kurze, allgemeinfassliche Darstellung der charakterischen Verschiedenheiten der architektonischen Stylarten*. Originally published 1859. Translated by W. Collett-Sandars. New York: D. Appleton, 1876.

——. "Die Bibliothek St. Geneviève in Paris." *Allgemeine Bauzeitung mit Abbildungen*, 16th yr. (1851): 66–68.

ROWE, COLIN. *The Mathematics of the Ideal Villa and Other Essays*. Cambridge, Mass.: MIT Press, 1976.

——, WITH FRED KOETTER. *Collage City*. Cambridge, Mass.: MIT Press, 1978.

RYKWERT, JOSEPH. *The First Moderns: The Architects of the Eighteenth Century*. Cambridge, Mass.: MIT Press, 1980.

——. "Lodoli on Function and Representation." *Architectural Review* 160 (July 1976): 21–26.

——. *On Adam's House in Paradise: The Idea of the Primitive Hut in Architectural History*. Museum of Modern Art Papers on Architecture. New York: Museum of Modern Art, 1972.

SADDY, PIERRE. *Henri Labrouste, architecte, 1801–1875*. Paris: Caisse Nationale des Monuments Historiques, 1977.

SANKOVITCH, ANNE-MARIE. "Structure/Ornament and the Modern Figuration of Architecture." *Art Bulletin* 80 (December 1998): 687–717.

SAUMAREZ SMITH, CHARLES. *The Building of Castle Howard*. Originally published 1990. New ed. London: Pimlico, 1997.

SCHAPIRO, MEYER. *The Unity of Picasso's Art*. New York; George Braziller, 2000.

SCHINKEL, KARL FRIEDRICH. *Collection of Architectural Designs, Including Designs Which Have Been Executed and Objects Whose Execution Was Intended*. New York: Princeton Architectural Press, 1989. Originally published 1819–40 as *Sammlung architektonischer Entwürfe, enthaltendtheils Werke welche ausgeführt sind, theils Gegenstände, deren Ausführung, beabsichtigt wurde*.

——. *The English Journey: Journal of a Visit to France and Britain in 1826*. Edited by David Bindman and Gottfried Riemann. New Haven, Conn.: Yale University Press, 1993.

SCHLEGEL, FRIEDRICH. *Dialogue on Poetry and Literary Aphorisms*. Originally published 1798. Translated and edited by Ernst Behler and Roman Struc. University Park: Pennsylvania State University Press, 1968.

SCHMARSOW, AUGUST. "The Essence of Architectural Creation." Originally published 1894. In *Empathy, Form, and Space: Problems in German Aesthetics, 1873–1893*, translated and edited by Harry Francis Mallgrave and Eleftherios Ikonomou, 281–97. Texts & Documents. Santa Monica, Calif.: Getty Center for the History of Art and the Humanities, 1994.

SCHNEIDER, R[ENÉ]. *L'Esthétique classique chez Quatremère de Quincy (1805–23)*. Paris: Hachette, 1910.

——. *Quatremère de Quincy et son intervention dans les arts (1788–1850)*. Paris: Hachette, 1910.

SCHULZ, JUERGEN. "Michelangelo's Unfinished Works." *Art Bulletin* 57 (September 1975): 366–73.

SCHULZE, FRANZ. *Mies van der Rohe: A Critical Biography*. Chicago: University of Chicago Press, 1985.

——, ED. *Mies van der Rohe: Critical Essays*. New York: Museum of Modern Art, 1989.

——, ED., WITH GEORGE E. DANFORTH, CONSULTING ED. *The Mies van der Rohe Archive: An Illustrated Catalogue of the Mies van der Rohe Drawings in the Museum of Modern Art*, part 2, *1938–1967: The American Work*. New York: Garland Publishing, 1992.

SCHUYLER, MONTGOMERY. "An Architectural Pioneer: Review of the Portfolios Containing the Works of Frank Lloyd Wright." Originally published 1912. Reprinted in vol. 2 of *American Architecture and Other Writings*, edited by William H. Jordy and Ralph Coe, 634–40. 2 vols. Cambridge, Mass.: Harvard University Press, Belknap Press, 1961.

——. "A Critique (with Illustrations) of the Works of Adler & Sullivan, D. H. Burnham & Co., Henry Ives Cobb." Great American Architects Series, no. 2. *Architectural Record* (February 1896).

——. "The Romanesque Revival in America." *Architectural Record* 1 (October–December 1891): 151–98. Reprinted in vol. 1 of *American Architecture and Other Writings*, edited by William H. Jordy and Ralph Coe, 200–25. 2 vols. Cambridge, Mass.: Harvard University Press, Belknap Press, 1961.

——. "The Skyscraper Problem." *Scribner's Magazine* 34 (September 1903): 253–56.

——. "The 'Sky-Scraper' up to Date." *Architectural Record* 8 (January–March 1899): 231–37.

SCHWARZER, MITCHELL. "The Emergence of Architectural Space: August Schmarsow's Theory of *Raumgestaltung*." *Assemblage* 15 (Fall 1991): 50–61.

——. *German Architectural Theory and the Search for Modern Identity*. Cambridge: Cambridge University Press, 1995.

——. "Ontology and Representation in Karl Bötticher's Theory of Tectonics." *Journal of the Society of Architectural Historians* 52 (September 1993): 267–80.

SCOTT BROWN, DENISE. "'A Worm's Eye View of Recent Architectural History.'" *Architectural Record* 172 (February 1984): 69–81.

SCULLY, VINCENT J., *Frank Lloyd Wright*. Masters of World Architecture. New York: George Braziller, 1960.

——. Introduction to *The Travel Sketches of Louis I. Kahn*, edited by Richard J. Boylen. Philadelphia: Pennsylvania Academy of the Fine Arts, 1978.

——. *Louis I. Kahn*. Makers of Contemporary Architecture. New York: George Braziller, 1962.

——. *Modern Architecture: The Architecture of Democracy*. Great Ages of World Architecture. New York: George Braziller, 1961.

——. *Modern Architecture and Other Essays*, edited by Neil Levine. Princeton, N.J.: Princeton University Press, 2003.

——. *The Shingle Style and the Stick Style: Architectural Theory and Design from Downing to the Origins of Wright.* Rev. ed. New Haven, Conn.: Yale University Press, 1971. Originally published 1955 as *The Shingle Style: Architectural Theory and Design from Richardson to the Origins of Wright.*

——. "Works of Louis Kahn and His Method." In *Louis I. Kahn: Sono zenbo,* edited by Toshio Nakamura. Special issue of *A+U: Architecture and Urbanism* (Tokyo, 1975): 286–99.

SEMPER, GOTTFRIED. *Style: Style in the Technical and Tectonic Arts: or, Practical Aesthetics.* Translated by Harry Francis Mallgrave and Michael Robinson. Texts & Documents. Los Angeles: Getty Research Institute, 2004. Originally published 1860–63 as *Der Stil in den technischen und tektonischen Künsten; oder, Praktische Aesthetik: Ein Handbuch für Techniker, Künstler und Kunstfreunde.*

SERRA, JOSELITA RASPI, ED. *Paestum and the Doric Revival, 1750–1830: Essential Outlines of an Approach.* Florence: Centro Di, 1986.

SHELL, WILLIAM S., WITH EDWARD A. DUCKETT AND JOSEPH Y. FUJIKAWA, EDS. *Impressions of Mies: An Interview on Mies van der Rohe, His Early Years, 1938–1958.* N.p., 1988.

SIRY, JOSEPH M. "Adler and Sullivan's Guaranty Building in Buffalo." *Journal of the Society of Architectural Historians* 55 (March 1996): 6–37.

——. *Unity Temple: Frank Lloyd Wright and Architecture for Liberal Religion.* Cambridge: Cambridge University Press, 1996.

SMITH, E[ARL] BALDWIN. *The Dome: A Study in the History of Ideas.* Princeton Monographs in Art and Archaeology 25. Princeton, N.J.: Princeton University Press, 1950.

SMITH, NORRIS KELLY. *Frank Lloyd Wright: A Study in Architectural Content.* Originally published 1966. Rev. ed. Watkins Glen, N.Y.: American Life Foundation & Study Institute, 1979.

SNODIN, MICHAEL, ED. *Karl Friedrich Schinkel: A Universal Man.* New Haven, Conn.: Yale University Press, 1991.

SOLOMON, SUSAN G. *Louis Kahn's Trenton Jewish Community Center.* Building Studies 6. New York: Princeton Architectural Press, 2000.

Soufflot et l'architecture des lumières. Paris: Ministère de l'Environnement et du Cadre de Vie, Direction de l'Architecture; Centre National de la Recherche Scientifique, 1980.

SPAETH, DAVID A. *Mies van der Rohe.* New York: Rizzoli, 1985.

SPENCER, ROBERT, JR. "The Work of Frank Lloyd Wright." *Architectural Review* (Boston) 7 (June 1900): 61–72.

SPEYER, A. JAMES. *Mies van der Rohe.* Chicago: Art Institute of Chicago, 1968.

SPIERO, SABINE. "Schinkels Altes Museum in Berlin: Seine Baugeschichte von den Anfängen bis zur Eröffnung." *Jahrbuch der preuszischen Kunstsammlungen* 55 (1934): suppl., 41–81.

STAFFORD, BARBARA MARIA. "Science as Fine Art: Another Look at Boullée's Cenotaph for Newton." *Studies in Eighteenth-Century Culture* 11 (1982): 241–78.

STANTON, PHOEBE. *Pugin.* London: Thames & Hudson, 1971.

STERN, ROBERT A. M. "The Doubles of Post-Modern." *Harvard Architecture Review* 1 (Spring 1980): 75–87.

STRALEN, MARIËTTE VAN. "Kindred Spirits: Holland, Wright, and Wijdeveld." In *Frank Lloyd Wright: Europe and Beyond,* edited by Anthony Alsofsin, 45–65. Berkeley: University of California Press, 1999.

STROUD, DOROTHY. *Sir John Soane, Architect.* London: Faber and Faber, 1984.

"The Studio-Home of Frank Lloyd Wright." *Architectural Record* 33 (January 1913): 45–54.

SULLIVAN, LOUIS. "The Tall Building Artistically Considered." *Lippincott's Monthly Magazine* 57 (March 1896): 403–9. Reprinted in *Inland Architect and News Record* 27 (May 1896): 32–34 and in *Louis Sullivan: The Public Papers,* edited by Robert Twombly, 104–13. Chicago: University of Chicago Press, 1988.

SUMMERSON, JOHN. *Architecture in Britain, 1530 to 1830.* Originally published 1953. 4th rev. and enl. ed. Pelican History of Art. Harmondsworth, Middlesex, England: Penguin, 1963.

——. *The Architecture of the Eighteenth Century.* London: Thames & Hudson, 1986.

——, ED. *Concerning Architecture: Essays on Architectural Writers and Writing Presented to Nikolaus Pevsner.* London: Allen Lane, 1968.

——. *Heavenly Mansions and Other Essays on Architecture.* Originally published 1949. New York: W. W. Norton, 1963.

——. *Sir John Soane, 1753–1837.* Architectural Biographies 4. London: Art and Technics, 1952.

——. *The Unromantic Castle.* London: Thames & Hudson, 1990.

SWITZER, STEPHEN. *Ichnographia Rustica, or, The Nobleman, Gentleman, and Gardener's Recreation.* 3 vols. Originally published 1718. Reprint, New York: Garland, 1982.

SZAMBIEN, WERNER. *Jean-Nicolas-Louis Durand, 1760–1834: De l'imitation à la norme.* Paris: Picard, 1984.

——. *Schinkel.* Paris: Hazan, 1989.

TAFURI, MANFREDO. *Architecture and Utopia: Design and Capitalist Development.* Originally published 1973. Translated by Barbara Luigia La Penta. Cambridge, Mass.: MIT Press, 1976.

——. "The Disenchanted Mountain: The Skyscraper and the City." In *The American City: From the Civil War to the New Deal,* by Giorgio Ciucci et al., 389–528. Cambridge, Mass.: MIT Press, 1979.

——. *The Sphere and the Labyrinth: Avant-Gardes and Architecture from Piranesi to the 1970s.* Originally published 1980. Translated by Pellegrino d'Acierno and Robert Connolly. Cambridge, Mass.: MIT Press, 1990.

——. "Storicità di Louis Kahn." *Comunità* 117 (February 1964): 38–49.

——. *Theories and History of Architecture.* Originally published 1976. Translated by Giorgio Verrecchia. Cambridge, Mass.: MIT Press, 1980.

——AND FRANCESCO DAL CO. *Modern Architecture.* Originally published 1976. Translated by Robert Erich Wolf. New York: Harry N. Abrams, 1980.

"Taliesin: 1911–1914." *Wright Studies* 1. Edited by Narciso Menocal. Carbondale: Southern Illinois University Press, 1992.

TAVERNE, ED, COR WAGENAAR, AND MARTIEN DE VLETTER. *J. J. P. Oud, Poetic Functionalist, 1893–1963: The Complete Works.* Rotterdam: NAi, 2001.

TEGETHOFF, WOLF. *Mies van der Rohe: The Villas and Country Houses.* Originally published 1981. Translated by Russell M. Stockman. New York: Museum of Modern Art, 1985.

TENTORI, FRANCESCO. "Il passato come un amico." *Casabella* 275 (May 1963): 26–28.

TOEWS, JOHN EDWARD. *Becoming Historical: Cultural Reformation and Public Memory in Early Nineteenth-Century Berlin.* Cambridge: Cambridge University Press, 2004.

TOKER, FRANKLIN. *Fallingwater Rising: Frank Lloyd Wright, E. J. Kaufmann, and America's Most Extraordinary House.* New York: Alfred A. Knopf, 2003.

TOYNBEE, PAGET, ED. "Horace Walpole's Journals of Visits to Country Seats, &c." *Walpole Society* 16 (1927–28): 9–80.

TRIANON, HENRY. "Nouvelle Bibliothèque Sainte Geneviève." *Illustration* 17 (January 10–17, 1851): 29–30.

TWOMBLY, ROBERT. *Louis Sullivan: His Life and Work.* New York: Viking, 1986.

———, AND NARCISO MENOCAL. *Louis Sullivan: The Poetry of Architecture.* New York: W. W. Norton, 2000.

TYNG, ANNE. *Louis Kahn to Anne Tyng: The Rome Letters, 1953–1954.* New York: Rizzoli, 1997.

VAN ZANTEN, DAVID. *Building Paris: Architectural Institutions and the Transformation of the French Capital, 1830–1870.* Cambridge: Cambridge University Press, 1994.

———. *Designing Paris: The Architecture of Duban, Labrouste, Duc and Vaudoyer.* Cambridge, Mass.: MIT Press, 1987.

———. *Sullivan's City: The Meaning of Ornament for Louis Sullivan.* New York: W. W. Norton, 2000.

VASARI, GIORGIO. *The Lives of the Artists.* Translated by Julia Conaway Bondanella and Peter Bondanella. Oxford: Oxford University Press, 1991. Originally published 1550–68 as *Le vite de' più eccellenti architetti, pittori, et scultori italiani, da Cimabue insino a' tempi nostri.*

VAUDOYER, LÉON. "Histoire de l'architecture en France." In vol. 2 of *Patria: La France ancienne et moderne, morale et matérielle, ou, Collection encyclopédique et statistique de tous les faits relatifs à l'histoire physique et intellectuelle de la France et de ses colonies,* 2113–2200. Paris: J.-J. Dubochet, Lechevalier, 1847.

———, AND ALBERT LENOIR. "Etudes d'architecture en France." *Magasin pittoresque* 7–21 (1839–53).

VENTURI, ROBERT. *Complexity and Contradiction in Architecture.* Museum of Modern Art Papers on Architecture 1. New York: Museum of Modern Art, 1966.

———, DENISE SCOTT BROWN, AND STEVEN IZENOUR. *Learning from Las Vegas.* Cambridge, Mass.: MIT Press, 1972; 2nd ed. rev., with subtitle *The Forgotten Symbolism of Architectural Form,* 1977.

VIDLER, ANTHONY. *Claude-Nicolas Ledoux: Architecture and Social Reform at the End of the Ancien Régime.* Cambridge, Mass.: MIT Press, 1990.

———. *The Writing of the Walls: Architectural Theory in the Late Enlightenment.* Princeton, N.J.: Princeton Architectural Press, 1987.

VILLARI, SERGIO. *J. N. L. Durand (1760–1834): Art and Science of Architecture.* Originally published 1984. New York: Rizzoli, 1990.

Viollet-le-Duc. Paris: Editions de la Réunion des musées nationaux, Ministère de la Culture et de la Communication, 1980.

VIOLLET-LE-DUC, EUGÈNE-EMMANUEL. *Compositions et dessins de Viollet-le-Duc.* Paris: Librairie centrale d'architecture, 1884.

———. *Dictionnaire raisonné de l'architecture française du XIe au XVIe siècle.* 10 vols. Paris: B. Bance, 1854–63; A. Morel, 1864–68.

———. *Lectures on Architecture.* 2 vols. Translated by Benjamin Bucknall. Originally published 1877–81. Reprint, New York: Dover Publications, 1987. Originally published 1863–72 as *Entretiens sur l'architecture.*

———. "Le Style gothique au XIXe siècle." *Annales Archéologiques* 4 (1846): 325–53.

VITRUVIUS POLLIO, MARCUS. *De architectura (On Architecture).* 2 vols. Edited and translated by Frank Granger. Loeb Classical Library. Cambridge, Mass.: Harvard University Press, 1945.

VOLBERTAL, J.-H. *Aux environs de Paris, un domaine célèbre. Ermenonville: Ses sites, ses curiosités, son histoire.* Senlis, France: Imprimeries réunies de Senlis, 1923.

VOGT, ADOLF MAX. *Boullées Newton-Denkmal: Sakralbau und Kugelidee.* Geschichte und Theorie der Architektur 3. Basel: Birkhäuser, 1969.

WATKIN, DAVID. *Sir John Soane: Enlightenment Thought and the Royal Academy Lectures.* Cambridge Studies in the History of Architecture. Cambridge: Cambridge University Press, 1996.

WEBB, GEOFFREY. "The Letters and Drawings of Nicholas Hawksmoor Relating to the Building of the Mausoleum at Castle Howard, 1726–1742." *Walpole Society* 19 (1930–31): 111–64.

WEINGARDEN, LAUREN S. "Louis H. Sullivan's Metaphysics of Architecture (1885–1901): Sources and Correspondences with Symbolist Art Theories." Ph.D. diss., University of Chicago, 1981.

WHISTLER, LAURENCE. *The Imagination of Vanbrugh and His Fellow Artists.* London: Art and Technics, B. T. Batsford, 1954.

WICKERSHAM, JAY. "The Making of Exeter Library." *Harvard Architecture Review* 7 (1989): 138–49.

WIEBENSON, DORA. *The Picturesque Garden in France.* Princeton, N.J.: Princeton University Press, 1978.

WIEGAND-HOFFMANN, NANY, ED. *Karl Friedrich Schinkel, Bauakademie: Essays 2003.* Berlin: Berliner Wissenschafts-Verlag, 2003.

WIJDEVELD, H[ENDRIKUS] TH[EODORUS], ED. *The Life-Work of the American Architect Frank Lloyd Wright.* Santpoort, Holland: C. A. Mees, 1925.

WILLIAMSON, TOM. *Polite Landscapes: Gardens and Society in Eighteenth-Century England.* Baltimore: Johns Hopkins University Press, 1995.

WITTKOWER, RUDOLF. *Architectural Principles in the Age of Humanism.* Originally published 1949. New York: Random House, 1962.

WOODBRIDGE, KENNETH. "Henry Hoare's Paradise." *Art Bulletin* 47 (March 1965): 85–116.

———. *Landscape and Antiquity: Aspects of English Culture at Stourhead, 1718 to 1838.* Oxford: Clarendon Press, 1970.

WRIGHT, JOHN LLOYD. *My Father Who Is on Earth.* Originally published 1946. New ed. Carbondale: Southern Illinois University Press, 1994.

WRIGHT, FRANK LLOYD. *Ausgeführte Bauten und Entwürfe von Frank Lloyd Wright.* Originally published 1910[–11]. Reprint, with English translation (*Studies and Executed Buildings by Frank Lloyd Wright*), Palos Park, Ill.: Prairie School Press, 1975.

——. *An Autobiography.* London: Longmans, Green, 1932. 2nd ed. New York: Duell, Sloan and Pearce, 1943.

——. "Form and Function." *Saturday Review of Literature* 13 (December 14, 1935): 6.

——. *Frank Lloyd Wright: Collected Writings,* edited by Bruce Brooks Pfeiffer. 5 vols. New York: Rizzoli, 1992–95.

——. "In the Cause of Architecture." *Architectural Record* 23 (March 1908): 155–221.

——. "Recollections: United States, 1893–1920." Part 1–4. *Architects' Journal* 84 (July 16, 1936): 76–78; (July 23, 1936): 111–12; (July 30, 1936): 141–42; (August 6, 1936): 173–74.

YOUNÉS, SAMIR, ED. *The True, the Fictive, and the Real: The "Historical Dictionary of Architecture" of Quatremère de Quincy.* London: Andreas Papadakis, 1999.

ZADOW, MARIO. *Karl Friedrich Schinkel.* Berlin: Rembrandt Verlag, 1980.

ZEVI, BRUNO, AND EDGAR KAUFMANN JR. *La casa sulla cascata di F. L. Wright: F. Lloyd Wright's Fallingwater.* Milan: ETAS/Kompass, 1963.

ZUCKER, PAUL. "The Paradox of Architectural Theories at the Beginning of the 'Modern Movement.'" *Journal of the Society of Architectural Historians* 10 (September 1951): 8–14.

ZUKOWSKY, JOHN, ED. *Chicago Architecture, 1872–1922: Birth of a Metropolis.* Chicago: Art Institute of Chicago; Munich: Prestel-Verlag, 1987.

——. *Karl Friedrich Schinkel, 1781–1841: The Drama of Architecture.* Chicago: Art Institute of Chicago; Tübingen: Wasmuth, 1994.

Index

Italic page numbers refer to figures. **Boldface** page numbers refer to primary discussions of specific architects or buildings.

Illustration Credits

The photographers and the sources of visual material other than those indicated in the captions are as follows. Every effort has been made to supply complete and correct credits; if there are errors or omissions, please contact Yale University Press so that corrections can be made in any subsequent edition.

Accademia, Florence, Italy, Scala/Ministero per i Beni e la Attività culturali/Art Resource, NY: 8.2

Albert Kahn Associates, Architects & Engineers, Detroit: 7.26

Alinari/Art Resource, NY: I.7, 2.24, 4.42, 8.24

© The Andy Warhol Foundation for the Visual Arts/Artists Rights Society (ARS), New York. The Andy Warhol Foundation, Inc./Art Resource, NY: 7.42

Archives Nationales, Paris: 4.21, 4.39

Courtesy of Art and Architecture Library, University of Michigan, Ann Arbor: 6.24, 6.25 (Photos: Henry Fuermann)

Art Institute of Chicago © 2009 The Willem de Kooning Foundation/Artists Rights Society (ARS), New York: 8.3

Avery Library, Columbia University, New York: 2.18, 8.37 (Photo: Louis H. Dreyer)

© Brad Bellows: 1.18, 6.19

Bibliothèque des Arts Décoratifs, Paris: 8.6

Bibliothèque nationale de France, Paris: 2.14, 2.16, 3.2, 3.4–3.7, 3.9–3.16, 3.19–3.21, 4.16

Bibliothèque Sainte-Geneviève, Paris: 3.17, 4.2, 4.15, 4.22, 4.23, 4.28, 4.32, 4.38, 4.40, 4.41

From Werner Blaser, *Mies van der Rohe: The Art of Structure*, 1965: 7.36, 7.37, 7.39

Nabil Boutros: 4.30

British Museum, London © The Trustees of the British Museum: 2.2

Caisse Nationale des Monuments Historiques, Paris: 4.34

Castle Howard Collection, with kind permission of the Hon. Simon Howard: 1.5, 1.7, 1.22, 1.27, 1.35

© Centre des Monuments Nationaux, Paris: 2.19 (Photo: Caroline Rose)

Courtesy of Chicago History Museum: 1.2 (Hedrich-Blessing Collection, HB-7327-D, Photo: Hedrich-Blessing), 7.34 (Photo: J. Sherwin Murphy), 7.38 (HB-13809-Q4, Photo: Hedrich-Blessing)

Collection Centre Canadien d'Architecture/ Canadian Centre for Architecture, Montréal: 2.26

Conway Library, The Courtauld Institute of Art, London: 4.27, 4.29 (Photos: James Austin)

Harold Corsini: 6.37

Country Life: I.5

From Arthur Drexler, *Ludwig Mies van der Rohe*, 1960: 7.15

English Heritage, NMR: 1.11, 1.12, 1.14, 1.26 (Country Life); 1.17, 1.19 (Photos: Herbert Felton)

Fine Arts Library, Harvard University, Cambridge, Massachusetts: I.1, I.8, 3.35, 7.32

From Doris Fouquet-Plümacher, *Mythos Bauakademie: Die Schinkelsche Bauakademie und ihre Bedeutung für die Mitte Berlins: Ausstellungskatalog*, 1998: 3.49

Foto Marburg/Art Resource, NY: 2.11, 8.8

Fototeca Unione, American Academy in Rome: 8.40, 8.46

© 2009 The Frank Lloyd Wright Foundation, Taliesin West, Scottsdale, Arizona: 6.4, 6.16, 6.28–6.30, 6.38, 6.43

© Frank Lloyd Wright Home and Studio, Oak Park, Illinois: 6.2 (Photo: Chester Brummel)

Henry Fuermann: 6.27, 6.31 (Private collection)

From Romaldo Giurgola and Jaimini Mehta, *Louis I. Kahn*, 1975: 8.48

Groeningemuseum, Bruges: 3.22

gta archives/ETH Zurich: 5.3

Thomas A. Heinz: 6.6, 6.12

From Henry-Russell Hitchcock, *In the Nature of Materials: The Buildings of Frank Lloyd Wright, 1887–1941*, 1942: 6.7, 6.11, 6.15

Houghton Library, Harvard University, Cambridge, Massachusetts: 1.4, 1.8, 1.33, 2.13

Image Collections Department, National Gallery of Art Library, Washington, D.C. (Clarence Ward Collection): 2.21

Louis I. Kahn Collection, University of Pennsylvania and the Pennsylvania Historical and Museum Commission, Philadelphia: 8.1, 8.14, 8.16, 8.17, 8.18, 8.20, 8.22, 8.23, 8.26, 8.27, 8.29, 8.35, 8.36, 8.38, 8.39

Kunsthalle Mannheim © 2009 Artists Rights Society (ARS), New York/VG Bild-Kunst, Bonn: 7.6

Kupferstichkabinett, Staatliche Museen zu Berlin, Berlin, Bildarchiv Preussischer Kulterbesitz/Art Resource, NY: 3.33 (Photo: Reinhard Saczweski), 3.40, 3.41, 3.51–3.54

Landesarchiv, Berlin: 3.44

Courtesy of Leo Castelli Gallery, New York © Jasper Johns/Licensed by VAGA, New York, NY: 7.41 (Photo: Rudy Burckhardt)

Neil Levine: I.6, 1.2, 1.10, 1.13, 1.16, 1.20, 1.21, 1.24, 1.25, 1.29, 1.30–1.32, 2.3–2.5, 2.7, 2.8, 2.10, 2.10, 2.20, 2.22, 2.25, 3.1, 3.29, 3.38, 4.5–4.9, 4.12, 4.14, 4.17–4.20, 4.24, 4.35, 4.36, 5.1, 5.4, 5.21, 5.30–5.32, 5.34, 6.9, 6.13, 6.18, 6.20, 6.23, 6.36, 6.42, 6.44, 7.7, 7.8, 7.10, 7.12, 7.35, 7.40, 8.4, 8.9, 8.12, 8.13, 8.15, 8.21, 8.44, 8.45, 8.51–8.53

Courtesy Frances Loeb Library, Harvard University, Cambridge, Massachusetts: 3.34, 3.37, 3.39, 3.42, 3.43, 4.1, 4.3, 4.10, 4.11, 4.13, 7.5

Courtesy of the Longaberger Company: 1.4

McCormick Library of Special Collections, Northwestern University Library, Evanston, Illinois: 3.46, 3.50

Courtesy of Max Protetch Gallery, New York: 7.13, 7.14 (Private collection)

Médiathèque de l'Architecture et du Patrimoine, Paris © Centre des Monuments Nationaux, Paris: 5.20, 8.7

David Mohney: 8.31, 8.32

Musée Carnavalet © Centre des Monuments Nationaux, Paris: 2.17

Museum of Foreign Arts, Riga: 2.9

The Museum of Modern Art, New York. Digital Image © The Museum of Modern Art/ Licensed by SCALA/Art Resource, NY: 6.1, 6.22, 7.4; 7.16–7.24 (Mies van der Rohe Archive; Gift of the architect); 7.25 (Photo: Hedrich-Blessing, 10199; Courtesy Mies van der Rohe Archive); 7.28, 7.30, 7.31, 8.41 (Mies van der Rohe Archive; Gift of the architect)

The National Gallery, London: 1.3

Collection of David R. Phillips, Chicago Architectural Photography Co.: 5.22 (Photo: Kaufmann & Fabry Co.), 5.35

2009 Estate of Pablo Picasso/Artists Rights Society (ARS), New York: 6.26, 6.35 (Private collection)

Courtesy Phillips Exeter Academy Library, Exeter, New Hampshire: 8.47 (Photo: Robert Wyer)

Research Library, The Getty Research Institute, Los Angeles: 2.6, 3.3

Réunion des Musées Nationaux/Art Resource, NY: 1.34, 2.15

RIBA Library Drawings Collection, London: 3.8

Cervin Robinson: 5.26

Paul Rochelau: 6.8, 6.14

© Roger-Viollet, Paris: 2.23, 4.26, 5.2

From Heinz Ronner et al., *Louis I. Kahn: Complete Works, 1935–1974*, 1977: 8.30

From Joseph Roux, *La Basilique St. Front de Périgueux: ses origines et son histoire jusqu'en 1583*, 1920: 8.25

Sandak, Inc.: 6.21, 6.33

Scala/Art Resource, NY: 3.18

Scientific Collections, Leibniz-Institut für Regionalentwicklung und Strukturplanung (IRS), Erkner: 3.48

From Michael Snodin, *Karl Friedrich Schinkel: A Universal Man*, 1991: 3.47

Stiftung Moritzburg, Halle (Saale) © 2009 Artists Rights Society (ARS), New York/VG Bild-Kunst, Bonn: 7.33

By courtesy of the Trustees of Sir John Soane's Museum, London: 3.23–3.28, 3.30–3.32, 8.5

V & A Images/Victoria and Albert Museum, London: 1.6

Courtesy of Western Pennsylvania Conservancy: 6.39–6.41 (Photos: Robert P. Ruschak)